de Gruyter Studies in Organization 67

The New Division of Labour

de Gruyter Studies in Organization

Organizational Theory and Research

This de Gruyter Series aims at publishing theoretical and methodological studies of organizations as well as research findings, which yield insight in and knowledge about organizations. The whole spectrum of perspectives will be considered: organizational analyses rooted in the sociological as well as the economic tradition, from a socio-psychological or a political science angle, mainstream as well as critical or ethnomethodological contributions. Equally, all kinds of organizations will be considered: firms, public agencies, non-profit institutions, voluntary associations, inter-organizational networks, supra-national organizations etc.

Emphasis is on publication of *new* contributions, or significant revisions of existing approaches. However, summaries or critical reflections on current thinking and research will also be considered.

This series represents an effort to advance the social scientific study of organizations across national boundaries and academic disciplines. An Advisory Board consisting of representatives of a variety of perspectives and from different cultural areas is responsible for achieving this task.

This series addresses organization researchers within and outside universities, but also practitioners who have an interest in grounding their work on recent social scientific knowledge and insights.

The New Division of Labour

Emerging Forms of Work Organisation in International Perspective

Edited by

Wolfgang Littek and Tony Charles

Walter de Gruyter · Berlin · New York 1995

Dr. Wolfgang Littek, Professor of Sociology of Work and Organizations, University of Bremen, Germany

Tony Charles, Professor of Sociology, Director,
School of Social & International Studies, University of Sunderland, England

With 5 figures and 19 tables

Library of Congress Cataloging-in-Publication Data

The new division of labour : emerging forms of work organisation in international perspective / editors, Wolfgang Littek, Tony Charles.
XIV, 514 p. 15,5 × 23,0 cm. -- (De Gruyter studies in organization ; 67)
ISBN 3-11-013972-3
1. Division of labor -- Europe -- Case studies. 2. Industrial organization -- Europe -- Case studies. 3. Comparative management. I. Littek, W. (Wolfgang), 1937– II. Charles, Tony, 1946– III. Series.
HD51.N475 1995
306.3'615'094--dc20 95-30413
CIP

Die Deutsche Bibliothek – Cataloging-in-Publication Data

The **new division of labour** : emerging forms of work organisation in international perspective / ed.: Wolfgang Littek ; Tony Charles. – Berlin ; New York : de Gruyter, 1995
(De Gruyter studies in organization ; 67 : Organizational theory and research)
ISBN 3-11-013972-3
NE: Littek, Wolfgang [Hrsg.]; GT

⊗ Printed on acid-free paper which falls within the guidelines of the ANSI to ensure permanence and durability.

Printing: WB-Druck GmbH. Rieden am Forggensee. Binding: D. Mikolai GmbH. Berlin. Cover Design: Johannes Rother. Berlin.

Preface

This book arose out of the growing internationalism, collaboration and exchange between researchers concerning the debate on the new division of labour. The research on new forms of work organisation includes contributions from many Western European countries as well as North America and Japan. One forum for debate on the new division of labour has been facilitated by the activities of the research committee on the sociology of work of the International Sociological Asssociation; a second forum emerged from increased collaboration between researchers working together on teaching exchanges in the ERASMUS Programme of the European Union; also, a few contributions were especially invited to complete the spectrum of themes in our book. In addition to international conferences and exchanges, day to day communication has increased via facsimile and the Internet. The main theme of the book — emerging forms of work organisation in international perspective — took shape as we reviewed the variety of contributions from different national contexts. Despite this variety, these international contributions converge upon our central theme and reinforce the need to revisit the theoretical debate and appraise developments that have taken place a decade after the first discussions about flexible specialisation and new production concepts. Because of limited space and the complexity of the subject matter we were not able to include the growing research output from other countries in Central and Eastern Europe, South-East Asia and South America. These developments would merit a second volume on the new division of labour in global perspective.

Producing such a book across geographical and language boundaries turned out also to be a learning process for the authors in a new division of labour. While we had set out to accomplish the editorship in a rational and logically laid out division of labour emphasising our respective expertise (language regions, blue collar and white collar work), reality and most of all time pressures destroyed all pre-planning and demanded a holistic, complex task from both of us.

We could not have completed this task without the invaluable involvement and assistance of Bernd Alpers and Christoph Schirmer. They provided the technical standardisation needed to cope with the diversity of contributions from different parts of the world. We wish to express our thanks to them as well as to Dr. Bianka Ralle from the publishers, De Gruyter, for her benevolent patience as the project proceeded. Finally we would like to acknowledge the perseverance of those contributors who have written in a language which is not their own. Whilst there has been extensive English editing we did not wish to loose the cultural distinctiveness of contributions which derive from the rich sociology of work in non-english speaking countries.

Wolfgang Littek
Bremen, Germany
May 1995

Tony Charles
Sunderland, England
May 1995

Contents

Introduction

Wolfgang Littek and Tony Charles

Contents

1 The Characteristics of the New Division of Labour

Widespread organisational restructuring, deregulation of labour markets, increased female participation in the labour force, the reduction of layers in organisational hierarchies, knowledge-based skill upgrading and the need for continuous learning to sustain the capacity for innovation are fundamentally changing the nature of work. New high skilled, knowledge intensive jobs in both manufacturing and services contrast with declining opportunities for the unskilled, increased unemployment and social exclusion. At the same time, the distinction between „permanent employment" and temporary work is eroded with increased casualisation (flexibility) of employment in the form of part-time, temporary jobs, and self employment. These changes are redefining the conventional classification of skilled, semi-skilled and unskilled jobs and also transform definitions of managerial, technical, and professional categories in the occupational structure. „De-layering" in organisations and the reduction in the numbers of middle management are changing the white collar concept of career and simultaneously placing higher performance demands upon white-collar operatives. The contributions to this volume examine the theories and evidence underlying these processes of change in work organisation and they converge upon the central issue of the book — the emerging shape of the new division of labour in different national contexts and in different industries and work settings.

A list of keywords which identify the new division of labour would include — skill enhancement, multi-skilling, team work, flexibility, flat hierarchies, trust, empowerment coupled with higher accountability, networking, flexible technology, quality, and organisational learning. Moreover, these concepts dominate the repertoire of human resource management training seminars throughout the advanced industrial countries. These keywords appear also in the chapters of this book but our emphasis is upon the social organisation of work-place relations and technology and upon the differences between rhetoric and empirical observation; in a nutshell, the contributions to this volume are concerned with the contradictory development of these concepts in the work place and their implications for both increased performance and improvements in the quality of working life and the democratisation of work. We do not subscribe to the view that little has changed compared to the old division of labour and that the new division of labour is simply a further extension of Taylorism or Fordism. Whilst the chapters in this book adopt different theoretical perspectives on the new division of labour, they demonstrate that cross-cultural comparative research can enhance our understanding of new forms of work organisation and inform the agenda concerning where the critical choices lie regarding the shape of new forms of work as we approach the end of the twentieth century.

The new division of labour at the level of the labour process, therefore, comprises a variety of ways in which new work practices transcend the separation of conception from execution which was predominant under Taylorism. At the same time we analyse the question of managerial control which was central to the labour process debate and Braverman´s (1974) thesis of de-skilling. Two major studies published ten years ago began to develop an understanding of new work forms which departed from Taylorism — in the USA the publication of Piore and Sabel´s *Second Industrial Divide (1984)* and in Germany, Kern and Schumann´s thesis concerning the *End of the Division of Labour (1984)*. The former initiated a long debate about flexible specialisation as the paradigm of new forms of work organisation and the latter produced extensive survey evidence concerning a reversal of Taylorism resulting from the introduction of new production concepts in Germany. With the benefit of ten years of subsequent research across diverse sectors of industry and in different countries this volume aims to assess the extent to which new forms of work have emerged and compare the conditions which have been favourable or unfavourable for their diffusion.

A further aim of this book is to indicate new directions for analysis of the division of labour and to underline the centrality of the division of labour for many features of social life which extend beyond the immediate labour process. This also has been recognised as the labour process debate (following the publication of Braverman´s book in 1974) ran its course and moved beyond work relations and control issues to analyse employment relations and occcupational structures. Indeed these are themes which were already central to the early sociological analysis of the division of labour. The critique of economic analysis was a key feature of Durkheim´s (1893) study of the integrative functions of the social division of labour and the non-contractual elements in contract. Similarly, Marx´s vision of the abolition of the division of labour under socialism was premissed on the critique of class relations under capitalism and the limits of the market and competition (Rattansi 1982). These issues remain vital today where the supremacy of markets contrasts strongly with the combination of trust, compliance and cooperation which underpins the day to day functioning of the modern division of labour. The terrain between the operations of the market and hierarchy or bureaucratic forms of control is an issue explored in several chapters of this book — the possibility of a „third way" between market and hierarchy and the relations between trust and compliance, collaboration and competition are given new prominence with the emergence of new forms of inter-firm networking and organisational interaction.

2 Why a *New* Division of Labour?

Modernity is associated, above all else, with industrialisation as the basis of wealth and economic development. The continuous introduction of new machinery in the labour process and the co-ordination of specialised functions in ever larger enterprises have brought about an unprecedented increase in the productivity of labour. Following the establishment of the factory system, *technology* has been permanently revolutionised over the past two hundred years. However, whilst technology is widely exploited, its potential to secure lasting profitability is increasingly limited. Likewise, reliance upon the traditional industrial strategies of increasing economies of scale and the search for lower labour costs is rendered less effective in today´s volatile economy, with strong competition on a global scale. The nature of work and the organisation of the labour process are undergoing fundamental change. *Human labour* has once more become the centre of attention. The focus has switched to human beings and human creativity which are no longer assumed to be replaceable by automation and computer programming.

The new division of labour in work organisations represents the effort to make use of the full potential of human labour, of tacit skills, energy and motivation. Nevertheless, this occurs with one intention in mind: to enhance productivity and to retain and enhance a competitive position in the market. Following the collapse of state socialism in the countries of central and eastern Europe, market mechanisms have also assumed an omnipotent position as the mode of organising workplace relations. The emerging new division of labour has not, therefore, derived in the main from quests for the humanisation of work or the quality of working life but from the assumed imperatives of economic rationality. The new division of labour derives from the continuous search for greater investment in „human capital" and the more effective exploitation and management of „human resources". In this respect there is a clear continuity with the old division of labour represented in Taylorist forms of work organisation. However, what is *new* is a sitution in which the interests of management are now clearly dependent upon the creativity of labour in a much more transparent fashion. Creativity and worker consent can no longer be obtained by control and coercion characteristic of the old factory regime. Whilst the trends of the 1980s and the Thatcher-Reagan-Kohl era moved in the direction of market liberalisation and labour market deregulation, the new division of labour within enterprises as well as between organisations depends upon increased collaboration and networking between all workers in the enterprise and between employees in different enterprises. This underlying tension is revealed in many of the contributing chapters to this book.

Insofar as the new division of labour incorporates work re-design towards more holistic tasks, higher skills, more autonomy, responsibility and decision making, does the power game between management and labour still rest upon a zero sum situation where the gains of one side are at the expense of the other? The new division of labour contains the potential for gains on both sides because required commitment as well as compliance towards higher performance will hardly be reached without concessions granted to labour. Whilst gains have to be fought for in the single case and new forms of labour compromise vary considerably between different countries, in the new organisation of work workers exist as active counterparts — the company cannot do without them voluntarily giving of their best. In this new form of organisational interdependence, coercion, command, tight supervision and control are no longer able to elicit major improvements in performance. The division of labour which is emerging contains a development which could be described as one towards *interactive work* — where workers as well as management know about the worth of competent performance and the necessity to find agreement about a voluntary delivery and adequate compensation (payment, career, recognition) for best performance.

3 Technology and the New Division of Labour

For two hundred years, the management of industrial work processes has attempted predominantly to eliminate everything specifically human in work and to realise a vision of machine-like performance: precise, reliable, predictable, totally controllable and rule-based. The possibility that management could not be in control over the work process was not considered. It was taken for granted that insight into the overall process in manufacturing or in the service sector and the capacity for decision making could only reside with management. The root of this approach derives from engineering: the vision was one of efficient but controlled mechanical performance, inspired by engineers like Frederick W. Taylor and Henry Ford and institutionalised by the scientific management movement which followed.

Today, machine-like performance no longer suffices — not in the factory and even less so in the office. Even under extreme forms of Taylorist work organisation, however, tacit human skills and work place co-operation were necessary to ensure production, but what was latent under the old division of labour is now manifestly at the centre of new forms of work organisation. After the concentration and effort to develop the use of technology and cheapen labour, the largest gains in the competitive struggle on the market are no longer expected here any more. The appropriation and social organisation of technology — once viewed as the „soft" side in the production process or in the provision of services have now assumed a central place. Indeed, the motto for the end of the century could well be that the organisation and intelligent development of labour brings more productivity than microelectronics. Or, to be more precise, the full potential of advanced technology can only be realised in conjunction with the full development of human skills and creativity.

At the same time, enterprise performance can no longer be based upon improvements in the output of isolated functions in the division of labour. The new division of labour embraces the whole production chain far beyond direct production and extends beyond the enterprise to include co-operation with suppliers and other service enterprises and reaches to interaction with customers. This transcends the boundaries of one single organisation if not the boundaries of one country. The scope of work restructuring now depends upon the development of extensive networks and even globalisation. With it, the operational scope of the division of labour has changed. The motor of development in the division of labour and enterprise performance has shifted from a narrow concern with efficiency and the cost of factors of production to the effectiveness of the whole organisation.

4 New Forms of Work Organisation

The slow demise of Taylorist forms of work organisation based upon traditional principles of engineering is accompanied by the decline of the traditional form of bureaucratic centralisation with its strict hierarchical divisions and its principles of direction and control. Enterprise leaders have begun to recognise that there is much more to human labour which has not been used, which has been left to waste and has not (this is true also) been exploited yet: creativity, imagination, flexibility, learning from mistakes and the potential to cope with the unforseen and deal with contingencies. Many of these qualities cannot be programmed in advance nor elicited by tight procedures of command and control or assigned to strictly prescribed tasks nor conserved in the software of computerised work.

Central to the debate on flexibility many of the contributions to this book focus upon the theoretical issues in the post-Fordist debate and address the more recent discussion of lean production in manufacturing (Womack et al.

1990). Informed by comparative research, the ideal type of lean production as the ascendant paradigm for advanced manufacturing is subjected to critical analysis. Case studies and detailed analysis of new forms of work organisation point to the need to demystify Japanese manufacturing practices and confront the underlying assumptions of lean production as a new „best practice". For example, team work and continuous improvement continue to operate within narrow limits of job discretion and tightly prescribed job descriptions in mass production industry. Similarly, the logic of lean production is rooted, like its Taylorist predecessors, in managerial strategies for cost reduction. Cross national comparative research also reveals that team work can only be understood in the institutional context within which it is embedded; thus European conceptions of group work and labour control contrast markedly with the team work principles of lean production. Comparison between different industrial sectors also reveals the dangers of concentration on the motor industry as the paradigm of new forms of manufacturing work organisation. Whilst new forms of advanced manufacturing undermine traditional distinctions between mass production, batch production and customisation, differences in skill profiles, the experience of work, and task discretion (between for example the machine tool industry and motor manufacturing) undermine the global claim for lean production as the ascendant paradigm for advanced manufacturing.

The development of the new forms of work organisation and the more demanding use of human labour which they entail reaches much more widely than direct production in manufacturing. The extensive rationalisation of direct production work has up-graded the skills required in the remaining production tasks together with a vast expansion of indirect work which encompasses producer services up-stream and down-stream of production, from design to marketing. At the same time, the expansion of management functions and the continued growth of personal services and the professions, including for example, banking, retailing and hospitals, has ushered in new forms of work organisation in service work. The potential for the continued rationalisation of routine service work up-grades the skills and productivity of employees in the service sector, whilst it reduces traditional conceptions of employment security, changes the concept of „career" and reduces the capacity of new service employment to compensate for unemployment in manufacturing.

The general consequences for employment have been double edged. In the advanced industrial societies we have witnessed a huge replacement of living human labour by machines in recent decades, stimulated by the potential of the new microelectronic information technologies. Consequently, job displacement and organisational down-sizing have exacerbated structural *unemployment* which has become the major problem in almost all the advanced industrial countries. So far, no really socially acceptable solution in economic and work policies has been found. In terms of the social division of labour and changes in the occupational structure, the tendency for capitalist economies to generate segmented labour markets has intensified — swelling the ranks of the socially excluded and the disadvantaged. Whilst womens´ employment has increased in all the advanced industrial societies, increased flexibility and the casualisation of employment continue to operate especially to the disadvantage of women and reproduce the gendered nature of workplace relations. The question of who benefits from the new division of labour requires a wider analysis of the relationship between the division of labour and social stratification. Several chapters allude to the changing social division of labour although the central focus is limited to workplace relations. Informal work, and non-waged work also lie outside the scope of this book but many of the chapters point to the contradictory implications of the new division of labour for the workforce as a whole and for the unemployed.

5 The New Division of Labour in International Perspective

The contributions to this volume focus in different ways on the main changes associated with the new division of labour for working conditions and work organisations. This central theme is put in an international context in the attempt to discover the extent to which new forms of work organisation are developing in different countries or different work settings (sectors of industry, production and service work). Several chapters confront the concepts of lean production, flexible specialisation and post-Fordist work organisation from a comparative perspective. A common theme which emerges from several of the contributions indicates that alongside more demanding and potentially more satisfying work and alongside increased autonomy and collaboration in the work place, new problems of stress and work intensity have emerged. Contributions which focus upon Japan, Europe and North America observe the ways in which, in different industrial cultures, trust and control, learning and monitoring, democratisation of work and empowerment are mediated by the cultural and institutional context within which they occur. In this sense, the new division of labour will take different forms across industrial societies and present new challenges to organised labour in response to developments which are largely management driven in the context of weakened trade union power in many countries.

Whilst we emphasise what is new about the division of labour we also recognise that the themes of this book have a long history in industrial sociology — emanating originally form the human relations tradition in the USA, socio-technical systems theory and the Tavistock research programme in the UK, the quality of working life movement in Sweden, human-centred and anthropocentric technology approaches of European origin, semi-autonomous working groups and the pre-war experiments in German „Betriebssoziologie" — to name several major examples from many (Rose, M. 1988; Corbett, J. et al. 1991). What is new is that, under conditions of increased global competition, new forms of work organisation are increasingly being put into practice in enterprises and new concepts have been diffused to a wider public — such as „lean production", Japanese manufacturing practices, the „empowerment" discussion and „re-engineering" in the United States, human-centred group technology and industrial networks in various European countries. Nevertheless, the case studies reveal that managerial resistance to change is still powerful and that much that was characteristic of the old division of labour still remains in many sectors. In sum, the chapters in this volume indicate where the key questions arise for the future of work and the agenda for future comparative research. Firstly, they demonstrate a need to develop a critical discourse about concepts such as empowerment and quality, team work and trust. Secondly, they point to the need to transcend discipline boundaries between, for example, industrial economics and organisation theory, sociology of work, economic geography and innovation theory. Thirdly, they highlight the importance of research which transcends the single enterprise to examine inter-organisational relationships and networks. Finally, they point towards research which goes beyond the boundaries of the nation state to understand the processes of globalisation and their impact on the division of labour in the workplace.

6 The Organisation of the Book

In order to approach the themes and issues we have raised concerning the characteristics and emergence of the new division of labour, the role of technology, new forms of work organisation and the extent to which they are becoming diffused across different nation states, we have arranged the chapters into three parts. We contribute a general and short introduction to each part in order to summarize the main objectives and the context of discussion of each chapter. In Part I, the contributions deal with the basic conceptual and theoretical issues which are prominent concerning the new division of labour; in Part II, each chapter discusses findings from international comparative studies or uses perspectives which include more than one country; in Part III, these broader discussions are complemented by shorter chapters which focus upon empirical research in one region or sector.

References

Braverman, H. (1974), *Labor and Monopoly Capital*, New York, Monthly Review Press.

Corbett, J., Rasmussen, L. and Rauner, F. (1991), *Crossing the Border,* London, Heidelberg, Springer.

Durkheim, E. (1893), *The Division of Labor,* Glencoe, Illinois, Free Press.

Kern, H. and Schumann, M. (1984), *Das Ende der Arbeitsteilung?*, Munich, Beck.

Piore, R. and Sabel, C. (1984), *The Second Industrial Divide*, New York, Basic Books.

Rattansi, A. (1982), Marx and the Abolition of the Division of Labour, in Giddens, A. and Mackenzie, G. (eds.), *Social Class and the Division of Labour,* New York, Cambridge University Press.

Rose, M. (1988), *Industrial Behaviour,* Harmondsworth, Penguin.

Womack, J., Jones, D. and Roos, D., (1990), *The Machine that Changed the World*, New York, Rawson.

Part I
Basic Issues in the New Division of Labour

Introduction to Part I

This part comprises chapters which deal with basic theoretical concepts and questions in the division of labour debate. They have a generalised focus though all of them emerge from a specific empirical background.

In **chapter 1** *Heisig* and *Littek* deal with the growing importance of *trust* as a medium to coordinate divided labour processes. Trust has emerged recently as a new issue in management literature. The authors, however, draw on their own empirical findings and maintain that trust is not a new medium, but an alternative to tight control. Trust has increased in importance with the spread of more complex work design, modern decentralised work organisation and the flattening of hierarches („lean production"/„lean management" and similar concepts). *Heisig* and *Littek* argue that trust relations represent the micro-sociological basis for new organisational structures and forms of work organisation. Such new forms are based on participation, responsibility and transfer of discretionary decision making to workers. In this approach immediate work behaviour is not controlled, rather the general performance of employees is subject to evaluation — for example, learning capability, flexibility, responsibility, and initiative. Such a system rests on a set of „instruments" to reward desired behaviour. These incentives comprise both symbolic and material rewards, from praise to bonus payments and career opportunities. The authors deal with the core elements of high trust relations and examine their consequences for the coordination of work processes including collective and individual bargaining. They also discuss *limits* to the organisation of trust which occur in the micro-politics of interaction. The chapter concludes with an evaluation, in the light of the trust concept, of recent economic developments in Germany with lasting mass unemployment, highly competitive markets and pressures from the international economy.

In **chapter 2** *Sabel* deals in a different way with the consequences of the new competitive, consumer oriented environment in a volatile economy. He calls for a new sociology of work which is capable of accounting for the emerging responses to the new competitive situation. Two principal arguments are advanced. One unfolds the features of new production structures called *meta-corporations* or *moebius-strip organisations*, characterised by blurred hierarchical distinctions within firms and boundaries between them.

Increased internal flexibility and opening of the borders between corporations create vulnerabilities which call for responses that work towards overcoming the distinction between *learning* and *monitoring* or *trust* and *control*. The second argument deals with the effects of the emerging organisational and technological ambiguities concerning employment, where the new situation is called an *open labour market* (as distinguished from craft labour markets, or internal labour markets of mass production industries). The acquisition of higher skills is required but because of the fluidity of corporate boundaries workers must learn to move from job to job, joining networks across company lines. Unfolding his arguments, *Sabel* presents in this chapter essential building blocks for a *new conceptualisation* of work some 10 years after the seminal (influential) study, *The Second Industrial Divide* (co-authored with *Piore*), where the authors envisaged the end of mass production and the emergence of flexible specialisation.

In Germany, the most influential and widely discussed research work on the new division of labour was based upon the *End of the Division of Labour* by Kern and Schumann in 1984. In **chapter 3**, *Schumann* and his colleagues revisit the issues first raised in that major work and present new research findings translated here in English for the first time. Based upon extensive empirical research in the car industry, the chemical industry and the machine tool industry, the authors examine the extent to which new production concepts have actually become diffused in German industry and their impact upon new forms of work organisation. Confirming the results of the earlier 1984 study, their findings indicate that the traditional Taylorist/Fordist type of organisation is on the way out along with the model of the fully automated factory without human intervention. In the sectors studied there is a search for new organisational forms involving team work and reduced division of labour based upon the key role played by the new *„systems regulators"* — the prototype of the new highly skilled autonomous and self-regulating worker.

However, despite widespread discussion of new organisational forms and lean production the trend towards new forms of work organisation is slow and uncertain. Horizontal and vertical divisions created by the old division of labour continue to produce resistance to fundamental changes in enterprise organisation and the prototype systems regulator represents only a small minority of production workers particularly in the car industry. Whilst the system regulator represents „the winner" in the rationalisation process with improved working conditions and career prospects, the authors note the contradictory consequences for work of new forms of inter-firm networking and the global reorganisation of production. The key issue for industrial sociology in the late 1990s is to examine the expanding category of „losers" in the rationalisation process — those employed in traditional manual work which is increasingly insecure in a more segmented labour market with high unemployment. The balance of positive and negative outcomes of current trends in work reorganisation will depend upon policy changes towards work which includea a new compromise between productivity, performance and improved working conditions.

No account of changes in work organisation and the division of labour can ignore the importance of the *sexual division of labour* and *gender issues* in the workplace. In **chapter 4** *Webster* takes up this challenge and reviews theoretical and empirical developments in understanding the relation between gender and technology. Starting with a critical analysis of the labour process debate initiated by Braverman´s (1974) *Labour and Monopoly Capital, Webster* demonstrates the weaknesses of labour process theory in failing to analyse the gendered nature of technology and women´s subordination in the „old" division of labour. Secondly, *Webster* finds little evidence that the sexual division of labour at work has been eroded by the „new" division of labour characterised by increased flexibility. Using evidence from feminist research in Britain, the U.S.A. and Australia, *Webster* notes that workplace relations and the control of technology in both factory and office work are shaped by gender relations and conceptions of women´s work. Technology it is argued, is masculine in its underlying values and reinforces patriarchal relations in the workforce. Despite the focus of more recent research on the impact of flexibility upon core and periphery segments of the labour market and increased casualisation of employment, the gendered nature of workplace relations is not adequately incorporated into the new division of labour debate. The issues raised by *Webster* are further explored in some of the empirical contributions to Parts II and III.

In **chapter 5,** *Gordon* takes up another major issue in the new division of labour and examines the implications of globalisation for the spatial division of labour and the labour process. *Gordon* distinguishes between three processes of internationalisation, multinationalisation and globalisation which structure the organisation of the world economy. Based upon research in Silicon Valley and its relationship to global production networks, *Gordon* argues that *globalisation* embodies a new logic of innovation which is different from either transnationalisation or internationalisation. Intensified competition in the world economy, the widespread diffusion of new information and communications technologies and the increasing costs of research and development propel firms to develop new forms of networking which transcend both market and hierarchy and encourage interdependent collaboration for permanent innovation. The result can be seen in the growth of new inter-firm relations and collaborative partnerships on a global scale. At the level of the labour process, global competition for innovation reinforces the social aspects of production organisation and potentially enhances the democratisation of work. Finally, this chapter considers the implications of globalisation for regional economies and the debate concerning industrial districts. Regional economies must increasingly participate in global networks to sustain innovation and at the same time globalisation is reshaping the international division of labour and redefining the relationship between core and periphery.

Finally in this part, *Bögenhold* (**chapter 6**) returns to the fundamental issues concerning the division of labour raised by the classical sociologists such as Durkheim and Weber and questions what is „old" and „new" in the division of labour today in terms of a longer historical perspective. As the title of this chapter suggests, *Bögenhold* searches for the continuities and discontinuities in industrial organisation, occupational structure and the economy and argues that the important disjunctions in the division of labour are not captured by the current discussion of the transition from Fordism to post-Fordism. Long-term changes in the occupational structure exhibit both a trend towards proletarianisation and also the emergence of new professional groups and knowledge workers in the service sector. Similarly, in industrial organisation, small enterprises were important even at the supposed peak of Fordism and they continue in importance in mature capitalist societies. Currently, an increasingly globalised economy and developments in information technology create new uncertainties for enterprises and a search for flexibility — a „new" division of labour based predominantly on the service sector. However, *Bögenhold* concludes that only an analysis which is historically informed and sensitive to sectoral and national variations can differentiate between fundamental new developments in the division of labour and the longer term continuities characteristic of capitalist development.

Chapter 1
Trust as a Basis of Work Organisation

Ulrich Heisig and Wolfgang Littek

Contents

1 Division of Labour, Control and Trust

Trust is a basis of work organisation which until recently has been widely underestimated in the sociology of work. The actual discussion of work reorganisation is also carried out largely under technological, material and organisational aspects, for example in lean production, flat hierarchies, total quality management and continuous improvement. Too little recognition is paid to the *social relations* underlying these aspects, which are relevant for the work process and for management-labour relations. The aim of this chapter is to examine the role which trust plays in labour relations and the growing importance which it gains in the new division of labour. We shall look shortly at the circumstances which brought up trust as a theme, consider the preconditions necessary for trust to evolve and then analyse the functioning of work relations under conditions of high trust. Such conditions sharply contrast with working behaviour under traditional Taylorist principles of work organisation which are based on low management trust towards workers.

Trust is closely connected with the division of labour. The more subdivided and complex a work process, the more organisational measures are required in order to achieve the coordination and integration of the process as a whole. Command or even coercion in combination with direct control come to mind immediately as means to enforce desired performance of the segmented workforce. But command and control is by no means the only principle of work coordination: Mutual trust is another one. Under the economic and technological changes of the recent years the conditions of work have changed dramatically. With it the need for other forms of work coordination became urgent. Under the new pressures of world market competition and selective consumer demands, companies in the highly developed countries have come to design work in a way that is relying much more on the motivation, competence, initiative and responsible autonomy of workers instead of command and tight control over a deskilled, dependent workforce. Thus trust emerges more clearly again as a basis of work organisation.

Under the industrial-capitalist regime *one* specific form of control over the labour force came to prevail out of a variety of possibilities, because it proved most successful under the historically given circumstances: the expansion of mass production industries. Its features were: fragmentation of tasks, separation of conception and execution of work, centralisation of command and control. Behind this lies a *fundamental distrust* of the workers. It was taken for granted that workers needed to be disciplined and tightly directed, that workers themselves would only be interested in how to shirk or avoid work. The history of establishing „*scientific management*" reflects the long enduring attempts of management to gain control over the labour process in private enterprises. This has been extensively described by Braverman in his well known study *Labor and Monopoly Capital* (1974). His study (which is only one among several others but became the most prominent one and triggered the continuing „labour process debate") shows how fundamental *distrust* of workers became the motor to develop and apply systems of work organisation which strip workers of their autonomy and decision-making over work performance. All conceptual and discretionary elements of a task had to be put into the hands of management which then directs the workers in the „one best way" of performance. This is the central idea of Frederick W. Taylor´s (1911) principles of work organisation.

To Taylor´s idea of work place efficiency Henry Ford added basic elements of industrial mass production with standardisation of products and work processes, and discipling workers through machine-pacing and conveyer belts. The ensuing *Taylorism* and *Fordism* are specific attempts to get the system of work performance watertight under established circumstances of distrust. With this background, factory work indeed was the target of attempts to reduce labour costs through standardisation and deskilling in mass production industries for decades (as is well documented in the vast literature on the degradation of work in capitalist industry).

As the sociology of work concentrated predominantly on production work, i.e. the execution of tasks at the shop floor level, distrust and the need for direct *control* gained a central place in the *sociology of work* as well. The narrow view merely of the „production process" led to a limited conceptualisation of the overall work process, of work performance and control. In consequence the sociology of work systematically overlooked that another relevant result of the enforcement of mass production and fragmented work on the shop floor was the *increase* of administrative jobs. These jobs are *knowledge based* and do not function like unskilled jobs. The expanding development, planning and supervising offices as well as management hierarchies were excluded from the predominate industrial sociological analyses. In the discipline the expectation obviously prevailed that demanding jobs which were the result of the separation of conception and execution would themselves become expropriated.

From this perspective which concentrated on the degradation of work in industry growing portions of work did not fit into this conception and went unnoted. Also, the majority of work in advanced „industrial" societies nowadays is no longer altogether industrial work. Direct goods producing work in the factory has dwindled to less then 20 or even 15% of all employment in the most advanced industrial societies, which have indeed become *service societies* by now (for overviews on the development of service work or white-collar work see W. Littek 1992; U. Heisig and W. Littek 1995, W. Littek and U. Heisig 1995). The focus of attention of empirical studies in the sociology of work remained with the dwindling minority of production workers and simply ignored the different work organisation in the vast field of professional and managerial functions or other skilled service work (or left it to specialised sub-sociologies such as the sociology of professions).

Before turning to the analysis of trust in work contexts, we shall deal with the question of how trust came to be an issue in our own empirical research findings, and how it emerged in recent discussions in the literature.

2 The Discovery of Trust as a Basis of Labour Relations

We came upon the concept of trust as a result of interpretation of our findings from an empirical research project on the working conditions of skilled white-collar workers in commercial and technical functions of large industrial companies (see W. Littek 1986; W. Littek and U. Heisig 1986, 1990; U. Heisig 1989). The subjective experience of work of our sample of white-collar employees revealed that they understood the work context as a cooperative relationship. For skilled white-collar workers, informal rather than formal agreements were relevant for the quantity and quality of their work load. Employees perceived that their performance would be rewarded over time. From their perspective the successful execution of tasks was their personal contribution to the success of the enterprise. Management saw itself urged to come up to these expectations because it was interested in such performance of employees. This way mutual expectations develop which rest on trust instead of coercion and tight control. Such trust relations are the result of a long-term process. The advantage emerging for both sides prevents each side from destroying this relationship for short-term profit.

In our case, employees obviously hoped to contribute to the security of their work place and to participate in the profits of the firm if prosperous. These expectations were understandable because the employees whom we interviewed were employed in firms which had been suffering from economic decline since the late 1970s. The firms had made financial losses and had been reducing personnel for some years. The employees thought that the depressed situation could only be overcome if staff and management stuck together and cooperated to achieve high performance. This view contradicted our initial expectation that strong disputes and conflicts would occur in the economic crisis and the antagonistic relation between capital and labour would become more obvious. Instead, *social relations* proved to be *stable* enough to effect the necessary changes.

The remarkable stability of social relations could be explained by the fact that the situation did not become markedly worse for those workers who remained employed. The decisive sacrifice was made by those who were made redundant, either by being dismissed (usually with compensation) or by being prematurely retired. The reduction of personnel on the contrary led to *positive* effects for those who stayed *within* the firm. Very often they moved more rapidly into higher ranks and better paid positions. In almost no cases did management attempt to transfer the difficult situation to the employees. Rather it retained the position of employees and recognised the rules of fairness.

Our research results revealed that in work restructuring *middle managers* and immediate superiors played a decisive role. They actively pushed through the decisions of top executives against their subordinates, but at the same time took care that the vital interests of the latter were not violated. Their important role was to *mediate* between the interests of top-management and employees and to function as agents of employees´ interest representation vis-à-vis top-management. (Similar findings are presented e.g. by Vicki Smith 1990 in her study on corporate restructuring in an American bank.) The employees at all levels of the hierarchy were obviously incorporated into a set of rules of conduct which regulated mutual intercourse. These rules were neither formalised nor even codified. They rather consisted of norms and values which were nevertheless highly mandatory.

In order not only to describe the discovered social relations but to explain them as expressions of an underlying social structure, we took up Alan Fox´s (1974) concept of *trust relations* for interpretation of our findings. Whilst employing the concept we discovered that it became a useful explanatory device if we combined it with the idea of a specific form of work organisation and social relations between capital and labour. This meant that trust relations, accordingly, need a form of work organisation which allows for margins of action and discretion for employees. In the enterprise this form of work organisation becomes stabilised by a system of remuneration which rewarded conformist and punished deviant behaviour.

In a subsequent research project, in which we examined the structure of trust relations at work again in skilled white-collar functions in another industry, our previous results were confirmed (see W. Littek and U. Heisig 1990,

1991; contributions in W. Littek et al. 1992; for more details on our empirical research work see also chapter 12 by W. Littek and U. Heisig in this book). In addition to our previous results, we found that the functioning of a trust system is closely tied to available *incentives and rewards*. Satisfaction and the readiness to work hard was highest in sectors of employment where the job structure was widely differentiated and personal engagement and efforts were rewarded with occupational advancement and career. In comparison with that trust relations only contributed to the satisfaction of employees, but did not stimulate high work efforts in departments where no or little incentives existed. If *trust relations* are to be used as organisational *means to improve performance and efficiency* they obviously have to be supplemented with an elaborated system of remuneration. *Incentives* are, as evidence showed, the central means of management to control employee behaviour within trust relations. Among these, higher payments play a prominent role, but not the only one. Incentives include a wide range of non-material rewards as well, from praise, the chance of more challenging work, a title of higher status to real advancement.

What we found then is, retrospectively, confirmed by the current discussion of Japanese „lean“ forms of work organisation (on the concept of „lean production“ see e.g. chapter 11 by U. Jürgens in this book; the original basic study by J.P. Womack et al. 1990). In the discussion of Japanese work organisation trust is not explicitely mentioned. Rather, organisational forms are indicated which lead to *effective performance of the overall system*. In these, delegation of responsibility and discretion play a prominent role. In order to make this function in practice mutual trust is needed as an indispensable pre-condition. The second important issue of the Japanese system emphasised in the discussion is the positive *sanctioning of adequate behaviour*. In the Japanese case it becomes evident that an elaborated *system of incentives* is needed to support trust relations. The great flexibility and efficiency of Japanese regular workers is generated by an extremely differentiated personal ranking „hierarchy“ which is independent of the concrete task a person performs (as Aoki 1990, for instance, demonstrates). The ranking system allows the continuous promotion of all quasi-permanent employees over a long time period. Although all employees move upwards within the ranking „hierarchy“, the speed of promotion within the firm differs strongly between them. Those who best fulfil the management´s expectations make rapid careers whereas bad performers only move slowly through the ranks. (For more comparisons between Western work organisation and the Japanese „lean production“ system see farther below.)

3 From Organisational Practice to Management Strategy

When we discovered during our research in the early 1980s trust relations as organisational principle and modality of interest regulation it was quite uncommon to speak about trust as a basic feature of work organisation and social relations. Other than Alan Fox´s study *Beyond Contract* (1974) we found no hints in the German and mainstream international industrial sociology literature that trust played a significant role within organisations. Even Fox himself had not taken trust as a distinct topic of empirical research. He rather used empirical findings that were generated in other theoretical contexts and reinterpreted them under the aspect of the predominance of trust or mistrust in social relations. Remarkable in Fox´s analysis is that his examples pick up trust relations at the moment at which they are violated and cease to exist. (This is one of the points of criticism of Fox by W.K. Roche 1991.) Obviously it is very difficult to analyse trust relations as long as they remain intact because they then do not come to the fore.[1]

Although the explanatory concepts which were presented by Fox could have opened new horizons his stimulating ideas were not then taken up in the scholarly discussion and did not lead to a distinct line of research. The industrial sociological debate of the 1970s and early 1980s (especially in Germany and other Western countries) was rather dominated by macro-sociological Marxist approaches which drew their concepts from political economy. The main reason why Fox´s attempt to introduce trust into industrial sociology and organisation theory failed was that it played *no practical role* in work and organisational design *at that time*. Until the early 1980s trust relations were the exclusive product of fortuitous practices and not a product of management strategies. They became stabilised if they proved to be successful.

[1] In general sociology *trust* is not a widely treated issue, but has found explicit recognition as a condtion of social relations by a few authors such as Georg Simmel, Niklas Luhmann (1988) and more recently Anthony Giddens (1990) and James Coleman (1983, 1990), though all of these authors deal with different dimensions of trust. (For a short treatment of the issue see H.-D. Gondek et al. 1992.)

Trust relations in work came to be an explicit topic in the early 1980s in the United States. They were then discovered as preconditions of the success of Japanese firms and were discussed in management literature (cf. T. Deal and A. Kennedy 1988; Th. Peters and R. Waterman 1982 which were most relevant for management practice).[2] This was the beginning of a thinking which accepted that there were serious alternatives to the until then unique Western model of „Taylorist" work organisation, which is built expressedly on distrust. The alternative model based work organisation on *responsible autonomy* (a concept which had been introduced into the labour process debate as an alternative model to „Taylorism" by Andrew Friedman 1977). Instead of being an outdated concept from the time before the application of „scientific management", organisational forms built on responsible autonomy proved to be more successful than social scientists and Western managers would have accepted.

The initial preoccupation with trust relations was to describe specific characteristics of successful companies and to point out their (real or supposed) success criteria. The organisational task, therefore, was to imitate those succcessful companies and to create a culture which would promote cohesion and identity within the organisation. There was a belief that every company would be able to create its own image which ought to contribute to cohesion and efficiency. However, the creation of corporate culture bore from the beginning an instrumental character. There was a failure to realise that in successful companies the *corporate culture* evolved from *year long* practices which in addition were not made explicit. What the corporate culture debate made clear was that it is not enough to proclaim common interests and cooperation between workers and managers, but that there is a real need to practice them.

Whereas the early corporate culture approach described and analysed the specific conditions of economically efficient firms it was later on attempted to make „culture" operational. Thus the casual character of success was dismantled, with the hope of being able to plan and design success. Management expected to realise this goal initially merely by ideological means. It was believed that formulating common interests and establishing a corporate consti-

[2] There is of course a longer history of *authors on management* with a wider range of theoretical concepts. Our intention is not to take up this academic discussion here, rather we want to point out the relevance cultural aspects gained in management practice.

tution was enough to integrate the workers and stimulate their efforts. In as much as this ideological offensive was not followed by adequate action and management itself did not adhere to the self-proclaimed rules, corporate identity proved to be insufficient. The current lean production/lean management campaign draws the conclusion that it is *not* enough to *speak* about reliable cooperation but that it has to be put into practice in restructuring work organisation. Common interests and commitment are now seen as results of a work organisation which allows workers to *practice* autonomy, to develop responsibility and to participate in work related decisions. Lean management thus means the construction of systems of action as systems of trust.

4 Alternative Work Cultures, Social Relations and Interest Representation

Under capitalist relations of production the interests of management and (blue- and white-collar) workers can never be structurally identical. Nevertheless management and workers have to work together within the labour process, if a useful and marketable product or service is to be manufactured. Cooperation and common effort within production, however, is only possible if participants find an arrangement for the concilliation of divergent interests which is acceptable to all involved. To reach such an agreement, management and workers have to accept that coordination and regulation of interests are necessary preconditions of successful work. As soon as they agree on this point more complex procedures can be developed which ensure that the interests of participants are considered and satisfied (at least to a certain degree). But even if procedures are established, the adjustment of interests is never a simple matter because the *subjective perception* of capital-labour relations by the actors, and their idea of appropriate remuneration and participation is crucial for the specific way in which conflicts and divergences are settled. (Typical differences of perception exist for example in Germany between blue-collar and white-collar workers. We shall deal with this later in the chapter.) As participants themselves always personally contribute to the structures which are established to define situations and to solve problems, there are no uniform but rather very specific forms of interest regulation which may differ from case to case within and between organisations.

The assumption of divergent work situations and social relations is inconsistent with the perspective of *traditional labour process theory* which assumed that a single logic of development existed within capitalist enterprises. This would lead to work structures and social relations in production of the same kind. Capital and labour here are treated as mere antagonists, and coercion is seen as the only adequate means of capital to control labour. From this perspective all qualitative aspects of labour (like e.g. different kinds of skill, knowledge and know-how) and social relations are reduced to mere quantitative variations. It is supposed that all different perceptible forms of waged labour will be eliminated in the long run and that qualified labour will inevitably also develop in the direction of unskilled and fragmented work. Thus all empirical particularities of labour and all possibilities of variant development of capital-labour relations are eliminated by theory.

The conception of invariant antagonistic relations between labour and management under capitalist relations of production was completed with the assumption that *scientific management* was the one and only appropriate way of capitalist control. But in fact Taylorism was only *one*, and an altogether bad, solution for the effective transformation of labour power into labour. The separation of conception and execution and the degradation of work in reality rather fostered the antagonism between capital and labour, made the coordination of interests less feasible and the reliance on coercive measures more necessary (cf. M. Burawoy 1985, p. 41). As Burawoy (1985) has indicated, scientific management thus *undermined* „the essence of capitalist control", which is the *obscuring* of surplus value and of the relations of exploitation between capital and labour.

The idea of a unilateral development of production relations was generated by the assumption that „the economic relation of capital to labour is zero-sum — the gains of capital are always at the expense of labour" (M. Burawoy 1985, p. 27). Capital in this concept is seen as an omnipotent institution that is solely interested in the crude exploitation and command of labour. In his prolific critique of this concept Burawoy (1985, p. 28) convincingly demonstrates that the relation between capital and labour indeed is always asymmetrical: because of the structural conditions of capitalist production the appropriation of profits turns out always to the advantage of capital. The share of capital is always greater than that of labour. But this does not necessarily mean that workers are left out in the cold. As much as increasing productivity leads to economic gains, there is room for concessions in the distribution.

After gains are produced, gains can be a subject of bargaining. Modern management knows very well that labour´s participation in the gains will secure its willingness to cooperate in the future. As cooperation is a productive force which creates extra profits a cooperative management will be able to distribute a larger cake. This allows for advantages on both sides and ensures that cooperation is to the advantage of employees as well.

The distribution of the gains of cooperation is not an arbitrary act which is fully at the management´s discretion. Rather employees expect to get a „fair share" of the receipts as an equivalent for their support and only continue to play the game if they believe it is not zero-sum for them. To observe the rules of this game is essential for the continuation of trust relations.

The extent and the way of cooperative behaviour do not come out of the blue: Rather they are embedded in enterprise traditions and corporate cultures. In addition, within one enterprise not only one single culture exists. Blue-collar and white-collar work sectors are characterised by *different* traditions of perception of the relations between labour and capital. Their different perception became institutionalised in the course of time. This finds its obvious expression in the modality in which the interest representation is organised. Whereas in blue-collar work areas, antagonistic perceptions and mutual distrust between capital and labour rule the social relations up to this day, social relations in skilled white-collar work are determined rather by mutual trust and common effort (cf. for an elaboration of the two different work „cultures" W. Littek and U. Heisig 1990). In the former case, trade unions and works councils are needed to restrict the *despotism* of capital, whilst the latter prefer to use individual strategies to pursue their personal interest instead of supporting collective action.

The typical blue-collar work situation, interest perception and bargaining procedures have been analysed frequently in the labour process literature, whereas white-collar work organisation has found almost no recognition until recently. The impression thus was created that labour relations based on give and take, trust and individual orientations did not exist in the world of work. Our text intends to correct this one-sided picture by outlining the latter form of work organisation. More recently trust in work relations has gained some attention, and the impression is created that this is a new phenomenon. However, trust has a long traditon in sectors of qualified employment. It only gained much greater importance with the expansion of all kinds of service work, the overall trend to work reskilling and the recent informatisation of production work.

5 The Distribution of Knowledge and Skills as a Foundation for the Formation of Trust Relations

5.1 Hierarchy and Knowledge Distribution

The way in which the labour process is organised and employee behaviour is controlled by management depends mainly on the nature of work: whether the definition of tasks and effort is part of the *job itself*, or the job is identical with the performance of *prescribed* qualitative and quantitative tasks. In the latter case employees are interested in the control of their work in order to create margins of action for themselves, in other words to control their working conditions against management´s access. (In the labour process debate this is dealt with under the heading „frontiers of control".) In the former case no explicit definitions of task execution exist, rather workers themselves define the outcome with their own standard of performance (being guided by generally stated aims; this is the essence of „management by objectives"). The outcome therefore depends highly on the employees´ competence and readiness to perform. In this case no limits exist regarding quantity and quality of work, because there is no other possibility to stand out against others and to prove one´s excellence. The resulting behaviour then is not an opposition *against* management but rather a definition of standards and aims *with* management.

Decisive for the form of work organisation and control is not the worker´s skill level per se, but the *distribution of skills* between levels in the hierarchy. This can be illustrated in a comparison between craft-based and modern functional work organisation. In organisational settings in which the manufacturing of goods and services is based on craft work the distribution of technical knowledge and know-how is hierarchically ordered. Here the master/supervisor generally has more skills of the *same* kind as the workers and therefore is able to competently judge their effort. The status organisation thus is *task continuous*. This type of work and status organisation, however, is completely *different* from the work organisation that is usually found in modern enterprises where management and workers, superiors and subordinates have skills and qualifications of a *different* kind. Knowledge and know-how thus are not vertically but laterally distributed, and work situations are characterised by a *task discontinuous status organisation* in which managerial authority and functional knowledge are separated. (The significance of this distinction was elaborated by C. Offe 1970.) Under such conditions the labour process cannot be technically controlled by rough bureaucratic structures.

In order to remain in „control" of the labour process in a *task discontinuous* work context *two* distinct *organisational concepts* which make sure that employees fulfil their duties adequately have been developed by management. The suitability of either one of the concepts largely depends on the kind of work which is needed to complete a task:

(1) If the way to manufacture goods or services is well known and invariant, the labour process is traditionally controlled by a „Taylorist" separation of conception and execution, supported in large industry by a „Fordist" arrangement of repetitive tasks to a work flow. Knowledge and know-how are centralised in specialised departments, the executing tasks are prescribed in great detail and the conduct of workers is monitored by specialised supervisors. Workers are reduced to mere labour power and the division of labour leads to many deskilled and fragmented jobs.

(2) The situation is completely different in organisational settings where the one best way to reach the officially defined aim is more or less unknown. In such an organisational setting work means to find ways to solve new problems. The completion of a task always includes a certain degree of self-organisation and discretion on the basis of personal knowledge and know-how. Even though work is divided into specialised functions, it is difficult or impossible to fragment it into standard repetitions, and qualification requirements remain high. Employees have methodological and procedural skills in common, they know how to proceed in problem solving. The technical knowledge which they have to apply in the different situations, on the other hand, varies widely. Complex problems can only be solved by *common effort*, by bringing together a variety of knowledge and expertise. Required here are informal ad hoc practices of intuition, interpretation, information, communication and adaption. Under such conditions the labour process cannot be organised simply from the top down by order and control; rather the information from the bottom up is more relevant for overall organisational efficiency (cf. e.g. N. Luhmann 1989).

The ascription of workers to one of the two work contexts tends to coincide *roughly* with the distinction between blue-collar and white-collar work although the distinction is not identical with the collar line. In as much as production work is confronted with high informatisation, as for example in the case of systems regulators, high trust becomes also a characteristic of the work situation of blue-collar workers. The work performance of systems regulators for example is no longer dominated by their chance to regulate stress and strain or financial compensation. Workers´ concern rather concentrates on work content and improvement of performance, if their expectations in autonomy and participation in the workplace are met. (For examples on such modern production work see M. Schumann 1992; see also the chapter 3 by M. Schumann et al. with the example of „systems regulators"). At the same time, certainly, not *all* white-collar work is knowledge based work. Parts which include less demanding tasks (auxiliary functions in retailing, offices etc.) tend to be regulated by low trust work relations. Our analytical distinction therefore basically coincides more precisely with the distinction between knowledge based and mere executing work and not with the collar line.

In situations where „intellective" skills (an expression by S. Zuboff 1988) and personal competence based on theoretical knowledge are essential, management generally does not have enough insight and is therefore unable to independently determine and control the labour process and its outcome. Management´s job here is not to prescribe work and to control workers *but to select and allocate personnel* — to put the right man/woman in the right place, to enable and motivate employees to communicate and cooperate, in other words to combine intelligently persons with different qualifications.

The phenomenon that personality traits and formal role requirements fall apart has often been described by organisation analysts as *tension between organisation and personality*. In earlier texts it was conceptualised as relation between formal structures and informal processes.

> From the standpoint of organisations as a formal system, persons are viewed functionally, in respect to their roles, as participants in assigned segments of the cooperate system. But in fact individuals have a propensity to resist depersonalisation, to spill over the boundaries of their segmentary roles, to participate as wholes (P. Selznick 1976, p. 263).

Organisations thus are cooperative systems which „are constituted of individuals interacting as wholes in relation to a formal system of coordination. The concrete structure is therefore a resultant of the reciprocal influences of the formal and informal aspects of organisation" (p. 267). On the basis of such considerations Selznick defines the *concept of organisation* as „a process of education, in which the winning of consent and support is conceived to be a basic function of leadership" (263).

Especially in knowledge based work sectors, uncertainty and unpredictability forces management to appeal to employees for their active cooperation. This leads in white-collar sectors to trust based work organisation. In blue-collar work there also exist segments of skilled work in which high trust work relations would be feasible. Traditional skilled workers, however, are embedded in a set of rules which are dominated by typical subcultural perception of antagonistic industrial relations, which prevent emergence of trust-based individualistic behaviour as a dominant form. If management here offers symbolic and material rewards and tries to motivate workers to take over responsibility, such bids are rejected in most cases by workers. Collective bargaining and interest representation by works councils and trade unions form thc frame of reference for labour relations and are indispensable for the blue-collar culture.

In skilled white-collar sectors on the contrary employees generally accept management´s offers and take over responsibility. In so doing they strengthen their position step by step with the effect that management becomes more and more dependent on their active support and cooperation. As a consequence we find

an enormous amount of vertical and horizontal interdependence among subunits which does establish practical and even fundamental common interests — such that all organisational actors share a common fate. This 'common fate' means that preferences overlap considerably, thereby mitigating extreme positions. But overlapping does not provide a specific identity; disagreement exists even when some goals are shared. And this condition gives rise to *precarious partnership or incomplete antagonism*" (R. Stout 1980, p. 109).

5.2 Resources of Bargaining Power in Organisations

It would be a mistake to overlook the fact that trust relations consist of power relations. Actors are only incorporated in trust relations who offer something relevant in exchange and who have sanctions at their disposal. Established stable trust relations in general represent an efficient social suprastructure which secures an adequate and accepted adjustment of interests. Employees only go back to the material foundations of trust, if they feel that relevant interests are disregarded. This always occurs if the norms and shared values are violated and the mutual consideration for rules of conduct and the idea of appropriate manners and attitudes is neglected (by management or competing groups). If members of the *high trust fraternity* feel that they are treated unjustly, they cancel the contract and renegotiate the terms of business.

Sources of power, thus, are at the core of trust relations. We can for the present identify four *sources of power* in organisation, which M. Crozier and E. Friedberg (1979) call „areas of uncertainty". Such conditions exist only for certain members of an organisation and can be used as resources in bargaining only by them. Sources of bargaining power are:

(1) the possession of a certain irreplaceable functional ability or specific knowledge and know-how;

(2) the control of relations between the organisation and the environment;

(3) communication and information between units and members of the organisation;

(4) the use of organisational rules. This last one is organisation related, whereas the first three are process related. It is a social construct which is mainly used as a response of the leadership to actions taken by employees. In the concept of Crozier and Friedberg rules are in principal used by management to control and eliminate the other „areas of uncertainty".

Against the predominant view of organisations as governed and totally controlled by hierarchy, Crozier and Friedberg accentuate the *interdependence* of organisation members. Thus they partly reverse the traditional perspective. In focusing on the real process of the production of goods and services they define *employees* as actors who are *in control* of the conditions of production. From this perspective formal hierarchies do not reflect the factual power structures. Rather the real power lies in the hands of the task performing staff.

This view, however, is certainly only partly true because management is in control of the *funds* of the organisation. Management controls the access of employees to the material and symbolic resources of the organisation: the assignment of interesting and demanding jobs, the award of prestige, the allocation of positions and the distribution of income. This allows managers to counteract and neutralise the influence of subordinates which they have as a consequence of their dominant role within the labour process. Because of this mutual dependence a *social exchange* takes place between management and employees. Social exchange is a specific form of exchange which does not respond with immediate rewards for behaviour. It rather is a necessary element of high trust systems which aims at rewarding desired behaviour in a middle- to long-term perspective. (The distinction between *social exchange* — typical for high trust relations — and *economic exchange* — typical for low trust relations — has been introduced by Blau 1974 and 1977.)

Up to this point we have dealt with the foundations of trust systems. In the following sections we shall describe, on the basis of our own empirical research (which has been undertaken in different functional departments of skilled white-collar work in large enterprises), some of the most relevant features of trust relations. Our statements derive mainly from interpretations of qualitative interviews with employees, managers at different levels, works councils and union representatives. In the meantime we have also received rather extensive feedback from practicioners of various companies.

6 Elements of High-Trust Work Systems

6.1 Trust Relationships, Responsible Autonomy, Work Performance and Working Time

A high degree of mutual trust manifests itself in a system of work organisation based on responsible autonomy. In this case employees are given room to take action and make decisions. As Zuboff (1988, p. 403) puts it: „The organising principle of such a workplace is based on the individual. People are held accountable for their particular jobs, and these jobs are treated as distinct elements that must be assembled in order to accomplish the work of the organisation." Employees are perfectly at liberty to diverge from the usual approach in their work, but they are expected to use their margin of manoeuvrability in a responsible manner and in line with the general company policy. Should difficulties and errors occur, this will in principle not be taken as evidence of personal insubordination, but instead as a result of unavoidable facts associated with the degree of difficulty of a given task. Should difficulties and errors become a frequent occurrence, this will first be blamed not on the person in question, but rather on the way in which the work was organised. Superiors and subordinates will then work *together* to seek out the causes and will change the circumstances which, in their view, were at the root of the problem.

In return for the trust shown, employees are expected to accept *responsibility*, to take initatives of their own and to show *personal commitment*. In order to demonstrate that they are worthy of the trust shown in them (in advance), employees do their utmost to carry out the duties entrusted to them in an independent manner. In the case of difficult duties of a labour-intensive and time-consuming nature, they will have to give their best and be prepared to work overtime. Such „demanding" and „energy-consuming" duties will not be shunned by white-collar staff; on the contrary, they will seek them out.[3] Such duties actually represent a real chance to prove one´s worth and to confirm one´s own place in the „high-trust community".

Accordingly, *hard work* in the skilled white-collar sector is viewed as entirely *positive*. It is the main means of stressing one´s wish for interesting and demanding duties. This alone often is enough to motivate good performance. In addition, it is a means of differentiation and an absolute prerequisite for making headway in one´s career, for promotion and for progressing up the social ladder. But good performance is no guarantee in itself of being considered for new duties and for promotion. Nevertheless, only those who deliver a good performance have any chance at all in that respect.

In jobs which attract a great deal of respect and are enjoyable to perform, physical demands, bodily exertion and mental concentration are not the first things to be considered by those who perform it. This is particularly true if the actual job offers *scope* for personal *development* and *identification*, if it compensates for the commitment shown in financial terms and if it involves chances of further skill development, promotion and career opportunities. This explains the success of the much used concept of *Management by Objectives* in areas of qualified activities, i.e the policy of targets, whereby it is not the working time that is fixed, but rather the work objectives. If a task attracts a great deal of recognition (from superiors and colleagues) and offers the possibility for occupational advancement in the long run, then even a job which at first glance offers meagre financial and symbolic returns is considered as attractive and onerous in the white-collar community.

In high trust systems for employees there is no question of defensive behaviour at work or of restraint in performance. On the contrary, „kindness" on the part of superiors in the form of allocation of uninteresting, unimpor-

[3] Such behaviour is part of the ambitious white-collar culture. It is well known in companies and shows in empirical research findings. Management tends to instrumentalise this behaviour for company goals, whereas works councillors and trade uninonists take a critical view of this and rather try to prevent it by formal regulations.

tant and tedious work is regarded as discrimination and punishment. If, indeed, this befalls any employee, he or she will no longer be seen by superiors and colleagues as qualified and significant member of the team. They will no longer be considered as equals and will not be taken seriously by others. Furthermore, if they are left completely in peace, then there is scarcely any reason to hope for a better future.

Performance policy is therefore one of the most important and explosive subjects in high trust systems. It is considered to be more or less good form among white-collar staff to „complain“ about the stringent demands and heavy pressure. This should not, however, be interpreted as a negative statement and as a criticism or a grievance. If a person says that he/she has a lot of work to do, this also means that the person is important, indispensable and significant. Moreover, an employee does not simply „complain“. If an employee really has too much work, then he or she must take the initiative and discuss it with a superior. If the employee then succeeds in convincing the superior that the grievance is justified, assistance will be forthcoming. But if someone complains about having too much work without being able to demonstrate that this is due to „objective“ factors, that person will quickly become known in white-collar circles as someone who is not up to the job.

Performance in the context of qualified white-collar jobs is often not clearly defined. It is very much dependent upon a process of negotiation, which is structured and regulated in policy terms by power relationships. It should, however, be borne in mind that employees implicated in this bargaining process are not always necessarily the weakest players at the start. The much maligned lack of transparency in the work context and the lack of clear rules governing performance also offer them a degree of protection. Qualified employees, in particular, call the shots in major „areas of uncertainty“ and can also derive benefits from this, if they are interested in doing so.

In principle, one may assume that a skilled white-collar employee has no greater interest in working overtime and weekends than a worker on the shop floor. But white-collar employees in responsible positions are always willing to be flexible about their working time, about overtime and about working at weekends, if they realise that this is really a necessity. This realisation is born out of the fact that the very way in which work is organised in their field of activities makes white-collar employees aware of their personal responsibility for getting their work done within the allotted time. The consequences of this feeling of responsibility is that white-collar employees often clash with the works council, which has its roots in the blue-collar sector of the workforce, if the question of fixed working hours and overtime comes up and if the works council wants to insist on rigid working hours and prevent overtime from being worked.

It should also be noted at this point that a white-collar employee who cannot manage to get his or her work done during „normal“ working hours is not necessarily considered particularly qualified by his or her superiors and colleagues. One of the things which a white-collar employee is expected to be capable of is organising his/her time in a way which means that work can be completed within the regular working hours.

It should be remembered that companies have no special interest in seeing their employees constantly overworked and putting in over-time, since this neither improves the „working climate“ nor does it help to generate quality work. If, nevertheless, it is more common for normal working hours to be exceeded in the white-collar sector than in the blue-collar sectors, this has its origin in the principles prevailing for work organisation in skilled white-collar functions, which limit staff flexibility. When, for instance, new staff are taken on, it is not a question of allocating a few individual tasks, but rather of reshaping whole specialised areas of work and of distributing duties within them. Thus, it is the way in which duties are apportioned, the way in which work is organised and the way in which social relations are constructed which prevent reaction to short-term fluctuations in the work load in the form of hiring more staff, transfers between areas and even redundancies.

Consequences of forms of work organisation which depend on acceptance of responsibility and trust are therefore:

(1) that there is no protection against high and even increasing demands in terms of performance;

(2) that there are areas of conflict which must be taken seriously, but which are nevertheless different from those areas of dispute dealt with by works councils and trade unions in low trust areas;

(3) that discussions consequently centre rather on the *cultural assessment*, the *image* and thus the associated *future prospects* of a job than the immediate relation between effort and payment.

We hold that disputes of this nature and the specific way in which they are settled will to an increasing extent influence developments in modern societies, whilst leaving the basic system of social relations intact.

6.2 Trust Relationships and Control over Work

The demand for trust implies doing away with forms of control which can be interpreted as expressions of mistrust. At the same time superiors, because of their responsibility for subordinates and their mistakes, must always be kept informed of, for instance, how a new member of the staff performs in the group or in the department. Much takes place at the microsociological and psychological level and will be perceived by superiors of this calibre as an increased challenge to themselves and occasionally as a heavy burden.

In addition, experience has shown that direct control of work performance to boost efficiency in qualified sectors of employment produces a strikingly opposite result, and that direct supervision of work is not advisable due to the social structure of jobs. Generalised supervision of skilled white-collar employees´ work via electronic data processing (EDP) systems would damage the recognised common standards for efficient organisation of work, disrupt social relations and question the relationship of trust. Skilled employees are very sensitive to close supervision and control. And they distinguish very carefully between technically necessary control and unjustified intervention. They are concerned with whether the person looking over their shoulder is interested in the progress of work or simply controls their conduct. (The difference between the *potential* and the *actual* use of personal monitoring via EDP is a finding mentioned frequently in recent studies of white-collar work.)

That is why management uses forms of supervision considered by the employees as legitimate, forms of supervision which are not directly related to persons, but rather to work. A system of supervision will be interpreted as being work-related if it ensures the correct and successful completion of a work process. Nowadays work is monitored mainly via the channels of cooperation between different workplaces and departments and largely through interactive data processing systems. Thus, supervision of work has abandoned the hierarchical approach and is now to be found in the *lateral* dimension (cf. U. Heisig 1988). In this way, it has become a central component of the work process and the relationships of cooperation between specialists. However, this form of supervision is frequently not perceived as such but is instead seen as a purpose-related exchange of information in which superiors are involved out of necessity.

Trust as a basis of work relations does *not* imply an *absence of control* (this would be called blind trust), to make sure. Control here is connected with a different logic, though, which in its basis implies the evaluation of trustworthiness. The traditional view on control in the labour process prevents from the beginning any adequate conceptualisation of the functioning of trust. The literature on organisation of the labour process for decades tended to emphasise almost exclusively the *dangers of misuse* of trust and delegated autonomy („empowerment“ in recent American management approaches) and undervalues the creative and productive potential.

Employees know, of course, that any system of supervision can be abused and a fear of such abuse is always present. The atmosphere of trust in relations between superiors and subordinates demonstrates, however, that such fears are not substantial. Fear presents no real threat because of the mutual trust. The fact that there are no direct, rigid control systems is, in addition, seen by *both* superiors and subordinates as an achievement. And, as long as an atmosphere of trust continues to work on an everyday basis, there will be no need for introducing controls. This treatment of „control“ demonstrates that control plays quite a different role in high trust and low trust work systems.

6.3 Trust Relationships and „Social Exchange“

Relationships of trust are reproduced every day, if they offer benefits to the persons and groups concerned. Once a link has been established and one of the parties involved has derived benefits from the relationship of social exchange, that party has an obligation to reciprocate and to ensure that the other side also benefits in return. Once the mutual interplay relationship has been established, a two-way process is set in motion, which leads to all parties involved benefitting more or less automatically in that it generates a system of mutual assistance. In addition, with the constant exchange of services, the *social bond* created by the social exchange between the parties is strengthend still further.

If then anyone falters within this structured context of action based on social relationships and fails to fulfil his obligations and return the favours received in one form or another, it is then up to the other party to take the initative in continuing friendly relations. Moreover, the person can quickly be accused of ingratitude. Since every voluntary service is accompanied by the expectation of a service in return, the very possibility of such an accusation is a social sanction, which in itself dissuades people from not meeting their obligations. An important point with these social exchange relationships is that through their very existence they have the immediate effect of indirectly bringing about coordination in terms of action. This is due to the ability of the „give-and-take" relationships to promote the establishment of conformity with social expectations via social approval and assistance. As soon as certain standards of conduct are widely recognised within a group, it is expected that they will be followed and this also means that value is attributed to conformity of behaviour. Conduct in line with expectations pays, because it will be rewarded via social approval. On the other hand, failure to live up to expectations or violation of those expectations goes unrewarded. The reaction to such behaviour will be social disapproval and condemnation.

The process of social exchange thus generates a strong measure of social pressure against practices deviating from the norm. Furthermore, this pressure only disappears if the deviant behaviour becomes recognised within a broader framework and meets with the approval of an increasing number of people. Once relations of trust and social exchange have been established, conformity follows almost automatically. The consequence of this is that the hierarchical structure in an organisation, which is based on relationships of trust, will function to a large extent without the need for direct sanctions and interference with the work process.

A social relationship based on give-and-take is accompanied by the expectation that good performance will be acknowledged. The simplest and least institutional form of reward is acknowledgement in the form of praise and criticism. Both, praise and criticism, constitute a direct confirmation of having been noticed. Employees expect a superior not to deck himself out with borrowed plumes but to appreciate the effort and success of his subordinates and to represent it to management.

Frequent praise, however, brings with it further pressure. Sooner or later, it must be transformed into comprehensible, material reward for the object of the praise. Here, there are three distinct possibilities. And, in all cases, a reward implies the allotment of increased trust in that

(1) anyone who has been singled out for a particular, difficult and demanding task is in a way placed on a pedestal;

(2) additional tribute is paid to the person in the form of better remuneration, better pay;

(3) the person is helped to rise through the ranks, thus acquiring more power and higher status.

6.4 Labour Relations and Interest Representation

Any social structure featuring relationships involving a high degree of trust aims at settling disputes that occur internally. If, however, the works council is brought in at any time, this is seen as an indication of failure of the relationships of trust. A qualified white-collar employee takes it for granted that he or she can solve any problems alone. If an employee has difficulties connected with work or has personal problems or worries, that person will first try to have a confidential talk with his or her superior. If the employee does not seek this of his own accord, the superior will as a rule be approached by colleagues about the „strange behaviour" of the employee and the superior will go and see him or her.

Immediate superiors in the white-collar sector are those who have a duty to represent the interests of staff under them *vis-à-vis* higher management. It is the superior´s job to protect them and to safeguard their interests. The superior is expected to get to the root of problems and to solve them *jointly* with the staff. Should a subordinate express an interest in a given issue (e.g. flexible working time, higher pay, in-company further training etc.), the superior must take the matter up, consider it and then refer it to „upstairs" or the appropriate department within the company. In addition, staff expect their superior to act decisively on their behalf and to safeguard their interests in dealing with the company management and with other managerial staff from other specialist divisions. If, in the eyes of the staff, a superior is felt to be not fulfilling this obligation or not adequately, then it is perfectly legitimate for them to involve a higher level (as a rule, this will be the departmental manager immediately above), the personnel department or a neutral assembly such as the works council.

However, it does not look good for a departmental supervisor to be bypassed by the staff, who turn frequently to the next level of management, the personnel department or even the works council. If this happens often, it will be apparent to everyone in the firm that this departmental supervisor is not living up to his or her obligations as prescribed in the established social order. The supervisor will be identified by superiors as not doing the job and in most cases will be replaced very soon. If, however, an individual employee in a department which otherwise functions well is constantly „running“ to the works council over „every little trifle“ and is constantly complaining, the backlash will be on that employee.

6.5 Limits to the Organisation of Trust

As a result of the shift in the hierarchical structure and the social stratification of different functions and areas of activity, we do *not* find a spirit of solidarity as an accepted part of the behavioural pattern among all employees in the white-collar sector. Rather we find discussions going on between different employees and groups of employees on cultural yardsticks and real competition over access to desirable workplaces in the different areas of employment where there are qualified demanding jobs, which are highly valued and therefore well paid.

Consequently, areas of activity where relationships of trust predominate are characterised *not* by harmony and the absence of disputes, but on the contrary by violent *micropolitical struggles* (cf. e.g. W. Küpper and G. Ortmann 1988 for the concept of micropolitics in work organisations). There are constant internal arguments over the yardsticks for evaluation of work, its worth and its inadequate remuneration.

Trust as an organisational principle makes for greater flexibility in terms of expectations and provides greater protection from disappointment. Employees must and can be more open with regard to their career strategies, for instance. But there is one thing that they must also learn and that is to deal with the vast und undiminishable vagueness concerning returns associated with this.

We cannot, however, ignore the overall limits on the extent to which relationships of trust can be organised. These are part of the *basic conditions* which quite simply have to be met and which are particularly necessary in connection with the establishment and maintainig of relations involving a high degree of trust: relative security of employment, a high level of social security, identification with the image of the product, cooperative approaches in the unions and corporate traditions. If these conditions are not met from the start or do not appear likely to be fullfilled in the near future, the chances of creating a „corporate culture“ based on trust are limited.

Qualified staff express an explicit interest in participation. They expect to be „involved“ as experts in the running of „projects“ designed to optimise everyday work routines or in the redesign of work processes and thus to be able to promote their ideas, interests and ambitions. Given this situation, it is clear that equal and confidential labour relationships will form across all lines of hierarchical demarcation. We may find a community where mutual trust prevails, where expertise is acknowledged and where collegial relations are nurtured. Thus, participation becomes a central ingredient in a relationship of trust as defined by employees.

The foundations for a workable system of trust relationships will, however, be rocked if one or more of the basic organisational conditions are damaged. This happens for example when

(1) employees are asked to sacrifice their professional future by doing work below their occupational level and below the level customary in a company without being offered any form of compensation;

(2) proving one´s worth through work and financial or symbolic rewards for effort is not possible;

(3) employees are not allowed to take part in the planning of their work and working conditions and have the impression of having no hope of influencing decisions made by the company management;

(4) the employees are neglected by their superiors and the management, receive little or no information and feel disappointed and deceived;

(5) superiors and management do not succeed in establishing a commonality of interests with qualified employees.

In such circumstances, there is little willingness to discuss individual disputes directly with one´s superior. In this case the works councils may become an important forum for qualified white-collar staff.

7 Trust Relations in Work Restructuring

The concentration of functional knowledge and know-how at the task performing level has relevant implications also for work restructuring. Superiors are generally aware that they cannot carry through technical and organisational changes *against* the will of their highly skilled subordinates. High trust social relations thus represent a *social infrastructure* which largely determines the way in which new technologies and new forms of work organisation can be implemented.

In a recent empirical research report on the introduction of microelectronically based production planning systems (PPS) M. Behr et al. (1991) found that apart from the very general expectations of management white-collar workers will in fact use the installed EDP-systems in *their* way to execute their tasks for which as a rule no detailed specifications for their use existed. Beyond that they found that available technologies in white-collar sectors can quite easily be undermined by competent actors through evasion and rejection (see also chapter 9 by P. Dubois et al. in this book). Thus, the efficient use of technologies depends much on individual willingness, active cooperation and support (which is different from the productive sector). The rationalisation of white-collar work therefore can only be successful, if conditions are created for employees´ own initiative and efforts. This will be accomplished best if the functional and social interests of qualified employees are taken into consideration.

This general problem gains in importance the more elaborated micro-electronically based work systems get. The more elaborate a system is, the more the likelihood that the general possibilities and the real degree of its application diverge. A complex EDP-system is consequently only as „good" — strictly speaking: as effective — as its users. End-users therefore have a considerable influence on what happens to the system. Their readiness to participate is therefore the key problem managers and EDP-promoters have to consider at all steps of the introduction and application of EDP-systems. And it is therefore in the interest of the EDP-promoters to come to an *agreement* with the end-users and to reach *consensus*. (In this respect the conditions in skilled white-collar office work differ decisively from those in direct production work.)

Acceptance of new technologies and cooperation of users within the labour process is, however, in most cases *not* reached by direct *active participation* and involvement of employees in the process of change. It is rather created by *prospective consideration* of employees´ interests by managers and rationalisation experts. Both have to take care that employees will accept the selected technology and implemented work organisation by considering their occupational aspirations and social interests starting at the level of job design.

To reach acceptance the protagonists of change first of all make sure that work restructuring will lead to (more) ambitious and (more) responsible jobs.

Ambitious qualified white-collar workers generally do not oppose technical and organisational change by overt resistance, outrage and collective action, even if their interests are not fully met. They rather try to correct negative effects by active cooperation, influence on superiors or individual obstruction. If, however, they often fail to influence management decisions and feel that their interests are arbitrarily violated, they ultimately quit and leave their unattractive job, their department, or even the firm behind. Another reaction is to quit internally, i.e. to withdraw commitment and to hold back effort.

The effect of this kind of *„hidden" resistance* is that „unattractive" departments or firms lose qualified personnel or respectively fail to attract new productive and motivated workers anymore. Those who remain reduce their achievements. This in the long run would lead to a decrease in productivity of the department and a deterioration in the quality of goods and services. If management wants to prevent or turn back the migration of qualified workers, it has to carry though measures which attract them (for an empirical example see the case in chapter 12 by Wolfgang Littek and Ulrich Heisig in this book).

8 Organisational Control via Promotion and Career Paths

Empirical evidence (from our own research as well as recent findings as reported in literature) shows that qualified employees prefer to work in departments or firms where work organisation is based on responsible autonomy, where work is challenging and their knowledge and know-how can be used. In order to meet these expectations, firms and departments need a functionally differentiated job structure and financial and social *incentives* in order to attract qualified workers. This allows management to reward efficient workers and to confirm and encourage personal commitment, cooperation and effort. If such material conditions do not exist, the readiness of skilled workers to engage in their jobs will gradually vanish.

Keeping this in mind one can easily identify *mobility chains* within enterprises, between firms and different industries in the course of which qualified employees move out of unattractive sectors of employment into sectors where their interests and aspirations are better met. Hence it is not collective action but rather *mobility* that forces management to take into account the subjective expectations of qualified employees.

Employees´ work performance and inter-job mobility are, as we have deduced, caused by organisational structures which closely tie personal status and income to the occupation of a certain work place. Within a firm all available tasks are evaluated and brought into a ranking system. This leads to the consequence that employees who wish to move upwards have to use these predefined job ladders in the internal labour market.

The internal position, status and income of employees, hence, are closely connected with the *task* in German firms (and Western firms in general). Over time, this moving step by step from low paid and less ambitious jobs to better paid and more ambitious ones creates some serious negative side effects: As jobs in certain departments and segments are valued lower than in other ones, the close link between status and task leads to the (unintended) consequence that the most active and efficient workers concentrate in sectors and departments where the value of tasks is high, whereas the less efficient, less skilled workers are found in unattractive sectors and departments. Motivated and efficient workers refuse to work there.

As a consequence the differences in productivity between different sectors and departments are significant, and they tend to grow over time. This is a consequence of the fact that status and influence of employees and departments are nearly identical with the official value system of the enterprise. Strong employees and departments thus can use *corporate culture* as a strategic resource within the firm´s public discourse und thus are able to tacitly carry through their interests in processes of change. In effect the already strong actors are almost always the winners of technical and organisational change.

By this process the *total effectiveness* of a company is strongly affected because the overall performance is hampered by the low productivity in the low performing sectors. Intentional change, however, is difficult to accomplish because to reverse the development would mean to completely reconstruct the company´s value system. This venture, however, is condemned to fail in most cases because those who are in control generally have no interest in restructuring a system from which they profit. (For an empirical case study on such disputes within a plant of a German automobile producer see H.-D. Gondek and U. Heisig 1991.) A redefinition of the value system in most cases only becomes feasible, if the legitimacy of dominant groups and coalitions is put into question by dramatic changes in the enviroment and by economic decline.

The actual lean production/lean management debate has made clear that the incentive structures of Japanese firms differ significantly from that of Western firms.[4] In the Japanese enterprise advancement and career are determined by a *personal* ranking „hierarchy". Here the status and income of workers is not tied to the work position which one occupies. Consequently, an internal labour market where workers can move upwards only by occupying more ambitious tasks does not exist. The *position* within the ranking „hierarchy" on the contrary *depends* exclusively on *personal criteria*, with the effect that employees of different status and pay may do, and in fact do, the same job. In Japanese firms, thus, quasi-permanent employees who originally started at the same level after a period of e.g. ten years are usually located at very different levels within the firm´s ranking „hierarchy". (This is unimaginable in German firms because it contradicts the existing value system and the rules of tariff agreements.)

In Japanese firms advancement and career are bound to persons and not to tasks. As personal income and status do not depend on the attractiveness of work and occupation of an ambitious workplace but rather on the readiness to move and the ability to fulfil any task, voluntary individual and group mobility is found in the Japanese firm throughout the whole work context. The most efficient employees and work groups are moved under mere functional aspects especially to areas and tasks where their special competence is needed most. As a consequence of the alternative incentive system the distribution of efficiency within the company is very different. The strong efficiency gap between low status and high status departments that characterises Western firms thus does not exist in Japanese enterprises. There is, indeed, no top performance in only some elitist departments but average high performance within all functionally relevant parts of the whole organisation. Thus the great manoeuvreabilty of labour power which is fostered by the ranking „hierarchy" significantly contributes to the overall good performance of the Japanese firm.

[4] Nowadays there is a vast literature on Japanese work organisation and the difference to Western companies. We draw our following arguments basically from Aoki 1990, also U. Jürgens 1992 (see also his chapter 11 in this book).

In contrast, in white-collar sectors of German firms the central means to control employee behaviour is the incentive structure which is closely bound to promotion within the job hierarchy. This leads, as pointed out, to the emergence of high performing and low performing sectors and therefore to strong productivity differentials and impairment of the overall productivity. Our rough comparison with the Japanese trust system shows that such negative effects can be prevented, if the incentive structure is constructed in an alternative way. This means that the starting point of business reorganisation and the strengthening of efficiency has to be the reorganisation of the incentive structure. The introduction of „Japanese" organisation principles thus cannot mean to establish „Japanese" work organisation but would rather require introduction of „Japanese" social relations, i.e. balanced mutual intercourse and remuneration of pure flexibility and cooperative behaviour.

9 Trust in Enterprises and Management Theory During the 1980s

Previously trust relations were, as we have explained above, emerging as a result of fortuitous practices. They were mainly based on *tacit* assumptions and practices. They were *informal* arrangements, which had (like the „indulgency patterns" D. Silverman 1978, p. 156, described in his reinterpretation of A. Gouldner´s wildcat strike study) „always been recognised by both sides as a non-negotiable issue, since even workers saw it to be of doubtful legitimacy and dependent on informal expectations which could not be revealed in public bargaining". Because of the unexplicated status of trust, struggles in white-collar sectors as well were nearly always fought over traditional issues like wages, working time and working conditions, even if the original reason for complaint was imbalance or disruption in the system of trust.

During the 1980s, however, trust relations gradually became recognised as efficient structures of social organisation and a key factor for the success of corporations (cf. T. Deal and A. Kennedy 1988; Th. Peters and R. Waterman 1982). Because of this, management then began to proclaim *„corporate culture"* and *„trust"* and layed down appropriate norms, values and rules of fairness as part of enterprises´ official policy. In this way management tried actively to *construct* trust relations and to use trust as a one-sided technique to manipulate employees´ behaviour.

In doing so, management obviously overlooked the fact that cooperation and consent cannot be commanded but that trust has to be *created* by polite mutual intercourse. (Even this is a very complex and long lasting undertaking.) Not realising this, corporate culture campaigns very often did nothing other than make the contradiction obvious between what managers said and what they actually did. The first thing managers had to learn in the early days of the campaign was that employees took promises literally and that words were measured by their actual deeds.

The process of implementing corporate culture was not without flaws, for in Germany at the same time an internationalisation of corporations and management took place. Many of the older top-managers were replaced by younger ones who were educated in a short-term American cash flow, hire and fire style. (Examples of the consequences of such changes are studied e.g. by H. Kotthoff 1992.) These new leaders were not handicapped as their predecessors by social considerations and feelings of responsibility and were not sensitive to the paternalistic traditions of *social relations* within German firms.

The temporary coincidence of these contradictory trends led to the strange effect that at the same time as corporate culture and high trust relations became recognised and offically proclaimed as effective ways to (re)organise social relations they were attacked by new „insensitive“ managers. This way the early corporate culture campaigns contributed considerably to the *explication of trust* as well as make employees more sensitive to the conditions of trust. Trust relations thus became more *institutionalised*.

The current situation within enterprises therefore is significantly different from the past, when employees had no chance to call for managements´ observance of the rules of trust. In as much as implications of trust were made more and more explicit, employees were able to refer to managements´ own principles. Employees in their fight for the continuation of trust relations today can explicitly refer to officially proclaimed norms and values; they can actively sue for their rights and bargain for the conditions of trust.

10 Economic Recession and the Future of Trust Relations

The transformation of trust relations seems to be accelerating and intensifying at present. This is due to the economic recession which hit Germany hard after the very first reunification boom (1990-1992) and the lasting problem of high unemployment and standing of a high-wages country in the world wide competition. The current crisis makes clear to all the urgent need for the restructuring of labour processes and social relations within enterprises and for restructuring the whole economy in both the eastern and western part of the country.

The pre-emptory diagnosis — nearly everybody agrees with — is that many enterprises and the national economy are too fat, too heavy and too expensive and that corporations as well as the ecomomic system have to become „leaner“ as fast as possible (cf. N. Piper 1993; K. Seitz 1993). In spite of the general consensus that restructuring has to be pushed ahead, specific issues of modernisation still constitute grounds for dispute among politicians, businessmen and trade unionists.

In the last three years the post-war compromise between capital and labour has been denounced. For the first time in the post-war period a collective wage agreement (in the East German metal and electrotechnical industry) was nullified unilaterally by the employers´ association in 1993 in the new eastern part, and later that year also in the old western States of the Federal Republic of Germany. By this, achievements reached during the 1980s in tariff agreements are put to disposition again. This concerns the general area-wide validity of agreements, working time and the arrangement of working hours, additional holiday and „Christmas“ payments (which often mean a thirteenth and sometimes even a fourteenth monthly payment), and the like. Moreover, at firm level voluntary extra payments, financial bonuses and social benefits have been cut or count towards the already settled increase of standard wages. In some cases these now are counted into the monthly wages (for example at Volkswagen, where this even has been reached in a compromise agreement between management and the IG Metall union). Large and prominent employers feel encouraged to unilaterally break the social consensus. Top managers obviously think that it is time to dismiss the idea of social obligation which the founders of German firms (like e.g. Robert Bosch and Werner Siemens) felt committed to and to risk once and for all the loss of social responsibility capital once had (cf. D. Lamparter 1993).

These developments indicate that in Germany at the moment a massive *struggle* over the distribution of the gains and losses is taking place, intensified by the repercussion of the unification process. Traditional living-standards of blue-collar and white-collar workers as well as the social security system are being called into question. In this context the federal government as well as employers´ associations are attempting to deregulate capital-labour relations, to reduce the area of application of collective agreements and to make them more flexible.

While at the macro-level political and ecomic struggles are taking place, management within firms is at the same time making great efforts to introduce lean production, lean management and lean administration structures. With decreasing demand, shrinking profits and reduction of personnel this is a rather complicated undertaking because management first of all needs the *active support* of qualified employees and trade unions in this process. Lean production concepts require a large amount of consent. By using the slogan: „less control, more trust" management makes propaganda for its campaign. But although management is explicitly speaking of cooperation and consent, it is, nevertheless, also pressing through tough organisational measures in the work context and is intervening aggressively in the social order. The actual process of restructuring is therefore characterised by two contradictory tendencies of consent in the pace and intensity of work on the one hand, and conflict over material rewards and working conditions on the other.

On the pretext of introducing lean production, lean management and lean administration German corporations have already begun to restructure the formal organisation of the manual and non-manual labour process. In order to reduce costs and to improve efficiency large, internationally well known firms (like Volkswagen, Mercedes Benz, Siemens or the Bosch-Group) are reducing personnel (in blue- and white-collar sectors), draw new distinctions between hierarchical and technical jobs and remove several levels of formal hierarchy.

The external observer at once gains the impression that management, while enforcing its rationalisation measures, is not handling social relations very sensitively. There is no recognition that the introduction of new formal structures will destroy historically evolved, functionally relevant social networks and informal structures which will be irretrievably lost. Management is obviously not pursuing a detailed plan but reacting to external constraints. Decisions are short-term and hasty and sometimes even contradict one another.

Management is muddling through volatile situations without knowing exactly what to do.

The rash, ill-considered introduction of „lean“ structures in many cases is *counter-productive* first of all because it undermines the system of trust by destroying two necessary elements of trust relations: informal bargaining procedures and the system of incentives and rewards.

At present top management in many large firms is eliminating hierachical layers and positions and thereby at the same time unintentionally removing established informal bargaining procedures. Thus, traditional cooperative structures (as described earlier for the typical trust relation) are *destroyed* and the mutual adjustment of interests is called into question. Thus top managers themselves undermine one central organisational precondition for the cooperative reality they want to establish by the introduction of lean organisation structures.

In addition, already existing trust relations are called into question by the reduction of incentives and rewards which to a certain degree are connected with hierarchical positions. The hierarchical construction of labour processes allowed for outstanding employees to be rewarded with a title or position. Promotion until now has been a widely accepted and welcomed remuneration for good performance and effort. As rungs of the career ladder are removed possibilities for reward are reduced.

Another consequence of the immediate reduction of hierarchical positions can be anticipated. Many individuals are personally downgraded as hierarchical positions are abolished. The demotion of former superiors (like departmental managers and group leaders) to simple employees („Sachbearbeiter“) will immediately lead to the demotivation of loyal and dedicated workers. Frustration will thus *irresistibly* spread among lower rank managers and hard-working employees who aimed at moving up the career ladder. For these employees the reduction of hierarchical positions calls into question their occupational ambitions and individual career perspectives.

The impulse to re-arrange relations of trust in nearly all cases comes from management which is unilaterally breaking the rules of the game. In effect struggles and quarrels and the need to redefine the rules of the high-trust game arise. Within many enterprises the question re-emerges of how cooperation and consent can be created in the future. This leads to a *transitory crisis* in the system of trust. The crisis will not be overcome before new informal or formal bargaining procedures and new methods of encouragement and praise are established. Without agreed upon modalities of interest regulation a sustainable and effective organisation cannot exist.

This unstable situation allows *works councils* and *trade unions* to become active players in the white-collar high trust game. Whereas the actual situation is rather favourable for works councils and trade unions, both institutions are, however, not very well prepared to seize the opportunity. Trade unionists and works councillors are themselves part of the traditional low-trust model of social relations if they feel and act as antagonists of capital. In most cases they are not willing to take over a new role within the system of trust. They have problems accepting the role of *referees* who ensure that the rules of the high-trust game are obeyed by participants and who mediate between opponents (cf. H. Kotthoff 1992; U. Heisig 1991, 1992). Playing this role would mean being part of a trust system.

Whereas in the traditional „antagonist" system unionists and works councillors execute the adjustment of interests for their members, in high trust systems employees act for themselves to push through their interests and try to come to an agreement with management. Under an established system of trust the function of union and works council representatives is to secure the maintenance of rules of fair play.

If works councils and trade unions do not succeed in taking advantage of the opportunity to actively participate in the definition of the rules of the new high trust game, disputes will sooner or later be settled without them because there is no better alternative in sight for coping with future challenges and uncertainties. In this case the new system of trust will of course certainly function again without them.

All the signs indicate that the „trust game" at the moment is undergoing a change which will lead to a new definition of the game. Concerning *participants*, the game so far has been played mainly between skilled white-collar workers and middle to top managers. With business reorganisation in the direction of lean production, flat hierarchies and „empowerment" of workers, the range of participants in high trust labour relations will presumably expand into production work. Due to the delegation of competence and responsibility to the shopfloor level, skilled blue-collar workers (e.g. the *systems regulators* described by Schumann et al. in chapter 3 in this book) will become incorporated into the game. Consequently, „antagonistic" perceptions, collective orientations and pugnacious strategies may play a more important role within the high trust game. On the other hand, business reorganisation which revalues operative functions against indirect administrative tasks threatens lower level and middle managers. In so far managerial functions of planning and control are transfered to workers, the position of those who carried out these tasks (and who have been a core group of the high trust fraternity) is weakened. To the extent that they are loosing their influential position a tendency towards stronger organisation in their particular interest representation groups could be expected (cf. M. Faust et al. 1994). This would also mean that for this group of players the style of conducting the game would be changed. Although high trust relations will increasingly constitute the basis of social relations in work organisation, the range of variations in playing the game will be widened.

References

Aoki, Masahiko (1990), *Information, Incentives, and Bargaining in the Japanese Economy*. Cambridge, Cambridge University Press.

Baethge, Martin and Herbert Oberbeck (1986), *Zukunft der Angestellten*. Frankfurt/Main and New York, Campus.

Behr, Michael, Martin Heidenreich, Gert Schmidt and Hans-Alexander Graf von Schwerin (1991), *Neue Technologien in der Industrieverwaltung*. Opladen, Westdeutscher Verlag.

Berger, Ulrike (1984), *Wachstum und Rationalisierung der industriellen Dienstleistungsarbeit*. Frankfurt/Main and New York, Campus.

Birke, Martin and Michael Schwarz (1990), Betrieb als arbeitspolitische Arena der Arbeits- und Technikgestaltung, in *Soziale Welt*, Vol. 41, No. 2: 167-182.

Blau, Peter M. (1974), *On the Nature of Organizations*. New York, Wiley & Sons.

Blau, Peter M. (1977), *Inequality and Heterogeneity*. New York and London, Free Press and Macmillan.

Braverman, Harry (1974), *Labor and Monopol Capital*. New York and London, Monthly Review Press.

Burawoy, Michael (1979), *Manufacturing Consent*. Chicago, University of Chicago Press.

Burawoy, Michael (1985), *The Politics of Production*. London, Verso.

Burawoy, Michael and Erik Olin Wright (1990), Coercion and Consent in Contested Exchange, in *Politics and Society*, Vol. 18 , No. 2: 251-266.

Burris, Val (1986), The Discovery of the New Middle Class, in: *Theory and Society*, Vol. 15, No. 3: 317-349.

Coleman, James S. (1983), Systems of Trust. A Rough Theoretical Framework, in *Angewandte Sozialforschung*, Vol. 10 , No. 3: 277-300.

Coleman, James S. (1990), *Foundations of Social Theory*. Cambridge/Mass. and London, The Belknap Press of Harvard University Press.

Crozier, Michel and Erhard Friedberg (1979), *Macht und Organisation*. Kronberg/Ts., Athenäum (French original: *L'Acteur et le Systéme*, Paris, Edition du Seuil 1977).

Deal, Terrence and Allen Kennedy (1988), *Corporate Cultures*. London and Harmondsworth, Penguin.

Faust, Michael, Peter Jauch and Christoph Deutschmann (1994), Mittlere und untere Vorgesetzte in der Industrie: Opfer der „schlanken Produktion"? In *Industrielle Beziehungen*, Vol. 1, No. 2: 107-131.

Fox, Alan (1974), *Beyond Contract. Work, Power and Trust Relations*. London, Faber & Faber.

Friedman, Andrew (1977), *Industry and Labour. Class Struggle at Work and Monopoly Capitalism*. London and Basingstoke, Macmillan.

Gambetta, Diego (ed.- 1988), *Trust. Making and Breaking Cooperative Relationships*. Oxford, Cambridge/Mass., Basil Blackwell.

Giddens, Anthony (1979), *Central Problems in Social Theory*. London, Basingstoke, Macmillan.

Giddens, Anthony (1990), *The Consequences of Modernity*. Cambridge, Polity Press.

Goldthorpe, John (1982), On the Service Class, its Formation and Future, in Giddens, Anthony and Gavin MacKenzie (eds.), *Social Class and the Division of Labour*. Cambridge, Cambridge University Press.

Gondek, Hans-Dieter and Ulrich Heisig (1991), Kulturelle Bewertungsmuster im Konflikt (am Beispiel von Ingenieurstätigkeiten), in Littek, Wolfgang, Ulrich Heisig and Hans-Dieter Gondek (eds. — 1991), *Dienstleistungsarbeit*. Berlin, Edition Sigma: 167-186.

Gondek, Hans-Dieter, Ulrich Heisig and Wolfgang Littek (1992), Vertrauen als Organisationsprinzip, in Littek, Wolfgang, Ulrich Heisig and Hans-Dieter Gondek (eds.), *Organisation von Dienstleistungsarbeit*. Berlin, Edition Sigma: 33-56.

Granovetter, Mark and Charles Tilly (1988), Inequality and Labour Process, in Smelser, Neil J. (ed.), *Handbook of Sociology*. Newbury Park, Sage: 175-222.

Hans-Böckler Stiftung and Industriegewerkschaft Metall (eds.- 1992), *Lean Production. Kern einer neuen Unternehmenskultur und einer innovativen und sozialen Arbeitsorganisation?* Baden-Baden, Nomos.

Heidenreich, Martin (1992), Informatisierungspolitiken und nationale Angestelltenkulturen, in Littek, Wolfgang, Ulrich Heisig and Hans-Dieter Gondek (eds.), *Organisation von Dienstleistungsarbeit*. Berlin, Edition Sigma: 263-287.

Heisig, Ulrich (1988), Organisational Change, New Technologies and the Development of Control. Paper presented at the 6th ASTON/UMIST Labour Process Conference on „Organisation and Control of the Labour Process", Aston University, Birmingham, 23-25 March, mimeo., Bremen.

Heisig, Ulrich (1989), *Verantwortung und Vertrauen im Großbetrieb*. Konstanz, Wisslit.

Heisig, Ulrich (1991), Angestellte und gewerkschaftliche Interessenvertretung. Ansätze zur Neudefinition eines problematischen Verhältnisses. (Representing Employee and Trade Union Interests. Efforts to Redefine a Problematic Situation.) Paper presented at the EURO-FIET „Industrial Employees" Committee meeting, Bad Kreuznach, 29-30 April, mimeo. Erlangen 1991/Geneva 1992.

Heisig, Ulrich (1992), Vertrauensbeziehungen und Interessenvertretung im Angestelltenbereich, in Bleicher, Siegfried and Eberhard Fehrmann (eds.), *Autonomie und Organisation*. Hamburg, VSA: 119-142.

Heisig, Ulrich and Wolfgang Littek (1989), Technological Change and Informal Participation: The Role of Competence and Control in Administrative Work, in Széll, György, Paul Blyton and Chris Cornforth (eds.), *The State, Trade Unions and Self-Management*. Berlin and New York, de Gruyter: 235-252.

Heisig, Ulrich and Wolfgang Littek (1995), Wandel von Vertrauensbeziehungen im Arbeitsprozeß, in *Soziale Welt*, Vol. 46, No. 3.

Hildebrandt, Eckart and Rüdiger Seltz (1989), *Wandel betrieblicher Sozialverfassung durch systemische Kontrolle*. Berlin, Edition Sigma.

Jürgens, Ulrich (1992), Lean Production in Japan: Mythos und Realität, in Institut für Arbeit und Technik, in IG Metall, Fraunhofer-Institut für Arbeitswissenschaft and Hans-Böckler-Stiftung (eds.), *Lean Production, schlanke Produktion*. Düsseldorf, Hans-Böckler-Stiftung: 25-34.

Kern, Horst and Michael Schumann, *Das Ende der Arbeitsteilung?* Munich, Beck.

Kotthoff, Hermann (1992), Qualifizierte Angestellte in high-tech Betrieben erobern den Betriebsrat, in Littek, Wolfgang, Ulrich Heisig and Hans-Dieter Gondek (eds.), *Organisation von Dienstleistungsarbeit*. Berlin, Edition Sigma: 179-200.

Küpper, Willi and Günther Ortmann (eds.- 1988), *Mikropolitik*. Opladen, Westdeutscher Verlag.

Lamparter, Dietmar H. (1993), Der Nimbus geht verloren, in *Die Zeit*, No. 15: 23.

Lane, Christel (1989), *Management and Labour in Europe*. Oxford, Basil Blackwell.

Lane, Christel (1992), Technologischer Wandel und kaufmännische Angestelltenarbeit in Großbritannien, in Littek, Wolfgang, Ulrich Heisig and Hans-Dieter Gondek (eds.), *Organisation von Dienstleistungsarbeit*. Berlin, Edition Sigma: 201-218.

Littek, Wolfgang (1986), Rationalisation, Technical Change and Employee Reactions, in Purcell, Kate, Stephen Wood, Alan Waton and Sheila Allen (eds.), *The Changing Experience of Employment*. Hounsmills, Basingstoke, Macmillan: 156-172.

Littek, Wolfgang (1991), Was ist Dienstleistungsarbeit? In Littek, Wolfgang, Ulrich Heisig and Hans-Dieter Gondek (eds.), *Dienstleistungsarbeit*. Edition Sigma, Berlin: 265-282.

Littek, Wolfgang (1992), Service Sector/Service Work, in Széll, György (ed.), *Concise Encyclopaedia of Participation and Co-Management*. Berlin and New York, de Gruyter: 743-755.

Littek, Wolfgang and Ulrich Heisig (1986), Rationalisierung von Arbeit als Aushandlungsprozeß, in *Soziale Welt*, Vol. 37, No. 2/3: 237-262.

Littek, Wolfgang and Ulrich Heisig (1990), Work Organisation under Technological Change: Sources of Differentiation and the Reproduction of Social Inequality in Processes of Change, in Clegg, Stewart R. (ed.), *Organisation Theory and Class Analysis*. Berlin and New York, de Gruyter: 299-314.

Littek, Wolfgang and Ulrich Heisig (1991), Competence, Control, and Work Redesign. Die Angestellten in the Federal Republic of Germany, in *Work and Occupations*, Vol. 18, No. 1: 4-24.

Littek, Wolfgang and Ulrich Heisig (1995, forthoming), *Soziologie der Dienstleistungsarbeit*. Stuttgart, Enke.

Littek, Wolfgang, Ulrich Heisig and Hans-Dieter Gondek (eds.- 1991), *Dienstleistungsarbeit. Strukturveränderungen, Beschäftigungsbedingungen und Interessenlagen*. Berlin, Edition Sigma.

Littek, Wolfgang, Ulrich Heisig and Hans-Dieter Gondek (eds.- 1992), *Organisation von Dienstleistungsarbeit*. Berlin, Edition Sigma.

Luhmann, Niklas (1988), Familiarity, Confidence, Trust: Problems and Alternatives, in Gambetta, Diego (ed.), *Trust*. Oxford, Cambridge/Mass., Basil Blackwell: 94-108.

Luhmann, Niklas (1989), *Vertrauen*. Stuttgart, Enke.

Molldaschl, Manfred (1992), Japanisierung der deutschen Industrie?, in WiSo-Führungskräfte-Akademie Nürnberg (ed.), *Lean-Management. Ideen für die Praxis. Erlangen*, Druckhaus Mayer: 35-74.

Offe, Claus (1970), *Leistungsprinzip und industrielle Arbeit*. Frankfurt/Main, Cologne, Europäische Verlagsanstalt.

Peters, Thomas J. and Robert H. Waterman (1982), *In Search of Excellence*. Harper & Row.

Peters, Tom (1992), *Liberation Management*. Alfred A. Knopf.

Piper, Nikolaus (1993), Zu dick, zu schwer, zu teuer, in *Die Zeit*, No. 12: 28.

Pirker, Theo (1991), Industriesoziologie, Büroforschung und die Kategorie der Arbeitsteilung, in Weiner, Rainer (ed.), *Theo Pirker — Soziologie als Politik*. Berlin, Schelzky & Jeep: 184-205.

Roche, William K. (1991), Trust Dynamics and Organisational Integration: the Micro-sociology of Alan Fox, in *British Journal of Sociology*, Vol. 42, No 1: 95-114.

Sabel, Charles (1991), Moebius-Strip Organisations and Open Labour Markets, in Bourdieu, Pierre and James S. Coleman (eds.), *Social Theory for a Changing Society*. Boulder, San Francisco, Oxford, Westview Press: 23-62.

Sabel, Charles (1992), Studied Trust: Building New Forms of Co-operation in a Volatile Economy, in Pyke, Frank and Werner Sengenberger (eds.), *Industrial Districts and Local Economic Regeneration*. Geneva, International Institute of Labor Studies: 215-250

Schienstock, Gerd (1991), Struktur, Politik oder soziale Praxis, in *Österreichische Zeitschrift für Soziologie*, Vol. 16., No. 2: 27-40.

Schumann, Michael (1993), Gruppenarbeit und neue Produktionskonzepte, in Binkelmann, Peter, Hans-Joachim Bracyk and Rüdiger Seltz (eds.), *Entwicklungen der Gruppenarbeit in Deutschland*. Frankfurt/Main and New York, Campus: 186-203.

Schumann, Michael (1992), Lean Production — kein Erfolgsrezept, in Institut für Arbeit und Technik, IG Metall, Fraunhofer-Institut für Arbeitswissenschaft and Hans-Böckler-Stiftung (eds.), *Lean Production, schlanke Produktion*. Düsseldorf, Hans-Böckler-Stiftung: 35-42.

Schumann, Michael, Volker Baethge-Kinsky, Martin Kuhlmann, Constanze Kurz and Uwe Neumann (1994), *Trendreport Rationalisierung: Automobilindustrie, Werkzeugmaschinenbau, chemische Industrie*. Berlin, Edition Sigma.

Seitz, Konrad (1993), Fortschritt fängt im Kopf an, in *Die Zeit*, No. 20: 23.

Selznick, Phillip (1976), Foundations of the Theory of Organisations, in Emery, F.E. (ed.), *Systems Thinking*. Harmondsworth, Penguin: 261-280.

Shapiro, Susan P. (1987), The Special Control of Impersonal Trust, in *American Journal of Sociology*, Vol. 93, No. 3: 623-658.

Silverman, David (1978), *The Theory of Organisations*. London, Heinemann.

Smith, Vicki (1990), *Managing in the Corporate Interest*. Berkeley, Los Angeles, Oxford, University of California Press.

Stout, Russel jr. (1980), *Management or Control? Bloomington and London*, Indiana University Press.

Taylor, Frederick W. (1911), *The Principles of Scientific Management*. New York, Harper & Row.

Wolf, Harald, Otfried Mickler and Fred Manske (1992), *Eingriffe in Kopfarbeit*. Berlin, Edition Sigma.

Womack, James P., Daniel T. Jones and Daniel Roos (1990), *The Machine that Changed the World*. New York, Rawson Associates (German edition: *Die zweite Revolution in der Autoindustrie*, Frankfurt/Main, New York, Campus 1991).

Zuboff, Shoshana (1988), *In the Age of the Smart Machine*. New York, Basic Books.

Zündorf, Lutz (1987), Einfluß, Vertrauen und Verständigung, in Seltz, Rüdiger, Ulrich Mill and Eckard Hildebrandt (eds.), *Organisation als soziales System*. Berlin, Edition Sigma: 33-56.

Chapter 2
Meta-Corporations and Open Labor Markets: Some Consequences of the Reintegration of Conception and Execution in a Volatile Economy

Charles Sabel[*]

Contents

1 The Vicissitudes of the Sociology of Work

Not so long ago, but in an easily forgotten time, the sociology of work was often seen as an academic master key to understanding industrial society. Grasp of the controlling logic of higher throughput, capital intensive and intricately connected production systems was thought a necessary and sufficient condition for understanding the changing organization of work and the corpo-

[*] This contribution was previously published in a sligthtly different version in Pierre Bourdieu and James Coleman, eds. (1991), *Social Theory for a Changing Society*. Boulder, Westview Press.
In writing this paper I have profited from discussions with Fabrizio Barca, Joshua Cohen, James Coleman, Ronald Dore, Gary Herrigel, Carlo Jaeger, Horst Kern, Richard Locke, Toshihiro Nishiguchi, Arthur L. Stinchcombe, Jonathan Zeitlin, and, especially, Michael Piore. The usual exculpations apply, although my debts are greater than usual.

ration, and their effects — reformist or revolutionary, according to the angle of analysis — on the way managers, workers, and trade unions of various kinds formulated their respective claims to authority. So pervasive was the belief in the connection between a determinate logic of technological progress on the one hand and organizational change and self-understanding on the other that business historians canonizing the rise of a new science of corporate management and Marxists conjecturing the emergence of collective revolutionary subjects — now skilled, now unskilled — in the very same corporations understood that they were speaking differently accented a version of a single lingua franca.[1]

Today that lingua franca is fast becoming a dead language, and for obvious reasons. Technology is commonly regarded as permissive rather than constraining: as much a tool for the realization of changing human ends as a machine imposing its rhythms on its tenders. Corporations, buffeted by markets which have become more volatile in part because technology is proving so malleable, are desperately trying to reduce their risks by transforming dedicated or special-purpose resources into general-purpose ones — whenever, that is, they cannot simply transform fixed into variable costs. In the process they are inventing organizational forms whose complexity and mutability often threaten to overwhelm those who design and execute them, as well as the sociologists and economists who struggle to understand their constitutional principles. „Work" now refers to such disparate and rapidly changing experiences that it is at least as reasonable to treat the word as a popular shorthand for the struggle for survival as to regard it as a category of activity which gives similar contours to our different understandings of life.

There have been two contrary responses to the breakdown of the linguistic whole. One is an effort to articulate separate languages for understanding at least some of the pieces. These investigations of diverse technological trajectories, patterns of work, and forms of corporate governance often produce a

[1] The most comprehensive version of the thesis that the rationalization of work deskilled almost all those active in production is Harry Braverman (1974). For a view of continuous-process control workers as potential revolutionaries, see Serge Mallet (1963). For the view that the acquisition of new skills by such workers will lead to novel forms of cooperation with management rather than conflict, see Robert A. Blauner (1964). For a history of the modern corporation consistent with the assumptions regarding technological development underpinning these first two works, see Alfred D. Chandler (1977).

vertiginous experience of diversity as the constitutive fact of social life.[2] Caricatured, the view is that societies consist of contradictory institutions whose historically specific heterogeneity is a precondition for survival in a changing environment. Context and contingency — national, local, or corporate — suddenly explain most things in a world with no grand rhythm or reason.

The second response is the search for new generalities amidst the apparent ruins of the old. The task here is to understand which parts of — and to whose benefit — the mass-production system and the vast areas of state and quasi-public institutions on which it rested would have to change in order to accommodate the demands of any of the many variously probable economic and political environments. This response can end in the intoxicating vision of a world not gone to pieces but rather stood on its head. In this view, universal materializing machines replace product-specific capital goods; small and effortlessly recombinable units of production replace the hierarchies of the mass-production corporation; and the exercise of autonomy required by both the machines and the new organizations produces a new model producer whose view of life confounds the distinction between the entrepreneurial manager and the socialist worker-owner.[3] Contingency and context determine only whether and in what precise way particular nations, regions, or firms manage the necessary handstands.

The aim of this essay is to adumbrate a sociology of work or production which does justice to the prudent version of these caricatures: to account, that is, for the diversity and similarity of efforts to adjust to the new competitive environment. It advances two principal arguments. The first is that a strategy of responding to turbulent markets by deploying general-purpose resources (or, in an equivalent formulation, the reintegration of conception and execution) must itself be hedged and complemented by deployment of less flexible ones. It is the shifting relation between the core strategy and its hedges and complements, the argument runs, which creates the impression of unruly va-

[2] Two excellent studies which illustrate this tendency are Bryn Jones (1990: pp. 293-309) and Robert Salais and Michael Storper (1990).

[3] Michael Piore and I have been cited enough as victims of this fantasy so that I would not dream of pointing the finger at someone else. Although many persons hold some part of the views caricatured in the text, no one, ourselves included, comes close to holding them all. But see Michael J. Piore and Charles F. Sabel (1984) and judge for yourself.

riety. One consequence of these risk redistribution strategies is the emergence of production structures which blur hierarchical distinctions within firms, the boundaries between them, and the boundary between firms in a particular area and the public and private institutions of the local society. I will call such production structures *meta-corporations* or *moebius-strip* organizations (section two): meta-corporations because they are designed to be easily redesigned[4] and moebius-strip organizations because, as with a looped ribbon twisted once, it is impossible to distinguish their insides from their outsides. Another consequence is a constant reordering of versatile and rigid technologies which reflects, among other things, guesses about the longevity of the parts of a product in relation to the whole as well as uncertainty about those guesses (section three).

The second argument concerns the effects of these organizational and technological ambiguities on the labor market. The claim is that the spread of the new production structures creates demand for skilled labor while undermining the fixity of any particular job. Workers under these circumstances must acquire skills, including the ability to cooperate in particular settings in order to be employable, yet cannot rely on long-term relations with any single employer. To learn what they need to learn in order to move from job to job in an economy in which boundaries between firms and between firms and society are blurring, they must join various networks that cross company lines and reach from the economy into social and family life. I will call this situation an *open labor market* to distinguish it from craft labor markets, which are based on traditional connections to particular materials or process, and the internal labor markets of mass-production industry, which are based on long-term employment in clearly bounded corporations. Because of Groucho Marx´s notorious fascination with ambivalent attractions, I will refer to the employers´ experience of open labor markets as the creation of *Groucho Marx identities* (section four).

So great are the mutual benefits of flexibility in the world of fluid organizations and open labor markets which I am about to describe that it may almost seem as if coercion in any form has no place within it. But flexibility of course creates or depends on vulnerability of the most diverse kinds, and vulnerability invites the exercise of power by the less vulnerable. Nor is there

[4] For an early discussion of institutions with related cababilities, see Arthur L. Stinchcombe (1965: pp. 34-35).

any reason to think that those excluded from the emergent flexible economies will accept exclusion without a fight. In the conclusion (section five), therefore, I underscore the novel aspects of conflicts within the new economy and between its beneficiaries and others — above all, the significance of the radical disjuncture between these two kinds of struggle.

2 The Meta-Corporation: Reconciling Learning and Monitoring

This section begins with a sketch of a new form of organization which hedges its risks not through portfolio diversification into unrelated activities, but by learning to move rapidly from declining markets or market segments to prosperous ones in the same or related industries. The precondition of this strategy is increased internal flexibility, and its consequence is the opening of the borders between corporations and between the economy and local society. But flexibility and openness create new problems of coordination. The second part of the section, therefore, argues that responses to these vulnerabilities are consistent with the reintegration of conception and execution, and depend on overcoming the distinction — traditional in theories of organization or the firm — between learning and monitoring or trust and control. For reasons of space, I limit discussion in this section to large firms in the manufacturing sector.[5] But the argument developed here applies to large service-sector

[5] When not otherwise indicated, the following composite account of the meta-corporation is based on interviews with managers in more than thirty American, French, Italian, Japanese, Swedish, Swiss, and West German multinationals between 1985 and 1990. The firms are leaders of the automobile, automotive parts, computers, chemical, electrical equipment, food-processing, garment, machine-tool, opto-electric, telecommunications, and textile machinery industries. Interviews with capital-goods manufacters in Baden-Württemberg (conducted with Gary Herrigel) in July 1986, with American and West German automobile and automotive parts manufacturers (conducted with Herrigel and Horst Kern) in January and July-August 1989, as well as with managers of a large Italian manufacturer of men's and women's clothing (with Richard Locke) between 1988 and 1990 were especially important in forming my views. For more on the firms surveyed and the results, see e.g. Horst Kern and Charles F. Sabel (1991: pp. 144-166). Many of the features of the meta-corporation have been described at length in the management literature. For representative references, see Charles F. Sabel (1989: fn. 65). Of the many recent portraits of large-firm reorganization, including decentralization of

firms, particularly in the banking, insurance, and retail merchandising.[6] Nor is it vitiated by the current wave of mergers and acquisitions. On the contrary: incomplete as it is, the evidence to date suggests that in the United States, at least, the redeployment of assets expidites the redistribution of operating authority described below.[7] Elsewhere I have presented convergent arguments regarding the organization of small- and medium-sized firms.

2.1 Market Fragmentation and the Logic of Development Costs

Imagine a world in which technology and consumer tastes are in continual but not spasmodic flux. Consumers are always wanting new kinds of cars, but are unlikely to abandon them all in favor of bicycles. Products and processes constantly appear which are superior to current ones in many ways; but it is rare for the improvements to be so great that existing goods simply lose all utility. Consumers are willing to pay a premium above the price for standard goods for differentiated products which satisfy their particular wants. Implicitly they evaluate their purchases as would users of investment goods: not by considering absolute cost, but by comparing the ratio of price to performance, understood precisely as the capacity to meet particular wants. Because of advances in flexible process technologies, it is possible to reduce the cost differential between standard and specialized goods so much that increasing

authority to quasi-independent units with responsibility for particular product lines or markets, intensified collaboration with outside suppliers, elimination of staff or its reintegration with line operations, one of the best is „Small Earthquake: IBM Slightly Hurt," which appeared in the *Financial Times* in installments on April 24, 25, 27, and May 2, 1990.

6 For restructuring in the service industry, see Martin Baethge and Herbert Oberbeck (1986), Thomas Bailey (1989), Lauren Benton et al. (1989), and Larry Hirschhorn (1988).

7 A recent and comprehensive study finds, first, that acquirers of the unbundled assets of firms which are taken over are already expert in the use of the assets they are buying. This suggests that companies are concentrating their efforts in particular lines of production, not diversifying risk through aquisition of unrelated businesses. The study finds, second, that the new owner companies tend to close the headquarters of firms they acquire and to lay off white-collar, but not blue-collar, workers. This suggests that the acquirer´s aim is to eliminate bureaucracy in general and to push responsibility for decisions down to the operating units in particular. Third, whereas headquarters are closed, production facilities are not. This suggests that the acquirer is not seeking to achieve economies of scale in production through consideration of plants. See Sanjai Bhagat et al. (1990).

numbers of investment-minded consumers are willing and able to pay the premium for the latter. As they do so they reduce the market for standard goods, raising costs to mass producers and forcing them ultimately to find ways to differentiate their own products — thus aiding in the improvement of flexible process technologies, further reducing the cost differential for customized goods, and setting the stage for further repetitions of the cycle.

In a world of stable markets, firms use dedicated or product specific resources — special-purpose machines and semi-skilled workers — to mass produce standard goods. Their chief problem is the amortization of the fixed costs of these resources. But under the circumstances just described, the corporation´s chief problem is the reduction of development time and costs.[8] By assumption, product runs are short, and physical investment goods (as opposed to the computer programs which often control them) can be reused because their flexibility dramatically reduces retooling expenses. Hence development costs are a rapidly increasing share of production costs. By the same assumption, goods are only marketable for a short period before successor products reduce their value. By any comprehensive accounting measure, therefore, it is pointless to reduce development costs unless development times can be reduced as well.

To reduce the burden of development costs it is necessary to reintegrate the conception and execution of production plans in the sense of redefining both as joint problems which must be solved simultaneously. Designs are only commercially viable if they facilitate manufacture at acceptable costs; profitable investment in small-batch manufacturing depends on an understanding of design sufficient to make well-informed estimates of the range of flexibility required to produce several generations of a product in all its variants. Because the problems are linked in this way, solutions to one suggest solutions to the other, and the expense of solving the joint problem can be reduced. From this it follows that „conception" and „execution" must be concurrent rather than sequential activities, with efforts to realize plans leading to their refinement, and these refinements facilitating their realization. Development costs and time can thus be simultaneously reduced because the same process which makes possible more efficient use of underutilized expertise also speeds its flow. A good illustration of these principles is the production of

[8] In a recent survey, some 400 chief executives of U.S. companies cited „shortened product-development cycles" as their first priority. See N.R. Kleinfield (1990: pp. 1-6).

low-budget, or, as they are called in the trade, fast-track, Hollywood films. Shooting often begins before the screenplay is complete; each day´s work on the set advances the story line for the next. In the mid-1980s, average development time for a new car was 48.2 months in Japanese producers, and 60.4 months for American car makers. Development work in Japanese automobile firms proceeds analogously.

At the limit, the drive to reduce development costs will lead to a blurring of the boundaries between, and the hierarchical distinctions within, firms. The first step is the administrative decentralization of the corporation. Responsibility for design, manufacture and sale of a narrowly defined range of products (small copiers, headlights as opposed to tail lights, large turbines, etc.) is assigned to quasi-independent operating units. The corporation often becomes in effect a holding company which makes strategic decisions, raises capital, allocates it among the operating units, and periodically monitors their general performance. By rotating promising managers through different kinds of jobs in different operating units, headquarters also forms a corporate elite which understands the needs of the concern as a whole. The corporate planning, accounting, research, and technical staffs are cut to the bone, if not disbanded or reorganized as wholly-owned subsidiaries which must sell their services to other operating units or outside firms. Thus, the corporation becomes more a federation of companies than a single organizational entity.[9]

A typical next step is for the operating units to reduce the risk, cost, and time of designing new products by seeking partners who take substantial responsibility for defining and manufacturing key components or aggregates of components — modules — of the final product. Collaborative arrangements allow the firm to learn from its partners´ experiences in their own and other industries without assuming responsibility for their survival; make it possible to shift direction rapidly should there be a truly revolutionary technical breakthrough; and — above all — concentrate scarce investment funds on ex-

[9] The reduction in size of corporate headquarters is documented in a recent study of the New York City economy, where 74 of the Fortune 500 companies were based in 1988. In one case presented as typical, a corporation with $2 billion of sales and 25,000 employees in 1989 reduced its headquarters staff from 500 in 1980 to 90 in 1989. Of those absented from headquarters, 300 were „dispersed to line companies“ and 110 were victims of „downsizing.“ For this and other examples, see Telesis (1989).

ploring those technologies which at any moment define the integrity of the firm and its products.[10]

Prominent examples of this kind of collaborative manufacturing are computer „systems" firms such as Sun Microsystems, a leading California maker of engineering workstations. Sun designs its own microprocessor (which is manufactured by several „process specialists"), writes software linking many commercially available components, and assembles the final product.[11] Many major automobile firms now develop the electronic control mechanisms which regulate engines, brakes, and the relation between these and other components of the car in collaboration with external suppliers. Many plan to or already enlist suppliers in the design and production of modules such as seats, instrument panels, brakes, doors or bumpers.[12]

At the limit, problems of reducing development costs for successive models shade into the problem of maintaining the firm´s long-term innovative capacity: its ability to learn of and profit from ideas which do not square with its organizational habits. Collaborative manufacturing grows out of and reinforces the assumption that it is no longer possible to distinguish between incremental improvements in product and process technologies and radical breakthroughs, or even to determine the relevance of research in one specialized area for work in another. Clues to great advances in one field can be found in apparently routine development work, or apparently distant research in another area. A large firm might therefore complement its new supplier relations with a minority stake in some of its key partners (a way of symbolically transforming repeated contractual exchanges into an enduring relation between entities with mingled identities and shared destinies). It might supplement them by diversifying and decentralizing its own core research and development facilities. This can be done by investing in firms experimenting in potentially relevant but unproven technologies, hiring a venture-capital firm to assemble a portfolio of such investments, creating internal ventures to

[10] For analysis of new subcontracting strategies regarding the U.S. manufacturing industry, see Susan Helper (1991). For subcontracting in Japan, and especially the growth in the subcontractors´ autonomy in relation to the customers´ efforts to increase flexibility, see Toshihiro Nishiguchi (1989).

[11] On Sun and similar firms, see Annalee Saxenian (1990).

[12] An extreme is BMW, which pays 75 percent of the total cost of components to outside suppliers and, but for considerations of prestige, would have subcontracted construction of cylinder heads, one of the most sophisticated components of its engines.

develop interesting ideas, or establishing design departments in the operating units. In the extreme case, which I will call collaborative manufacturing, producing a component or conducting research in a particular area become ways of learning what needs to be known to choose and monitor the external partners who assume the full burden of production and investigation.

By the same logic, hierarchical distinctions within corporations blur as conception and execution are integrated to encourage projects that can be rapidly produced and production set-ups that can accommodate new projects. *Integrated engineering* is the American term of art for the interpenetration of design and production engineering described a moment ago. Closer to the shop floor, supervisors and the work groups they lead assume responsibility for many of the residual industrial engineering tasks required to complete the translation of design into efficient manufacturing practice. Within the work team, increasingly skilled workers assume some of the responsibilities for set-up, maintenance, logistics (particularly control of work flow), and quality control which were parcelled out to specialized departments in the mass-production system.

The explosive proliferation of project groups or teams in firms of all sizes and branches is perhaps the best expression of the blurring of internal hierarchical distinctions and company boundaries. Whereas the aim of interdisciplinary committees in the mass-production corporation was to harmonize the application of standard operating procedures in different parts of the organization, the role of the new project teams is almost the reverse: to introduce new procedures, production methods, and products in precisely those situations where current practice inhibits innovation. The teams are typically composed of specialists from a variety of disciplines and companies, and distinguished by large nominal differences in hierarchical rank. Thus a team responsible for introducing a flexible manufacturing system for one family of components might include design and production-planning engineers, programmers, skilled workers, and representatives from sales and marketing as well as from the vendors of the capital goods and network software to be used in the new system. Teams of this sort often undertake projects lasting 5 or more years; many managers, technicians, and workers make their careers by moving to successively more responsible jobs in different teams. To the extent that the project teams are empowered to combine disciplines in ways which produce analogous but otherwise unachievable changes in the larger organization, they are the institutional emblem and indispensable agent of the meta-corporation.

A final consequence of the reintegration of conception and execution, and one which further blurs the boundary between firms and between the economy and society is the formation of regional economies: clusters of firms with different specialties working in various combinations to serve common markets.[13] First, the more volatile markets become, the riskier it becomes to hold inventory. Hence the need for just-in-time logistics, which require that suppliers put production units, warehouse facilities, or transportation hubs, close to their major customers´ plants. Second, the more volatile the markets and technology, the more likely it is that timely knowledge is embodied in everyday experience — the more likely it is, in other words, that knowledge becomes local knowledge. Living together in the sense of learning to speak a common technical or commercial language becomes a precondition for working together. Once firms value such conviviality, they must be present where this expertise is grounded. Call this the localization effect of firms — or of members of a community of producers — on each other. Third, the more specialized a firm becomes, the more it depends on the collective provision of training, research, hazardous-waste disposal, supplemental unemployment or medical protection, environmental monitoring, market information, or warehousing which it cannot provide itself. Many such services can be supplied by private vendors, but in any particular case, some are almost certain to be provided by, or in partnership with, local authorities. If firms rely on public provision of crucial services, however, they become part of the local political community. Their survival depends on its prosperity. Call this the localization effect of providing a public exoskeleton to specialized firms.

Note, however, that the foregoing does not require all key operations needed to manufacture a complex product to be located in a single region. Some must be, for the reasons just given. But a company often prefers to collaborate with a supplier in a distant network rather than establish a local producer of a key subassembly. Hence regionalization and internationalization of production may proceed hand in hand; the more robust a local economy, the more it attracts and is attracted to complementary foreign localities. The decisive point is that, whatever the regional distribution of activities, firms in each region have similar relations to their neighbors and local institutions.

[13] For more on the formation of such economies, see Charles F. Sabel (1989).

2.2 Trust and Mistrust in the Meta-Corporation

What is, of course, missing from this account of the meta-corporation is reference to the conflicts which make such organizations so hard to construct and maintain. Imperiled corporate staffs can raise the self-interested but legitimate question: What, in their absence, will secure the integrity and coordination of the decentralized operating units? In the same spirit, design engineers, plant managers, and workers told to collaborate with outsiders in the production of subassemblies for which they had exclusive responsibility may warn against the dangers of being too dependent on a collaborator of unproven loyalty. The subcontractor has reason aplenty to fear closer relation with an overbearing partner. Or a plant manager asked to contribute to a local training program may prefer an in-house program which directly benefits company and only company employees. And even when there is agreement in principle to decentralize authority, collaborate with outsiders, or share the costs of public goods, fights over who wins and loses from the application of the principle — or even squabbles over how much and by what rules the winners will be paid — are often violent enough to undo the agreement. The upshot is that the benefits of collective learning may be unobtainable because of considerations of factional or personal vulnerability and advantage.

The practical problems are theoretically vexing as well. The reason is that innovation in general and the meta-corporation in particular seem to depend on the fusion of two well established but contrary principles of organization. Indeed, given the available theories, the puzzle about the meta-corporation is not that it is ramshackle, but that it can stand at all. In the rest of this section, therefore, I want to suggest how learning organizations address their vulnerabilities by creating novel forms of governances which create the impression of a fusion of opposites.

As all those familiar with debates in this area have already guessed, the contrary principles in question are those of markets and hierarchies. On the one hand innovation seems to require that the actors, individual or institutional, enjoy the entrepreneurial autonomy to act as they see fit and reap the full rewards of their initiative. Otherwise, they will have neither the ability nor the motive to create something novel. On the other hand, insofar as innovation requires complementary, project- or product-specific investments, success seems to depend on organizational coordination of all the necessary activities. Otherwise each potential investor would be paralyzed by the fear that, having dedicated resources to the common project, he or she would be at the mercy of partners who might decide to abandon the enterprise, seek other collaborators, or use the threat of doing either as a weapon in renegotiating the bargain. The problem, therefore, is how to induce the coordination without stifling the initiative.

One school of thought, originating in the work of Ronald H. Coase and Oliver E. Williamson, argues that autonomy can be organized if the form of organization is supple enough. In the simplest variant, which virtually no one believes adequate to the case of innovative institutions, control is by means of hierarchical authority: Do as I say because, as my subordinate, you have agreed to follow my instructions.[14] In a second variant, principals control their agents by means of complex incentive systems: Do what I would want you to do if I had your knowledge of the situation, because your performance is observable and success will be rewarded.[15] A still more general variant emphasizes the control powers of property understood as the right to decide matters not formally agreed between collaborators: Exercise your freedom in my interest, or else I will deny you the use of the physical capital I own, and without which your autonomy is useless.

But just as every new tax produces unintended consequences, including new forms of tax evasion, so every control strategy produces surprises, including elaboration of a counter strategy. That bureaucratic rules can be used as instruments of individual or group privilege at the expense of the institutional good is among the most common of sociological commonplaces.[16] But elaborate incentive schemes are hardly a solution. It can also be shown that in complex situations, defined by multiple and often conflicting goals, incentive schemes concentrate efforts on activities which the principal regards as less important than those which self interest has led the agents to pursue. Finally, the history of innovative, small-firm start-ups in industries as diverse as steel, semiconductors and computers suggests that, given broad capital markets, it is hard to control collaborators by holding hostage the physical capital they use.

A contrary school of thought resolves the problem of coordination by ob-

14 For a nuanced presentation of this view, see Oliver E. Williamson and William G. Ouchi (1981: pp. 347-370).

15 For examples of this kind of argument, see John W. Pratt and Richard J. Zeckhauser (1985).

16 For one of the best statements of the view, see Michel Crozier (1964).

serving that, under certain conditions, all potential collaborators rightly assume that each will forebear from exploiting the others´ vulnerability. The assumption of mutual forbearance is called trust. Once trust has been established, the parties can assume that they will fairly share the burdens of problems which arise by definition whenever economic exchange is also an occasion for reciprocal learning. Hence they have nothing to lose and everything to gain from engaging in such exchanges. The origins of trust are obscure in this analysis. Where it is not treated as a social datum, it is regarded as the result of the historical, hard fought formation of a national, ethnic, religious, or political identity; and the limits of trust in economic affairs coincide with the boundaries of these collective identities. Some of the Nordic analysis of economic networks,[17] and many discussions of relations among groups of small- and medium-sized firms in the Italian industrial districts are examples of this line of argument. If the maxim of the first school is something close to Lenin´s view that trust is good but control is better, the maxim of the second, especially in its Italian variant, is that trust is enough.

The difficulty of this line of argument is that by drawing such a firm distinction between trust and mistrust, it overstates both the robustness of trust relations and the difficulty of establishing them in the first place. But those who depend on trust relations are also most aware of their fragility, and most vigilant in protecting them. The vitality of industrial districts — in Italy and elsewhere, today as in the nineteenth century — depends on their ability to establish arbitration boards and joint councils to resolve the constant conflicts that arise between labor and capital, large firms and small, and public providers of collective goods and the firms.[18] The Nordic networks of firms are under the collective tutelage of the trade unions, government, political partners and, increasingly, local authorities. Conversely, the rapidity with which Japanese managers and Americans following their lead have been able to establish trust relations within plants and between customers and suppliers in

[17] Jens Laage-Hellman (1987: pp. 26-83) and Jan Johanson and Lars-Gunnar Mattsson (1987: pp. 34-48). But note that the network school has an ambivalent view regarding the origins of trust. It is treated both as datum — the result, essentially, of „a similar cultural and educational background“ — and as the outcome of increasingly complex and demanding exchanges with various partners. See for both views Laage-Hellman, „Process Innovation“ (1987: pp. 63-64).

[18] For the rule of such organizations in modern Italian industrial districts see Carlo Trigilia (1990: pp. 160-184).

the United States strongly suggests that, given the right incentives, trust can be built where it was not found.[19] Pursuit of self-interest, in sum, can lead out of but also into relations which are not purely self-regarding; and arguments which see control as a substitute for trust or vice versa fail to do justice to that fact, and therefore fail as solutions to the coordination problem of innovation.

Between these two positions there are, however, intermediate ones which take better account of the complex relation between trust and self-interest. The simplest of these positions resolves the difficulties of the other two by creating a category — often called the relational contract — which combines descriptive features of the first two while purging them of their troubling theoretical connections. The result is a more believable account of the mixture of vigilance and vulnerability which in fact characterize long-term collaborative exchanges. But here description is a substitute for analysis: Relational contracts work when and because they work. Pressed to explain the why and where of the matter, proponents of this view typically recur to just the kinds of culturalist or group identity explanations characteristic of the trust school. Dore´s analysis of subcontracting relations in the Japanese textile industry or Ouchi´s discussions of the network clans which occupy the typological space between markets and hierarchies are examples.

Another strand of the intermediate position, and the one I will follow, cuts deeper by attacking the distinctions between trust and mistrust and the corresponding forms of governance. One theme, as developed by Jeffrey L. Bradach and Robert G. Eccles, is that the shortcomings of one form of governance can be overcome if it is combined with another possessing compensating strengths. A fast-food chain, for example, can learn much from its franchises, but it finds their behavior hard to monitor. The situation is the reverse with its wholly owned outlets. By owning some outlets and franchising others, therefore, the company learns both how to innovate and how to monitor the risks of innovation. A related theme in their work and that of Arthur L. Stinchcombe is that apparently distinct governance structures can make (different) use of the same features or institutions. The existence of a market can thus facilitate the creation of trust relations by providing price information which serves as a self evident, mutually agreeable boundary condition on

[19] For an evaluation of the striking success of the Japanese transplants and American firms applying Japanese organizational principles, see J.P. Womack et al. (1990: pp. 85-87).

an exchange which is already subject to strain through constant renegotiation of its other aspects (Stinchcombe: pp. 121-171). This deconstruction of governance structures and the categories of trust and mistrust explains why, for example, in Dore´s characterization of large Japanese firms „cooperative pursuit of common goals“ goes hand in hand „with vigilant monitoring to ensure that the costs and benefits of achieving those goals are fairly shared“ (Dore, 1989: p. 6). The argument can also be extended historically to show how trust relations can be built and destroyed, although I will not do so here.[20]

What I want to claim here is that the meta-corporation is pressing this intermediate argument towards its radical conclusion. The effort to group governance structures with complementary strengths is accompanied by an effort to create institutions in which the distinction between learning and monitoring is reduced to the point of imperceptibility. Thus, as noted earlier, production in a system of collaborative manufacturing is both a means of learning how to make things better and a way of learning how to select and monitor partners. The transformation of central technical staffs into quasi-independent companies serves the same double end. The rotation of managers through different jobs in different operating units is a variation on this theme. It forms a corporate elite which is good at monitoring complex tasks because of the variety of what it has learned, and has learned the importance of learning through its diverse experiences in monitoring. Notice, however, that the creation of institutions and careers which blend learning and monitoring does not imply the end of corporate conflict. There will still be more or less self-interested fights about organizational integrity, vulnerability and equity. The meta-corporation´s hope, I believe, is simply that the new governance structures increase the likelihood that the parties to the disputes will have come to an understanding of themselves and the organization which favors a resolution in the latter´s interest.

The meta-corporation is in its infancy, and study of it has hardly begun.

[20] A related argument derived from the theory of repeated games shows how firms can lower the cost of establishing trust relations by acquiring a reputation for reliability through forbearing behavior; how fear of jeopardizing this reputation also checks opportunism; and even how the need to assure that all employees act accordingly leads to formulation of a corporate „culture“ understood as the injunction not to exploit the vulnerability of partners. In a fuller treatment of the problem of the passage from mistrust to trust and back, it would be necessary to connect this last variant to the second. See for this David M. Kreps (1990: pp. 90-143).

But for present purposes, I think, baby steps will do. If the foregoing suggests how organizations´ reintegration of conception and execution converges with their reconciliation of monitoring and learning, the stage is set for another aspect of the argument: consideration of the way moebius-strip organizations use technology.

3 Technological Diversification

Whereas almost all students of organizational behavior or corporate strategy agree that something fundamental is going on, and then proceed to argue about the interpretation of widely agreed, stylized facts, observers of technology are divided as to whether there is much new to talk about, and whether the apparently new is truly novel. At issue is the interpretation of the variety of production forms intermediate between mass production and the caricature of universal materializing machines. Are they renovations of the former? Anticipations or variants of the latter? Or hybrids which reflect market conditions which are themselves intermediate between mass and specialized production? As in the last section, the claim is that the actors have realized the dangers of pursuing either of two strategies long regarded as mutually exclusive and exhaustive (there, monitoring or control as against learning and trust; here, the use of rigid, dedicated equipment as against flexible, programmable machines) and discovered how to combine elements drawn from both.

3.1 Three Views of Flexible Technologies

Three views of the deployment of new technologies dominate current debate. The first of these emphasizes the continuing primacy of the large firms, either because technological innovation is being assimilated to existing organizations and patterns of authority, or because technical or economic barriers block diffusion of flexible automation equipment (or networks of such equipment) to smaller firms.[21] These arguments regarding the limitations of small

[21] Giancarlo Cainarca, Massimo G. Colombo, and Sergio Mariotti (1987). Yet another variant asserts that large firms will dominate the economy because of the need to

firms simply do not stand close empirical scrutiny, as we will see in a moment. The problem with the others is that in their haste to answer the undoubtedly important question of who is in control, they overlook the possibility that the new system might operate according to a logic of its own.

The second current in the debate is concerned to show the plasticity of technology and the way its use depends on the economic and organizational setting into which it is introduced. Sociologists such as Hans-Jürgen Ewers, Carsten Becker, and Michael Fritsch (1989) as well as Arndt Sorge and his colleagues (Sorge et al., 1982) find that — other things being equal — small-batch specialized production favors the use of versatile, programmable equipment operated by skilled workers, whereas high-volume production favors more rigid uses of such equipment by much less skilled workers. In conjunction with Eckart Hildebrandt and Rüdiger Seltz´s monograph on the West German machine-tool industry (1989), this work establishes the capacity of small firms to adopt single pieces of flexible technology, and increasingly to connect them by computer into networks.[22] The limitation of these studies is that in emphasizing local situations — and particularly the extreme ones — they obscure the crucial influence of the whole of any production system on the formulation of each of its parts.

A third, business-school current describes best-practice cases and draws conclusions about the relation of skill and sophisticated technology for managers. The surprising result of the work of Ramchandran Jaikumar (1986: pp. 69-76), and John F. Krafcik and John Paul MacDuffie (1989) is that the rigid, low-skill use of the new technology appears to be much more expensive — perhaps prohibitively so — than the context school´s finding suggested. These scholars argue that the *real* choice firms face-off is between a high-productivity, high-quality, flexible, high-skill system, and a low productivity (because frequently broken) low-quality, low-skill one. But here, too, the focus on a general lesson — that skill is a precondition for effective

coordinate innovation through hierarchy. For this view, see Cristiano Antonelli (1989: pp. 33-45). The preceding discussion suggests that if „big" firms are needed to solve complex coordination problems, they will be „big" in a sense radically different from the traditional understanding of the large firm which informs this line of argument.

[22] „The introduction of the newest computer technologies depends ever less on the financial strength and organization potential of large firms. The building blocks of systems rationalization (the connection into networks of discrete pieces of computer-controlled equipment) are also affordable for middle-sized firms" (Hildebrandt and Seltz 1989: pp. 439-440).

use of the new technologies in all settings — has distracted attention from the ways different uses of technologies influence one another.

3.2 Mechanizing Flexible Production

There are two principal methods of mechanizing flexible production. Each can be deployed to produce a fixed number of variants of a single product (flexible mass production), to accommodate an unpredictable number of variants of related products (what I will call fully flexible manufacturing or flexible specialization). In some situations, the two methods are fungible, and firms choose the one with which they have had the most experience. In many others, however, considerations of cost in relation to various kinds of uncertainty lead firms to prefer one over the other, or a combination of both to either.

The first method of mechanizing flexible production is by means of versatile or programmable equipment. At its most rigid, this system resembles a programmable variant of the traditional mass-production transfer line: a sequence of single-purpose machines linked by an automatic conveyance system operating at a fixed rhythm. If the individual machines are more versatile, and less rigidly coupled, the set-up becomes what is typically called a flexible manufacturing system. These are capable of manufacturing a range of parts defined by, say, a common size and prismatic geometry. At their most versatile, automation systems of this first type consist of general-purpose capital goods linked by re-routable transfer mechanisms.

In machining operations, flexibility in this type of automation is typically achieved with programmable machining centers, which literally transform themselves from one type of machine tool to another through automatic tool changes: a lathe becomes a mill, which becomes a borer, and so on. In assembly the latest robotics makes possible equally versatile equipment which might by analogy be called assembly centers. These are batteries of from 10 to 30 independently programmable robots which together position, clamp, weld, or otherwise fasten an extraordinary variety of complex parts or subassemblies. They too transform their mechanical identity through tool changes. Conveyance is by systems which route parts individually from work station to work station, either by automatically guided vehicles (robot carriers) controlled by magnetized strips buried under the factory floor), or by self-powered monorail carriers moving along an overhead track system. By decoupling the progress of the work pieces, these systems make it easy to manufacture different models in arbitrary sequences, reconfigure the flows of production when new models are introduced, and to divert parts from disabled to operating machines or to buffer stations.

The second method of mechanizing flexible manufacturing is by what I will call snap-on capital goods. By these I mean machines and machine attachments such as jigs or dies which can be incorporated in a matter of minutes, if not seconds, into the production process as the need arises. Snap-on machines typically occupy an intermediate position between dedicated and versatile equipment. One example would be a press with a restricted operating range, but not optimized for production of a particular part at a given speed and pressure; another would be a small spray-painting unit capable of covering pieces of a given size with a limited number of coatings. Snap-on machine attachments are built according to norms which facilitate their rapid substitution and lower their production costs. Dies for stampings, for example, will be of a standard height so as to speed insertion into the press; and design elements common to a family of dies will be inventoried by computer and reused as needed in the construction of new attachments. Here, too, conveyance among machines ranges from a rigid conveyor to a re-routable mechanical transfer system to a push cart.

Used most restrictively, snap-on capital goods simply reduce the set-up times necessary to change from one variant of a product to another on a traditional mass-production manufacturing line. If many different, easily substitutable specialized machines are grouped so that by altering the flow of the work piece it is possible to perform a wide range of constantly varying operations, the system becomes a snap-on variant of fully flexible manufacturing. Between these extremes are what the Japanese call U-shaped or horseshoe lines. These are sequences of easily replaced or retooled specialized machines. The number of machines exceeds the number of persons serving them. Operators select those machines required to manufacture particular pieces, and the composition of the machine park changes as the product range is altered. The horseshoe configuration simply reduces the effort required to move the work pieces through the appropriate sequence. The U-shaped line is the snap-on equivalent of the flexible manufacturing system.

The choice between versatile and snap-on technologies depends on expectations about the volatility of product mix and the length of model life as well as the relative prices of machinery of each type. These, in turn, are related to certain principles of product design and investment characteristics of the two types of flexible automation in ways which pattern the deployment of technology in a flexible economy.[23]

Take first the question of product design. In the last section we saw that modularity — the conception of products as a system of systems — emerged as an answer to the problem of cutting development costs and time. But modularity is also a means of reducing the costs of producing many variants of a single product by, in effect, extending the life of some of its components. The greater the range of end products, the greater the benefits in reduced production costs of creating variety through combinations of parts drawn from a limited number of part families[24] (components of different dimensions but showing fundamental geometric characteristics and produced with the same equipment) or subassemblies, each of which can be varied without compromising its compatibility with the others. Subassemblies, moreover, can be decomposed into easily recombinable subunits or components. But of course the expected longevity of particular parts or modules varies greatly with respect to the life expectancy of the end products of which they are components, and in a world of short product life-cycles, these differences determine whether they are provided in high or low volumes. Barring a truly revolutionary technological breakthrough, for example, a family of car engines produced in one facility might be expected to power two or three model generations over the course of 15 to 20 years. A brake family might be expected to equip one generation of models in all their variants during a seven-year life. A door or seat assembly might change every year or two to accommodate new styles in interior design.

Take next the investment profiles of versatile as against snap-on mechanization. All else being equal, programmable equipment requires greater initial investment per unit output than does a snap-on system. Decisions regarding the moment-to-moment choice of machines and tools are made manually in the latter, and by a combination of hard- and software in the former. And

[23] Notice, however, that the cost estimates in turn depend on the relationship between the design of the final product and the firm´s automation strategy. The added cost of the complex cells performing many operations is compensated, in theory, by the relaxation of design constraints needed to assure efficient manufacture in a greater number of simpler steps.

[24] A good discussion of „parts family“ or „group“ technologies is Peter Brödner (1990).

what is true moment-to-moment is all the more true for long periods. The product range of all snap-on systems can be modified piecemeal as needed. Programmable systems must accommodate from the first production of parts for which demand may emerge near the end of their productive lives. The higher initial costs of programmable systems are offset by lower operating costs; but whether the initial difference in investment can be recouped depends naturally on total production during the lives of the respective installations.

Hence two very simple rules of thumb. First, the longer the life of the part family or module, the more likely it will be built by programmable rather than snap-on equipment. Second the less predictable the range of output, the less tightly coupled — the closer to being fully flexible either type of system will be. Several examples will illustrate this double calculation at work, although they are hardly an exhaustive catalogue of the possibilities. (The fully flexible variant is an exception, because it is anticipated that machines with new characteristics will be introduced into the system.)

One point of reference is the engine plant. The product, however variable by comparison to earlier standards (when a change in the number of cylinders meant junking a whole production line), is still relatively homogeneous. Output levels are high, so rapid operations are of the essence. Investments in sophisticated capital goods that are both versatile and fast can be amortized over a long period. Under these conditions the preferred solution is flexible mass production: a line of programmable but specialized machines — programmable boring machines, not machine centers — linked by a fast-moving conveyance system.[25]

Final assembly facilities illustrate the opposite pole in the application of programmable technologies. The final assembly is the module of all modules, and the plant which can connect all subassemblies should be usable for all modules of any current generation and for many successive generations of a product. What we should expect here is precisely what, as anticipated in the preceding discussion, we see: the rapid introduction of programmable assembly cells or loosely coupled sequences of programmable work stations.

[25] There is, however, nothing immutable about such a solution. If the cost of versatile capital goods sinks rapidly enough, it may prove efficient to build smaller, more dedicated facilities serving one assembly plant rather than many, or more flexible plants, which dramatically increase the range of engine variants offered by any one company. See Richard P. Hervey (1987-88: pp. 15-19).

Fiat managers, for example, estimate that they will be able to reuse at least 80 per cent of the capital goods in the new Cassino plant south of Rome in the manufacture of cars yet to be designed. They are confident, moreover, that it will be possible to use flexible routing systems and shift work to introduce new models into the plant without ceasing production of currently saleable ones. They, like managers at Volkswagen at Emden, also claim on the basis of experience to date that all of the firm´s current models could be produced in any desired combination at their respective plants.

Headlight production illustrates the typical setting in which snap-on technology dominates. The product will be altered every year or two to give a more stylish look to a range of models and variants which will be fundamentally renewed only once every 7 or 8 years. In addition, the number of variants of the subassembly produced for any type of car is likely to be large because, for example, the trim and other design elements of the subassembly must match those of the rest of the car. Total production volumes will be high, and ideally the subassemblies will be produced and delivered in the sequence in which they will be installed on the final assembly line. Hence the headlight producer needs high-volume production facilities whose capacity to vary the mix of current products does not limit the capacity to change the components of that mix at short intervals.

The U-shaped line meets these requirements. Some stations are bays of 2 or 3 machines of the same type, equipped to produce a production of different variants of the subassembly. A single worker loads the appropriate machine as required. Other stations consist of scaled-down versions of continuous process equipment (machinery for heat treatment or applying coatings or finishes) which has been adapted in-house to suit the requirements of the materials being worked. By reducing the size (and generally the operative range) of, e.g., the general-purpose painting equipment, and painting the subassembly in the production line rather than in a distinct painting department, the firm reduces the complexity of its logistics. This arrangement also creates the optimal conditions for learning how to improve this kind of manufacturing operation. Given that the basic principles of miniaturization (and much of the necessary hardware) in any particular process area are likely to change rather slowly, the costs of developing successive generations of equipment are modest.[26]

[26] Managers typically acknowledge the dangers associated with dedicated equipment, but argue that in many cases of module production, rewards in efficiency more than outweigh the risks.

Similar considerations govern the choice of technology used to manufacture the various types of capital goods themselves. Thus, versatile, programmable machines tend to be produced by flexible manufacturing systems, whereas snap-on machines or machine attachments are produced with versatile equipment deployed as in the fully flexible factory. The more flexible the capital goods, the smaller the risk to owning them, and thus the greater the manufacturer´s potential market. General purpose machines, particularly if they are lower or medium-priced, will therefore tend to be produced in relatively long runs with a limited range of variants. Various flexible manufacturing systems are well suited to producing the different geometrically defined families of parts from which successive generations of such equipment are built. And in fact, Japanese producers of large numbers of programmable lathes or machining centers for small- to medium-sized job shops typically favor such systems for their high-volume products.

Taken as a piece, the discussion so far illustrates one cross section of the technological strata of an economy in which products are short-lived, but demand is still stable enough to make confident guesses about the relation between average product life and the longevity of its chief components. In the automobile industry, to continue with our dominant example, the top stratum — the one closest to the final consumer — consists of flexible assembly plants using a combination of robotic assembly cells and sequences of discrete, programmable equipment, the balance between the two depending on the design of the car. At the next level are the suppliers of high-volume modules. Producers of relatively long-lived modules favor flexible mass production, producers of short-lived modules favor snap-on equipment arranged in U-shaped or horseshoe lines. At a still lower stratum are the capital-goods suppliers. Some of these will be using flexible manufacturing systems to produce versatile equipment such as assembly robots and the machining centers. Other capital-goods producers will be using fully-flexible technologies to produce snap-on machines and machine attachments. A more complete cross-section would of course have to include references to the technological choices of the high-and low-volume subassemblers´ own suppliers, including those in steel and other process industries.

But even if it were thus extended, there would remain a fundamental limitation to this attempt to match types of flexible technology to positions in a production system governed by a global logic of market diversification and technological malleability. Firms are in fact often not as certain in their estimates of product and component longevity as I have assumed. Not are they as sure about the relative costs, much less *trends* in the relative costs, of versatile as against disposable technologies.

The consequence of these additional uncertainties is that the technological hedging strategies — the firm´s choice of a particular type of mechanized flexibility as the least risky given the concurrent choices of other firms in the same economy, is itself hedged. An obvious way to do this is to create hybrid solutions: production systems which combine, say, versatile and snap-on technologies in a way which facilitates subsequent changes in the balance between them. Such hybrids can be observed in the constitution of individual machines, the composition of single production lines, or the simultaneous pursuit of different technological strategies by different plants making similar products in the same firm. It is more and more common, for example, to see presses or complex grinding machines which are both programmable and designed for use with snap-on attachments. The U-shaped line, with its characteristic combination of loosely coupled, disposable machinery and scaled-down general-purpose equipment is — in principle — also such a hybrid, although I have emphasized the dominant role of the easily replaceable specialized machines. Fiat plans to build several plants on the Cassino model to accommodate short-run models and fluctuations in demand. The cars that can be sold in higher, more predictable volumes will be produced at less flexible facilities. In practice, U.S. firms seem to arrive at these hybrids as they try to eliminate the defects in technologically thoroughbred systems or correct unambiguous and incorrect bets on the future. Western European and Japanese firms, in contrast, arrive at them by combining, as in the U-shaped line, isolated pieces of diverse technologies and strategies, each introduced for reasons of its own.

But in any case there is now substantial agreement in all three advanced manufacturing zones that with regard to choices of technology or organizational design there are guiding principles — those, namely, which follow from hedging guesses about the implications of the logic of flexibility — but few principled solutions in the sense of the thoroughbred models presented thus far. And even when firms *do* choose thoroughbred solutions, they tend to hedge the choices by making sure that they have access to alternatives through contact with suppliers, other divisions of the company, or consultants. This kind of virtual diversification ensures that, at a minimum, no sequence of decisions in favor of one type of technology accidentally becomes irreversible.

Looked at from afar, therefore, the technologies deployed in a flexible economy will seem an assortment of hybrids, with only loose associations between types of equipment and types of production. Looked at from the inside, however, any one of the hybrids or selected clusters of them will appear to result from the application of straightforward principles of technical choice under uncertainty to a limited set of equipment types, all more flexible than traditional mass-production machinery and more productive than the repertoire of traditional flexible machines.

This is the place, finally, to say a word about skill. Studies done at the *Soziologisches Forschungsinstitut* in *Göttingen* and the *Institut für Sozialwissenschaftliche Forschung* in *Munich* document clearly the extent to which workers operating versatile capital equipment require ever more fundamental knowledge of a greater variety of disciplines to do their jobs.[27] In the case of workers who program their own equipment or maintain complex systems, traditional distinctions between blue- and white-collar work are breaking down. It is plain that workers tending machines in the bays of U-shaped lines are less skilled than workers programming machining centers, although in some cases they may be as skilled as the operators of flexible manufacturing systems. But it is easy to make too much of these absolute differences in skill level. What is perhaps more interesting is the fact that, whatever their current jobs, workers in different positions in these production systems are plainly having to extend their skills in overlapping ways. The worker in the U-shaped line must start off adept at several jobs, learn to set up or program this or that piece of equipment, and to manage the ever-changing work flow in his or her area.[28] The craft worker using a versatile machine has to become more adept at managing logistics when that machine is linked with others, and so on. What they face in common is the continuing need to augment and adapt their skills to the changing needs of the work place. Peer Hull Kristensen´s studies of work in small- and medium-sized Danish metalworking plants shows a similar pattern as well (1987).

The need for skilled adaptability of this kind is, furthermore, the common

27 Two good examples of the current research are Klaus Düll and Burkart Lutz (1989), and Martin Baethge et al. (1989).

28 For a good discussion of the relationship between increased flexibility in routing work in progress and the need to „cross train“ operators in a variety of jobs, see Thomas Bailey (1989).

finding of recent studies of emergent types of employees in a variety of work settings and countries. Research by Thierry J. Noyelle, Larry Hirschhorn (1988: pp. 19-38), and Lauren Benton and colleagues (Benton et al., 1989) on the reorganization of the service sector calls attention to the abandonment of internal job ladders in banking, insurance and retailing firms. As part of a strategy of permanent innovation, these internal labor markets are being replaced by a system of „horizontal" recruitment of generally trained persons with various specialties into project groups; and extensive programs of continuing education equip the group members for new tasks. „We want to hire people who have a general capacity to become specialists, over and over again," a bank official told Benton and her collaborators. The work of Eckart Hildebrandt and Rüdiger Seltz (1989: p. 149) on the introduction of computer-controlled machinery in the West German machine-tool industry shows that design and production engineers are making „spiral" careers by advancing from project group to project group in different firms, rather than by the traditional climb up the hierarchy of a single firm. Rosabeth Moss Kanter´s study (1989), of managerial career patterns in recently reorganized U.S. corporations uncovered a great variety of ways of getting ahead, including some similar to this last one, all predicated on the impossibility of progressing step by step up a hierarchy — typically because hierarchies of the familiar type no longer existed.

The limitations of such studies are well known.[29] But they are all we have,

[29] There is little aggregate evidence of increased inter-firm mobility of skilled workers, technicians or managers in the large-firm sector in those countries, notably the Federal Republic of Germany and Japan, where these firms are expanding. The large firms are hoarding such employees precisely because they value their scarce skills. But the studies do not explore the possibility that the firms are retaining skilled personel precisely by offering them opportunities for self-development normally achievable only through job changes. A high official of a leading Japanese opto-electronics firm told me, for example, that in his company, engineers collaborated in project teams with outsiders, and entered joint ventures with them. To offset these fissiparous tendencies, the company planned to turn itself into the center of opto-electronic research in Japan, not least by creating a kind of internal research university. „If we succeed in that," he said", anyone who wants to realize a technological dream in this industry will have to maintain an institutional association with us." In any case, surveys report that the newest entrants to the work force seem more disposed to change jobs than their counterparts in earlier cohorts. See generally Christoph Büchtemann (1990) and Ronald Dore et al. (1989: pp. 55-66). It is worth noting, finally, that the business press is beginning to advise managers to acquire a portfolio of skills that make them marketable outside as well as inside the large corporation throughout their entire working lives. See Charles Handy (1990).

and they tell a common story. In the next section, therefore, I want to draw out the implications of the need to constantly acquire new skills in an uncertain institutional environment for the employer´s relation to work.

4 Open Labor Markets and Groucho Marx Identities

The characteristics of labor markets and the experience of work in the world of the meta-corporation are shaped by two related paradoxes that follow directly from the drive to reintegrate conception and execution. The first is that the same considerations which lead to increasing demand for skill make it increasingly difficult to fix the definition of particular jobs and give them a secure institutional place. Skill is the ability to execute incomplete or indicative instructions; and the meta-corporation´s reintegration of conception and execution plainly depends on the cooperation of skilled persons in sales, design, manufacturing, and the outside suppliers, all with an intimate, almost instinctive knowledge of the corporation´s needs. But reliance on the skills of outsiders, especially the constantly shifting but more intimate relation to subcontractors (the systems suppliers) and consultants (the former staffs reconstituted as independent firms, or complete outsiders operating on the open market) make it impossible to say what will go on inside the firm, what outside: Just as the outer edge of a moebius-strip flows into its inner edge, so activities inside these organizations can move outside, and vice versa.[30] And when the status of whole production or research units can change in a matter of months, or when everyone anticipates this possibility, production workers, technicians, and engineers most constantly wonder how they will survive if they are „on the market" for a job.

[30] For wide-ranging discussion of a limiting case of this kind of labor market, see Arthur L. Stinchcombe and Carol A. Heimer (1988: pp. 179-204).
For an argument that the gains in learning which this kind of career mobility makes possible can outweigh such costs as additional training and disruption of authority, see Gene I. Rochlin et. al. (1987: pp. 76-90). There is an almost 100% turnover of the crews of the U.S. Navy´s aircraft carriers every 40 months. Service tradition prescribes constant rotation of sailors and officers. Because almost everyone except a small core of senior enlisted specialists is constantly learning a new job, the situation encourages just the general willingness to collaborate in mastering surprises necessary to maintain high-tempo flight operations under conditions, which, given changes in technology and sea conditions, could not be stabilized in any case.

Hence a characteristic ambiguity in employees´ identity. They must be loyal to the work group or corporation to execute concepts while reconceptualizing them. But to whom, in the moebius-strip organization, is this loyalty owed? Conversely, the meta-corporation owes its employees *its* loyalty. Why else would they accept the uncertainty of permanent reorganization? But given permanent reorganization, to whom is the meta-corporation promising this loyalty? Recall Groucho Marx´s observation that he would not want to be a member of any club that would want him for a member. As it tries to retain the freedom to recombine resources without destroying its employee´s loyalty, the meta-corporation is becoming the kind of club which Groucho Marx would always *consider* joining.[31]

The second distinguishing paradox of the open labor market is this: Work in the restructured economy simultaneously increases and limits the employees´ autonomy in the world of life outside it. Employees who are encouraged to think of themselves as entrepreneurs, to treat their employer as a market, and to pay attention to hazardous materials, are forced to manage resources and risks in ways which make it easier to imagine changing the conditions of their lives. The conceivable changes range from going into business for oneself to becoming much less tolerant of environmental threats at home. But this enhanced autonomy is simultaneously qualified by the same situation which produced it. Just as the firms form networks with one another and their environment in order to keep abreast of local knowledge, so too individuals secure their long-term employability through participation in neighborhood groups, hobby clubs, or other professional and social networks outside the firm. Only those who participate in such multiple, loosely connected networks are likely to know when their current jobs are in danger, where new opportunities lie, and what skills are required to seize them. The more open corporate labor markets become, the greater the burden these networks will have to bear, and the greater the economic compulsion to participate in the social activities they organize.

Hence, just as it is becoming harder to say for whom one works, it is be-

[31] In discussing their attachments to their work, middle managers in U.S. corporations are beginning to speak of „commitment“ (to particular projects or work groups) rather than loyalty (to an imprecisely defined corporate entity). This change reflects fear that they could be the next victims of restructuring. But in part, it may also reflect a change in the way obligations to employers as persons and institutions are conceptualized generally. See Charles Heckscher (1990).

coming harder to say when one is working. Activities at work become preparation for turning the family into a family enterprise which absorbs all leisure; family and leisure activities become preconditions of employability. Anticipation of these possibilities itself undermines the distinctions between „work", „leisure" and „family". A limiting case is the two-earner household, which could not enter the labor market at all if it did not participate in the community life of day-care centers, schools, or neighborhood improvement associations, and whose double dependence on the local labor market can only be managed by careful use of all the information about employment this participation provides.

5 In Search of a New Language of Power

At the outset, I said that power might almost seem to disappear from the world of the meta-corporation, but that this appearance would be deceiving. By way of a conclusion, I want to distinguish the power struggles within the restructured economy from power struggles between it and the persons and firms it excludes. My purpose is to underscore the novelty of the relation between these two kinds of conflicts and to point towards an understanding of that relation by showing how it escapes traditional categories of analysis.

The discussion of trust and governance structures has foreshadowed the analysis of conflicts within the meta-corporation. Wherever there are bilateral monopolies — wherever, that is, two parties benefit from an exchange relation which neither can easily carry on with a third — the party which ultimately depends less on the relation can extract the greater share of the total benefits. To do so is to exercise power in the familiar sense of bargaining power.

By making everyone dependent on the expertise of everyone else, the meta-corporation creates a web of bilateral monopolies. Governance structures which simultaneously encourage learning and monitoring limit these conflicts but do not eliminate them. The many open questions in this regard are obvious. Will suppliers be able to use their growing expertise to augment their margin of manoeuvre by establishing independent relations with the market? Will managers put their expertise at the service of outside stakeholders or their co-workers? If the latter, will employees use their increasing skills to play a sustained and concerted part in shaping the large questions of corporate strategy or even national economic policy? Certainly the disparities in labor´s power in different systems of mass production — compare the rules of trade unions in Sweden and the United States in the 1960s and 1970s — strongly suggest that nothing in the logic of any particular industrial order determines the outcome of such bargaining conflicts or the composition of the alliances to which they give rise. In this sense, context and contingency — local, regional and national — matter.

The conflicts between those inside and those excluded from the world of the meta-corporation are different. These groups are not mutually dependent in the sense that each requires the cooperation of the other to achieve its ends. In a learning economy workers must possess substantial skills to acquire more. The unskilled, therefore, have little chance to set foot in the factory; neither do they have value as a labor reserve, nor even as a reservoir of purchasing power. Markets are more likely to be international than national. Without global management of aggregate demand, a skilled worker or engineer in one town will have a greater interest in the earning power of his or her counterparts in other countries than in that of an unskilled neighbor. When, as here, conflict becomes disentangled from the possibility of mutually advantageous exchange, the exercise of power becomes a clash of wills, an existential struggle between friends and foes in which the control of resources is seen as a precondition of collective survival.

In the traditional sociology of work, there was a clear connection between the two kinds of power: the exercise of bargaining power ended in existential struggle. The archetypal case was of course Marxism, in which the proletariat is dispossessed, deskilled, immiserated and emarginated before rising up against the investor class to reclaim its possessions, prowess, and social place. Even absent a determining logic of technological development, and despite the differences between mass-production and moebius-strip corporations, it is tempting to categorize potential conflicts in the new economy by analogy to these familiar tropes.

The first possible outcome evokes the idea of proletarianization. The ins stay in and the outs stay out, maintained by welfare systems and casual employment which guarantee their physical survival while sapping their capacity to change their situation. In the meta-corporations, small groups of workers use their market power to extract privileges at the expense of the excluded or their co-workers, further decreasing the chance of any redistribution of rights in favor of the outsiders. The suggestion is that if there is any justice in this world, the social tensions which these divisions produce will eventually lead to chaos or the effort to construct a more inclusive alternative.

This second, inclusive outcome corresponds to the classic idea of the socialization of the means of production. In this alternative, the struggles for power in both senses are linked in a way which weakens the grip of the owners of capital on the meta-corporation while widening the circle of the flexible economy to include more and more of the unskilled. The key to this solution is the formation of a new kind of labor movement, born of the existing trade unions or other organizational experiences. Instead of directly regulating conditions of work in firms or industries, this labor movement would help employees acquire the skills and knowledge of the labor market they need to move from job to job, while also enabling them to manage the changing relation between work and the rest of life. By providing these services, it would become as indispensable to the meta-corporation as other systems suppliers, while encouraging older firms, daunted by skill shortages, to reorganize as meta-corporations. To succeed nationally, the new labor movement would seek allies by pressing for legislation facilitating the redistribution of resources from prosperous regions to those that needed to restructure. It would also have to build a popular constituency by pressing for the protection of individual and group rights to self-determination at the workplace, and becoming the paladin of an educational and vocational training system open to all. Here is a new bloodless version of the revolutionary victory of reason and solidarity.

Many now argue that we in the United States have already begun to inhabit the first world. There is a widening debate with the West European Labor movement directed toward achieving some version of the second.[32] Yet despite this versimilitude, I think these evocative analogies obscure what is most novel and conceptually disorienting about the new economy: the chasm between insiders and outsiders, and the amorphous relation of insiders to one another.

Thus, to associate exclusion from the meta-corporations with proletarianization is to invite confusion of abandonment with exploitation. The association suggests that the losers in the new economy are insufficiently compen-

[32] For a fuller statement of the argument and further references, see Horst Kern and Charles F. Sabel (1990).

sated for their contribution to production, whereas we have seen that what they are losing is the possibility to make any contribution to the economy at all. Throughout the history of industrialization the unskilled were recruited from farming, petty commerce, or artisan workshops into the factories. They or, more likely, their children learned the skills they needed by doing successively more demanding jobs. Whether such employees were justly compensated for their contributions is, of course, open to debate. That the barriers between the high-skill economy and the subsistence borderlands have been raised is not. Exclusion may be more inhuman than exploitation insofar as the winners´ absolute indifference to the losers is more brutalizing than even a master´s twisted reliance on a slave. But to raise that possibility it is necessary to acknowledge the difference between the two. Surely one task of a new sociology of work will be to inquire into the connections, if any, which family ties, political allegiances, welfare rights, and other circuitous exchange relations create between insiders and outsiders in the new economy. Or, to put the point the other way around, what barriers will questions of gender, ethnicity, and social origins create between them.

Association of the second, inclusive outcome to the idea of the socialization of the means of production likewise tends to forclose discussion of troubling questions. The association suggests not only that the more inclusive economy would be less vulnerable to social conflict than the exclusive one (which seems plausible enough), but also that it might well be without significant conflict at all (which hardly follows). The world of inclusive meta-corporations might be a world of cabals and cliques in which the struggle for an honorable place *within* the community of production constantly threatens the forms of cooperation on which productive flexibility depends.[33] Or to avoid this danger it might be a world in which workplace autonomy was combined with, even dependent on, forms of social conformity which persons of my generation once associated with the post-war American suburbs and Americans now associate with Japan. What would be the role of women in either of these societies? Of men? Or the meaning of citizenship?

Notice, however, that this inclusive world does not correspond to the idea of a pluralist society, at least in its American variant. Pluralists believe the identity of each individual is the composite of the vector of his or her attach-

[33] See Marcel Mauss (1990: pp. 7-8; 35-37) for the view that the struggle for honor can be socially disruptive as the struggle for wealth in a monetary economy.

ments to groups of different kinds.[34] But the identities of these groups are fixed by ethnicity, religion, or place in the division of labor. In the meta-corporate world I am describing, individuals form and reform identities by reference to groups whose own identities are constantly in flux. Individuals are thus not the „natural“ result of the accidental combination of „natural“ collective self-understandings. Surely, a second pressing task for a new sociology of work is, therefore, to better characterize the substance of solidarity within the meta-corporation.

A world in which the boundaries within firms, among them, and between the public and private are blurring is not a world without boundaries. New boundaries, indeed new kinds of boundaries, are being drawn as the old fade. To detect them, we need not only a new language of analysis, but new concepts of equality and fairness. And by the oldest paradox in the book, once we have such a language and such concepts, we will begin to change the very boundaries we discuss.

References

Amin, Ash and Kevin Roberts (1990), Industrial Districts and Regional Development: Limits and Possibilities, in Pyke, Frank; Giacomo Becattini and Werner Sengenberger (eds.), *Industrial Districts and Inter-firm Cooperation in Italy*. Geneva, International Labour Organisation.

Antonelli, Cristiano (1989), Capitalismo flessible o capitalismo organizzato? *Politica ed Economia,* no. 6: 33-45.

Baethge, Martin; Rolf Dobischat; Rudolf Husemann; Christiane Schiersmann and Doris Weddig (1989), Gutachten über Forschungsstand und Forschungsdefizite im Bereich betrieblicher Weiterbildung unter besonderer Berücksichtigung der Belange der Mitarbeiter und darauf aufbauend Erarbeitung einer zukunftsweisenden Forschungskonzeption. *SOFI Research Report.* Göttingen.

Baethge, Martin and Herbert Oberbeck (1986), *Zukunft der Angestellten. Neue Technologien und berufliche Perspektiven in Büro und Verwaltung*. Frankfurt, Campus.

Bailey, Thomas (1989), Technology, Skills, and Education in the Apparel Industry. Technical Paper 7, Conservation of Human Resources. New York, Columbia University.

Becattini, Giacomo (1990), The Marshallian Industrial District as a Socio-Economic Nation, in Frank Pyke, Giacomo Becattini and Werner Sengenberger (eds.), *Industrial*

34 On pluralism as defined in American political science, see David B. Truman (1953). British pluralists had a view of the reciprocal constitution of individual and group closer to the one suggested above. See Paul Hirst (1989).

Districts and Inter-Firm Cooperation in Italy. Geneva, International Labour Organisation: 37-51.
Benton, Lauren; Thomas Bailey; Thierry Noyelle and Thomas M. Stanback (1989), *Jr. Training and Competitiveness in U. S. Manufacturing and Services: Training Needs and Practices of Lead Firms in Textile, Banking, Retailing, and Business Services.* Conservation of Human Resources. Columbia University.
Bertrand, Oliver and Thierry Noyelle, Employment and Skills in Financial Services: A Comparison of Banks and Insurance Companies in Five OECD Countries. The Service Industries Journal, vol. 8, no. 1: 7-18.
Bhagat, Sanjai; Andrei Shleifer and Robert W. Vishny (1990), Hostile Takeovers in the 1980s: The Return to Corporate Specialization. Brookings Paper. Graduate School of Business, University of Chicago.
Blauner, Robert A. (1964), *Alienation and Freedom.* Chicago, University of Chicago Press.
Block, Fred and Larry Hirschhorn (1979), New Productive Forces and the Contradictions of Contemporary Capitalism: A Post-Industrial Perspective. *Theory and Society: Renewal and Critique in Social-Theory,* vol. 7, no. 3: 363-395.
Bradach, Jeffrey L. and Robert G. Eccles (1989), Price, Authority, and Trust: From Ideal Types to Plural Forms. *Annual Review of Sociology*: 97-118.
Braverman, Harry (1974), *Labor and Monopoly Capital: The Degradation of the Work in the Twentieth Century.* New York, Monthly Review Press.
Brödner, Peter (1990), Computersysteme: Ersatz oder Hilfsmittel des Menschen in der Produktion. Working Paper, Institut Arbeit und Technik. Gelsenkirchen, May.
Büchtemann, Christoph (1990), Employment Security Policy in Europe: Some Lessons from the West German Experience. Paper prepared for the ILO/IILS/WZB International Conference on Workers´ Protection and Labor Market Dynamics. Berlin, May 16-18.
Burt, Ronald (1988), The Stability of American Markets. *American Journal of Sociology,* vol. 94, no. 2: 356-395.
Cainarca, Giancarlo; Massimo G. Colombo and Sergio Mariotti (1987), Innovazione e diffusione: il caso dell automazione flessible: *L´Industria,* no. 4.
Chandler Jr., Alfred D. (1977), *The Visible Hand: The Managerial Revolution in American Business.* Cambridge, Harvard University Press.
Clark, Kin, B., Takahiro Fujimoto and W. Bruce Chew (1987), Product Development in the World Auto Industry. *Brookings Papers on Economic Activity,* no. 3: 729-776.
Crozier, Michel (1964), *The Bureaucratic Phenomenon.* Chicago, University of Chicago Press.
Dore, Ronald (1983), Goodwill and the Spirit of Market Capitalism. *The British Journal of Sociology,* vol. 34, no. 4: 459-482.
Dore, Ronald (1989), The Management of Hierarchy. Paper presented to the NOMISMA Conference, Industrial Policy, New Issues and New Models, the Regional Experience. Bologna, Italy, November 16-17.
Dore, Ronald; Jean Bounine-Cabalé and Kari Tapiola (1989), *Japan at Work: Markets, Management and Flexibility.* Paris, OECD.
Düll, Klaus and Burkart Lutz (eds. -1989), *Technikentwicklung und Arbeitsteilung im internationalen Vergleich.* Frankfurt, Campus.
Eccles, Robert (1981), The Quasifirm in the Construction Industry. *Journal of Economic Behavior and Organization,* vol. 2: 335-357.
Ewers, Hans-Jürgen; Carsten Becker and Michael Fritsch (1989), Der Kontext entscheidet: Wirkungen des Einsatzes computergestützter Techniken in Industriebetrieben, in Schett-

kat, R. and M. Wagner (eds.), *Arbeitsmarktwirkungen moderner Technologien.* Berlin, Walter de Gruyter: 25-63.

Fligstein, Neil (1990), *The Transformation of Corporate Control.* Cambridge, Harvard University Press.

Fujimoto, Takahiro (1989), Organizations for Effective Product Development: The Case of the Global Motor Industry. Unpublished Ph.D. dissertation, Graduate School of Business Administration, Harvard University.

Granovetter, Mark S., The Strength of Weak Ties. *American Journal of Sociology,* vol. 78, no. 6: 1360-1380.

Handy, Charles (1990), *The Age of Unreason.* Cambridge, Harvard Business Scholl Press.

Hart, Oliver (1989), An Economist´s Perspective on the Theory of the Firm. *Columbia Law Review,* vol. 89, no. 7: 1757-1774.

Heckscher, Charles (1990), The Managerial Community. Unpublished paper. Graduate School of Business Administration, Harvard University.

Hervey, Richard P. (1987-88), Engine Manufacturing Strategies for the 1990s. *AiM Newsletter.* Michigan Modernization Service, Winter: 15-19.

Hildebrandt, Eckart and Rüdiger Seltz (1989), *Wandel betrieblicher Sozialverfassung durch systemische Kontrolle? Die Einführung computergestützer Produktionsplanungs- und steuerungssysteme im bundesdeutschen Maschinenbau.* Berlin, Edition Sigma.

Hirsch, Joachim (1985), Fordismus und Postfordismus: Die gegenwärtige gesellschaftliche Krise und ihre Folgen. *Politische Vierteljahresschrift,* vol. 26, no. 2: 160-182.

Hirschhorn, Larry (1988), The Post-Industrial Economy: Labour, Skills and the New Mode of Production. *The Service Industries Journal,* vol. 8, no. 1: 19-38.

Hirst, Paul (ed.- 1989), *The Pluralist Theory of the State: Selected Writings of G.D.H. Cole, J.N. Figgis, and H.J. Laski.* London, Routledge.

Holmstrom, Bengt and Paul Milgrom (1990), Multi-Task Principal-Agent Analyses. Yale School of Management, New Haven, unpublished.

Hull Kristensen, Peer (1987), Udkanternes industrielle miljo. Institute of Economic and Social Policy. Copenhagen, unpublished.

Ikeda, Masayoshi, Shoichiro Sei and Toshihiso Nishiguchi (1980), U-Line Auto Parts Production. International Motor Vehicle Program. Paper, M.I.T., October.

Jaikumar, Ramchandran (1986), Postindustrial Manufacturing. *Harvard Business Review,* November-December: 69-76.

Johanson, Jan and Lars-Gunnar Mattsson (1987), Interorganizational Relations in Industrial Systems. *International Studies of Management and Organization*, vol. 17, no. 1: 34-48.

Jones, Bryn (1990), New Production Technology and Work Roles. A Paradox of Flexibility Versus Strategic Control? In Loveridge, R. and M. Pitt (eds.), *The Strategic Management of Technological Innovation.* New York, John Wiley & Sons: 293-309.

Kanter, Rosabeth Moss (1989), *When Giants Learn to Dance.* New York, Simon and Schuster.

Kern, Horst and Charles F. Sabel (1990), Gewerkschaften in offenen Arbeitsmärkten: Überlegungen zur Rolle der Gewerkschaften in der Industriellen Reorganisation. *Soziale Welt*, no. 2: 144-166.

Kleinfield, N.R. (1990), How „Strykforce" Beat the Clock. *The New York Times*. Business section, March 25: 1, 6.

Krafcik, John F. and John Paul MacDuffie (1989), Explaining High-Performance Manufacturing: The International Automotive Assembly Plant Study. Working Paper. International Motor Vehicle Program, MIT, Cambridge.

Kreps, David M. (1990), Corporate Culture and Economic Theory, in Alt, James E. and Kenneth A Shepsle, *Perspectives on Positive Political Economy.* Cambridge, Cambridge University Press: 90-143.

Laage-Hellman, Jens (1987), Process Innovation through Technical Cooperation, in Håkan Håkansson (ed.), Industrial Technological Development. London, Croom Helm: 26-83.

Mallet, Serge (1963), *La Nouvelle Classe Ouvriere.* Paris, Editions du Seuil.

Mauss, Marcel (1990), *The Gift.* New York, W.W. Norton.

National Center on Education and the Economy (1990), *America's Choice: High Skills or Low Wages.* Rochester, National Center on Education and the Economy.

Nishiguchi, Toshihiro (1989), Strategic Dualism: An Alternative in Industrial Societies. Unpublished Ph.D. dissertation. Subfaculty of Sociology, Nuffield College, Oxford.

Noyelle, Thierry J. (1987), *Beyond Industrial Dualism: Market and Job Segmentation in the New Economy.* Boulder, Westview Press.

Noyelle, Thierry and M. Stanback (1989), Training and Competitiveness in US Manufacturing and Services: Training Needs and Practices of Lead Firms in Textile, Banking, Retailing and Business Service. Typescript, Columbia University, DRAFT.

Ouchi, William G. (1980), Markets, Bureaucracies, and Clans. *Administrative Science Quarterly* 25: 129-141.

Piore, Michael J. and Charles F. Sabel (1984), *The Second Industrial Divide: Possibilities for Prosperity.* New York, Basic Books.

Powell, Walter W. (1987), Hybrid Organizational Developments: New Form or Transitional Development. *California Management Review,* Fall: 67-87.

Pratt, John W. and Richard J. Zeckhauser (eds.- 1985), *Principals and Agents: The Structure of Business.* Boston, Harvard Business School Press.

Rochlin, Gene I.; Todd R. La Porte and Kathlene H. Roberts (1987), The Self-Designing High-Reliability Organization: Aircraft Carrier Flight Operations at Sea. *Naval War College Review,* Autumn: 76-90.

Sabel, Charles F. (1982), *Work and Politics: The Division of Labor in Industry.* Cambridge, Cambridge University Press.

Sabel, Charles F. (1989), Flexible Specialization and the Re-emergence of Regional Economies, in Hirst, Paul and Johnathan Zeitlin (eds.), *Reversing Industrial Decline? Industrial Structure and Policy in Britain and Her Competitors.* Oxford, Berg: 17-70.

Salais, Robert and Michael Storper (1990), One Industry, Multiple Rationalities: Flexibility and Mass Production in the French Automobile Industry. Working paper D901. School of Architecture and Urban Planning. University of California at Los Angeles.

Saxenian, Annalee (1990a), The Origins and Dynamics of Production Networks in Silicon Valley. Working Paper no. 516. Institute of Urban and Regional Development, University of California at Berkeley.

Saxenian, Annalee (1990b), Regional Networks and the Resurgence of Silicon Valley. *California Management Review,* vol. 33: 89-112.

Schmitt, Carl (1976), *The Concept of the Political.* Rahway, Rutgers University Press.

Sorge, Arndt; Gert Hartmann; Malcolm Warner and Ian Nichols (1982), *Mikroelektronik in der Industrie: Erfahrungen beim Einsatz von CNC-Maschinen in Grossbritannien und der Bundesrepublik Deutschland.* Frankfurt, Campus.

Stinchcombe, Arthur L. (1965), Organization-Creating Organizations. *Trans-Action,* vol. 2, no. 2.: 34-35.

Stinchcombe, Arthur L. (1985), Contracts as Hierarchical Documents, in Arthur L. Stinchcombe and Carol A. Heimer, (eds.), *Organization Theory and Project Management.* Oslo, Norwegian University Press: 121-171.

Stinchcombe, Arthur L. and Carol A. Heimer (1988), Interorganizational Relations and Careers in Computer Software Firms. *Research in the Sociology of Work,* vol. 4: 179-204.

Storper, Michael and Bennett Harrison (1990), Flexibility, Hierarchy and Regional Development: The Changing Structure of Industrial Production Systems and Their Forms of Governance in the 1990s. Working paper D902. School of Architecture and Urban Planning, University of California, Los Angeles.

Telesis (1989), A Strategic Audit of Manufacturing in the New York-New Jersey Metropolitan Region, September, n/p.

Trigilia, Carlo (1990), Work and Politics in the Third Italy´s Industrial Districts, in Frank Pyke, Giacomo Becattini and Werner Sengenberger (eds.), *Industrial Districts and Inter-Firm Cooperation in Haly.* Geneva, International Labour Organisation: 160-184.

Truman, David B. (1953), *The Governmental Process: Political Interests and Public Opinion.* New York, Alfred A. Knopf.

Williamson, Oliver E. (1975), *Markets and Hierarchies, Analysis and Anti-Trust Implications.* New York, The Free Press.

Williamson, Oliver E. (1985), *The Economic Institutions of Capitalism: Firms, Markets, Relational Contracting.* New York, The Free Press.

Williamson, Oliver E. and William G. Ouchi (1981), The Markets and Hierarchies Program of Research: Origins, Implications, Prospects, in Van de Ven, Andrew and William Joyce (eds.), *Perspectives on Organizational Design and Behaviors.* New York, John Wiley & Sons: 347-370.

Womack, James P.; Daniel T. Jones and Daniel Roos (1990), *The Machine that Changed the World.* New York, Rawson Associates.

Wood, Stephen (1989), The Transformation of Work?, in Stephen Wood (ed.), *The Transformation of Work?* London, Unwin Hyman: 1-43.

Zahavi, Gerald (1981), Negotiated Loyalty: Welfare Capitalism and the Shoeworkers of Endicott Johnson, 1920-1940. *The Journal of American History,* vol. 71, no. 3: 602-620.

Chapter 3
New Production Concepts and the Restructuring of Work

Michael Schumann, Volker Baethge-Kinsky, Martin Kuhlmann, Constanze Kurz, Uwe Neumann
(translated by Brian Barton)

Contents

1 Introduction — Structural Change in Industrial Work

Our article presents the results of a recently concluded empirical investigation on structural changes in industrial work. The project „Trend Report on Rationalisation — Structural Change in Industrial Work in the Car Industry, Machine Tool Manufacture, and the Chemical Industry" (Schumann et al., 1994) was financed through the Association for Technological Research in the Social Sciences by the Federal Ministry for Research and Techology (BMFT) and was carried out between summer 1986 and winter 1992. The radical change in industrial rationalisation emerging in the late 1970s and early 1980s and the debate on „The End of the Division of Labour?" were the starting points for this research project. The question was whether new production concepts really were becoming established and what effects the changes in rationalisation were having for work structures. In a methodical mixture of intensive studies and „overall work structure analyses“ we investigated this issue in the three sectors of the initial study, taking a broadly based empirical approach. In the car industry we investigated factories in three companies, where we covered a total of 29 rationalisation projects in all the key processes of car manufacture (58 workplace observations, 193 interviews with workers, and 264 discussions with experts). In the chemical industry we looked at four companies and seven factories, where we conducted detailed research on 18 rationalisation cases (25 workplace observations, 83 interviews with workers, 180 discussions with experts). In the machine tool industry we included a total of 27 companies in the investigation by use of postal and telephone research; in 10 cases we investigated rationalisation cases on the spot (13 workplace observations, 25 interviews, 57 discussions with experts). Our analyses of overall work structures in which we obtained structural data on how activities in production work and the level of qualifications are changing, covered 79,200 manufacturing jobs in the car industry, 12,000 in the chemical industry, and 4,400 in machine tools. So far we have published results which focused on both the methodological approach (Schumann et al., 1989) and provisional results of the empirical surveys. (Schumann et al., 1990) and the final report (Schumann et al., 1994). In our article we concentrate on a few controversial issues, making specific reference to relevant findings and assessments from other recent studies.

2 The Point of Departure: Marking Out and Narrowing the Field of Study

In spite of all the continuing uncertainties about the effects on the social structure of capitalist economies, few would now dispute that since the late 1970s or early 1980s radical changes have been taking place in the nature of company rationalisation. But a change which ten years ago was just starting to emerge and seemed to point in a clear direction is turning out to be a development which in many areas is extremely sluggish, with many ramifications and counter-movements. Only in a few areas can these trends be anticipated with any degree of reliability; in others predictions can at best be highly provisional. For the world-wide debate on this change in the paradigms of rationalisation[1] the interim résumé by Robert Boyer, based on varied and international comparative material, is of particular interest because it warns us so emphatically against the „widespread over-valuing of the speed of change“ (Boyer, 1992: 66) and because it gives particular emphasis to the contradictory trends in the current process of transformation in company rationalisation. Boyer regards the 1980s solely as a period of incubation with „transitory developments“, in which, because of the changes occurring in socio-economic conditions for action, the limits of the Taylor-Ford concepts as well as the contours of new „principles“ are becoming recognizable. During the transition into the 1990s the only certainty for him is that the old concept can at best only offer defensive, sub-optimal solutions; at the start of the decade, however, the essential conditions and elements for a „new, coherent management style“ are, he suggests, taking shape. Only now, he suggests, can we see these basic principles starting to be translated and adapted in accordance with the particular features of companies, sectors and nations.

According to our results, the phasing of this development is demonstrated in an impressive way by the history of rationalisation in West German industry over the last ten years. The radical change in rationalisation has become established in Germany too, especially as far as its initial premises are concerned; developed policy concepts, however, are still in short supply and are limited to specific areas within individual sectors.[2] The current Lean Production craze has, it is true, nourished hopes among the implementers of rationalisation and even more so among the managers, who seem to think there might exist a generally applicable „new best practice“, but disillusionment is already on its way.

What the „Lean Production“ debate in Germany underlined above all was that the new approaches to rationalisation all go beyond the immediate production process; they are concerned with total concepts that regard the organisation of work and the organisation of the company as a unity. They are concerned with reconstruction not only in the production process but also in

1 In the Federal Republic of Germany, where this debate was stimulated by the argument on „New Production Concepts“, a number of different objections were documented fully in the anthology of Malsch/Seltz (1987).

2 The sector reports on rationalisation can also be used to illustrate the upward and downward trends in this respect (cf. Pries et al., 1989, 1990; Voskamp et al., 1989; Hirsch-Kreinsen et al., 1990; Seltz/Hildebrandt, 1989; Jürgens et al., 1989).

the broad spectrum of research and development, manufacturing within and outside the firm, production planning and organisation, through to ideas about distribution. The sights are set on overall strategies in which organisation and technology, personnel and products, market relationships and control conditions represent the instruments as well as the framework. A feature of today´s structural changes in industry is precisely that it is all-embracing. In the direction it points, it does not leave out any of the various functions and areas of the company, it increasingly relates them systematically with each other and requires strict co-ordination. To this extent it is a change in management philosophy, though its centrepiece is labour policy — dynamic teams and group work are above all what will make it possible to slim down the factory.

This state of affairs takes the heat out of those debates in German industrial sociology that were concerned with setting priorities in such questions as: In what areas and with what means does the structural change in company rationalisation mainly occur; and what importance should be attached to the individual components? „New production concepts" were set against „systemic rationalisation" (Altmann et al., 1986), „labour-centred" concepts against „technology-centred" ones (Bergmann et al., 1986; Hirsch-Kreinsen et al., 1990; Bechte/Lutz, 1989). In our judgement there is little sense in continuing this debate. We now find at any rate broad agreement that industrial sociological analysis has to take this entire process into account by broadening its perspective, if it is adequately to comprehend the new quality of the process. It seems wrong to us, moreover to present a „new type of rationalisation" or „new production concepts" as alternatives; they should be thought of as complementary lines of development. To take up the thoughts of Wittemann and Wittke (1987) on this issue, the debate about new production concepts and the new type of rationalisation can be regarded not as differences in concepts and interpretation but as a division of labour within the field of study. Since there is no developed theory or extended empirical research, the new production concepts analyse the companies´ rationalisation actions in the arena of actual production — so long as advanced production technology exists, a change in the policy of labour deployment is observed. The new rationalisation type, on the other hand, is concerned with the integration of production systems between different areas of the company and the wider networking of whole companies — based essentially on the progress in data-processing technology. The new production concepts seem to be centred on the traditional fields of rationalisation, whilst the new rationalisation type has as its theme the broadening of the dimensions of the industrial rationalisation process — redefining the interfaces between the departments within the company, the increasingly fluid boundaries between companies (relationship between end manufacturer, supplier, machine manufacturer), the integration of companies with their social environment (political organisations, state institutions, private associations), relocalisation of production (new regional groupings), and at the same time new forms of the national and international division of labour — all of these factors influence the direction which the transformation in manufacturing technology and organisation takes in the companies, and are in a reciprocal way affected by these changes.

If we also in the „Trend Report“ (Schumann et al., 1994) focus on the changes in production and the associated changes in the use of labour, this is mainly for pragmatic research reasons, i.e. a research design accessible to empirical methods. We do not, however, overlook the fact that in the follow-up to our 1984 study too we are thereby making an empirical study of only one (admittedly highly relevant) part of the overall rationalisation process and that the results have to be interpreted accordingly. This means that our analysis and its location in terms of the total process has the following serious limitation.

Systemic rationalisation (in the sense of initiatives going beyond the realm of actual production) has, in the past few years, limited the validity of evidence obtained through surveys in the „key“ companies of the „key“ sectors. The division of labour between companies imposed in the context of „inter-company production networks“ (Bieber, 1992) and the reduction of vertical integration are accompanied by considerable restructuring of employment and they explain a tendency for the key sectors to become leaner. This means that analyses of the „key“ areas encompass ever diminishing parts of the totality of industrial labour. In terms of content the studies conform to the logic of a supply network that is organized in pyramid form: it seems certain that, as a result of the industry-wide division of labour, and the consequent trends towards polarisation and segmentation in the key industries, attention becomes focussed precisely on that end of the spectrum that represents the „winners“ in the transformation process. To this extent we can say that when research focusses on these sectors the negative consequences of the new strategies remain systematically under-exposed. It is important that this limitation on the shape of the empirical investigation be taken into account when the findings of the „Trend Report“ are interpreted.[3]

There is today a considerable level of agreement on the points mentioned above; however, the radical change in company rationalisation together with its reception and interpretation by social scientists still seems to us to be controversial in areas concerning the development of industrial work in the key sectors themselves, where the issue is the conceptual change and its effects on work. Significant differences of opinion can be summarized in the following three points:

(1) Insofar as explicit statements on industrial work are made in relation to a new type of rationalisation, these tend to point towards two sets of conclusions. On the one hand it is indicated that labour as both an object and as an instrument of industrial rationalisation strategy is increasingly losing importance the new technologies of information, organisation and control provide a higher potential for elasticity which, it is argued, ensures that the company is able to respond to the increased pressures for greater flexibility and efficiency, and integration of the „entire company system“; consequently the focus on labour from a human resource perspective is reduced to the „implementation phase“ of a new type of process structure. On the other hand, stud-

3 D. Bieber in particular pointed out the limited range of findings from the key industries, with specific reference to the „Trend Report“, in his essay on „Systemic Rationalisation and Production Networks“ (1992). We do not deny this. Bieber, however, also emphasizes the need to retain empirical studies of production processes, because more global interpretations all too easily suffer from the fact that they are having to argue with infirm assumptions about developments on the level of production processes (p. 274). Building on the premise of an expanding industrial-sociological perspective on rationalisation, we are trying — to some degree at least — to take account of the previous omission (which applies to the „Trend Report“ too) in a follow-up project to the „Trend Report“. In this, we concentrate on the one hand on a single industrial „key complex“ (car and supply industry), on the other hand we see in this reduced sectoral focus opportunities to engage in primary empirical analysis of the effects on work of cross-over within the firms (especially to the technical white-collar areas) and inter-company networks (supply firms). In considering any broadening of the analytical framework we need to keep sight of the dilemma in research methodology, namely that the need for a broader approach does not mean that the reduction problem of any empirical investigation can be overlooked. It remains inevitable that sharpening the focus of empirical research will result in only parts of the overall context being dealt with. This imposes corresponding restrictions on the scope of empirical research and its interpretation.

ies may lead us to assume that the effects on work remain largely „uncertain“ and „open“ the concepts of systemic rationalisation evolved through technology and so the planning of their systems occurs in this medium. The deployment of labour is therefore a separate issue and since it is in itself not a „goal“ in the calculation, it is not conceptually determined or measurable by analysis.

These arguments remain in our view contentious. Our counter-argument is that precisely in the use of advanced technologies the effects of production rationalisation on work are no longer the „results“ of other intentions, but deliberate deployment concepts, and are to that extent inferable results of detailed company strategies. We will develop this argument more closely through analysis of labour and company organisation and of the concepts underlying the use of automated production as well as the new forms of system regulation that occur as a result. It should, however, be noted here, that we also consider the accuracy of our judgement to be underlined by recent debates in industrial sociology. Our central argument in „The End of the Division of Labour?“ was that the goals that firms sought to achieve through the use of new technologies — an increase in their capacity for innovation and flexibility, increased use of machines, process optimisation as well as the achievement of company-wide system links — can only be achieved by (cost-benefit) changes in the policy of labour deployment in the direction of a human resource orientation. This is because the algorithm-driven appropriation and remodelling of nature comes up against material barriers, and the increasing technical complexity constantly creates new „left-over problems“ which provide the labour force with the new strategic function of closing these „gaps in manufacturing´s capacity to become technically autonomous“. This assessment of the imperfection of technical solutions is now shared by many industrial sociologists. The „Ironies of Automation“ and the image of the hydra, which is inherent in the technical domination of all further progress, are concrete expressions of this situation. Recent empirical studies[4] confirm that the human capacity for work does not lose its importance as a

[4] Recent studies relating to the sectors or production processes that we highlight here include in particular those of Moldaschl (1991), Böhle/Rose (1992), Dörr (1991) and Wittke/Voskamp (1993). These refer to the workplace level using their own empirical approaches and make reference to work situations and their perception by the employees.

productive force even in automated production processes. Because of the limits to which processes can be controlled by technology, human working activity remains essential in order to secure process continuity and the effective use of capital-intensive production technology. What is stressed is not just the continuing importance, but in fact the growing importance of human labour for automated production processes. At the same time there is broad support for the assertion that the kind of activities that are created here involve production work of a technically demanding level. This leads to the „rehabilitation of human labour", to cite Gerhard Brandt´s early summing-up of the debate in industrial sociology (Brandt, 1987).

In addition recent studies are agreed that the tasks that can be observed in automated production processes are ones which are marked by a specific characteristic of work activity. Böhle/Rose (1992) attribute to the jobs of „plant operators" in automated manufacturing processes a fundamentally different character from that of manual production work and have developed the concept of „subjectifying" work to describe the particular mode of cognitive and practical activity involved. Moldaschl also emphasizes the growing importance of qualitative factors in work activity and draws particular attention to the changed time structure of work (Moldaschl, 1991: 370-374).

With the new results from the Trend Report we are able to confirm and substantiate those assessments and findings that have already probed the issues of „loss of meaning in work" and the „lack of concepts" in labour deployment. Moreover, the MIT investigations of Krafcik (1988) and Womack et al. (1990), and particularly their reception in the companies (irrespective of how we ourselves view these studies in detail) confirm, in our view, that it is difficult to sustain the allegation that systemic rationalisation concepts are „indifferent" to related questions of labour usage and the structuring of working activity. The central message of Lean Production lies in the policy of linking integrative rationalisation measures with a re-evaluation of the work actually carried out; this message is regarded by all parties involved as an idea that points the way forward and as a call for new structural approaches.[5] In the practice of German companies these implications for labour policy are debated mainly with regard to the restructuring of manual produc-

[5] This does not imply, however, that it already established to what extent these structural concepts result in exclusively positive — or even mainly positive — effects on the work situation of the employees.

tion work in the mass manufacturing areas, because this is where the priority need for action is seen in view of the continuing legacy of the Taylor-Ford production model. Even though, in the initiatives inspired by Lean Production it is becoming increasingly obvious that the structuring plans they contain do not represent any convincing break with this legacy, nevertheless the focus on these areas of the firms underlines the continuing importance of a labour-related conceptualisation of company rationalisation.

(2) More recent studies in industrial sociology contain critical assessments of the effects on working practice of the current rationalisation process in (at least partially) automated manufacturing processes; these are directed against the assertions made in „The End of the Division of Labour?“ and relate mainly to the potential in new technologies for monitoring performance and the possibilities offered for extending performance-policy procedures in automation work. In particular, in investigations on the introduction of PPS (production planning systems) in mechanical engineering it is argued that through information and communication technologies, supervision of the production process and (as a result) the work process is reinforced (Manske, 1987, 1991; Dörr, 1991; various contributions at the Sociology Conference in Glatzer 1991: 159-178). According to these, the companies are establishing a new form of monitoring. The way in which this occurs is not so much that the (skilled) machine operators´ scope for action is restricted through a strengthening of the division of labour and more precise constraints concerning the way in which the central task is carried out, but rather that work becomes more transparent and more intense through new ways of representing and controlling the timing and nature of work routines through information technology.[6] Moldaschl (1991) argues on the basis of investigations into high-technology processes in the electrical industry that the connections that are usually assumed to exist between increased qualification requirements, relatively relaxed monitoring procedures and greater opportunities for performance regulation break down. In his view, however, the basis for this is not

[6] A divergent interpretation is given in the machine tool industry study of ISF Munich, which sees Taylorist-inspired rationalisation strategies at work in a whole series of companies — strategies which, through the imposition of technocratic rationalisation projects and an intensification in the division of labour introduce a cycle of successive dequalification (Hirsch-Kreinsen et.al., 1990).

the new quality of information technologies but new forms of performance policy.[7]

(3) New stresses and dangers in the field of modern automation work are emphasized by Böhle (1992, 1993) or Böhle/Rose (1992) and set against what is in their view too „reconciled“ a description of work in our earlier investigation. According to Böhle however the effects of stress relate only partially to the consequences of a specific performance policy; the key factors are the effects of structuring organisations and technology in ways which are not sufficiently geared to the specific working capacities of production workers and to the process requirements of automated production systems. Companies are accused of being „blind“ to the growing strategic importance of experiential knowledge to ensure the functioning of automated systems. Böhle adheres to the notion that the effects on work result from this situation and anticipates new ways in which the problems relating to automation workers will become more acute: „Our argument is that the debate about the intensity of performance demands that was characteristic of the Taylorist syndrome is moving on to a debate about the experiential knowledge that is actually demanded of workers and the risks to which this knowledge is exposed“ (Böhle, 1992: 126).

In the following sections we will relate the results of the „Trend Report“ to these three open questions in the current debates in industrial sociology and to the problems raised over the results in „The End of the Division of Labour?“, and in so doing we intend to justify our divergent position. This debate relates exclusively to automated work, but the lean production concept — which has tended to be ignored by industrial sociology but has had significant effects in company practice — does influence the structuring of work processes, particularly in manufacturing assembly work. For this reason we shall also, in a concluding section to characterize the current form of rationalisation in these areas and question the range and scope of the new forms of work organisation.

[7] Regarding the monitoring aspect of control routines rationalized through information technology, Moldaschl (1991: 376-377) makes precisely the opposite argument: „Performance problems and stresses for the workforce — this has been shown by our stress analyses — result far more from the functioning problems, or the non-functioning, of these systems in the control of time critical processes, and not so much from the possibilities of using information technology to carry out detailed control of work routines and work performance.“

3 Empirical Findings on Industrial Rationalisation and its Effects on Work

3.1 New Concepts of Rationalisation, New Work Patterns, Re-evaluation of Production Work

When Boyer (1992) states as a motto for the 1990s: „Organisation results in more productivity than micro-electronics“ (p. 72), he hits upon a view that is undoubtedly widespread in companies at present; however, with this he is lending support to a judgement which is false at least for German industry, one which pretends that it really is a question of technology-led *or* organisation-led rationalisation strategies. The truth is, rather, that the decision to adopt technology depends in fact to a considerable extent on whether there are accompanying effective organisational concepts that can be expected to bring about economically successful technological solutions. It is precisely in this uncertain relationship between technology and organisation that the new rationality of company rationalisation strategies lies. In particular, this calculation (which may turn out differently in each individual case) is the reason that explains why in the three sectors investigated by us the strategies for technological development differ substantially from each other.

In the car industry automation trends in the1980s are limited essentially to automating key processes in paint-spraying and welding and to perfecting peripheral aspects (tool and part handling) of the traditionally mechanized processes (stamping and mechanical parts production), while in the final assembly plants (with the well-known exception of Workshop 54 at VW) there is no automation except at specific points. In machine tool making, a gradual change from conventional to CNC (computer numerically controlled) manufacturing is taking place, usually in the form of free-standing individual machines and processing centres; only among larger programme manufacturers does this take the form of flexible manufacturing units and systems. In the chemical industry continuous processes with conventional instrumentation are increasingly being converted to digital process control systems. These kinds of control systems are already beginning to be used today in discontinuous batch processes.

In many of the companies in all three sectors these automation processes are integrated into the expanded use of CIM (computer integrated manufacturing) components: computer-aided control of the production flow and the installation of central control rooms in the car industry, the use of production planning and control systems in the mechanical parts production shops of the machine tool industry, the installation of high-level computers for process and production control in many production firms of the chemical industry, to name just a few examples. Nowhere, however, do these individual components fit together to form a CIM system. This visionary notion of production without human involvement is in fact generally regarded as having failed.

Despite the universally high level of process automation and the integration of information technology, the firms in the 1980s do not become involved in particularly ambitious technical projects. If we consider automated assembly, which had been presented as the main task of engineers in the car industry, or central manufacturing control and networking concepts in the machine tool industry, or large-scale process automation in the chemical industry: in each case further developments are rather slow to appear. Even in process organisation, firms abstain from introducing controlling principles that might take too firm a stranglehold on the existing and necessary capacity for independent control of the production systems. The new information technologies serve above all to provide an improved overview of the process data and to co-ordinate the systems as a whole, rather than to take overall control.

The state of technology-orientated rationalisation in the late 1980s and early 1990s can be summed up as follows. In significant areas of manufacturing it has been possible to transfer the execution of the process to the (controlling) system and thereby to get beyond the phase of high mechanisation (control still requires permanent human guidance). Production work that is understood as „system regulation“ is, however, also an expression of the company´s recognition of the fact that, even if the production processes have become more scientifically organized and modelled, there remain gaps in the optimisation, control and guaranteed functioning of those processes. That is to say, human intervention remains necessary to compensate for technical imperfection.

This realisation promotes in all of the sectors investigated by us the search for organisational concepts by which the smooth integration of these systems into the overall context of industrial production can be guaranteed. The focal point of these organisational concepts is the *„system regulator“*, the automation worker who has close experience of the process and whose work complements and develops the engineering design of the production system. Originally this type of production worker was often limited in his/her prescribed activity mainly to regulatory interventions in a production process that was regarded as being autonomous; increasingly, however, the system regulator is forming a central focus of a broader rationalisation calculation, in which the time-critical factor regarding usage of available capacity has been extended to areas and functions that are tangential to the actual production process, and in which rationalisation in the sense of the optimal utilisation of plant increasingly becomes a priority task. Continual process and product innovations mean that the clearly defined time scales for the introduction and optimal utilisation of machinery or product changes become less fixed and more open-ended, and consequently there is inevitably a demand for on-the-spot production expertise that is flexible and available at any time.

Nevertheless our sample reveals — partly determined by specific sectoral characteristics — that quite different approaches to labour policy exist side by side. The approaches differ in the degree to which a division of labour occurs, or a hierarchical structure is imposed on regulatory activities within the production process; they also differ in the extent to which engineering, planning and traditionally indirect functions (quality, maintenance) are integrated (cf. Figure 1). In industrial reality these organisational concepts are used to form links between specific situations in which the system regulators work or act. The common characteristic of the regulators remains in all cases their new relationship to the process, but the breadth and depth of their responsibilities for the process vary according to the work organisation and to labour policy that have been adopted, thus constituting differing (work) forms of system regulation.[8]

The „Traditional Work Organisation" (Type 1) and „Hierarchical Expertise" (Type 1a) both stand for a concept in which the production area concerned is not regarded as a component of an „innovative system" and does not have any independent contribution to make in order to become better integrated into the production process as a whole. The type of organisation referred to as „traditional work organisation" ignores to a large extent the problem of modernisation through production technology and information

[8] We differentiate between the following types of regulator in terms of their work situation:
Regulator Type 1/2: „System regulation with limited allocation of tasks/process competence";
Regulator Type 3: „Qualified system regulation";
Regulator Type 4: „High level system regulation".

technology as well as the new demands which are thereby imposed on the organisation of the company and of the work. In the machine tool industry this means that a work planner is formally responsible for the preparation of the programme, which in reality cannot be sustained. In the car industry the „fitter/operator" model is continued; the higher-level tasks are fulfilled by the former fitter, and simple monitoring tasks by a low level regulator. In the chemical industry on the other hand regulatory functions are carried out in a hierarchically structured way within the framework of the „semi-skilled worker" model, in which the production workers can „climb up the ladder" to the higher levels as they gain experience. Here, the programming is essentially a task for engineers, adjustments are made by means of co-operative „consultation" with the process expert higher in the hierarchy (usually the foreman). The working situation of the regulator is therefore in this organisational model generally determined by a restricted set of tasks and an extremely small area of responsibility for the process, his main function being the monitoring of the production process from the point of view of fault analysis and fault elimination. Regulatory tasks are polarized internally. This type of regulator occupying an extremely precarious position can also be found in the type of organisation named „hierarchical expertise". Although here — at least as far as the chemical industry is concerned — beside the less complex regulatory functions there are also some requiring higher skills. The „hierarchical expertise" type of organisation regards itself as responding to the challenges of the integration problems that are brought about by production and information technologies, but remains firmly attached to the Taylorist paradigm.

The outstanding characteristic of this type of organisation is the use of „specialists" to cope with production-related planning and programming tasks that occur with computerisation — specialists who form a special department in the organisation or else represent a new hierarchical level in production: maintenance staff or system engineers in the car industry, or in the case of the chemical industry a chief regulator or „production engineer" who is not a member of the actual production team.

What we understand by „Limited Integration" (Type 2) is that type of organisation which has already been described in „The End of the Division of Labour?" and in the meantime is frequently found as a „starter solution", introducing integration concepts in the car and chemical industry. In this model the separation of regulatory and indirect tasks is maintained in the company

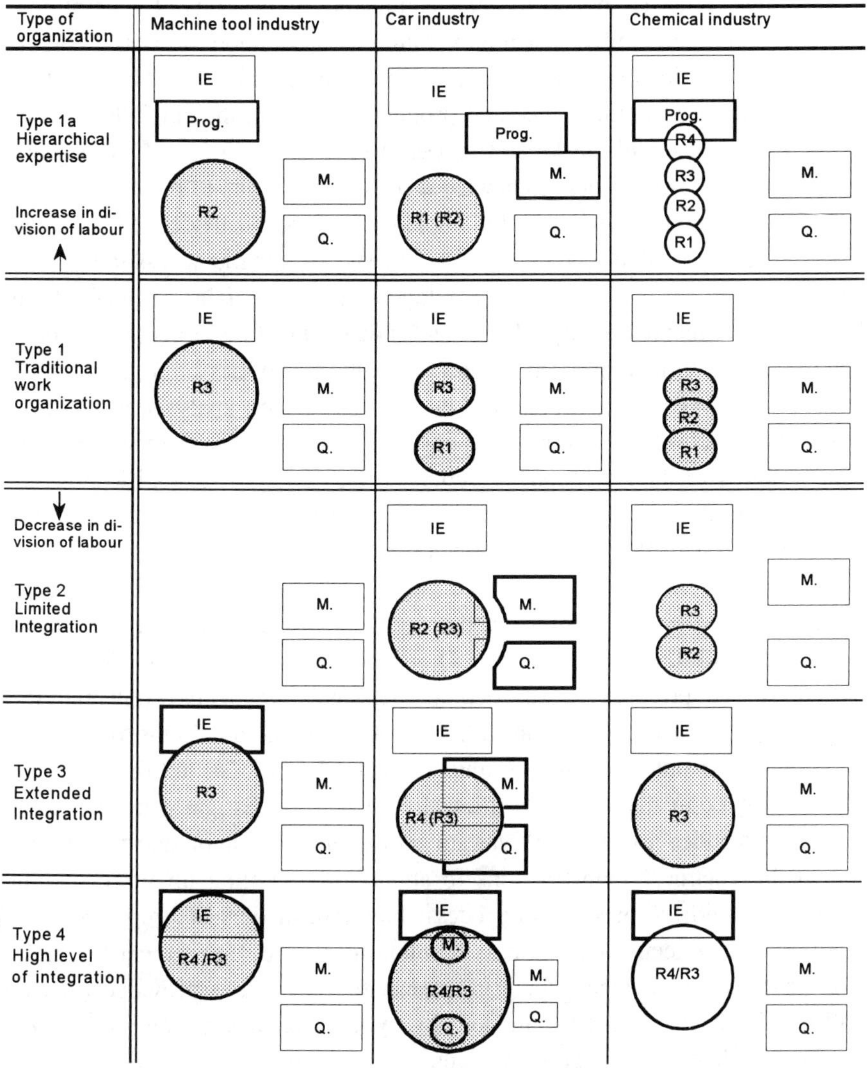

Figure 1: Types of Work Organisation and Labour Deployment in (at Least Partially) Automated Manufacturing*

* Function: system regulation work.

Keys: M = Maintenance; Q = Quality; IE = Industrial Engineering, Planing; Prog. = Programming.

R1 to R4 Levels of system regulation: R1 = System regulation with very restricted task allocation; R2 = System regulation with limited task allocation/process competence; R3 = Qualified system regulation; R4 = High-level system regulation.

organisation. What is abolished either completely or in terms of general policy direction is the differentiation within the production process between regulatory activities that have different degrees of complexity. The adoption of indirect tasks of maintenance and product control (in the car industry) remains limited to simple tasks and serves largely to use more of the regulator´s free time. This model, somewhat inconsistently, fails to provide any appropriate framework conditions for implementing the clearly stated intention of allowing the regulating team as a whole more systematic access to the production process. It is true that the employees are given rights to intervene in the production technology and the variables that control the process, but these powers remain limited and are reduced to routine activities on a semi-skilled level. This is particularly noticeable in the case of fault analysis and correction. When it comes to problem-solving tasks, the regulators repeatedly encounter limits to their freedom of action on the grounds of qualifications or their place in the hierarchy. This is particulary true in the case of more fundamental „large-scale" faults, which process specialists are (of necessity) called upon to remedy.

The organisation types referred to as „extended integration" (Type 3) and „High Level of Integration" (Type 4), by comparison, leave no doubt that considerable importance is attached to the regulating teams´ potential for mastery of the process and innovation — a potential that stems from their permanent confrontation with the functioning of the process and the machine. Today many companies in all of the sectors that we investigated have already put the „Extended Integration" variant into effect. The approach to integra tion in the chemical industry aims to abolish the splitting up of regulating functions within the production process; hierarchical tiers are replaced by a genuine team concept. The team as a whole meets the requirement for high-level process competence (which in organisation Type 2 is provided by specialists). In machine tool production this type designates a strategy of integration which organizes process planning (i.e. creating and optimising the programme) on the basis of co-operative work-sharing relationships created in work preparation and workshop activities. In the car industry the boundaries that traditionally tend to exclude indirect areas such as maintenance and quality assurance are made more fluid; as a result the production team is not just allocated the routine elements of indirect functions. Instead, indirect tasks are deliberately given broader definitions (for example, the ability to make an initial diagnosis when a fault occurs) in order to allow the regulators to grasp the overall connections between processing (methods) parameters and quality parameters and the way in which the technical installation „behaves". This high degree of process competence (in the sense of broad access to the relevant process variables) and the professional nature of the tasks involved distinguishes this type of qualified system regulation from those at the semi-skilled level. The regulators can and should intervene on their own initiative in the control programmes and the machine technology and for this they possess an appropriate systematic and theoretical knowledge which they are able to use together with their experiential knowledge and their overview of the process in order to maintain the optimal functioning of the production process.

The „High Level of Integration" type of organisation represents certainly the most radical break with traditional forms of company and work organisation; it is the most far-reaching attempt to utilize production expertise and one which promotes the interlinking of theoretical knowledge and practical experience. In this type, those functions which were traditionally rooted in various parts of the organisation and which were needed to optimize process operations or plant availability are all brought together under the „roof" of the production department in largely homogeneous „teams". In the machine tool industry this approach is linked to the concept of „Operator Programming".[9] In the chemical industry it now includes participation in developing and optimising the programme. In the car industry the task of optimising the links between the process/processing methods and the machine technology becomes a joint task of the working group composed of a mixture of production mechanics, fitters, electricians and electronics specialists. With this type of organisation the only planning and optimisation functions that are excluded from the range of tasks of the regulating team are those which, as a result of their time structure, would tend to conflict with the regulating function: full repairs on replaced machine parts, pre-planning of complex processing operations, or systematic quality analyses of the processes for which there are no suitable instruments on the spot. However, this model of labour deployment brings about new equal and co-operative relationships with these expert areas (which include the engineers of the planning departments). With the

[9] Attempts to create „manufacturing island" types of organisation should be included here, although we did not find this idea properly developed in any of the firms we investigated.

„Extended Integration“ type of organisation holistic utilisation of the employee is already clearly a central demand, yet the work pattern still in some respects is organised in a way that planning and rationalisation is first of all the privileged business of central planning authorities. In the case of „Full Integration“, on the other hand, rationalisation in the sense of constant process improvement (through the programme and the technology) finally becomes a central task of the production workers.

What our findings show concerning the durability and likely expansion of the individual organisational types is the following. Organisation Type 1 is without doubt a model that is being phased out, for it is the expression not so much of a conscious structural intention but rather of a conservative business policy or a lack of any organisational concept, resulting from an inability to anticipate problems. In the long term this is something that no company can afford. This is not quite so clearly true of the „Hierarchical Expertise“ type of organisation. At any rate, the reason why it is adopted only to a limited extent — at least in our fields of investigation — is not simply that it represents an organisational philosophy that is in retreat. As a concept that promises (but does not guarantee) success it is only possible in cases where a process that is more or less guaranteed to be fault-free keeps the degree of specialist intervention within strict limits; and/or where passive regulatory functions can be combined relatively smoothly with remaining manual functions in a task portfolio. These are conditions which in the sectors we investigated are rarely found but in other sectors may possibly be more common. Even if, therefore, this type is against the „principles“ of new production concepts, it cannot be generally assumed that it is on the point of „dying out“.

There are sound reasons for regarding the „Limited Integration“ type of organisation as a transitional category which sooner or later will merge into the „Extended Integration“ type. When we were conducting research in the early 1980s, we came across the first pilot projects of „Limited Integration“. At the start of the 1990s the trend is quite clearly going in the direction of „Extended Integration“; in the companies limited variants on integration are often explicitly treated as starter solutions by which they can gain experience before risking the next step. Once this type of organisation is linked to the concept of skilled worker deployment, an additional dynamic for change to the more advanced organisational type is created.

It is difficult to judge, on the other hand, whether this „rising“ curve of integration will in the long term extend as far as the „High Level Integration" type of organisation. From the point of view of optimal utilisation of plant, the best solution would undoubtedly be a way of using system regulators that overcomes both horizontal divisions in work relating to maintenance and quality assurance and vertical barriers to team planning. Putting this solution into practice, however, means uprooting many traditional company practices. Resistance is also aroused over the question whether the improvements in system availability and optimisation that can be gained by such advanced organisational concepts always justify such high and (in relation to the overall set of tasks) inevitably „excessive" personnel qualifications. According to our results, at any rate, hurdles have to be overcome before „High Level Integration" can become general practice.

Depending on how far automation has advanced in the companies, as well as on the sector and process involved, the new type of work represented by the system regulator is more or less characteristic of the new industrial structures.

In all of the industries we investigated, the system regulator represents today 8% of the production workers in car manufacturing, 10% in machine tool making, and 47% in the chemical industry. These proportions are very much higher in the technically advanced areas of production: 27% in the machine works and press shops of the car industry; 27% in the machine divisions of machine tool making; 88% in refineries. In particular, tasks which are so far just „mechanized" are constantly being transformed into „automated" processes; the *operation* of machines for example currently applies to 29% of production workers in the chemical industry, 20% in machine tools, and 1% in the car industry (see Table 1). As a result of this the proportion of system regulators will rise considerably in some areas in the next few years.

The system regulator as a category, however, as the various organisational models have shown, does not yet necessarily mean that production work acquires an enhanced value and will be skilled. The level of qualification is determined by the organisation form that is chosen. The type of organisation we have called „Traditional Work Organisation" as well as the „Limited Integration" type corresponds in its qualification requirements to the „semiskilled model", even for system regulator functions. Only with the more advanced approaches to integration does the skilled worker or the highly skilled worker become dominant (see Table 2). In the beginning of the 1990s, only 50% of the system regulator jobs in the car or chemical industry were skilled

Table 1: Forms of Activity in Production Work According to Sectors and Processes/Product Typ
(in %)

Level	Machine tool industry			Car industry				
	Total (n=3,908)	Machine Work	Assembly	Total (n=64,694)	Press Shop	Machine Work	Body Shop	Paint Shop
Manual works on/ with products	66	9	100	70	2	5	71	87
Manual work on machines	4	12	-	21	73	65	23	6
Machine operating	20	52	-	1	-	3	-	1
System regulation	10	27	-	8	25	27	6	6
Total	100	100	100	100	100	100	100	100

* Along the axis „Technical level of production" and „form of work organisation" we distinguis between 4 types of production activity according to the main focus of work: „Manual work c the product" (in pre-mechanized manufacturing); „Manual work on machines" (in mechanize and partially automated manufacturing — according to selected form of work organisation „machine operating" (in mechanized production without computerised process control); „syste regulation" (in — at least partially — automated production with computerized process control

Table 2: Qualification Structures in Production Work According to Sectors and Processes/Produ Type (in %)

Level*	Machine tool industry			Car industry				
	Total (n=3,908)	Machine work	Assembly	Total (n=64,694)	Press shop	Machine work	Body shop	Paint shop
Basic unskilled work	5	7	4	59	49	43	58	64
Higher semi-skilled work	11	15	8	29	32	30	33	29
Skilled work	51	55	48	10	16	17	8	7
Highly skilled work	33	23	40	2	3	10	1	-
Total	100	100	100	100	100	100	100	100

* We grade the qualification requirements in four levels according to the nature and duration o the (professional) training process: „unskilled work" (short introduction, on the job learning u to one year); „semi-skilled work" (systematic learning lasting several months, on the job learr ing up to three years); „skilled work" (apprenticeship or several years systematic job training „highly skilled work" (apprenticeship plus additional specialized training).

** The figures differ from those in the table on forms of activity because of the inclusion of shi foremen.

?ar industry, cont.)			Chemical industry				
ub assembly ?ngine, gear- ?ox, axles)	Final assembly	Total (n=10,728)	Refinery	Chemical based materials	Chemical intermediate products	Chemical products for industrial/ agricultural use	Pharmaceutical products
80	94	4	-	1	12	1	12
11	5	20	5	11	25	22	28
-	-	29	7	25	35	28	36
9	1	47	88	63	28	49	24
100	100	100	100	100	100	100	100

?ar industry, cont.)			Chemical industry				
?b assembly ?ngine, gear- ?x, axles)	Final assembly	Total (n=11,447)**	Refinery	Chemical based materials	Chemical intermediate products	Chemical products for industrial/ agricultural use	Pharmaceutical products
49	66	19	2	15	27	16	32
38	25	36	8	39	32	38	39
10	8	30	39	31	27	33	23
3	1	15	51	15	14	13	6
100	100	100	100	100	100	100	100

or highly skilled. If, however, these advanced integration concepts — as we expect — become established in automated production, then the skilled worker will become the standard type of employee appointed in these areas of the key sectors.

3.2 Extended Freedom of Action and Self-Monitoring

An inherent feature of the system regulator´s work is the relatively open scope for action which is the result of the remaining imperfections and instabilities in the (partially) automated processes and which limits the extent to which working activity can be planned. Through the increasing degree of task integration that is involved in the organisational models described, production work in automated processes becomes upgraded in terms of qualification levels and this tends to be accompanied by a growing scope for individual action and increased opportunities for self-organisation by the working group.

Despite this overall positive evaluation we too in our investigations were able to observe some individual instances of what Manske and Dörr for example have described as the concept of a „new form of monitoring". These kinds of situations were, it is true, only typical in the machine tool industry, and here mainly in those areas of (highly) mechanized — but not automated — production, where the manual nature of human work makes its mark on the overall situation. Because production improvements are related to repeated manual actions such as preparing materials, tightening and controlling, the performance and output achieved remain directly linked to the amount and qualitative characteristics of the productive effort that is invested. Intensification here, therefore, is the result of „closing the pores" of the production process and the direct linkage between production work and work in the sense of manual labour.

We have found, however, that the kinds of problems that occur in highly mechanized manufacturing processes as a result of this work pattern lose some of their force when the transition is made to CNC machines. But we also consider that work on CNC machines in the machine tool industry represents a transitional category, shifting from manual work to systems control, monitoring and regulation. The work involved is characterized by a predominantly *temporal* disengagement of production process and work process. The process no longer needs to be „taken by the hand" and carried out manually.

In a practical sense, however, production and work are still connected. It is still necessary to carry out the process „mentally“ but on the whole this does not form part of any objective process organisation by the companies. The production workers, whose central characteristic continues to be their competence in the relevant work processes, are thus offered opportunities for „subjective“ disengagement which they are able to utilize by extending their freedom of action and controlling their expenditure of physical effort.

When more advanced automation also involving the periphery takes place, on the other hand, i.e. when there is a change-over to processing centres and „systems“, the question of work intensification as a factor harmful to workers´ interests becomes more marginal; this is the case both in the machine tool industry and the automated areas of the other sectors studied. Here, the fact that disengagement of production process and work process has objectively occurred or is subjectively possible provides the chance of a resolution to the conflict of interests between the „business of rationalisation“ and the fear of work intensification.

In stating this we do not wish to deny that new information technology has created the possibility of new forms of monitoring. Overall, however, we have found in our analyses of the work situation few indications that these are actually being used in the form of stricter and more systematic surveillance of work and performance.[10] The primary goal of the technological options adopted is not monitoring of behaviour but surveillance of processes and diagnosis of faults. The actions of workers that are recorded in this way are often documented in a form which at best could only provide feedback on an individual´s performance by means of very complicated evaluation procedures. Even if information relating to performance monitoring is available, as in particular in some documentation systems that are used in the chemical industry, there is a substantial agreement in the companies that the directed use of the potential of information technology for performance monitoring is not only unlikely to achieve success (compared with the effort expended) but would have counter-productive effects. The fear is then that the system regulators refuse to accept responsibility or to co-operate in process optimisation

[10] There are variations in the extent to which automated systems for capturing process and machine data are used; they are certainly used most widely in the chemical industry, where any interventions in the control systems are usually recorded. In many cases, however, data input by the employees themselves still plays a large role.

and collectively reject all active involvement with the installation, the process and the IT aids that are provided. The fact is that the system regulators themselves are the most frequent users of these information systems and — depending on the system structure — have great influence on the quality of the data through their inputs.

The increased use of information systems for targeted investigation into the causes of faults does, it is true, contain for the system regulators the concealed risk that thereby their own wrong actions will be uncovered. This issue is raised, often in a critical way, in the interviews we carried out; not, however, to criticize petty supervision aimed at making the work more intensive but in relation to the pressure to have to avoid making mistakes or alternatively to have to take responsibility for them. At the same time, however, reference is made to the new opportunity opened up by IT to use unambiguous data evidence to prove innocence when unjustified accusations are made.

In our interviews about a third of the system regulators express dissatisfaction or criticism related to the potential use of technology for monitoring purposes. The issue of monitoring has least importance among the Type 4 regulators who are equipped with high powers of intervention; it is, therefore, an issue which declines in significance in the course of the transition to more advanced organisational concepts.

In terms of performance monitoring the situation of the system regulators is marked by a relationship that is based on professional standards and in which employees have substantial freedom of action to organize their work and use this freedom to keep the production process functioning effectively. The condition which makes this arrangement possible (and it is scarcely feasible in traditional manual work because of the quite different performance situation) is that the demands which result from this task definition can be accepted by the employees without significant damage to their own interests and that they even provide scope for development of specialist skills. From the point of view of the companies such a „self-managed“ form of monitoring represents an effective means of building up and integrating the employees´ commitment.

Phenomena such as the „idealisation of technical mastery of the process“, „gradual minimisation of personnel allocations“ or „revaluation of personnel monitoring“, which become central points of analysis in the study by Moldaschl (1991), did not play any significant role in the areas investigated by us. Among the production managers interviewed by us the susceptibility of highly technical installations to faults was taken for granted as part of their experience and justified for them the enhancement of production work in the form of the system regulators. Also the minimisation of staffing levels was, in the automated production areas we investigated, not a priority strategic goal of the companies. On the contrary we often found a situation in which the figures on staffing levels that had been originally planned were gradually increased — as a result of practical experience at the workplace and corresponding negotiations with the employees or the Work´s Council. Their strong strategic position in the companies ensures that the system regulators are well placed in these negotiations. Increasing performance requirements by withdrawal of personnel is therefore generally a difficult policy to push through.

Finally we were not able to observe any revaluation of staff monitoring in the sense of increased external supervision by superiors. In relation to the role of the foremen the situation in automated processes is in fact the reverse, i.e. that their disciplinary and monitoring role tends to be weakened. Because of the complexity of the tasks they are often hardly in a position to keep up with qualified system regulators in terms of detailed specialist knowledge. In practice this leads to a situation in which the system regulators to a large extent organize and co-ordinate their work autonomously. The foremen hardly ever intervene in these processes, limit themselves to representing the group externally, co-ordinate matters of general concern and within the group act if necessary only in relation to social problems.

3.3 New Stress Factors, Old Stress Levels

With regard to the assertion that new types of stress and new risk factors are emerging, evidence can also be found in our analyses to support certain specific findings. We do not, however, share the argument put forward by Böhle and Rose that an internal company debate concerning „objectifying" or „subjectifying" forms of working activity acquires a structurally decisive importance. According to our own results the consequences of stress do not, from the employees´ viewpoint, play the prominent role in the assessment of their working situation which Böhle and Rose seem to suggest.[11] In this particular respect the results of our interviews confirm our own workplace observations. For about half of those questioned stress factors do not form a point of reference which they themselves prioritize in assessing their own work situation, and only a minority of 14% (car industry) or 9% (chemicals) name stress factors as a specific negative feature of their work. Only one third classify the stresses of their work as „serious" — and these refer mainly to shift work. On the question of whether they regard the stress factors over the rest of their working lives as bearable, there are clear divergences between the views of the regulators in the car and chemical industries. An unconditional affirmative response to this question is given by just under 60% of the regulators in the car industry but only one third in the chemical industry. This difference is quite clearly the result of the stress caused by shift work which is typical of the chemical industry, and it demonstrates that traditional stress factors play a greater part in the regulators´ perception than new kinds of stress problems resulting from the restructuring of work and technology.

Our critique of recent studies on the stress situation of production workers in highly technical production processes relates above all, however, to the question : what is the characteristic feature of the system regulators´ work situation? And what importance does stress in general have for their work situation? In our view the key to understanding the work situation of the system regulators lies not in new forms of stress or the employees´ need to come to terms with new performance policy measures or new monitoring technologies. The decisive element is rather the way in which the system regulators´ scope for action has changed compared with traditional forms of manufacturing work.

For the system regulators the questions that are central to their assessment

[11] This is not to say that we reject the differentiation or consider it irrelevant. The description of subjectifying working activity seems indeed to us to coincide with important features of the working activity of system regulators. To that extent it can claim to provide a more exact representation and analysis of the specifics of actions that are tied to experience. We would stress rather more strongly than Böhle/Rose (1992), however, that qualified system regulators manage to integrate and mediate different ways of thinking and acting. Particularly when from the point of view of the employees there are organisational deficiencies and stresses, then the lack of opportunities for getting formal qualifications, lack of knowledge of production technology and production processes, as well as limited authority and powers to act still represent the crucial factors.

of their working situation are those concerning the degree of autonomy they have in their work and the professional dimension of their working situation. These are the determining factors in their overwhelmingly positive judgement of their working situation and their future prospects (as indicated in Table 3, section A).

It is also characteristic of their perception of work that in higher level forms of system regulation (where there are improved opportunities for professional development of working skills as well as greater autonomy in the action sphere) there is also a distinctly more positive attitude not only to the skill situation but also to the effects of company rationalisation. The employees see themselves predominantly in a „professional" working situation and count themselves among the „winners" in the rationalisation process (See Table 3, sections B and C).

Our assumption is that among the system regulators the traditional conflict of interests that is reproduced through the work process has become weaker in important respects. This certainly does not mean, however, that it has ceased completely. Even system regulation is not a conflict-free form of work in which clashes of interests between the two poles of capital and labour have entirely disappeared. Conflicts of interest in the case of system regulators however, had to be divided into two sets.

(1) The traditional conflicts about the amount of remuneration, the number of employees, working conditions and questions of working hours remain virulent. Understaffing, shift work, overtime and traditional kinds of stress such as noise and health hazards represent also for system regulators potential violations of their interests. These factors can sometimes actually increase in highly technical areas, and in the context of a work situation which has otherwise improved, they are then perceived in a particularly negative way.

(2) A comparatively new line of conflict is in the process of being drawn along an axis that includes the weakening in the division of labour, the granting of greater freedom of action, changes in the styles of monitoring, and especially the creation of opportunities for acquiring skills and for professional development. Here, from the point of view of the system regulators, the changes in the companies do not go fast enough or far enough. In particular the change in company organisation is in their view still incomplete. The benchmark they use consists of their own opportunities for participation in planning and their own autonomous implementation of optimisation meas-

ures. In addition there is the question of the provision of company resources in the form of time, money and facilities for further developments that seem necessary. This second line of conflict causes just as many problems for the companies as the traditional one. If the issues are not heeded, the resulting dissatisfaction may cause the best and most „marketable“ workers to leave and to go whatever individual ways are open to them to gain further training or promotion.

Table 3: Perceptions of Work: Systems Regulators*

	System Regulators					
	Total (n=182)	Chemical Industry overall (n=54)	Car industry overall (n=117)	Type R2 (n=42)	Type R3 (n=44)	Type R4 (n=28)
A Assessment of overall work situation						
Positive	59	59	58	40	64	75
Ambivalent	31	33	31	36	30	25
Negative	10	8	11	24	6	-
B Own position in rationalisation process						
„Loser“	7	7	8	4	11	6
Ambivalent	23	21	25	21	36	12
Advantages but not „winner“	12	16	10	21	4	12
Winnner	58	55	58	53	49	70
C Basic assessment of work in professional terms						
Self-developing work	12	12	13	7	16	18
„Interesting“ work	71	72	71	62	74	78
Work not interesting	15	14	14	25	10	5
„Explicitly boring“; insufficiently demanding	2	2	3	7	-	-

* Tables 3 and 4 are derived from in-depth interviews (1.5 to 2.5 hours) concerning system regulators´ and assembly workers´ perceptions of work.

3.4 Manual Work — Continuing Traditions, Open Developments

The dynamics of rationalisation have to be evaluated quite differently in those areas where work still means manual labour. In areas of manual work — which still determine working structures in the car industry[12] — the traditional questions and problems concerning work and performance remain on the agenda. But even in the manual work areas it is not simply a matter of pursuing traditional Taylorist mass production principles. In all of the car-making companies that we investigated we found attempts to take up experiences and principles of work organisation that featured in the discussions of the 1970s with slogans like „New Work Forms" or „Job Re-Design". In most cases, however, these notions involved very limited areas of deployment and narrowly defined restructuring measures. In spite of the growing awareness of the inadequacies of Taylorist working structures and procedures on the assembly lines, no fundamentally new concepts were introduced in these areas during the 1980s. There were technology-based moves away from the assembly line with a broadening of the range of work; detailed ergonomic improvements; internally rotating work groups with a continuation of short-cycle work; integration of material handling; reintegration of individual testing procedures in accordance with the slogan formulated in the 1970s, „Quality is produced, not controlled" — but there was very little else.

At the end of the 1980s therefore manufacturing work was still dominated by traditional short-cycle work in types of organisation marked by hierarchical structures and a continuing division of labour. The picture is for the most part one of continuity in labour policies and the only spots of colour come from a small number of pilot projects. These variants can be grouped in four basic types and form the basis for classification in Table 4.

(1) In the variants described by us as „modified production-line work" the production line is replaced by individual carriers; in this way flexible and variable assembly work sequences are created and stationary assembly is made possible. From the viewpoint of the companies this assembly layout takes account of the increased flexibility requirements in the assembly areas

[12] Within the framework of the „Trend Report" we looked into the new developments in „manual work" principally in relation to final assembly work in the car industry. This part of our article therefore abandons the over-view of different sectors and refers exclusively to the car industry.

and in addition makes it easier to organize the details of the work processes from the time-management aspect.[13] However, in this type of assembly work organisation there is still an adherence to the principle of a centrally controlled line production. There are hardly any possibilities for buffers to be created and the employees are not given the opportunity to establish time accounts. What emerges from this is a phasing of work similar to that of the production line. In the range of tasks this type also remains traditional. The assembly cycles remain short (2 to 5 minutes), indirect activities are hardly ever handed over to the employees concerned and organising tasks remain in the hands of the supervisors. The latter even have to fulfil additional disciplinary tasks in performance monitoring in the case of parallel flows, since the controlling discipline of the conveyor belt is no longer there. The employees are granted hardly any opportunities to organize their own work; in this respect too, the variants summarized here remain traditional, and directed towards the labour deployment policy of the Taylorist production line organisation.

(2) In the second type, „Group Work with modified line organisation", there are significant advances in the withdrawal of horizontal and vertical division of labour and also some moves to break with the functional logic of repetitive work. The technical basis is also a conveyor system which allows stationary non-phased work to take place. The assembly cycles themselves remain short; groups are formed, however, whose field of activity comprises pre-assembly, re-work and simple indirect functions. In addition there is self-organisation on a group basis by means of elected group spokespersons and fixed „time out" periods, thus permitting the groups to undertake planning activities. Self-organized rotation, buffers and training opportunities, as well as negotiated performance conditions still do not lead to any notable enhancement in the professional level of work, but nevertheless bring significant improvement in the working situation.

(3) The third type „Off-line assembly work with extended range of work" also relates to assembly „islands" that permit stationary non-phased assembly work. Here, however, the assembly cycles are significantly higher (10 to 20 minutes) than in Types 1 and 2. In the variants observed by us the work groups (3 to 4 employees) carried out simple indirect tasks in addition to di-

[13] The main aim here, as in all forms of non-line, stationary assembly work, is to reduce losses resulting from bad line-balancing and to reduce handling and transportation times.

rect assembly work. Group work in the sense of defined opportunities for self-organisation and the taking over of planning tasks was, however, not yet achieved in this type of organisation — the vertical division of labour remains intact.

(4) Finally, we found in one case a type of assembly work organisation which in terms of the job dimensions and task definition goes far beyond the traditional pattern of assembly work in mass manufacturing. In the case of „Integrated Assembly Work“ the job cycle was large (60 to 100 minutes) and functionally coherent, and indirect functions were also involved. In this case the work groups still did not have any formal powers of self-organisation, but informally the principle of a stable group formation was practised and the groups were granted the scope for independent organisation of work, performance and training. It is possible in this type to get away from the constraints of an inflexible production line organisation not only by buffers, but also by the large work cycles. Whilst Type 3 already required more qualified employees than the traditional type of assembly organisation, Type 4 represents a sustained upgrading to the level of „semi-skilled work“. Those characteristics of large series assembly work that still remain (high degree of specialized pre-planning, little involvement in problem solving, highly repetitive tasks) mean, however, that this type still does not represent genuine skilled work.

The results of our work analyses and interviews make it clear that along with the different types of assembly work identified by us there are clear differences in the work situation and the way in which it is perceived (see Table 4, sections A and B). Summing up the argument and narrowing it to the central aspect, the assessment of the various types of assembly work by the employees is that the work situation improves in relation to the extent to which the horizontal and vertical division of labour is broken down, and to which the inflexible production line principle is abandoned to create scope for performance regulation.[14]

[14] To this extent our investigations confirm the results of Altmann et al. (1982), who in relation to restructuring projects of the 1970s argued that inadequate structural experiments that are too traditional in their design do not lead to any improvment for the employees and have ambivalent or even negative effects. Altmann et al stressed the negative effects of traditional policies on performance and remuneration and the half-hearted abandonment of production-line principles and traditional personnel policies (inadequate

Table 4: Perceptions of Work: Assembly Workers*

	Assembly work — car industry			
	Type 1 (n=11)	Type 2 (n=8)	Type 3 (n=21)	Type 4 (n=14)
A Assessment of overall working situation				
Positive	9	38	43	64
Ambivalent	36	38	24	14
Negative	55	24	33	21
B Basic assessment of work in professional terms				
Self-developing work	9	13	-	7
„Interesting" work	36	38	38	50
Work not interesting	36	38	48	21
„Explicitly boring"; insufficiently demanding	18	13	14	21

* Tables 3 and 4 are derived from in-depth interviews (1.5 to 2.5 hours) concerning system regulators´ and assembly workers´ perceptions of work.

The judgement of the specific nature of the activity and of the overall working situation becomes all the more positive when there is a more marked enrichment in terms of the range of tasks and the opportunities for self-organisation. Along with group „self-organisation", performance demands are seen as more achievable and the regulatory opportunities are regarded more favourably. It is noticeable that the opportunity for self-organisation can clearly compensate to some degree for drawbacks of the work in terms of the task definition.

In the perception of stress factors it should on the one hand be emphasized again that assembly work in the car industry is to a high degree perceived as an activity that wears down the capacity to work and represents a danger to physical well-being. The stresses here result largely from the activity itself. On the other hand it becomes clear even here that the seriousness of the

training, retention of the vertical division of labour). Also the results of the study by Berggren (1991) in Sweden are in accordance with our findings on pilot projects in the German car industry. According to Berggren, the working situation improves, the more the principle of function-integrated complete assembly is followed and the more autonomy is created in the work groups.

threat is assessed differently according to the type of assembly work. Powers of self-organisation, functioning group structures and acceptable performance conditions have a positive effect particularly in relation to the long-term ability to cope with stress.

The growing awareness of increasingly strong international competition, together with the results of Womack et al. (1990) indicating serious productivity weaknesses particularly in these areas of the German car industry, and the knowledge that final assembly work will remain a work-intensive area for the foreseeable future: these factors accelerated the search for viable solutions at the start of the 1990s. In all German car firms reorganisation of assembly production — though based on differing concepts and methods — is on the agenda for the 1990s. The focus is becoming the more or less universal introduction of various forms of group work.[15] It is intended that within the framework of group work concepts not only a new ability and willingness to achieve better performance should be mobilized; the main point is to arrive at a system of continual improvement of production processes which is basically sustained by the assembly workers. The production system that is overall more flexible, logistically more closely integrated and provided with fewer safety buffers increases the demands on the reliability and commitment of the employees in all areas of production. With specific reference to system regulators we have given reasons why process optimisation in technically advanced production areas appears attractive even from the viewpoint of the employees and why the greater commitment on the part of the employees is usually forthcoming. In manual work, on the other hand, attempts at fundamental reorganisation which seek to involve production workers more intensively in rationalisation processes are faced with particular problems because of the work situation in those areas.

Organisational concepts which seek to establish a fundamentally new way of dealing with employees, to create new performance potential and to involve all production employees more closely in a permanent process of optimisation — such concepts encounter in the manual labour areas long-established structures based on traditional labour policies and conservative work orientations (Schumann et al., 1982). Accordingly, production workers reject

[15] At this point we can only refer to the discussion on the concepts employed here. Cf. in particular Muster (1990), Berggren (1991), Jürgens et al. (1989), Jürgens (1990), Turner (1991), Scherrer/Greven (1993).

any change in their work in principle, because it endangers the status quo into which they have settled and with which they feel familiar.

If organisational initiatives are aimed exclusively at cultural and social integration[16] or are limited to the establishment of higher performance standards in the context of favourable general conditions (particularly an economic crisis, a slack labour market, limited representation of workforce interests), then they are likely to achieve only small or temporary effects. The traditional attitude of the employees to their work is too strongly rooted in experiences and interests relating to their working situation and is, in addition reinforced by the existing company structures.

A new attitude to work could only arise through a change in policy towards work and performance. This is the objective of current efforts at reorganisation in which increases in productivity *and* improved working situations are promised.[17] Whether this will work and what changes it will lead to in the companies and for the employees[18] should become one of the central fields of investigation for industrial sociological research in the 1990s.

On the basis of our analyses of work and interviews we consider that the effects that are hoped for will only occur if:

(1) innovations occur on the level of work and performance organisation;

(2) there are serious attempts to shift power to the level of those performing the work;

(3) this is accompanied by a general restructuring of the plant organisation;

(4) the employees achieve a real improvement in terms of their working situation and the requirements and conditions relating to their performance;

(5) a fair and lasting compromise is achieved on the issue of performance and productivity increase.

[16] The individual components of such a strategy are described by Deutschmann (1989).

[17] In German companies, and also internationally, the slogan „work smarter not harder" seems to be gaining acceptance for this approach.

[18] Empirical studies that illuminate the consequences of team concepts practised in North America are collected in Lüthje/Scherrer (1993). For the Federal Republic of Germany there are so far only some initial attempts at empirical research into the effects on work of new organisational concepts: Minssen et al. (1991).

4 Problems Beyond the Reach of our Empiricism

Our argument so far remains limited to those questions that we are more or less „certain" of being able to answer through our trend report. But rationalisation at the present time extends far beyond the topics we have identified. In our following remarks we wish to at least suggest areas where we ourselves consider it necessary to broaden the perspective.

The new working and professional role of the *system regulator* is starting to become established in terms of professional standards if it is compared to traditional manual labour or to the early phase of integrated process and work organisation. At the same time the traditional performance conflict and with that the question of old and new models of monitoring for the system regulator have declined in importance. The aim is to be able to fulfil professional, communicative and expressive (i.e. subjective) demands in work and through work, and although the current organisational models do not always achieve this in an optimal way, the opportunities offered are clearly becoming greater.

It is possible to find evidence of a process of „increasing normative subjectivisation of the immediate working process" (Baethge), which is both desired by the subjects involved and promoted by workforce-oriented concepts; to make this assertion, however, does not imply any intention to present a miniature picture of the industrial worker liberated from all control and production constraints (Bergmann, 1990). The working actions of the system regulator remain part of the „factory regime" with its functional principles relating to time and practice, its divisions of labour and imbalances of power; they certainly do not present „liberated" work in Gorz´s sense (Gorz, 1989). We should not underestimate the fact that experiences at work *help* to create a trained, autonomous, independent type of worker who can make his/her presence felt in disputes within the firm and at the same time has developed social competences and sensitivity (Kern/Schumann, 1988). However, precisely because the working situation is increasingly determined by subjective factors, individual (though not per se „conformist") interests (Bergmann, 1990) carry much weight and can easily dominate collective or social orientations. At the same time the consequences of modernisation represent a risk to the world in which we work and live and thus also to the need for subject-centred thinking. Time will tell whether the system regulator is willing and able to use his „surplus" activity and critical ability to support ecological changes in production and living conditions both within the company and in society.

The privileged situation of the *system regulator* should not allow us to forget that for the majority of production workers in manual work, where the exploitation of labour is still the order of the day, „subject-centred work concepts“ are still far away. The resulting divergence of interests between manual workers and system regulators has given rise to an extremely precarious situation for the works councils in the early 1990s. Segmentation between different groups in the work force is hardening and is difficult to deal with in a fundamental way by means of training and retraining programmes or quota systems. A re-structuring policy that targets these fields is concentrated primarily on the already well-established winners in the high-tech areas. In the low-tech areas on the other hand there is (still) an overriding need for traditional protection and performance policies. As the industrial worker overall cannot therefore be made into a standard reference unit for group representation policies in the firm, the only labour policy that the workforce representatives can conduct for the time being is a kind of balancing act between a modern policy of reprofessionalisation and maintenance of the status quo.

To what extent substantial changes can be expected here as a result of the new concept in labour policy and how far the problem of segmentation might — to some degree — resolve itself must remain an open question for the moment. The answer will depend to a large extent on whether, and on what conditions, the firms are willing actually to establish an independent „problem-solver“ (Voskamp/Wittke, 1992), for workers with much broader tasks in thc areas of manual work, too. The special conditions affecting the way in which the timing and nature of repetitive work are structured do not provide any clearly viable way of doing this. On the other hand it is not impossible that if improvements in work and increases in performance can be successfully reconciled, a revaluation of assembly work can occur which helps to bridge the currently wide gap between skilled production workers and workers performing repetitive single tasks.

The reorganisation of privileges and discrimination within the companies in the key sectors can be explained not only as the results of the process of technological change and the consequent change in manpower deployment. The reorganisation of production into world-wide networks is influencing the shape and speed of the process by which production structures are becoming more heterogeneous. Systemic rationalisation measures that are intended to create internal and external flexibility signal the integration of work routines carried out within the firm and between firms; at the same time, however, they also induce processes of „vertical disintegration“ (Leborgne/Lipietz, 1990) which shake up the employment and social structures, working relationships, and not least the spatial structure in an extremely unpredictable way.

Insecure manual work may be hived off to the next layer in the supply pyramid whilst at the same time work at the „main factory“ is upgraded; employment relations may become more flexible and deregulated or there may be (collectively arranged) offers of extended participation; de-industrialisation on the one hand, the promotion of peripheral regions to become new growth centres on the other; world wide versus national sourcing versus local production systems: development trends such as these can be found (with very contradictory effects on work) within and alongside each other in international, national and local economic areas, and only to a limited extent can they be brought together to form convincing development models (Krätke, 1991).

Industrial sociology has difficulty in seeing beyond the micro-level of the firm — summing up „in a nutshell“ the disparate, contradictory features of economic, social and spatial restructuring. It is the „external“ processes, however, that are affecting the micro-level to an increasing extent and they are forcing research to include movements beyond the „command centres“ in their field of vision. It is obvious that because this perspective has to be adopted in industrial sociology, we run the risk of allowing „our own object of investigation and that which makes it socially significant slip through our fingers“ (Bechtle/Lutz, 1989: 79). Yet the call for increased interdisplinarity and new „risk-taking research strategies“ remains unsatisfying so long as the responses to „original“ industrial-sociological aspects of the complex processes of change — for example in terms of their effects on employment and industrial relations — remain comparatively thin in their empirical content.

In contrast to what occurred in the 1980s, it is also important to identify much more the expanding groups of „losers“. For one thing is obvious: whereas previously the regular workforce was relatively secure in terms of employment policy, even if their chances of sharing in the modernisation process may have varied, these workers will now fragment further into „key“ and „marginal“ groups. Patient observers will become „losers“, not least in the supply firms. Many see themselves as being in the „shadow of working society", faced — not in the short term but certainly in the medium to long term — with the risk of permanent exclusion from the labour market and with a no-win situation (Kronauer et al., 1993). In turning to the „losers" and the unemployed our task is to acknowledge their growing social importance much more emphatically than in the 1980s, and to take up their particular problem situations as part of a critical research perspective in industrial sociology.

References

Altmann, N., Z. Binkelmann, K. Düll and H. Stück (1982), *Grenzen neuer Arbeitsformen — Betriebliche Arbeitsstrukturierung, Einschätzung durch Industriearbeiter, Beteiligung der Betriebsräte*. Frankfurt/New York, Campus.

Altmann, N., M. Deiß, V. Döhl and D. Sauer (1986), Ein „Neuer Rationalisierungstyp" — neue Anforderungen an die Industriesoziologie, in *Soziale Welt*, 37(2/3): 191-206.

Baethge, M. (1991), Arbeit, Vergesellschaftung, Identität — zur zunehmenden normativen Subjektivierung der Arbeit, in Zapf, W. (ed.), *Die Modernisierung moderner Gesellschaften — Verhandlungen des 25. Deutschen Soziologentages in Frankfurt am Main 1990*. Frankfurt/New York, Campus.

Bechtle G. and B. Lutz (1989), Die Unbestimmtheit post-tayloristischer Rationalisierungsstrategien und die ungewisse Zukunft industrieller Arbeit — Überlegungen zur Begründung eines Forschungsprogramms, in Düll and Lutz (1989).

Berggren, Chr. (1991), *Von Ford zu Volvo — Automobilherstellung in Schweden*. Berlin, Springer.

Bergmann J. (1989), „Reelle Subsumtion" als arbeitssoziologische Kategorie, in Schumm (1989).

Bergmann, J. (1990), Einige Anmerkungen und Fragen zur Göttinger Arbeitssoziologie, in Lösche (1990).

Bergmann, J., H. Hirsch-Kreinsen, R. Springer and H. Wolf (1986), *Rationalisierung, Technisierung und Kontrolle des Arbeitsprozesses. Die Einführung der CNC-Technologie in Betrieben des Maschinenbaus*. Frankfurt/New York, Campus.

Bieber, D. (1992), Systemische Rationalisierung und Produktionsnetzwerke, in Malsch and Mill (1992).

Böhle, F. (1992), Grenzen und Widersprüche der Verwissenschaftlichung von Produktionsprozessen, in Malsch and Mill (1992).

Böhle, F. (1993), Objektivierendes und subjektivierendes Arbeitshandeln — Rationalisierung und Risiken bei neuen Formen qualifizierter Produktionsarbeit. Munich, unpublished paper.

Böhle, F. and H. Rose (1992), *Technik und Erfahrung — Arbeit in hochautomatisierten Systemen*. Frankfurt/New York, Campus.

Boyer, R. (1992), Neue Richtungen von Managementpraktiken und Arbeitsorganisation, in Demirovic, A., H.-P. Krebs and Th. Sablowski (eds.), *Hegemonie und Staat — Kapitalistische Regulation als Projekt und Prozess*. Münster, Verlag Westfälisches Dampfboot.

Brandt, G. (1987), Fragen der betrieblichen Arbeitsgestaltung im Kontext der technisch-wissenschaftlichen Entwicklung, in Brandt (1990).

Brandt, G. (1990), *Arbeit, Technik und gesellschaftliche Entwicklung — Transformationsprozesse des modernen Kapitalismus. Aufsätze 1971-1987*. Frankfurt, Suhrkamp.

Deutschmann, Ch. (1989), Reflexive Verwissenschaftlichung und „kultureller Imperialismus" des Managements, in *Soziale Welt* (3): 374.

Dörr, G. (1991), *Die Lücken der Arbeitsorganistion. Neue Kontroll- und Kooperationsformen durch computergestützte Reorganisation im Maschinenbau*. Berlin, Edition Sigma.

Düll, K. and B. Lutz (eds.- 1989), *Technikentwicklung und Arbeitsteilung im internationalen Vergleich. Fünf Aufsätze zur Zukunft industrieller Arbeit*. Frankfurt/New York, Campus.

Glatzer, W. (ed.- 1991), *25. Deutscher Soziologentag. 1990. Die Modernisierung moderner Gesellschaften*. Opladen, Westdeutscher Verlag.

Gorz, A. (1989), *Kritik der ökonomischen Vernunft — Sinnfragen am Ende der Arbeitsgesellschaft*. Berlin, Rotbuch.

Hildebrandt, E. and R. Seltz (1989), *Wandel betrieblicher Sozialverfassung durch systemische Kontrolle?* Berlin, Edition Sigma.

Hirsch-Kreinsen, H., R. Schultz-Wild, C. Köhler and M. Behr (1990), *Einstieg in die rechnerintegrierte Produktion — Alternative Entwicklungspfade der Industriearbeit im Maschinenbau*. Frankfurt/New York, Campus.

Jürgens, U. (1990), Der japanische Produktivitätserfolg, in Muster and Richter (1990).

Jürgens, U., K. Dohse and T. Malsch (1989), *Moderne Zeiten in der Automobilfabrik — Strategien der Produktionsmodernisierung im Länder- und Konzernvergleich*. Berlin, Springer.

Kern, H. and M. Schumann (1984), *Das Ende der Arbeitsteilung? Rationalisierung in der industriellen Produktion*. Munich, Beck.

Kern, H. and M. Schumann (1988), Kontinuitätsbrüche, verschobene Problemlagen, gewandelte Orientierungen — Herausforderungen an eine Gesellschaftspolitik in den 90er Jahren, in *Die Neue Gesellschaft* (4): 300-308; (5): 471-480.

Krafcik, J.F. (1988), Comparative analysis of performance indicators at world auto assembly plants. Boston, unpublished paper.

Krätke, S. (1991), *Strukturwandel der Städte. Städtesystem und Grundstücksmarkt in der „post-fordistischen" Ära*. Frankfurt/New York, Campus.

Kronauer, M., B. Vogel and F. Gerlach (1993), *Im Schatten der Arbeitsgesellschaft. Arbeitslose und die Dynamik sozialer Ausgrenzung*. Frankfurt/New York, Campus.

Leborgne, D. and A. Lipietz (1990), Neue Technologien, neue Regulationsweisen: Einige räumliche Implikationen, in Borst, R.; S. Krätke, M. Mayer, R. Roth and F. Schmoll (eds.), *Das neue Gesicht der Städte. Theoretische Ansätze und empirische Befunde aus der internationalen Debatte*. Stadtforschung aktuell, Vol. 29. Basel/Boston/Berlin, Birkhäuser.

Lehner F. and J. Schmid (eds.-1992), *Technik — Arbeit — Betrieb — Gesellschaft, Beiträge der Industriesoziologie und der Organisationsforschung*. Opladen, Westdeutscher Verlag.

Lösche, P. (ed.- 1990), *Göttinger Sozialwissenschaften heute — Fragestellungen, Methoden, Inhalte*. Göttingen, Schwartz.

Lüthje, B. and Chr. Scherrer (eds.- 1993), *Jenseits des Sozialpakts — Neue Unternehmensstrategien, Gewerkschaften und Arbeitskämpfe in den USA*. Münster, Westfälisches Dampfboot.

Lutz, B. (1987), Wie neu sind die „neuen Produktionskonzepte"?, in Malsch and Seltz (1987).

Malsch, T. (1987), „Neue Produktionskonzepte" zwischen Rationalität und Rationalisierung — mit Kern and Schumann auf Paradigmensuche, in Malsch and Seltz (1987).

Malsch, T. and U. Mill (eds.- 1992), *ArBYTE — Modernisierung der Industriesoziologie?* Berlin, Edition Sigma.

Malsch, T. and R. Seltz (eds.- 1987), *Die neuen Produktionskonzepte auf dem Prüfstand. Beiträge zur Entwicklung der Industriearbeit*. Berlin, Edition Sigma.

Manske, F. (1987), Ende oder Wandel des Taylorismus? — Von der punktuellen zur systemischen Kontrolle des Produktionsprozesses, in *Soziale Welt* (2): 166-180.

Manske, F. (1991), *Kontrolle, Rationalisierung und Arbeit — Kontinuität durch Wandel: Die Ersetzbarkeit des Taylorismus durch moderne Kontrolltechniken*. Berlin, Edition Sigma.

Minssen, H., J. Howaldt and R. Kopp (1991), Gruppenarbeit in der Automobilindustrie — Das Beispiel Opel Bochum, in *WSI-Mitteilungen* (7): 434-441.

Moldaschl, M. (1991), *Frauenarbeit oder Facharbeit? — Montagerationalisierung in der Elektroindustrie II*. Frankfurt/New York, Campus.

Muster, M. (1990), Team oder Gruppe? Zum Stand der Sprachverwirrung über die „Gruppenarbeit", in Muster and Richter (1990).

Muster, M. and U. Richter (eds.- 1990), *Mit Vollgas in den Stau*. Hamburg, VSA.

Pries, L., R. Schmidt and R. Trinczek (1990), *Entwicklungspfade von Industriearbeit — Chancen und Risiken der Produktionsmodernisierung*. Opladen, Westdeutscher Verlag.

Pries, L., R. Schmidt and R. Trinczek (eds.- 1989), *Trends betrieblicher Produktionsmodernisierung — Chancen und Risiken für die Industriearbeit*. Opladen, Westdeutscher Verlag.

Scherrer, Ch. and T. Greven (1993), Für zu schlank befunden — Gewerkschaftliche Erfahrungen mit japanischen Produktionsmethoden in Nordamerika, in *WSI-Mitteilungen* (2): 87-97.

Schmid, J. and U. Widmaier (eds.- 1992), *Flexible Arbeitssysteme im Maschinenbau — Ergebnisse aus dem Betriebspanel des Sonderforschungsbereichs 187*. Opladen, Westdeutscher Verlag.

Schmiede, R. (1989), Reelle Subsumtion als gesellschaftstheoretische Kategorie, in Schumm (1989).

Schumann, M., V. Baethge, U. Neumann and R. Springer (1989), Arbeitstypologische Bestandsaufnahme. Zum methodischen Ansatz der Untersuchung: „Strukturwandel der Industiearbeit — Entwicklungen in der Automobilindustrie, im Werkzeugmaschinenbau und in der chemischen Industrie", in *Mitteilungen des Verbunds Sozialwissenschaftliche Technikforschung* (5): 25-35.

Schumann, M., V. Baethge-Kinsky, M. Kuhlmann, C. Kurz and U. Neumann (1992), Neue Arbeitseinsatzkonzepte im deutschen Automobilbau — Hat lean production eine Chance?, in *SOFI-Mitteilungen* (19): 15-27.

Schumann, M., V. Baethge-Kinsky, U. Neumann and R. Springer (1990), Breite Diffusion der neuen Produktionskonzepte — Zögerlicher Wandel der Arbeitsstrukturen, in *Soziale Welt* (1): 47-69.

Schumann, M., E. Einemann, Ch. Siebel-Rebell and K. P. Wittemann (1982), *Rationalisierung, Krise, Arbeiter — eine empirische Untersuchung der Industrialisierung auf der Werft*. Frankfurt, Syndikat.

Schumann, M., V. Baethge-Kinsky, M. Kuhlmann, C. Kurz and U. Neumann (1994), *Trendreport Rationalisierung: Automobilindustrie, Werkzeugmaschinenbau, chemische Industrie*. Berlin, Edition Sigma, Rainer Bohn.

Schumm, W. (ed.- 1989), *Zur Entwicklungsdynamik des modernen Kapitalismus: Beiträge zur Gesellschaftstheorie, Industriesoziologie und Gewerkschaftsforschung. Symposium für Gerhardt Brandt*. Frankfurt/New York, Campus.

Seltz, R. and E. Hildebrandt (1989), Rationalisierungsstrategien im Maschinenbau — systemische Kontrolle und betriebliche Sozialverfassung, in Pries et al. (1989).

Turner, L. (1991), *Democracy at work — Changing world markets and the future of labour unions*. Ithaca/London, Cornell University Press.

Voskamp, U., K.P. Wittemann and V. Wittke (1989), *Elektroindustrie im Umbruch. Zur Veränderungsdynamik von Produktionsstrukturen, Rationalisierungskonzepten und Arbeit*. Interim report. Göttingen, SOFI.

Voskamp, U. and V. Wittke (1992), Junge Facharbeiter in der Produktion — eine Herausforderung für betriebliche Arbeitspolitik, in *SOFI-Mitteilungen* (19): 28-34.

Voskamp, U. and V. Wittke (1993), Neue Anforderungen an HdA? Zum Verhältnis von neuen Entwicklungslinien in der Rationalisierung und der Anforderungen and HdA am Beispiel der Elektroindustrie. Final report. Göttingen, SOFI.

Witteman, K.P. and V. Wittke (1987), Rationalisierungsstrategien im Umbruch? — Zu den Auswirkungen von CIM und Just-In-Time auf industrielle Produktionsprozesse, in *SOFI-Mitteilungen* (14): 47-86.

Wittke, V. (1989), Systemische Rationalisierung — Zur Analyse aktueller Umbruchsprozesse in der industriellen Produktion, in *SOFI-Mtteilungen* (17): 41-52.

Womack, J.P., D.T. Jones and D. Roos (1990), *The machine that changed the world*. New York, Rawson Associates.

Chapter 4
Gender and Technology: An Appraisal of the Labour Process Debate

Juliet Webster

Contents

1 Introduction

The publication in 1974 of Braverman´s seminal work, *Labor and Monopoly Capital*, together with the emergence in the late 1970s of information and communication technologies (ICTs), has prompted a huge resurgence of interest in technologies and their effects upon social and industrial divisions of labour. The „labour process debate" which ensued concerned itself with understanding the precise nature of changes in management strategy, work organisation, and the deployment of technology in late twentieth century capitalism.

When Braverman´s book first provoked the labour process debate, general criticisms were made about his presentation of both the working class and capital as homogenous groups undifferentiated by sectional interests or individual strategies for maintaining or securing control over the labour process. Many labour process writers after Braverman have therefore attempted to develop and refine labour process concepts of the degradation of work, the application of new techniques, skill and deskilling, and managerial control

(Friedman 1977; Edwards 1979; Burawoy 1979; Elger 1982; Wood and Kelly 1982).

Feminist labour process writers presented further criticisms of the labour process analysis. They were concerned about Braverman´s failure to account for the specificity of female wage labour within monopoly capitalism (Baxandall et al. 1976; Beechey 1977; Gardiner 1977; West 1978; Barrett 1980). Their objections can be summarised as being twofold. First, they argued that Braverman´s account was unable to explain the source of female subordination at work in terms other than their role in domestic reproduction and consumption. Such an account failed to address processes operating *within* the workplace which created and perpetuatued a ghettoisation of women in low-grade jobs and the sex-typing of particular jobs (Beechey 1983; Liff 1986). In particular, the various managerial control strategies elaborated by Braverman and others (for example, Friedman 1977 and Edwards 1978) failed to address the specific ways in which female workers were controlled in the workplace — not only by capitalist management but also by men. The concept of patriarchy was advanced to explain why women rather than men were concentrated in deskilled, low-paid work at the bottom of the hierarchy of production and to provide an understanding of the specific control strategies to which women were subject (Hartmann 1976; Barker and Downing 1980; Walby 1986). Patriarchy was thus „not simply an ideology legitimising the status quo but an institutionalised system for the control of female labour, operating in the interests of men — ordinary men" (West 1990:246). Feminists thereby issued a challenge to labour process theory to take account of forms of domination, oppression and exploitation based on both gender and class.

Second, they pointed out that Braverman´s conception of „skill" and „deskilling" was based on an ideal-type of craft work, which has historically been monopolised by men who enjoy significant bargaining power to the exclusion of women. This meant that „skill", as well as denoting technical expertise and control over the labour process, was a concept „saturated with sexual bias":

> far from being an objective economic fact, skill is often an ideological category imposed on certain types of work by virtue of the sex and power of the workers who perform it (Phillips and Taylor 1980:79).

The consequence of this bias has been that the craft-based concept of „skill" predominant in much labour process theory fails to encapsulate the competences of women at work (Phillips and Taylor 1980; Beechey 1982). Moreover, the labour process concept of „deskilling", reliant as it is upon this conventional notion of skill, equally leaves unexplained changes in women´s labour processes. For these changes to be properly addressed, a more complex definition of skill is required which takes into account not only manual dexterity and control over the labour process, but also the labour market position and (lack of) bargaining power of different groups of workers.

These, then, have been some of the general criticisms of the labour process approach raised by feminists. In their turn, they have initiated an intense debate, for example, about the precise explanatory status of „patriarchy" in understanding women´s subordination, and about the relationship between gender, class and race divisions of labour — a debate which remains unresolved (Knights and Wilmott 1986). However, in addressing the deficiencies in orthodox labour process theory, feminist writers have drawn attention to the fact that its understanding of women´s subordination in the workplace is as yet comparatively poorly developed, and that much labour process theory has overlooked the position of women workers or has assumed that female workers are subject to the same processes as male workers.

This chapter outlines the major insights contributed by feminist research to the labour process debate. It focusses particularly upon the debate in Britain, the U.S. and Australia, showing how feminist research in these countries has highlighted the gender/technology relationship as a topic which is central to our understanding of developments in the labour process, rather than being marginal to it, as labour process writers too often seem to assume. Having considered the ways in which „old" divisions of labour are shot through with gender differentiations, the chapter examines the so-called „new division of labour", searching for evidence of gender awareness in the flexibility debate and questioning whether this literature is any more sensitive to gender issues than the labour process literature.

2 Technology and the Labour Process: A Growing Recognition of Gender Issues

Until the influence of feminist analysis gained ground, labour process studies of technological change also remained remarkably sex-blind, reflecting a general complacency about gender divisions and relations within industrial sociology, labour economics and industrial relations. Many of the early studies concentrated solely on the impacts on men´s jobs (e.g. Noble 1979; Wilkinson 1983), or made generalisations about the impacts of technological change on men´s jobs which assumed that these were applicable to *all* jobs. A major deficiency of all of these early studies was their ignorance of the ways in which gender relations are not only affected by technology, but are actually to be found at the centre of the process of technological change. As Arnold and Faulkner have pointed out:

> Precisely because men do dominate most of our social institutions, any analysis of technology which does not take gender into account runs the risk of largely analysing relations between men (1985:2).

Recent feminist research has set out to provide a corrective to this state of affairs. At an empirical level, it has been concerned to understand the effects of technological change on women´s work and gender relations in the workplace. Also, and at a more theoretical level, it has sought to articulate the relationship between gender and technology, and particularly to analyse the ways in which technologies, similarly to jobs, come to be gendered — that is, to have gender relations and divisions of labour embedded within them.

2.1 Technological Change: The Impact on the Sexual Division of Labour

Conventional labour process theory has assumed that, at the macro-level, technical change would result in an increasing degradation of labour and the substitution of male labour with cheap, unskilled female labour. Women were seen as constituting a „Reserve Army of Labour“, an army which could easily be drawn into or repelled from waged work at a relatively low cost to capital. As well as securing the subordination of this section of the labour force, the existence of a reserve source of labour, it was argued, had the additional advantage of holding down wage levels of those in employment.

The explanation for women´s subordination in production was to be found in women´s actual or assumed role in the family (Beechey 1977).

Studies of occupational shifts associated with technical change in the U.K. reveal numerous difficulties with this concept (Hakim 1978, 1981). They do not indicate that the introduction of technology has led to jobs historically done by men now being carried out by women — in other words, to the replacement of male labour with cheap female labour. Instead, they suggest a remarkable degree of stability in the sexual division of labour, with women remaining concentrated in low-grade, low-paid jobs, most notably in the service sector and within service occupations (such as clerical occupations) in the manufacturing sector (Liff 1986).

Feminist analysis has, however, drawn attention to other shifts in the division of labour, at the regional and global levels. It has highlighted the part played by ICTs in the location of corporate activities away from the more expensive regions in the First World, either to less favoured regions within the same countries (Henwood and Wyatt 1986; Goldstein 1989), or to entirely different countries in the Third World (Grossman 1979; Fuentes and Ehrenreich 1983; Mitter 1986; Posthuma 1987; Common Interests 1991). Capitals are manufacturing ICTs, or using ICTs to carry out manufacturing or data entry functions, in areas where labour and other overheads are cheap. Occupations in the clerical, textile and electronics sectors appear to be the ones most affected in this respect. However, again, this does not represent a shift in the sexual division of labour, for these are occupations in which women have traditionally been concentrated, so much as a shift in the global and regional division of labour. In other words, the gendering of these jobs has remained intact, despite their geographical relocation.

Similarly, research into the growth of homeworking has identified continuing disparities between the working conditions of men and women, disparities which reflect the sex-typing of the work being done from home and the differential levels of bargaining power which men and women in these jobs enjoy. Huws´ (1984) study of clerical homeworking found that the majority of homeworkers were married women in their mid-1930s. In addition to the routine and intense nature of the work itself, the women in her study were low-paid, isolated, un-unionised and uncertain as to the status of their employment. Routinised and increasingly intense labour processes, together with low-pay and lack of unionisation are conditions of work which are typical of women´s clerical work in general, but for homeworkers these conditions were exacerbated by their isolation from other workers and their inability to organise collectively in any way. Wajcman and Probert´s (1988) study examined both male and female homeworkers. They found that the sexual division of labour operating in society at large was reproduced in the types of homeworking jobs that men and women did, and they found marked differences in working conditions between them. Men were to be found mainly in professional occupations (such as management, computer programming and systems analysis) working from home, while women were located largely in clerical occupations. Most of these women, too, were married with young children. Like female homeworkers in the traditional sweated industries, they were typically paid at piece rates and earned substantially less than comparably skilled workers working in offices, and in addition, they had to meet their own overhead costs — heating, lighting, and power for machines. The male professionals, on the other hand, were typically self-employed, and were able to exploit the skill shortage in their type of work, earning more working at home than working from an office and with lower overhead costs.

Workplace ethnographies of women´s work have also enhanced our knowledge about women´s position in the social division of labour. These have attempted to provide a corrective to the predominance of labour process studies which focussed exclusively on male labour and the changes wrought upon it by the implementation of technology, particularly in the engineering and assembly industries. By contrast, studies of women´s labour processes have focussed mainly on jobs in which women are predominant, in an attempt to understand how women workers are organised and controlled, and how the process of technical change affects their work.

The rich picture that emerges from these various studies does not provide us with any definitive conclusions as to whether a fundamental shift is occurring in the sexual division of labour and in the allocation of men and women to particular jobs. However, they do reveal a strongly gendered division of labour based on assumptions about women´s „natural" manual dexterity and their aptitude for handling technology. Pollert´s (1981) study of Churchman´s tobacco factory, for example, describes a highly segregated long-established division of labour between the highly mechanised, capital intensive tasks performed by men and the non-mechanised, labour intensive work performed by women. In both her study and Cavendish´s (1981) research into the production of components for car assembly, the work performed by women, though requiring a considerable degree of manual dexterity, was defined as less skilled than men´s work. A similar pattern of allocating men to „high-technology“ occupations and women to „low-technology“ ones is noted by Armstrong (1982), who argues that labour-intensive work is inherently more insecure than capital-intensive work, due to short-term changes in demand and to long-term pressures for automation.

Research into clerical occupations confirms the comparatively low status of women, and highlights a particular set of managerial practices designed to control and subordinate these workers. Clerical, and particularly secretarial, jobs are of course ones that have traditionally been sex-typed, that is performed almost exclusively by women. The implementation of information technology, specifically in the form of word processing, seems to have had little impact on this organisation of office work along gender lines. This can be explained, of course, by the fact that, perhaps more than any other „female“ occupation, the successful performance of secretarial work requires „an apprenticeship in womanhood“ (Barker and Downing 1980:75). The tasks which many secretaries are called upon to perform are often less connected with formal office activities and more with the domestic, servicing role that men expect them to fulfil — in other words, the role of the „office wife“ (Benet 1972).

According to Barker and Downing (1980), female office workers have traditionally been subject to a particular form of patriarchal control by management and male office workers alike which has sought to secure their subordination, loyalty and hence devotion to duty. They predicted, however, that the introduction of new technology into the office would bring about the demise of these patriarchal relations of control and their replacement with more „mechanical“ control structures, together with a deskilling of secretarial work similar to that identified by Braverman in relation to male craft work. More recent research on the automation of the office, however, indicates that this „homogenisation“ of office work and manual work has not occurred (Webster 1990). Instead, patriarchal control of women office workers persists, and this, somewhat perversely, has permitted many of the technical skills and the control over the labour process that these women formerly exercised by virtue of the loopholes in managerial control practices to remain in place. This does not mean that women´s office work has ever attracted the label of „skilled“, despite the fact that many typing tasks do indeed require technical training and competence. Women´s office work has always provided a strong example of how women´s work comes to be devalued simply because it is women who perform it. Nevertheless, it alerts us to the need to be cautious about assuming that changes in the labour processes of men brought about by technological change will be necessarily be parallelled by changes in the labour processes of women.

Crompton and Sanderson´s (1990) research, by contrast, is optimistic about the potential that new technology creates for women in the financial services industries to move into new areas of employment. They suggest that employers in this sector are using computerised network technologies to bring about a new organisation of work, centred around customer-responsiveness and customer care. According to Crompton and Sanderson, the interpersonal skills which are traditionally regarded as the particular province of women are becoming more highly valued in these industries, with the result that new career structures based upon the provision of personal services to the customer are opening up to women. Similarly, Rhodes and Carter (1993) draw attention to the way in which, in the textile industry in India, new technologies, coupled with flexible patterns of work organisation, may have the potential for transforming the low-grade and menial, though technically skilled, tasks of women textile workers into multiskilled and more varied and responsible activities. However, again, neither of these scenarios provide evidence of the sexual division of labour within these industries actually being eroded; rather, they can be seen as representing the creation of fundamentally new areas of work that, from the outset, draw upon stereotyped notions of women´s appropriateness to fit them and thus from their very inception come to be gendered.

The most prominent and thoroughgoing attempt to theorise the relationship between technological change and gender in the workplace has come from Cynthia Cockburn. Cockburn provides, first, descriptive case study evidence of the impact of technical change upon the sexual division of labour and the deployment of skills, particularly in the printing industry (Cockburn 1983). Secondly, she highlights the way in which the process of technological change is itself conditioned by struggles by skilled men to retain the basis for their exclusive craft privileges. Thirdly, she articulates at a theoretical level the construction of male and female gender identities in relation to technological competence and asserts the masculinity of technology as a social product (Cockburn 1985).

Cockburn´s (1983) research into technological change in typesetting describes attempts by newspaper employers to replace hot metal typesetting —

work traditionally carried out by skilled craftsmen and from which women had always been excluded — with cold electronic composition. The employers saw this technical change as enabling them to replace the men with cheaper women workers. The male compositors fought to defend their position by having sole rights to use the computer typesetting equipment, and their strategy of resistance continued to centre around the exclusivity of their skills and the barring of women from the trade. In many workplaces, they succeeded, though the old material basis of their craft had now been eliminated. Gone was the old apprenticeship system which had conferred upon these workers their particular expertise with hot metal, and gone was the need for physical strength or bodily knack required for the moving of heavy and mechanical parts. The new electronic composition involved touch-typing on a QWERTY, or typewriter-style, keyboard. Not only was this a much lighter physical activity, but it entailed „women´s" typing skills, and the men were taught to use these new keyboards by female typing instructors. Moreover, it signified a shift of activities from those of the factory to those associated with the office. On a number of levels, then, the craftsmen experienced these changes as highly emasculating.

Cockburn demonstrates how the introduction of computerised typesetting with QWERTY keyboards formed part of a longer term strategy by the employers to abolish the requirement for craft workers with particular, hard-won skills and high wages, to render typists (mainly women) and hot metal operators (mainly men) equal competitors for the new machines, and thus to enable the use of relatively cheap female labour. The very design of the new machinery, therefore, had built into it the wherewithal to undermine the traditional allocation of skilled jobs to a powerful group of highly unionised male craft workers, and thus their exclusive rights to this craft. Despite the fact that the male workers resisted the incursion of women into their craft preserve in the short run, Cockburn acknowledges that the particular setting in which her study was carried out, the London newspaper industry, is somewhat unusual, and she sees women entering the unique preserve of typesetting in the long run. As this happens, the traditional „gendering" of typesetting work, through the physical power involved and the exclusive trade union control, will be eroded.

Cockburn´s later (1985) work develops her ideas about the construction of male identity in terms of technical competence and skills. In general, physical strength, initiative, and technological competence materially distinguish the work of men and women. Women, she asserts, are not typically found in jobs using technological skills. However, for Cockburn, there is nothing „natural“ in this state of affairs. Men have appropriated these skills, not because they are inherently more adept with technologies, or because the physical requirements of work are pre-determined, but rather because of social processes which define men as technologically-capable and also because of their historically greater ability to organise to secure rewards in the labour market. Social and cultural relations within and outside the workplace — male camaraderie, competitiveness and definitions of women as non-technological — rather than direct discrimination, have served to exclude women from technological know-how. The exclusive access of men to technological competence has been a key source of men´s power over women and of their capacity to command higher incomes and scarce jobs. Thus, while social assumptions about masculinity and „men´s work“ are actively reproduced in the workplace within a patriarchal exclusionary culture of aggression, male drive, total commitment to the job and long hours of overtime, so too are assumptions about women´s lack of technological capability played out through the sexual division of labour and the cultural relations of work. Men and women, therefore, have very different relationships to technical knowledge and to machinery, and it is these relationships which in part consitute their gender identities:

Technology enters into our sexual identity: femininity is incompatible with technological competence; to feel technically competent is to feel manly (Cockburn 1985:12).

Even in jobs where tcchnology features, there is a sexual division of labour between designers and fixers (male) on the one hand, and operators (female) on the other. „With few exceptions, the designer and developer of the new systems, the people who market and sell, install, manage and service machinery, are men. Women may push the buttons but they may not meddle with the works“ (1985:11-12).

While men have appropriated the technological sphere at the expense of women, Cockburn is careful to distinguish between this deployment of technology to sexual advantage by men, and the overall *control* over the means of production which is exercised by capital. Nevertheless, it is this aspect of her analysis which attempts to interrelate class and gender that has recently invited some critique. In particular, her tendency to underplay the differences between men´s jobs and thus to overstate the distinctions between men´s and women´s work has been found problematic (West 1990; Wajcman 1991). As West points out, there is a great deal of difference between the control over the labour process and the technical competencies that are exercised by skilled craftsmen and those that are exercised in semi-skilled, machine-paced jobs. Moreover, not all men are technologically competent, a point recognised by Cockburn herself. Even if it is not men but masculinity which has this bond with machinery, as Cockburn argues, this bond may be less resilient than class domination because it is not the mechanism through which economic production is socially organised (West 1990: 259).

In Cockburn´s analysis gender identity has obliterated class position, leading, according to West, to inadequate attention to the ways in which gender identity is itself class structured: „it is perhaps too easily assumed that masculinity welds together those whose class position is in fact quite distinct" (1990: 259). Similarly, Wajcman´s reservation about Cockburn´s analysis is that „Male employees themselves vary considerably in their capacities to control and benefit from technological innovations. It is important to remember that ... technology is also used by some men to dominate others" (1991:39). Moreover, Wajcman observes, technological competence has different connotations for different groups of men. While the cult of masculinity revolving around physical prowess is closely associated with shop floor manual workers, middle class men possess a different kind of abstract technological know-how. So, class differences (and also ethnic and generational differences) give rise to different versions of masculinity, such that it may be more useful to think in terms of „masculinities" (Wajcman 1991:40). This point, of course, also highlights the importance of an issue which is all too often overlooked: that the terms „gender", and „gendered jobs" do not refer only to women and their employment position, but equally denote the processes by which men come to occupy the positions that they do.

Nevertheless, Cockburn´s analysis is generally regarded as path-breaking, not least for its detailed empirical content, its theoretical incisiveness and its formulation of gender relations as not simply the passive recipients of change brought about through the introduction of technology, but as themselves critically shaping the process of technological change, the institutions and the practices involved. This is an aspect of the debate on gender and technology which we shall return to later in this chapter.

This aspect aside for the moment, we can summarise the contribution by feminists to the study of technological change as broadly focussed upon a number of related questions: How has the introduction of technology affected the sexual division of labour within occupations and within the economy overall? How has it affected the nature and experience of women´s work? Have women and men had differing experiences of technological change?

Given that feminist research into the introduction of technology has been so varied in both focus and scope, it is hard to identify a consensus on these issues. However, the pattern of evidence emerging suggests that technical change has not substantially undermined sexual divisions in the labour market or the segregation of occupations between men and women. Instead, it would seem that the sexual division of labour has been left very much intact by the introduction of technology. According to Liff, the evidence does not bear out a simplistic reading of labour process theory, „which sees the manufacturing sector developing, via technical change and the introduction of women, towards a goal of a largely unskilled, unorganised, undifferentiated and cheap workforce" (1986:88). Liff suggests that this is in part because labour process theory has failed to fully take account of male worker resistance to such changes, in particular to defend their interests over the allocation of work and a social organisation of the reproduction of labour power which is heavily dependent on a sexual division of labour. In addition to this, the evidence indicates that managements do not regard men and women as undifferentiated, substitutable groups, and that, through the process of technological change, they are drawing women into *new* jobs rather than *changed* jobs. Thus, the original sex-typing of jobs seems to persist.

In jobs which have historically been allocated to women, there is also less evidence for radical changes in the nature of work than conventional labour process theory would lead us to expect. Here, the technical division of labour — that is, the organisation of a job into component tasks — seems to be the principal determinant of the nature of work and of the level of skill deployed (Webster 1990). New technology may alter the *type* of skills used in carrying out particular tasks so that, for example, word processing a document may involve less skill in touch typing accurately and rapidly but more skill in deploying the varied functions of the machine. However, it is far from certain that it alters the *level or amount* of skill needed, or results in a significant loss of overall control over the labour process for the typist or secretary. Moreover, as I have argued elsewhere (Webster 1990), job fragmentation and deskilling are processes set in motion by managerial decisions concerning their desired organisation of work and technical division of labour, not exigencies of technological change alone. The question that then has to be addressed is, why have company managements not used the process of technological change to secure control over, and thus cheapen, female labour in the same way that they have used it to secure control over and cheapen male labour?

Given what we know about the relative cost of female labour and managerial control over that labour, the answer to this question would seem to be obvious. Women, as we have seen, are concentrated in low-paid, low-status occupations, and this concentration has been little, if at all, altered by the introduction of technology. In this context, it makes little sense for managements to embark on expensive and disruptive programmes of work rationalisation in order to achieve productivity gains that may not offset the costs of such programmes. In other words, there is little to be gained from attempting to cheapen labour that is already very low in price. Indeed in Britain, the only area in which employment is rising is in part-time women´s work, while the twin forces of technological change and recession have resulted in precisely the opposite scenario for men. Moreover, female labour, as we have also seen, is subject to its own particular form of patriarchal control in the workplace which is far more cultural than mechanical. This form of control over women by management (and, we might add, by male workers) is deeply embedded in and reinforced by the social institutions and practices of everyday life. It is effective as a means of control because it goes far beyond the confines of the workplace, depending heavily upon social assumptions and expectations of women´s roles (including those held by women themselves), upon an educational system which perpetuates sexual stereotyping, and upon the place of women within the domestic division of labour. Women workers have therefore historically been subject to a markedly different type of workplace control to that of men, and, given this situation, it would be perverse to assume that this type of control should suddenly be swept away with the introduction of new technology, or that techniques used to control women should inevitably be brought into line with techniques used to control men.

This accumulated evidence has prompted a re-evaluation of the Reserve Army of Labour thesis, not least by Beechey herself (Beechey 1983). Difficulties in applying the concept in the light of recent trends in male and female employment have been identified by Anthias (1980), Liff (1986), and West (1990). The concept has particularly failed to explain the continuing ghettoisation of women in low-grade occupations, and the general principle of job sex-typing which seems to transcend economic imperatives and which overrides the economic benefits of substituting women for men. Couched as it is in terms of the supply characteristics of women workers and their role in domestic production and reproduction, it focusses too strongly on the labour market at the expense of a consideration of the labour process. In other words, in locating the source of women´s inequality of employment in the domestic sphere, it fails to address the ways in which gender divisions of labour and patriarchal social relations are produced and reproduced *in the workplace*. The feminist project has therefore recently reasserted the importance of „exploring the interconnections of gender and class relations at the point of production" (West 1990:246).

2.2 Engendering Technology: Reversing the Focus

With a few notable exceptions (Cockburn 1983; Noble 1984), an area in which labour process theory has been remarkably weak has been in the analysis of the role of social relations in *shaping*, rather than simply being affected by, the process of technological change. Labour process theorists have all too often taken technology for granted, treating it as given, and have ignored the range of factors — social, economic, political, cultural, organisational and gendered — which have conditioned the process of technological change (Williams and Edge 1992). Many feminist analyses within the labour process tradition, too, have concerned themselves almost exclusively with the *impact* of technological change upon the sexual division of labour and gender relations. Yet there is a reverse aspect to this relationship, namely, the way in the sexual division of labour itself shapes the creation and consumption of technologies. And it can be argued that it is impossible to sufficiently grasp the impacts of technological change without attending to the factors generating such change in the first place. Evidence arising from an accumulation of empirical studies in this area has prompted an increasingly explicit articulation of this relationship.

Feminist interest in the gender relations of technology developed out of an analysis of the exclusion of women from science and of the gendered nature of scientific knowledge and activity. Following from this, feminists began in the 1980s to examine the position of women in technological jobs, and the wider question of the impact of gender relations on the design and production of technology and hence the gendered nature of technology.

First, it has been shown that occupational sex-typing provides the basis for the design of technologies applied to particular jobs. In some cases, this has generated technologies which embody the features of work done primarily or exclusively by women, in other words, technologies which are designed and marketed for use by women workers. For example, histories of the typewriter and, more recently, the word processor have shown how established working patterns and skills in „women´s" office jobs have come to be embedded in the tools which are developed for them (David 1985; Knie 1992; Webster 1993). Features like the size and weight of typewriters, the QWERTY keyboard, and functions keys on dedicated word processors, all reflect the sex-typing of office jobs, assumptions that they will be used primarily by women with touch-typing skills and assumptions about the „light" character of the work that women are fitted for.

Technologies may also be designed in order to undermine the sex-typing of certain occupations. We have already examined Cockburn´s (1983) work on the development and application of computerised typesetting systems in the printing industry. The salience of this study is that it reveals how these systems were designed expressly to depart from the old linotype devices which relied on skilled, male craft labour, marked by long apprenticeships, strong trade union organisation, and which required a combination of physical strength and manual dexterity for their operation. There was nothing inevitable about this new design. Electronic circuitry could have been used in conjunction with the old linotype keyboards, and indeed, Linotype did manufacture such a device. As we have seen, the purpose (even if not the initial outcome) of designing electronic systems with smaller, light-to-operate, QWERTY-style keyboards was to deskill male craft labour and ultimately to replace it with relatively unskilled female labour.

If gendered divisions of labour are involved in the conception and design of technologies, then they are certainly involved in the actual production of them. In information technology, there is a sharp sexual division between men, who are principally involved in the design, development, marketing, selling, installation, management and servicing of systems, and women, who are concentrated in the low-skilled assembly of them (Goldstein 1989; Cockburn and Ormrod 1993). Again, essentialist assumptions of men´s and women´s „natural" abilities underlie this division. On the one hand, as we have seen, men are seen as having an inherent affinity with technology, while on the other, it is supposed that women have the nimble fingers and patience necessary for the microscopic assembly of minute components. Moreover, in the employment of women in the Third World in sweated, routinised, integrated circuit assembly work, racial stereotypes are heaped upon gender stereotypes and economic imperatives. While the electronics multinationals clearly perceive the cost benefits of this cheap source of labour, together with the absence of trade unionism or worker militancy, they are also attracted by the particular „docility" of South East Asian women (Grossman 1979; Fuentes and Ehrenreich 1983).

Gender relations have also profoundly affected the pace and direction of technological change in the workplace. As we have seen, the conditions of women´s paid employment — the casualised, unskilled and relatively cheap nature of female labour in certain industries, together with use of labour control practices which are primarily patriarchal in nature — have often cut across moves towards the rationalisation of these production processes through automation. This has meant that the diffusion of technologies has often been slower in many jobs in which female labour is concentrated than it has been in jobs dominated by men.

Most fundamentally, however, feminist analysis has pointed to the gendered nature of technology in general. Rather than examining how women could be more equitably treated by an essentially neutral technology, many feminists now argue that Western technology itself embodies patriarchal values. In particular, the strong military-industrial orientation of modern technology is seen as being symptomatic of the male dominance of technology, and of the masculinity of technological processes and products. Technology is seen as dceply implicated in the masculine project of the domination and control of women and nature. According to Arnold and Faulkner (1985), for example,

> Technology is central to the immense productive dynamism of capitalism ..., but it is also more than this: it is a vital aspect of modern patriarchy. It enables men to exercise unprecedented domination over the natural world and over society. In the capitalist period, more than any other previous epoch, technology has excluded and alienated women; it has become *masculine* (1985:22, emphasis in original).

Technology is seen as masculine, first, in the institutions and processes which generate and perpetuate it, and second, in the values which underlie it. Socialist feminists have reminded us that the relations of production are constructed as much out of gender divisions as class divisions. In this vein, Cockburn (1983, 1985) and Faulkner and Arnold (1985) see women´s exclusion from technology as a consequence of the gender division of labour and the male domination of skilled trades that developed under capitalism. The gender division of labour which developed in the factory, in which women were excluded from craft skills and from access to technology, meant that the machinery introduced was designed by men with men in mind, either by the capitalist inventor/entrepreneur, or by skilled craftsmen. Industrial technology from its origins thus reflected male power as well as capitalist domination.

The masculine culture of technology is fundamental to the way in which the gender division of labour is still being reproduced today. „The social institutions of technology are, like most institutions in society, dominated by men“ (Arnold and Faulkner 1985:18). Feminists have pointed to a variety of barriers to women´s access to technology, from social attitudes, to girls´ education, to the teaching of engineering and technology in post-school education, to the employment policies of firms. In the light of the resulting sex-stereotyped definition of technology as an activity appropriate for men, Cockburn (1985) has suggested that women, as well as finding themselves barred from opportunties in this area, actively resist entering technological fields because of its cultural incompatibility with femininity.

In addition to the institutional domination of technology by men, it has been asserted that technology is redolent with „male values“. Cooley (1980), one of the most prominent writers on technology and the labour process, argues that technology has the male values of objectivity, rationality, strength, competition, and domination built into it and is starved of the so-called female values of intuition, subjectivity, tenacity and compassion. Similarly, eco-feminists, though coming at the question from a very different perspective, equate women with a closeness to nature. They contend that the technologies that men have created are based on the domination of nature paralleling their domination of women. Their analysis focusses particularly on military technologies, which they see as „products of a patriarchal culture that speaks violence at every level“ (King 1983:126).

Does the problem lie in men´s domination of technology, or is technology inherently masculine? The difficulty with the second approach, as Wajcman (1991) has pointed out, is that it views „male“ and „female“ values as natural biological and psychological attributes, and fails to examine the ways in which, through socialisation and social processes which restrict women to the private domain, men and women have become associated with these values in the first place. Nevertheless, the strength of this approach is that it goes beyond the usual conception of the problem as being women´s exclusion from the processes of innovation and from the acquisition of technical skills. Despite the difficulties with this „essentialist“ approach, an analysis of technology as embodying patriarchy points at the very least to a serious lack of regard to women´s needs and priorities in technological innovation and design. It also raises the intriguing prospect that different technologies would emerge in a society not organised along patriarchal lines.

2.3 New Divisions of Labour: The Flexibility Debate

Feminist studies of the development and use of technologies raise, therefore, fundamental questions about the ability of the orthodox labour process perspective to account either for sexual divisions of labour or for the gendering of technologies. Revision of the labour process approach has come, though, from another quarter — from the flexibility literature.

The work of Piore and Sabel (1984) on the demise of mass production and the rise of flexible specialisation, together with the work of Atkinson (1984) on flexible labour markets, predicts transformations in production methods, skills and divisions of labour, and calls attention to the potential of the latest generations of programmable automation to facilitate new work systems. It has been subject to some sustained critique, most notably for its assumptions about radical breaks with past work systems (Williams et al. 1987; Hirst 1989), and for its romanticisation of craft labour and the small firms sector (Murray 1987; Jenson 1989; Pollert 1988). Is the „flexibility thesis“ (to represent crudely a complex and disparate set of writings) any more sensitive to the dynamics of gender and technological change than the labour process debate was?

In relation to the sexual division of labour and women´s employment, the flexibility thesis revisits old themes. In particular, it resuscitates the concept of segmented labour markets first described by flexible specialisation theorist Piore some thirteen years before the publication of *The Second Industrial Divide* (Doeringer and Piore 1971; Berger and Piore 1980). It identifies primary and secondary labour markets, and a reserve army of labour composed of women workers (in Atkinson´s formulation this reserve army is known as a „peripheral“ labour force).

Some feminist research has uncovered evidence to support the notion of employment flexibility. Walby (1989) points to the growth, particularly in Britain, of peripheral part-time work for women. However, she sees this type of employment as an increasingly integral and permanent feature of the labour market, rather than as a temporary measure designed to attract and repel a reserve army in times of crisis of labour supply. This, for Walby, is not evidence of a peripheral reserve army of labour, but of a long-run process of employment restructuring in which old forms of patriarchal structures are replaced by new ones.

Pollert (1988) suggests that many of the employment practices identified in the concept of periphery, particularly concerning the use of temporary work, homeworking and subcontracting, are far from new. She cites evidence to show that in some sectors, these are well-established forms of employment. The conclusion one must draw is that there is nothing innovatory about the sexually segmented labour market (indeed, Piore´s own long-running focus on this topic surely confirms this view), or in the location of women in the „peripheral“ or secondary sector, but that instead we are witnessing a consolidation and crystallisation of these phenomena in permanent employment structures.

The trouble with the flexibility thesis is that the fundamentally gendered quality of these divisions in the labour market is never really made explicit, or if it is, it is merely described and not integrated into the analysis. Core workers tend to be equated with males, while peripheral workers tend to be equated with females (Walby 1989:131). There is a profound gender-blindness in the analysis of the flexibility theorists — a gender-blindness which has serious implications for their ability to adequately theorise the social relations prophesied for the future. The enthusiasm of Piore and Sabel for a new order of craft production dominated by the small firms sector fails to consider whether women and men are located in the labour force in such a way that they will benefit similarly from any new emphasis on skilled labour (Jenson 1989:141). Indeed, the entire flexible specialisation thesis treats the concept of „skill“ as totally unproblematic — a treatment that is all the more surprising given the wealth of evidence demonstrating that „skill“ is social construct, contested just as much by women and men as by capital and labour (Phillips and Taylor 1980; Cockburn 1983).

The flexible specialistion thesis, therefore, remains unable to answer questions about the roles of men and women in the new labour processes or about their relationship to technologies. In fact, it provides little convincing evidence that gendered divisions of labour have fundamentally altered, or that the technology/gender relationship has been transformed. Given continuities in the sexual division of labour and in the social construction of skill — continuities which are largely ignored in the flexibility literature — it comes as no surprise to find that women continue to find themselves in semi-skilled jobs and isolated from technology. Numerous studies have highlighted the persistence of the mass production industries in which women are maintained in labour-intensive production, assembly and packing jobs (Herzog 1980; Pollert 1981; Cavendish 1981; Westwood 1984). These industries seem to have been little touched by „flexible specialisation", and the gender segregation of employment within them remains.

The flexibility thesis is therefore just as guilty of gender-blindness as were labour process accounts. Both perspectives treat all workers identically and fail to distinguish between male and female workers, or employers´ strategies for controlling and organising them. Both fail to distinguish between the labour costs of women and men, and particularly to address the ways in which employers might make use of differentially-priced labour power in particular circumstances, often using women as a cheaper or more reliable option than machinery (Pollert 1988; Webster 1990). Instead, labour market divisions are treated in purely functional terms, and no attempt is made to theorise the origins and dynamics of these divisions. In both perspectives, the notion of the craft worker is equated with the male artisan/mechanic and is grossly romanticised (Beechey 1982). And in both perspectives, tendencies towards deskilling/reskilling are presented as if they were even across the economy and the labour force. In all, the flexibility thesis offers no better insights to the position of women workers than the labour process literature before it did.

3 Conclusion: The Future of the Debate on Gender and Technological Change

Overall, then, feminist analysis has pointed out some of the deficiencies of conventional labour process theory, and also latterly, theories which posit new divisions of labour based around flexibility of production and of employment. In particular, it has suggested that a simple reading, in which the process of technological change is associated with a straightforward breakdown of the sexual division of labour, fails to take account of the very real differences in women´s and men´s relationships to technology and to the organisation of paid work.

Most usefully, feminist analysis has begun to point to the ways in which the gendered nature of society influences technological development, and by implication, the impact of technologies. It has shown that technological artefacts have gender relations actually embedded within them, and also that the institutions of technology, the acquisition of technological know-how, and indeed the very culture of technology itself, have come to be dominated by men at the expense of women. An identification of the processes whereby technology has become „masculine" provides some explanation as to why the introduction of technologies has had differential impacts on women´s and men´s jobs, and why it has been experienced differently by men and women. It also alerts us to the fact that technologies are no more gender-neutral than they are neutral in any other sense. Analysis of the development and impact of technologies upon work must therefore take into account not only the class relations within which they are introduced, but also the gender relations of the workplace, of technology itself, and of society at large. We are rightly sceptical of technological determinism, with its mistaken emphasis on the autonomy of technology from social relations; we must also be sceptical of any account which does not place gender divisions — as a critical component of those social relations — right at the heart of its analysis.

References

Anthias, F. (1980), Women and the RAL: A Critique of Veronica Beechey. *Capital and Class*, 10: 50-63.

Armstrong, P. (1982), If it´s Only a Women it Doesn´t Matter so Much, in West, J. (ed.), *Work, Women and the Labour Market*, London, Routledge.

Arnold, E. and W. Faulkner (1985), Smothered by Invention: The Masculinity of Technology, in Faulkner, W. and E. Arnold (eds.), *Smothered by Invention: Technology in Women´s Lives*. London, Pluto.

Atkinson, J. (1984), Manpower Strategies for Flexible Organisations. *Personnel Management,* August: 42-75.

Barker, J. and H. Downing (1980), Word Processing and the Transformation of Patriarchal Relations of Control in the Office. *Capital and Class*, 10: 64-99.

Barrett, M. (1980), *Women´s Oppression Today: Problems in Marxist Feminist Analysis.* London, Verso.

Baxandall, R., E. Ewen and L. Gordon (1976), The Working Class has Two Sexes. *Monthly Review*, 28, 3: 1-9.

Beechey, V. (1977), Some Notes on Female Wage Labour in Capitalist Production. *Capital and Class,* 3: 45-66.

Beechey, V. (1982), The Sexual Division of Labour and the Labour Process: A Critical Assessment of Braverman, in Wood, S. (ed.), *The Degradation of Work? Skill, Deskilling and the Labour Process*. London, Hutchinson.

Beechey, V. (1983), What´s so Special About Women´s Employment? A Review of Some Recent Studies of Women´s Paid Work. *Feminist Review*, 15: 23-45.

Benet, M.K. (1972), *Secretary: An Enquiry in the Female Ghetto*. London, Sidgwick and Jackson.

Berger, S. and M.J. Piore (1980), *Dualism and Discontinuity in Industrial Societies*. Cambridge, Cambridge University Press.

Braverman, H. (1974), *Labor and Monopoly Capital.* New York and London, Monthly Review Press.

Burawoy, M. (1979), *Manufacturing Consent: Changes in the Labor Process under Monopoly Capitalism.* Chicago, University of Chicago Press.

Cavendish, R. (1981), *Women on the Line*. London, Routledge.

Cockburn, C. (1983), *Brothers: Male Dominance and Technological Change*. London, Pluto.

Cockburn, C. (1985), *Machinery of Dominance: Women, Men and Technical Know-how.* London, Pluto.

Cockburn, C. and S. Ormrod (1993), *Gender and Technology in the Making*. London, Sage.

Common Interests (1991), *Women Organising in Global Electronics*. London, Women Working Worldwide.

Cooley, M. (1980), *Architect or Bee? The Human/Technology Relationship*. Slough, Langley Technical Services.

Crompton, R. and K. Sanderson (1990), *Gendered Jobs and Social Change*. London, Unwin Hyman.

Crompton, R. and G. Jones (1984), *White-Collar Proletariat: Deskilling and Gender in Clerical Work*. London, Macmillan.

David, P.A. (1985), Clio and the Economics of QWERTY. *Economic History*, 25, 2: 332-337.

Doeringer, P. and M. Piore (1971), *Internal Labour Markets and Manpower Analysis*. Lexington, Mass., Heath.

Edwards, R. (1979), *Contested Terrain: The Transformation of the Workplace in the Twentieth Century*. London, Heinemann.

Elger, T. (1982), Braverman, Capital Accumulation and Deskilling, in Wood, S. (ed.), *The Degradation of Work? Skill, Deskilling and the Labour Process*. London, Hutchinson.

Faulkner, W. and E. Arnold (eds.- 1985), *Smothered by Invention: Technology in Women´s Lives*. London, Pluto.

Friedman, A. (1977), *Industry and Labour*. London, Macmillan.

Fuentes, A. and B. Ehrenreich (1983), *Women in the Global Factory*. Boston, South End Press.

Gardiner, J. (1977), Women in the Labour Process and Class Structure, in Hunt, A. (ed.), *Class and Class Structure*. London, Lawrence and Wishart.

Goldstein, N. (1989), Silicon Glen: Women and Semiconductor Multinationals, in Elson, D. and R. Pearson (eds.), *Women´s Employment and Multinationals in Europe*. London, Macmillan.

Grossman, R. (1979), Women´s Place in the Integrated Circuit. *South East Asia Chronicle*, 66: 2-17.

Hakim, C. (1978), Sexual Divisions with the Labour Force: Occupational Segregration. *Employment Gazette,* November, 1264-1268.

Hakim, C. (1981), Job Segregation: Trends in the 1970s. *Employment Gazette*, December, 521-9.

Hartmann, H. (1976), Capitalism, Patriarchy and Job Segregation by Sex, in Blaxall, M. and B. Reagan (eds.), *Women and the Workplace*. University of Chicago Press.

Henwood, F. and S. Wyatt (1986), Women´s Work, Technological Change and Shifts in the Employment Structure, in Martin, R. and B. Rowthorn (eds.), *The Geography of De-industrialisation*. London, Macmillan.

Herzog, M. (1980), *From Hand to Mouth*. Penguin, Harmondsworth.

Hirst, P. (1989), After Henry, in Hall, S. and M. Jacques (eds.), *New Times: The Changing Face of Politics in the 1990s*. London, Lawrence and Wishart.

Huws, U. (1984), *The New Homeworkers: New Technology and the Changing Location of White Collar Workers*. London, Low Pay Unit.

Jenson, J. (1989), The Talents of Women, the Skills of Men: Flexible Specialization and Women, in Wood, S. (ed.), *The Transformation of Work?* London, Hutchinson.

King, Y. (1983), Toward an Ecological Feminism and a Feminist Ecology, in Rothschild, J. (ed.), *Machina ex Dea: Feminist Perspectives on Technology*. New York, Pergamon Press.

Knie, A. (1992), Yesterday´s Decisions Determine Tomorrow´s Options: The Case of the Mechanical Typewriter, in Dierkes, M. and U. Hoffman (eds.), *New Technology at the Outset: Social Forces in the Shaping of Technological Innovations*. Frankfurt/New York, Campus.

Knights, D. and H. Willmott (1986), Introduction, in Knights, D. and H. Willmott (eds.), *Gender and the Labour Process*. Aldershot, Gower Publishing.

Liff, S. (1986), Technical Change and Occupational Stereotyping, in Knights, D. and Willmott, H. (eds.), *Gender and the Labour Process*. Aldershot, Gower Publishing.

Mitter, S. (1986), *Common Fate, Common Bond: Women in the Global Economy*. London, Pluto.

Murray, F. (1987), Flexible Specialisation in the „Third Italy“. *Capital and Class,* 33: 84-95.

Noble, D. (1979), Social Choice in Machine Design: The Case of Automatically Controlled Machine Tools, in Zimablist, A. (ed.), *Case Studies on the Labor Process*. New York, Monthly Review Press.
Noble, D. (1984), *Forces of Production: A Social History of Industrial Automation*. New York, Knopf.
Phillips, A. and B. Taylor (1980), Sex and Skill. Notes towards a Feminist Economics. *Feminist Review*, 6: 79-88.
Piore, M.J. and C.F. Sabel (1984), *The Second Industrial Divide: Possibilities for Property*. New York, Basic Books.
Pollert, A. (1981), *Girls, Wives, Factory Lives*. London, Macmillan.
Pollert, A. (1988), Dismantling Flexibility. *Capital and Class*, 34: 42-75.
Posthuma, A. (1987), The Internationalisation of Clerical Work. Sussex, University of Sussex Science Policy Research Unit Occasional Paper No 24.
Rhodes, E. and R. Carter (1993), EDI and Supply Chain Innovation: Emerging Production Options in Textiles and the Implications for Changing Patterns of Gender and Skill in Apparel Manufacture. Paper presented to PICT/COST Workshop on Electronic Data Interchange/Inter-Organisational Networks, Edinburgh, April.
Wajcman, J. (1991), *Feminism Confronts Technology*. Pennsylvania, Pennsylvania State Press.
Wajcman, J. and B. Probert (1988), New Technology Outwork, in Willis, E. (ed.), *Technology and the Labour Process. Australian Case Studies*. Sydney, Allen and Unwin.
Walby, S. (1986), *Patriarchy at Work*. London, Polity Press.
Walby, S. (1989), Flexibility and the Changing Sexual Division of Labour, in Wood, S. (ed.), *The Transformation of Work?* London, Unwin and Hyman.
Webster, J. (1990), *Office Automation: The Labour Process and Women's Work in Britain*. Hemel Hempstead, Harverster Wheatsheaf.
Webster, J. (1993), Women's Skills and Word Processors: Gender Issues in the Development of the Automated Office, in Probert, B. and B. Wilson (eds.), *Pink Collar Blues: Work, Gender and Technology*. Melbourne, Melbourne University Press.
West, J. (1978), Women, Sex and Class, in Kuhn, A. and A. Wolpe (eds.), *Feminism and Materialism*. London, Routledge and Kegan Paul.
West, J. (1990), Gender and the Labour Process: A Reassessment, in Knights, D. and II. Willmott (eds.), *Labour Process Theory*. London, Macmillan.
Westwood, S. (1984), *All Day Every Day*. London, Pluto.
Wilkinson, B. (1983), *The Shopfloor Politics of New Technology*. London, Heinemann.
Williams, K., T. Cutler, J. Williams and C. Haslam (1987), The End of Mass Production? *Economy and Society*, 16, 3: 405-439.
Williams, R. and D. Edge (1992), The Social Shaping of Technology: Research Concepts and Findings in Great Britain, in Dierkes, M. and U. Hoffman (eds.), *New Technology at the Outset: Social Forces in the Shaping of Technological Innovations*. Frankfurt/New York, Campus.
Wood, S. and J. Kelly (1982), Taylorism, Responsible Autonomy and Management Strategy, in Wood, S. (ed.), *The Degradation of Work? Skill, Deskilling and the Labour Process*. London, Hutchinson.

Chapter 5
Globalization, New Production Systems and the Spatial Division of Labor

Richard Gordon

Contents

1 Introduction

The catalogue of forces, processes and organizational changes whose confluence, in one combination or another, ostensibly has generated a new process of globalization is now well established. The fusion of telecommunications and computer technologies (or telematics) makes possible the low-cost global transfer of information and data in real time, provides a basis for new forms of world-wide interaction and control, and liberates organizational structure from spatial constraints (Castells, 1989). The unprecedented exposure of national economies to trade in foreign goods and services transforms their relative insulation into mutual interdependence (Keohane, 1984). Deregulation of financial markets and the vast mobility of international capital has expanded the autonomous power of global financial networks newly liberated from the tutelage of either national policy, or international regulatory, regimes (Altvater, 1993). At still another level, not only has the integrative power of multinational corporations continued to augment, but intensified competition between them has generated even more elaborate forms of world-wide business activity and new levels of foreign organizational penetration of domestic markets (Cowhey and Aronson, 1993; Barnet and Cavanagh, 1994). Products formerly the relatively discrete output of particular national economies or individual firms are increasingly produced as „global composites“ (Reich, 1991), the combined output of diverse firms of different nationalities. Research and development, or, more broadly, the accumulations of knowledge underlying technological innovation, appear increasingly to issue from global networks of enterprises and associated institutions (Mowery and Rosenberg, 1989). At the outer reaches of the new globalization paradigm, some postulate the appearance of a „global civil society“ (Lipschutz, 1992), prospective political unification at a global level (Held, 1993) and a globalization of perception and consciousness (Ruigrok and van Tulder, 1993).

It is undeniable that each of these lineaments of the proposed new global order embodies dynamics that, in some respects at least, push beyond the limits of national or regional territorial and institutional frameworks within which economic activity has been predominantly confined for most of the millennium. It is equally clear, however, that such a catalogue, however commonplace, lacks in specificity what it captures in scope. Do all these phenomena transcend national boundaries in the same respects or in the same manner? Do they all incorporate the same logic of „globalization“ or do they follow different, even divergent or contradictory, logics? Is the new global economy an homogeneous and evolutionary entity or, on the contrary, a radically discontinuous and internally differentiated unity? Despite the rhetorical force of their sequential recitation, do these various forces, processes and organizations manifest themselves in fact at the same spatial scale? Is the relation of globalization to other spatial levels (nation-state, region) simply one of immanent transcendence or is there a more intricate connection between them? Specifically, what is the relationship between the still conceptually unsynthesized processes of globalized and territorialized industrial development? Finally, we should ask, even at the risk of apparent absurdity, what are the spatial coordinates of the new global economy?

This chapter will attempt to support several contentions in the context opened up by these questions. First: it will suggest that the contemporary world economy is not a singular unity but a multi-layered or even „multiply-dominated“ (Swyngedouw, 1992), global space comprised of intersecting processes of *internationalization, multinationalization* and *globalization*. Second: following Petrella´s (1989, 1991) critical injunction (if not necessarily his precise line of reasoning), it will suggest that these three processes are quite distinct, embodying divergent implications for the globalization of economic life. Third: it will argue that each domain of the world economy is governed by a specific dominant logic — internationalization by a *logic of exchange*, multinationalization by a *logic of production*, and globalization by a *logic of innovation* — and that these logics embody different organizational frameworks for the world economy as a whole.[1] Fourth: since these logics follow opposing dynamics at many points, the world economy exists as a contradictory unity projecting multiple alternative trajectories of development. Finally: the spatial implications of each logic are equally varied. In contrast with internationalization and multinationalization, globalization neither effaces space nor subsumes it as a factor to be exploited but, on the contrary, valorizes the specificity of regional innovative milieux and mobilizes their particular attributes within global innovation processes.

One final introductory observation should be made. It is obvious that the technological infrastructure provided by telematics is especially fundamental to the reconfiguration of the contemporary world economy. However, it is imperative to resist the kind of technological determinism that commonly links new communications and control systems automatically with globalization *per se*, for, at the macro-level, as at the micro-level, information technologies can be structured within a variety of organizational forms (Nora and Minc, 1980; Zuboff, 1984). As a consequence, far from imposing any particular structure on the world economy, telematics simultaneously provides an objective basis for quite distinctive processes of internationalization, multinationalization and globalization and the ultimate significance of this technical infrastructure must be seen as deriving from the specific politico-economic logic within which it is embedded.

[1] It goes without saying that exchange, production and innovation are intimately linked in reality: the idea of a „dominant logic“ here denotes which of the three intertwined forces serves as the organizing principle of their intersection within a particular realm of the contemporary world economy.

2 Internationalization

The present discussion will focus principally upon the question of globalization. But it is not mere convenience that dictates separating discussion of internationalization, multinationalization and globalization into distinct sections: this separation also is intended to support the common presumption that globalization introduces a qualitatively new dimension to the world economy. Both internationalization and multinationalization are older phenomena, the former evident at least since the seventeenth century, the latter since at least the late nineteenth century: by contrast, globalization must be considered a relatively recent development, one inaugurating another substantive structural phase in the history of capitalism. Indeed, while their contemporary manifestations reveal important new elements in their historical evolution, the underlying logics of internationalization and multinationalization remain essentially unchanged and may even serve as fetters on the further extension of globalization proper.

Internationalization is premised upon the core principle of *exchange* — the cross-national transfer of information, goods and services or production factors between economic agents or units that remain quite discrete, a process regulated principally through a system of relative prices governed by supply and demand.[2] The dynamics of contemporary internationalization, however, are driven not simply, as in the past, by the spatial extension of markets but by the vertical deepening and horizontal intensification of market transactions.

At the level of the exchange of goods and services, market deepening is constituted as the appearance of new markets in the products made possible by the information revolution, the fragmentation of markets typified by the expansion of intra-industrial trade and the explosion of international trade in services as a quasi-independent complement to more traditional markets in goods. Horizontal intensification in this sphere is constituted by the new salience of global competition in both international and domestic markets, the

[2] Braudel (1981, 1982, 1984) remains the finest analysis of the emergence and historical trajectory of this phenomenon. As Braudel observes, in contradistinction to many other perspectives, this level of the world economy, originally based precisely upon the separation of production and exchange, remained a „vast but superficial" layer of economic life as a whole until the late nineteenth and twentieth centuries.

incipient abolition of traditional product cycles and the increasing significance of permanent innovation.

Intensified internationalization in the exchange of goods and services is exhibited in a number of intersecting registers. The overall volume of trade has experienced an historically unprecedented expansion. The postwar „golden age“ of dynamic capitalist economic growth stimulated an extraordinary rise in world trade marked, until the mid-1970s at least, by simultaneous growth in the volume of trade issuing from advanced industrial economies as Europe and Japan sought to catch up to the U.S. and from the Third World generated by the massive expansion in demand for cheap raw materials and other primary products. A new layer of international competition, financed in large part by the liberation of international credit, emerged by the 1980s from the export-oriented industrialization of the NICs. Since the 1960s world trade consistently has expanded more rapidly than the gross output of world production (Storper, 1992). Expanding mutual interdependence among the world´s economies, in large part the consequence of state policy at the international (the Bretton Woods accord) and national (the boosting of „national champions“) levels, enlarges the role of exports and imports in economic activity. The level of internationalization of economic activity consequently expands for each country as exports and imports assume more significant shares of total GNP and internationalization in turn intensifies competition within both domestic and international markets (OECD, 1992). The increasing specialization of production has resulted in a growing proportion of international trade, particularly within and between advanced economies, being devoted to intra-industrial exchange of goods and services (Dosi et al., 1990; Archibugi and Pianta, 1992): both intermediate and final goods markets are becoming more and more internationalized as a consequence. The effective abolition of the product cycle in advanced product markets means that new products can no longer be sequentially phased into international production and sales but must enter all markets more or less simultaneously if the rents accruing to innovative leadership are to be captured successfully.

In the financial sphere, the now seemingly incessant creation of new types of market or „market pyramiding“ (Collins, 1990) is almost totally dependent on the mathematical ingenuity to convert abstract rights or terms of trade into indices, values or prices and on the computer´s capacity both to regulate the new markets and to link them into a system of increasingly speculative transactions in these new „cyber-commodities“. Vertical deepening in this sphere, therefore, occurs whenever a new underlying asset (an amount of currency, a security, „new commodities" such as bundles of home mortgages or auto loans, a payments stream such as the value of air traffic in predictable travel corridors, or performance in a particular market such as time-constrained differences or convergences in relative exchange rates) can be converted into quantifiable indices and specifiable proprietary rights and/or new financial instruments (swaps, forwards, puts, caps, floors, collars, etc.) can be created in order to trade them, thereby giving rise to a new layer in the pyramid of exchange.[3] The horizontal intensification of market transactions results from the application of Fordist throughput logic to the system of exchange such that the computerized ability to facilitate and regulate real-time transfers dramatically expands both the speed and volume of transactions. As this dynamic is self-reinforcing, it also constitutes one source of continued market expansion.

The postwar international monetary system was regulated as an extension of the national economy: within a system of fixed exchange rates, adjustments had to be made at the level of the domestic economy. Domestic monetary regulation and international stabilization in turn linked the international financial system strongly to industrial production and to trade as well as mitigating against disorder induced by speculation. Beginning with the first stirrings in the liberation of international credit arising with the offshore accumulation and circulation of Eurodollars and petrodollars, through the eventual disintegration of the Bretton Woods regulatory system and culminating in the advanced deregulation of financial markets and capital flows in the past two decades, the international financial system has rapidly de-coupled itself from direct dependence on the real economy (Block, 1977; Altvater, 1993). Once disengaged, it has become possible, particularly with the application of new technological capabilities, to create a relatively pure system of exchange whose awesome expansion and unregulated independence is perhaps best evidenced in the fact that the total combined foreign currency reserves of the G7 powers amounts to less than the value of a single day´s trading on foreign currency markets.[4]

[3] It is emblematic of this process that the electronic ability to create new „products" and new sources of information is hastening the demise of the older bank-based trading system traditionally mediated by (slower-moving) personal relations: see Kurtzman (1993).

[4] The value of three days currency trading in New York exceeds the total annual output of U.S. companies (Kurtzman, 1993). Other data in this domain are equally impressive:

The international financial system is an increasingly self-referential system of exchange. New financial instruments are constructed not on the transfer of products (trade in goods and services) but on the proliferation of media of exchange (money, credit card debt, equipment leases and a range of other financial assets) and the ability to create markets in the terms of trade (future interest rates on outstanding loans, currency rate movements) themselves. Ever-more ingenious forms of securitization essentially constitute platforms for the continuous mass production of credit. The critical objective in these markets has shifted from developing opportunities for investment to devising new means for proliferating transactions *per se:* the primary aim of these exchanges is less to channel capital to corporate investment or to broker the transfer of goods than continually to shift electronic monetary resources between transactions and markets, a compulsion constantly enhanced by the multiplication of opportunities for making transactions engineered by increasing throughput in the system of exchange as a whole.

The almost unlimited possibilities for securitization, the increasing volatility of the markets which accompanies their increasing dissociation from the real economy, the continual elaboration of new hedging strategies to offset the higher risks involved and the capacity to capitalize electronically on even minute or momentary shifts in market values or conditions all multiply the pace and volume of economic activity in these markets. Their very efficiency — the ability to respond instantaneously to new information — institutionalizes volatility (as a consequence, large fluctuations in interest rates, equity markets and currency values are now commonplace in the world economy) and these fluctuations serve in turn as the structural foundation for new transaction opportunities and further market expansion. Incessant oscillation, even crisis, are instrumental to the logic of profit-making exchange in these markets as movements of money and capital now respond primarily to developments within the monetary realm itself.

e.g. international bank lending (i.e. cross-border and domestic lending in foreign currency) has expanded from $324b in 1980 to $7,5tr in 1991, the latter figure approximately the combined GDP of the leading 24 OECD industrial nations in 1980; the global stock of derivatives, a core pyramiding strategy, has increased from $1,1tr in 1986 to $6,9tr in 1991; foreign exchange turnover, up from $650b per day in 1986 to more than $900b per day in 1992 amounts to 40-50 times the value of daily world trade; U.S. securities transactions involving foreigners, the equivalent of only 9% of U.S. GDP in 1980, had expanded to 93% of GDP by 1990 (and similar increases were evident in Germany, Japan and elsewhere): see The Economist, September 19, 1992.

The international monetary system imposes potent constraints on economic growth patterns at the level of the nation-state and at the level of global innovation strategies. Since international monetary transactions respond less to the rates of return on real capital or to shifts in the markets for goods and services than to differences in the price of money (interest rates, exchange rates), national monetary regimes are increasingly compelled, as national interest rates are driven to converge around the highest world levels, to exercise a form of macroeconomic discipline that imposes deflationary constrictions on domestic economies (and on all economies at more or less the same time).[5] As both Notermans (1993) and Bruno (1993) have observed, national *policy choices* to prioritize counter-inflationary strategies, external balances and international capital flows further ensure the subordination of national economies to the logic of the international financial system rather than, as in the earlier period of Bretton Woods, the reverse. The incipient disintegration, or at least transcendence, of national systems of investment linking household savings, regulated banking systems, industrial investment priorities and public policy support for domestic production objectives effectively subordinates political logics (whose principal objective is the provision of public goods and the fulfillment of social goals and collective well-being) and industrial logics (oriented to long-term national economic growth) to the short-term market considerations of financial logic (guided only by the search for profitability levels relevant to the efficient utilization of capital) (Muldur, 1991). The increasingly speculative character of corporate strategic perspectives — whether manifest in the trading of foreign currencies, issuing commercial paper, the leveraged buyout phenomenon or the reduction of long-term industrial investment (particularly in R&D) in favour of financial transactions — represents the gradual conversion of corporate organizations to prioritizing the logic of exchange over the more fundamental objectives of production or innovation.[6]

[5] The recent (early-mid 1994) bidding-up of U.S. interest rates is merely the latest example of this constraint. This system also encourages the transfer of capital — whether in the form of potential inward investment or domestic capital flight — from the Third World.

[6] As Muldur (1991) observes, the primacy accorded high short-term returns on investment results in the devalorization of „unprofitable“ operations, workers and regions, thereby reinforcing the resulting crisis of traditional production forms.

The spatial dynamic of internationalization tends towards genuine spacelessness. The movement of goods and, to a far lesser degree, services is necessarily defined in terms of spatial constraints, though the advent of information technology — its embodiment in infrastructure, products and processes — and the intensification of competition at all levels currently speeds the velocity of circulation of goods and services through the international economic system. The overwhelming preponderance of the financial circuit within the contemporary international economy, however, involves an historical deepening of the logic of exchange in that transactions within the international financial system effectively surmount spatial barriers altogether, converting the tyranny of distance into spaceless flows.[7]

Yet, not only should this logic of internationalization be differentiated from multinationalization and globalization, but each of these three processes contends against important counter-movements designed to reconfigure world-economic trends into dimensions more manageable by the traditional nation-state. In an epoch in which „national capitalism has ceased to be the only coherent form of organization of capital" (Group of Lisbon, 1993: 22), national space attempts to re-assert itself, through these counter-movements, against world space. The principal counterpoint to tendencies leading towards the abolition of spatial constraints in the new international system is constituted by the re-assertion of *explicitly spatial systems of control* in the incipient emergence of *re-continentalized economies* or *regional blocs*.[8] Though some blocs might exhibit pretensions to supra-national forms of political integration, it seems fair to conclude that, with the partial exception of the European Union, contemporary blocs are unified principally at the level of trade and financial relations (where tendencies exist to concentrate such relations within the bloc) (Frankel, 1992). That is, blocs, insofar as they exist as coherent entities at all, manifest their presence at the *international* level.[9] As such,

[7] Of course, even these flows are still anchored in particular spatial locations (see Sassen, 1991; Roberts, 1994; Martin, 1994) and some dimensions of international financial movements (e.g. equity investment) are more locationally specific than others (see Frieden, 1991).

[8] Space constraints preclude extended development of this issue here. For a more complete treatment of this, and other state-centred counter-movements mentioned in this chapter, see Gordon (1994).

[9] This phenomenon should not be exaggerated. Hirst and Thompson (1992), for example, go too far in declaring that the „most significant post-1970s development, and the most enduring, is the formation of supra-national trading and economic blocs".

they constitute not a „revenge of geography" (cf. Lipietz, 1993) tied to the ostensible spatial requirements of just-in-time and flexible production[10] nor the emergence of new supra-national political forms, but the „revenge of the state": in each of the leading blocs, the incipient „continental" economy is under the leadership, if not the outright control, of a single dominant power (the Federal Republic of Germany, the U.S., Japan) which, insofar as it acts within this framework, attempts to maintain control over phenomena that threaten to establish a separate zone of autonomy in the international system by channeling them instead within a specific hegemonic geographical framework. Given the long-term crisis of the different production models in the leading economies of Japan, the U.S. and Germany (Lehner et al., 1994), spatial extension of their respective economic zones also constitutes a new set of minimum scale requirements for a state-centred solution.[11]

3 Multinationalization and Transnationalization

Intensification of processes of international mobility, transfer and exchange constitutes a distinct, quasi-autonomous mechanism of the new world economy. However, quite apart from the fact that the presupposition of these flows is the objective *separation* (as opposed to the global integration) of national/individual economic units, globalization *per se* remains illusory in this sphere by virtue of the fact that, in reality, the volume of transactions constitutive of international financial dealings and world trade has been spatially *contracting*, not expanding: triadization (the increasing concentration of trade and investment in the United States, Europe and Japan) simultaneously involves a „de-linking" of advanced industrial economies from many other regions of the world (Group of Lisbon, 1993). Perhaps globalization is more

[10] As will be seen in section 5 below, the link between flexible production forms and localization has been greatly exaggerated. Japanese plants located in Mexico, to take an extreme example, effectively operate just-in-time production systems (maintaining around one to four days inventory) even though 95% of their production inputs are shipped from Japan. That is, even if, ceteris paribus, manufacturers might prefer supplier localization, it is quite possible to run JIT and other flexible systems with supply lines that are global in extent.

[11] As Lipietz (1993) notes, each of these zones also has its own built-in „centre-periphery" structure.

effectively synthesized in the indubitably expansive phenomenon of multinationalization?

Multinationalization involves the organized direction and control of cross-national economic activities by corporations that remain fundamentally anchored in *national* economic systems: if internationalization is constituted by flows between distinct economic units in different countries, multinationalization is demarcated by the *centrally coordinated* activities of specific corporate organizations extended to multiple countries (e.g. Kindleberger, 1969; Chandler, 1977; Hymer, 1979; Dunning, 1981).

The origins of multinationalization lie in the late nineteenth and early twentieth centuries when access to raw materials inputs and the need for high volume market outlets stimulated the first wave of cross-national manufacturing operations. In the earliest period of multinational development, emergent mass production techniques required permanent access to low cost materials and supplies, while optimal benefits from economies of scale necessitated a constant search for new markets. In this phase, the primary purpose of companies operating abroad consisted in protecting both competitiveness and market share in their home country and the power of a multinational enterprise (MNE) was evidenced precisely in its ability to marshal international resources to its *domestic* advantage (Perlmutter, 1968).

A concatenation of forces — accumulated organizational experience, expanding export sales, oligopolistic competition, inter-country structural distortions, communications constraints on real-time centralized management — fueled the continued transfer over time of MNE resources abroad, with the intention of building export-substitution capacity in diverse national markets. Subsequently, as international competition increased within both domestic and global markets, the share of foreign income in the total activity of MNEs augmented substantially and MNEs were compelled further to expand their foreign operations and transfer even more resources to overseas enterprises. As the significance of diverse foreign markets expanded, overseas MNE subsidiaries began to acquire greater autonomy in design, production and marketing for local requirements and needs.

Innovation, with respect to both fundamental research breakthroughs and the more incremental elaboration of existing technological trajectories, is obviously important to contemporary multinationalization processes (Bartlett and Ghoshal, 1990). But, in contrast with globalization processes which are systematically focused on the ability to create *permanent innovation* (see section 4 below), multinationalization is constituted fundamentally as a *logic of production*, oriented to the stabilization and coordinated articulation across global space of the various activities necessary to convert innovation into a worldwide process of production and distribution: multinationalization involves manufacturing on a world scale. Foreign direct investment (FDI) in this context is activated by the gains embodied in diffusing innovation initially developed within domestic headquarters locations across space or by the ability to utilize specific locational advantages and know-how embodied in foreign operations of the firm to adapt such innovations to different conditions thereby facilitating the marketability of products. Mobilization of the advantages inherent in corporate control — size, market power, ownership — specific and location — specific advantages — depend upon the appropriation of potential rents involved in production on a worldwide basis.

The power of the MNE is evidenced in its capacity for extensive foreign market penetration and its technological and organizational superiority with respect to host country competitors. However, objective organizational, communications and control deficiencies meant that overseas branches or subsidiaries characteristically retained substantial autonomy and that cross-border transactions between individual branches, or between overseas branches and the parent company, were relatively restricted. This traditional „multi-domestic" strategy (Porter, 1990) tended to presume that multinational operations operated with limited cross-national coordination: multinational strategies, despite their pretensions to global integration, essentially comprised aggregate domestic strategies.

In the past two decades in particular, the pace of multinationalization has intensified to the point of initiating further qualitative structural change, unleashing a further evolution towards genuine transnationalization. Vertical and horizontal integration within the ranks of multinational corporations has been advanced by expanding growth rates of mergers and acquisitions. Industrial concentration has increased in many sectors, and this has served largely to intensify, rather than to diminish, oligopolistic competition within the world economy (Amin and Dietrich, 1991; OECD, 1992). The control and communications potential inherent in global information technology networks have dramatically enhanced central coordination capabilities within trans-national organizations. But the most significant indicator of a new phase in the evolution of multinationalization is the recent and rapid proliferation of foreign direct investment within the world economy.

The expansion of FDI results from a number of causes. Declining regulatory barriers to overseas investment, uncontrolled domestic and international capital markets and reduced communications costs all render foreign investment both easier and cheaper. Shifts in international technological advantage create new sources of offensive FDI (as evidenced in the growth of European and Japanese FDI and the conversion of U.S. status from home to host country for FDI), while oligopolistic competition drives waves of defensive FDI as followers emulate first mover investments in new locations (Graham and Krugman, 1989; Schoenberger, 1990). Continuing ownership-specific and location-specific advantages constitute incentives both to expand further and strategically to restructure foreign investments.

For these, and other, reasons, FDI has expanded phenomenally in recent years, increasing four times faster than world GNP in 1983-1988 and three times faster than international trade in the same period (OECD, 1992). Julius (1990) anticipated a further doubling in the global stock of FDI prior to 1995.[12] Even by the early 1970s, the degree of global MNE expansion was relatively limited: in 1973, 44.9% of MNEs had operations in only one country, 39.8% in only two to five countries (Howells and Wood, 1991). As a result of the recent acceleration in FDI, an increasing number of firms now have large proportions of their total operations outside their domestic base and, in a growing number of cases, firms are becoming economically dependent on the higher profitability of their overseas activities (Carnoy, 1993).

The most important aspect of this phenomenon, however, is the fact that expansion of FDI has driven the process of world economic integration well beyond the structural parameters of the international trading system. Indeed, trade-based analysis provides an increasingly misleading conception not only of inter-national competitiveness but of the core structures of the world economy. In the United States and Japan, for example, more than one-half of all imports and exports are FDI-related „trade" (i.e. *intra-firm* shipments) and in advanced industrial societies generally the trend is for overseas branches and divisions to generate far greater sales than cross-border exchanges: U.S. subsidiaries abroad sustain sales three times greater than U.S. exporters (a large proportion of U.S. exports, of course, deriving from the same multina-

[12] The deepening of the economic crisis in the advanced capitalist world, particularly in Japan and Europe, has undoubtedly led to a slowdown in the rate of growth of FDI in the early 1990s, however.

tional companies) and, by the late 1980s, this was true also of Japanese subsidiaries in the U.S. (Encarnation, 1992). Foreign subsidiaries, moreover, are increasingly serving third-country, and even home-country, markets from their offshore production and distribution platforms.

Thus, it is clear that trade flows are increasingly subordinate to, and are shaped by, investment flows (Julius, 1990; Ostry, 1990): hierarchy subsumes market. So substantial is this transformation that, if U.S. product flows are re-calculated on the basis of changes of ownership (i.e. accounting for FDI-related trade) and not simply in terms of when goods cross borders (i.e. ignoring FDI-related trade), the nation´s infamous trade deficit is converted into a substantial *surplus* (Julius, 1990). Still more important, since intra-organizational transfers replace market transactions and, in particular, provide multinationals with greater security against the foreign exchange fluctuations associated with market-based transfers, the expansion of FDI must be seen ultimately as engineering a structural reversal: as financial internationalization exacerbates uncertainty and risk for production organizations, FDI represents an attempt to de-link the world of production from market forces and insulate processes of production more securely within new macro-level transnational hierarchies.

The voluminous increase in the total stock of foreign direct investment and its simultaneous spatial extension to new geographic locations represents a multiplication and deepening of linkages between national economies. It constitutes as well a shift away from the economic primacy of domestic comparative advantage (the core of trade-based relations) to the primacy of global organizational superiority at the level of the world economy. Unfortunately, there is no method available for distinguishing the uses of FDI more precisely. Some substantial share of total FDI is undoubtedly deployed to maintain or extend traditional *multinational* operations and practices. But, in line with the shifting dynamics from market to hierarchy in the world economy as a whole, FDI is increasingly financing the transformation to *transnational* production organization.

In a process gathering momentum over the last decade, MNEs have begun to establish truly transnationally integrated production networks in which overseas facilities are brought more directly within the ambit of a singular centralized strategy (Dicken, 1992; Barnet and Cavanagh, 1994). Multiple geographic operations or divisions are merged into single global operating units.[13] Each unit in the overall corporate organization now performs a specialized function for the group as a whole: the differentiated products manufactured and distributed by localized units are replaced with centers dedicated to specific product development for worldwide distribution. Specifically regional operations are replaced by global product development teams. Instead of being largely autonomous, dispersed operations are integrated across national borders and are collectively guided by a single global accumulation strategy (Kogut, 1990; Amin and Dietrich, 1992). Functional flows and linkages are established between formerly discrete sites. Strategically, *transnationalization* involves the re-assertion of strong internal central coordination and an articulated portfolio of facilities in sites determined by comparative locational advantage, the whole directed predominantly by a concern for eliminating duplication and other inefficiencies, reducing the costs of development, materials and components by optimizing single sourcing capabilities, exploiting global economies of scale, and increasing response time within regional markets.[14] Transnationalization manifests itself, that is, in the consolidation of a world-wide *intra-firm* division of labor. As such, it constitutes the ultimate terminus of the multinational project: in the final analysis, transnational networks are coordinated essentially as self-contained *intra-firm* projects of enterprises that, however extensive their global reach, are still singularly corporate, if not still national-corporate, in character.

[13] Ford, for example, recently merged its North American and European operations into a single unit and plans to integrate its Asian-Pacific and Latin American operations into the same unit at a later date.

[14] The spatial organization of the transnational network is not determined by labor costs alone, but as Grunwald and Flamm (1985) emphasized, by a number of inter-related variables. Schoenberger (1990) observes that U.S. direct investment in Western Europe has gravitated towards areas with comparatively high wage rates and high levels of unionization, indicating the primary salience of market access considerations and other non-price-based performance criteria (improved turnaround times, more efficient supplier relations, customer support). Factor prices in S.E. Asia would dictate investment in Indonesia, Thailand and the Philippines and not in Singapore, Malaysia and South Korea where it is in fact concentrated (Rasiah, 1990). The concept of spatially-segmented labor markets organizing docile production labor in the Third World and research-intensive employment in core industrial regions is far too undifferentiated to account for the widespread establishment of advanced technical functions in „peripheral“ regions and the employment of large quantities of semi-skilled immigrant labor in „core“ regions like Silicon Valley (Gordon and Kimball, 1985; Sassen, 1990).

Petrella (1991) has observed that this process tends to reverse long-standing relationships between MNEs and the state. In the postwar period, MNEs everywhere benefited from state policies designed to expand the influence of their respective „national champions“ and the development of multilateral interdependence was, in large measure, the objective outcome of competing national policies. In contrast, transnationalization strengthens the autonomy of multinational organizations with respect to the state and, as it increasingly makes critical decisions regarding technological progress, economic development and social well-being, transnational capital gains legitimacy even over the state. The ability of transnational firms to operate in an integrated way on a worldwide scale increasingly places states on the defensive. Yet, as Petrella carefully emphasizes, relations between the state and transnational capital presently remain ambiguous: the pendulum has not swung to the other side definitively.

In this context, the counter-movement to the process of transnationalization is evidenced in attempts by the state to retain its leadership role in the mobilization of national production capabilities which are focused in policies of national competitiveness and strategic trade. The basic orientation in the fusion of trade and industrial policy that characterizes strategic trade is towards creating *national* mastery of new technological trajectories and establishing position within international markets on the basis of an asymmetric distribution of technological capabilities between competing firms and countries. With respect to the core industrial sectors which define the leading edge of international competitiveness or which enhance the national welfare through their impacts on wages, job creation and skill distribution, government intervention through strategic trade policy may be deployed as a „profit-shifting device“ to capture a larger national share of the returns to innovation in international markets (Stegemann, 1989; Richardson, 1990).[15] Through conversion to the doctrine of strategic trade, the state can hope to remain a critical mediator of transnational economic processes in the world economy, deflecting the tendency for transnationalization to bypass the limits of state intervention back into a mold that remains focused on *national*, as an alternative to purely transnational, technological mastery and economic welfare.

[15] Within strategic trade theory, the difference between enhancing national welfare, and the welfare of particular groups is left deliberately vague, occluded by the designation of certain industries as „strategic“ in the national security sense.

4 Globalization and New Production Systems

However sophisticated the degree and character of internal control, and whatever their undoubted advantages over business organization that remains purely national in scope, multinational and transnational enterprises encounter severe structural limits in a world of intensified oligopolistic competition. First: transnationalization involves a reinforcement of hierarchy as the dominant organizational principle of world-economic activity in a period in which new logics of innovation invalidate the strategy of ever more comprehensive vertical integration for even the largest, wealthiest and most capable corporations. As market forces successfully intensify competition on a global scale, diversify demand and increase the speed of economic transactions to a pace approaching the real time satisfaction of desires, the structure of the independent firm, ostensibly ideally suited to the logic of pure competition, becomes increasingly problematic, indeed even prospectively obsolete. Fundamental transformations in the cost and complexity of innovation and production expose the excessive rigidity of vertically integrated organizational structure.

Second: the trade-off between the coordination of space and the organization of product manufacture[16] tends to be resolved in favor of higher levels of standardization (the „world car") and the subsumption of space within hierarchical strategy, although it should be noted that certain forms of „mass customization" (Swatch, Benetton) geared at least to the differentiation of demand (if not to the valorization of other localized innovation capabilities) are possible on this scale as well. In the final analysis, the aim of transnationalization is to *reduce*, if not to eliminate, forms of differentiation that resulted from the higher levels of local autonomy attained within traditional multinational production.[17] The spatial dynamics of transnationalization tend towards

[16] As Dicken (1986) has observed, multi-divisional organizations constantly confront a difficult choice between facilitating the coordination of product lines across space (at the expense of engaging the localized advantages of a given geographical zone) or encouraging localized product variation (at the expense of efficient transferability across space).

[17] This is also why, for example, the high cost structures typical of Japanese domestic production systems tend not to be recapitulated within offshore Japanese manufacturing organizations. A recent survey of Japanese manufacturing facilities in California (Milkman, 1992) found little evidence of transplanting characteristic forms of Japanese production and work organization: Japanese plants in the U.S. and Mexico tend, with some exceptions, to be quite Fordist in character: see also Adler (1993).

a differentiated homogenization of space: in principle, locations for multinational operations are increasingly substitutable (a function of the routinization and standardization of products and processes, widening locational choice resulting from infrastructural improvements and global economic development and the substitution of internal, for place-specific, assets) while substantive distinctions between locations derive not from the specific character of regionalized production systems but more or less completely from corporate determinations of internal need. Third: though following an autonomous dynamic, the movement of foreign direct investment mirrors developments at the level of international trade and finance in that its integrative impetus is experienced over a *narrowing*, rather than an expanding, terrain of the world economy. Three-quarters of global FDI is concentrated within the G5 economies — FDI is even more concentrated within the Triad than trade — and, in the last decade, FDI in the less developed countries has declined both relatively and absolutely (OECD, 1992).

In contrast, *globalization* properly so-called is propelled by a new social-organizational *logic of innovation*.[18] The creation of new technologies is currently an exceedingly complex task. Some technologies issue more or less directly from basic scientific research as delineated in the traditional linear model of technology development. The reverse process of generating new technologies incrementally from existing practices and techniques through „learning-by-doing" constitutes a critically important source of innovation as well. However, fundamental changes in the material logic of modern production — the appearance of new core technologies, the widespread diffusion of advanced technological capabilities and dramatic convulsions in long-standing patterns of international competition, the complexity and pace of technological change, technological convergence, massive increases in development costs, ubiquitous organizational, technological and market uncertainty —

[18] Tyson (1992) has observed that the extent of globalization should not be exaggerated because national parent companies still control the bulk of total MNE assets, sales and employment. In a different but related vein, Krugman (1994) suggests that competitiveness still depends principally on domestic productivity as opposed to international competitiveness. While correct so far as they go, both of these arguments seriously neglect the issue of innovation, the extent to which both „national" firm assets, sales and employment and domestic productivity increasingly depend on the ability of firms to establish systems of permanent innovation and the degree to which the creation of new technology currently rests on global presuppositions.

have prompted both theoretical and practical re-assessment of the innovation process in advanced industrial societies.[19]

R&D commitments now transcend the resources even of firms with the highest levels and shares of research expenditure. Performance constraints imposed by firm-specific technology trajectories are exacerbated as international competition and technological convergence expand the range and complexity of the technologies a firm must monitor in order to produce innovation. The rapidity and complexity of technological change in all sectors necessitate closer and more flexible relationships with both customers and suppliers. As applications-specificity and customization assume greater salience in new product development, demand no longer exists as a generalized abstraction for producers: rather, demand must be integrated into the earliest stages of the innovation process, *in an anticipatory way*, as a specific schedule of functional requirements, design features and product characteristics. As a consequence, collaborative relations between producers and clients are now central to the innovation process. Similarly, the increasing inability of producers to track developments in a wide range of interdependent technologies places greater pressure upon suppliers to act as independent sources of creativity in a process of joint technology creation. The heightened importance of design specificity and operational complementarity simultaneously reduces the efficacy of both market supply (the commodity status of inputs assuming less salience than their specific functional attributes) and vertical integration (the inability to track a wide range of component technologies at the leading edge of innovation invalidating attempts to supply them internally). Arms-length transactions preclude the elaboration of long-term collaborative inter-relations while vertical integration reduces informational diversity and multi-directional creativity. Abbreviated product cycles and the necessity for simultaneous access to world markets expose inevitable shortcomings in corporate marketing expertise and distribution networks. New technology combinations alter the boundaries between sectors, plunging firms into unfamiliar activities outside the scope of their normal operations.

These developments, both severally and collectively, increasingly invalidate the traditional organizational alternatives of „market“ and „hierarchy“ (Williamson, 1985, 1986): explosive technical and economic change dramati-

[19] For analyses treating these phenomena in more detail, see Amendola and Gaffard (1988); Gordon (1990a); Camagni (1991); Freeman (1991); Imai (1992).

cally enhance the level of uncertainty and risk associated with market transactions, while the pace and cost of adaptability militate against a strategy of vertical integration. *Innovation for any firm in these circumstances is necessarily dependent upon external transactions, yet structural change negates the efficiency and adequacy of market provision.* Firms, both large and small, are coping with this contradiction by elaborating *new non-market forms of inter-firm coordination.* That is, both large and small firms increasingly focus their own enterprise on core capabilities and delegate interdependent functions (formerly provided in-house or purchased on the market) to the complementary specialization of autonomous firms organized in a collaborative and inter-dependent chain of production.

Innovation is no longer endogenous to the single firm but presupposes constructing a new relationship between the firm and its environment (Gordon, 1990a, 1992; Amendola and Bruno, 1990; Bruno and de Lellis, 1994). Firms organized according to this logic comprise an interdependent network in which the production strategies of individual actors are determined in part by their position within the chain and, hence, by the organization of relations between the constituent components. Technology design, transfer and use cannot be seen as discrete stages within a given firm or as independent functions embodied in separate firms. Rather innovation is a composite process in which the activities of other members of the production chain exert critical independent impact upon innovation in each function. Research and learning occur at all levels of this collaborative organization and innovation is no longer a function of R&D capacities and expenditures alone but depends on the accumulation and appropriation of learning throughout the organization as a whole. The reciprocal dependence of each stage of production upon the others means that the mode of organization adopted decisively both the primacy and the relative autonomy of the organizational process created to coordinate the various elements of the new innovation flow.[20]

Innovation from this standpoint tends to be neither radical exogenous invention (as in the linear model) nor narrowly path-dependent incremental change (as in the evolutionary model). Far more frequently, innovation tends to occur in the unilluminated space between these options: that is, while proceeding substantially within existing frameworks of knowledge and practice

[20] For an analysis of the articulation of technology design, transfer and use in terms of differential „cultures of learning", see Gordon (1990b). See also Lundvall (1988).

rather than initiating or requiring fundamental breakthroughs in science and technology, innovation nonetheless commonly tends to push at the margins of established organizational, technical and economic practice as opposed to operating within a more restricted field of „normal“ problem-solving routines.[21] Innovation in this context, therefore, is not simply a matter of adjusting to known environmental constraints or independently applying existing technical routines (static flexibility), but of modulating constantly uncertain environmental change through organizational creativity in cooperation with others (dynamic flexibility): the critical issue is not the allocation of given resources but *the creation of new resources* (Amendola and Gaffard, 1988).

This shift in the material logic of contemporary innovation and production confronts all firms — large and small, domestic and international — with the need for substantive organizational adjustments. In the present context, it is perhaps most instructive to focus on the challenges posed to the prevailing internalized logic of innovation within the traditional MNE. In the first place, each element of the firm´s organizational structure must assume responsibility for quasi-autonomous contributions to innovation. Within firms committed to the logic of globalization, the multinational network has to be operated not as a hierarchy but as a *heterarchy* (Bartlett et al., 1990) or as a set of globally interdependent, spatially dispersed innovation centers. Core strategic activities and coordination roles are themselves dispersed beyond the headquarters locality or home country; foreign subsidiaries play a strategic, not a subordinate, role within the corporation as a whole, and the multi-centered network tends to be organized around horizontal, rather than vertical or hierarchical, linkages. The fundamental objective of these new global networks involves not simply the traditional goals of channeling information and delegating authority throughout the hierarchical structure but, on the contrary, the *creation* of new research, manufacturing and organizational knowledge and the management of permanent innovation through the mobilization of inter-organizational learning.

This transformation is particularly evident in the organization of MNE R&D.[22] Traditionally, R&D units have exhibited a certain locational rigidity

[21] For more detailed observations on this issue, see Gordon (1990a, 1992, 1993a); Henderson and Clark (1990); Imai (1992); Lehner et al. (1994).

[22] Multinational corporations account for 75% all industrial R&D in OECD countries and the five largest firms in the U.S., Japan and the U.K. collectively support R&D ex-

with regard to proximity to headquarter sites or core business operations as a result of low mortality rates, the need for close linkages between research and headquarter decision-making functions, scale economies associated with research concentration and the spatial logic of typical corporate divisions of labor. Dispersed R&D operations tended to be related to specific product divisions or confined to the modification for host markets of products developed elsewhere in the company. Currently, however, the increasing scope, scale and specialization of research activity combined with the widespread diffusion of R&D capabilities throughout the world economy and the significance of tacit over generic knowledge within the R&D process itself are generating an increasing globalization of R&D activities (Howells, 1990; Warrant, 1991; Guelle, 1989; Malerba et al., 1991).

R&D departments and facilities in foreign locations serve as a basis for interaction with a wide range of localized scientific and technical expertise: overseas locations function not simply as modalities of technology transfer from transnational corporations to host economies but as environments for technology sourcing into the multinational firm itself (Chesnais, 1988). Precisely because of the predominantly non-generic and localized nature of technological knowledge, overseas R&D units are transformed from superficially embedded support facilities into quasi-independent and locally integrated research organizations, while their position within the firm shifts from a subordinate status to a more truly interdependent relationship with other similar operations (Sakakibara and Westney, 1992; Pearce, 1992). These collaborative arrangements are spreading precisely in order to transcend the constraints on producing new technology combinations inherent in intra-firm incrementalism.

A second dimension of this globalization process concerns the formation of collaborative partnerships between firms (an incipient socialization of capital) on a global scale. In the 1980s particularly, there occurred a profound elaboration of cross-national and trans-organizational strategic alliances, particularly in sectors impacted by information technology. Global cooperative agreements linking producer and users, design centers and manufacturing operations or vendors and marketing outlets are particularly prevalent in the semiconductor industry. Similarly extensive agreements exist in the computer

penditures larger than the total social resources devoted to R&D in the 15 OECD economies with the lowest levels of R&D activities (Archibugi and Pianta, 1992).

branch, both among manufacturers for technical cooperation and distribution and with suppliers of components and software. Telematics is another field experiencing large-scale inter-sectoral alliances designed to absorb technological convergence and establish control over standards. Transnational alliance structures, formed to overcome the strategic limitations of the „national" multilocational corporation are carving out vast areas of cooperation among the alliance partners, while competitive strategies cut across discrete national territorial frameworks and inter-national trade disputes to center increasingly upon rival transnational alliance formations. Alliance structures have diffused rapidly in other advanced technology sectors: commercial aircraft, automobiles, biotechnology (Chesnais, 1988; Cowhey and Aronson, 1993; Gordon, 1992, 1993a; Mowery, 1988; OECD, 1992).

The proliferation of strategic alliances is a relatively new phenomenon: inter-firm coordination within this framework often remains relatively experimental. The forms taken by inter-firm partnering are manifold. Some partnering arrangements do not proceed far beyond traditional forms of instrumental exchange (licensing agreements, technology transfer, distribution arrangements). Others undoubtedly manifest concealed forms of hierarchical dependency and serve as preludes to subsequent mergers. In these cases, alliances are merely modified forms of traditional mechanisms of resource control. But the attempt to traditionalize new types of relations is unlikely to succeed. New production logics require new organizational strategies: the form of business organization chosen by an enterprise or industry affects its economic success quite independently of the market.

The form of alliance most appropriate for contemporary production needs involves genuine structural interdependence: firms leverage their own strengths through integration with the strengths of others. Partners are not merely instrumental allies: in fact, each serves as an essential *presupposition* of the other´s ability to achieve its own objectives. While strategic alliances involve agreements between autonomous firms, and are oriented towards strengthening the competitive position of the network and its members, inter-firm relations *within* the alliance itself tend to push beyond traditional market relations. Permanently contingent relationships mediated by strict organizational independence and market transactions — the arms-length exchange structure of traditional short-term linkages — are replaced by long-term relations intended to endure and which are mediated by highly personalized and detailed interaction. R&D capabilities relate not simply to the production of innovation within the firm´s own learning parameters, but, on the contrary, enhance its capacity to identify, assimilate and deploy external knowledge from the firm´s environment (Cohen and Levinthal, 1989). Extensive organizational integration is often achieved within alliance relationships: duplicate management and research teams from each partner engage in frequent interaction, including long periods of on-site work in each other´s plants. Unplanned individualistic market coordination is replaced by collectively specified goals. Competitive secrecy gives way to the mutual sharing of confidential business information and long-range plans. Ongoing collaborative communication flows facilitating reciprocal innovation are substituted for contacts activated by standardized production needs and immediate market signals. Contracts are not necessarily specified rigidly and, in an increasing number of instances, contractual agreements between partners are rudimentary or even non-existent. Cooperative trust, shared norms and mutual advocacy overcome antagonistic independence and isolation.[23] Even where they have been set up for limited, instrumental purposes alliances, when they are successful, tend to extend to all aspects of a firm´s operations over time and to shift their focus from particular outcomes to more permanent interactions designed to produce a continuing stream of innovations. In other words, *in the social-organizational model, innovation is a product of the inter-organizational creation of a viable long-term innovation process.*[24]

The logic of innovation at the core of the globalization process also casts light on the relationship between new technologies and trends in the social and industrial division of labor, issues discussed at length in other contributions to this volume.

Whether elaborated from the standpoint of attributes necessarily embodied in new technologies, the logic of capitalist workplace control or the organization of the labor process, formulations of this relationship generally have

[23] It would be incorrect to assume that partnering relationships commonly derive from trust: on the contrary, trust is usually the result of continuous collaborative interaction and improvements in mutual understanding that emerge from long-term interactions within the relationship.

[24] The state-led counter-movement to the globalization of innovation is encapsulated in the concept of the „national system of innovation“ (see Lundvall, 1992; Nelson, 1993) and its concomitant evolutionary theory of innovation (Dosi et al., 1988, 1990). Without at all denying the importance of this mode of innovation, it remains too constricted to stand as a general theory of technology creation: for a broader critical treatment, see Gordon (1990a); Amendola and Gaffard (1988, 1993); Lehner et al. (1995).

adopted a dichotomous mode, one set of approaches insisting upon a unilinear tendency towards the strengthening of management control systems, the technological programming and standardization of production scheduling and operating practices, and the deskilling or elimination of human labor while opposing approaches insist upon a trend towards more flexible forms of work organization, enhanced worker decision-making autonomy and upgraded skills.

In fact, no unilinear trend exists in any of these spheres. Research into specific technological applications as well as more synthetic analyses of available data reveal empirical manifestations of both deskilling and reskilling associated with similar technologies, task structures and occupations.[25] Indeed, these variations suggest that, far from embodying any particular determinate outcome, information technologies in fact broaden the range of alternative possible forms of work organization and skill composition and impose only the necessity of making a socio-political choice within this range of alternative combinations.[26] Capitalist control strategies may work as effectively through the hierarchical decentralization of decision-making and responsibility (as in the Japanese system) as through the maintenance of more traditional forms of centralized power. In a particularly cogent argument, Walker (1989) has observed that typically reductionist labor process analysis obscures the complexity of the labor process itself, the irregular procession of automation across the various dimensions of the labor process and the fact that the application of new technologies may have diverse impacts in each sphere of the labor process. The divergent constraints imposed by different manufacturing environments, the varying dynamics of product and process

[25] For extremely useful assessments of available research, see Hartmann et al. (1983); Hirschhorn (1984); Shaiken (1984); Adler (1987, 1992); Clark et al. (1988); Hodson and Parker (1988); Spenner (1988); Wood (1989); Adler and Borys (1989); Warner et al. (1990); and Sayer and Walker (1992).

[26] In line with this observation, it is important to note that change frequently takes more complex forms than straightforward improvement or degradation of existing skills. Jobs may be deskilled while the workers performing them are upgraded. Elimination of lower-skilled positions resulting from automation effectively raises the average skill level of the remaining workforce. The transfer of some work performed by higher-level workers to personnel below them in the occupational hierarchy has the effect of upgrading both groups. Workers may gain on one dimension (autonomy or system responsibility) while simultaneously losing on another (control over work pace or task specialization).

transformation and the inevitable unevenness of new technological applications generate extensive heterogeneity in the outcomes of labor process automation.

The independent impact of the kind of materials deployed in a given manufacturing process, the type of product produced, the specific historical form of development in an industrial sector, the presence of different generations of technology at the shop or plant level and the subtle reciprocal impacts of autonomous changes in product or process technologies all shift the focus of analysis from particular technological applications or the labor process as a privileged site to the organization of production as a whole (Sayer and Walker, 1992; Walker, 1989). Indeed, the analysis of technology design, work organization and skills must be situated within a more comprehensive examination of decisions concerning the integration of the various phases of production, the control and management of information flow in the enterprise, the occupational distribution of work tasks and responsibilities and the relationship established between authority and expertise in the operation of the production system as a whole (Gordon and Krieger, 1992).

At this level, it is important to emphasize that new technologies, far from initiating a singular shift from mass production to flexible specialization (Piore and Sabel, 1984), in fact make possible a variety of forms of flexible production: modes of flexible mass production (potentially culminating in the manufacture of essentially customized products from highly standardized components or „mass customization") remain as viable as small-scale flexible specialization, while a broad range of intermediate forms, derived from the technological relaxation of the once rigid distinction between efficiency and flexibility and the new capacity to restructure around a subtle and rich profusion of scale-scope combinations, comprise equally plausible forms of contemporary production organization.[27] In addition, the newly problematic nature of the self-sufficient vertically-integrated company serves as a reminder that the configuration of a particular production system increasingly may take the form of an *inter-firm* organization.

[27] It is pertinent also to note that clear distinctions between „rigidity" and „flexibility" can be quite misleading. Classically „rigid" mass production systems utilized highly flexible external labor market strategies, while, as Dore (1987) and Streeck (1985) have suggested, certain institutional „rigidities" have facilitated the successful implementation of flexibility in Japan and Germany.

It is in this context that commitment to the logic of permanent innovation constitutes an important axis of differentiation with respect to the impact of new technologies on work organization and skills. Analysis of technological and organizational transformation in the U.S. machine tool, semiconductor and auto industries has found that leading competitive firms in each sector are linking structural change and novel logics of collaborative innovation with new modes of skill-oriented work organization, while less competitive firms tended to remain oriented to neo-Fordist forms of industrial organization and self-defeating modes of incremental change that limit the scope of innovation at all levels of the company (Gordon and Krieger, 1993). Successful technological and organizational innovation was correlated with the simultaneous and systematic expansion and upgrading of workforce educational requirements, learning capabilities, social and organizational, as well as technical, skills, and worker decision-making responsibilities at the level of both particular tasks and the organization of work as a whole (whereas trends in these areas tended to be uneven and contradictory in non-innovative firms).

Neither the internal nor the external environment of the permanently innovative firm is stable: the technical characteristics of the production system, the social organization of production activities and the formation of human resources are all continually modified or transformed as part of the process of generating each round of new product development. Inside the firm, the orientation to continuous innovation means that variations in product characteristics and product mix require frequent process changes or adjustments. Contrary to technocentric expectations, integrated automation systems operating in an environment of constant change are not governed cybernetically but by the necessity to deal with contingency as the essential element of the production environment (Hirschhorn, 1984). Higher levels of uncertainty in the production system demand greater decentralization of expertise and authority to those individuals or groups most immediately executing work functions (Adler, 1987, conceptualizes this process as „local mastery") and correspondingly higher levels of adaptiveness and creativity on the part of such workers. Relations between R&D, production planning and marketing departments must become more tightly and reciprocally integrated and, as part of this process, both vertical and horizontal coordination between formerly distinct workers and workstations must become far more interactive (Aoki, 1988). Personnel increasingly take responsibility for the operation of the system as a whole, not only for particular tasks (Gordon and Kimball, 1985).

Accelerated rates of technological change reduce the viability of external labor market solutions (and places a premium on extensive prior work experience where they remain significant) and compels firms to institute more advanced and more frequent training of the in-house labor force. Collaborative inter-firm innovation, through the pressure of reciprocal demands for new forms of creativity from each member of the chain of production, ensures that parallel changes will articulate throughout the inter-firm production system as a whole. Contemporary logics of innovation, in other words, impose important structural tendencies towards magnifying the transparency of the social character of production organization and enhancing the democratization of work.[28]

5 Globalization and the Spatial Division of Labor: The Case of Silicon Valley

A fourth critical dimension of the globalization process concerns its spatial organization. It has become commonplace to assert that, in contradistinction to the global „footlooseness“ of MNEs, technological development has been reconcentrating in regionalized production complexes or industrial districts. In the first instance, a combination of enhanced uncertainties generated by transformations in final product markets and new opportunities engendered by technological change is presumed to magnify the inefficiencies of hierarchical organization and to promote the fragmentation of industrial production systems into smaller establishments capable of absorbing rapid adjustments in processes and products. Second: both vertical disintegration and input variation establish the predominance of non-standardized, irregular and cost-intensive transactions between enterprises. Third: the trust-based relations essential to constant reorganization of the production system and the reduction

[28] These tendencies obviously do not go unopposed: the important point, from a political perspective, is that the struggle between new forms of control and new expressions of worker autonomy and power (at all levels of the organization) is increasingly centered on the micro-level of the immediate work situation. For powerful observations on the importance of this development for labor movement strategy as a whole, and on the need for new forms of „innovative militancy“, see Allen (1990).

of distance-dependent transaction costs require the spatial agglomeration of the producers constituting the industrial system. Fourth: these industrial districts of flexible producers exist as independent centers of comparative specialization and their principal external relations consist of straightforward market exchanges.[29]

For the most part, these propositions remain entirely speculative, the product primarily of theoretical deduction. Empirical confirmation has been relatively slight and quite selective, generally focusing only on activities and relationships that appear to confirm the theory and ignoring the need for a broader contextualization of firms and regions. Comparative analysis has been negligible, except paradoxically to assimilate quite diverse regions and sectors to the same model of industrial change. Most of this work more or less completely ignores the relationship of regionalized production systems to the global dimension of contemporary economic change.[30] In fact, neither the assertion of a geographical reconcentration of production nor its underlying assumptions above, hold with the kind of self-evident force that advocates of flexible specialization seem to assume.[31]

Even if we leave to one side the question of whether either market transformations or technological change necessarily eradicate specific competitive advantages of large firms or preclude conversions to flexible forms of mass production, the preceding analysis suggests that flexibility is less a function of size *per se* — the chains of production constructed to absorb the technical and economic requirements of permanent innovation almost invariably comprise both large and smaller firms — and more a product of organizational structure transcending the alternatives of market and hierarchy. Second, while the choice between scope and scale economies may serve to distinguish the activities of some firms, innovative enterprises more generally attempt to remain at the leading-edge by elaborating complex *combinations* of scale and scope. Flexible specialization constitutes merely one, and by no means the most prevalent form, of flexible production organization. Third: neither non-

[29] The literature on these questions is now vast: for the principal works establishing the preceding propositions, see Piore and Sabel (1984); Scott (1988a, 1988b, 1993); Sabel (1989); Pyke et al. (1990); Storper (1992).

[30] Storper (1992) treats the issue in the most depth, arguing that relations between „technological regions“ are governed by trade.

[31] For a detailed critique of the flexible specialization argument, see Gordon (1990a, 1991, 1994), and the many sources cited therein.

routinized and transaction-intensive linkages nor trust-based relations are confined to localized territorial boundaries or complexes: on the contrary, the inter-organizational creation of viable long-term innovation processes increasingly presupposes the extension of precisely such relations beyond the region. The assumption that flexible specialization builds upon a spatially constrained infrastructure of supply and support services (and, even more, the assumption that clients, suppliers and subcontractors are predominantly localized) ignores the increasing globalization of economic activity for suppliers and subcontractors as well as for their own manufacturing customers. Finally, while new organizational structures for innovation result in part from strengthening linkages *within* territorial production complexes, permanent innovation increasingly rests upon the primacy of *extra-regional* relationships. Globalization, in other words, presupposes a reconstruction of the spatial division of labor creating new forms of articulation between global and regional levels that move well beyond one-dimensional portraits of global „footlooseness" (in which the region is subsumed within a corporate division of labor, something which, as we have noted in section 3 above, is still characteristic of transnational strategies) or putatively autonomous industrial districts (in which the global dimension is derived as a market-based outcome of inter-regional trade).

Since it has been almost universally considered as the original model of the *self-contained* industrial district, analysis of the Silicon Valley region is particularly appropriate in the present context.[32] If we consider the trajectory of innovation in Silicon Valley´s high technology industry it can be seen that in fact high technology development has not been driven by purely localist (or, indeed, by purely global) processes but has been based *upon changing articulations of regional processes and dynamic external linkages*. Each serial transformation in the structural preconditions of innovation, while absorbing preceding forms, has been dominated by a specific logic of economic governance which has precipitated basic changes in the articulation of industrial and spatial organization.[33]

[32] As the OECD has recently observed (OECD, 1992), the globalization process is obscured further by the relative paucity of systematic studies concerning the organization and location of innovation per se in the global economy.

[33] These observations are drawn from extensive analysis of the changing industrial structure in Silicon Valley elaborated in Gordon (forthcoming).

In the first stage of its growth, extending broadly from the postwar invention of the transistor to the construction of manufacturing routines for integrated circuits by the early to mid-1960s, the embryonic microelectronics industry emerged in the U.S. and in Silicon Valley not, as universally accepted mythology would have it, from localized entrepreneurial initiative, but from a conjunction of innovation in established firms and extensive state (i.e. federal government) intervention.

The state was involved in every aspect of the microelectronics industry´s emergence and early development. Advanced military and aerospace demand provided the principal market for microelectronics, established research priorities in product and process innovation, stabilized high profits for successful companies and underwrote the risks of new product development.[34] The vast majority of scientists, engineers and technicians in the microelectronics industry acquired state-of-the-art theoretical and practical knowledge in government-financed university or corporate research and development programs. The performance specifications of the world´s hegemonic military power pushed development continually beyond existing technological frontiers into more advanced miniaturization and higher levels of performance. Government funding significantly extended to development of the manufacturing equipment and technologies facilitating the transition of device R&D into commercial production capability. Defense support was also critical in the establishment of the learning economies which governed the subsequent evolution of the industry: since market growth and expanded production volumes resulting from military sales accelerated cost reductions, U.S. firms were able to move faster and earlier than their foreign competitors down the learning curve towards more consistent quality, higher yields and lower prices. Government policy also provided a bridge between traditional industrial leadership and new entrants for, while established firms did receive substantial military funding for microelectronics R&D, defense contracts (including contracts for the construction of production facilities) were also awarded to smaller start-up companies, helping to diversify the structure of the emergent semiconductor industry. Military demand, therefore, was instrumental in creating and maintaining U.S. market leadership in electronics (for

[34] In 1962, military sales consumed 100% of integrated circuit, and almost 40% of overall semiconductor, production. By 1977, military sales constituted only 7% of IC, and 12% of total semiconductor, output.

more detail on the preceding summary, see Gordon and Krieger, 1992, Gordon, 1993b, and the numerous sources cited therein).

It was under the auspices of this state-led dynamic that Silicon Valley emerged as a high technology complex. Silicon Valley´s subsequent expansion, however, did not proceed simply as an outgrowth of agglomeration economies associated with defense contracting (such as occurred in Los Angeles) or as a linear expansion of existing locational attributes, but necessitated a basic shift in the prevailing technological paradigm and a corresponding transformation in the character and integration of internal and external innovation relations. The introduction of the integrated circuit (and, subsequently, the personal computer) transformed the institutional preconditions of leading-edge innovation from political interdependencies to *hegemonic market linkages*. Demand for the explosion of new applications resulting from the new technologies generated investment for new rounds of technical development which in turn generated markets for new products. Learning economy barriers simultaneously constrained competitors and allowed leaders to push technological frontiers forward. Global market power was deployed as a source of internal growth, the region reaping superprofits derived from capturing world markets against inferior competing technologies (Markusen, 1985; Storper and Walker, 1989). This transition from „state" to „market" provided the basis for a flourishing entrepreneurialism which was a *consequence*, not a cause, of the region´s global hegemony. State intervention and commercial hegemony mediated technological innovation in Silicon Valley to produce a process of regional agglomeration based principally upon evolutionary learning, industrial diversification, informal information flows and predominantly arms-length, market-based inter-firm transactions.

In the past decade, changing patterns of global competition, market organization and industrial structure have threatened this particular articulation of external and internal dynamics, and Silicon Valley has again reconstructed relations between the regional production system and the extra-regional environment. Detailed research into several different sectors within Silicon Valley´s economy (Gordon, forthcoming) reveals two fundamental transformations in the current linkage structure of Silicon Valley companies.

First: there has been a wholescale organizational conversion to the establishment of collaborative strategic alliances. In the semiconductor industry, surveyed firms almost unanimously concurred that partnerships had become essential to their very survival as they have attempted to shift the logic of competition with Japan away from mass production capacity and cost reduction to product specialization and design innovation. Though alliances with suppliers, clients and marketing partners are prevalent among semiconductor firms, their principal focus is R&D and manufacturing or, more precisely, the interface of design expertise, process technology and manufacturing. The most common form of partnership in this sphere involves not simply the straightforward exchange of process technology for manufacturing capacity (an exchange often thought to constitute the yielding of technological expertise to foreign competitors) but rather utilization of the relationship as a means to develop new paths to permanent product and process innovation. Strategic alliances are similarly proliferating among high technology SMEs in Silicon Valley: ninety% of all firms surveyed had established operational partnering arrangements. Motivations for these alliances are complex. Market needs — gaining access to market outlets or acquiring more accurate determinations of customer requirements — are paramount (32% of all reasons). The use of alliances as a means of reducing costs, avoiding risk or acquiring equity financing provide their principal economic rationale (23%). Technological (16%) or production (16%) needs constituted important motivations for SMEs seeking access to complementary technologies, technical expertise, shortened production cycles or expanded manufacturing flexibility. Even industrial supplier firms in Silicon Valley are increasingly oriented to extra-regional markets and, in conjunction with this shift, are subject to more intense demands for collaborative relationships with producers.

The second transformation of fundamental importance to the changing organization of the Silicon Valley production complex is that, contrary to the core assumptions of flexible specialization and industrial district theory, research discloses the increasing salience of *extra-regional* relationships precisely for the most technologically sophisticated, non-standardized and transaction-intensive interactions of regional high technology firms.[35] These, and other, critical transformations indicate that, over time, Silicon Valley has moved from „state“ to „market“ to „network“ as the animating principle of

[35] Two of many examples of this change in the spatial organization of innovation are that in both semiconductor firms and the high technology SMEs, around three-fifths of inputs technologically critical to recent innovation were acquired from outside Silicon Valley and the majority of firms considered that their supplier base was becoming more internationalized over time. In both cases, clients, predominantly external to the region, were considered to be the most significant actors in the innovation process.

regional innovation. The notion that this latest wave of collaborative innovation in Silicon Valley represents the reincarnation of a territorially agglomerated system of „flexible specialization“ reminiscent of the region´s early development (Saxenian, 1990, 1994) is to misinterpret Silicon Valley´s past, present and future as well as to misunderstand the contemporary logic of high technology innovation which increasingly demands *extra-regional* linkages as the essential precondition for technology creation in the contemporary world economy.[36]

At the same time as Silicon Valley firms are globalizing their own innovation relations, research on inward investment by European and Japanese firms is beginning to establish the changing significance of the Silicon Valley innovative milieu for global firms and networks.[37] Traditional foreign investment strategies, particularly the establishment of research-oriented „listening posts“ and market access, remain salient in the Silicon Valley context. However, overseas firms locating in Silicon Valley are now moving well beyond these goals to establish a more systematic and integrated involvement with regional innovation capabilities. Foreign operations in the region place greater emphasis on R&D and technological development and tend to enjoy greater independence in pursuing new lines of innovation. Silicon Valley is important to these firms because it provides access to the highest levels of development in numerous high technology fields and because of the localized availability of advanced scientific and technical skills and infrastructure. Location within the region also provides an opportunity for closer relationships with the leading-edge clients of overseas firms. FDI is also being deployed increasingly as a basis for the creation of long-term collaborative partnerships with Silicon Valley firms which are articulated, in turn, with the global network structures of both partners. In the majority of cases, foreign firms were now participating in the Silicon Valley milieu in order to create new research, manufacturing and organizational knowledge for the global inter-organizational networks of which they were members. In each

[36] The policy implications of this development for all other high technology regions are also transparent: if a region with all the agglomeration advantages of Silicon Valley can no longer produce innovation through localized relations within its own territorial framework, the industrial district strategy is unlikely to be successful elsewhere.

[37] See Teece (1992) and Gordon and Boronat (1993). Evidence with respect to Japanese FDI in Silicon Valley is derived from an ongoing study undertaken by the Center for the Study of Global Transformations at the University of California, Santa Cruz.

instance, it is precisely the specific innovation know-how embedded in the region that is being mobilized in these collaborative relationships. As Teece (1992) cogently argues, FDI in this context can only be properly understood if attention is given to the organizational requirements of the innovation process: foreign investment here is not linked to the question of oligopolistic rents in identifiable product markets (the focus of strategic trade policies) but to the inter-organizational creation and accumulation of learning capabilities essential to permanent innovation.

It is clear, therefore, that technological innovation can no longer be considered within a self-contained or purely localized spatial framework. Industrial systems do have critically important territorial dimensions: collaborative learning dynamics, the „relational capital“ involved in locationally-specific institutional interdependencies, the provision of collective services and other regionally-specific assets, and the presence of agglomeration economies are some of the critical territorial elements that provide a coherence to regional production systems that extends beyond the mere aggregate of firm-level dynamics.[38] At the same time, these territorial mechanisms alone are increasingly insufficient either to initiate or to sustain creative activity as technico-economic complementarities force production chains to incorporate extra-regional sources of innovation.[39] On the one hand, industrial districts or innovative milieux are compelled to integrate extra-regional contributions *as an essential component of the regional innovation process itself.*[40] On the other hand, the globalization of industrial networks increasingly involves a transcendence of traditional approaches in which internationalization is propelled by the search for comparative factor advantage or internal transnational investment strategies. Rather, FDI is directed towards regions in which multinational firms can *valorize*, rather than simply *exploit*, the specific at-

[38] The most extensive and detailed comparative empirical work on regional innovative milieux is contained in the various projects conducted by the European Research Group on Innovative Milieux (GREMI): see the numerous studies collected in Aydalot (1986); Aydalot and Keeble (1988); Camagni (1991a); Maillat and Perrin (1992); Maillat et al. (1993).

[39] New GREMI research analyzing this question is contained in Ratti et al. (forthcoming).

[40] That is, in contrast with the argument in Storper (1992), the increasing uncertainty associated with the process of technology creation in fact turns firms outwards to make extra-regional connections (rather than reinforcing localization) and relations between regions are based primarily upon the organizational dynamics of innovation (and not simply upon trade).

tributes of territorial production systems in their attempt to forge new logics of innovation.

In this new global context, localized agglomeration, far from constituting an alternative to spatial dispersion, becomes the principal basis for participation in a global network of regional economies. At the same time, the viability of regional economies is a product of their ability to articulate a coherent organizational presence within a global milieu. Regions and networks in fact constitute interdependent poles within the new spatial mosaic of global innovation. Globalization in this context involves not the leavening impact of universal processes but, on the contrary, the calculated synthesis of cultural diversity in the form of differentiated regional innovation logics and capabilities.[41]

6 Conclusion

Simultaneous processes of internationalization, multinationalization and globalization are profoundly reconfiguring the spatial organization of the world economy.[42] Traditional conceptions of center and periphery convey little genuine meaning when the „center" can simultaneously reconcentrate itself electronically within cyberspace and „de-center" either into new core areas (Silicon Valley, Tokyo-Osaka, Third Italy) or into the „periphery" itself

[41] It should be noted that, in this context, current EC innovation policy, which aims simultaneously to strengthen local networks of production and create trans-European or multinational industrial networks, operates fundamentally at cross-purposes: regionally introspective policies to build transportation and communications infrastructure, local entrepreneurship, the innovative capabilities of SMEs and local collaboration lack any explicit extra-regional dimension, while efforts to create supra-national corporate networks are still guided primarily by traditional science-based innovation theory and lack explicitly regional dimensions. Fundamental reformulation and re-articulation of both strategies is required if they are to promote European competitiveness in a complementary, and not contradictory, manner. For pertinent observations on this problem, see Bianchi and Miller (1995); Amin (1992); Quevit (1993); Perrons (1992); and Lehner et al. (1995).

[42] As observed throughout this analysis, state-led counter-movements to each of these processes also have important spatial implications. Equally significant opposing, and essentially political, processes of national fragmentation and decomposition are beyond the purview of the present exercise.

(NICs) and when the „periphery" can upgrade itself to a central location, establish itself as a zone within the center (New York, Los Angeles) or, conversely, more or less disengage from world economic circuits almost entirely (as is the case in sub-Saharan Africa, parts of Latin America and the Caribbean and, prospectively, areas of the former Soviet Union and Eastern Europe) (Watts, 1994).[43]

Where it does not simply rule over space as a supremely whimsical financial overlord, internationalization tends to perpetuate a collection of separate, internally self-sufficient regions increasingly unable to maintain pace, on the basis of exchange alone, with the global innovation capabilities of the world economy.[44] Processes of multinationalization and transnationalization, where they do not perpetuate versions of the traditional spatial division of labor based on the desire to lower costs tend at best, often in conjunction with the state, to create „islands of innovation" or „archipelagos" (Hilpert, 1992) which maintain more inter-relations with each other than with their own regional economies, and consequently exacerbate, rather than dilute, existing regional inequalities.

In contrast with the processes of internationalization and multinationalization which predominantly perpetuate traditional dependent relations (or perhaps even worse, eliminate linkages altogether) between advanced industrial societies and less developed countries (LDCs), and force local and national authorities into self-destructive competitive bidding wars for new investment, the process of globalization and its systematic integration of inter-firm networks and differentiated regional innovation capabilities, offers potential for a restoration of coordinated and reciprocal economic development in both advanced and less developed economies.

The globalization of innovation in all its dimensions (from the decentralization of R&D to the incorporation of client demand into design processes),

[43] Goodman (1995) refers to the fact that different processes are operating simultaneously at diverse spatial scales with both contradictory and complementary effects and that „mediation occurring at different scales can generate dynamic feedback effects, which actively and continuously modify the characteristics and operation of spatial processes at all scales, amplifying, cushioning or decreasing their impact, as the case may be, through succeeding rounds and periods".

[44] This is precisely the fate of many of the Third Italy regions now in substantial decline as a result of their inability to open up their regional innovation systems to the external world: see Camagni (1991b); Rabellotti (1994); Camagni and Rabelotti (forthcoming); Harrison (1994).

far from dictating a reversal of comparative advantage in favor of core economies, in fact provides a basis for an interaction with specific territorialized capabilities and the location of more sophisticated research, design and production operations outside core areas. Their more recursive approach to innovation imposes a greater necessity upon global companies to reconcentrate inter-related functions rather than to disperse them as is common in transnational firms pursuing a more linear strategy of innovation. The necessity for externalization within the social-organizational model of innovation encourages global firms to create localized technological linkages and supply networks. The establishment of regionalized overseas export platforms oriented to manufacture for global markets increasingly necessitates the local use of best practice technologies, processes and work organization. The global firm´s orientation to collaboration as the cement of long-term innovation relations includes substantive transfers of expertise, financing and managerial assistance to local firms and support for the upgrading and consolidation of local technological and human resource capabilities.

Recent research on areas as diverse as Mexico (Morales, 1994; Shaiken, 1990, 1994), Malaysia (Ernst and O´Connor, 1989; Rasiah, 1990), Singapore and Hong Kong (Henderson, 1989) and Wales (Ashcroft, 1993; Morgan, 1993) reveals a number of common themes. Each of these regions is experiencing a substantial upgrading of operations and functions in the regional units of global companies. Assembly operations are being converted from partial to complete assembly and/or are being expanded to fully integrated manufacturing. Upstream research and design facilities and downstream marketing and distribution functions are being added to existing manufacturing entities. More advanced production technologies, including sophisticated automation, are being applied even to low value-added manufacturing. Local labor is also being re-evaluated. Global firms utilize an increasing complement of scientific, engineering and technical labor in LDC locations in addition to the traditional employment of low-skill labor. The qualifications of local manufacturing workers are being raised by higher levels of training and other procedures enhancing skill formation. Forms of flexible work organization common to advanced industrial labor are being adapted in some cases to offshore facilities. As a consequence of these and other transformations, it has become possible for plants in LDC locations to achieve levels of product quality, labor productivity, technical efficiency and even, to some degree, skill formation in advanced manufacturing production of high technology products equivalent to those attained in best-practice facilities in headquarter locations.[45]

Successful globalization strategies at the regional level confront a complex dialectic. The co-existence of three overlapping and contradictory processes of world-economic reorganization indicates that the potential benefits of globalization do not flow automatically, and that prior conversion to a truly global strategy at the corporate level remains an essential precondition of their appearance.[46] Even where a firm acts as a global, and not merely an international or transnational, actor tensions will invariably exist between the company´s worldwide operations and any specific regional embodiment of its activities. The attractiveness of a given region to global firms rests upon a demonstrable capacity for regional participation in innovation networks (on the basis of territorially-specific production know-how and capabilities) and the formation of such regional capacities in turn, as the Silicon Valley example discloses, increasingly presupposes an articulation of the regional economy with the external world. Spontaneous processes, from both the global and regional level, are important to potential success in developing a mutually beneficial set of innovation linkages, but so complicated a dance of cause and effect cannot be articulated without conscious direction. Global companies must be encouraged to establish the kinds of regional operations that will lead to strong local linkages and raise the productivity of local resources (skills, efficiency of resource utilization and capacity for innovation) while the effectiveness of local resources and the ability to achieve genuine forms of cooperation with global networks must be developed from within the region itself at the same time. In other words, at the regional level, this process calls for a steering mechanism, one whose role will be a new form of *interstitial intervention* focused on optimizing the beneficial outcomes of market, hierarchical and collaborative linkages while minimizing the costs and fail-

[45] As Shaiken (1994) in particular observes, the fact that broader social and political conditions tend to keep wages down in these economies, and that wage levels as a result tend to be disconnected from productivity, adds yet another dimension to the growth potential of these regions, albeit one with more negative implications for the local labor force.

[46] In a paper in progress examining the conceptions of the global corporation held by company managers, Michel Perriard confirms the meaningfulness of the distinction between international, multinational and global operations to these decision-makers.

ures of each.[47] Contrary to the almost universal clamor for the liberation of pure market forces, successful globalization processes — those truly interconnecting diverse capabilities on a broad global basis in a common enterprise of mutual growth — absolutely require state intervention, albeit the intervention of a state able to chart a new course between regional isolation and capitulation to the international and multinational forces of illusory globalization.

References

Adler, P. (1987), Automation et qualifications: nouvelles orientations. *Sociologie du travail*, 29, 3: 289-303.

Adler, P. (ed.- 1992), *Technology and the future of work.* New York, Oxford University Press.

Adler, P. (1993), Time-and-motion regained. *Harvard Business Review*, January-February: 97-108.

Adler, P. and B. Borys (1989), Automation and skill: three generations of research on the NC case. *Politics and Society*, 17, 3: 377-402.

Allen, C. (1990), Trade unions, worker participation and flexibility: linking the micro to the macro. *Comparative Politics*, April: 253-272.

Altvater, E. (1993), *The future of the market.* Verso, London.

Amendola, M. and S. Bruno (1990), The behaviour of the innovative firm: relations to the environment. *Research Policy*, 19, 5: 419-433.

Amendola, M. and J.-L. Gaffard (1988), *The innovative choice: An economic analysis of the dynamics of technology.* Basil Blackwell, Oxford.

Amendola, M. and J.-L. Gaffard (1993), Changes in structure and relations between productive systems. Paper presented to the „International congress on the European periphery facing the new century“, IDEGA, Santiago de Compostela, Sept. 30 — Oct. 2.

Amin, A. (1992), Big firms versus the regions in the Single European market. *Cities and regions in the new Europe: the global-local interplay and spatial development strategies.* Dunford, M. and G. Kafkalis (eds.). London, Belhaven Press.

Amin, A. and M. Dietrich (1991), Deciphering the terrain of change in Europe. *Towards a new Europe?* Amin, A. and M. Dietrich (eds.). Edward Elgar, Aldershot.

Aoki, M. (1988), *Information, incentives and bargaining in the Japanese firm.* Cambridge, Cambridge University Press.

Archibugi, D. and M. Pianta (1992), *The technological specialization of advanced countries.* Dordrecht, Kluwer.

[47] Interstitial intervention, in other words, focuses less on direct substantive support for, and hierarchical organization of, specific projects than on organizing the interface of relatively independent sources of innovation.

Ashcroft, B. (1993), External control and regional development in an integrated Europe. Paper to the „International congress on the European periphery facing the new century", IDEGA, Santiago de Compostela, Sept. 30-Oct. 2.

Aydalot, P. (1986), *Milieux innovateurs en Europe.* Paris, GREMI.

Aydalot, P. and D. Keeble (eds.- 1988), *High technology industry and innovative environments: the european experience.* Routledge, London.

Barnet, R. and J. Cavanagh (1994), *Global dreams.* New York, Simon & Schuster.

Bartlett, C. and S. Ghoshal (1990), Managing innovation in the transnational corporation, Bartlett et al. (1990).

Bartlett, C., Y. Doz and G. Hedlund (eds.- 1990), *Managing the global firm.* London, Routledge.

Bianchi, P. and L. Miller (1995), Systems of innovation and the EC policy-making approach. *Working together for growth: Systems of innovation.* Bianchi, P. and M. Quere (eds.). Dordrecht, Kluwer.

Block, F. (1977), *The origins of international economic disorder.* Berkeley, University of California Press.

Braudel, F. (1981, 1982, 1984), *Civilization and capitalism: 15th-18th century.* New York, Harper and Row, 3 volumes.

Bruno, S. (1993), Boosting European growth: Strategies for integration and strategies for competition, Paper to the International congress on the European periphery facing the new century, IDEGA, Santiago de Compostela, Sept. 30-Oct. 2.

Bruno, S. and A. de Lellis (1994), Innovative systems: The economics of ex ante coordination. *Working together for growth: Systems of innovation.* Bianchi, P. and M. Quere (eds.). Dordrecht, Kluwer.

Camagni, R. (ed.- 1991a), *Innovation networks: A spatial perspective.* London, Pinter/Belhaven.

Camagni, R.(1991b), Local „milieu", uncertainty and innovation networks: towards a new dynamic theory of economic space. *Innovation networks: A spatial perspective.* Camagni, R. (eds.). London, Pinter: 121-144.

Camagni, R. and R. Rabellotti (forthcoming), Footware production systems in Italy: A dynamic comparative analysis. *La dynamique des milieux.* Ratti, R., R. Gordon and A. Bramanti (eds.).

Carnoy, M. (1993), Multinationals in a changing world economy: whither the nation-state? *The new global economy in the information age.* Carnoy, M., M. Castells, S. Cohen and F. Cardoso (eds.). University Park, PA, Pennsylvania State University Press.

Castells, M. (1989), *The informational city.* Oxford, Blackwell.

Chandler, A. (1977), *The visible hand.* Cambridge, Cambridge University Press.

Chesnais, F. (1988), Multinational enterprises and the international diffusion of technology. *Technical change and economic theory.* Dosi, G., C. Freeman, R. Nelson, G. Silverberg and L. Soete (eds.). London, Frances Pinter: 496-526.

Clark, J., I. McLoughlin, H. Rose and R. King (1988), *The process of technological change: New technology and social choice in the workplace.* Cambridge, Cambridge University Press.

Cohen, W. and D. Levinthal (1989), Innovation and learning: the two faces of R&D. *The Economic Journal,* 99, September: 569-596.

Collins, R. (1990), Market dynamics as the engine of historical change. *Sociological Theory,* 8, 2: 111-135.

Cowhey, P. and J. Aronson (1993), *Managing the world economy: The consequences of corporate alliances.* New York, Council on Foreign Relations Press.

Dicken, P. (1986), *Global shift: Industrial change in a turbulent world.* London, Harper and Row.

Dicken, P. (1992), *Global shift.* New York, Guilford Press.

Dore, R. (1987), *Flexible rigidities.* London, Athlone Press.

Dosi, G. (1988), Technical change and industrial transformation. London, Macmillan. *Technical change and economic theory,* Dosi G., C. Freeman, R. Nelson, G. Silverberg and L. Soete (eds.). London, Frances Pinter.

Dosi, G., C. Freeman, R. Nelson, G. Silverberg and L. Soete (eds.- 1988), *Technical change and economic theory.* London, Frances Pinter.

Dosi, G., K. Pavitt and L. Soete (1990), *The economics of technical change and international trade.* New York, Harvester.

Dunning, J. (1981), *International production and the multinational enterprise.* London, Allen and Unwin.

Encarnation, D. (1992), *Rivals beyond trade: America versus Japan in global competition.* Ithaca, Cornell University Press.

Ernst, D. and D.O´Connor (1989), *Technology and global competition.* Paris, OECD.

Frankel, J. (1992), Is Japan creating a Yen bloc in East Asia and the Pacific? NBER Working Paper No. 4050, National Bureau of Economic Research, Cambridge, MA.

Freeman, C. (1991), Networks of Innovators: A Synthesis of Research Issues. *Research Policy,* 20: 499-514.

Freeman, C. and J. Hagedoorn (1992), *Globalization of technology*, FAST, Brussels, 3, June.

Frieden, J. (1991), Invested interests: the politics of national economic policies in a world of global finance. *International Organization*, 45, 4: 425-451.

Goodman, D. (1995), International political economy and new directions in agro-food studies. *World scale processes and agro-food systems: Critique and agenda. The international agro-food system: Global restructuring and local change*. Ward, N. and R. Almas (eds.). London, Fulton.

Gordon, R. (1990a), Systèmes de production, réseaux industriels et régions: les transformations dans l´organisation sociale et spatiale de l´innovation. *Revue d´Economie Industrielle*, 51, 1: 304-339.

Gordon, R. (1990b), Innovation, Cultures of Learning and Modes of Flexible Production: U.S., Europe and Japan. Unpublished ms. prepared for the International conference on industrial culture and human-centered systems, Tokyo.

Gordon, R (1991), Innovation, industrial networks and high technology regions. *Innovation networks: A spatial perspective*. Camagni R. (ed.), London, Pinter.

Gordon, R. (1992), PME, reseaux d´innovation et milieu technopolitain: la Silicon Valley. *Entreprises innovatrices et developpement territorial.* Maillat D. and J.-C. Perrin (eds.). Neuchatel, EDES.

Gordon, R. (1993a), Alternative logics of innovation and global competition in the U.S. electronics industry: a comparative assessment. *New perspectives on global science and technology policy.* Okamura S., F. Sakauchi and I. Nonaka (eds.). Tokyo, Mita Press: 329-357.

Gordon, R. (1993b), Structural change, strategic alliances and the spatial reorganization of Silicon Valley´s semiconductor industry. *Reseaux d´Innovation et Milieux Innovateurs.* Maillat D., M. Quevit and L. Senn (eds.). Neuchatel, EDES.

Gordon, R. (1994), State, milieu, network: systems of innovation in Silicon Valley. *Working together for growth: systems of innovation*. Bianchi, P. and M. Quere (eds.). Dordrecht, Kluwer.

Gordon, R. (forthcoming), *Silicon Valley, Global High Technology and the Politics of Economic Change.*

Gordon, R. and P. Boronat (1993), Collaborative linkages, transnational networks and new structures of innovation in Silicon Valley´s high technology industry (III). French multinationals in Silicon Valley. Report prepared for DATAR, Paris.

Gordon, R. and L. Kimball (1985), High technology, employment and the challenges to education. Silicon Valley Research Group, University of California, Santa Cruz, Working Paper, No. 1.

Gordon, R. and J. Krieger (1992), Anthropocentric production systems and U.S. manufacturing models in the machine tool, semiconductor and auto industries. FAST APS Research Paper Series, 18, Commission of the European Communities, Brussels.

Gordon, R. and J. Krieger (1993), Technological change, production organization and skill formation in the U.S. machine tool. semiconductor and auto industries. Report prepared for the Office of Work-Based Learning, U.S. Department of Labor, Santa Cruz, Center for the Study of Global Transformation, University of California.

Graham, E. and P. Krugman (1989), *Foreign direct investment in the United States.* Institute for International Economics, Washington, D.C.

Group of Lisbon (1993), *The limits to competition.* Manuscript.

Grunwald, J. and K. Flamm (1985), *The global factory.* Washington, D.C., The Brookings Institution.

Guelle, F. (1989), L´internationalisation et la délocalisation de la R.D. des grands groupes japonias. *Revue d´Economie Industrielle*, 47, 1: 197-208.

Hagedoorn, J. and J. Schakenraad (1991), *The role of interfirm cooperation and agreements in the globalisation of economy and technology.* FAST FOP 280, Institute on Innovation and Economics. University of Limburg, Maastricht.

Harrison, B. (1994), *Lean and mean: The changing landscape of corporate power in the age of flexibility.* New York, Basic Books.

Hartmann, G., I. Nicholas, A. Sorge and M. Warner (1983), Computerized machine tools, manpower consequences and skill utilization: A study of British and West German manufacturing firms. *British Journal of Industrial Relations*, XXI, 2: 221-231.

Held, D. (1993), Democracy: from city-states to a cosmopolitan order? *Prospects for democracy.* Held, D. Stanford, Stanford University Press.

Henderson, J. (1989), *The globalization of high technology production.* London, Routledge.

Henderson, R. and K. Clark (1990), Architectural innovation: the reconfiguration of existing product technologies and the failure of established firms. *Administrative Science Quarterly*, 35: 9-30.

Hilpert, U. (1992), *Archipelago Europe: Synthesis report.* Brussels, FAST.

Hirschhorn, L. (1984), *Beyond mechanization: Work and technology in a postindustrial age.* Cambridge, MA., MIT Press.

Hirst, P and G. Thompson (1992), The problem of „globalization“: international economic relations, national economic management and the formation of trading blocs. *Economy and Society*, 21, 4: 357-396.

Hodson, R. and R. Parker (1988), Work in high technology settings: A review of the empirical literature. *Research in the Sociology of Work*, 4: 1-29.

Howells, J. (1990), The internationalization of R&D and the development of global research networks. *Regional Studies*, 24, 6: 495-512.

Howells, J. and M. Wood (1991), *The globalization of production and technology.* FAST, Brussels.

Hymer, S. (1979), *The multinational corporation.* Cambridge, Cambridge University Press.

Imai, K. (1992), The Japanese pattern of innovation and its evolution. *Technology and the wealth of nations.* Rosenberg, N., R. Landau and D. Mowery (eds.). Stanford, Stanford University Press.

Imai, K. and Y. Baba (1989), Systemic innovation and cross-border networks: Transcending markets and hierarchies to create a new techno-economic system. Paper to the „International seminar on the contributions of science and technology to economic growth", OECD, Paris.

Imai, K. and A. Yamazaki (1992), Dynamics of the Japanese industrial system from a Schumpeterian perspective. Working Paper No. 3. Kyoto, Stanford Japan Research Center.

Julius, D. (1990), *Global companies and public policy.* London, Pinter.

Keohane, R. (1984), *After hegemony: Cooperation and discord in the world political economy.* Princeton, Princeton University Press.

Kindleberger, C. (1969), *American business abroad.* New Haven, Yale University Press.

Kline, S. and N. Rosenberg (1986), An overview of innovation. *The positive sum strategy.* Landau, R. and N. Rosenberg. Washington, D.C., National Academy Press: 275-305.

Kogut, B. (1990), International sequential advantages and network flexibility. Bartlett et al. (1990).

Krugman, P. (1994), Competitiveness: a dangerous obsession. *Foreign Affairs*, March-April: 28-44.

Kurtzman, J. (1993), *The death of money.* New York, Simon & Schuster.

Lehner, F., R. Gordon, T. Charles, M. Hirooka, F. Naschold and F. Niwa (1995), *Global production: Strategic issues for industry in Europe, the United States and Japan.* FAST, Brussels.

Lipietz, A. (1993), Les nouvelles relations centre-peripherie: les exemples contrastes Europe-Amerique. Paper to the „International congress on the European periphery facing the new century", IDEGA, Santiago de Compostela, Sept. 30-Oct. 2.

Lipschutz, R. (1992), Reconstructing world politics: the emergence of global civil society. *Millenium*, 4, 3: 389-420.

Lundvall, B.-A. (1988), Innovation as an interactive process. *Technical change and economic theory.* Dosi, G., C. Freeman, R. Nelson, G. Silverberg and L. Soete (eds.). London, Frances Pinter.

Lundvall, B.-A. (ed.- 1992), *National systems of innovation.* London, Pinter.

Maillat, D. and J.-C. Perrin (eds.- 1992), *Entreprises innovatrices et développement territorial.* Neuchatel, EDES.

Maillat, D., M. Quevit and L. Senn (eds.- 1993), *Réseaux d´innovation et milieux innovateurs.* Neuchatel, EDES.

Malerba, F., A. Morawetz and G. Pasqui (1991), *The nascent globalization of universities and public and quasi-public research organizations.* FAST FOP 278, Brussels.

Markusen, A. (1985), *Profit cycles, oligopoly and regional development.* Cambridge, MA., MIT Press.

Martin, R. (1994), Stateless monies, global financial integration and national economic autonomy: the end of geography? *Money, power and space.* Corbridge, S., N. Thrift and R. Martin (eds.). Oxford, Blackwell.

Milkman, R. (1992), The impact of foreign investment on US industrial relations: The case of California´s Japanese-owned plants. *Economic and Industrial Democracy*, 13: 151-182.

Morales, R. (1994), *Flexible production.* Cambridge, Polity Press.

Morgan, B. (1993), Foreign direct investment and regional economic growth. Paper to the „International congress on the European periphery facing the new century", IDEGA, Santiago de Compostela, Sept. 30 — Oct. 2.

Mowery, D (1988), *International collaborative ventures in manufacturing.* Cambridge, MA., Ballinger.

Mowery, D. and N. Rosenberg (1989), *Technology and the pursuit of economic growth.* Cambridge, Cambridge University Press.

Muldur, U. (1991), *Le financement de la R&D au croisement des logiques industrielle, financière et politique.* FAST, Brussels.

Nelson, R. (ed.) (1993), *National innovation systems: A comparative analysis.* New York, Oxford University Press.

Nelson, R. and S.G. Winter (1982), *An evolutionary theory of economic growth.* Cambridge, MA., Harvard University Press.

Nora, S. and A. Minc (1980), *The computerization of society.* Cambridge, MA., MIT Press.

Notermans, T. (1993), The abdication from national political autonomy: why the macroeconomic policy regime has become so unfavorable to labor. *Politics and Society*, 21, 2: 133-167.

OECD (1992), *Technology and the economy.* Paris, OECD.

Ostry, S. (1990), *Governments and corporations in a shrinking world.* New York, Council on Foreign Relations.

Pearce, R. (1992), *The internationalisation of research and development by multinational enterprises.* London, Macmillan.

Perlmutter, H. (1968), Super giant firms in the future. *Wharton Quarterly*, 3, 2: 8-14.

Perrons, D. (1992), *The regions and the Single Market, Cities and regions in the new Europe: the global-local interplay and spatial development strategies.* Dunford M. and G. Kafkalis (eds.). London, Belhaven Press.

Petrella, R. (1989), La mondialisation de la technologie et de l´economie. *Futuribles*, 135: 3-25.

Petrella, R. (1991), Internationalisation, multinationalisation and globalisation of R&D. Paper to the „International seminar on changing technology, issues and policy research trends", Seoul, Korea, Oct. 30-31.

Piore, M. and C. Sabel (1984), *The second industrial divide: Possibilities for prosperity.* New York, Basic Books.

Porter, M. (1990), *The competitive advantage of nations.* New York, The Free Press.

Pyke, F., G. Becattini and W. Sengenberger (1990), *Industrial districts and inter-firm cooperation in Italy.* Geneva, ILO.

Quevit, M. (1993), Réseaux de partneriats technologiques et milieux innovateurs. *Réseaux d´innovation et milieux innovateurs.* Maillat D., M. Quevit and L. Senn (eds.). Neuchatel, EDES: 119-148.

Rabellotti, R. (1994), Footwear industrial districts in Mexico and Italy: A comparative study. Labor Institutions and New Industrial Organization, Discussion Paper No. 65, International Institute for Labor Studies. Geneva.

Rasiah, R. (1990), The role of foreign manufacturing firms in industrial development: A study of Malaysia. Phd. dissertation, Faculty of Economics and Politics. University of Cambridge.

Ratti, R., R. Gordon and A. Bramanti (eds.- forthcoming), *La dynamique des milieux.*

Reich, R. (1991), *The work of nations.* New York, Knopf.

Richardson, J. (1990), The political economy of strategic trade policy. *International Organization*, 44, 1,: 107-135.
Roberts, S. (1994), Fictitious capital, fictitious spaces: The geography of offshore financial flows. *Money, power and space*, Corbridge, S., N. Thrift and R. Martin (eds.). Oxford, Blackwell.
Ruigrok, W. and R. van Tulder (1993), The ideology of interdependence. PhD thesis. Amsterdam, University of Amsterdam.
Sabel, C. (1989), Flexible specialization and the re-emergence of regional economies. *Reversing industrial decline?* Hirst, P. and J. Zeitlin (eds.). Oxford, Berg.
Sakakibara, K. and D. Westney (1992), Japan´s management of global innovation. *Technology and the wealth of nations*. Rosenberg, N., R. Landau and D. Mowery. Stanford, Stanford University Press.
Sassen, S. (1990), *The mobility of labour and capital*. Cambridge University Press, Cambridge.
Sassen, S. (1991), *The global city:* New York, London, Tokyo, Princeton, Princeton University Press.
Saxenian, A. (1990), Regional networks and the resurgence of Silicon Valley. *California Management Review*, 33, 1: 89-112.
Saxenian, A. (1994), *Regional advantage: Culture and competition in Silicon Valley and Route 128*. Cambridge, MA., Harvard University Press.
Sayer, A. and R. Walker (1992), *The new social economy*. Cambridge, MA., Blackwell.
Schoenberger, E. (1990), U.S. manufacturing investments in Western Europe: Markets, corporate strategy, and the competitive environment. *Annals of the Association of American Geographers*, 80, 3: 379-393.
Scott, A.J. (1988a), *New industrial spaces*. London, Pion.
Scott, A.J. (1988b), *Metropolis*. Berkeley, University of California Press.
Scott, A.J. (1993), *Technopolis*. Berkeley, University of California Press.
Shaiken, H. (1984), *Work transformed: Automation and labor in the computer age*. New York, Holt, Rinehart and Winston.
Shaiken, H. (1990), Mexico in the global economy: High technology and work, organization in export industries. Center for U.S. Mexican Studies. University of California, San Diego.
Shaiken, H. (1994), Advanced manufacturing in Mexico: A new international, division of labor. Latin American Research Review, 29, 2: 39-71.
Spenner, K.I. (1988), Technological change, skill requirements, and education: The case for uncertainty. The impact of technological change on employment and economic growth. Cyert, R.M. and D.C. Mowery (eds.). Cambridge, Ballinger.
Stegemann, K. (1989), Policy rivalry among industrial states: What can we learn from models of strategic trade policy. International Organization, 43, 1: 73-100.
Storper, M. (1992), The limits to globalization: Technology districts and international trade. Economic Geography, 68, 1: 60-93.
Storper, M. and R. Walker (1989), The capitalist imperative: Territory, technology and industrial growth. New York, Blackwell.
Streeck, W. (1985), Industrial relations and technical change in the British, Italian and German automobile industry: Three case studies. Discussion Paper, Wissenschaftszentrum Berlin, IIM/LMP: 83-85.
Swyngedouw, E. (1992), The Mammon quest. 'Globalisation', interspatial competition and the monetary order: the construction of new scales. *Cities and regions in the new Europe: The global-local interplay and spatial development strategies*. Dunford, M. and G. Kafkalas. London, Belhaven Press.

Teece, D. (1992), Foreign investment and technological development in Silicon Valley. *California Management Review*, Winter: 88-106.

Tyson, L. (1992), *Who´s bashing whom? Trade conflict in high technology industries.* Washington D.C., Institute for International Economics.

Walker, R. (1989), Machinery, labour and location, the transformation of work? Wood (1989).

Warner, M., W. Wobbe and P. Brodner (eds.- 1990), *New technology and manufacturing management: Strategic choices for flexible production systems.* Chichester, John Wiley and Sons.

Warrant, F. (1991), *Déploiement mondial de la R&D industrielle: facteur et garant de la globalisation de la technologie et de l´economie?* FAST FOP 276, Brussels.

Watts, M. (1994), Development II: The privatization of everything. Unpublished paper.

Williamson, O.E. (1986), *Economic organization: Firms, markets and policy control.* Wheatsheaf Books, Brighton.

Williamson, O.E. (1985), *The economic institutions of capitalism.* New York, The Free Press.

Wood, S. (ed.- 1989), *The transformation of work? Skill, flexibility and the labour process.* London, Unwin Hyman.

Zuboff, S. (1984), *In the age of the smart machine.* New York, Basic Books.

Chapter 6
Continuities and Discontinuities in the Sociology of the Division of Labour

Dieter Bögenhold[*]
(translated by Sonja Meier and Alan Spencer)

Contents

1 Introduction

The aim of this contribution to the debate is to address some general aspects of the sociology of the division of labour and in so doing to advocate the thesis that in the areas of the sociology of work, organisation and industry, we would be well advised not to take too narrow a view of the matter or to limit the time-frame unduly. The scientific practice, which has generally been adhered to, has ceased to have any validity due to a great extent to these very mistakes. New topics and theses are continually being generated to replace those which preceded them and it is very often difficult to see any substantial gain in terms of scientific progress.

Instead it would be more sensible to refer more often, during current discussions, to the classic sociologists and their original questions about the di-

* I am indebted to Wolfgang Littek, not only for having prompted me to make this contribution but also for having followed it through its various versions and for having made constructive criticism. The final version was conceived during my stay in the working group „Transformation Processes" of the Max Planck Society.

vision of labour and to also have the time period which has passed since Marx, Durkheim, Schmoller and Weber, up until the posing of our present day questions, as a temporal pattern of the development of modern times.

Otherwise, and this is a serious defect of current discussions about the division of labour within society, one becomes too much orientated towards short-term topic cycles. It is important to keep an analytical eye on the dovetailing of social and economic structural levels. Only then does the secular trend of proletarianisation become apparent, alongside the simultaneous differentiation of social and occupational structures. This is eclipsed by the continuous progress and increase of production in society, the continuing rise in the general qualifications of the workforce and the proportion of formal school and college education, as well as by the integration of female workers into the labour market. The process of proletarianisation has progressed incessantly during the last hundred years but its results are contradictory: waged employment became the fate of the masses, however this „fate of the masses“ is not uniform but destandardized and fragmented. The sociology of the division of labour — and that is the thesis — must include its dual processes of universalism and differentiation.

The usual discussion of today about the evolved change from so-called Fordism to Post-Fordism, are all, in the light of the perspectives of a century, only the naive playthings of colleagues, who want to group the complexities of the creation of modern economies into one perspective. Behind this idea lies the acceptance of the „one type enterprise“ or „one type economy“, as the case may be which is in fact completely unjustified. There are not only so many different enterprises within the sectoral margins of an economy, all with their own specific production processes of goods and their different performances, but in the vertical margins of the size-structure of enterprises too, there are such different companies, with an astonishingly high proportion of small and mini enterprises that have to be taken into account in the empirical and theoretical calculation. Otherwise one remains dependent on such regressive formulations as Fordism, which in its lack of clarity is an ideology which contributes little to a modern and adequate understanding of the forms and variations of the division of labour in developed capitalist market economies.

2 Interdisciplinary and Historical Perspectives: The Age of Proletarianisation

Whoever thinks about the „new division of labour“, at a time when a century and a millennium are drawing ever more rapidly to an end, must inevitably ask themselves what the frames of reference now are, for the „old“ and the „new“. This simultaneously raises the question as to what the criteria for them are and what is now the norm in the sense of what is known and trusted and what on the other hand are referred to as deviations from the trend, modifications or even mutations. Even in antiquity the Greek Heraklites formulated his credo „Everything flows“. Most contemporary workers have the feeling that in their case it is flowing especially fast now. This is because of the divergence of the subjective views held by those actively involved with the subject and the objective historical position of such perceived social phenomena in the framework of social evolution.

In dealing with the division of labour we are tackling a subject which is simultaneously being dealt with by a variety of academic disciplines. Joseph A. Schumpeter said of the basis of economic sociology that it is a discipline which lies somewhere between economics and sociology, and that it is an area „in which neither economists nor sociologists can move without frequently treading on each others toes“.[1] Interdisciplinariarism is known to have advantages as well as disadvantages, and through the plurality of perspectives and subject specific methods on the one hand, cognitive synergy effects can be achieved, however, on the other hand, mutual ignorance also prevails from which mistaken appraisals and half truths result.

We have in the sociology of work and industry the same situation which is found in other parts of sociology, namely the very problematic relationship which exists between what we on the one hand call theory and on the other, empiricism. If we not only aspire to achieving particular descriptions through the collation, evaluation and analysis of data, but at the same time wish to apply the results in such a way as to achieve a gain for sociological theory, then there is the important question, to what extent the social circumstances observed in one country at any given point in time are typical of other geographical and historical areas and structures (economic systems and cultures,

[1] Josef A. Schumpeter, cited in Kaufmann (1981).

regions, branches of industry, ethnic groups etc.). In other words, the question is to what extent do specific cases of empirical observation represent some generality in social universality in sociological terms, or are they the exception to the rule?

Unfortunately this question is very seldom asked: instead we are more likely to experience a culmination of very specific individual studies — and often these are „only“ case studies — which try to suggest through their findings that they represent the whole picture. In the long term this is by no means satisfactory. For this reason we must remind ourselves more often, in our conception of research, to keep sight of the connecting links to economics,[2] anthropology and history[3] and most of all to draw comparisons and to do this nationally and internationally and also historically. This basically represents the methodological approach called for by Durkheim in his „Règles“ (1964) in which he describes the comparative method as sociology´s only adequate one.

In his work „Big Structures, Little Processes, Huge Comparisons“ Charles Tilly (1984) brilliantly advocates inter-temporal comparison for understanding the present (and the future) and puts forward the thesis that only those who have at least an adequate knowledge of historical precedences since the nineteenth century can sensibly reflect on present day social work and economic structural conditions. The basis for his argument is as follows:

> First, those shifts formed the context in which our current standard ideas for the analysis of big structures, large social processes, and huge comparisons among social experiences crystallised. Second, they marked critical moments in changes that are continuing on a world scale today. Understanding those changes and their consequences is our most pressing reason for undertaking the systematic study of big structures and large processes. We must look at them comparatively over substantial blocks of space and time, in order to see whence we have come, where we are going, and what real alternatives to our present condition exist. Systematic comparisons of structures and processes will not only place our own situation in perspective, but also help in the identification of causes and effects (Tilly 1984: 10-11).

Instead of following such a methodological perspective, we experience in sociology an entirely different practice: at least every five years new topics and

2 The book by Granovetter and Swedberg points to a list of classic sociological perspectives, which look in the direction of economics (edited 1992). Fundamental questions are also addressed by Stinchcombe (1978) Granovetter (1985) and Swedberg (1987).

3 Cf. in reference to the fundamental contribution by Stinchcombe (1978) and more recently, Goldthorpe (1991).

theses turn up and replace those hypotheses which preceded them. A cycle of discussion is displayed which in certain ways is similar to the changes in clothing fashion. The most obvious thing about it is that topical categorisations take place with ever changing accentuations, which try to interpret and intellectually rationalise the social world from one viewpoint. However, precisely this categorisation presents the danger of single-mindedness being idolised and of plural realities, in the sense of different empirical phenomena co-existing being ignored. For example we are currently experiencing a lively discussion about questions of flexibility of enterprises and their strategies of increasing autonomy, about new concepts of management, organisation of production and administration of industrial enterprises and about the (supposed) evolving change from Fordism to Post-Fordism.

In my view these topics and the basis of their discussion are an example of how narrowly confined perspectives and hypotheses are becoming, both in terms of time and of their relevance so that a reality „sui generis“ is produced because of it, which is in the end both theoretically and historically uninformed: If instead we take a historic birds eye view (as was advocated by Charles Tilly) and bracket a century as the time period to be viewed analytically, then a completely different relief of important features and turning points is produced.

Take for example the Erfurt Programme (1891) of the (German) Social Democrats which was ratified a little more than a hundred years ago. This programme followed the lines of thought of the agenda, which the Communist Manifesto (1848) had formulated barely half a century earlier. If we look at the period diagnoses of that time and the prognoses related to them for the near future at that time, a decidedly hazy picture emerges and correspondingly pessimistic assessments regarding further development. One observed the rapid process of proletarianisation which advanced hand in hand with capitalism and expected that this development would continue in the same way. Among other things, this idea was perpetuated by the assumption that the bigger and largest enterprises would have comparatively high production capabilities and would emerge as the dominant enterprises. This „focus on size“ united proponents from otherwise incompatible schools of thought through the world wars up to the present day.

So not only was the assumption of polarisation and the hardening of the two blocks within society (proletariat and bourgeoisie) as well as their internal levelling effect popular a hundred years ago, but there was also talk of a

„Naturnotwendigkeit“ (Kautsky), a logical necessity, with which the demise of small companies became a foregone conclusion. This represented in the critical thinking of the day the straight- jacket of historical theory and its political contents and consequences.

3 The Vicious Circle of the Market

Indeed such a rapid development in the change of the permanence of enterprises did take place a hundred years ago, that the bleak future prophesied in social and cultural terms is sociologically extremely plausible. The economy and society of that time changed at such a rapid rate that it must have appeared as if the demise of small enterprises was just a matter of time. All developments headed purposely in one and the same direction, namely towards a capitalist industry, which was squeezing out all other forms of work and production in society, and thus the discussion of the future of the twentieth century to a large extent predicted that mass production would bring with it the large enterprises. These would become the „fate of the masses“ and people´s living conditions would visibly become similar.

Without doubt much has changed in this century, and many conditions would be worth addressing systematically in a longer essay, but we are only concerned here with what has changed or remained the same in the structures of enterprises, occupations and the economy. In so doing, hypotheses about different aspects will be formed.

In the light of various points of view we will find — according to the research presented here — lines of continuities and changes interlaced with each other. Wherever the process of standardisation and of levelling takes place on the surface, there is beneath the surface a counter current in the direction of fragmentation and differentiation. What Gordon, Edwards and Reich (1982) describe in the examination of social structural development in the USA as the contra flowing double motion of homogenisation and segmentation, can be verified more or less for all advanced market economies. In the course of the last hundred years we have experienced a process of increasing proletarianisation — even though it may have progressed in different ways and different degrees — in all of these countries in which the number of self-employed people decreased and that of waged employees increased.

In individual cases this development was dependant upon national prerequisites, the speed of the modernisation process of the economy of a country and the type of structural change in agriculture. The historical advance of the regime of waged employment occurred in the 20th century as the result of industrial capitalism, which had imposed itself radically and widely even before the Second World War[4] and had become more widespread comparatively due mainly to the continued shrinking of the agricultural sector.

In his reflections on the sociology of legislation Max Weber had introduced the „Janus-like double-headedness" of the formal „liberal" type of employment contract (Weber 1972: ch. VII), which effectively obeys the law of the strongest. The process of advancing proletarianisation and with it the development of the „impregnable cocoon" of the objectified world (Weber 1979: 188), must be seen as one of the most significant innovations of this century in those countries considered „developed", such as (western) European, (north) American as well as some Asian countries. Karl Polanyi (1944) described this in his own — brilliant — way from a different perspective as the „great transformation", which with its (anonymous) vicious circle of the markets first created a system of (market) economy in society.

However, the establishment of the rationality of capitalism was simultaneously „diagonally" affected by changes in the structure of occupations and social conditions in another direction. Those changes were not always fully comprehended and reflected upon: The process of proletarianisation did indeed result in the decimation of self-employment and the advance of waged labour dependant on the labour market — but that did not mean, as many contemporaries of a hundred years ago assumed that the living, working, and social conditions of people became ever more uniform.[5] There wasn´t only the liquidation of (old) sectors of trade and occupations but new sectors and occupations frequently emerged. New technical developments went hand in hand with the differentiation of occupational structures as was the case, when the electric motor replaced the steam engine at the turn of the last century. We only have to look at the automobile and currently at micro-electronics to

[4] Also see in this connection, the more recent theses of Runciman (1993).

[5] In the 1930s, Götz Briefs had already pointed out, as waged employment became more and more widespread, so it became less and less sensible to describe all wage dependant workers as proletarians. Otherwise those high-flyers at the top of the salary scale, would have to be counted as belonging to the proletariat. That would make a nonsense of the term proletariat (Briefs 1931: 458).

get an idea of the spillover effects which stimulate the coming into existence of new sectors and occupation profiles.

Alongside the trend of the standardisation of social and working life, we simultaneously also find diverse processes of differentiation, which with the increasing complexity of labour within society increase rather than decrease. Most of all the historically important process of the increase in productivity in the manufacture of goods in the last hundred years, created secular changes in social, occupational and economic structures, which did not adequately register. If more can be produced and more quickly with an ever decreasing input of labour, then inevitably the significance of transport, trade, consumerism and (individual) leisure time increases. In Germany in 1892 for example the ratio of employment in production to employment in transport and commerce changed from 9.2 to 1 in 1882 to 2.4 to 1 in 1990. This clearly shows, among other things, the increased significance of economic circulation within the economy. The fact that people on average have more (free) time and income creates more demand in the areas of what we colloquially call the entertainment and tourist industry, which produces facilities to meet the (historically new) emotional demands/needs of people.

Marx did indeed acknowledge the whole area of the so-called service industries. Mostly, in later work, the third volume of „Das Kapital", we find various expositions and references to, for example, modern shareholder companies, to productive and non-productive labour, to the question of the production of surplus value and to the medium of circulation and the merchant´s capital. But because Marx wanted primarily to show, that most importantly, social conditions are a reflection of economic conditions, his references to the effects of the increase of production in the tertiary sector represent only a glimpse of the whole subject.

Sociology has only started to tackle the question of this phenomenon in a more systematic manner from different perspectives in the twentieth century. Since Emil Lederer wrote about „Private Sector Clerical Workers in Modern Economic Development" (1912),[6] various works have examined in one way

[6] Lederer emigrated from Germany to the U.S.A. in 1933 and worked in the graduate faculty in the New School of Social Research in New York until his death in 1939. Although, mainly in his later years, he published in English too, he remained to a large extent unrecognized in the U.S.A. An introduction to the work of Lederer can be found in Lederer (1979).

or another the „new created legions“ of wage dependant office workers. This includes for example studies of ownership and control in mature economic organisations (Burnham 1972), of clerical workers and the so-called middle-classes (Mills 1952), and of the increase of (specialised) knowledge within society (Etzioni 1968), and of the trend towards a tertiary economy and its problems of the corresponding semantic classification (Fuchs 1968; Bell 1973; Gershuny 1978).

With increasingly more thought being given to tertiary dimensions,[7] the advances in productivity that evolved from the division of labour as already picked out as a central theme by Adam Smith and Karl Marx, were pursued from a specific angle, indeed like it or not radicalised, particularly within the universal logic of the expansion of the kind of dependant work that does not create a surplus value and is not directly productive, located in the economic system. This constituted the key point of the dynamic development of social and economic structures in modern market economies.[8]

The tendency towards tertiarisation is parallelled by two further secular trends: on the one hand the feminisation of dependant work and on the other, the ever-increasing standard of education in advanced industrial societies. The growing integration of women into the (formal) labour market can be observed without exception internationally, but there are differences in the speed of integration and the standard of female participation in breadwinning. A second important course of development is the increasing qualification and graduate employment in the workforce.

Looking back over the century we see with the rapid increase of knowledge in the form of school and university education a creeping revolution in the sense of a fundamental change in social and work structures, to which the technical developments in the economy and the demands which have grown out of them have certainly contributed. Those professional groups that Max Weber (1972: 179) had described as the „poor Intelligensia and with specialised knowledge“ , are meanwhile now well on the way to becoming the central majority of society. Basically, what we see here are various social and

7 At the end of the 1980s between 55 and 70% of wage-earners in most OECD. countries were employed in the tertiary sector (measured by the sectoral concept). On the question of social structure convergence and divergence, cf. extensively Haller (1988).

8 For the differing perspectives on the individual phenomena of service and office work, cf. both volumes by Littek et al. (edited 1991, 1992).

work structural fragments of a new picture of the division of labour with various accentuations but principally of the same tendency, which presents itself at the end of the twentieth century as a splendid display of the interdependence of homogenisation and differentiation.

4 Continuities and Discontinuities

What is apparent at social and work structural levels, reveals itself in a similar form from the point of view of the company and economic structure: Capitalism has established itself as a universal logic. But the position that has existed for more than a hundred years, regarding the incessant advance of large and multi-concerns that has united Marxist and a large part of non-Marxist arguments up until the present day, has not proved itself.

It was based on the axiom that the increasing size of enterprises correlated positively with their output and that in this way a selection favourable to large enterprises and a resulting squeezing out of small enterprises occurred as a result of competition. This assumption of the (technical) superiority of large enterprises, emerging form the appraisals of the efficiency of the increasing division of labour since Adam Ferguson, had introduced too few questions, in respect of the human factor and the ability to plan and the standardisation of stages of production, into the calculation.

Still today we find a high proportion of small and mini concerns in almost all markct economies. For instance, in 1987 more than 95% of all firms in the private sector in (West) Germany had between 1 and 49 employees.[9] Furthermore, this proportion represents an increase rather than decrease since 1970. The rapid and mainly synchronised development of industrialism and capitalism has clouded the view that the speed of events during the change of the structure of industries does not always continue at the same speed.

9 Most small businesses are in the hands of self-employed wage-earners and vice versa, most self-employed people have small and medium-sized businesses. Relating to conditional factors of the development of self-employment, cf. Bögenhold and Staber (1991) including a look at employment data, Bögenhold and Staber (1993) too, for the inclusion of additional dimensions for the importance of small and medium-sized businesses in the economies of various OECD countries, cf. data in Segenberg and Loveman (1987).

Table 1: Number of Enterprises in the Federal Republic of Germany

Size of enterprise (=number of employees)	1-49	50-499	500+	Cumulative
Year	in 1,000			
1950	---	---	---	1,923.6
1961	2,148.8	39.0	3.3	2,191.2
1970	1,861.7	39.8	3.6	1,905.1
1987	2,056.9	37.6	3.3	2,097.9
	%			
1950	---	---	---	100
1961	98.0	1.8	0.2	100
1970	97.0	2.8	0.2	100
1987	97.2	2.6	0.2	100

Source: Own calculations according to work place statistics ("Arbeitsstättenzählungen"), Statistisches Bundesamt, various years.

Table 2: Number of Employees in Enterprises in the Federal Republic of Germany

Size of enterprise (=number of employees)	1-49	50-499	500+	Cumulative
Year	in 1,000			
1950	---	---	---	12,157.4
1961	8,360.8	4,958.1	7,387.6	20,706.5
1970	8,066.5	5,154.1	8,035.0	21,255.5
1987	9,591.1	4,800.3	7,525.1	21,916.6
	%			
1950	---	---	---	100
1961	40.4	23.9	35.7	100
1970	37.9	24.3	37.8	100
1987	43.8	22.0	34.4	100

Source: Own calculations according to work place statistics ("Arbeitsstättenzählungen"), Statistisches Bundesamt, various years.

A conclusion of the history of the twentieth century is that not only were the (Marxist) theories of the collapse of capitalism in the corresponding way not realised, but it can in no way be said that, in spite of all the tendencies toward Internationalisation and Globalisation in the financial markets and in spite of all the tendencies towards creating oligopolies by capital, the small and above all the smallest companies have now absolutely or relatively disappeared — on the contrary. In contrast to this impressive continuity of small business production in capitalist market economies the proportion of small firms in the socialist planned economies decreased considerably more, because inherent within the planning philosophy of the one time communist countries lay the fascination with supposed economic potential of large industries as most western theorists believed.[10]

The centrally controlled planned economy in communist societies was always based on the misconception that centralisation equalled productivity. This historical anachronism lies in the fact that the development which had been prognosticated as the future of capitalism by socialist-marxist theorists, namely the inevitable tendency towards an ever decreasing and more powerful number of large and multi industries and the vanishing of small decentralised production, was based on political suppositions which defined the development of the real existing socialism. Thus we experience today the attempt at the administrative re-establishment of the industrialist class within the transformation processes of former planned economies towards market economy type organisation (Offe 1991: 281).

As far back as the last century, there were within (German) social science theorists who through systematic reasoning and reference to empirical studies in contrast to the mainstream of the discussion had argumentatively named the limits of the „tendency towards large industries". Gustav Schmoller (1838-1917) and Werner Sombart (1863-1941) were for example two of these theorists, both of whom had pointed to the necessity of the differentiation based on economic sectors in the argument with the Marxist theorists.[11] Thus they formulated relatively early — well founded — theses about the increasing cumbersomeness of enterprises due to the increasing organisational difficulty, about questions of efficiency and flexibility and the unusual economic features in various areas of the economy, without the present sociology of work and industry having even taken it up to any great extent.[12]

[10] For examples of the enormous fascination of the Taylor system (and of Taylor the person), cf. W.I. Lenin, in Hughes (1989: ch.VI).

[11] For an excellent overview of these perspectives, cf. Barkin (1970). For the present day reappraisal of Schmoller, cf. Schiera and Tenbruck (1989). For the multiple works of Sombart, cf. vom Brocke (1987).

[12] Cf. here for example Schmoller (1892), who puts great value on the observation of empirical analyses, as did Sombart at a later date. The neglect of the empirical dimension was one of Schmoller"s criticisms of Durkheim"s book on the division of labour, which he reviewed shortly after it appeared. Cf. Schmoller (1984). For all of Sombart"s colossally extensive works, cf. Sombart (1987, Vol. III).

The discussion about work and the division of labour has instead been oriented towards stereotypical discussions about the (capitalistic) company — the (capitalist) economy as the case may be, as if there were neither size groups of companies nor different economic sectors with specific peculiarities. Large parts of the debate about the „future of work" oriented themselves for this reason exclusively towards the question, at what rate technology is replacing the human work force. In well known books too, such as those by Georges Friedmann (1949) or Harry Braverman (1974) the dominance of these rationalisation perspectives is reflected. Only the „Labour Process Debate" (Wood 1982; Littler 1982; Thompson 1983; for a summary see Charles 1989) taken up by sociologists in the 1980s introduced an element of doubt as to whether such a simple paradigm of rationalisation is appropriate to the complex social reality of the economy and what is happening therein.

Had the sociological discussion been directed much more toward theoretical questions of organisation and management, that were much more adequately dealt with in the American *Administrative Science Quarterly* or in the European magazine *Organization Studies*, and if first and foremostly the temporal spectrum of perception and reflection had (only) encompassed a hundred years of history instead of only including five or at best ten years of historical knowledge, then it can be supposed that this discussion within sociology would not have raised such passions.

The same is true of the so-called evolved change from Fordism to Post-Fordism (compare: Aglietta 1979; Lipietz 1986), proclaimed in the 1980s which in my view was an invention of the authors who tried to define the complexity of the economy in a single concept — regardless of the fashionable prefix „post-" — while not even being aware of the discussion about „Fordism" in Germany in the 1920s. One asked oneself at that time, where industrial production and the economy were generally heading. It was clear to most people, that the economy of the future meant ever more industrial production. And this inevitably raised the question as to how this was to be judged in a politically-normative way.

In the preface of his second edition of a collection of essays the German Gottl-Ottlilienfeld got to the heart of the matter: „We are not dealing here with how things really look in America or in the heart of Ford but only with the question as to whether Fordism as an ideology is free of internal contradiction and as a result can still continue to be thought of as a new „limit" towards which the development of current economy is moving, so that therein perhaps lies the „way to the freedom" from our present constraints" (1926: preface).

If Fordism had been thought of in this sense as a „limit" in the sense of an ideal, one would inevitably have to ask, if it established itself in principal in such a way, that one could talk of a „Fordist" economy after the second world war. The answer is of course that the difficulties with this terminology and its inherent implications are too great. And so I am not able to go along with the popular semantic which wants to intellectually domesticate the economic happenings of a developed market economy and the complex social structures of the population: Not only were 95% of all companies small and mini enterprises with a maximum of 50 employees practising specific production processes that had nothing in common with industrial mass production, but also their numbers have not decreased since 1970 but have in fact increased.

Of course with such sparse data a careful interpretation is called for: this data for example does not give any information about general questions in the area of the concentration of finance and wealth. They are restricted to only one aspect namely that of the distribution of enterprise. Additional differentiations have to be made without any doubt but the second step cannot be made before the first. Nor can we agree with the popular conceptions of dualism as for example those of Averitt (1968) or Bowring (1986):[13] it makes little sense analytically to describe one or two percent of all enterprises as the nucleus and the other 95% as the „periphery" of the economy. The network of power of the enterprises of the different size groups is far too complex to simplify it in such a comparison. As early as 1892 Schmoller had conceded to large enterprises a „kind of public character" in view of their strong position with reference to regional labour markets, the budget of cities and councils and the network of their suppliers.

It is an ideology which attempts to bring the different congregations of capitalist market economies into the concept of Fordism. The same is true of the supposedly now following era of Post-Fordism. Concealed behind that are short-lived methods of categorisation which in the end appear to be relatively uninformed in the area of the sociology of the division of labour.

[13] In spite of all the strengths of his work, Edwards (1979), who impressively transformed the above mentioned advocacy for a historical perspective also comes ever closer to the dichotomizing trivialisation of periphery and monopoly sector, through haste.

At the end of his „objectivity essay", Max Weber had pointed out in 1904, that in every science the definition and treatment of its area of research and its methods follow their own independent course. Weber: „At some time or another things change: the importance of points of view which have been utilised but not fully considered becomes uncertain, we remain in an area of twilight while the light of central cultural topics draws further away" (Weber 1973: 214). When the present discussion about „new" questions of the division of labour loses its course, or when theorems of Post-Fordism are applied, then developments that are also selected in the discussion about new management concepts and the so-called lean production come to the forefront (Dertouzos et al. 1989; Womack et al. 1990). Changing and in an economic sense fast-moving times create new imperatives. If an enterprise or an economic system is not comparably flexible, in the long term it will inevitably lag behind.

Enterprises have always tried to optimise in various ways, mostly by processes of trial and error of limited rationality. But it is apparent in a long-term observation how large enterprises had increasingly shown preference for a divisional type organisation above other types of organisation. (Chandler 1962; Dyas und Thanheiser 1976). That is certainly principally due to an increased awareness of the control problems of the human factor. But especially since the 1970s it appears that environmental factors have had to be taken much more into account than ever before.

Thus the framework of economic systems has changed fundamentally. The regional focus of the internationalised and globalized world economy has shifted, new industries in expanding economies appear with greater frequency (Korea, Taiwan, Singapore, Malaysia), the demand for goods has also changed fundamentally, technological developments especially in the area of microelectronics revolutionised production processes and working practices, a change in fluctuating economic trends influences the length of the validity of planning and of investment decisions, the termination of the Bretton-Wood´s agreement in the late 1960s led to fluctuating (and uncertain) rates of exchange in the money markets. It appeared that in general terms the complex changes led to new areas of uncertainty in decision making, which created greater competition but at the same time they showed that taking chances and risks is at the heart of all business.

The task of enterprise strategy is to overcome the increasing uncertainties and to find appropriate solutions.[14] There is much to indicate that large enterprises are tending to trim down in order to attain greater flexibility through internal decentralisation or expansion into new markets. These developments that can be empirically reconstructed in individual countries, form the present basis of the discussion about a „new" kind of division of labour. Above all we must not forget, to what extent the economy is intertwined with general changes in social and working structures. They too are rapidly developing in the direction of an economy increasingly based on the service industry sector.

5 Conclusion

At this point I would like to try to clarify the background of this essay and to point out the nucleus of the argument. Whosoever would like to make general statements about types and levels of division of labour in society and their modification and mutation, needs — and that is the initial thesis — a relevant structure that within a cognitive frame of reference can separate the chaff from the wheat. The thesis was put forward that in the sociological search for social universalities it seems to be necessary to use an international as well as inter temporal method of research. Contrary to that the majority of our present day sociological studies and those of work and industry implicitly and also explicitly concentrate on a single society model of single countries in the present day.

For this reason I am not only advocating research methods which are more oriented towards international comparison, but also perspectives which have their basis in history and which include the developments in the social and

[14] It was Knight (1971), who pointed out, in his dissertation on economics, the certainties and uncertainties in economy. The basic problem in modern economy is: „How do I proceed in spite of uncertainty." The adoption of a perfect competition in which everyone has all the relevant information, would not be the right thing to do according to Knight. „With uncertainty absent, man"s energies are devoted altogether to doing things: it is doubtful whether intelligence itself would exist in such a situation; in a world so built that perfect knowledge was theoretically possible, it seems likely that all organic readjustments would become mechanical, all organisms automata. With uncertainty present, doing things, the actual execution of activity, becomes in a real sense a secondary part of life; the primary problem or function is deciding what to do and how to do it" (1971: 268).

economic structures and the structures of work at least during the last hundred years. Only those people who „look back" in such a way and have done the necessary groundwork are capable of making a statement about the „future of work" — although there are still a lot of prognostic uncertainties — as is the practice today without reflecting on some kind of theory or methodology.

Whosoever looks back over the last hundred years will see a peculiar balance of continuities and discontinuities that goes hand in hand with the establishing of capitalism as an economic system and as a universal rationality. Really we see in the majority of „developed" market economies convergent processes of the interlocking of homogenisation and segmentation that affects the areas of occupation and enterprise to exactly the same extent.

The black apocalyptic theories which were used at the turn of the last century to foretell the future have not been proven correct to the extent that people today work at the same (low) level in large enterprises. The enormous advances in productivity of the manufacturing sector over this century were also not taken into account, which continuously further undermined industry with the expansion of the tertiary sector which to different extents was taking place in the individual countries. For this reason it is not always easy to separate, on one hand, the irreversible secular trends and on the other the effects of enterprise strategies seen as a whole because they can be interlocked and thus can no longer be separated into cause and effect.

One of the axes of development is the (historic) saturation of society by „free" waged labour which clearly is ambivalent in as much as the contingent of the dependent workers meanwhile includes the whole spectrum of social classes and income groups in society. Another one is the slowly occurring shift within economic sectors, which not only occurs at an occupational level but also at enterprise level. In addition to this, internationalisation and globalisation is taking place which makes it ever more problematic in sociological terms to direct the analysis only within the confines of national boundaries (Bornschier and Chase-Dunn 1985; Chase-Dunn 1989). In spite of the centralisation of financial centres, regional locations have become increasingly less restricted during the second half of the twentieth century due to the introduction of new information technology and means of transport (Chandler 1990).

With the internationalisation of production and distribution in economy and society, the system of „capitalism" has become dominant over past decades, especially in the light of the background of the transformation processes towards a capitalist market economy which are currently taking place in former communist countries, which set sociology the new tasks of diagnosing and categorising the social world.

In dealing with the sociology of the division of labour we have to be both careful and daring at the same time. Care is required with respect to the emergence of new (fashionable) topics which try to suggest that everything is completely different now or is becoming so. A German proverb says: „Nichts wird so heiß gegessen, wie es gekocht wird." It means that a little patience can often help us to avoid getting our fingers burnt. Courage is required when dealing with the observation of longer periods of time and then to recognise in the supposed discontinuities the continuities. Such a careful mixture of consideration and courage promises the biggest gains for future research into the division of labour within society.

References

Aglietta, Michel (1979), *A Theory of Capitalist Regulation. The US Experience* (French Orig. 1976). London, New Left Books.

Averitt, Robert T. (1968), *The Dual Economy: The Dynamics of American Industry Structure*. New York, Norton.

Barkin, Kenneth D. (1970), *The Controversy over German Industrialization, 1880-1902*. Chicago, University of Chicago Press.

Bell, Daniel (1973), *The Coming of Post-Industrial Society. A Venture in Social Forecasting*. New York, Basic Books.

Bögenhold, Dieter and Udo Staber (1991), The Decline and Rise of Self-Employment, in *Work, Employment and Society*, 5 (2): 223-239.

Bögenhold, Dieter and Udo Staber (1993), Social Continuity and Change: The Contextual Environment of Self Employment, in H. Klandt (ed.), *Entrepreneurship and Business Development*. Aldershot, Avebury: 221-224.

Bornschier, Volker and Christopher Chase-Dunn (1985), *Transnational Corporations and Underdevelopment*. New York, Praeger.

Bowring, Joseph (1986), *Competition in a Dual Economy*. Princeton, Princeton University.

Braverman, Harry (1974), *Labor and Monopoly Capital. The Degredation of Work in the Twentieth Century*. New York, Monthly Review Press.

Briefs, Götz (1931), Proletariat, in Alfred Vierkandt (ed), *Handwörterbuch der Soziologie*, 2nd Volume. Stuttgart, Enke: 441-458.

Brocke, Bernhard vom (ed.- 1987), *Sombarts „Moderner Kapitalismus"*. Munich, DTV.

Burnham, James (1972), *The Managerial Revolution: What is Happening in the World?* (Orig. 1941). Westport (Conn.), Greenwood Press.

Chandler, Alfred D. Jr. (1962), *Strategy and Structure. Chapters in the History of the American Industrial Enterprise*. Cambridge, Harvard University Press.
Chandler, Alfred D. Jr. (1990), *Scale and Scope. The Dynamics of Industrial Capitalism*. Cambridge, Harvard University Press.
Charles, Tony (1989), New Technology and the Future of Work, in: Tony Charles (ed.), *New Technology and Work in the Future*. New Dehli, Gian Publishing House: 1-20.
Chase-Dunn, Christopher (1989), *Global Formation. Structures of the World Economy*. New York, Basil Blackwell.
Daniels, P.W. (1985), *Service Industries. A Geographical Apraisal*. London and New York , Methuen.
Dertouzos, Michael L., Richard K. Lester and Robert Solow (1989), *Made in America. Regaining the Productive Edge*. Cambridge, MIT Press.
Durkheim, Emile (1964), *The Rules of Sociological Method* (French. orig. 1895). New York, The Free Press.
Dyas, Gareth and Heinz Thanheiser (1976), *The Emerging Enterprise*. London, Basingstoke, Macmillan.
Edwards, Richard (1979), *Contested Terrain: The Transformation of the Workplace in the Twentieth Century*. New York, Basic Books.
Etzioni, Amitai (1968), *The Active Society. A Theory of Societal and Political Processes*. New York, The Free Press.
Friedman, Georges (1949), *Problèmes Humaines du Machinisme Industriel*. Paris, Gallimard.
Fuchs, Victor R. (1968), *The Service Economy. National Bureau of Economic Research*. New York, Columbia University Press.
Gershuny, Jonathan (1978), *After Industrial Society? The Emerging Self-service Economy*. London-Basingstoke, Macmillan.
Goldthorpe, John H. (1991), The Uses of History in Sociology, Reflections on Some Recent Tendencies, in *The British Journal of Sociology*, 42 (2): 211-230.
Gordon, David M., Richard Edwards and Michael Reich (1982), *Segmented Work, Divided Workers. The Historical Transformation of Labor in the United States*. Cambridge, Cambridge University Press.
Gottl-Ottlilienfeld, Friedrich von (1926), *Fordismus. Über Industrie und technische Vernunft* (Third edition). Jena, Gustav Fischer.
Granovetter, Mark (1985), Economic Action and Social Structure, The Problem of Embededness, in *American Journal of Sociology*, 91: 481-510.
Granovetter, Mark and Richard Swedberg (eds.- 1992), *The Sociology of Economic Life*. Boulder, San Francisco, Oxford, Westview Press.
Haller, Max (1988), Grenzen und Variationen gesellschaftlicher Entwicklung in Europa — Eine Herausforderung und Aufgabe für die vergleichende Soziologie, in *Österreichische Zeitschrift für Soziologie,* 13 (4): 5-19.
Hughes, Thomas P. (1989), *American Genesis. A Century of Invention and Technological Enthusiasms*. New York, Penguin.
Kaufmann, Franz-Xaver (1981), Wirtschaftssoziologie I: Allgemeine, in *Handwörterbuch der Wirtschaftswissenschaft*. Stuttgart and Tübingen, Fischer and Mohr: 239-267.
Knight, Frank H. (1971), *Risk, Uncertainty and Profit* (Orig. 1921). Chicago, The University of Chicago Press.
Lederer, Emil (1912), *Die Privatangestellten in der modernen Wirtschaftsentwicklung*. Tübingen, Mohr.
Lederer, Emil (1979), *Kapitalismus, Klassenstruktur und Probleme der Demokratie in Deutschland 1910-1940*. Göttingen, Vandenhoeck and Ruprecht.

Lipietz, Alain (1986), *Miracles and Mirages*. London, Verso.

Littek, Wolfgang, Ulrich Heisig and Hans-Dieter Gondeck (eds.- 1991), *Dienstleistungsarbeit. Strukturveränderungen, Beschäftigungsbedingungen und Interessenlagen*. Berlin, Edition Sigma.

Littek, Wolfgang, Ulrich Heisig and Hans-Dieter Gondeck (eds.- 1992), *Organisation von Dienstleistungsarbeit. Sozialbeziehungen und Rationalisierung im Angestelltenbereich*. Berlin, Edition Sigma.

Littler, Craig, R. (1982), *The Development of the Labour Process in Capitalist Societies*. London, Heinemann.

Marx, Karl (1976), Das Kapital. Kritik der politschen Ökonomie, Volume 3 (Orig. 1894), in Karl Marx, *Marx-Engels-Werke* (MEW 25). Berlin, Dietz.

Mills, C. Wright (1951), *White Collar. The American Middle Classes*. New York, Oxford University Press .

Offe, Claus (1991), Das Dilemma der Gleichzeitigkeit. Demokratisierung und Marktwirtschaft in Osteuropa, in *Merkur*, 45 (4): 279-292.

Polanyi, Karl (1944), *The Great Transformation*. Boston, Beacon Press.

Runciman, Walter G. (1993), Has British Capitalism Changed Since the First World War?, in *British Journal of Sociology*, 44 (1): 53-67.

Schiera, Pierangelo and Friedrich H. Tenbruck (eds.- 1989), *Gustav Schmoller in seiner Zeit: Die Entstehung der Sozialwissenschaften in Deutschland und Italien*. Berlin, Bologna, Duncker and Humblot, Società editrice il Mulino.

Schmoller, Gustav (1892), Über die Entwicklung des Großbetriebes und die soziale Klassenbildung, in: *Preussische Jahrbücher*, 69: 458-462 und 467-480.

Schmoller, Gustav (1894), Review of Emile Durkheim: Chargé d´un cours de science sociale à la Faculté des Lettres de Bourdeaux: De la division du travail social, etude sur l´organsation des societes superieures. Paris : Felix Alcan 1893, in: *Jahrbuch für Gesetzgebung, Verwaltung und Volkswirtschaft im Deutschen Reich*: 286-289.

Sengenberger, Werner and Gary Loveman (1987), Smaller Units of Employment. A Synthesis Report on Industrial Reorganisation in Industrial Countries. Discussion Paper, International Institute for Labour Studies. Geneva.

Sombart, Werner (1987), *Der moderne Kapitalismus*, 3 volumes (Reprint of the third, revised, edition 1927). Munich, DTV.

Stinchcombe, Arthur L. (1978), *Theoretical Methods in Social History*. New York, Academic Press.

Stinchcombe, Arthur L (1983), *Economic Sociology*. New York, Academic Press.

Swedberg, Richard (1987), Economic Sociology: Past and Present, in: *Current Sociology*, 35 (1): 1-221.

Thompson, Paul (1983), *The Nature of Work*. London, Macmillan.

Tilly, Charles (1984), *Big Structures, Large Processes, Huge Comparisons*. New York, Russell Sage Foundation.

Weber, Max (1972), *Wirtschaft und Gesellschaft* (Fifth edition, orig.1921). Tübingen, Mohr.

Weber, Max (1973), Die Objektivität sozialwissenschaftlicher und sozialpolitischer Erkenntnis (Fourth edition), in Max Weber, *Gesammelte Aufsätze zur Wissenschaftslehre*. Tübingen, Mohr: 146-214.

Weber, Max (1979), Askese und kapitalistischer Geist (Fifth edition), in Max Weber, *Die protestantische Ethik*. Gütersloh, GTB.

Womak, James P., Daniel T. Jones and Daniel Roos (1990), *The Machine that Changed the World*. New York, Rawson.

Wood, Stephen (ed.-1982), The Degradation of Work? London, Hutchinson.

Part II
The New Division of Labour in Comparative Perspective

Introduction to Part II

In this part the emphasis of chapters is on an international comparative perspective. By comparing work structures in two or more countries the authors elaborate the factors which are responsible for variations in work design, the uses of technology and organisational practices. Despite technology transfer and worldwide knowledge of new forms of work, the division of labour and its consequences are found to exhibit considerable variation. In their comparative analyses the authors pinpoint the most important factors which underpin national variations.

In **chapter 7,** *Charles* uses the results of two major cross national European research projects on the diffusion of anthropocentric production systems and industrial development to discuss the new division of labour in Europe. Rejecting the binary contrast between Fordism and post-Fordism, this chapter focuses upon the importance of different modes of institutionalisation of work and management relations which characterise the diversity of industry in Europe. Comparative research results indicate the uneven diffusion of new forms of work organisation in Europe. Anthropocentric production systems (a combination of human skills, collaborative work organisation and adaptive technologies) have developed in the more favourable institutional context of Germany and Scandinavia where there are supportive infrastructures of general education, vocational training and participative forms of industrial relations, compared to the „Anglo-Saxon" industrial culture of the U.K. and more taylorised forms of work organisation in France, Spain and the less industrialised member states of the EU. Comparison of different industrial sectors also reveals variations in the diffusion of new production concepts and, in this context, the spread of „lean production" in the car industry does not reveal a straightforward trend towards improvements in the quality of working life or the democratisation of work. Finally, this chapter examines the relationship between changes in the technical division of labour in the workplace and the wider process of social transformation in Europe. Whilst European traditions of social welfare and the humanisation of technology offer the possibility of a new division of labour based upon high skills and employee involvement, increased unemployment and the casualisation of labour threaten the development of European integration with increased social exclusion.

In **chapter 8** *Mok* and *Geldorf* discuss trends in several branches of service work in a number of European countries. Conclusions are drawn from an internationally coordinated research project including conditions of work in banking, hospital laboratories and retailing. The authors emphasise the peculiarity of *service work* which, because of the interaction with customers or clients in many spheres, is particularly sensitive to the introduction of new technologies. Looking at the lower end of the skill hierarchy, several findings of growing rigidity and loss of former job content in task performance are reported with computerisation. But, nevertheless, there is a general trend towards higher skill requirements on the labour market as automation is taking over simpler standard tasks. With mechanisation the *personal service relationship* is found to change and even to disappear widely. Overwhelming is the finding of *organisational conservatism* meaning that in almost all cases the potential of the new electronic information technologies is not used for fundamental work reorganisation. Rather, higher efficiency is sought within the old organisational forms.

In **chapter 9** the international research group GIFT with *Dubois, Heidenreich, La Rosa* and *Schmidt* take the example of the introduction and use of production planning systems (PPS) in three European countries to show and explain variations in work design, performance and flexibility. They find companies have to deal with growing uncertainty due to external contingencies (changed market conditions and consumer demands in a volatile economy). This, in their analysis, means a *„politicisation of industrial change"*. A solution like the traditional „one best way" no longer exists, instead there is a „conceptual rivalry" in the processes whereby production planning systems are developed and used. Experience-based knowledge and informal work relationships are depicted as essential „non-computerised preconditions of computerisation processes". The shift to increasingly *„communicative rationalisation"* means a change in the relationship between management and employees. Higher skilled „systemic qualifications" are increasingly required which call for an individualised reward system with opportunities for promotion. The new work context is based on high trust relations, which they find limited by a new form of *„controllable autonomy"*. In their culturalist approach the authors depict different institutionalised forms including educational and vocational training systems as explanatory factors. But they warn that a mere cultural determinism in the explanation of the division of labour has to be avoided.

Two further chapters in Part II extend the scope of comparative research and focus upon the current widespread preoccupation with forms of work organisation in Japan. In **chapter 10** *Maurice* compares the role of professional engineers in the division of labour in France and Japan and their respective roles in the process of technological innovation in firms. This study applies the „societal analysis“ approach developed by researchers at LEST (Laboratoire de Economie et Sociologie du Travail) in order to understand the „social construction“ of French and Japanese engineers in the context of different logics of innovation in each country. The societal analysis approach is contrasted to both functionalist cross-national research and contingency theory in terms of its methodological assumptions and analytical framework. This approach focuses on the social relationships and mediations between the firm and society which shape the social status of engineers and their role in the division of labour. The élite training of graduate engineers in France and their social distance from either technicians or the manual workforce is contrasted to the Japanese system. The long process of career development for Japanese engineers corresponds to the horizontal employment structure in Japan contrasted with the more hierarchically ordered employment system in France. Consequently it is argued that engineers and manual workers collectively „appropriate technology“ in Japanese industry which facilitates incremental innovation and cooperative learning. Conversely, in France the more hierarchical division of labour creates problems of integration and weaknesses in the firms capacity to develop research and development into marketable new products. *Maurice* argues that the strength of the French innovation system is rooted in support for science and basic research. The Japanese division of labour in enterprises is further from the Taylorist model in its capacity to valorise the contributions of both engineers and shop floor workers in the process of innovation. Whilst Western firms are now trying to imitate the Japanese success in continous innovation the question for Japan is whether it can strengthen its capacity for basic research which is considered a weakness of the Japanese system.

In **chapter 11** *Jürgens* develops a critical analysis of the lean production model. This chapter begins with an analysis of the main arguments of the MIT study — *The Machine that Changed the World* (Womack, Jones and Rose, published 1990) in order to compare the claims of the MIT report and its enthusiastic reception by Western companies with the evidence concerning production processes and work organisation in Japanese industry. Firstly,

Jürgens argues that lean production cannot fully explain the superior performance of Japanese companies since it ignores questions of capital costs, labour costs and industrial relations issues. At the heart of the German debate on lean production, *Jürgens* finds the concept vague and the performance comparisons potentially misleading. Secondly, the chapter focuses upon two key elements of the lean production system — namely team-work and „*Kaizen*" or continous improvement . German concepts of group work are contrasted with forms of teamwork in Japanese factories. *Jürgens* finds little evidence of democratised working relations nor is there an absence of hierarchy in Japanese enterprises. Japanese teamwork is based upon the pressures of continous improvement, a comprehensive system of personnel appraisal and work which is closely tied to production cycles. Whilst Japanese workers are „multi-skilled" in their ability to switch between short-cycle production tasks there is little opportunity for self regulation. *Jürgens* concludes that the system of lean production in Japan is nearing its limits and is undergoing strain and further evolution due to labour shortages, increased automation and high labour turnover. Consequently, „post-lean" concepts are already discussed in Japan which take account of the need to humanise work and come to terms with computer-aided manufacturing.

Chapter 7
The New Division of Labour in Europe

Tony Charles

Contents

1 Introduction — Europe and the New Division of Labour

In January 1994 the members of the European Community became citizens of the European Union. The establishment of European Citizenship de jure with the final ratification of the Treaty of Maastricht may signal the political vision (on behalf of some of the member states) of an eventual European political union. Nevertheless, European citizenship and identity de facto can hardly be said to exist since the experience of everyday life and of the work place remains socially constructed by institutions and forms of social relationships which are fundamentally national in character if not local in terms of social experience.

The overriding logic of integration from the Treaties of Rome to Maastricht, together with the completion of the single market, proceeds from economic integration and monetary union: the process of Europeanisation is, in this sense, primarily the development of an open and competitive market which transcends national borders. Despite the inclusion of the Social Chapter in the Maastricht Treaty, industrial relations, education systems, work practices and welfare continue to exhibit strong national characteristics.

The heterogeneity of European countries — differences of culture, language and institutions — in contrast to the „melting pot“ of United States federalism or the greater homogeneity of Japanese society means that European unity takes a fundamentally different form — based upon diversity and subsidiarity. The European Union has progressively established the conditions for a single market and the free mobility of capital, goods and labour, but this is no guarantee either that production will be harmonised or that poorer member states will be able to emulate the industrial performance of the richer countries of the north of Europe. At the same time, the evolving conception of European integration will exclude the countries of Central and Eastern Europe until at least 2005 as well as Russia (which is considered too large to be part of Europe) and Turkey (which is considered „too Asian“). The „European archipelago“ of Union member states is confronted at its borders by the low wage economies of the Mediterranean and Eastern Europe. From a sociological perspective these wider issues concerning Europeanisation reflect longstanding concerns with the relations between economic and social development, citizenship and social identity.

Whilst sociology was a product of the European enlightenment and industrialisation in Europe its object of study has remained the nation state as the defining feature of „society“ and, likewise, the sociology of work in Europe has reflected national diversity. The different research traditions of the sociologie du travail, Arbeitssoziologie, sociologia de trabajo and British sociology and their lack of significant interaction are a clear illustration of nationally based frames of reference. This diversity is reflected in the predominant empirical focus of research in the sociology of work in different European countries. Examples include: the emphasis in Germany on new production concepts in the 1980s (Kern and Schumann, 1984) where the focus has been upon the centrality of the skilled worker, the strength of the German system of vocational education and training and institutionalised forms of co-determination in the workplace; the focus upon industrial districts, new inter-firm networks and „flexible specialisation“ in „the third Italy“ and enterprises in these countries (Pyke and Sengenberger, 1992; Piore and Sabel, 1984); also, the long and continuing debate in British sociology over the labour process since the 1970s linked to a British history of more adversial industrial relations, the common concerns of „Anglo-Saxon

Industrial Sociology" across the Atlantic and more pronounced tendencies to deregulation of labour markets in the British case.

This list could be extended to include other European countries but it suffices to illustrate the significance of national distinctiveness in the institutional arrangements which constitute the social organisation of production. At the same time, strong commonalities exist with respect to the theoretical issues which surround the analysis of the new division of labour concerning the demise of Taylorism and the much debated binary contract between Fordism and post-Fordism.

Whilst empirical research continues to pinpoint the significance of diversity between industrial cultures the wave of new management literature deriving from the North American business schools points in a different direction — reminiscent of the sociological debate of the 1960s concerning convergence between industrial societies. The proponents of „lean production" (Womack et al., 1990) predict a universal convergence in the car industry towards management practices and forms of work organisation which have their origins in Toyotaism — propelled by the need for competitive advantage in world markets, Technology and knowledge transfer in the global corporations stimulated by transplants, new supplier relationships with indigenous firms and the emulation effect lead, it is assumed, to the diffusion of „best practice" in the adoption of new forms of work organisation in much the same way that Fordist production models spread from the USA since the 1940s. Convergence theory in the 1960s was based on a form of technological determinism in terms of the functional exigencies of modern production: rooted in the ascendancy of American capitalism (Giddens, 1973); in the same way, post-Fordism is ushered in, it is argued, by the exigencies of the market and the flexibility afforded in advanced manufacturing by programmable technologies, shorter product life cycles, increased product variety, and economies of scope as opposed to scale — these define the new parameters of advanced capitalist production.

The market and the search for competitiveness become the only driving forces following the collapse of state socialism and command economies in the former Soviet Union and Eastern Europe. In the midst of such complexity the temptation in the social sciences is to rely upon binary concepts which capture some elements of the transition; the alternative (by no means new in industrial sociology) falls back upon empiricism, indeterminacy and contingency in the face of the diversity of new forms of work organisation. This paper suggests that some insights into the emerging forms of the new division of labour in Europe can be gained from the comparative study of the interplay between the wider processes of Europeanisation and the contingent circumstances of locality, region and nation state which structure forms of work organisation.[1] In other words, how do different regions and industrial sectors in Europe and different industrial cultures mediate, respond to and in turn shape new forms of work and advanced manufacturing technology?

This chapter is based upon research conducted across the member states of the European Union and the attempt to transcend the confines of nationally based research through the comparative analysis of the diffusion of new production concepts in Europe and their implications for the technical and social division of labour. The research was sponsored by the European Commission´s FAST (Forecasting and Assessment in Science and Technology) programme between 1989-1992 and subsequently extended to an analysis of the future of industry in Europe in a project completed between 1991-1993.

The chapter begins with a discussion of the research findings of the FAST project on new production systems in Europe in the context of the wider debate concerning the new division of labour, new forms of work organisation and the changing technical division of labour in the work place. The second part returns to issues raised concerning Europeanisation in the introduction and the implications of changes in the division of labour in the work place for the wider processes of social transformation in Europe; namely — changes in occupational structures, social divisions and the relation between manufacturing and services.

2 New Forms of Work in Europe

2.1 Models of Industrial Change — A Post-Fordist Europe?

The binary contrast between Fordism and post-Fordism claims the theoretical high ground in the analysis of the dynamics of advanced industrial societies. The cornerstone of the Fordist/post-Fordist model comprises an analysis of

[1] See also: chapter 5 by Richard Gordon in this volume which examines the implications of globalisation for the new division of labour.

the „crisis of Fordism" identified in most western capitalist societies in the late 1960s which progressively made way for radical new developments in the labour process towards „flexibility", and a widespread re-appraisal of manufacturing strategies and work organisation (OECD, 1992). Fordism, in the narrow sense of a production system, was based upon a Taylorist labour process involving the fragmentation of semi and unskilled labour, and the production of standardised goods for mass markets via economies of scale using dedicated machinery for assembly line production. In the broader sense, developed by the French „regulation school", Fordism denoted a type of economic system with a specific regime of accumulation and mode of regulation (Aglietta, 1979; Lipietz, 1987). Fordism as a total economic system included large scale business enterprises, the welfare state in its various forms and Keynesian demand management supported by an international framework established via the Bretton Woods agreement for international exchange. Theorists of post-Fordism variously locate two sets of factors as responsible for the crisis of Fordism — namely, limits internal to the Fordist labour process due to the rigidities of assembly line mass production, declining rates of profit and exhaustion of economies of scale, and heightened labour resistance to the de-skilling and monotonous character of assembly work; secondly, the inability of Fordist production methods to respond to rapidly changing market, heightened world competition, and ultimately markets saturation for mass produced goods.

Theorists of Fordist development disagree over whether the emerging „new economic order" constitutes an evolution within the Fordist framework (neo-Fordism) or whether there is a „second industrial divide", and whether the consequences of the emerging forms of work organisation are progressive or regressive for labour (Aglietta, 1979; Piore and Sabel, 1984). Post-Fordism embraces a variety of distinct but inter-related trends of which the most important concern changes in the labour process towards increased flexibility — namely, a reversal of the process of de-skilling with skill enhancement and multi-skilling, greater significance of trust and responsible autonomy in work relations, team working, reduced hierarchical levels and „worker empowerment". These trends are further facilitated by flexible technology and the use of new production methods such as just-in-time systems which facilitate shorter production runs, increased product variety and quality, continuous innovation and rapid response to changed market conditions. Economies of scope replace economies of scale in the search for competitive advantage.

Changes in the labour process are accompanied by fundamental changes in the firm´s external relations — company down sizing to core functions and increased sub-contracting and long term supplier relationships for just in time production (Boyer, 1993). The story thus far is well known and does not require further elaboration here. The fullest exposition of the post-Fordist ideal type is of course the model of „flexible specialisation“ derived from studies of the „third Italy“ based upon craft work, advanced technology and networks of co-operation between small firms in localised agglomerations (Piore and Sabel, 1984; Brusco, 1982). Of equal, if not greater importance than the third Italy model is the ascendancy of Japanese manufacturing and industrialisation in the NIEs (new industrialised economies) of East Asia. Japanese dominance in world markets for motor vehicles and electronics has provoked wide spread interest in Japanese production methods and associated models of „best practice“ in world manufacturing. Japanese practices such as long-term contracting, team working, just-in-time and continuous improvement, once denounced by western management as „rigidities“ are now taken seriously as an alternative to western capitalism (Dore, 1987). Thus flexible specialisation is the exemplar of the revival of small batch production and small firm networking whilst Japanese manufacturing is the exemplar of flexibility in mass production.

Fordism, post-Fordism, flexible specialisation and lean production are ideal-types, and, as such, we would expect empirical research to reveal both their usefulness and their limitations. This is conceded, for example, in the work of Harvey (1989) who is careful to note the continuities in the transition from Fordism to a new mode of flexible accumulation. Thus the increase in flexibility via sub-contracting, temporary and self-employment is a recurring feature of capitalism and occurs under Fordism; new organisational forms based on flexible technologies are limited in their diffusion in the same way that the earlier mode of Fordist production was never hegemonic. Harvey´s analysis is based on a careful historical analysis of the forces which undermine Fordism at the global level with the formation of new financial markets (Harvey, 1989: 141-172). However, the catalogue of limitations to the Fordist/post-Fordist binary opposition is now so large as to call into question its continued utility for an understanding of new forms of work in Europe in a global context. I am inclined to agree with the conclusion of Sayer and Walker that our principle objection to the mass production/flexible specialisation contrast which underpins the post-Fordist debate: the superior industrial performance of Japan or West Germany over the United States and Britain is not so much a question of their relative commitment to mass production or flexible specialisation but has to do with broader „environmental“ characteristics which cut across labour process and production scale distinctions. In this respect comparative studies may serve us better than binary histories (Sayer and Walker, 1992: 223).

Three major points serve to warrant this conclusion: firstly, in the European context mass production was never fully Fordist and the British case involved a higher incidence of mass/batch production suited to its more diverse product markets (Smith, 1988). In the British case only 12% of employment in manufacturing involved assembly line work at the supposed high point of Fordist production in 1968 (Alan and Massey, 1988). Additionally, the different industrial relations systems in Britain and Germany imposed constraints on the rigid application of Fordist production methods. Secondly and conversely, the current diversity in manufacturing strategies and work organisation does not confront enterprises with a stark choice between mass production and flexible specialisation — as the Japanese case reveals, mass production continues to dominate in sectors such as motor vehicles and consumer durables but advanced manufacturing organisation allows a combination of both scale and scope economies and increased product variety (Gordon and Krieger, 1992). Thirdly, the major impetus for change in the direction of a new „techno-organisational revolution“ has come from the competitive advantage and superior performance of Japanese manufacturing, intensified world competition with new market entrants from East Asia, and the saturation of mass markets without corresponding growth in new sectors. The demise of Fordism is synonymous with the decline of the United States industrial hegemony and the declining competitive position of the old industrial heartlands of Europe — with slower rates of growth, increased unemployment and declining shares of export markets (European Commission, 1994).[2]

In the European context, whilst fundamental changes are underway in terms of experimentation with new forms of work organisation they do not fit comfortably into one homogenised model of post-Fordism or lean production „best practice“; instead, they bear the historical imprint of different modes of institutionalisation of work and management relations and contrasting

[2] For a detailed discussion and critique of the post-Fordist model see Sayer and Walker (1992) and Wood (1989).

strengths and weaknesses in the capacity for industrial innovation which are explored below.

2.2 Technology and Work in Advanced Manufacturing

From the early development of mechanisation in the industrial revolution to the first phase of process automation in the 1960s and the ascendancy of mass production technologies to the current age of information technology and computer integrated manufacturing the dominant engineering paradigm and management philosophy has placed technology and human labour in opposition. Technology in manufacturing embodied the principles of natural science — exactness, predictability, calculability, objectivity, optimality of engineering solutions and control of the environment; in contrast, human labour represented a source of unpredictability in the production process, a source of error and subjectivity. Such a perspective also included a unilinear model of technological progress as science-driven and a conception of technological rationality in which technology was value-free and exogenous in the process of industrial development.

These fundamental presuppositions have, until recently, exerted a profound influence upon both the design and implementation of new technology in manufacturing, reaching their zenith in the juxtaposition of mass production with scientific management. Their imprint is still strongly evident in the goal of progressively higher automation leading to the „peopleless factory" of the future and computer integration of the whole production process, within what has been described as a „technocentric paradigm" (Brodner, 1990).

According to this technocratic perspective, the development of CIM (computer-integrated manufacturing) in the 1980s presupposed the progressive exclusion of remaining manual tasks from the production process, extending control of uncertainty and complexity through the more and more elaborate formulation of production rules based upon algorithms (Cooley, 1987). Research into artificial intelligence and expert systems supposedly extends rule-governed decision making beyond the domain of direct production to the whole enterprise and promises greater flexibility and control for both mass production and batch production.

However, the promise of new programmable technology for a renaissance of American or European manufacturing has failed to live up to expectations.

The supposed „flexibility“ of programmable technologies owes more to human skill and organisational innovation than features internal to the technology. Numerous studies in the USA and Europe indicate that the effective development of the potential of new technology is dependant upon human skill and the social organisation of production. For example, Jaikumer´s (1986) comparison of FMS (flexible manufacturing systems)in Japan and the USA reveals the inflexible use of FMS in the USA where they are used primarily to reduce costs compared to the higher product variety achieved in Japan. Similar studies in Europe report high „failure rates“ with FMS where technological solutions have been sought for production problems which are really rooted in work organisation and the previous manual system (Haywood and Bessant, 1990; Fix-Stertz and Lay, 1987).

Similarly industrial robots in their second and third generation have not evolved into general purpose machines but have become more specialised. Despite improvements in sensory capabilities, the majority of robots are still used for limited spot-welding and pick and place operations in mass production, although their use for more complex assembly is increasing, particularly in Japan (Tidd, 1991). Likewise, assessments of the performance of production and materials planning systems show that a majority of packages fail to conform to expectations after implementation. A common problem is noted in many cases: a predisposition to search for technical solutions to production problems. The learning process involved in implementation involves a continuous process of transforming the technology and trial and error which requires co-operation between designers and users to make the technology work effectively (Webster, 1990). The importance of users´ tacit knowledge in the process of implementation is as much a process of innovation as the original design of technology.

2.3 New Production Concepts in Europe

European industry is characterised by its diversity. Strong variations exist in production philosophy, national institutional infrastructures of industrial relations, education and training and corporate governance in addition to marked sectoral differences in production from mass to small batch and customised manufacturing. German industry alone accounts for 20% of EC manufacturing gross domestic product and, together with the UK, France and Italy comprises 80% of EC industrial output (European Commission, 1992a). Large enterprise dominance in vehicle assembly, aerospace and chemicals contrasts strongly with medium and small enterprise importance in mechanical engineering and textiles. Small and medium-sized enterprises in the European Union contribute 65% of gross national product and more than 75% of employment. Much of this industry has developed from earlier craft origins and is based upon batch production of high quality goods (Cooley et al., 1989; European Commission, 1992a). Research and development intensive production in the Northern member states also contrasts strongly with low wage labour textile production in Portugal. This diversity is, on one hand, perceived as a weakness in terms of the problems of uneven development and the distributive consequences of the single market; on the other hand, diversity is also recognised as a source of competitive advantage in rapidly changing markets (Cooley et al., 1989). It is in this context of diversified quality batch production that anthropocentric approaches have taken root.

Anthropocentric production systems evade precise definition as a manufacturing blue-print. Rather, they refer to a manufacturing philosophy where production is dependent upon a balanced integration between human skills, collaborative work organisation and adapted technologies. They are manufacturing principles which rely upon human skills and creativity to develop the potential of new technologies. Founded upon the different forms of the post-war „labour compromise" which took different forms in European industrial relations institutions, a wider tacit social contract and independent trade unions (Lash and Urry, 1987), anthropocentric production systems make the quality of work a prerequisite for advanced, competitive manufacturing and successful innovation.

Reflecting the diverse origins of the concept in Scandinavia, Britain and Germany there is no pure model of such a system. UK research traditions emphasise human-centred technology with a concern for the humanisation of technology as such. Scandinavian approaches stress the role of worker participation in technology design and German approaches emphasise both socially compatible forms of technology as well as improved performance and competitiveness deriving from production systems which incorporate some or all of the principles of anthropocentric production systems. French perspectives have focused upon technology and work attitudes and issues of participation (Rose, 1975). This approach to manufacturing represents a convergence of research traditions in the human sciences, engineering and socio-technical systems. R&D programmes in the European Commission and member states together with practical experiences in industry with new production systems provide examples of European developments. It is hardly surprising that no universal pure model exists in the same way that lean production is an abstraction in management text books rather than a precise description of the trial and error learning experiences of actual organisations.

There is a strong continuity between current conceptions of anthropocentric production or human-centred technology and earlier research in the human relations and socio-technical approaches of the Tavistock Institute of the 1950s and even earlier roots in the human factor industrial psychology of the 1920s (Rose, 1975). Despite this strong continuity with socio-technical systems design, anthropocentric or human-centred approaches comprise a more critical analysis of the „black box" of technology and systems architecture (Corbett et al., 1990; Warner et al., 1990).

In the FAST studies the principles of anthropocentric production were investigated using a variety of indicators, including:

(1) the development of a learning organisation utilising the tacit skills of operators and „learning by doing";
(2) changes to organisational structure and culture which reduce hierarchy, decentralise control and transform authority relations from command to participative and collaborative forms;
(3) continuous training to increase skill levels and develop multi-skilling;
(4) participative systems design and implementation;
(5) development of new forms of semi-autonomous group work;
(6) interactive, decision support information systems including shop floor programming.

Surveys in all the member states as well as Japan and the USA also examined the significance of the wider socio-economic context for the take-up of such systems as well as obstacles which prevent organisational innovation. These factors include technical infrastructure, work organisation, skills education and training, industrial relations systems and public policy.

Research results provide some evidence that the distinctive characteristics of European industry facilitate the take-up of such systems to produce new forms of production organisation which differ from either Japan or the USA. The reasons for this are as follows: firstly, the relative importance of small and medium batch production in sectors such as mechanical engineering where scope for organisational innovation may be greater than in mass production. Secondly, the important role previously mentioned for SMEs in European industry which have built upon traditions of craft production and customisation. Thirdly, certain European countries such as Germany and Sweden contain strongly supportive infrastructures of general education, vocational training and participative forms of industrial relations (Lehner, 1992).

In contrast, obstacles to the development of anthropocentric production are stronger in what can be described as the „Anglo-Saxon" industrial culture of the USA and Britain and the stronger vetical division of labour in French enterprises (Lane, 1989; Linhart, 1991; Gordon and Krieger, 1992; Charles and Roulstone, 1991; Tidd, 1991). The institutional mode of industrial organisation in Britain differs in important respects from continental Europe. UK industry is more internationalised, more predatory and more polarised between a concentrated corporate sector and the SMEs (Ramsey, 1991). The former is biased towards consumer goods and overseas investment whilst the SMEs are weaker than their continental counterparts, employ less skilled workers and focus upon production of standardised goods of medium to low technology content (Lane, 1989). The absence of a formal institutional basis for employee participation, a free-market labour policy which has encouraged „numerical" rather than „functional flexibility" (Pollert, 1991) and strong horizontal boundaries between occupations combine to limit organisational innovation and changes in work organisation (Charles, 1993). Corporate strategy, as in the USA, is governed by short-term criteria of performance which favour cost reduction as a strategic objective for the introduction of new technology.

Other, less industrialised member states in Europe, including Ireland, Portugal and Greece also exhibit very limited experimentation with new production concepts. Obstacles in these countries include limited education and training for new skills, low skill levels and the inability of enterprises to research and develop new production technologies (O´Siochru, 1990). In sum, therefore, surveys of European industry reveal slow and uneven development of new production systems. However, surveys are incomplete without case studies of developments in the direction of human-centred technology. An expanding list of cases across the main manufacturing sectors report changes to work organisation such as group work, and increased operator involvement (Brandt, 1991; Kidd, 1991). Notable cases include the machine tool industry in Germany with increased diffusion of operator-controlled NC machines and semi-autonomous work groups (Bandemer et al., 1991). Similar cases are documented in Denmark, Sweden, Italy and the UK but, nevertheless, the majority of cases rarely extend increased shopfloor control to a more fundamental re-organisation of the whole enterprise.

„The Swedish model" still represents the best example of anthropocentric production, but examples from Germany (especially in the machine tool industry) from Denmark and from Northern Italy reveal alternative forms of development in a similar direction (Lehner, 1992). In Germany, the active role of trade unions through the system of work´s councils supports new experiments in group work on the basis of industrial democracy and a compromise between productivity increase and improvement in working conditions. Indeed, the introduction of group work is becoming widespread in German industry as is support for new forms of work organisation which appropriate some of the elements of lean production but adapt them to the German institutional and cultural context, with the slogan — „don´t work harder, work more intelligently" (Schumann et al., 1994). However, cases of increased participation and group work are modest, even in European countries with legally codified and neo-corporatist systems of industrial relations: this observation is especially pertinent to early participation in technology and organisation design as revealed in European surveys of worker participation (Cressey and Williams, 1990).

These, in brief, were the research results concerning the diffusion of new production concepts in Europe up to the end of the 1980s.[3] The second FAST study on the future of Industry in Europe (Lehner et al., 1994) whilst not replicating the earlier study, notes the wide spread reappraisal of manufacturing strategies of work organisation and the increasingly prevalent rejection of Taylorist management in theory if not in practice and the increased importance attributed to organisational change in management circles as opposed to the earlier search for technological solutions to problems of competitiveness. Amongst the car producers in Europe the fascination with lean production (Womack et al., 1990) and the attempt to emulate Japanese manufacturing performance has resulted in a variety of attempts to re-organise the technical division of labour. A survey of German engineering firms in Baden-Würt-

[3] For detailed analysis of the research results the reader is referred to the country reports of the FAST studies — European Commission (1991).

temberg found extensive experimentation with new forms of team work, new supplier relations and R&D collaboration although this remained within an overall framework of rationalisation and a philosophy of cost reduction (Cooke, 1992). High automation strategies have been reversed in favour of a balance between human skills and advanced technology; relevant examples here include: Daimler-Benz at its new plant in Rastatt which has abandoned the assembly line, VW which has reduced the level of assembly automation and the new FIAT plant at Malfi which has reduced robotisation and increased group work (Wobbe and Charles, 1994). In Britain, the manufacturing malaise has received a piecemeal response in terms of new initiatives for training supported by a national system of vocational qualifications (NVQs) and growing diffusion of management methods of American origin such as TQM (Total Quality Management) and re-engineering (Charles, 1993). A major vehicle for changes in work practices in Europe and Britain in particular has been the effect of Japanese transplants — directly in terms of transplant factories and indirectly via their effect on local economies, supplier relationships and competition with existing manufacturers in Europe. In the next section we examine briefly the effects of Japanese direct investment for changes in work practices in Europe.

2.4 Transplants and the Diffusion of New Production Concepts

The rapid increase in Japanese foreign direct investment in the 1980s created a cumulative total of $40 billion of manufacturing direct investment in the USA by 1991 and $12 billion in Europe — still modest in comparison with cumulative North American direct investment in Europe but second to Britain in terms of foreign investment in the USA. In Europe, with the completion of the Single market, there was a major increase of Japanese investment and, by 1990, a total of 592 new production plants or laboratories had been established. In the USA there are now 250 component factories and 12 assembly plants (Mair, 1993). These changes represent the changed position of the USA in the world economy and the process of triadic globalisation (Petrella, 1991), but the focus here is upon the transfer of technology and new forms of work organisation — frequently perceived as „Japanisation".

The relative success of Japanese transplants in Europe and the USA would appear to confirm the view that „lean" principles can be applied outside the

Japanese social structure. However, the evidence[4] from transplant studies reveals a complex process of adaptation to local conditions rather than simple transfer of practices. A process in which Japanese production concepts are applied selectively in much the same way as the earlier wave of US foreign direct investment entailed the diffusion of Fordism from the 1930s. Mass production under Fordism was developed and adapted to specific European conditions, often accompanied by considerable conflict over working practices (Littler, 1982).

Case studies of Japanese transplants do not reveal a uniform process of transfer of work organisation and employment practices from the parent company — neither NUMMI, the GM-Toyota joint-venture in the USA, nor Nissan, UK offer „lifetime employment“ for example although employment security is a high priority for management. However, team-working and „kaizen“ (continous improvement) are practised extensively in the car industry transplants. JIT does not match Japanese performance although it is a longer-term management objective dependent upon the development of adequate supplier relations and infrastructure, as in the Honda plant at Ohio. Similarly, industrial relations structures have varied between anti-union policies and single-union enterprise representation. Nissan is non-union in Tennessee but single union in the UK. The result, in both cases, is to remove unions from traditional issues of job control (Mair, 1993).

2.5 Nissan UK — A Case Study

The case of Nissan, Sunderland, UK has become a key example of „lean production“ in Europe. The wheel has turned full circle with a certain irony in the case of Nissan — in 1952 the Company manufactured cars under license from Austin, UK; in 1986 Nissan started European production of Japanese cars at Sunderland in the UK. With a production capacity of 200,000 cars and 3,500 employees in 1992, Nissan UK is the largest Japanese investment in Europe. Built upon a large 730 acre greenfield site with space for suppliers factories, total development costs were in the region of £670 mil-

[4] See for example, studies in the USA and Mexico — Shaiken (1990); Milkman (1992); Mair et al. (1988). Studies in Europe include: Oliver and Wilkinson (1989) and the review of the „Japanisation“ debate by Wood (1991).

lion (including £112 million of UK development grants). The new plant includes a press shop, body assembly, paint, engine and final assembly. R&D facilities are located at Sunderland and Cranfield, UK — focusing on design for the European market.

According to Moriyama, Personnel Director, Nissan, Tokyo,[5] the Nissan strategy for globalisation includes a policy of localised management and an adaptation of Japanese production philosophy to local conditions whereby transplants incorporate the best aspects of Japanese production practices and, in the case of Nissan UK, the good points of British manufacturing practice. This is a process of two-way learning in which Moriyama notes — Nissan Japan is also modifying its corporate strategy with greater mobility of white-collar staff and specialists since company based training alone creates a certain inertia. Nissan UK has adopted a „tripod“ of Japanese practices — teamwork, quality consciousness and flexibility (Wickens, 1987). Wickens (Nissan UK Personnel Director) considers Japanese practices weaker in the human resources area — „single-status“ employment was introduced in Sunderland but not in Japan, whereas the Japanese were stronger in quality, kaizen and organisation of manufacturing technology. At Sunderland the production team and the team leader are the core of work organisation. Team working is more individualistic in conception than in Japan. Teams are multi-skilled without detailed job classifications and work practices involve a combination of standardised mass production operations and a smaller latitude of task discretion to facilitate quality improvement and kaizen.

The Nissan philosophy is based upon employee involvement — a combination of „control and commitment“ (Wickens, 1992). Whilst a single union is recognised, its role in job control is limited compared to the Company works council. Wickens acknowledges that work is intensive at Nissan in a system of lean production where waiting times are progressively eliminated in the production process. JIT is being introduced gradually as relations with suppliers are built up — 80% European sourcing is claimed for the plant. Nevertheless Nissan UK is already a major example of JIT deliveries in the UK and operates JIT within the factory production flow. The advantage of the greenfield site, modular assembly and single-sourcing has reduced inventories of European parts to 1.6 days with 195 suppliers (27 based in NE England).

[5] Based on a series of interviews and plant visits to Japan, Nov. 1991.

Compared to the older ZAMA plant in Tokyo, JIT practices are better facilitated by the transport system in NE England than Tokyo. In-company training is extensive as workers build up a range of skills relative to their team. Unlike many indigenous UK companies, the wider organisational structure at Nissan also reverses several features of management authority relations — direct production work is central and the role of accounting and personnel assumes a „service“ function rather than financial control. Sunderland management judge the new plant a success with build hours for the two production models the best in Europe — 12.5 hrs and 10.5 hrs for the smaller car. Whilst the greenfield site and a plentiful supply of young workers contribute to performance in the factory, Mair (1993) notes that Nissan also cite the importance of the newest technology design for ease of manufacture, and new factory layout in combination with lean production work organisation.

Does Nissan, UK therefore combine the best of lean production efficiency with a European emphasis on the quality of working life? Critics note the high work stress, „compulsory overtime“, weak trade unionism, consensus building and teamwork which shades into „the management of consent“ and paternalistic management control via continuous improvement (Oliver and Wilkinson, 1988; Garrahan and Stewart, 1992). A situation in which employer´s power is increased without the cost of lifetime employment. Nissan management (Wickens, 1992) see a combination of Japanese production concepts and a European approach to teamwork and employee relations. Anticipating the critics, Wickens observes that production is lean but still mass production in the car industry with much of the standardisation characteristic of Taylorism.

The Japanese car transplants remain a political issue in the USA and Europe — particularly over the question of local sourcing. In the case of Honda in North America, Mair et al. (1988) note the tendency for Japanese component suppliers to follow the major manufacturers and supply high value — added parts, but both in the case of Honda, USA and Nissan UK the evidence does not confirm the view that transplants are merely „screwdriver plants“. No doubt issues of protectionism, access to markets and surplus capital have been important factors for Japanese foreign direct investment (FDI) but there is no reason to consider Japanese multi-nationals as different in this respect from the first wave of US and European FDI (Sayer and Walker, 1992).

The focus upon car transplants in the debate on lean production is, however, misleading in terms of the more general diffusion of new production concepts. Studies of Japanese transplants in the electronics industry, metal products and food (Milkman, 1992; Henderson, 1991; Shaiken and Browne, 1991) in the USA, Mexico, Europe and SE Asia indicate that they incorporate few of the features of lean production and approximate more closely to conventional low-skilled mass production based upon cheap wage labour and casual employment. In Southern California Milkman (1992) found that few Japanese firms adopted Kaizen, quality circles or team work — they conform more closely to North American style non-unionised management practice. Thus conventional Fordist mass production continues to operate extensively in sectors based upon simple mass assembly.

Turning to the indirect effects of Japanese production performance on learning and emulation by European and US companies we also find a diverse range of experimentation with new forms of work organisation and management practice. In the UK the selective application of elements of Japanese production concepts such as JIT and quality circles was widespread in the 1980s but the majority have collapsed due to a failure to incorporate such changes into more fundamental organisational and cultural change and resistance to new practices based upon „organisational inertia“. This is not the case for transplants with new management on greenfield sites. In short, elements of lean production have been implemented selectively and in a piecemeal fashion.

3 European Production in a Global Context

Industry in Europe is currently enmeshed in the wider and more uncertain processes of globalisation of production.[6] As the centre of gravity of industrial production moves to East Asia and newly industrialising economies rapidly upgrade their labour force for global production, and as the significance of direct labour costs declines in assembly production in the new knowledge based industries, firms are under continuous pressure to innovate and valorise worker creativity in the production process. Trust relations and

[6] See chapter 5 by Gordon in this volume.

employee involvement, formerly the preserve of white collar workers, are now actively explored in the process of direct production. The dilemmas of bureaucracy and vertical integration for organisational innovation have long been a research issue in organisation theory — the problems of bureaucracy in the form of rule governed behaviour were contrasted with „organic organisations", „clan" and market managerial forms of control (Burns and Stalker, 1961; Ouchi, 1980). Long standing dilemmas of organisation design are now being re-cast in the search for new forms of managerial control and coordination in turbulent environments.

The implications of these changes are far from clear and in each part of the „triad" (US, Europe and Japan/East Asia) new contradictions emerge in production systems. In the USA the old paradigm of high technology in mass production once the basis of world hegemony is a source of inertia and still exaggerates cost reduction as a source of competitive advantage. The implementation of automation to reduce labour and extensive resort to company restructuring, rationalisation and increased casualisation of labour on the periphery remain predominant management strategies in the USA. In Japan, the limits to lean production are becoming evident — the future of life-time employment is questioned in terms of declining employment security, the contraction of the section of the work force covered by this system and a more individualistic dimension to career structures which favours individual performance and merit pay over seniority (Kumazawa and Yamada, 1989). In terms of wages and conditions of work, there is a steep gradiant between large corporations and small company suppliers further down the tiers of the production chain (Williams and Haslam, 1992). Loss of domestic market share and world recession has also forced plant closures in Japan leading to early retirement programmes and displacement of workers into subsidiary companies. Excess capacity therefore creates the same problems for high volume lean producers as their mass production predecessors. Similarly, restructuring in the German SMEs (Cars and Electronics) industry is leading to contraction in the numbers of suppliers. Continuous improvement in the „long run" requires expanding markets to sustain the employment security of core workers which is a pre-requisite for higher trust employee relations. Similarly just-in-time manufacturing both in production and supplier relations requires sustained market demand for high volume throughput in the factory. JIT cannot function fully without standardisation in work tasks. Indeed it is suggested that fully operational JIT is only applicable to mass production but much less so to small batch and one-of-a-kind production characteristic of SME manufacturing — the mainstay of manufacturing output and employment in Japan and in Europe (Sayer and Walker, 1992).

Lean production therefore remains a system of mass production subject to the same market limitations as Fordism. In terms of environmental constraints there is a paradox in the „rationality" of production efficiency to reduce waste in manufacture whilst the increase in motor vehicle output, shorter lead times and JIT exacerbates „externalities" in terms of environmental problems. JIT deliveries in Japan intensify road congestion and pollution and frequent model changes increase product waste. Already elements of the Toyota system of production have been modified to reduce the number of components via modular assembly, product variety has been reduced, product life cycles extended and some buffers introduced into the JIT system (Nomura, 1992). Strains in Japanese manufacturing practices have also surfaced in problems of work intensification, stress, compulsory overtime and long hours of work (Tokumoto, 1991). Rising absenteeism and labour shortages have resulted in Japanese corporations such as Toyota reducing product variety and increasing product life cycles. These are serious problems for a system which relies upon worker involvement and commitment. A strategic question for Japanese industry is the extent to which lean production can accommodate improvements in the quality of working life, rising expectations of the Japanese work force and the globalising influence upon Japanese social values of stylised individualistic consumer consciousness. The latter is increasingly difficult to reconcile with the collectivism and company orientation in the sphere of production.

In Europe, the much discussed third Italy model of industrial districts and localised networks which became a symbol of international production success in the 1960s and 1970s also faces limitations and problems of adaptation. Escalating costs of R&D and the pressure for inclusion in global networks of production present a challenge to the self contained model of industrial districts (Gordon, 1995).

4 The New Division of Labour in Europe: Economy and Society in Transition

This paper has focused primarily on the technical division of labour — that is to say the sub-division of work tasks at enterprise level, hierarchies of skill and power in work organisation; by way of conclusion this final section assesses in tentative fashion the implications of new forms of work organisation for the wider social division of labour in Europe — namely, changes in occupational structure, labour market changes and the relationship between work and other forms of social life. In the leading industrial sectors of Europe it is clear that the slowly emerging trend is towards forms of labour utilisation which regard labour as a creative resource over and above a cost of production. The new division of labour involves team working, skill enhancement, the ability to perform more than one function and the delegation of decision making further down the organisation to direct workers. Such trends are, however, less evident in sectors such as textiles and clothing which, to take the UK as an example, employs 80% female workers. Skill divisions are based on gender with women predominantly employed in machining (which is classified as less skilled). The changes in the social organisation of work in clothing manufacture have led to both de-skilling and new skilled jobs for technicians and „systems controllers". Technology winners have been the new core, male white collar workers with computer skills; whereas skilled male craft workers and women machinists face labour displacement and greater casualisation via sub- contracting (Phizacklea, 1990). This sector therefore contrasts strongly with the male dominated machine tool industry in Europe and the car industry.

For the shrinking minority of core workers in high quality and high skilled jobs in mechanical engineering, the chemical industry and aerospace the new division of labour becomes a bargaining terrain over the distribution of rewards — industrial democracy as opposed to managerially defined „empowerment", work intensification as opposed to worker autonomy over the pace of work. In this bargaining process trade unions redefine their role in the new forms of work organisation and employee relations.

At the other extreme are those permanently excluded from the labour process by restructuring, resulting in sharp increases in long term unemployment in Europe. 28% percent of unemployed people in the UK have been without jobs for over a year, 60% in Ireland, 45% in Germany and 38% in

France (ILO, 1994). The trend to labour market segmentation is most pronounced in the UK where „numerical flexibility" has resulted in rapid growth in part-time employment — replacing job loss in male full-time employment. 30% of employees now work part-time in the UK (CBI, 1994); high labour costs are pushing the more regulated labour markets in Germany and France in the same direction (European Commission, 1994). In short, skill enhancement and new forms of work organisation in manufacturing are over shadowed by increased unemployment due to „re-engineering". The decline of male full-time employment is compounded with the decline of the labour intensive European industries of coal, steel and shipbuilding, with over capacity in world production and recession leading to increased levels of unemployment.

The new division of labour in Europe and the USA therefore incorporates a high proportion of technology and rationalisation losers (Kern and Schumann, 1984). Whilst male employment has fallen over the past two decades in Europe, female employment has increased to such an extent that in the UK in 1994 there will be more women employed than men. A full account of these changes is beyond the scope of this paper but no account of the changed social division of labour can ignore the changes which have taken place in the service sector. The second dimension of the new division of labour involves a new form of relationship between manufacturing and services. The decline of direct employment in manufacturing is accompanied by an extension of indirect work — particularly in the form of producer services.

In all three world regions of the triad it is the producer or business services which have shown the largest relative increase since 1970 (both in terms of employment and value added). Whilst employment in transport, communication and distribution sectors has tended to stagnate in the 1980s together with personal consumer services, growth in financial and producer services has been rapid (European Commission, 1992b). This growth reflects a changed division of labour in which service inputs increase at each stage in the chain of production (Charles, 1995). Similarly finance, marketing and sales services which link producer and consumer have also developed. Whilst the separation of „knowledge work" from the practical skills of production is misleading and artificial (Cooley, 1987) the former has become a central input complementing direct production — from R&D and design services to more complex management and information systems for co-ordination and monitoring of the whole process of production. Services have expanded up stream and down stream of production. Intermediate producer services have increased in strategic importance for manufacturing industry — a phenomenon described in the EC/FAST programme of research as „meta-industrialisation" (Olivry, 1986). This brief over-view of the role of producer services points in the direction of a re-definition of services. No longer can services be classified as „unproductive" or residual — based upon manufacturing as the „motor of the economy". Manufacturing is dependant upon service provision where services are provided with goods and used in direct production. At the same time most services have no function without corresponding goods. The case of hardware and software illustrates well this form of interdependence. However the importance of non market services for absolute employment levels is still more significant than producer services. Public services, including health and education account for over one third of service employment in the European community, followed by the retail and distribution sectors which provide a further 25% of employment (European Commission, 1992b).

The introduction of information and communications technologies has been extensive in major service sectors such as banking, insurance, retailing, hospitals and public administration since the 1960s. This „modernisation" and „industrialisation" of services has followed a similar technological logic to manufacturing automation. Trends towards lean management, company down-sizing, and office automation raise a question mark as to the capability of service sector growth to counteract the loss of employment in direct manufacture. With a high productivity manufacturing sector and rising social costs the future mix of manufacturing and service employment becomes a critical public policy issue. In Japan, the combination of high performance manufacturing for export and an „inefficient" service sector sustains near full employment. The three ideal type models of social welfare — Sweden, USA and Germany exhibit different dilemmas for future employment and the relation between work and welfare. The state led social welfare model in Sweden is experiencing the increased strain of public debt. In Germany, the system of state welfare operates to reduce labour supply and restrict service employment growth, whereas the US market based welfare model creates a mix of high quality jobs in business services and a large supply of low skilled jobs in personal services (Esping-Anderson, 1990).

Thus in Europe social exclusion and uneven development in the regions exist hand in hand with the new division of labour in manufacturing. Industrial dynamism, R&D and innovation is restricted largely to the industrial districts and high technology regions of northern Europe (for example, Grenoble, Catalonia, the Rhine corridor, the M4 corridor, and Baden-Württemberg) whereas the poorer regions of southern Europe reveal limited potential for advanced manufacturing development in enclaves of industrial development often supported by inward foreign direct investment. Whilst the goal of European level policies is to promote convergence via the structural funds and the cohesion funds provided by the treaty of Maastricht, the single market logic is concerned only with securing „equal conditions for competition". The challenge for the future division of labour in Europe concerns the extent to which the current pre-occupation with competitiveness can incorporate environmental concerns and the quality of life and welfare as defining features of European competitiveness. As prospectively the world´s largest market and trading region, European industry is potentially in a position to set the standards for social welfare, labour and environmental quality. The European traditions of social contract, social welfare, and the humanisation of technology — currently under threat from social transfer costs, rising labour costs, and market de-regulation nevertheless, open up the possibility of a new division of labour based upon active citizenship and the quality of working life.

References

Aglietta, M. (1979), *A Theory of Capitalist Regulation*, London, New Left Books.

Allen, J and D. Massey (1988), *The Economy in Question*, London, Sage.

Bandemer, S. J. Hennig and J. Hilbert (1991), *Prospects of Anthropocentric Production Systems in West Germany*, Brussels, FAST, EC.

Boyer, R. (1993), New Directions in Management Practices and Work Organisation, in OECD (ed.), *Technological Change as a Social Process,* Paris, OECD.

Brandt, D. (1991), *Advanced Experiences with APS*, Brussels, FAST, EC.

Brodner, P.(1990), *The Shape of Future Technology*: *The Anthropocentric Alternative,* London, Springer.

Brusco, S. (1982), The Emilian Model: Production Decentralisation and Social Integration, *Cambridge Journal of Economics,* 6 (2): 167-184.

Burns, T. and G. Stalker (1961), *The Management of Innovation*, London, Tavistock.

CBI (Confederation of British Industry) (1994), *Report on the UK Economy*, London, CBI.

Charles, A. and A. Roulstone (1991), *Prospects for Anthropocentric Production Systems in Britain,* Brussels, FAST, EC.

Charles, A. (1993), Großbritannien, in Grebing, H.W. and Wobbe (eds), *Industrie und Arbeitsstrukturen im europäischen Binnenmarkt*, Cologne, Bund Verlag.
Charles A. (1995), Advanced Economies: A New Pattern of Manufacturing and Services, in Lehner et al. (1995).
Cooke, P. (1992), *The Experience of German Engineerning Firms in Applying Lean Production Methods*, Geneva, ILO.
Cooley, M. (1987), *Architect or Bee? The Human Price of Technology,* London, Hogarth Press.
Cooley, M., A. D'Iribarne, T. Martin, J. Ranta and W. Wobbe (1989), *European Competitiveness in the 21st Century,* Brussels, FAST, EC.
Corbett, M., L. Rasmussen and F. Rauner (1990), *Crossing the Border,* London, Springer.
Cressey, P. and R. Williams (1990), *Participation in Change — New Technology and the Role of Employee Involvement,* Dublin, European Foundation for the Improvement of Living and Working Conditions.
Dore, R. (1987), *Flexible Rigidities, Industrial Policy and Structual Adjustment in the Japanese Economy,* London, Athlone Press.
Esping-Anderson, G. (1990), *The Three Worlds of Welfare Capitalism,* Cambridge, Polity Press.
European Commission (1991), FAST Series on *The Prospects for Anthropocentric Production Systems in Europe,* Vols. 1-27, Brussels, EC.
European Commission (1992a), *EC Panorama of Industry*, Luxembourg, EC.
European Commission (1992b), *Employment in Europe*, Luxembourg, EC.
European Commission (1994), *White Paper: Growth, Competitiveness, Employment,* Luxembourg, EC.
Fix-Stertz, J. and G. Lay (1987), *Flexible Manufacturing Systems and Cells in the Scope of New Production Systems in Germany,* Brussels, FAST, EC.
Garrahan, P. and P. Stewart (1992), *The Nissan Enigma,* London, Mansell.
Giddens, A. (1973), *The Class Structure of the Advanced Societies,* London, Hutchinson.
Gordon, R. (1995), Industrial Districts — A Self Contained Future?, in Lehner et al. (1995).
Gordon, R and J. Krieger (1990), *Prospects for Anthropocentric Production Systems in the United States,* Brussels, FAST, EC.
Harvey, D. (1989), *The Condition of Post Modernity*, Oxford, Basil Blackwell.
Haywood, B. and J. Bessant (1990), Organisation and Integration of Production Systems, in Warner et al. (1990).
Henderson, J. (1991), The Globalisation of High Technology Production, London, Routledge.
ILO (1994), *Annual Report for 1993,* Geneva, ILO.
Jaikumer, R. (1986), Post-Industrial Manufacturing, *Harvard Business Review,* 64 (6): 69-76.
Kern, H and M. Schumann (1984), *Das Ende der Arbeitsteilung,* Munich, Beck.
Kidd, P. (1991), *Organisation, People and Technology in European Manufacturing,* Luxembourg, EC.
Kumazawa, M. and Yamada, J. (1989), Jobs and Skills Under the Lifelong Nenko Employment Practice, in: Wood, S. (ed.), *The Transformation of Work?*, London, Unwin-Heinemann.
Lane, C. (1989), *Management and Labour in Europe*, Aldershot, Edward Elgar.
Lash, S. and J. Urry (1987), *The End of Organised Capitalism*, New York, University of Wisconsin Press.

Lehner, F. (1992), *Anthropocentric Production Systems: The European Response to Advanced Manufacturing and Globalisation,* Luxembourg, EC.

Lehner, F., S. Bandemer, V. Belzer; T. Charles, J. Hilbert, M. Kleinschmidt, J. Nordhanse-Janz, W. Potratz, B. Widmaier (1994), *The Future of Industry in Europe*, FAST (FOP 365), Brussels, EU.

Linhart, D. (1991), *Le Torticolis de l´autruche,* Paris, Editions Seuil.

Lipietz, A. (1987), *Mirages and Miracles: The Global Crisis of Fordism,* London, Verso Press.

Littler, C. (1982), *The Development of the Labour Process in Capitalist Societies,* London, Heinemann.

Mair, A. (1993), Globalisation and Governance: The Politics of Japanese Automobile Transplants, in Wobbe, W. and M. Nakashima (eds.), *Proceedings of the EC-Japan Conference (Essen)*, Brussels, FAST, EC.

Mair, A., R. Florida and M. Kenny (1988), *The Geography of Automobile Production: Japanese Transplants in North America*, Economic Geography, 64: 352-373.

Milkman, R. (1992), The Impact of Foreign Investment on U.S. Industrial Relations: The Case of California´s Japanese Owned Plants, *Economic and Industrial Democracy*, 13: 151-182.

Nomura, M. (1992), *Fairwell to Toyotism?,* Paris, GERPISA.

OECD (1992), *Technology and Economy: The Key Relationships*, Paris, OECD.

Oliver, N. and B. Wilkinson (1988), *The Japanisation of British Industry,* Oxford, Basil Blackwell.

Olivry, D. (1986), *Services to the Manufacturing Sector,* Brussels, FAST, EC.

O´siochru, S. (1990), *Prospects for Anthropocentric Production Systems in Less Industrialised Member States — A Synthesis Report*, Brussels, FAST, EC.

Ouchi, W. (1980), Markets, Bureaucracies and Clans, *Administrative Science Quarterly*, 25: 120-142.

Petrella, R. (1991), *Four Analyses of Globalisation of Technology and Economy,* Brussels, FAST, EC.

Phizacklea, A. (1990), *Unpacking the Fashion Industry*, London, Routledge.

Pollert, A. (1991), *Farewell to Flexibility? Questions of Restructuring,* Oxford, Basil Blackwell.

Pyke, T. and W. Sengenberger (eds.- 1992), *Industrial Districts and Local Economic Regeneration*, Geneva, ILO.

Piore, R. and C. Sabel (1984), *The Second Industrial Divide,* New York, Basic Books.

Ramsey, H. (1991), The Commission, the Multi-National, its Workers and their Charter, *in Work, Employment and Society,* 5 (4): 541-566.

Rose, M. (1975), *Industrial Behaviour*, London, Penguin.

Sayer, A. and R. Walker (1992), *The New Social Economy,* Oxford, Blackwell.

Schumann, M., V. Baethge-Kinsky, M. Kuhlmann, C. Kurz and U. Neumann (1994), *Trendreport Rationalisierung,* Berlin, Sigma.

Shaiken, H. (1990), *Mexico in the Global Economy: High Technology and Work Organisation in Export Industry*, San Diego, University of California.

Shaiken, H. and Browne, H. (1991), Japanese Work Organisation in Mexico, in Szekely, G. (ed.), *Manufacturing Across Borders and Oceans: Japan, the United States and Mexico,* San Diego, University of California Press.

Smith, C. (1988), Flexible Specialisation, Automation and Mass Production, *Work, Employment & Society*, 2 (4): 274-275.

Tidd, J. (1991), *Flexible Manufacturing Technologies and International Competitivness*, London, Pinter.

Tokumoto, T. (1991), Competition and Co-operation in a Borderless World: Important Issues for Labour Unions, in Wobbe, W. (ed.), *1st Euro-Japan Conference, Tokyo and Kanagawa: The Future of Industry in the Global Economy*, Brussels, FAST, EC.
Warner, M., W. Wobbe and P. Brodner (eds.- 1990), *New Technology and Manufacturing Management,* Chichester, Wiley.
Webster, J. (1990), The Social Shaping of Software Systems in Manufacturing, Edinburgh, PICT Working Paper, no.17.
Wickens, P. (1987), *The Road to Nissan,* London, Macmillan.
Wickens, P. (1992), *Lean, People Centred Mass Production,* Geneva, ILO.
Williams, K. (1992), Against Lean Production, *Economy and Society,* August: 321-54.
Wobbe, W. (1992), *Anthropocentric Production Systems: A Strategic Issue for Europe,* Luxembourg, EC.
Wobbe, W. and A. Charles (1994), Human Roles in Advanced Manufacturing Technology, in Karzowski, W. and G. Salvendy (eds.), *Organization and Management of Advanced Manufacturing*, New York John Wiley and Sons.
Womack, J., D. Jones and D. Roos (1990), *The Machine that Changed the World,* New York, Rawson.
Wood, S. (ed.- 1989), *The Transformation of Work?*, London, Hutchinson.
Wood, S. (1991), Japanisation and — or Toyotaism?, *Work, Employment and Society* 5 (4): 567-600.

Chapter 8
The Changing Face of Service Work in European Countries

Albert L. Mok and Dirk Geldof

Contents

1 Introduction

The service sector is historically and culturally embedded like no other branch of human activity, and in it the life styles and the social differentiation of a society become visible. The service relation is expressed in interaction between people, often within the context of a *network*, a regular set of contacts or connections between people or groups (Granovetter and Swedberg, 1992, p. 10). Even if there is a machine which mediates between server and client, like the automated teller machine in banking or self-service in retailing, the service relation is expressed in interactions within a network. The service transaction involves a high element of trust, shared beliefs and moral obligations, which give it more of the charateristics of the interactions in a collective, such as the *clan*, than of a market transaction (Butler, 1991, p. 32).

The retail trade is a telling example of the embeddedness of service in society. For centuries the small shop, privately owned by independent artisans and entrepreneurs, dominated the scene. The retailer was the focal point in the local network and an important source of information about life in the community. The 19th century saw the start of important changes in retailing, with the coming of the department store, first in the United States (Salt Lake City, Utah, 1849) and later in that century in Europe too. The department store catered more luxurious goods to the rising middle classes. After the turn of the century the newly emancipated „Fordist“ workers became the mass consumers who bought the mass produced goods in large quantities and more cheaply at multiple retail outlets (chain stores), cooperatives, and later, after World War Two, in the emerging self-service stores and supermarkets. Now, nearing the end of the 20th century, we can see a further development of structures, of products and of commercial strategies, with more specialization by products and segments of customers and a new emphasis on quality of service (Kruse, 1993, p. 146).

But whatever the structural context, the act of buying and selling is expressed in interaction between buyer and seller (which may both be an enterprise and/or a person). That means that changes in the division of labour and in the organization of service work will have consequences for the server and the customer alike, and not only for the agency that renders the service. We can see this more clearly when we regard the service interaction as embedded in the context of a network.

Developments in the society or the community effect the service relationship in an important way. This is true for the whole of the service sector, including the non-profit part of it, like health care. The CEDEFOP-report on training in the retailing sector (Kruse, 1993) has indicated that the service sector in all countries of the European Union will be particularly effected by five societal trends:

(1) an overall aging of the population;
(2) more sophisticated consumer demands;
(3) increasing competition between firms;
(4) internationalization;
(5) extensive use of information technologies.

We want to analyze the changing division of labour and new forms of employment and server-customer relations in Europe in the light of the above mentioned trends. We concentrate on banking, retailing and hospital work because of their importance in the service sector as a whole and because they reflect most clearly the embeddedness in the life of a society: daily needs, finance and health care.

In most European countries there is a rise in the proportion of women workers in services, reflecting an increasing participation of women in the labour market as a whole. Many women entering or re-entering the labour market via the service sector do so with *precarious contracts*, these are contracts with non-standard forms of work which bind workers only temporarily and flexibly. The amount of flexible, part-time work in the service sector is on the increase. Although the precariarization of work in the service sector is not confined to women, quantitatively they form by far the majority of the precariously employed workers. In conjunction with this there is a *polarization* of the work force in services, that is a growing dualism between the routine jobs at the lower end of the task structure of firms and the more interesting and demanding jobs at the higher end of the job hierarchy. This dualism in the skill structure reflects the two trends which we will dwell upon in what follows: deskilling of tasks on the one hand and reskilling on the other hand. These changes, we will argue, reflect the growing importance of Information Technology (IT) for the rendering of services and for the server-customer network. Everywhere there is a tendency for simple, repetitive tasks to be automated. This, together with fierce competition between service establishments (including hospitals and other health care institutions) which has made them more cost conscious, has led to a slowing down of or even a stop in the growth of the service sector in most European countries.

In 1991 in the twelve countries of the European Union 62% of the civil workforce was employed in the service sector, 31.8% in industry and 6.2% in agriculture. There are, however, important differences between the European countries. The service sector is most developed in the United Kingdom (70.4% of the civil workforce), the Netherlands (69.9%) Belgium (68.8%), and Denmark (68.1%). The countries of Southern Europe have a much smaller service sector: 49.8% of the civil workforce in Greece, 48.7% in Portugal, 56.3% in Spain. Agriculture and industry still remain more important in these countries.

On the other side of the ocean the service sector has grown even further,

Table 1: Proportion of Sectors of Economic Activity (in %) in Total Employment, 1981-1991

Country	Agriculture		Industry		Services	
	1981	1991	1981	1991	1981	1991
Belgium	2.9	2.7	32.2	28.5	64.8	68.8
Denmark	7.7	5.5	26.7	26.4	65.6	68.1
F.R. Germany	5.4	3.4	42.5	39.2	52.1	57.4
Greece	29.2	21.6	27.5	28.6	43.3	49.8
Spain	18.0	10.7	34.0	33.1	48.1	56.3
France	8.2	5.4	34.3	29.5	57.5	65.1
Ireland	17.1	13.8	31.7	28.9	51.2	57.1
Italy	13.1	8.5	36.5	32.3	50.4	59.2
Luxemburg	5.0	3.1	37.1	29.6	58.0	67.3
Netherlands	4.8	4.5	29.3	25.5	65.9	69.9
Portugal	26.1	17.5	35.7	33.7	38.1	48.7
United Kingdom	2.6	2.2	35.4	27.5	62.0	70.4
European Union	9.2	6.2	36.0	31.8	54.8	62.0
Sweden*		3.2		28.2		68.4
Norway*		5.9		23.7		70.9
USA*		2.9		25.3		71.8
Canada*		4.5		23.2		72.3
Japan*		6.7		34.4		58.9

Source: Eurostat.
* No Eurostat data available for 1981.

Table 2: Proportion of Employment in Banking and Retailing Sectors in Total Service Employment (in %), European Union, 1987-1991

Country	Retailing (nace 64/65)		Banking (nace 81)	
	1987	1991	1987	1991
Belgium	7.8	9.2	4.4	4.7
Denmark	10.4	9.1	4.6	4.2
F.R. Germany	13.0	15.9	4.8	5.0
Greece	19.3	9.4	3.0	4.4
Spain	12.3	13.0	5.2	4.4
France	11.5	11.4	3.9	3.7
Ireland	13.5	14.7	4.4	4.8
Luxemburg	14.2	14.9	12.3	12.8
Netherlands	11.2	11.3	3.4	3.0
Portugal		12.8		4.1
United Kingdom	14.4	16.3	3.8	4.3

Source: Eurostat (figures for Italy and for Portugal in 1987 not available).

employing 72.3 % of the civil workforce in Canada and 71.8 % in the USA. The service sector in Japan on the other hand employs 58.9 % of the civil workforce, which means that its relative importance is small compared to the European Union as a whole, but certainly compared to the United States or Canada (Eurostat, 1993, see Tables 1 and 2).

The larger the service sector, the less adequate the concept „service sector" is to describe the economic activity. Service activities are *heterogeneous*, ranging from the commercial to the social, from the transportation of people from the home to the transmission of information into the home, and from work aids to leisure activities. However, not all work in the service sector is service work. It is therefore important to know how we define the service sector (section 2).

The technological evolution in the service sector in the 1980s and 1990s has been enormous. We focus mainly on banking, hospital laboratories and retailing in some European countries (Belgium, Germany, Hungary, Italy, Netherlands, Sweden and the United Kingdom) to describe the principle innovations. Finally we will explore the question whether there is a new division of labour in service work and if so, what the effects are on the internal as well as on the external labour market.

2 What is Service and Service Work?

Despite its increased importance, „service sector" is still not an operational concept. It is usually defined *per negativum*. Littek complains that there is actually no satisfactory definition of what „services" and „service work" mean. Negative characteristics prevail, merely indicating that service „differs from" industrial production modes (Littek, 1992, p. 745). But in what respect?

In order to identify the key differentiators within the service activity, the Research Team on Micro-electronics in the Service Sector (the collaborators on the MESS-project) distinguished between three dimensions of service activities (Child and Loveridge, 1990, pp. 35-37).

The first concerned the *service relationship*: whether the service is provided directly or indirectly to the public. Loveridge (1984) distinguished *personal* services, which have descended from pre-industrial forms rooted in domestic or gentlemanly service to property owners, from *impersonal* services, which derived from the emergence of a bureaucratic division of labour accompanied by the creation of clerical tasks and modern professions.

A second dimension of service arises from the *function* that is attached to the service work: whether the service is provided on a *commercial* or a *public* service basis. Since the coming of the welfare state more and more services are being provided on a non-commercial, public service basis. With the gradual erosion of the welfare state as a result of budget deficits in most of the countries of the European Union, public services are being privatized with increasing speed. This means not only that the public is made to pay individually for services which used to be collective and gratis, but also that essentially collective protective functions, such as for the aged, for those incapable to work and for the chronically ill, are being shifted back from communal provision to private care (Berghman and Cantillon, 1993).

A third dimension of service activity concerns the codification and diffusion of *knowledge* bearing upon the service transaction: the extent to which information and knowledge involved in the service transaction is available to the consumer or confined to service-providing staff. If the *client* is to play his (or her) part in the service-rendering, the technology involved will have to be adapted to this participation and the division of labour will have to be changed accordingly.

The differentiation in service activities results in a differentiation of service work. In industry the process of introduction of new technologies has varying outcomes: substitution of labour by machines, diminishing worker control and deskilling in some cases, and creation of new jobs, enhancement of worker control and reskilling in others (Francis, 1986). But can such an industrial scheme be applied to the service sector? The picture as a whole is mixed, complex and difficult to predict without detailed knowledge of the particular situation. Information Technology (IT) is a malleable, adaptable technology, open to many uses. It is far more flexible than the so-called flexible manufacturing systems (Child and Loveridge, 1990, pp. 44-45).

Our theoretical perspective is therefore concerned with the reciprocal nature of the networks involving the use of technology within and between service organizations. It is a refusal of a simple technological determinism, because this determinism neglects the differences between people, sectors, organizations and countries. Ours is not a culture-free perspective on technology which stresses convergence (Kerr et al., 1960), but a culturally specific perspective which has an anthropological point of departure (Clegg, 1990; Crozier, 1963).

The institutional and legal arrangements for labour relations, employment contracts and the labour market differ greatly across Europe (Hartog and Theeuwes, 1993), as does the extent of the informal sector in the context of which so many of the services rendered take place. These differences condition rather than determine the different contents and modes of service work in the countries studied.

3 Changing Relations between Server and Customer

In service work new technology brings with it a shift in the role of the worker as well as of the client: from the tool and its use and guidance, to the system and its maintenance, regulation and control. In answering the MESS research question why so many service organizations have so readily adopted new technology, most of the managers of these organizations gave the answer that investment in Information Technology is the only way to survive in an ever more competitive consumer market. The changes in work structures, staff qualifications and work organization, including the new worker-client relationship which this entails, has to be dealt with in the context of the internal and external labour markets and of the industrial relations system. The more sophisticated the machine-service relationship is, the more limited is the contribution of the worker (Davis and Taylor, 1990, p. xiii) and the more important the quality of the service which is being rendered becomes for the relationship between service organization and client.

For the new service relationship a change in „work habitude" is needed, that is a change in the way service workers deal with the instruments and modes of their work situation (Baethge and Oberbeck, 1986, p. 33). Increasingly the intermediary between service organization and customer is not the worker, but automated control. Given the necessary information, the customer may serve himself. This is a distinctive change from a traditional situation in service provision.

Perhaps paradoxically this change in service rendering has in some European countries been conducive to a more customer centered as opposed to product centered approach on the part of service organizations, be it banks (Stroeke, 1990, p. 99), supermarkets or hospitals. Now, in the middle of the 1990s, there are many more small bank branches and retailing outlets then ever before. There is growing pressure to take the service of banks right into the home of the customer (home banking). Even the increased tendency for day hospitalization comes under this heading. Small operations, like eye surgery, and other medical treatments are performed without the patient being hospitalized for longer than one day. The role of client and even that of patient is changing rapidly.

New consumer markets are being discovered and new segments of the market are being broached. There is a stiff competition between firms within branches of the service sector like in banking, retailing and even medical services. Partly as a result of this, writers on developments in the service sector discovered a new attitude of managers and customers alike towards automated services. Managers are more likely to take the social and psychological aspects of the new service concepts into account, like user participation in the decision making about service technology. Expectation of customers about what is possible in the service relationship have risen greatly. Nowadays customers are a force to be reckoned with. Training for these new developments should have top priority, but that does not seem to be the case in all of the service sector. For instance in retailing a lack of training facilities may in the long run lower the quality of service rendering (Kruse, 1993). We feel that works councils, where they exist, could exert pressure on managements to improve the quality of service rendering by providing more and better training to the work force.

4 Worker Participation

Knowing how much work in the service sector is conditioned by new technology, workers councils have been drawn into this decision making process more and more. There is an important difference between European countries in the formal provision of worker participation in the decision making about new forms of work organization. For instance, this provision is relatively high in Sweden, Germany, the Netherlands and Italy, lower in Belgium and almost non-existent in Britain. Users have received special training to be able to cope with the new developments, but even here important differences between countries exist, with a much older tradition of in-firm on-the-job training in Germany and Sweden as compared to Belgium, Britain and the Netherlands (Child and Loveridge, 1990).

„User" here means „member of staff", but the ultimate beneficiary often is the customer. Because the customer does not have a say in the way services are rendered and organized, and in general did not receive a special training to participate in its operation, the manner of service rendering must be customer-friendly. To that end managers must leave their „ivory towers" of decision making and must take social and psychological factors into account, as well as economic and financial ones. This makes service organizations more dependent upon customer judgement and in that sense makes the service renderer more vulnerable. Quality control is absolutely essential in the competitive world of services.

All this has led to new forms of work organization, in many cases (but by no means always) beginning with a reduction in and at the same time an upgrading of part of the staff and a stricter division of labour between the „think" jobs and the „do" jobs. Front office workers have to work more commercially, have to perform a wider range of tasks (banks) or have become more specialized (Point of Sale [POS] workers in retailing). Residual work remains, like administrative work in banks, rack filling in supermarkets and nursing aids in hospitals. In all of those cases a new „work habitude" is needed, as was already mentioned before. This new work habitude, according to Baethge and Oberbeck (1986) who coined the concept, entails a new way of interacting with automated equipment as well as a new way of behaving towards customers, treating them not as objects of service, but as subjects as it were, drawing the customers into the service relationship in an active, cummunicative way. That is not to say one can generalize this point to apply to all European countries.

5 The New Division of Labour in Comparative Perspective

The customer has indeed become part of the organization of the seller, as predicted by Chester Barnard as far back as 1938 (Barnard, 1958), which makes for a more user-friendly trend in the architecture of Information Technology in services.

In general, computers in the 1990s have become more powerful, less expensive and more user-friendly. As a result the use of computers has become more and more widespread in the service sector. The number of employees working with computers has increased enormously, as has the amount of information available to them. As a result the impact of Information Technology on the work process and the division of labour has increased. Much front office work is done on stand-alone machines (although linked to main-frame computers) and work posts are more isolated physically than used to be the case. Customer expectations of the quality of the services rendered have risen. However, the consequences of the introduction of new technology can vary a lot between countries, sectors, organizations in the same sector as well as different parts within one organization. What do we know about the impact of new technology on the labour process? And how do we analyze the changes?

Although within their respective sectors banks, retail firms and hospitals introduced basically very similar technologies, there were differences in the way they organized people to operate those technologies (Child and Loveridge, 1990, p. 309).

The utmost care must be taken if one wants to use the outcomes of studies conducted in *industry* for the *service* sector. One of the main tendencies in industrial work in Europe is to do away with individual work posts and assembly line work as much as possible in favour of teamwork. Kern and Schumann (1984) refer to this in their seminal book on *The End of the Division of Labour*. Employment contracts are mostly of a collective kind. In the service sector there is the opposite tendency of individualization of work and of employment contracts. Another important difference between industrial and service work is the amount of part-time work. In the Netherlands, for instance, 85% of workers in industry is employed full-time, against only 55% in the service sector. The Netherlands is the absolute champion in Europe as regards *part-time work*: in 1994 35% of all workers worked part-time. In Belgium this figure stood at 13%, in Germany 20% and in the United Kingdom 25%. The number of part-time workers is increasing everywhere in Europe, especially among female workers in retailing, catering and financial services. Flexibility in industry is more of the functional type (rotation of tasks), in services is mainly numerical (differing working time, on-call contracts).

5.1 The MESS-Project

The Micro-electronics in the Service Sector (MESS) research group in the 1980s investigated the introduction of information technology in the service sector. Originally nine countries were included: Belgium, the United Kingdom, the Federal Republic of Germany, Italy, Sweden, Hungary, Yugoslavia, Poland and China. Unfortunately there were no data from Poland and only partially usable data for Yugoslavia and China. The research was inspired by seven *assumptions*, based on previous research.

(1) The introduction of new technology in organizations is a process in which various groups potentially participate and seek to influence decisions.
(2) At the different stages of the decision making process there are different degrees of opportunity for interested parties to exercise influence.
(3) Different groups will tend to share their own perspectives on the new technology (linked with their possibilities to influence the decisions on new technology).
(4) The introduction of new technologies involves a learning process and offers a range of new organizational design possibilities. The introduction process will therefore be characterized by uncertainties and the need to make design choices.
(5) These choices are (at least partially) determined by economic and other pressures.
(6) A wider involvement of different interested parties in the preparation of specifications for technology selection and systems design at an earlier stage in the process is expected to have a greater chance of promoting innovative solutions utilizing technological possibilities.
(7) The introduction of new technology creates elements of irreconcilable conflict between the interests and values of different groups within the organization (Child and Loveridge, 1990, pp. 32-33).

The importance of these assumptions is that they offer a framework for a more differentiated approach to the introduction of new technology, with special attention for the position of the different groups in the labour process.

Before we pay attention to the impact of new technologies on the division of labour, it is necessary to provide a brief description of the technological changes in the parts of the service sector which were investigated.

5.2 Banking

In the sector of (retail) banking the introduction of new technologies can be divided into three phases. In the 1960s and 1970s investment in centrally located mainframe computers permitted the centralization of customer accounts. This made Electronic Fund Transfer (EFT) possible.

From the 1970s onwards new technologies were introduced into the branches, with front and back office terminals. A further step was the introduction of customer operated terminals in the 1980s, in a first stage only automated teller machines, nowadays often allowing more complex transactions and orders (so-called self-banking).

A third phase of retail banking automation in the 1980s and 1990s concerned the introduction of Electronic Fund Tranfer at the Point Of Sale (EFT/POS) and the promotion of home banking. EFT/POS allows retail store customers to pay for goods at the point of sale through electronic transfer of funds from their bank account to the store´s bank account. Leading countries in the introduction and generalization of EFT/POS were Belgium, France, Germany and the United Kingdom. The Netherlands and the countries of southern Europe were relative latecomers in this particular field. Home banking (sometimes called phone banking) allows customers to obtain information and carry out transactions from terminals (or simple telephones) located in their homes which are connected with the bank´s computer via the telecommunications network.

The decision to introduce new technology in retail banking is never taken at the local offices. It is always a central decision, emanating from the head office, sometimes even taken abroad. The outcomes of the MESS-project made clear that the organization of bank branch work around a particular type of technology permits a variety of job designs and that there is a possibility of choice. Upgrading as well as deskilling and skill polarization appeared. Nowhere was there an overall deskilling. There was considerable variety in the division of labour and the content of jobs across the sample of branches. Some tellers performed only „residual" tasks at automated machinery like in the example given above, others had their tasks upgraded by adding commercial activities (see also *Chapter 13* by Tremblay on the Canadian Banking Sector).

This enables front office staff to concentrate more on commercial activities, like loans and insurance. In general there is a „polarization" between two main functions in the structure of work in retail banks, at least on the very important local level. On the one hand there is the old cashier function (tellers and administrative employees combined) and on the other hand the newer commercial function, with a stress on recruiting new clients and the marketing of (new) services (Stroeke, 1990, p. 116). Even the local bank manager has undergone a change of function, in the sense that his external activities (like deciding on credit lines of clients) have increased and his internal functions (like the managing of the bank branch´s personnel) have become less important. Internal checks on employee performance can easily be done with the help of the computer data. This also applies to the retailing sector.

There is no consistent relationship between the level of automation (the degree of computer support) and the level of task specialization within the categories of branch employment. It is not technology itself, but rather what Gerwin (1981) terms „system design“, namely the configuration of technology and work organization, which has a direct bearing upon employees´ experience of work. Similar equipment can be used to support different system designs. Job content does not change along single trajectories of upgrading or downgrading, nor along those of increased or diminished control. Different categories of staff do not necessarily experience new technology in the same way (Child and Loveridge, 1990, pp. 124-156).

Together with the introduction of new technologies in the Dutch banking sector in the 1980s there was an increasing educational level of the bank employees (Bilderbeek and Buitelaar, 1992, p. 59). Partially the banks achieved this by internal training courses and internal promotion. Human resources management became more important. However, it was clear that the internal labour market became a problem for those working in the banking sector. In order to find higher qualified personnel there was a shift from the internal to the external labour market (Tijdens, 1989, pp. 249-274).

5.3 Hospital Laboratories

One of the important technological changes in the hospitals studied was connected with the introduction of new technology in laboratories. Innovation in the hospital laboratories concerned the way the analyses are processed. Manual analyses were replaced by automated analysing processes. The technology used is the automated analyser, possibly linked to a wider network of information processing. These are all „black-box“ chemistries where the chemical analysis is completely automated (Child and Loveridge, 1990, p. 272). The task of the laboratory technician is to put blood and urine samples into the auto-analyser, add the reagent, close the lid and let the centrifugal mechanism do its work. He or she (mostly she) has become an observer of his or her own work. In this way up to 2,000 samples per hour may be analyzed, as opposed to 5 per hour when performed manually. In essence the same technology is applied in all laboratories, although the size, workload and integration in a network may differ.

An interesting difference between the countries of the MESS project was found in the structure of their health insurance system. In Sweden a national health insurance system exists with a very centralized decision-making. In Britain there is a national health insurance system in existence, but decisions are made locally. In Germany and Belgium there is a compulsary social insurance in operations, where prospective patients choose the hospital at which they want treatment on a free market basis. Here hospitals and doctors are in fierce competition and the system is very localized, albeit under the general supervision from a central authority. Despite the fact that technology was more or less the same everywhere, the decision-making process showed great differences (Child and Loveridge, 1990, pp. 245-247).

The influence of the producers and suppliers of technology equipment on the hospital laboratory has increased. Not only does the machine exactly prescribe the activities of the worker, laboratory assistants have also become dependent on the suppliers of reagents which in most cases are the same as the suppliers of the hardware. The laboratory staff is not acquainted anymore with the formulas of the reagents. In view of the great variety of tests that can be carried out by the automated equipment, there is an increasing demand for reagents of better quality and a longer life. Reagents can therefore no longer be made by the laboratory technicians themselves, which is an important element in the deskilling process in hospital laboratories. In all but three of the laboratories investigated, working with automated analysers was experienced as deskilling by the workers. The inability of automated analysers to present laboratory technicians with any challenge in terms of using their qualifications was a commonly expressed theme (Child and Loveridge, 1990, pp. 279-289; Mok and De Decker, 1990, p. 35).

The MESS-project also focused on the size of the laboratories and the vertical and horizontal division of labour. Hierarchy did not appear to be affected by the application of new technology: in none of the cases did the number of hierarchical levels change after new technology had been implemented. Hierarchy was obviously much more related to national characteristics, such as qualification structures, and possibly hospital corporate traditions, than to technological innovation. There were also considerable differences in the division of labour between jobs within laboratories. Formal authority structures appeared to be more affected by national cultures than by technology. They were more resistant to change than were the horizontal divisions of labour and job structures.

Laboratory work organization seemed to vary not only in the way that it is formally structured, but also in the allocation of identifiable and comparable tasks between job holders. This variation equally could not be ascribed to the laboratory technologies employed.

5.4 Retailing

Since consumption has become a much more important, or even dominant aspect of European life-style, the significance of retailing has increased. Much of the post-war expansion in retail employment has been accompanied by an increase in feminization of the workforce and in part-time work.

In the MESS-project eight modes of retailing were identified: home shopping, discount warehouses, department stores, service multiples, hypermarkets/superstores, supermarkets, specialist traders and convenience stores. The classification was based on three contingent features: the product range, the range of transactional locations and the perishability or durability of the goods sold (Child and Loveridge, 1990, pp. 168-169). Nowadays the different types of retail-stores often belong to the same national or multinational groups.

The most important technological development was the use of EPOS (Electronic Point of Sale) cash registers in the 1980s, with the introduction of laser-scanning of bar-codes or Universal Product Codes. The break-through of this technology happened much later in Europe compared to the United States and Japan.

The EPOS-terminals potentially — and in an increasing number of places effectively — form the front end of totally integrated computer based retailing systems. The terminal generates not only the bill for the customer, but the computer system initiates stock-keeping as well as book-keeping, and it automatically produces orders for delivery of products to the stores.

Another innovation is the decreasing importance of cash money. Cash is being replaced by Electronic Fund Transfer at the Point of Sale (EFT/POS) and by the use of credit cards. Here similarly information technology becomes more and more important.

In the case studies of the MESS-project it was difficult to distinguish differences in the deployment of technology that could not be attributed to a broadly economic rationale or to differences in organizational size. Examination of five representative clusterings of jobs under the general title of rack-filler, sales assistant, invoice clerk, in-store manager and head office staff revealed that the changes in the content of jobs following the introduction of EPOS were relatively small (Child and Loveridge, 1990, pp. 217-226). Boonstra concluded in a study of the Dutch retailing branch that the consequences of the introduction of new technology were influenced by the previous organizational choice for centralization or decentralization. In fact the new technologies merely reinforced the previous strategic choices (Boonstra, 1991).

The reasons most consistently mentioned in the MESS-project for the introduction of new technologies were to improve management control and operational information. In all cases it involved a growing realization of the degree to which organizational change and an intellectual comprehension of information and potential analytical capacity available to strategic management lagged far behind the development of machines (Child and Loveridge, 1990, pp. 198-210).

Staff rationalization was another explicit goal of executive management in all cases (except the Hungarian ones), and this was usually achieved through a process of attrition. Insofar as all managements succeeded in rationalizing their staff over the early years of EPOS, and at least maintaining or improving their turn-over, a productivity gain must be assumed. The deployment of remaining staff resulted in greater task interchangeability and the acquisition of new skills (Child and Loveridge, 1990, pp. 231-232).

5.5 Organizational Conservatism

One of the outcomes of the MESS-project was the influence of organizational conservatism. In the case histories opportunities for organizational innovation appear to have been realized very infrequently. It has become evident that learning to secure the *full potential* of new technology is a process that is shaped and bounded by forces of a social and political nature in the sense that the people who are involved have a concern to preserve or extend organizational arrangements with which they are comfortable. The controlled and contested nature of organizational learning is of theoretical significance for an understanding of how technology and organization come to be configured together (Child and Loveridge, 1990, pp. 355-359).

This conclusion is confirmed by more recent investigations, for example in the Dutch retailing sector (Boonstra, 1991, p. 25). Here organizational structures have hardly changed, in spite of the radical changes of the market and of the technological possibilities. The information technology potential is insufficiently put to use as a result of tenaciously hanging on to the existing organizational models by those responsible for organizational design (Bilderbeek and Buitelaar, 1992, p. 57). „Organizational conservatism" is human conservatism as visible in organizations.

Heming´s conclusions are similar. During the planning and the start of automation processes *social and organizational consequences* are seldom discussed. In the decision making on the system design these elements do not play an important role. Heming concludes that if one wants the introduction of information technologies to lead to changes in the organization and division of labour, it is necessary to formulate this as an explicit goal of the project in advance and to pay attention to this goal from the earliest stages of the innovation project onwards. Once the project is underway the possibilities to implement these changes in the work organization will only diminish. It is also essential that a specific member of the organization is clearly responsible for the realization of these goals during the process of introduction of new technologies (Heming, 1992, pp. 188-189).

In other words labour relations influence — directly as well as indirectly — the degree to which the information technology potential is used (Van Ruysseveldt, 1991), or to put it in another way: the degree to which the old division of labour is maintained after the introduction of the new information technology. This is also evident from the case studies in Britain, Germany and Sweden quoted by Francis (1986, pp. 79-103).

6 Consequences for the External Labour Market

In times of recession, high unemployment and technological progress it is fitting to pay extra attention to the relationship between automation and employment. The number of surveys and theories on this subject are increasing, as are the often contradictory conclusions and prognoses.

In general it seemed that on the microlevel the direct loss of jobs in the service sector by IT is generally speaking insignificant, certainly when compared with some predictions of the 1970s. Fröhlich et al. (1993) argue that in their European sample they find evidence that on the company level the introduction of IT had in most cases no influence, or even a positive influence on employment.

At least one group of professionals clearly benefited from the growing weight of information technology. The information and computer specialists in the different service sectors have become more and more numerous and important. This development is accompanied by a loss of low-skilled jobs. If the introduction of new technologies did not cause a direct exclusion of lower qualified employees, it caused an indirect exclusion on the external labour market.

The indirect effects of IT on employment are, however, much harder to measure. IT mostly leads to an increased productivity and in that way — in the best situation — causes a smaller growth of the number of jobs, against the background of an increasing supply of job seekers in the labour market.

Whereas the outcomes for employment on the company level (microlevel) were rather positive, more negative employment consequences might be expected at the mesolevel (economic sectors and regions) as well as on the macrolevel. Introduction of information technology in one company may stimulate the closure of other, less equiped companies. The exact correlation between the use of IT and increasing unemployment remains vague. But there certainly is an influence of IT on the profile of the unemployed. IT made it possible to replace large numbers of low skilled jobs by machines. The design of IT, the implementation, the maintainance and to a large extent even the use of IT requires middle or even highly skilled employees.

As a result unemployment became a qualitative as well as a quantitative problem. Low skilled unemployed do not only have problems in gaining access to the labour market because of the shortage of jobs, but also because their skills are no longer required. The increasing demand for better qualified people in most service sectors caused a supply surplus of low skilled workers. The skill demand rose faster than the educational level of the potential employees. Although the development of IT is not or not entirely responsible for the rise in unemployment, there is a clear influence on the demand for the qualifications of the unemployed population.

7 Conclusion

In the 1970s a negative view of the introduction of new technologies was dominant, stressing deskilling processes and often resulting in technological determinism. Strange as it may sound, these negative ideas were almost entirely due to the book by Harry Braverman, published in 1974. Braverman´s radical ideas had a profound influence on researchers in the field. Although his ideas have been effectively challenged by other scholars (Francis, 1986), the fact remains that they have been of seminal importance. Braverman laid much stress on the fragmentation of tasks in the capitalist labour process, also and even specifically in the service sector (Braverman, 1974, pp. 359-373), and on the need for managements to control and discipline workers by organizational and technological means (Taylorism). In this respect the radical marxist Braverman was a real functionalist.

Today, in the 1990s, the picture is less clear. Some negative trends have come true, others have not. However, the resistance against the introduction of information technology, which existed in some union circles and amongst some groups of (militant) workers, has been broken. Information technology has been, and still is, introduced on a large scale in the service sector. Discussions nowadays concern the extent of automation, the speed of innovation, the need of flexibility and the social support or compensations, but very seldom its (negative) outcomes. This is probably due to the low union density in service occupations.

Due to organizational conservatism the consequences for the organization of the labour process were smaller than many authors expected in the 1970s. Nevertheless the overall penetration of new technologies was accompanied by changes in the division of labour.

Inspite of what was expected in the 1970s, it is nowadays impossible to find a clear outcome of the changes in the labour process after the introduction of IT in the service sector. On the internal labour market reskilling as well as deskilling appeared. The introduction of new technology must be seen against the background of the culture of the organization, the structure of the service sector, the nature of the service provided and the country concerned. The historical and cultural embeddedness of the service sector is more important than a simple technological determinism.

Since the consequences of the introduction of IT are not always negative, some authors claim today a greater influence of workers on the design of new technology as a tool for change in the workplace. The post-Fordist production strategies in which paradigms will tend to place greater emphasis on technological development which improves the effective use of an increasingly skilled and responsible workforce are based on this belief (Badham and Mathews, 1989).

The question remains, however, whether the opportunities for improving the work situation are given to service workers. On the internal labour market we noticed a shift towards more qualified jobs. In large parts of the service sector this has been solved by internal training. Job losses often have been minimized by an increasing workload, job increase stopped however. The post-Fordist approach seems too optimistic. The well qualified and responsible workforce remains a small elite. The emphasis on the work situation of this group hides the problem of deskilling of other, larger groups. It hides as well the growing unemployment as an external labour market consequence.

On a macro-level, however, labour market problems increase. Substitution effects occur, certainly in recruitment policy, excluding low skilled workers and thus causing further labour market segmentation.

With an increasing attention for productivity in the service sector and systematic attempts to reduce the cost of the production factor labour — against the background of the recession of the early 1990s — the growth of employment in the service sector has halted in several European countries. If the service sector is no longer capable of compensating for the reduction of employment in European industry (and agriculture), does this not mean that a rethinking of the division of labour in general is necessary?

More and more people are nowadays victims of *social exclusion* (Vranken and Geldof, 1993): they have lost their position on the labour market and joined the large group of almost 17 million officially unemployed (and an even larger number de facto) in the European Union. These socially excluded are not only confronted with an income reduction and dependency on social security benefits. In a society in which a job still remains a major tool for social integration, being unemployed remains a stigma, as was shown in a recent study of values in Europe (Mok and Van Goethem, 1992, pp. 70-71).

In order to stop this progressing social exclusion, a more radical division of labour between employed and unemployed seems to become necessary, including a drastic reduction of working time. Or, as Gorz has put it: let´s work less in order to have work for all (Gorz, 1991). In that case it is not only the changing face of service work in European countries, but the changing face of work, and thus of the European societies in globo.

References

Badham, R. and J. Mathews (1989), The new production systems debate, in *Labour and Industry,* Vol. 2, No. 2: 194-246.

Baethge, M. and H. Oberbeck (1986), *Die Zukunft der Angestellten. Neue Technologien und berufliche Perspektiven in Büro und Verwaltung.* Frankfurt/New York, Campus.

Baethge, M. and H. Oberbeck (eds.- 1992), *Personalentwicklung im Handel. Zwischen Stagnation und neuen Perspektiven.* Frankfurt/New York, Campus.

Barnard, C. (1958), *The functions of the executive.* Cambridge, MA, Harvard University Press (originally 1938).

Berghman, J. and B. Cantillon (eds.- 1993), *The European face of social security.* Aldershot, Avebury.

Bilderbeek, R. and W. Buitelaar (1992), Bank computerization and organizational innovations: the long winding road to the bank of the future, in *New Technology, Work and Employment,* Vol. 7, No. 1: 54-60.

Boonstra, J. (1991), Technologische en organisatorische vernieuwing in de detailhandel, in SISWO (ed.), *Informatietechnologie en arbeidsorganisatie in de dienstensector.* Amsterdam, SISWO: 11-34.

Braverman, H. (1974), *Labor and monopoly capital. The degradation of work in the twentieth century.* New York, Monthly Review Press.

Buitelaar W. and R. Bilderbeek (1991), Bankinformatisering en organisatieverandering. Over technologie, bedrijfsorganisatie en arbeidsverhoudingen, in SISWO (ed.), *Informatietechnologie en arbeidsorganisatie in de dienstensector.* Amsterdam, SISWO: 35-51.

Butler, R. (1991), *Designing organizations. a decision-making perspective.* London/New York, Routledge.

Child, J. and R. Loveridge (1990), *Information technology in european services. Towards a microelectronic future.* Oxford/Cambridge, Basil Blackwell.

Clegg, S.R. (1990), *Modern organizations. Organization studies in the postmodern world.* Newbury Park/London/New Delhi, Sage.

Crozier, M. (1963), *Le phénomène bureaucratique.* Paris, Seuil.

Davis, L. and J. Taylor (eds.- 1990), *The design of jobs.* Harmondsworth, Penguin.

Eurostat (various years), Basisstatistieken van de Gemeenschap, vergelijking met enige Europese landen, Canada, USA, Japan en de USSR. Luxembourg, Eurostat.

Francis, A. (1986), *New technology at work*. Oxford, Clarendon.

Fröhlich, D., C. Gill and H. Krieger (1993), Informatietechnologie en werkgelegenheid in de Europese Gemeenschap, in *Tijdschrift voor Arbeidsvraagstukken*, No. 1: 90-101.

Gershuny, J. (1978), *After industrial society: the emerging self-service economy*. London, Macmillan.

Gerwin, D. (1981), Relationships between structure and technology, in Nystrom, P.C. and W.H. Starbuck (eds.), *Handbook of organizational design*, Vol 2. Oxford, Oxford University Press.

Gill, C. and H. Krieger (1992), The diffusion of participation in new information technology in Europe:survey results, in *Economic and industrial democracy, an international journal*, Vol. 13, No. 3: 331-358.

Gorz, A. (1991), *Métamorphoses du travail: quête du sens. Critique de la raison économique*. Paris, Editions Galilée.

Granovetter, M. and R. Swedberg (eds.- 1992), *The sociology of economic life*. Boulder/San Francisco/Oxford, Westview.

Hartog, J. and J. Theeuwes (eds.- 1993), *Labour market contracts and institutions. A cross-national comparison*. Amsterdam, North-Holland Publishers.

Heming, B. (1992), Kwaliteit van de arbeid, geautomatiseerd... Een studie naar kwaliteit van arbeid en de relatie tussen automatisering, arbeid en organisatie. PhD Thesis, Delft, University of Delft.

Kern, H. and M. Schumann, M. (1984), *Das Ende der Arbeitsteilung? Rationalisierung in der industriellen Produktion: Bestandsaufnahme, Trendbestimmung*. Munich, Beck

Kerr, C., J. Dunlop, F. Harbison and C. Myers (1960), *Industrialism and industrial man: the problems of labor and management in economic growth*. Cambridge MA, Harvard University Press.

Kruse, W. (1993), *Training in the retail sector. A survey for the FORCE programme*. Berlin, CEDEFOP.

Laurijs, S. and A.L. Mok (1989), *The politics of policies: insurance and new technology*. Antwerp, University of Antwerp.

Littek, W. (1992), Service sector/service work, in G. Szell (ed.), *Concise encyclopaedia of participation and co-management*. Berlin/New York, Walter de Gruyter: 743-755.

Littek, W., U. Heisig and H.-D. Gondek (eds.- 1991), *Dienstleistungsarbeit: Strukturveränderungen, Beschäftigungsbedingungen und Interessenlagen*. Berlin, Sigma.

Littek, W., U. Heisig and H.-D. Gondek (eds.- 1992), *Organisation von Dienstleistungsarbeit. Sozialbeziehungen und Rationalisierung im Angestelltenbereich*. Berlin, Bohn.

Loveridge, R. (1984), Micro-electronics and the growing polarisation of service employment, in *Proceedings of the labour process conference*. Birmingham, Aston Business School.

Loveridge, R. and A.L. Mok (1979), *Theories of labour market segmentation. A critique*. The Hague/Boston/London, Martinus Nijhoff Social Sciences Division.

Mathews, J. (1989a), *Age of democracy. The politics of post-Fordism*. Melbourne/Oxford/Auckland/New York, Oxford University Press.

Mathews, J. (1989b), *New technology and the democratisation of work*. Sydney, Pluto Press.

Mok, A.L. and K. De Decker (1990), Workers´ reaction to new technology in professional work, in *The Polish Sociological Bulletin*, No. 2: 27-36.

Mok, A.L. and W. van Goethem (1992), Werken in de prestatiemaatschappij, in Kerkhofs, J., K. Dobbelaere, L. Voyé and B. Bawin-Lagros (eds.), *De versnelde ommekeer. De waarden van Vlamingen, Walen en Brusselaars in de jaren ´90*. Tielt, Lannoo: 70-71.

Nisbet, P. (1992), Enterprise size, information technology and service sector — the employment implications, in *New Technology, Work And Employment,* Vol. 7, No. 1: 61-70.

Regtering, H. and H. Doorewaard (1991), Is organisatorisch conservatisme een rem op integraal automatiseren?, in SISWO (ed.), *Informatietechnologie en arbeidsorganisatie in de dienstensector*, Amsterdam, SISWO: 53-70.

Stroeke, J.H.M. (1990), Informatietechnologie bij banken, in Horn, L.A. ten, and F.R.H. Zijlstra (eds.), *Informatietechnologie in de maatschappij. Toepassing, beleid, perspectief.* Leiden/Antwerpen, Stenfert Kroese: 99-117.

Tijdens, K. (1989), *Automatisering en vrouwenarbeid. Een studie over beroepssegregatie op de arbeidsmarkt, in de administratieve beroepen en in het bankwezen.* Amsterdam, Uitgeverij Jan van Arkel.

Tijdens, K. (1991), 25 jaar automatisering van het betalingsverkeer. Een empirisch onderzoek naar product- en procesinnovaties in het bankwezen, in SISWO (ed.), *Informatietechnologie en arbeidsorganisatie in de dienstensector.* Amsterdam, SISWO: 127-156.

Van Ruysseveldt, J. (1991), Arbeidsverhoudingen, arbeidsruilrelaties en technologische innovatie: gezichtspunten vanuit cross-nationale en inter-sectorale vergelijkingen, in SISWO (ed.), *Informatietechnologie en arbeidsorganisatie in de dienstensector,* Amsterdam, SISWO: 71-103.

Vranken, J. and D. Geldof (1993), *Armoede en sociale uitsluiting. Jaarboek 1992-1993.* Leuven/Amersfort, ACCO.

Chapter 9
New Technologies and Post-Taylorist Regulation Models: The Introduction and Use of Production Planning Systems in French, Italian, and German Enterprises

*Pierre Dubois, Martin Heidenreich, Michele La Rosa and Gert Schmidt**

Contents

* This joint paper from the German-Italian-French Research Team (GIFT) on New Technologies has been translated from the German by Jonathan Harrow, Bielefeld University. Other members of GIFT are Luigi Benedetti (ISFEL and University of Bologna, Italy); Giancarlo Cerruti (IRES di Torino, Italy), Maura Franchi (Regional administration of the Emilia Romagna, Italy), Stefan Heiner (Villazzano, Trento, Italy), and Solange Montagné-Villette (University of Poitiers, France). A reader with nine articles based on our common empirical work (11 case studies on the basis of 145 interviews with production controllers, systems developers, top managers and shop stewards) has been edited by Heidenreich (1993). The 11 companies are indicated by abbreviations like C1I. The first letter refers to the branch (clothing or electronics industry); the second to the country where the company is located.

1 Introduction: „Post-Taylorist“ Models of Production

The combination of increased competition on the world market, new technological developments, and changes in the labour resources of society has led to changing patterns of industrial development in the leading Western industrialized nations. Economists, political scientists, and sociologists — while using different formulae — have conceived these as a radical break and as a structural change of any Taylor-Ford regulation model that has essentially characterized the industrialization of the last 50 years. In Western European countries, industrial and organizational sociologists have in recent decades repeatedly discussed the social, organizational, and technical implications of the Taylor-Ford regulation model and — especially since the 1980s — its possible transformation into post-taylorist models of work organization. Sociologists became increasingly aware of the fact that the supposed „one best way“ of an extreme parcellization and routinization of work was probably limited only to a specific phase of capitalist production: the era of standardized mass production with semi-skilled workers for large, price-competitive markets.

In the context of a new, international division of labour between old and newly industrialized countries and an increasing globalization of industrial competition, West European industries are no longer confronted with the classical alternative between homogeneous, cheap products on one side or custom-built high quality, high flexibility products on the other side. The classical mass producers and the producers of diversified quality products (like the machine tools industry) have to reduce their unit costs, increasing at the same time the quality, the innovativeness, and the diversity of their products. The transformation of the classical alternative between „economies of scale“ and „economies of scope“ into simultaneously to be achieved aims eroded the distinction of mass production and craft production concepts as well. Enterprises in advanced industrial countries are looking for possibilities to combine the two, formerly opposed logics of industrial organization — either deskilled, routinized jobs in low-trust organizations or qualified, autonomous tasks under high-trust conditions: The „lean production“ concepts of Japanese car makers (Womack et al., 1990) or the „new competition“ between highly industrialized countries (Best, 1990) are characterized by huge production lots of customized, modularized, innovative products. The required flexibility and the increased interdependencies of R&D, engineering, production, production control, and marketing increased the possibilities for broader task structures, higher job discretion, a reduced division of labour and non-hierarchical forms of coordination (e.g. in project groups, quality circles, production teams; cf. Kern and Schumann, 1984; Piore and Sabel, 1984; Reich, 1992).

This means that „post-Taylorist" models of production are not simply the „opposite" of Taylorist models but new, tentative, and instable forms of work organization which are only partly based on previous, Taylorist or craft-based forms of organization and social integration. The flexible spezialization is not simply a return to the past of pre-Taylorist principles (as Piore and Sabel seem to indicate) but an attempt to create new, competitive, flexible, and socially acceptable forms of production which transcend the former opposition of Taylorist and craftbased principles of organization. This can be discussed in the following three dimensions which refer to central organizational, social and cultural aspects of the emerging models of post-Taylorist forms of production:

(1) Ideal-typical Taylorist companies were — in line with the model of a rationally structured, bureaucratic organization — divided into functionally differentiated domains to which were assigned specific, precisely defined subtasks within the production of huge quantities of homogeneous products. The coordination between different domains followed a previously set plan. The need for coordination and negotiation between individual departments was low, as the „systemic rationality" of the work process was defined a priori and was not the result of permanent processes of negotiation and agreement. On the ideological level, the hierarchical and functional organization of companies — true to the „machine model" of rationally constructed and operated organizations — was justified by technological or economic pressures or by unequivocal scientific findings that were considered to be sufficiently instructive for designing the construction process.

New ways of coordination are not based on the return to the small batches of the craft-based types of production; neither the relative independance of autonomous professional workers nor the corresponding, informal synchronization by qualified work groups are sufficient to coordinate the huge production series of increasingly diversified products. Instead of this, new information and communication technologies (ICT) are used to monitor the required and available material, the production schedules, the production operations already completed, the relevant quality indicators and the time until the finishing of a production lot etc. But these technologies do not solve all the internal coordination problems. In lateral, non-hierarchical forms of cooperation and consultation, especially in project groups, employees have to develop and maintain — as a „non-computerized requirement of computerization processes" — a synthetic, shared view of the organizational processes. This corresponds to a decentralization and de-hierarchization of responsibilities for the interdepartmental coordination of work processes.

(2) The dominant model for the use of labour was „low-trust relations" (Fox, 1974): Ideal-typical Taylorist companies did not rely systematically on the skills, creativity, and motivation of labour, but attempted to prestructure the work processes as precisely as possible and design them to be controllable. The social integration of labour was based on the logic of an „economic exchange" (P. Blau) guaranteed through directly measurable, short-term gratifications and sanctions (production bonuses, piecework systems, dismissal).

The new patterns of social integration cannot be characterized as a simple shift to high-trust relations. Even if ICT systems are not used for the direct and permanent monitoring of employees behaviour — the initial fear of the so-called „transparent man" proved to be an exaggeration — the transparency of individual and collective achievements has been increased by new ICT technologies and by an increased accountability of „profit centres", departments and factories. This leads not to a „responsible autonomy" — as Friedman (1977) supposed — but to a kind of „controllable autonomy", a higher degree of self- and group-control and to „self-created" stress which is less the result of direct hierarchical supervision than the consequence of organizational promotion politics and habitualized forms of work behaviour and commitment.

(3) In line with the minimal social integration of the employees, the impact of sociocultural contexts for Taylorist (but not for professional or craft-based) forms of work organization was low. Taylorist companies referred to societal norms and values (built into different institutions as the industrial relations systems or the national systems of education or vocational training) only to a limited extent. This reference normally was limited to extrafunctional norms such as meticulousness, discipline, high motivation, punctuality, respect for authority, cooperative forms of bargaining, which facilitated the passive subordination under the organizational order. Large mass producers of standardized goods were able to be autonomous from their societal environment be-

cause they designed the work tasks to be as simple and repetitive as possible and controlled them directly.

The shift from direct control to a higher, but controllable autonomy corresponds to a higher organizational dependence on external, socio-cultural forms of social integration (Lane, 1994; Hickson, 1993). The problem is that the stability of institutionally embedded norms and values — like the professional orientations transmitted in the system of vocational education or cooperative forms of conflict resolution typical for some systems of industrial relations — can no longer be taken for granted in front of the pluralization und individualization of life styles and professional biographies (cf. Beck, 1986). This is even true for Japan where the long working hours, the high work intensity, and the low wages especially in smaller firms are no longer regarded as „natural" aspects of the Japanese traditions. National cultures of work and management are no longer — if they have ever been — a type of „iron cage" determing the work behaviour in culturally embedded work organizations but they become more and more a sort of „toolkit" (Swidler, 1986) which are used by culturally embedded, but not culturally determined, individuals in shaping their actions, creating and recreating organizational structures and cultures. Managers confronted with such a „detraditionalized" use of culture must abandon the vision of an integrated, homogeneous „corporate culture" (as a new sort of a „one best way") and can only hope to arrange the context in a way which allows the continuous (partially computer-based) control of organizational performance.

In a cross-national study of computerization processes in eleven Italian, French, and West German clothing and electronics companies we tried to analyze some aspects of the emerging post-Taylorist models of work organization. We concentrated on the redefinition of work roles, organizational structures and organizational cultures. We were interested both in the general, transnational aspects of new regulation models of industrial work as in country- and culture-specific patterns of „post-Taylorist" forms of work organization and social integration. Three aspects of new, post-Taylorist and post-bureaucratic regulation models will be discussed on the basis of our empirical evidence: (1) The politicization of computerization processes as a consequence of the open, contingent nature of systemic, interdepartmental rationalization processes; (2) a different place of human labour in industry; and (3) a different impact of national cultures for the forms of social integration at the enterprise level.

2 Computerization and Industrial Concepts of Production Planning

An important characteristic of current business strategies is a change in the way they deal with external, above all market-related contingencies. „Turbulent“ market conditions are no longer broadly ignored in order to assemble a small range of highly standardized products as cheaply as possible, but the organizational flexibility, the organizational „requisite variety“ has significantly increased. This leads to a higher degree of uncertainties to be dealt with within the company. These contingencies are „handled“ within the organization in power and exchange relationships; instead of bureaucratic rules, hierarchies, or „economic or technical necessities“, complex decisions are taken (in an incremental way) in open negotiation and exchange processes. This has been labelled the „politicization of industrial change“ (Heidenreich and Schmidt, 1990).

This politicization is an important feature of the processes in which production planning systems are developed and used. There is no „one best way“ for the implementation of these systems because they represent a specific view of the organization materialized in algorithms and data structures. This computerized representation of organizational information and communication processes is dependent on a previously created, shared view of these processes which has to be developed in interest-based communication and negotiation processes between system developers, production planning and control departments, and production departments. First of all, such a shared, partially homogeneous view of organizational processes instead of the partial views of each department is a necessary basis for the development of interdepartmental information systems; secondly, for the „reasonable“ use and interpretation of decontextualized data and control procedures the users have to rely on a non-computerized conception of overlapping, cross-departmental processes. In the following sections, we shall describe the politicized development of information systems, their openendedness, their dependence on company- or even department-specific power constellations, and the legitimization of the respective strategies that lead to a „conceptual rivalry“ (Wiedemann, 1989) between different rationalities and logics.

Empirically, four different steps in the development of production planning can be differentiated. In these phases, two logics of production planning, the logic of global, ex-ante optimization and the logic of situational, ad hoc optimization, are combined in a different manner (cf. Table 1). This corresponds to different roles and strategies of the two main protagonists of industrial production planning concepts — production managers and foremen on one side and production planning and control departments and systems development on the other side.

Table 1: Global Control and Situational Control

	Global control (ex ante optimization)	Situational control (ad hoc optimization)
Logic	Production prescriptions based on deductions from abstract goals (deductive/top-down)	Locally optimizing production decisions, suitable to the given situation
Protagonist of the control concept	Mainly separate production control departments, as well as central EDP and organizational departments	Mainly employees in production but also time and methods departments
Knowledge of production control	In decision algorithms and data banks	Bound to persons, only to a certain extent amenable to systematisation; information system as source of data
Means of control	Formalized orders on the basis of bureaucratic rationality (written information and other forms of documentation)	Informal exchange of information (e.g. between foremen); personal contact valued highly
Strong point	Systematic consideration of all relevant and available information (in the ideal case)	Flexible response to unforeseeable situations and changing production requirements

2.1 Production Planning and Control by Foremen

The classical model of production planning and control by foremen is based on the practical experience and knowledge of the foremen who are directly responsible for production, their overview of the process of production, and their informal contacts with other foremen. A prerequisite for foreman planning are (hidden) reserves of flexibility in production, such as discontinuously required personnel or machine capacities, intermediate stores of raw and semi-manufactured goods, and the possibility for the foreman to select between a larger number of orders (in the interests of a minimizing setting up costs). More systematic and comprehensive forms of production planning play only a marginal role in this model; the Taylorist time and motion departments were above all responsible for working out production times and defining work methods. The importance of the computer departments for defining, developing, and implementing new production planning methods is also very low in this phase — in spite of their generally very strong position — as available programmes are predominantly batch programmes for processing mass data in the administrative and commercial departments.

In view of the increasing demands for temporal, material, and social flexibility, this model has reached economic and organizational limits in most branches.

2.2 Upgrading the Status of Product Planning Departments and Centralized and Deterministic Planning Concepts

One answer to these attendant deficits in production planning is the introduction and utilization of comprehensive production planning systems that are generally used in the dialogue mode. The implementation of integrated information systems has frequently been accompanied by a major upgrading of the status of production planning departments that is documented in (1) an expansion of personnel; (2) the recruitment of personnel with higher formal qualifications; and (3) in a higher position in the hierarchy for the corresponding departments (extending as far as the establishment of logistics directors).

Frequently, the first attempts to set up production planning through external departments were initially based on a centralistic and deterministic planning concept. An attempt was made to develop an abstract, global model of industrial processes and to translate this conception into software structures. This was based on the assumption of an ideal model of industrial processes in which all production planning decisions could either be performed automatically or could be taken over by the planning departments; the role of the foreman was restricted purely to the implementation of the pre-given decisions.

In many cases, however, the limits of comprehensive planning and control concepts very soon became apparent as „in the early, deterministic production planning systems, a decisive 'shot of empiricism' and close-to-practice problem-solving capacity was repeatedly necessary in order to meet deadlines and keep the workshop and the personnel busy“ (Hildebrandt and Seltz, 1989, p. 287; translated). The intrinsic rigidity of computer systems thus continues to require the autonomous control activity of those responsible for production in order to guarantee the course of real-life production behind the facade of rationally organized computer-assisted processes.

2.3 Complementarity and Juxtaposition of Detailed Production Planning and Experience-Based Production Control

A third phase of industrial production planning models can be characterized by a more or less conflict-laden „coexistence" between a computer-assisted framework planning and a detailed, incremental control of the production managers. In such companies, production programmes are typically preset by planning departments, while the planning of capacity (and thereby the production schedules) and particularly the coping with unforeseen production breaks (missing parts, insufficient workforce, quality problems, machine breakdowns etc.) are predominantly in the hands of the foreman.

This differs from the second model of production planning, on the one hand, in that the production planning systems are more efficient, decentralized, temporally more precise, and generally work in a dialogue mode. On the other hand, it is precisely detailed planning that reveals the limits of their planning capabilities to the planning departments. This often results in the acceptance of „spheres of uncertainty" that cannot be planned systematically and, thus, areas in which the foreman is active in planning and control. Precisely because of experiences with the „all-powerful claims" of the earlier deterministic systems, the foremen can now more self-consciously emphasize their contribution to production planning and control against the „imperialism" of the planning departments.

We consider the juxtaposition of global production planning systems, with which the necessary time and materials for the production process can — even if not very precisely in detail and time — be planned in advance combined with experience-based, locally optimizing, ad hoc decisions by the foreman, to be at present the quantitatively most significant form of industrial production planning. It ensures both the autonomy of decision and action of those responsible for production as well as the status of the planning departments, just as, to a certain extent, it permits a more flexible reaction to market conditions. Its advantages are an increase in productivity and transparency: Increasingly more and smaller orders can be processed within the company without additional clerical staff, and precise information on orders and materials can be determined on a computer screen, that is, without time-consuming personal or telephone contacts.

2.4 On the Way to Increased Integration of Computerized and Experience-Based Production Planning?

Only when the deficits and weaknesses of computer-assisted framework planning — that „normally“ are exploited as uncertainty zones and power resources of production departments — become too onerous to the production managers (stress) or too expensive for the company (increasing stocks, insufficient flexibility, difficulties of dealing with always shorter cycles of product innovation and decreasing production lots) is an attempt made to break up the juxtaposition of the second and third phases by other, better integrated solutions.

Such an open situation was revealed in some of the companies studied; these could be the starting point for a search for new planning conceptions that are characterized by a stronger integration of abstract ex-ante and experience-based ad-hoc forms of production planning.

In one West German electronics company (E2G), for example, efforts are being made to decentralize the production planning systems and increase the participation of foremen. It is being considered whether production cannot be reorganized so that the foremen are no longer just responsible for certain work procedures but can take on responsibility for the production of a specific product — and thereby for several, previously separate work procedures. The goal of such a conception is to upgrade the foreman´s task and to develop a sort of computer-based foreman planning.

This is also the goal of the rigorous reorganization of a French personal computer assembly plant (E1F) according to Japanese kanban and just-in-time principles. Through a very „lean“ and transparent design of the production flow, and through the consistent dismantling of buffers within production, the technological and organizational conditions for upgrading the role of the foreman and for the repression of complex, computer-assisted production control systems were established. This solution should be supported by a new production planning system (PPS) aimed at controlling continuous production flows.

Another strategy is being followed in two French clothing companies

(C1F; C2F). Because of the deficits in the central production planning concentrated in Paris, the managers in the provinces developed their own computer-assisted solutions. This led to a juxtaposition of centralized and decentralized computer-assisted solutions.

A similar strategy, which aims at having a high degree of autonomy from the directives of external, central production planning, was observed in a West German electronics group (E1G). Here the single plants developed a great deal of their own computer capacity. The development of systems that were not integrated throughout the entire company provided the opportunity to develop planning methods that were better adjusted to local problems.

Regardless of whether responsibility is shared between production and production planning, or is exclusively assigned to production, the result in each case is a more strongly integrated concept of production planning in which the abstract, formalized, comprehensive production planning data of the external departments is combined with the concrete, particular, experience-based knowledge of the foreman and some production controllers that is based on informal relationships. This knowledge is an essential, „non-computerized precondition of computerization processes".

The concrete form of these production planning concepts is to a large extent shaped by the specific negotiation processes within the company or even the department that can often last for years. These risky, uncertain, and open-ended processes, in which the „right" planning models are selected, are generally legitimized by visions and rationalities whose validity has to be asserted in a concept rivalry with other departments. These concept rivalries replace the analysis of a universal logic of rationalization and industrialization, the well-known „one best way". Some examples of such concept rivalries follow:

(1) In an Italian electronics company (E1I), the developers of an automatic assembly line started with the vision of a deterministic course of production that could not be, and did not need to be, modified by the foremen or the workers but was completely controlled by computers. Only after an „experimental phase" lasting several years with major optimization and integration problems could those responsible for production — who previously were „wordlessly" confronted with this „modern and innovative" vision — develop their own proposals. Their concept was oriented more toward the real variances of the production process and aimed at a higher flexibility and

a weaker computer-technological integration of the individual areas of production.

(2) In a French personal computer assembly plant (E1F), it was intended to introduce a new production planning system to demonstrate the functionality of the company´s own production planning systems. Because of previous bad experiences with a similar system, the assembly department was very resistant to this proposal from the company´s central management. Instead, some of the employees developed their own vision — the vision of a very simply organized kanban assembly requiring the support of a production planning system that would have to be principally constructed in a different way. After more than two years of negotiations with the central management, they were permitted to implement this vision.

(3) In a West German clothing company (C2G), the chief manager tried to push through his vision of a deterministic, completely automatic production control without any human intervention. Only after the shortcomings of this vision became obvious, were participative introduction and inservice training courses developed by a department manageress and introduced despite the policy of the top management.

In all, it would appear that the global, comprehensive, „systemic", and often technocratic visions of the 1970s and 1980s (compare, e.g. the MAP and Saturn programme at General Motors or the robotized FIAT factories) are losing ground to less perfectionist and less totally integrated visions that also leave space for particular, simple solutions and which are explicitly dependent on the support from „below", from foremen, experienced production controllers and other users. The concept rivalry between different departments and groups of employees illustrated in the examples point to a remarkable change in production control concepts. With increasingly less success, internal uncertainties and the corresponding conception rivalries can be „absorbed" or settled by directives from above. Instead of a hierarchical mode of coordination („order and obedience"), decisions and compromises between different rationalities and action logics particularly have to be justified by the adequacy of their content and their social implementability. In this way, „competence" and „consensus" become a decisive foundation for legitimizing the results of power struggles and for guaranteeing the indispensable support „from below" for the adequate development and use of information systems.

To summarize — the design of industrial computerization processes is the outcome of open-ended and company-specific negotiation processes and the particular action strategies followed in each case are also legitimized by their promoters through reference to commonly shared values and norms. This means that information systems are only a partial solution to increasing demands of flexibility, quality and accountability; without the support „from below“ and the „intelligent“ use of production planning systems these objectives cannot be achieved. Therefore, we will discuss in the following section ways in which the commitment of the employees has been assured in the different firms of our sample.

3 Computerization and the Utilization of Labour

The change in industrial computerization and organization concepts is not only linked to a greater impact of power and exchange relationships and concept rivalries. It is simultaneously accompanied by a different and broader use of the competences and the commitment of the employees. This aspect of the computerization processes — which points to a changing relationship between organizations and their members — will now be described in the dimensions of changing qualificational and motivational requirements and different patterns of coordination.

The change in dealing with the labour force can be understood as a form of coping with contingencies just like the increased impact of unofficial power and exchange relations outlined above. The company depends on the voluntary engagement of its employees, on their contribution to the development of adequate algorithms, and on their „willingness to engage actively“ in the development of complex information systems and their meaningful integration into previous work routines.

In concrete terms, this means that in all successful processes of system development, some white-collar workers and lower management have actively been committed to „filling the system with life“, smoothing out errors, adapting it to fit the demands of their departments, and teaching their colleagues how to use the system. This (voluntary, non-enforceable) commitment is absolutely essential for a successful system implementation, because, on the one hand, the computer departments do not possess the necessary, detailed, task-specific knowledge to develop a system that fits the needs of its users, while, on the other hand, a comprehensive, optimized production planning, and thereby an „intelligent“ use of the system cannot be dictated but has to be voluntarily provided by the users — even if this voluntariness has to be guaranteed by adaequate qualification, recruitment, promotion, and gratification policies. The increasingly „communicative rationalization“ (Heidenreich and Schmidt, 1990) of work has to be supported by adequate personnel policies.

This also means that the problem of participative system implementation strategies is not „acceptance“ in the sense of a passive willingness to follow but active „commitment“. The „systemic qualifications“ required in such processes can be classified as follows:

(1) The ability to analyze one´s own work routines systematically so that they can be modelled as computer programmes.

(2) Knowledge of the „sense“ and meaning of programme structures once they are developed and the data is stored, in order to recognize the suitability (and the limitations) of programme structures that are nothing other than rigid and decontextualized „micro-worlds“ (Dreyfus, 1985).

(3) The comprehensive utilization of production planning systems as well as their development requires a general understanding of the work processes in other departments. This is even more true since the length of production runs in most companies is greatly shortened, and this leads to increased interdependencies between different departments.

(4) Data input in networked systems must also be very carefully performed as the chances of detecting incorrect input are low.

From an organizational perspective, the demands of communicative rationalization correspond to a changed mechanism of coordination that is partially based on nonhierarchical forms of concertation. An example of this are project groups that are normally responsible for the development and implementation of computerized systems. In formal or informal ways, in project groups or ad-hoc discussions among production managers, production controllers, and systems developers, a kind of public space was created in which the relevant actors could express their visions of the system to be developed, in the end creating a relatively homogeneous, consensually shared concept which was incorporated into the algorithms and data structures of the production planning and control system („hierarchy“, however, does not lose its function in this case, as consensual decisions often cannot be implemented if the project group leader doesn´t have a high status in the enterprise).

The reward for participating in communicative rationalization processes is the opening up of individual opportunities for promotion. In this respect, companies do not just control work activity directly (by orders or directives) but also and above all by personnel policies shaping the ambitions and opportunities of employees.

It can be concluded that the uncertainties linked to turbulent environmental conditions and open-ended computerization strategies lead to changes in the relationship between companies and employees: While in the Taylor-Ford regulation model, the major emphasis was on the differentiation between the labour force and the individual person reducing the dependance on subjectivity, creativity and commitment, on hierarchically structured paths of communication and highly routinized work tasks, a stronger integration of professional and personal identities, non-hierarchical forms of coordination, and more open, less precisely prestructured work tasks are now coming to the fore.

This, however, does not mean a shift to completely individualized career patterns, a clear, unambiguous improvement of working conditions, or a trend to unlimited „trust“ — in the sense of the complete abolishing of all control mechanisms.

The individualization of career patterns does not lead to a world of qualified and committed white-collar workers pursuing their individual career strategies and thus increasing the overall performance of the enterprise. Individual career strategies and personal engagement are embedded in a network of institutionalized norms and expectations. We only have to recall the payment schemes and the rules protecting against dismissal established in collective bargaining or by law, the rights of works committees, the protection against the technical supervision of work behaviour and productivity, and so forth. In general, these rules are respected even without an explicit reference to them because their violation would shake the „high-trust relations“ that are typical for qualified white-collar workers (see Fox, 1974; and Littek and Heisig, 1991).

The tacit recognition of collective norms and expectations in apparently individual strategies can be illustrated by analyzing the hidden impact of industrial relations. A common pattern in nearly all of the eleven companies studied was the extremely limited impact of trade unions and shop stewards on the computerization process. Union representatives in all three countries were not informed in advance, they did not press for the thorough training of users, and they did not request „ergonomic“ terminals and workplaces. Union representatives were unable to prevent the development of new lines of social segmentation (especially between old and young, skilled and unskilled employees), and they did not alleviate the increased employee stress related to the implementation and use of production planning systems. They did not press management to avoid layoffs. Despite the unions weakness and shortcomings, we did not observe attempts by management to take advantage of this situation through strategies designed to exclude unions from, or reduce their influence on, the computerization process. Management was more interested in strengthening and using the cooperative aspects of industrial relations — even in Italy, where management thus helped to redefine the traditionally conflictual culture of industrial relations. In Germany, in particular, this emphasis led to the intensification of traditionally cooperative relations. German „Betriebsräte“ (a kind of shop steward) generally obtained all the information they desired, even without insisting on their legally guaranteed information rights; if they opposed the storage of data related to individual workers, these data were not stored; if they insisted on appropriate training, their demands were met; if they insisted, at the instigation of the national union, on company-wide agreements concerning the introduction of new technologies, these agreements were concluded (in three of the four companies studied), although they later fell into disuse. This cooperative attitude cannot be explained as simply the continuation of traditional forms of industrial relations, however. The shop stewards did not actively participate in the computerization process, often due to their own reluctance to become involved in this new, unknown field. Instead of responding to union initiatives, management tried to anticipate and avoid union complaints — especially by maintaining an active information policy and by avoiding the storage of individual data. The non-interference of unions was crucial for employee acceptance of the new information systems. Although employees normally did not rely on the union to represent their interests, they viewed the shop stewards as a collective security net, there to protect them if their usual, more individualistic strategies failed.

A second argument against the vision of a world of highly motivated, individualized and socially integrated white-collar employees are the important ambivalences and ambiguities of communicative rationalization processes. Thus, clerical personnel report that the other side of the higher personal responsibility and the more interesting work tasks is an increase in stress and psychological strain. Furthermore, there are segmentation lines within the departments in which computer technologies are implemented — as a rule, between younger employees with a higher level of education and older employees with lower formal school qualification (the former are often forming a new kind of „participation elite" using the possibilities of participation and commitment for the sake of their own career). The privileged working conditions of the employees surveyed in comparison to those employed in small supplier companies or even the unemployed also indicate social exclusion processes.

Thirdly, the erosion of the classical, Taylorist forms of „low-trust relations" does not necessarily mean the complete dismantling of hierarchical forms of domination and control. Between „direct control" and a „responsible autonomy" (Friedman, 1977) based on an intrinsic, professional control of work behaviour arises a new form of „controllable autonomy" which is characterized by a high transparency of production flows and therefore of work results. Even if employees and their work groups are performing their tasks in a more autonomous way (especially in white-collar departments, where simple, routinized administrative tasks have been reduced), their performance can be controlled and measured more easily. With production planning and material requirement systems it becomes easier to control the stock of unfinished materials in production, the level of the production quality, the lost time due to supply problems, the degree of equipment utilization etc. This increased accountability explains the coincidence of decentralized responsibilities, and increased autonomy and the increased stress employees are reporting.

It can be concluded that the greater reliance on the commitment, the voluntary engagement and the systemic qualifications of white-collar workers and more individualized career patterns does not mean that collective rules are increasingly becoming useless and dysfunctional and that the social consequences of computerization processes are unambiguous. Such a positive vision would neglect the transformation of organizational patterns of control because computers increase the possibilities of a combination of a high local autonomy and job discretion and a central supervision of the increasingly transparent production processes.

4 National Patterns of Computerization Processes and Socio-Cultural Contexts

Up to now, we have discussed two modes of coping with uncertainties, namely, their transformation, on the one hand, into „policy" in the sense of internal, organizational processes of power and exchange, and, on the other hand, into „participation" in the sense of greater involvement of employees in communicative rationalization processes. We were able to observe these patterns of change in all three countries; this points to a broad erosion of the Taylor-Ford regulation model on the organizational level. The myth of the rationally structured organization is reaching its limits. New forms of coordination and social integration (which are characterized by an increased openness and politicization of organizational processes and a higher impact of non-hierarchical forms of coordination) are emerging.

Our thesis therefore was (with particular reference to Lutz, 1976; Maurice et al., 1986): the politicization of industrial change and the increased reliance on the commitment and the qualifications of the employees is accompanied by an increasing impact of national cultures of work and management which are institutionally embedded, e.g. in the different systems of industrial relations and the vocational training systems. We supposed that organizational structures were shaped according to the patterns of cooperation and conflict resolution, the type of skills and status hierarchies incorporated in these national institutions thus facilitating the need for higher degrees of social integration. We supposed that the „elective affinity" between national and organizational work cultures would explain national patterns of computerization processes.

This required first of all the analytical construction of these national patterns on the basis of our limited empirical evidence. Even if it is not possible to test — on the basis of only eleven case studies — the hypothesis of the existence of national patterns of computerization, we were able to construct on our empirical basis three ideal-typical patterns by distinquishing two different dimensions of computerization processes. Besides the dimension explained in Table 1 we asked whether the relevant decisions were taken by just one actor — either the organizational and data processing department or the production managers — or shaped in bargaining and exchange processes between different groups of actors.[1] (See Figure 1.)

[1] In monocentric, centralized forms of production control, homogeneous production plans and planning methods are imposed by a central computer and production planning

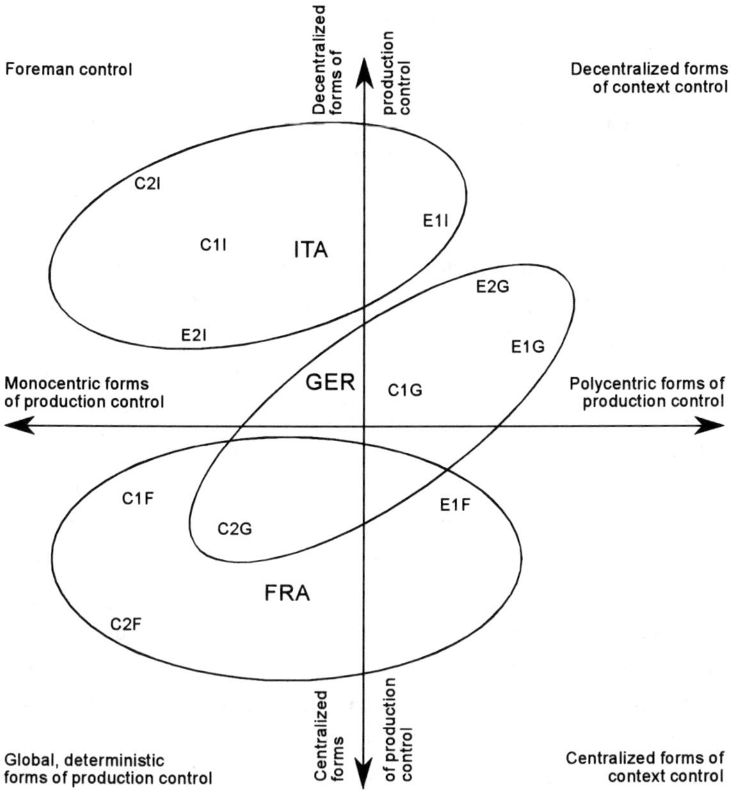

The first letter indicates the branch: C=Clothing industry; E=Electronic industry.
The number specifies the companies of a branch and a country.
The last letter indicates the country: I=Italy; G=Germany; F=France.

Figure 1: Production Control Concepts in 11 Italian, French and German Enterprises in the Clothing and Electronics Industry

department, in decentralized, monocentric forms of production control the foreman retain the essential role in determining the job order, the capacity planning etc. In polycentric, contextual forms, production control plans result from negotiation, communication and exchange among the various local production and production control units and the central department. The central department defines general production control methods and production schedules (thus guranteeing a companywide homogenity of production plans and data bases), while local production controllers and foreman are responsible for optimizing decisions locally. In decentralized forms of context control even the company-wide production control methods result from bargaining processes between different production departments, local production control departments and central production planning units.

The most important difference between the computerization processes in the three countries studied consists in the way in which incomplete planning („missing parts“) is dealt with in the relation between production and planning. The typical combinations of model-oriented global production control and empirical production control procedures we observed in the West German, French and Italian companies where we did our case studies can be briefly summarized in what follows. Then we will propose a „cultural“ explanation for these national patterns of computerization policies.

In Germany a widespread means of dealing with new production control technologies is characterized by reservations about comprehensive, abstract production control concepts in favour of practicable production control concepts. After conflict-ridden and generally unsuccessful attempts to introduce comprehensive, centralized concepts of production control, many of the companies investigated adopted computerization concepts that are not based on comprehensive „top-down“ integration.

Instead, the experiences of the foremen and their resistance towards abstract, central production control methods leads to more integrated solutions. The consequence of decentralized production control systems is an enhancement of the position of the foremen in questions of information technology and organization. Typical is a permanent, unspecular, day-to-day contact between production control and production departments.

Characteristic for the French companies we investigated is a considerable technical, social and even spatial distance between production control and production. The factories are located in the countryside, while the headquarters, the sales, EDP and production planning departments are located in Paris (or some other large city).

As a result of the spatial and social distance and the completely different cognitive orientation of the main actors, the two aspects of production control activity are separated: below and alongside the work of the main-frame computers and the abstract production control models a world of PCs and practically applicable production control data arises. The organizational and technical separation of production and production control leads to a minimal connection between the systemic and the „practice-related“ aspects of production control. This separation finds its expression in such contrasts as: production control and production; mainframe computers and PCs; theoreticians and practitioners; the company headquarters in Paris and the factories in the countryside; academic education versus training within the company; younger, formally more highly qualified employees versus older, more experienced employees etc...

What is striking about the computerization processes in the four Italian firms investigated is the temporal and technical divorce of the processes of systems development and of systems use: In a firm we investigated (E1I), for example, the conception of an automatic assembly line was worked out within a few months by a four-man project group and then the necessary equipment was purchased. This group designed the system without the participation of the middle-level foremen, the workers, the union representatives, or the maintenance and repair sections. Since the systems developers did not depend on cooperation with those who would be using the system there was no strong conflict between the two groups, but the development of a kind of side-by-side existence. This eventually resulted in a mutual blocking that led to frequent work-stoppages and the year-long minimal use of the system. In the other investigated firms, too, comprehensive material requirement planning systems were developed that left the practical work of the control and production sections largely untouched. In one firm (C2I), on the occasion of the introduction of a planned new development, the former production control system was turned off without serious consequences; in another firm (C1I) production control was actually carried out using handwritten index cards and documents; and in a third company (E2I) it was the foremen who, for the most part, actually ran production control. This parallelism of computerized ex-ante and experience-based ex-post production control (contrasted with opposition, as in France, or cooperation, as in Germany) is typical for the Italian firms of our sample.

The decisive question for the form of future planning concepts could therefore be how far production is granted a strategic role in the development of planning conceptions. The second aspect of our central „cultural" hypothesis is that national patterns of computerization are also shaped by sociocultural factors, for example by national differences in the social ranking of „mental and manual work" (differences which are certainly more pronounced in France than in West Germany). One consequence of the greater social proximity of production and planning departments in West German firms could be the stronger emphasis on the inclusion and integration of production in comprehensive planning concepts, as the computerization of production planning can more easily be dealt with as a shared project because of the greater professional and social proximity.

Such a culturalistic approach may lead to voluntarist explanations. Given the overwhelming variety and heterogeneity of norms and values it is difficult to determine in a systematic way the relevant and stable characteristics of the broader societal context. Therefore, we decided to concentrate on the institutionalized forms of national cultures, expecially on the different systems of general education or vocational training (for other institutional variables and their impact on computerization processes cf. the different articles in Heidenreich, 1993). The concentration on institutions has been justified by Child (1981, p. 329) pointing out that institutions are the result of past interest and legitimation struggles and the cultural embodiment of lines of compromise reached in past conflicts and debates.

In Germany, the national system of vocational training was initially aimed primarily at blue-collar workers, but now about half of the apprentices are trained for white-collar positions. Apprentices undergo a period of „dual" training, typically three years in length, involving both part-time study in a vocational or professional school and part-time work with an employer in the relevant field. Thus, apprentices acquire not only abstract knowledge, but also professional skills, norms, values, and patterns of behaviour which can be put to immediate use in the workplace. Significant social esteem is accorded to the official certificate („Facharbeiterbrief") awarded for completion of an apprenticeship. The holder of such a certificate is generally classified as a skilled worker, and thus obtains the corresponding pay level and status in the enterprise according to industry-wide collective agreements. The vocational certificate also opens the way to further professional training programmes, which are credentialed by a foreman diploma („Meisterbrief") or even a university degree („Diplom-Ingenieur/Fachhochschule"). This apprenticeship is the most important form of initial professional or vocational training — for both blue- and white-collar workers. Even with the expansion of higher education since the 1960s, about two thirds of each age-group begin their careers with an apprenticeship.

In France, there is a very close connection between the level of academic education and the status within an organizational hierarchy. In the absence of a developed, company-based vocational training system, emphasis is placed on mastery of abstract knowledge acquired through the educational system, while practical experience and applied knowledge are devalued. Socially recognized credentials are available only for abstract, theoretical knowledge, in the form of technical and university degrees. The low social recognition of applied knowledge is at least partially due to the fact that executive blue-collar jobs are mostly filled by employees who failed in early phases of their school career. Differences in levels of success in a highly selective school system, and in types of knowledge, deepen the cleavages between the occupational groups who design information systems and those who use the information systems in the production and production control departments.

In Italy, employees´ status and responsibilities within organizations are largely decoupled from professional schools or academic institutions. There are at least three reasons for this.

Firstly, due to the extreme heterogeneity of Italian schools, companies are reluctant to grant a nationwide, general recognition of educational diplomas or certificates.

Secondly, a high youth unemployment rate reduced the chance for young employees to claim a higher classification than older, more experienced, but formally less qualified employees.

Thirdly, in small and medium-sized enterprises (which have employed an increasing proportion of the labour force since the 1970s) scholastic achievement and formal diplomas are less important than personal relationships and non-standardized, individual credentials and qualifications. In Italy, the meritocratic coupling of school diplomas and organizational status typical of French enterprises (and — with reference to professional degrees — of German ones as well) is lacking; scholastic qualifications have only a minor impact.

Why would national differences in the relationship between educational attainment and status within organizations lead to differences in the organizational forms and processes surrounding the introduction of new computer technology? We explained previously that the exploitation of their „systemic" capabilities depends to a considerable extent on the involvement of the users and their practical knowledge of the functioning of the organization. Therefore, a condition for successful implementation is an intense, open-ended cooperation among data processing departments, production planning and control services, and production lines. The integration of experience-based forms of knowledge and abstract, company-wide control methods of production control is a crucial issue for the success of the computerization process. This „problem of reference", located at the interface of production, production control, and EDP and organization departments depends upon whether young, highly and abstractly qualified, white-collar production controllers and computer experts can cooperate with their older, formally less qualified, but experienced blue-collar colleagues in the production and production control departments.

In German firms, the development of production control systems that are closely adapted to the production process is facilitated by the presence of both employees with practical experience in production and white-collar employees with commercial or technical training. Both groups have experienced a similarly structured programme of vocational training. Moreover, logistics and EDP experts cannot simply impose their abstract, theoretical knowledge on foremen and production controllers, whose practical, experience-based knowledge is also formally recognized and enjoys high social esteem. In contrast, in the three French firms investigated, a professional and social distance is maintained between the EDP and administrative departments, on the one hand, and the production control and production areas, on the other. This distance reflects the different types of knowledge — abstract and general versus empirical and application-oriented (cf. Lutz and Veltz, 1989) — characteristic of French employees with higher and lower levels of education. In both German and French companies, the competition between younger and older employees leads to the mutual limitation of purely abstract and purely pragmatic methods of production planning and control. The integration of both logics into a unified, comprehensive and efficient information system is less likely in French than in German firms; French employees are more inclined to choose strategies of separation and distinction (cf. Bourdieu, 1984).

In the four Italian firms, there were no open power struggles and conflicts between the production, production control and systems development departments, but rather a parallel development of the two approaches to production control, resulting frequently in a year-long isolation of the new information technologies. Once the limitations of abstract, global production control became apparent — when management realized that the support of the foremen was crucial — an intense and informal cooperation sometimes developed. The difficulties in establishing cooperation between proponents of pragmatic and abstract approaches may be explained by the fact that in Italy there are no „modernized", institutionalized and socially accepted patterns of cooperation and behaviour such as the crafts model in Germany. As a result, cooperation between the production, production control and systems development departments is not blocked by status hierarchies based on education, as it is in France, but neither is it facilitated by a vocational training system in which the majority of both white- and blue-collar employees participate, as it is in Germany.

However, the use of national institutions to operationalize culture may lead to an overestimation of the internal coherence and consistency of national cultures and to a minimization of its internal cleavages. It may also promote an undue focus on nationally specific aspects of culture and obscure important transnational cultural elements (Rose, 1985). An even more radical critique points to the implicit cultural determinism of the institutionalist approach. Culture is less a kind of iron cage which determines individual behaviour; social actors can always reformulate or even re-invent „traditions". Institutions can be used in new ways by actors facing new challenges, or can even be changed.

The most important examples of a non-traditional, individualized use of cultural patterns were nearly „invisible", taking place as part of open-ended, non-hierarchical and politicized computerization processes. In project groups and other „open" bargaining arenas, traditional status differences and formally certified qualifications were less important than the ability to communicate, to structure problems, to persuade, and to reach agreement. Especially for young employees with a higher education, this opened new opportunities to demonstrate to their older colleagues (who generally had a higher hierarchical status, but a lower education) their personal and professional abilities. Because of the openness and indeterminacy of the political processes related to computerization, it was possible for these employees to define their own tasks and create new channels for upward mobility. For example, some production controllers — due to their close involvement in the development of information systems — became experts in the practical analysis of organizational and informational systems, knowing how to transform practical knowledge into algorithms and data structures. In small and medium-sized companies, in particular, it was often the case that one such expert, often young, enthusiastic, and communicative, who had been socialized within the company and who was intimately acquainted with its problems and power structures, became the key person for the organization of computerization processes. Members of project groups were sometimes able to move to different departments (e.g. from production to production management), due to their new contacts. This created „diagonal" chains of mobility across department boundaries, reducing the importance of traditional vertical mobility patterns and employees´ dependence on their immediate supervisors. In sum, computerization processes are often associated with a decrease in the importance of hierarchical, professional and status-based social divisions and an increase in the importance of individuals´ active use of their individual social and cultural competences — which are also shaped (but not determined) in local or national institutions.

It can be concluded that with the reduced impact of the classical agencies of socialization in the industrial society, the relevant sociocultural contexts of industrial companies also have to be determined anew. Modern societies seem to be characterized by the progressive erosion of external sources of legitimation and normative integration; the „non-contractual elements of contracts" (Durkheim) must increasingly be produced by the contractors themselves. Due to the limits of „low-trust relations" and bureaucratic forms of integration, organizations are experiencing an increasing demand for policies that actively promote social integration but they can rely less on external, institutionalized pattern of cooperation, participation, and conflict resolution.

On the other side, it is not clear whether a corporate culture can really be created, modified or maintained by top management or by human resources departments. Rather than attempting to impose uniformity on the diversified, culturally embedded interpretations and behavioural patterns of employees, management could follow a more promising approach by limiting its focus to the definition and strategic modification of relatively autonomous organizational arenas. Management can only attempt to shape the context for the autonomous, culturally embedded strategies of employees in such a way that the enterprise will survive in an increasingly turbulent environment. That is exactly what is happening in project groups: managers try to understand and evaluate the outcomes of these groups without interfering with the open, indeterminate processes of negotiation and re-interpretation taking place within them.

The increased reliance on a higher normative integration of the employees and the difficulties of assuring this integration by the creation of a homogeneous „corporate culture" or the use of external sources of legitimation points to another central difference to the Taylor-Ford regulation models of the postwar period which can be characterized by a reduced dependency on national cultures of work.

5 Conclusion

In summary, the previous empirical „impressions" regarding some aspects of new, post-Taylorist models of work organization and social integration should once more be contrasted in a simplified manner with the three dimensions of the Taylor-Ford regulation model mentioned above on a company level:

(1) Instead of bureaucratic, rationally structured organizations, there is an increase of openended negotiation processes and „concept rivalries" that extend beyond set areas and hierarchies.

(2) Alongside low-trust relations as a dominant paradigm of the use of labour, there is a broader access to labour´s capabilities and willingness to participate which should not be taken as unconditioned high-trust relations because the relative autonomy of employees is situated within the frame of an increased transparency and accountability and the social consequences of the increased autonomy and job discretion are far from unambiguous.

(3) Instead of a minimal normative integration of the workforce and besides the use of institutionally embedded and relatively stable norms and values of the „broader society" (such as those in trade unions, vocational training systems, and structures of social inequality), a „detraditionalized" use of culture arises. Especially younger employees use their social and cultural competences in a more individualistic way — beyond the boundaries of professionally defined competences or competences assigned to a specific hierarchical status — to support the systemic rationalization processes in enterprises and to facilitate their own promotion.

Neither the increasingly indeterminate, flexible task structures nor the more educated, qualified and self-conscious work force accustomed to making their own choices (and to taking the responsibility for them) will facilitate the continuation of the old top-down forms of organizational coordination. Post-Taylorist models of work organization and social integration will rather be characterized by broader task structures, a higher but controllable autonomy of employees, an increased participation of employees in politicized, communicative processes of rationalization, a reduced importance of hierarchical forms of coordination and control, and more individualized patterns of inequality between younger, higher qualified, sometimes even female „participation elites" and older, sometimes foreign, less qualified workers.

A new incentive for such new forms of organizational coordination and social integration will result from the emerging new division of labour between Eastern and Western Europe. Labour-intensive operations, traditional products and the classical mass production tasks can and will be delegated to the adjoining Eastern sites which can offer low wages but suffer from serious infrastructural disadvantages (in transport, telecommunication, research and development know-how, supplier networks). Only with a flexible, qualified and intrinsincally motivated workforce and increasingly flexible forms of coordination within and between enterprises can West European enterprises survive in a new, global competition on prices, quality, innovation, and flexibility.

References

Beck, U. (1986), *Risikogesellschaft. Auf dem Weg in eine andere Moderne*. Frankfurt/M., Suhrkamp.

Best, M.H. (1990), *The New Competition. Institutions of Industrial Restructuring*. Cambridge, Mass., Harvard University Press.

Bourdieu, P. (1984), *Distinction: A Social Critique of the Judgement of Taste*. Cambridge, Mass., Harvard University Press.

Child, J. (1981), Culture, Contingency and Capitalism in the Cross-National Study of Organizations, in *Research in Organizational Behavior*, Vol. 3: 303-356.

Dreyfus, H.L. (1985), From Micro-Worlds to Knowledge Representation: AI at an Impasse, in Brachman, R.J.and H.J. Levesque (eds.), *Readings in Knowledge Representation*. Los Altos, Morgan Kaufmann: 71-94.

Fox, A. (1974), *Beyond Contract: Work, Power and Trust Relations*. London, Faber and Faber.

Friedman, A. (1977), Responsible Autonomy versus Direct Control over the Labour Process, in *Capital and Class*, No. 1: 43-57.

Heidenreich, M. and G. Schmidt (1990), Neue Technologien und die Bedingungen und Möglichkeiten ihrer betrieblichen Gestaltung, in *Kölner Zeitschrift für Soziologie und Sozialpsychologie*, Vol. 42, No. 1: 41-59.

Heidenreich, M. (ed.- 1993), *Computers and Culture in Organizations. The Introduction and Use of Production Control Systems in French, Italian, and German Enterprises*. Berlin, Sigma.

Heidenreich, M. (1995), *Informatisierung und Kultur. Die Einführung und Nutzung von Informationssystemen in italienischen, französischen und westdeutschen Unternehmen*. Opladen, Westdeutscher Verlag.

Hickson, D.J. (ed.- 1993), *Management in Western Europe. Society, Culture and Organization in Twelve Nations*. Berlin, New York: Walter de Gruyter.

Hildebrandt, E.and R. Seltz (1989), *Wandel betrieblicher Sozialverfassung durch systemische Kontrolle? Die Einführung computergestützter Produktionsplanungs- und -steuerungssysteme im bundesdeutschen Maschinenbau*. Berlin, Sigma.

Kern, H. and M. Schumann (1984), *Das Ende der Arbeitsteilung? Rationalisierung in der industriellen Produktion*. Munich, Beck.

Lane, Ch. (1994), Industrial Order and the Transformation of Industrial Relations: Britain, Germany and France Compared, in Hyman R. and A. Ferner (eds.), *New Frontiers in European Industrial Relations*. Oxford, Blackwell: 167-195.

Littek, W. and U. Heisig (1991), Competence, Control, and Work Redesign: Die Angestellten in the Federal Republic of Germany, in *Work and Occupation*, Vol. 18, No. 1: 4-28.

Lutz, B. (1976), Bildungssystem und Beschäftigungsstruktur in Deutschland und Frankreich — Zum Einfluß des Bildungssystems auf die Gestaltung betrieblicher Arbeitskräftestrukturen, in Institut für Sozialwissenschaftliche Forschung e.V. (ed.), *Betrieb — Arbeitsmarkt — Qualifikation*. Frankfurt/M., Munich, Aspekte: 84-151.

Lutz, B. and P. Veltz (1989), Maschinenbauer versus Informatiker — Gesellschaftliche Einflüsse auf die fertigungstechnische Entwicklung in Deutschland und Frankreich, in Düll, K. and B. Lutz (eds.), *Technikentwicklung und Arbeitsteilung im internationalen Vergleich. Fünf Aufsätze zur Zukunft industrieller Arbeit*. Frankfurt/M., New York, Campus: 213-285.

Maurice, M., F. Sellier and J.J. Silvestre (1986), *The Social Foundations of Industrial Power*. Boston, MIT-Press.

Piore, M.J. and C.F. Sabel (1984), *The Second Industrial Divide. Possibilities for Prosperity*. New York, Basic Books.

Reich, R.B. (1992), *The Work of Nations. Preparing Ourselves for 21st Century Capitalism*. New York, Vintage Books.

Rose, M. (1985), Universalism, Culturalism and the Aix Group: Promise and Problems of a Societal Approach to Economic Institutions, in *European Sociological Review*, Vol. 1, No. 1: 65-83.

Swidler, A. (1986), Culture in Action: Symbols and Strategies, in *American Sociological Review*, Vol. 51, April: 273-286.

Wiedemann, H. (1989), *Mitarbeiter richtig führen. Motivation, Partizipation, Kommunikation (2nd edition)*. Ludwigshafen, Kiehl.

Womack, J.P., D.T. Jones and D. Roos (1990), *The Machine that Changed the World*. New York, Rawson.

Chapter 10
The Social Foundations of Technical Innovation: Engineers and the Division of Labour in France and Japan

Marc Maurice

Contents

1 The Research Context

Since the end of the 1970s, technological innovation has become a major factor in international competitiveness, both for governments and for firms. This is certainly not a new question, but it is now being asked in different terms. Thus the hitherto widely accepted concept of technological innovation as a phenomenon arising in a linear fashion from scientific progress is now being challenged. There seems to be a rather complex network of relationships between scientific development and innovation, mediated through numerous processes of feed-back and myriad loop systems. In consequence, it may be considered that technological innovation, because of its relationships to the market, „pulls“ scientific research as much as scientific research „pushes“ technological innovation. Such a change of perspective is not without consequences for the way in which firms conceive the organisation and management of research and development in its relationships with the firm´s different functions, in particular, the production and marketing of products.

However, other changes should also be mentioned here, for they too have an influence on the way in which firms today organize innovation. These changes are a product of the crisis in the model of the firm classed as Taylor-Fordist that has been evident since the late 1970s particularly in the United States and in Europe. Thus firms facing new demands in the market are obliged to seek new forms of organisation and management that enable them to be more flexible and manufacture their products in smaller runs while at the same time improving quality. This change has called into question the type of „rationality“ hitherto associated with the Taylorian-Fordist model of the firm which predominated throughout the thirty years of sustained economic growth between 1950 and 1980. Indeed, since the beginning of the 1980s we can observe a change in the technological paradigm associated with change in the model of the firm. It is sufficient to mention here the publications of Kern and Schumann (1984) and the contributions by Schumann et al. and Sabel in this volume. These different publications introduced new ways to analyse the classical issue of technology and work. However, the „societal analysis“ developed between 1977 and 1982[1] by researchers at LEST (Laboratoire de Economie Sociologie du Travail) differs from the previous approaches mentioned above. The „societal analysis“ approach is more global, analysing the firm within society and emphasising the indigenous character of the development of technology and the development of the professionalism of actors in the firm. We present here an application of that approach to analyse the process of innovation.

We shall return to these questions in our conclusion. They are mentioned briefly here because they indicate the socio-economic and scientific context in which our own research „approach“ has developed since the end of the 1970s (e.g. Maurice et al. 1987).

[1] Discussion of the „societal analysis“ approach can be found in Maurice et al. (1986).

2 The Societal Analysis of Innovation

The research on which the following observations are based has its roots in a methodology and an analytical mode first implemented in a comparative study of French and German firms conducted in the late 1970s (cf. Maurice et al. 1986). The research programme (1992) to which we refer here enabled us to compare the role of engineers in the technological innovation process in French and Japanese companies in the electrical, electronics and chemicals industries.[2]

Although the results of this latest research project will not be presented in their entirety, reference will be made to them in order to illustrate some of the characteristics of the societal analysis to technological innovation.

This will also help us to locate this analysis in relation to the comparative research that has been conducted for more than ten years by several teams in the United States, England and Japan, notably by Hull et al. (1984). These researchers were inspired partly by the analysis of the Aston School of which David J. Hickson was the inspiring force. It is not our wish to repeat here the criticisms of both content and method that we have made of this type of analysis of which some of these authors have themselves described as „culture free thesis“ (Hickson et al. 1974), and we prefer to stress the particular contribution of *societal analysis* to our understanding of technological innovation as it is organised and implemented in and by firms (Maurice 1979, 1989).

However, before developing this last point, we should mention briefly what characterises *societal analysis* in relation to other international comparative analyses (Maurice 1989).

The societal approach (AS) characterises the two most common contexts of research in this field: functionalist-universalist (FU or „cross-national“) and culturalist-particularist (CP or „cross-cultural“).

International comparative analyses show the start of a relationship between macro-social phenomena (institutions, social structures, organisations) and micro-social phenomena (for example, actors and their immediate context of action or labour). The different approaches are defined, on the one hand, by the

[2] This joint research project was carried out between 1988 and 1991 by a team of researchers from LEST-CNRS: Caroline Lanciane, Marc Maurice, Hiroatsu Nohara and Jean-Jacques Silvestre, in cooperation with researchers from the Japanese Institute of Labour in Tokyo: Ishii Toru, Ito Minoru, Kameyama Naoyuki, Yahata Shigemi.

way they treat the macro-level and micro-level analysis, and on the other hand, by the status they give to the comparability of the observed phenomena in each country (see Figure 1).

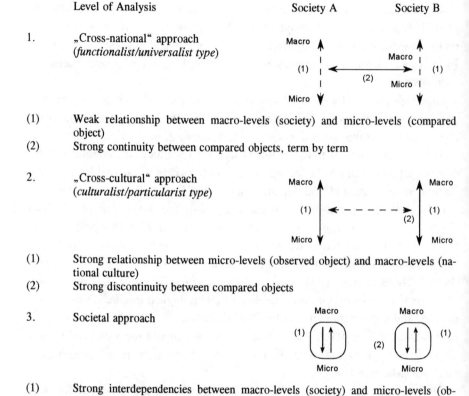

Level of Analysis | Society A | Society B

1. „Cross-national" approach (*functionalist/universalist type*)

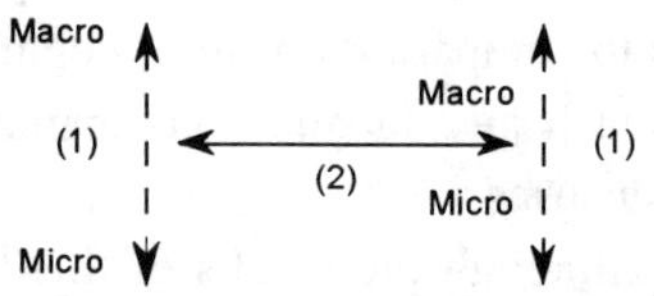

(1) Weak relationship between macro-levels (society) and micro-levels (compared object)

(2) Strong continuity between compared objects, term by term

2. „Cross-cultural" approach (*culturalist/particularist type*)

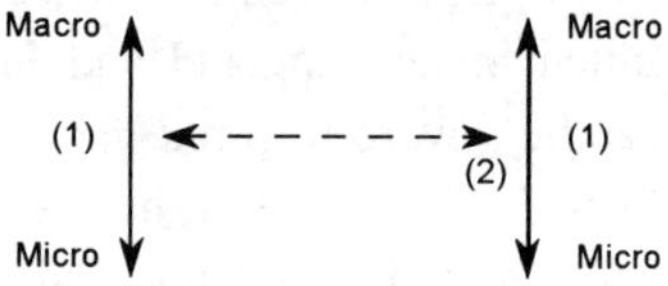

(1) Strong relationship between micro-levels (observed object) and macro-levels (national culture)

(2) Strong discontinuity between compared objects

3. Societal approach

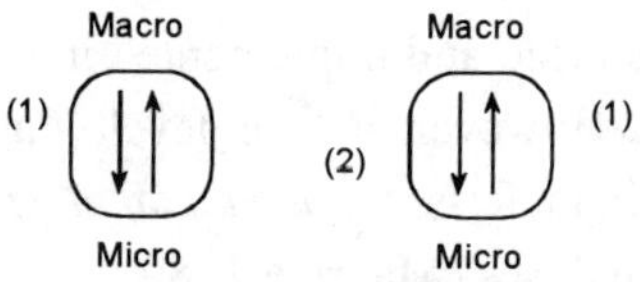

(1) Strong interdependencies between macro-levels (society) and micro-levels (observed object)

(2) Comparison of societal groups (socialized objects) founded on the paradox of non-comparability term by term of the elements of which they are constituted.

Figure 1: International Comparative Method

Thus, with regard to the relationships between the macro and micro levels of analysis:

(1) The FU approach tends not to problematise the contextualisation of the compared phenomena in each country, since this is not considered a key component in the analysis.

(2) However, the CP approach considers the „national culture“ affect on the phenomena studied in each country of paramount importance.

(3) As for the societal analysis, it attaches great importance to the relationship macro/micro, to the point of considering it as a principal analysis: the compared phenomena from one country to another are first analysed as a „social construct“ in each society.

The status of the comparison will therefore be different in accordance with each of the previous approaches.

(1) The FU approach postulates a strong continuity between the observed phenomena from one country to another, insofar as it refers to „national“ models of interpretation and to evaluation criteria that give them a universal status.

(2) However, the CP approach introduces a strong discontinuity between the compared objects by the status that they give to „national culture“.

(3) The societal analysis characteristic differs from the previous approaches, yet again, in „socialising“ the objects of analysis on account of the importance they give to the macro/micro relationships. However, in this case, these relationships are not determined by „national culture“: it is the analysis of the social process that is specifically shown that in each society contributes to the constitution or construction of the observed objects (for example, the social identity of actors, their professionalism, or their social relationships).

Consequently, comparability necessitates factors of differentiation, and the social construction of actors is possible in accordance with the different processes in each society and the factors of generalisation. The national specificities from a limited combination of components highlight the societal configurations of a majority of the observed phenomena which in this case are not postulated as rational or universal; more precisely, they are factors of a societal majority and studied in the analysis of the particularity of nation states.

In other words, even if engineers, as a category of actors in the firm, in each society are constructed by the social relationships between the education system and the production system; it remains to be said that in Germany and Japan these relationships are of a different nature, conveyed by specific processes of socialisation and organisation.

In the case of societal analysis, comparison is carried out on „societal groups", that is to say on the „contextualized" and „socialised" objects arising from relationships of interdependence between the macro-level and the micro-level. Thus, with regard to firms, it is not enough to consider them in relation to their „environment" (as is the case with contingency theory). The societal analysis treats them as already existing in society (in this sense, by multiple mediations, society exists in firms), which tends to give a different significance to environment or context notions. It is this procedure of analysis, schematised here, that was applied to the comparison of French and German firms (Maurice et al. 1986) stressing, in particular, the construction of actors and hierarchical structures (organisational and salary). We were able to show this more easily in the France/Japan comparison of technological innovation: the introduction of numerical machine-tools (Maurice et al. 1988) and the growth of professionalism of actors in technical innovation: the case of engineers (Maurice 1992a).

In this initial research project, we will present several factors established on the status of engineers in the division of labour and the innovation process in firms.

Although the results of this research project will not be presented here in their entirety, we shall highlight the framework of the analysis and the various dimensions (macro/micro) which contribute to „constructing" French and Japanese engineers and the space of technical innovation in firms. (Figure 2 outlines our approach.)

The construction of this space and its actors are therefore understood in the relationships and mediations that the firm has with society. We will present here only the factors relevant to this research project, such as the status of engineers within the innovation process and the types of division of labour. The aim of this paper is to prove that technological innovation is a complex phenomenon and that it cannot be understood by simple observation of the firm alone. It can, however, be understood when observed within society (as shown in Figure 2).

We will present here some of the dimensions that structure innovation space in firms:

(1) The R&D policy in France and Japan and, in particular, the importance of public and private research respectively.

(2) The logic of industrial growth in each country.

(3) The status of engineers in both countries, their place in the division of labour and the progress of their capacities.

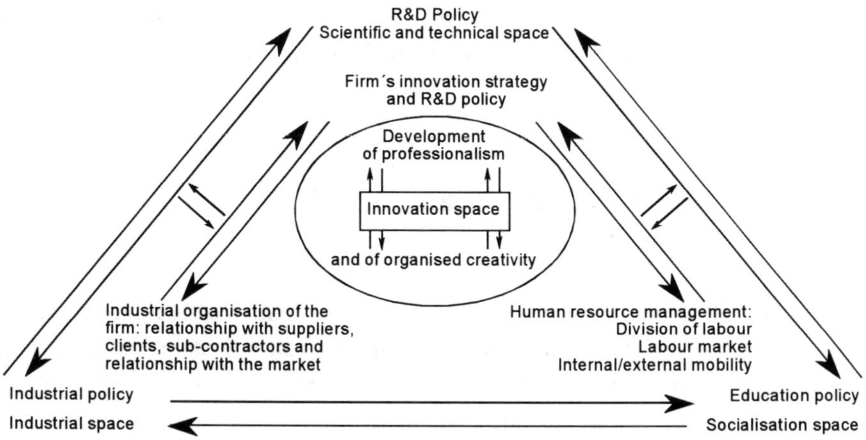

The larger triangle represents the firm´s societal context; the firm itself is represented by the inner triangle, in the center of which is the innovation space. This space is produced by the interpedendencies between the development of „technical professionalism“ (particularly that of engineers) and „organised creativity“. The innovation space is thus constructed within the interdependencies between „actors“ and „spaces“ at the level of both the firm and society.

Figure 2: The Relationships between the Firm and Society: The Construction of the Innovation and Professional Space

To conclude, we shall highlight the societal analysis contribution by a better understanding of technological innovation. This analysis is in a way „socialised“ instead of being limited to its technical dimensions (product innovation or innovation process). In this sense, societal analysis gives a larger and greater significance to the technical innovation notion whilst considering it as a social construct with different actors within firms, types of division of labour and organisation that these actors are involved in.

Consequently, the engineer often considered until now as a symbolic figure of „technical progress“ must be considered as one of the emergent actors of the innovative firm, at the same time the product and creator of an innovation which tends to convey a new form of rationality of the firm itself (Lanciano et al. 1993).

On the whole, this paper does not try to constitute a real application of societal analysis on innovation in the firm. It represents rather a test for this type of analysis which must therefore be further developed in a systematic manner in the future. These initial reflections are published along these lines.[3]

3 The R&D Situation in France and Japan, and Recent Developments

Attention will focus here on the principal characteristics of the current situation in respect of R&D in each country, taking national statistical data as a starting point. In our view, such indicators represent questions to be resolved rather than an answer to our quest for insight into the process of innovation. There are striking differences between the forms of R&D in the two countries, particularly in the roles played by industry and the state. Of the main OECD countries, France now occupies fourth place in the R&D league table (measured by domestic expenditure on R&D — DERD — as a percentage of gross domestic product — GDP). In 1990, this ratio (DERD/GDP) was 2.34 in France, behind Germany (2.88) and the United States (2.82).

However, the greatest difference between France and Japan is undoubtedly the relative contributions of industry and the state to the R&D programmes; this difference has a number of implications, as we shall see. The state still plays a considerable role in France, even if the state´s share in the R&D programme has been in relative decline since the beginning of the 1980s, as is the case in most countries.[4] In contrast, the strength of the Japanese R&D system is based on the important role played by the private sector both in the financing and realisation of research and development. This has consequences for the relative importance in each country of basic research and applied research and development (to use the categories commonly used in R&D). Thus, France leads the four main OECD countries in the financial support it gives to basic research and, to a lesser extent, to applied research. Conversely, Japan has

[3] We note that in an attempt to point out the principal tendencies in a detailed empirical research, the reflections may appear too stylized, and that each country has an image which is too coherent. The author is aware of this type of restriction.

[4] However, France is still the OECD country where government support for R&D is greatest, even if the proportion of money reserved for defence is excluded (38.8% compared with 19.3% in Japan in 1989).

seemed until now to give a certain degree of priority to development, in which it excels: As might be suspected, this also means that the universities and state research organisations play a relatively greater role in R&D in France that in Japan, where research tends to be concentrated in companies. For example, in Japan, 64% of researchers are in industry, compared with a figure of 43% for France.

The difference in the distribution of resources in each country is also reflected in differences in industrial dynamics. France is strong in those sectors that have been able to benefit directly or indirectly from state aid : the aerospace industry, electronics and computers, chemicals and the nuclear industry. These sectors are complemented by state research organisations in which a significant proportion of researchers are concentrated (30% in France, compared with 6% in Japan), not including the universities, which account for 25.3% of researchers in France and 28.5% in Japan).[5] The importance attached to development in Japan means that the country is better able to distribute its resources evenly throughout the whole of the industrial structure, both in large companies and in small and medium-sized enterprises (SMEs). These latter benefit from the highly decentralised network of technical centres located in the prefectures. Of course Japanese industry also has its strong sectors — these include electronics, chemicals, electrical machinery (including the so-called „mechatronics" sectors) and transport equipment (including the automobile industry).

In both France and Japan, the R&D situation indicated by these statistics might give the impression of a certain degree of stability over time, as if each country were condemned to its own history. This is absolutely not the case. It is certainly no accident that both countries are now seeking to strengthen what they see as the weak points in their R&D systems. France has been trying since the mid-1980s to strengthen its industrial research, particularly by supporting SMEs in their quest for greater access to technological resources. Similarly, through joint ventures between industry and government research organisations (including the universities), the government is attempting to encourage firms, whatever their size, to make better use of resources available for basic and applied research in order to develop new products with high value added. In this way, the state is seeking to compensate to a certain extent for the weak-

[5] It should be noted that France has a total of 45.4 researchers per 10,000 members of the labour force compared with 69 in Japan (source: OECD 1989).

nesses of the private sector in the area of research and for dis-equilibriums in the diffusion of technological resources in the industrial structure as a whole. Japan, conversely, is in a strong position because of its ability to develop new products which it has frequently acquired through the purchase of foreign licences, is now seeking to further develop its basic research capacity in order to gain greater independence. This is an issue of considerable importance for a country seeking to maintain its position both in the international market place and in world politics. Nevertheless, if both countries are manifesting a certain degree of dynamism and a desire to develop their R&D systems, this can only be done within the limits of the capacities they have acquired in the course of their histories.

4 The Logic of Industrial Development in France and Japan

Remaining on the macro-social level, let us highlight briefly some of the characteristics of each country´s industrial development considered in terms of a socio-economic logic associated with its own history. This is not an attempt to use historical interpretation as a principle for analysing the process of technological innovation that can be observed today in French and Japanese companies. The purpose of this brief historical survey is rather to highlight some of the characteristics of the „social construction" of the actors involved in innovation. In this sense, technological innovation is itself a „social construct", as is the „engineer" category in both France and Japan.[6]

Like other European countries, but in its own characteristic way, France has been able to ensure its industrial development and technological independence thanks to scientific advances to which it has contributed at its own level. The role of the state has been decisive in this regard; even more so perhaps than in other countries after the initial phase of industrial take-off. France is also characterised by the importance accorded to science as a principle of rationality in all areas of life, far beyond the industrial or economic spheres. Thus there are constant references in the French education system to the „exact sciences", to

[6] The following reflections concern, in particular, the status of science in the industrial development in both countries, notably by Gilpin (1975); Long (1975); see also Nakayama (1984).

the point where they form the basis for the training of élites. The training of engineers in France constitutes a significant feature of the French system: the first engineering schools were military institutions, and they were to remain oriented towards the training of an élite whose sphere of competence was to go far beyond the needs of industry. The research system is itself imbued with a certain „scientism“ which prevailed during the age of Enlightenment. It is from science that technological progress „naturally“ flows. Consequently, the development of science appears to be associated with state control and assistance, to the extent that the state controls both the universities and public research organisations. It is also the state that fosters the notion of large-scale research programmes and the idea that a certain degree of economic planning is desirable. If we add to these various characteristics the importance that the state in France attaches to defence, both in terms of industrial production and as a key factor in foreign policy, we may be able to explain both the role played by the government in the whole R&D system and the strengths and weaknesses of one part of France´s industrial activity.

Our argument, shown here as a hypothetical framework analysis that remains to be founded more systematically, is based on the notion that Japan´s development has its own specificity and that what is now known as the „Japanese model“ of the firm contains the principal characteristics of the Japanese logic of development. More precisely, the R&D system, with the characteristics that differentiate it from the French system, is itself derived from the logic of development. Although we cannot yet develop this argument at length, we can put forward the essential factors. Thus the industrial development of Japan may be divided into three main historical phases:

(1) a phase of imitation and borrowing, from the Meiji period onwards;

(2) a phase dominated by development, which culminated during the period of post-war expansion (1950-1980);

(3) a phase dominated by the strengthening of basic research (from the mid-1980s onwards) (see Figure 3).

We should stress that our aim here is not a historical one and from this point of view this cut-off is probably in part arbitrary as far as the important periods are not taken into account (such as the Zaibtatsu levels in the 1930s).[7]

[7] The following reflections are inspired from the works of: Dore (1973); Yui and Nakagawa (1989), Lehmann (1982) and Levine and Kawada (1980).

We wish to evoke here the logic of a principle process that contributes to construct in time the space of the actors in the Japanese enterprise. Consequently, the main point is that these three phases did not follow each other sequentially, as if each phase had developed by cancelling out the previous one. On the contrary, the three phases overlapped each other, with the result that each one assimilated the gains of its predecessor, as if they were each a stage in a long learning processs. We shall note here only the gains made in each of these phases and their contribution to the system of production and the R&D system that can be observed today. The phase of imitation and borrowing marked the beginning of industrialisation. With assistance from the state (particularly the Ministry of Industry), Japanese firms first had to bring in Western experts (engineers, technicians, even skilled workers) in order to install machinery and equipment purchased mainly in Europe. Similarly, Japanese experts were sent abroad to draw inspiration from the organisation of the main European institutions (legal system, police, army, universities, etc.).

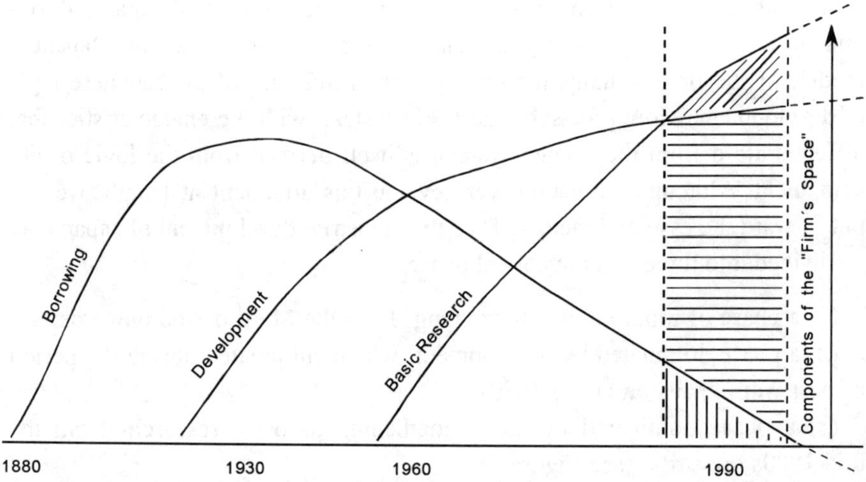

Abstract from Maurice (1992c).

Figure 3: The Three Stages of Japanese Industrial Development. How the „Japanese Model" of the Firm Has Been Built through Time

At that time, workshops in large firms appeared to be veritable „crucibles" in which engineers (recently recruited from the first universities) and manual workers dismantled and re-assembled machines imported from abroad, with each group exchanging their particular competences and know-how, both theoretical and practical. Even though engineers occupied an increasingly high status in Japan at that time, they remained in close contact with the shop floor and manual workers, which encouraged cooperation between the two groups in the exercise of their functions and skills.[8] Thus this phase, which was to continue for as long as Japan purchased its technologies on a massive scale from abroad, can be considered as an initial collective learning process, during which the technology was appropriated. Japan has sometimes been described as an „imitator" of Western technologies. It would be more accurate to use the term „developer", since from the very beginning of this lengthy collective learning process the actors in Japanese firms enhanced those same technologies by creating value added. This became even more evident in the subsequent phase.

4.1 The Development Phase

This phase, located essentially in the inter-war period, reached its zenith in the 1960s in a period of rapid growth. The period dominated by the purchase of machines and the process of learning to use their technologies was followed by one characterised by the large-scale purchase of licences from abroad (firstly from Europe, then from the United States). This period was crucial to Japan´s future, since the largest Japanese companies were to acquire particular competence in the science and understanding of „development". Indeed, in the 1970s and 1980s, numerous „missions" were sent from Europe and the United States to learn this science of development which seemed to be poorly understood in those countries.

„Developing" products by using „technologies" purchased under licence means making the transition from a „project" to a product that can be marketed. Here also, Japanese companies were able to contribute their own value added to this development process, which combined technological efficiency, product quality and the art of relating to both clients and the market.

[8] It should be noted that the leading universities in Japan had developed (perhaps for the first time) engineering faculties and institutes that were to outstrip science faculties in both numbers and resources. In France in particular, the universities concentrated more on natural sciences than on engineering.

4.2 The Basic Research Phase

Japan certainly did not wait until the 1980s and 1990s to develop its basic research capability in its universities and research institutes. However, the new factor that has emerged since the mid-1980s, and particularly since the beginning of the 1990s, is the priority now being given to the development of basic research, which is seen as one of the major issues for the 21st century and the imminent „globalisation“ of the economy. This emphasis on such an objective reflects of course the political need to acquire the genuine independence and scientific and technological autonomy appropriate to the position Japan is aiming for in the increasingly competitive world economy. Something else that characterises Japan in this sphere (and this is a further contrast with the French situation) is that this new challenge cannot be met today without the participation of the major industrial companies or groups. This has given rise to a debate among Japanese experts: is it the role of firms to run the risks inherent in basic research? Is this not rather the role of the universities or of public-sector research institutes?[9] The questions remain unresolved at present.

What should, in particular, be noted is the fact that the three preceding phases have overlapped and merged with each other in the course of Japan´s industrial development; the most striking feature of which is its rapidity rather than its lateness. Japan´s industrial „success“ has been secured over a period of slightly more than a hundred years; and the pace of this development has quickened incessantly over the years; particularly in the last thirty years.

This overlapping of the phases, the periodisation of which is undoubtedly somewhat arbitrary, has certainly contributed to the development of what is now called the „Japanese model“ of the firm. In order to illustrate this, it is sufficient to refer to the schematic outline of the model given in the appendix, which shows both the overlapping of the three phases and a cut-off point (1990) which enables us to understand how the „Japanese model“ of today has developed by combining successive forms of learning process in accordance with a logic that is different from the one found in France and the other European countries.

[9] When it is realised that the five largest firms in the Japanese electronics industry have a total R&D budget comparable to that of the CNRS in France, it is hardly surprising that they can also afford to take that risk!

The current „model“ is in fact made up of a basic collective learning process in the course of which engineers and manual workers learn to cooperate and to share their own particular competences; a science, or rather an art of development, by means of which the transition from R&D to the industrialisation and marketing of products can be effected; and, finally, basic research, which in the case of firms undoubtedly still has a specific purpose and which can be transformed, through the constant relationship with the market, into industrial applications and new products, even if it entails the company diversifying its product range. All these elements within the firm lead to the creation of conditions favourable to technological innovation, which takes place in accordance with a logic that differs from the one in which science, research laboratories and engineers are almost the exclusive sources of the new technologies.

Some experts have certainly questioned the ability of Japanese firms to take on board basic research, which might well, in the best of cases, call into question a „model“ of the firm that developed initially from the bottom up, in contrast to the opposite tendency observed in Western firms — notably in France in which the principle of hierarchical and vertical coordination is predominant. Conversely, it might equally well be wondered whether the relative stability or continuity of the „institutional actors“ (such as the education system, the R&D system, the organisation of the „Keiretsu“, the existence of networks of subcontractors, etc...) and the closeness of the relationships between them will not have the effect of adapting and thus sustaining the „bottom-up“ principle, together with the equally important principle of multiple forms of horizontal coordination.[10] Similarly, it has already been observed that several of the large Japanese companies have found an answer to the above-mentioned risks by turning their basic research laboratories into subsidiaries, as if they had had a feeling that this might disrupt the homogeneity of their organisation and give rise to damaging changes in the internal logic of their innovation processes.[11] In other words, it is impossible to separate the potential for change within firms from the institutional and relational

[10] It is through the proximity of engineers to the production process and to the market and their mobility within their company that the conditions favourable to such diversification are created. We shall return to this point in discussing the notion of „technological fusion“.

[11] Thus „basic research“ is, as it were, externalised in this case; although privileged links are maintained with the other R&D laboratories in these firms.

context in which those firms are themselves immersed or embedded, which is not to deny that changes may also take place within that context. However, history teaches us that they generally occur over long periods and they are seldom radical.

The differences we have highlighted in the R&D systems and the logics underlying the innovation process in France and Japan must be linked to those that have been revealed in a category of actors of considerable importance to technological innovation, namely engineers.

5 The Status and Position of Engineers in the Innovation Process and in the Division of Labour

5.1 The Training and Status of Engineers

It might be thought that the category of engineer is a relatively universal one, particularly if it is assumed to be essentially a graduate profession. In fact, even making a comparison between France and Japan proves to be a difficult exercise, and any attempt to estimate the number of engineers in these two countries is a risky undertaking. It is estimated that in 1989 the annual flow of graduate engineers (4-5 years´ post-baccalauréat study) in France was 15,658. If approximately 8,000 advanced technicians (2-3 years´ post-bac study) are added to that figure, the total rises to 23,658. In Japan, the flow of graduate engineers for 1993 can be estimated at approximately 122,000 (of whom 94,600 had been in higher education for 4 years, and a further 12,200 for 5 to 6 years). Similarly, the flow of graduate engineers per thousand inhabitants was 0.23 in the case off France and 0.59 in that of Japan.

However, such comparisons have to be taken with a very large pinch of salt! The length of study is not always comparable from one country to another, any more than the content of that study. In Japan, for example, the number of engineers holding a doctorate in engineering science who obtained their qualifications in the course of their professional lives is almost as high as the number of those who obtained their doctorates at the end of their university careers. Similarly, the proportion of students training to be engineers in Japan is much higher than the proportion pursuing courses in science (22% and 18% respectively), whereas in France the proportion of students studying science is relatively greater (23% to 24%).

Thus, in Japanese firms it is always more difficult to identify who is an „engineer“. The notion of „Gijutsusha“ is relatively imprecise and does not necessarily correspond to the job of a university graduate. In certain cases, it might equally well correspond to the French notion of „technician“. Such differences go well beyond the limited criteria of educational levels or the content of university courses mentioned above. Firms´ management and organisational practices contribute to the differences in the „construction“ of this category, as does the social status that each society (France, Japan) confers upon engineers and which is reproduced to a greater or less extent by firms themselves.

5.2 The Training of Graduate Engineers in France

As we saw above, engineers enjoy a relatively high social status in France as a result of the particular status of the élite engineering schools such as the Ecole Polytechnique, the Ecole Centrale and the Ecole des Mines and the existence of the great bodies for which some of them are destined, along with graduates of the prestigious Ecole Nationale d´Administration. The engineering schools[12] differ from university science faculties, which traditionally tend to train future researchers. These schools (and the associations dependent on them) play an important role in defending the title of engineer, which is protected by law. Admission to these schools is regulated by competitive examinations, with each school having its own entry threshold. This partly explains the relatively small number of engineers in France compared with Japan.

Nevertheless, this numerical weakness (which is associated with certain Malthusian sympathies in the major engineering schools) is associated with the more extensive development in France than in other countries of the „technician“ category, which is also difficult to identify in Japan. Moreover, this category, which is long established and defined and protected in sector-level collective agreements, has developed rapidly in the past twenty years, more rapidly than that of engineer. The time required to qualify as an „advanced technician“ is relatively short (2 or 3 years postbac. study), and

[12] Although an increasing number of less prestigious schools have emerged over the past twenty years, these do benefit to a certain extent from the status of the élite schools, which stand apart from the universities.

firms are keen to recruit them, seeing them as a way of fulfilling, at lower cost, their growing need for technical staff that cannot be met by the shortage of engineers. However, in France (compared to Japan), going beyond the economic argument, one can estimate that the importance is attached to the „technician" category that corresponds to the forms of division of labour (social and technical) and the social relationships between engineers and technicians; as recently confirmed in recent surveys by LEST carried out in electrical and chemicals firms.

Thus the initial training of engineers in France is less oriented towards manufacturing industry than in Japan, and when graduate engineers do decide upon a career in industry they find themselves in managerial positions more quickly than their Japanese counterparts, as we shall see. Even the élite engineering schools produce „generalists" rather than real „professionals" with particular technical competences. From this point of view, these engineers are comparable to those graduating from Japanese universities. However, firms´ practices create significant differences between French and Japanese engineers.

5.3 The Management of Engineers by Firms and their Place in the Innovation Process

In order to understand the place of engineers in the process of technological innovation in firms, it is necessary to characterise the forms of recruitment and the career paths followed by engineers in the two countries.

Socialisation through the education system is reinforced by the multiple forms of socialisation that engineers experience within firms. These forms of socialisation seem in their turn to parallel the way in which firms plan the organisation of R&D in conjunction with their other functions, as well as the relationships (and division of labour) between engineers, technicians and production workers; taken as a whole, these managerial and organisational characteristics generally reflect the dominant forms of the internal or external labour market. This is the broad thrust of the research we carried out in French and Japanese firms, of which only some aspects will be presented here. Thus analysis of innovation as we conceive it leads us to take account of professional socialisation as well as of organisation, division of labour — seen particularly from the perspective of engineers´ career forms and mobility — and personnel management practices.

However, as has already been indicated, such essentially micro-social analyses are themselves related to the essentially macro-social forms (actors and institutions at national level) that characterise each society. This can be seen, for example, when a comparison is made between the forms of education and training and the forms of socialisation and organisation implemented by firms. We shall limit ourselves here to presenting some of the features of engineers´ career paths and forms of mobility in each country, which will serve to illustrate this approach. We will then be able to show the extent to which these forms of socialisation, of organisation and of division of labour between the various categories of personnel may encourage the development of technological innovation within firms. Similarly; these innovative practices will be related to the R&D system as conceived and institutionalized in each society.

5.4 The Career and Mobility of French Engineers

In order to understand the characteristics of engineers´ careers in France, it is necessary to consider them in the context of the employment system and labour market specific to that country.

It is only recently that the French have become aware both of the weakness of industrial research (as carried out by companies) and of the need to strengthen skills in the technical departments of firms, particularly as far as the development and manufacturing of new products is concerned, or in other words, in effecting the transition from research to the industrialisation of products, a weakness of the French system, although it is strong in basic research. In order to overcome these difficulties, the tendency is to strengthen the existing occupational stratification. Broadly speaking, the French employment system moves vertically (hierarchically) rather than horizontally (unlike the Japanese system). At the top of the company, in their posts as managers, are engineers trained in the élite schools; then come the engineers and middle managers, and between them and the manual workers and supervisory staff come the technicians, who have a sort of intermediate role between production workers and the engineers in charge of technical functions such as design; development, methods and scheduling. In other words, *the division of labour* between these categories is relatively well defined by collective agreements and the job classification system and the organisational structure of the firm conserves this employment system as it incorporates it into its own management system.

Thus the recruitment of engineers (which takes place case by case depending on the short-term needs of the firm) creates a correspondence from the outset between the hierarchy of functions — and the probable careers of engineers — and the hierarchy of engineering schools. Research laboratories usually have their own recruitment rules, to the extent that they stand somewhat apart from the firm´s other functions. In principle, they recruit university graduates; and researchers in large firms are relatively immobile (except for those intended for a career in senior management, who have to serve their apprenticeships in research). All engineers advance more rapidly in the early stages of their careers than is the case with their Japanese counterparts, with this rapidity often being a function of the status of the school where they were trained.

A further difference between French and Japanese engineers is the possibility open to the former of formulating a genuine career strategy for themselves. Firms are thus obliged to take account of these strategies in their own management practices, knowing that an engineer (or a middle manager) can always change company in the course of his career.[13] In this sense, French engineers seem to enjoy greater autonomy than their Japanese counterparts in respect of career management; this is consistent with the absence in France of the lifetime employment rule that can be observed in large Japanese firms, although this notion has to be interpreted in the context of the management of those firms, as we shall see. In this respect, career planning does not seem as important in France as it is in Japan, where it is more closely integrated into the management system, particularly into the continuing training programmes that firms themselves provided (as Catherine Maurice 1991 points out in her thesis).

This type of career, mobility and job allocation has a series of consequences that are not always favourable to the development of innovation and

[13] Surveys carried out in relatively similar French and Japanese companies have often shown that French engineers and middle managers change company more frequently in the course of their careers than their Japanese counterparts.

which require firms to make certain „intangible investments“ in order to achieve their efficiency targets. Thus the professional distance between engineers, the privileged providers of the company´s technical skills and functions, and production workers (shop-floor technicians, supervisory staff and manual workers) is relatively great. In order to compensate for this difficulty, firms have for several years been recruiting advanced technicians (techniciens supérieurs), and a very recent development is the training of new categories of engineers (sometimes called „technologists“) who will be destined for careers in production or the technical departments close to the shop floor. Although such measure may have positive effects, they will further reinforce the stratification of jobs within firms and increase the need for them to invest in means of improving the communication and coordination between the various levels of the company hierarchy.

5.5 The Career and Mobility of Japanese Engineers

One initial difference must be noted at the outset: in France, a person can lay claim to the title of engineer as soon as he or she graduates from an engineering school empowered to award the appropriate qualification. In Japan, firms recruit „university graduates“ at a fixed date every year; they will continue to train these new recruits in accordance with their needs, and some of them will be destined to become engineers (mainly those who have graduated in engineering). In other words, the status of engineer is acquired in Japan in the course of a career and in accordance with the firm´s wishes. The fact that Japanese „engineers“ belong to numerous associations also contributes to the professional recognition of their status, which is further enhanced by the company itself.

This social and professional „construction“ of engineers is a lengthy process. A recent article by Kazuo Koike (1991) highlights the difference between the „slow-speed careers“ of Japanese graduates and the „high-speed careers“ of their foreign counterparts (and the careers of graduate engineers in France certainly fall into this latter category).

Japanese graduates (who will gradually be recognised as engineers in the course of their careers) are initially allocated to peripheral technical tasks selected from a much wider range of tasks; these peripheral tasks would often be entrusted in France to technicians or experienced manual workers.[14] Then, depending on how they develop, they will gradually be entrusted with more complex tasks, even if that means allocating them to areas requiring new if not wholly unrelated technical skills. This gradual extension of tasks and competences amounts to a genuine apprenticeship, management of which is rigourous and the subject of coordination between management and the central personnel department. This apprenticeship is of course a collective one, in the sense that future engineers are integrated into a group made up of more experienced employees where they receive „on the job" training which alternates with „off the job" training in courses organised by the firm. The collective nature of engineers´ career development is further reinforced by the fact that firms recruit their graduates at a fixed time every year, so that the new recruits constitute a cohort whose members maintain close relationships with each other.

Graduates take ten years on average to reach the first rungs of the middle management ladder (namely Kakaricho, or head of section, and Kacho, or head of service). This brings us back once again to the notion of „crucible" mentioned above, in which young graduates work together with more experienced employees (manual workers, supervisory staff, engineers) and then, having been rotated through a series of different jobs and having in the process accumulated a fairly wide range of skills and know-how, eventually acquire greater autonomy.

The logic underlying this kind of career development is very different from that experienced by the majority of French engineers. In the Japanese case, there is a crucial period of socialisation into the functioning of the company, its organisation and its products, on both the professional and social levels. As far as the processes of innovation are concerned, new recruits will be taught all the tasks that contribute to them; taking those tasks as a starting point, they will then use their abilities collectively in order to improve products and the production process. They will not be expected at the beginning to have any particular technical prowess, nor will they be entrusted with risky ventures, as they are in French firms, where graduate engineers are often „put to the test" in order to check their „potential" and „position" them on a

[14] This also explains why the notion of engineer is a hazy one in Japan and the technician category is relatively informal.

career path along which they can progress rapidly towards management responsibilities.

Japanese firms, which adopt a longer-term perspective in their management of human resources, base their relationships with their employees on the notion of reciprocal exchange and confidence: they grant employees a certain degree of job security and offer them training, and in return require them to show equal commitment to their work and to accept the rules by which the company operates. For the first ten years, which constitute an intense period of learning and socialisation, the difference between the pay of graduates and non-graduates is relatively slight. Pay differentials are still greater in France than in Japan. According to M. Aoki (1988), the smaller wage differences observed in Japan reflect one of the important characteristics of companies in that country, namely horizontal coordination, which Aoki contrasts with the hierarchical or vertical coordination that is more common in the West (particularly in France, in our view). This horizontal coordination reflects both the „crucible“ effect described above, particularly during the first ten years of an engineer´s career, and also the fact that technological innovation itself is a „bottom-up“ process, in which the actors work collectively to appropriate new technologies and develop new products.

Differences in pay (between graduates and non-graduates) become particularly evident after this period, when engineers reach managerial positions in the hierarchy. Nevertheless, it should be noted that this rise through the hierarchy is, as it were, legitimated by the acquisition of competences and know-how during the long period of collective apprenticeship. Selection exists, of course but in this case it is objectified and legitimated by the performance of those involved and by the assessment of their capabilities, in which different managers will have played a part during this period. Moreover, there is fierce competition surrounding the initial promotion to the rank of Kakaricho or Kacho. And if engineers´ careers seem to be more closely „controlled“ by the company, the commitment of individual engineers to their work is no less important and is subjected to a great deal of „incentive“, through both the system of virtually continuous assessment, in which both their peers and their direct supervisors play an informal part, and the „implicit contract“ which binds them to the company and which is based on a certain sharing of interests and obligations (on this subject, see also M. Aoki 1988).

5.6 Engineers in the Innovation Process

We have mentioned here only a few significant aspects of management of engineers (others were dealt with in our 1992 research report: Maurice 1992a). However, taking these observations on career development and mobility as a starting point, it is possible to highlight their links with the role of engineers in the innovation process.

5.6.1 The Relationship to Technology

It would undoubtedly be necessary here to make a distinction between various types of technologies and products. Nevertheless, it can be assumed that the position of engineers within a company and their career profiles have an effect on their relationship to technology. Thus in France, technology often seems to have been „parachuted“ into production departments by engineers, whose exclusive preserve it remains. „Engineering sciences“ is the term readily used to denote their sphere of competence. This characteristic is reinforced by the high degree of stratification observable in job categories, which leads to greater distance between engineers and manual workers in production departments than is the case in Japan. In this situation, it is the technicians who act as go-betweens; however, it can be assumed that they do not manage completely to fill the gap between the various types of knowledge and competences (both theoretical and practical), which tend to conflict with each other. In this case, technology imposed from above reduces the opportunities for establishing a continuous chain of knowledge and competences that would encourage the development of innovation (with respect to both product and process) and their continuous refinement, as can be observed in Japanese companies.

In this latter case, the development and refining of technology can be considered to come „from the bottom up“, to the extent that the „crucible“ effect means that engineers and manual workers collectively appropriate technology by considering each product or production process in its totality. In consequence, the technology is not considered to be foreign to those who have to implement it. Moreover, a strong contribution to this collective appropriation of technology and the competences underlying it is made by the multiple forms of mobility and transfer of knowledge and know-how that exist between R&D, production and marketing. In this sense, the sequence of human mobility is parallelled by the sequence by which knowledge and know-how are transferred, with engineers playing a strategic role in both cases.[15] This also has consequences for the position of engineers in the organisation and the development of their competences. Similarly, this collective appropriation of technologies leads to a genuine endogenisation of technology for main actors within the firm, meaning that it is no longer the exclusive preserve of a few specialists.

5.6.2 The Capacity for Innovation and the Development of Competences

In French firms, engineers seem to be either generalists, where they occupy managerial positions, or specialists, where they may well be isolated within their own particular technical competence. Some engineers manage to be both in succession, but a managerial position is in fact irreversible. This explains why, in an organisation in which hierarchical (i.e. vertical) relationships predominate over horizontal relationships (cf. Aoki 1988), firms feel it necessary to establish „teams“ or „project groups“ in order to overcome the risks of compartmentalisation, or non-communication, which are prejudicial both to the development of new products and to the process of innovation.

Such „project teams“ also exist in Japan, but they do not seem to function as ad hoc organisational solutions or tools to the same extent as they do in France. Project teams in Japan are not such unusual phenomena as they are in France, but fit much more „naturally“ into firms´ organisational style. Moreover, a project team will usually be led by an engineer in a managerial position (Kacho) whose authority and technical competence are recognised in equal measure.

Although it exceeds the scope of the present text to do so, it would be apposite here to analyse the formation of authority (or of hierarchy) in the two countries. In Japan, hierarchical position is based on the gradual accumulation of competences (cf. the first ten years of an engineer´s career), which gives engineers both an extended field of specialisation based on a specific technical competence and an overall vision of the various technologies used in a given product. The (hierarchical) authority of engineers is thus legiti-

[15] Furthermore, it should be noted that engineers (who are only a minority) can often follow a project from R&D to production and then return to their research or development laboratory, which necessarily enhances both ends of the sequence described here (cf. on this point C. Maurice1991).

mated by the authority they acquire in their own spheres of competence. This provides the foundations for the establishment of engineers´ relational capacities, which are of obvious importance for the efficiency of the system of knowledge transfer which underpins the innovation and product development processes. In this case; in short, to refashion slightly Aoki´s notions (1988), it might be said that vertical (or hierarchical) coordination is constructed on the basis of horizontal coordination (the development of a sphere of competences).

In the French case, as we have seen, the rapidity with which careers unfurl and the attractiveness of managerial positions tend to decrease the importance of horizontal coordination in favour of vertical coordination. As a consequence, authority relationships are based more on hierarchical power than on recognised competences. Specialist engineers themselves have an authority that is undoubtedly recognised, but it may in certain cases lack „power“.[16]

As these few observations show, the process of developing competences is not based on the same logic in both countries. This in turn has consequences for the logic underlying the innovation process in the two cases. Japanese specialists in management and organisation have put forward an image to describe the innovation process observed in Japanese firms (ideally opposed to the one used to describe Western firms). In the first case; the logic is that of a rugby team, while in the second it is that of a relay race. It is not difficult to understand that the qualities expected of the players will not be the same in the two cases.

6 General Conclusion

We shall underline here briefly two types of issue that deserve to be developed further at a later date:

(1) some characteristics of a societal approach to innovation;
(2) in what respects does this approach differ from those based on contingency theory?

[16] Or it will be relatively isolated from the day-to-day functioning of the firm: the competences of those engineers will be called upon as needed to solve difficult questions.

As we noted at the beginning of this paper, the societal approach to innovation tends to emphasise the interdependencies between the macro and micro levels of analysis. This aspect has merely been sketched here, and will be developed in a forthcoming publication. We shall confine ourselves here to observing that in this respect there is a certain degree of consistency in each country between the characteristics of their R&D and innovation systems, both at national and company level. It is not a question in this case of simple structural homologies or simple institutional or political particularities. It is a question rather of different logics underlying the „construction of spaces" in which actors interact (cf. Figure 1).

Thus, the „strength" of the French system lies both in the importance of the basic scientific research carried out with state aid in public-sector organisations and in the „qualities" of the engineering schools which confer on engineers a relatively hegemonic position within firms and in French society. These two characteristics may give rise to certain perverse effects which the government and French companies are now seeking to overcome. The weakness of the French system lies particularly in industrial research, as if firms placed too much reliance on the state to develop R&D (which is also true of vocational training). This weakness is compounded by the stratified, hierarchical organisation of French companies, which makes it more difficult to integrate functions (from R&D to industrialisation to marketing) although this is now essential for technological innovation and product diversification. This organisational phenomenon is itself associated with the „élitiste" training of engineers (particularly graduates of the élite grandes écoles) and the importance of the technician category in France. The knowledge and skills of engineers, which tend to be located in the upper reaches of the company, are associated with a division of labour that tends to impoverish the knowledge and skills of shop-floor workers. The question of how to combine effectively the competences of engineers and those of manual workers has not yet been answered, except in a few firms that have invested resources in the search for an answer. This also reflects an hegemonic concept of science that has developed historically, to the detriment of a notion of technological development more closely tuned to the needs of customers and the market.[17]

[17] These perverse effects have now been identified and changes are being made in an attempt to offset them, both in firms and among government authorities.

The strength of the Japanese system lies rather in its ability to develop, industrialize and market new products. Innovation, in this case, tends to be a gradual process and is implemented through continuous improvements to products as much as to processes. In a country with a liberal tradition, research has not been concentrated in state organisations (although they also exist); rather, firms have taken responsibility for the development and financing of R&D. This has undoubtedly made a great contribution to the development of the „Japanese model", some features of which have been outlined above with reference to engineers. The weakness of the Japanese system, which has only recently been recognised and is now being tackled, is that basic research is inadequately developed, at a time when Japan is seeking to gain real autonomy, including in this sphere. Questions are being posed in this respect, even by Japanese experts. How can basic research be strengthened without undermining those characteristics that have hitherto constituted the originality and efficiency of Japanese firms? Will the bottom-up logic hold out against the logic of a research programme that would reverse the innovation process that Westerners are now trying to imitate? The question remains unresolved.

As regards the logic of societal analysis to innovation, it tends to differ from other approaches mentioned in the bibliography. It opens a particular path between a „particularist/culturalist" approach and a „universalist/rationalist" approach that is beyond opposition. This type of approach, illustrated here by a comparison of engineers in the innovation process in France and Japan, is not restricted to noting the different choices or strategies adopted by firms in these countries when confronted with similar problems. It consists rather of identifying elements which are often comparable when taken in isolation but which combine differently with each other in each country. The existence in Japanese firms and in those in other countries, of such specific combinations highlights both the universal nature of the search for (an always limited) rationality and the variability, from one society to another, of the routes and means by which that goal is achieved. In this sense, the „rationality" of the Japanese firm and that of its French counterpart may turn out to be different.

Thus the variability of the forms of managing and organizing the innovative firm and R&D is not merely a „temporal" phenomenon (for example, that associated, in the case of Japan, with the „development lag" relative to the USA and other Western countries); from the perspective of the societal approach, this variability may equally well be a „spatial“ phenomenon (i.e. existing between countries at equal levels of development).

As Figure 2 in respect of the phases of Japan´s economic development shows, such spatial variability is itself constructed in time and is thus susceptible to transformation or evolution.

Thus the innovation space within the firm, as observed at any given moment, corresponds to a certain temporality. Consequently, each national innovation space (conceived in terms of the interdependencies between the firm and society) is itself constituted within a time/space system characteristic of each society.

Such an approach offers not only greater insight into the processes that constitute the innovation space observed today but also into the processes that may contribute to future changes in that same space.

References

Aiken M. and J. Hage (1971), The Organic Organization and Innovation, *Sociology*, 5.

Aoki M. (1988), *Information, Incentives, and Bargaining in the Japanese Economy*. Cambridge University Press, Cambridge.

Aoki M. (1990), Towards an Economic Model of the Japanese Firm, *Journal of Economic Literature*, March.

Brossard M. and M. Maurice (1974), Existe-t-il un modèle universal des structures d´organisation?, *Sociologie du Travail*, 4. (Translation: „Is there an Universal Model of Organization Structure?“, *International Studies of Management and Organization*, 3, 1976.)

Burns T. and G.M. Stalker (1961), *The Management of Innovation*. Tavistock, London.

Clark P. (1987), *American Innovation*. De Gruyter, Berlin, New York.

Coriat B. (1991), *Penser à l´envers : Travail et organisation dans l´entreprise japonaise*. Christian Bourgeois, Paris.

Dore P. (1973), *British Factory, Japanese Factory : The Origins of National Diversity in Industrial Relations*. Allen and Unwin, London.

Gilpin R. (1975), Science, Technology and French Independence, in Dixon T.L. and Ch. Wright (eds.), *Science Policies of Industry Nations*. Praeger, London.

Hickson D.J., C.R. Hinings, Ch. MacMillan and J.P. Schwitter (1974), The Culture-free Context of Organization Structure, *Sociology*, 8.

Hickson D.J., Ch. MacMillan, K. Azumi and D. Horvath (1979), Grounds for Comparative Organization Theory: Quicksands or Hard Core?, in Lammers C.J. and D.J. Hickson (eds.), *Organizations Alike and Unlike*. Routlege and Kegan Paul, London.

Hull F., J. Hage and K. Azumi (1984), Strategies for Innovation and Productivity in Japan and America, *Technovation*, 2.

Kern H. and M. Schumann (1984), *Das Ende der Arbeitsteilung?* Beck, Munich.

Koike K. (1988), *Understanding Industrial Relations in Modern Japan.* MacMillan, London.

Koike K. (1991), Le développement professionnel des „cols-blancs", *Sociologie du Travail,* 1.

Lanciano C., M. Maurice, H. Nohara, J.J. Silvestre, T. Ishii, M. Ito, N. Kameyama, T. Kudo and S. Yahata (1991a), Innovation : acteurs et organisations. Les ingénieurs et la dynamique de l'entreprise. Comparaison France-Japon, Research report LEST-CNRS, 500, Laboratoire d'Économie et de Sociologie du Travail, Aix-en-Provence.

Lanciano C., M. Maurice, H. Nohara and J.J. Silvestre (1991b), Innovation : acteurs et organisations. Les ingénieurs et la dynamique de l'entreprise. Comparaison France-Japon, Report LEST-CNRS, 42, Laboratoire d'Économie et de Sociologie du Travail, Aix-en-Provence.

Lanciano C., M. Maurice, H. Nohara and J.J. Silvestre (1993). L'analyse sociétale de l'innovation: genèse et développement. LEST-CNRS, Working paper, 35, Laboratoire d'Économie et de Sociologie du Travail, Aix-en-Provence.

Lehmann J.P. (1982), *The Roots of Modern Japan.* Macmillan, London.

Levine S.B. and H. Kawada (1980), *Human Responses in Japanese Industrial Development.* Princeton University Press, Princeton.

Long D.T. (1975), The Dynamics of Japanese Science Policy, in Dixon T.L. and Ch. Wright (eds.), *Science Policies of Industry Nations.* Praeger, London

Marsh R. and H. Mannari (1976), *Modernization and the Japanese Factory.* Princeton, Princeton University Press.

Maurice C. (1991), Culture et rationalité dans les formes de gestion des ressources humaines. Le cas des ingénieurs de l'électronique. Une comparaison France-Japon, Doctoral thesis. Institute for Political Studies, Paris.

Maurice M. (1979), For a Study of the „Societal Effect": Universality and Specificity in Organization Research, in Lammers C.J. and D.J. Hickson (eds.), *Organisations Alike and Unlike, International and Inter-institutional Studies in the Sociology of Organisations.* Routledge and Kegan Paul, London.

Maurice M. (1989), Méthode comparative et analyse sociétale : les implications théoriques des comparaisons internationales, *Sociologie du Travail,* 2.

Maurice M. (1992a), L'organisation et la dynamique de la R/D dans les entreprises japonaises, Working paper LEST-CNRS, Centre National de la Recherche Scientifique, Aix-en-Provence.

Maurice M. (1992b), Le transfert des techniques de gestion est-il possible?. Le cas des techniques de gestion associées au „modèle japonais" de l'entreprise, Paper to the Actes du Séminaire Condor, Ecole Polytechnique, Paris.

Maurice M. (1992c), The Social Bases of Innovation. Research report, LEST-CNRS. Centre National de la Recherche Scientifique, Aix-en-Provence.

Maurice M., F. Eyrand, A. d'Iribarne and F. Rychner (1987), Des entreprises en mutations dans la crise, Research report, LEST-CNRS, Centre National de la Recherche Scientifique, Aix-en-Provence.

Maurice M., H. Mannari, Y. Takeoka and T. Inoki (1988), Des entreprises françaises et japonaises face à la mécatronique : acteurs et organisation de la dynamique industrielle, Research report, LEST-CNRS. Centre National de la Recherche Scientifique, Aix-en-Provence.

Maurice M., F. Sellin, and J. Silvestre (eds.- 1986), *The Social Foundations of Industrial Power,* MIT Press, Boston.

Nakayama S. (1984), *Academic and Scientific Traditions in China, Japan and the West,* University of Tokyo Press, Tokyo.

OECD (1989), *Science and Technology Indicators Report*. OECD, Paris.
Sakakibara K. and E. Westney (1985), Comparative Study of the Training, Careers and Organization of Engineers in the Computor Industry in the United States and Japan, *Hitotsubashi Journal of Commerce and Management,* 1.
Yui T. and K. Nakagawa (eds.- 1989), *Japanese Management in Historical Perspective.* University of Tokyo Press, Tokyo.

Chapter 11
Lean Production in Japan: Myth and Reality

Ulrich Jürgens

Contents

1 The Messages of the MIT Automobile Study

The German debate on new production concepts in the 1980s, initiated by Kern and Schumann (1984) revolved around the „Facharbeiter“ (skilled worker) as the central figure of work re-organisation in Germany. More recently, this debate has been confronted with the advent of lean production concepts in the early 1990s. The Japanese oriented model of lean production seems to stress similar issues to those raised in the debate of the 1980s such as task integration and group work, but at the same time both approaches differ fundamentally.

However, the ensuing comparison of these two models has been flounded upon misconceptions and the many myths which surround the role and the functioning of lean concepts such as team work in Japanese production plants. The purpose of this contribution is to discuss some of these myths and to elaborate upon some of the cross-national differences between the approaches towards group work which derive from the discussion of new forms of work in the 1980s and the current lean production debate. Japan — as removed as it is from Western Europe, and not only in the geographical sense — has always been fertile ground for myths. Thus there is a tendency on the part of Western observers here to sensationalise and glorify individual phenomena, without any closer analysis of either their characteristics or the conditions required for their effectiveness.

The lean production debate is largely sustained by the „Japanese Myth", with many arguments drawing their persuasive force from here. This also applies to the report by the MIT (Massachusettes Institute of Technology, USA) authors, Womack, Jones and Roos (1990), entitled „The Machine that Changed the World". Because the study fails to deal with differences between companies or changing trends in the concepts observed, their description of Japanese reality is pallid and often stereotyped. In view of the massive potential and many attractions of the concept of lean production this is clearly unsatisfactory. Lean production, the back-cover text promises, „welds the activities of everyone from top management to line workers, to suppliers, into a tightly integrated whole that can respond almost instantly to marketing demands from consumers. It can also double production and quality, while keeping costs down. Its adoption, as it inevitably spreads beyond the auto industry, will change almost every industry and consequently how we work, how we live, and the fate of companies and nations as they respond to its impact." For the traditionally organised Western manufacturers, the message thus reads „change or die", and this is certainly the bottom line of the MIT study.

The discussion on lean production is now taking place on several levels, and these must be dealt with separately in any critical examination. First, we have the level of reality, primarily that of the Japanese companies, which the MIT authors describe using this concept. Then there is the MIT report, which proclaims lean production is a revolutionary new concept.Finally there is the reception level — the study has led many to eagerly pour old wine into the new bottles. So what do the MIT authors mean by „lean production", and to what extent does Japanese reality reflect their interpretation?

Regarding the above questions, the following two basic elements of the lean system will be discussed by way of illustration: teams and continuous improvement (kaizen), in an attempt to try to refute a few myths and misunderstandings. But first a further misconception will be dealt with and another essential message of the MIT study should be addressed. A misunderstanding heard frequently in the current discussion is that lean production explains the competitive strength of Japanese companies. This amounts indeed to a *misrepresentation* of the concept of lean production and its explanatory power.

The MIT study itself contains no economic indicators such as costs or profits. It is astonishing at first that the MIT authors have almost entirely neglected this aspect, given that there are other factors at play here which are further consolidating Japan´s competitive edge. A few of these will be touched upon briefly:

(1) The study deals neither with the issue of capital costs nor with the conditions for the mobilisation of capital for investment purposes. Yet there were huge differences in these respects in the past: the cost of capital for large enterprises in Japan amounted to around 2%, while the figure for western firms was 6-8%. The reasons for this difference can be traced to the exceptional savings behaviour of Japanese households and to the special organisational structures of the Japanese economy, the *keiretsu*, or corporate alliances of banks, commercial and industrial enterprises, and the ring of suppliers dependent upon the final-product manufacturers. Of course the crucial role these networks play is not restricted to questions of capital costs or mobilisation, and the special ties should also be considered which exist between the state and business, with the Ministry of International Trade and Industry, MITI, at the hub.

(2) A further point which the study fails to address is the issue of personnel costs. Here, the famous pyramid system of suppliers comes into effect, in which wage rates on the lower level amount to just over half the rates paid by the final-product manufacturers. However, according to the recent VDA data, as far as overall wage costs are concerned, average rates in Japan and the Federal Republic of Germany have gradually come into line.[1]

(3) Disparities in taxes and other contributions to the state are overlooked.

(4) Finally, the MIT study also disregards for the most part collective bargaining and questions concerning industrial relations. Differences in working hours, for instance, are not addressed. During the 1980s, the gap between Germany, with approximately 1,500 annual working hours per employee, and Japan, with around 2,300 hours, remained almost constant;[2] due to the recession working hours were down at 1959 hours in 1993 (1,399 in Ger-

[1] According to these data, in 1994 the labour cost differentials were DM 57.06 in Germany versus DM 45.47 in Japan (*VDA Pressedienst,* January 31, 1995, Overview 12).

[2] Estimates suggest that 10 million of the 60 million employees in Japan work 3,000 hours per year (see Mineshige 1992, p. 29).

many). In addition, there is the almost unlimited flexibility in Japan regarding overtime, which itself can be considered an integral component of lean production.

Moreover, direct costs resulting from the industrial relations system, such as release from duties for works councillors and works meetings, are not mentioned.

These and other factors should certainly be taken into consideration when seeking to identify the reasons underlying Japan´s competitive edge. The lean production concept *alone* does *not* suffice as an explanation. These factors, central to the current discussion on German competitiveness, were left out of the equation, as it were, by the MIT authors but, in the light of their objective, this can be justified. What mattered to them was targeting the study´s message — and its inherent demand for action — unambiguously to the proper quarters, namely management. Their message to management was: it is not the state with its taxes, nor is it the unions with their pay and other demands, which are at the root of the problem; rather, it is *management* and the system it has created, and it is here that the changes must be initiated. The MIT study does not allow management to pass the buck. In this sense the international debate on lean production is on a different plane from the current domestic German discussion on the country´s competitiveness, and it must be recognised that German management accepts the message at the heart of the MIT report.

2 Criteria for Lean Production in the MIT Study

So what exactly do the MIT authors mean by lean production? A close reading of the study with this question in mind elicits more difficulties than one would have expected, considering the enthusiastic reception given to the study. Nowhere in the report is there a clear definition of the necessary and sufficient conditions for lean production. The concept remains vague and in need of interpretation, and hence it is no surprise that it is currently being used to legitimise all kinds of measures (the planned reduction of capacity in General Motors in North America, for example, was termed „leaning up“ by GM´s president) (Zola 1992, p. 3). More precise criteria for lean production were in fact developed in the course of the MIT project itself. This was done in connection with the distinction between production systems as either *fragile/lean* or *robust/buffered*; Japanese firms were found to correspond most closely to the type „fragile/lean“ while production organisation in western firms was closer to the type „robust/buffered“.

The determining factors were divided into three groups:

(1) Those concerning company practices related to the orientation towards „no errors, no buffers“ in the organisation of production: proportion of rework area to the total production area, buffer zone capacity, stock-keeping policy.

(2) Features of the working system: percentage of employees working in teams, percentage of employees in representative groups, improvement efforts, and a few indicators pertaining to responsibility, mobility, etc.

(3) Features relating to personnel development: selection of employees in recruitment, performance-linked payment, etc. (MacDuffie 1989).

It appears that the management index: whether a company is lean or not lean, is essentially determined by the variables for the working system, primarily by the existence of teams and improvement efforts.

Krafcik, who together with MacDuffie carried out the assembly plant survey for the MIT project, devised a simplified management index for his calculations in order to measure the characteristics for lean or not lean. This index has four dimensions:

(1) The size of the rework area as an expression of the extent to which the manufacture of the product is accomplished correctly and flawlessly from the start.

(2) The degree of visual control over the production process; here, there are four different influential factors: constant feedback to the workforce, on quality and output for example; the level of utilisation of statistical process control to ensure quality; the general level of order and cleanliness in the factory, and the stock-keeping system in operation (storage on high shelves along the belts, for example, is not considered compatible with the principles of lean production). The classification of the firms in these categories was carried out based on subjective judgements after site visits to the plants.

(3) Distribution of teams; here, evaluation was based on a scale of one to three. Grade One was given to plants in which the majority of divisions had

been organised in teams for at least one year, and each team had a team leader who also worked in production; Grade Two was given if some divisions were organised in teams, and team leaders performed only some production work; Grade Three, finally, was used to denote plants in which no division was organised in teams.

(4) The fourth and final criterion is the rate of unplanned absenteeism.

MacDuffie and Krafcik apply their definitions for lean production within the context of their worldwide comparative study of assembly plants and their attempt to explain the differences in performance observed. The authors of the summary report (Womack et al. 1990) use the term comprehensively for the entire process chain, from product development and supplier relations to dealer-customer relations, and this usage is naturally at the expense of its analytical precision. However, it is the results of the assembly plant comparison that lend the study its explosive nature. Shocking above all are the differences in the productivity of mass producers which have been quoted again and again in the ensuing discussion. Japanese-run assembly plants in Japan require an average of 16.8 hours to produce a motor vehicle (and the transplants in North America are not far behind); 35.5 hours, by comparison, are required in plants belonging to European manufacturers in European locations. Differences in quality are less pronounced, but follow the same pattern.

These differences in performance can partly be explained by the characteristics of the management index (from lean to buffered), as Krafcik demonstrates in his calculations. Table 1 presents these calculations in relation to productivity and quality, with additional reference to the level of technology in the assembly plant in question. These figures, which were not included in the book of Womack et al. (1990) — perhaps because the results proved to be somewhat less spectacular — are more telling with regard to the relationship between management strategy and performance than the figures mentioned above. Here, the differences in performance are not as strongly characterised by the „Japan Effect“. The relevant difference for a Japan-Germany comparison lies in the company type „high tech-robust/buffered“, which is characteristic for traditional work organisation in Germany, and „high tech-fragile/lean“, which, according to the MIT study, is predominant in (though not only native to) Japan. The differences in performance are still considerable when the technological level is taken into account — e.g., the productivity differential is around 40% — but they are no longer in the region of the 100% superiority which the MIT authors like to trace back to the lean production concept.[3]

Table 1: Performance Levels by Technology/Management Categories

	Productivity (average hours/vehicle)	Quality (average assembly defects/100)
Low tech-robust/buffered	40.0	104.9
High tech-robust/buffered	29.6	80.4
Low tech-fragile/lean	29.5	86.5
High tech-fragile/lean	21.1	59.8

Source: MacDuffie and Krafcik (1989, p. 13).

3 The Team Concept in Japanese Production Organisation

The team concept quite clearly plays a key role in the lean production system. This is where the veracity of the lean production system in Japan must be dissected. According to the MIT study, an average of almost 70% of Japanese assembly plants were organised in teams in 1989, compared to only 0.6% of European plants (Womack et al. 1990, p. 97).

We have already reviewed the definition of „team" underlying these figures. This definition is tailor-made for the Japanese context, where the *„hancho"* position traditionally represents the first step on the career ladder. The „hancho" in Japanese plants is a „playing leader" and is not exempted from production work. His function corresponds most closely to that of the „Kolonnenführer" (small group leader), a traditional job desription in German factories quite similar to the „hancho". The title in fact directly implies the existence of a team: „han" means a small group in Japanese, „cho" denotes a leader. The „hancho" is thus an easily identifiable indicator for the existence of teams; however, if there is no hancho, it does not necessarily follow that the organisation of work is not based on teams.

[3] Cf. the study´s back-cover quoted at the beginning of this paper and passim in the text itself.

Just as one would be correct in hesitating before interpreting the existence of gang leaders as indicators of team-based work organisation in British firms, one could have the same doubts about Japan. In this respect, the team definition discussed above is an oversimplification. This should not imply that teamwork is not widespread in Japanese factories. However, the type of teamwork that exists in Japan differs considerably from the conception prevalent in Germany in the 1980s (see on group work Roth and Kohl 1988; Minssen, Howald and Kopp 1991; Steinmann, Heinrich and Schreyögg 1976; Muster 1990; Lieske 1992).

The MIT study does not in fact tell us much about the characteristics of teamwork — what is emphasised is high flexibility in labour deployment, the range of skills of individual team members (multiskilling), the level of task integration, and the degree of autonomy afforded to the teams. A sweeping definition spares the authors the difficulty of distinguishing between the different notions of group work which exist in Japan and in the transplants on the one hand, and in traditional western conceptions on the other. This vagueness has its advantages for trade-union supporters of group work too, since demands for group work can now be justified by a reference to Japan and its competitive strength. But this support will be based, most probably, on a conception of group work as the result of socio-technical systems design of process and jobs, of an appropriate restructuring of tasks, of „time sovereignty" for the group with regard to the pace of the work and of a certain degree of autonomy of the group within its area of responsibility.

Group work in Japan is not linked with certain task characteristics or socio-technical systems design. It is related to personnel department. The *group* is the vehicle for social integration in the firm and for further training. A worker´s behaviour in the group is decisive for promotion, wage, and personal development opportunities; the group penalises unseemly behaviour; it is both a social network and sanctioning authority. We should not, however, over-emphasise the cultural influences or the alleged „innate" team spirit of the Japanese. This team spirit is also the product of precisely coordinated „social technologies". *Three forces*, in particular, should be mentioned in this regard (for the following cf. the description of the „Toyota philosophy" as a system in Jürgens et al. 1993, pp. 40-51):

(1) The organisation of a comprehensive just-in-time approach to all processes in the factory. Without the frequent support and help of colleagues, individuals would not survive daily working life. The whole basis of the just-

in-time (JIT) system is that it constantly seeks to reduce buffers of material and personnel, the limits to this process being determined by analysing the effects on quality, and to induce continuous improvement to eliminate bottlenecks. This leads to constant and severe strain on the individual in the form of „process pressure“, and this is one of the main reasons for the solidarity found in the teams.

(2) The hierarchical structure and the supervisory levels on the Japanese shopfloor. It is simply not true that Japan is a paragon for the eradication of hierarchies. This is shown in Table 2.

We can see that on and near the shopfloor there are many hierarchical levels. The authority of these superiors is not restricted by self-regulation rights for the group. Thus „self-organisation“ in the sense of ideas about democratising working relations does not exist on the shop floor. All scope for decision-making, ostensibly in the hands of the group, actually lies within the responsibility of the superior. The structure is really one of multiple supervision, which also contributes to cohesion within the group.

Table 2: Management Levels and Organizational Units on the Japanese Shopfloor*

Hancho („team leader“)**	403 1:6 WA	„team“
Kumicho („group leader“)**	140 (148)*** 1:17 WA	„group“
Kocho or Kakaricho (foreman)	8 (14)*** 1:297 WA	„group area“
Kacho (head of department)	4 1:593 WA	„department“
Bucho (senior head of department)	1	„central department“

* Data based on a study of a Japanese car assembly plant; cf. Jürgens and Strömel (1987, p. 109).
** Translation from the Japanese used in the company brochures.
*** Number of deputies.

(3) The personnel evaluation system, which starts with the individual. We often underestimate the role of the personnel evaluation system, since we are used to looking for incentive functions primarily in the pay system. Japanese sociologists, in contrast, believe that the evaluation system, which has a very differentiated approach to work attitudes and habits, plays an essential guiding role in group organisation. The results of the personnel assessments con-

ducted twice a year have considerable influence on the pay cheque especially on bonus payments, and are primarily decisive for the speed of advance on the very narrow-runged career ladder, which apart from formal promotion positions, offers many informal managerial and prestige posts. All members of the core workforce progress up this ladder from more or less the same starting point with greater or lesser speed; the continuity between the bottom and the top is much higher than in western firms. All core workers — to emphasise this point once again — are expected to attain lower management positions in the course of their working life. The personnel evaluation systems are structured in such a way that individual output is less important than criteria such as group orientation and involvement in improvement efforts. The personnel evaluation system is thus central in explaining the high degree of shop discipline and group orientation in Japanese factories.

The enormous differences between the Japanese concept of a team and the understanding of teamwork in Germany in the 1980s should already be becoming clear. Table 3 presents a summary of the different models of production organisation, and helps to point out other differences.

Table 3: Models of manufacturing strategy

„German“	„Japanese“
skilled worker in production	semi-skilled workers, usually with a high initial qualification
uncoupled to production cycle	coupled to production cycle
increase in job content	high flexibility of deployment
mixed teams	homogeneous teams
high partial autonomy of teams through technological design	low partial autonomy of teams through JIT design

A review of the debate in Germany in the 1980s (see Jürgens, Malsch and Dohse 1993) indicates that a model of work organisation for the future has developed here which has the following characteristics:

(1) An endeavour to use under-utilised skilled labour potential and the maximum possible deployment of skilled labour in manufacturing jobs. At the same time, this led to pressure from these workers, who expected that work structures in production should accordingly be appropriate to skilled labour.

(2) Decoupling of human work from the production cycle, in particular by eliminating assembly line work as far as possible through automation, or by

establishing manufacturing islands, box manufacture and other forms of work organisation.

(3) Expanding job content with a view to creating more challenging activities offering opportunities for learning and personal development.

(4) Creation of mixed teams comprising specialists and workers performing „simple" tasks, who share the same area of responsibility, but have limited possibilities for mutual replacement and task rotation, thereby avoiding excessive training efforts and claims for higher pay.

(5) Partial functional autonomy through process and technological design, so that the usage of time to confine one´s duties is at the worker´s discretion.

The most important motivators in this new style of work organisation were considered to be meeting the desire for enriched job content as well as responsibility and partial functional autonomy in the execution of work. The concept was strongly influenced by the approaches developed in the course of the Swedish discussion.

These characteristics stand in stark contrast to the *principles of work organisation in Japanese firms* (see Fujimoto 1993):

(1) Here, there is no skilled-worker status. Production workers have the same initial qualification and development possibilities as skilled blue-collar and white-collar workers.

(2) Work is closely coupled to production cycles; the assembly line remains the backbone of production and work organisation — and here one-minute cycles are the norm; functional procedures are highly standardised, and only the kaizen process affords individuals some degree of freedom.

(3) The endeavours are not targeted towards broadening job content, such as has been achieved in Swedish factories, but rather towards increasing deployment flexibility through on-the-job training and job rotation; thus, the aim is not to design jobs such that the task performed corresponds to the skills of the worker, rather, the worker should be able to switch between different short-cycle tasks in a given time period.

(4) The teams are homogeneous, the aim being to ensure mutual replaceability.

(5) The teams have negligible partial autonomy with regard to their control over the way tasks are performed. Control over the pace of work does not exist, due to the restrictions inherent in the just-in-time production system.

The motivating factors in this style of work organisation are not job content and partial functional autonomy. Whatever the motivating factors in Japan may be — and this is a complicated issue — we should be clear about these conceptual differences when talking about the adoption of lean management.

As we have seen, the process design and the hierarchical structure afford the team neither free disposal over time nor opportunities for self-regulation. On the contrary, procedures are highly standardised and discipline in maintaining these standards is considered of prime importance (thus, Japanese assembly workers are not able to „work ahead of their work station" in order to gain time for a break later). So in what sense do the teams in Japan have creative scope? This question leads us to the second key concept of lean production.

4 Continuous Improvement Practices — Kaizen

The answer is not to be found in the performance of production tasks themselves, but rather in the contribution made to improvement efforts. Japanese teams do not have a significant amount of discretion with regard to Kaizen either. The problems and the approaches to them underlying the improvement efforts are mainly given by the prevailing circumstances: the MIT authors also stress that „simply going through the motions of mass production with one´s head down and mind elsewhere quickly leads to disaster with lean production" (Womack et al. 1990, p.103). The no-buffer, no-error target demands constant improvement efforts and the employees do in fact have opportunities for qualified participation in problem-solving in their respective areas. One can go so far as to say that daily work consists at all times of *extremely repetitive* and *highly standardised* tasks; an enormous amount of discipline and pressure is exerted in order to maintain standards. The creative scope of the teams lies in their freedom to change these standards and in this sense to develop solutions to problems. The teams´ suggestions, after a formal though unbureaucratic process, set the new standards which will determine the daily routine in the future.

The MIT study is, it has to be said, perfectly clear on this point. Despite this awareness, the authors insist that the system is both „humane" and a model for the future. In perhaps the most important passage in the study they assert: „We agree that a properly organized lean-production system does indeed remove all slack — that´s why it´s *lean*. But it also provided workers with the skills they need to control their work environment and the continuing challenge of making the work more smoothly. While the mass-production plant is often filled with mind-numbing stress, as workers struggle to assemble unmanufacturable products and have no way to improve their working environment, lean production offers a creative tension in which workers have many ways to address challenges. This creative tension involved in solving complex problems is precisely what has separated manual factory work from professional „think“ work in the age of mass production“(Womack et al. 1990, pp.101-102; see for a similar argument: Kenney and Florida 1993).

The authors pursue this idea a little further: „We believe that once lean production principles are fully instituted, companies will be able to move rapidly in the 1990s to automate most of the remaining repetitive tasks in auto assembly — and more. Thus by the end of the century we expect that lean-assembly plants will be populated almost entirely by highly skilled problem solvers whose task will be to think continually of ways to make the system run more smoothly and productively“ (Womack et al. 1990, p.102).

The authors couple this vision with a criticism of the supposedly humanistic nature of the Swedish model.[4] Yet, with their vision of the fully automated factory, all the MIT authors have done is to neatly conceal the snag in the lean system. Despite all the anti-Tayloristic emphasis on ending the division between brain-work and manual work, at no point do they enter into any detail about the fact that the reality of production work in the lean assembly plants in their investigation embodies, for the most part, manual assembly on the production line. Looking first for technical solutions simply does not accord with the „Think Leaner“ motto, western management has correctly learned from Japan. Japanese firms were thus much more hesitant in pursuing the path of assembly-line automation than were their German counterparts, and, in their plans for the future, they are likewise proceeding only with caution in this direction. The vision of fully automated final assembly by the end of the 1990s allows the MIT authors to neglect a more in-depth investigation of prevailing working conditions. This vision corresponds to the all too familiar western idea of progress through technology.

4 „Screwing many parts together in a long cycle instead of few parts in a short cycle is a very restricted vision of job enrichment“ (Womack et al. 1990, p. 102). The MIT authors themselves carried out no investigation of teamwork in Swedish plants.

The vision of fully automated assembly plants and a staff that consists exclusively of qualified problem solvers represents a euphemism of unjustifiable proportions for the reality in both the assembly plants in Japan and in the transplants (Japanese-organised factories outside Japan). The involvement of the Japanese shopfloor employee in solving problems is an important element of the attractiveness of work. A black-and-white picture of soul-destroying stress versus creative suspense as respective characteristics of Taylorism and „Toyotism“ would, however, certainly be an oversimplification. Auto manufacturing in Japan is highly repetitive, often short-cycle, highly intensive work under extreme pressure. And this is the case every long working day. As a rule, and to a large extent, there is little or no time for problem-solving in the face of the daily routine. Meetings for problem solving in many plants can only take place during the five-minute afternoon tea-break. This is only one side of the argument, but it too must be stated.

The other side of the argument is that individual employees can be confident that they will not have to put up with these working conditions for the rest of their lives. This refers to the system of personnel development for the core work force in most of the leading companies even for the average employee up to lower supervisory positions. Even before these positions are reached task alternatives and job rotation prevent a person from being tied to a certain job for a long time. Under prevailing conditions, the improvements which can be carried out alongside the daily routine can only be minimal; however, if more is required, e.g., quality-circle activities, etc., weekend and after-hours work is often necessary. Some employees have even been known to move in a hotel room in order to work on some problem. But this is not the rule. Everyone is expected to make suggestions for improvement — and indeed the number of submitted suggestions per employee is high (61.6 per employee per year compared to 0.4 in European factories, according to the MIT authors´ inquiries). But while in Europe the savings achieved due to improvements are seen as a decisive criterion, in Japan it is the commitment and identification with company objectives underlying these suggestions which counts. Improvements which lead to greater savings, by contrast, are initiated and implemented in Japan by rationalisation experts, usually engineers, as is the case in Europe.

The „everyone does their bit“ mentality, so fundamental to the Japanese kaizen concept, is certainly susceptible to friction, and it would appear that this friction is increasing. It results firstly from time coordination problems, for the activities of the quality circles have further aggravated the overtime problem. Secondly, due to the increased utilisation of computer-aided systems and more sophisticated production control systems, specialised skills and expertise play an increasingly important role. Thus, there is a tendency to place stronger emphasis on those improvements initiated by the experts, even if, verbally, great importance is attached to the small group efforts at the shopfloor level, because of their considerable ideological significance in the Japanese context.

5 Concluding Remarks

This chapter has been limited itself to two important aspects of lean production — teamwork and continuous improvement. In both cases, the MIT authors´ depiction tends to distort Japanese reality. The tensions which are becoming apparent in Japan — protests, contradictions and frictions — are disregarded as are both differences within Japan itself and development trends, from which predictions regarding the limits to the stability and/or intensification of the existing model could be made. The MIT authors have, in this writer´s opinion, glossed over these matters in typical Western fashion in the passage quoted above, by placing lean production within the context of a vision of the fully automated factory. Yet a typical characteristic of lean production is that technology should be implemented only so far as the employees on the job consider themselves capable of using it, and, further, that the creation of „islands“ of automation is rejected because this necessitates the establishment of buffers and leads to discontinuity in production.

The problems which have become apparent in Japan as a consequence of increased levels of automation in some assembly plants merits further investigation. In practice, however, firms are currently much more cautious in this regard than the MIT authors suggest, so that the duality between repetitive and monotonous work closely coupled to production cycles, on the one hand, and efforts geared towards improvements, on the other, will also be characteristic for future forms of production organisation in Japan (see Fujimoto, T. 1993).

Is the lean production system the manufacturing strategy of the 21st century, as the MIT authors claim? If it is pursued along the lines and under the conditions which we currently find prevailing in Japan and in the transplants, this is by no means a foregone conclusion. Certain features of the Japanese system are somewhat attractive to western employees and do represent progress over Taylorism. But the system is reaching its limits in Japan, and the restrictions on such concepts are even tighter in the European context (see Nomura 1992).

These limits have become ever more evident in recent times and are giving great cause for concern, both to Japanese firms and MITI (see Fujimoto 1993). The consequence is that the discussions in Japan tend to focus on „post-lean" *concepts*; this is where new solutions are being sought.

The factors underlying this development are the chronic manpower shortage which afflicted Japan right through the 1980s, a change in values among the younger generation due both to contact with Western moral concepts and growing prosperity, and finally, indisputable evidence of burn-out, particularly amongst the privileged core workforce of the leading firms in the Japanese economy during the „bubble gum" years at the end of the 1980s. The result was a severe recruiting problem both for the leading firms, and in particular for suppliers, who were increasingly competing with the former for manpower. A further result were increasing labour turnover rates, which attained, in some areas, Swedish proportions. The economic recession in the years after provides only partial relief in this respect.

In view of these problems, Japanese firms now find themselves forced — whether they like it or not — to take measures, some of which they would certainly prefer to avoid (see Nomura 1992; Fujimoto 1993; Shimizu 1993):

(1) The first is a forced automation of production processes and the incorporation of computers in areas where previously the flexibility of human resources was particularly appreciated. Thus, one hears these days of projects for assembly automation, in which automation levels similar to Hall 54 at Volkswagen and beyond are being pursued.

(2) Secondly, both the legal and sometimes illegal employment of guest workers who are constantly pouring into the country is affected. The suppliers, in particular, would be helpless without this reserve .

(3) And finally, measures towards „humanising" production work are also affected. The assembly line is increasingly being called into question. In the Honda factory for the NSX, the Swedish Udevalla plant might have served as a model in some areas: assembly work as skilled production work with long

work cycles and a wide range of deployment possibilities for the assembly group.

The problems and the measures taken to resolve them are now clearly leading to the erosion of the basic principles of Japanese production and work organisation. With forced automation, the necessity arises to carry out intensive training of personnel for the operation and maintenance of equipment, while, at the same time, foreign workers are tending to take over simple manufacturing tasks. Will there now be a development towards polarised structures of work organisation and status differentiation? Perhaps the Japanese will make the same mistakes as we did, but they face an enormous challenge. The question must be asked: To what extent are they capable of developing post-lean concepts which incorporate the basic principles of lean management in order to meet new targets of making work more attractive, while at the same time coping with the demands of computer-aided manufacture? It would be quite wrong if we concluded that the competitive edge of the Japanese had blunted, and that Western companies should proceed more complacently in their efforts to devise new forms of work organisation. They still have much to catch up on with regard to the basic principles of lean production, which will certainly remain key elements of post-lean concepts, too.

References

Berggren, Ch. (1991), *Von Ford zu Volvo: Automobilherstellung in Schweden*. Berlin, Springer.

Fujimoto, T. (1993), Strategies for Assembly Automation in the Automobile Industry. Paper presented at the International Conference on Assembly Automation. Tokyo, Hosei University.

Jürgens, U., Th. Malsch and K. Dohse (1989), *Moderne Zeiten in der Automobilfabrik. Strategien der Produktionsmodernisierung in Länder- und Konzernvergleich*. Berlin, Springer.

Jürgens, U., Th. Malsch and K. Dohse (1993), *Breaking from Taylorism. Changing Forms of Work in the Automobil Industry*. Cambridge, Cambridge University Press.

Jürgens, U. and H.-P. Strömel (1987), The Communication Structure between Management and Shopfloor. A Comparison of a Japanese and a German Plant, in M. Trevor (ed.), *The Internationalization of Japanes Business. European and Japanese Perspectives*. Frankfurt-on-Main, Boulder, Col., Campus, Westview Press: 92-110.

Kenney, M. and R. Florida (1993), Beyond Mass Production. Production and Labour Process in Japan, in Kato, T. and R. Steven (eds.), *Is Japanese Management Post-Fordism?* Tokyo, Mado-Sha.

Kern, H. and M. Schumann (1984), *Das Ende der Arbeitsteilung*. Munich, Beck.

Krafcik, J.F. (1988), *A Methodology for Assembly Plant Performance Determination*. Cambridge, MIT, IMVP Papers, October.

Lieske, H. (1992), Vom Kollektiv zum Team — Neue Strukturen in Eisenach, in *Industrieclub 2000: Tagungsband der Konferenz „Zukunftsorientierte Team- und Gruppenarbeitskonzepte"*. Stuttgart, Industrieclub 2000.

MacDuffie, J.P. (1989), *Worldwide Trends in Production System Management: Work System, Factory Practice,and Human Resource Management*. Cambridge, MIT, IMVP International Policy Forum.

MacDuffie, J.P. and J. F. Krafcik (1989), *Explaining High Performance Manufacturing: The International Automotive Assembly Plant Study*. Cambridge, MIT, IMVP International Policy Forum.

Mineshige, M. (1992), Tod durch Überarbeitung — genug ist genug, in *Japan Magazin*, No. 1, pp. 28-29.

Minssen, H., J. Howald and R. Kopp (1991), Gruppenarbeit in der Automobilindustrie. Das Beispiel Opel Bochum, in *WSI-Mitteilungen*, Vol. 44, No. 7: 434-441.

Muster, M. (1990), Team oder Gruppe. Zum Stand der Sprachverwirrung über die „Gruppenarbeit", in Muster, M. and U. Richter (eds.), *Mit Vollgas in den Stau*. Hamburg, VSA.

Nomura, M. (1992), Toyotismus am Ende? Zur Reorganisation der „Schlanken Produktion" in der japanischen Autoindustrie, in Hans-Böckler-Stiftung and IG Metall (ed.), *Lean Production*. Baden-Baden, Nomos.

Roth, S. and H. Kohl (eds.- 1988), *Perspektive Gruppenarbeit*. Köln, Bund.

Shimizu, K. (1993), *Un Nouveau Toyotisme. Actes de GERPISA*, No. 8, November. Evry, University of Evry.

Steinmann, H., M. Heinreich and G. Schreyögg (1976), *Theorie und Praxis der selbststeuernden Arbeitsgruppen*. Cologne, Hanstein.

Womack, J.P., D.T. Jones and D. Roos (1990), *The Machine that Changed the World*. New York, Oxford, Rawson Associates etc.

Zola, D.E. (1992), GM to Downsize in U.S.; Will „Lean Up" Overseas Too, *Ward´s Automotive International*, January, p. 3.

Part III
Case Studies on the New Division of Labour

Introduction to Part III

This part presents case studies of new forms of work organisation in different countries and different branches of the economy. Its purpose is not primarily to inform the reader about the specific branch in a specific country, rather, the cases are meant to put more „meat to the bones" of the theoretically and conceptionally inclined chapters in Parts I and II. Guiding questions for this part are — whether the new division of labour is to be found in the same way in comparable industries of different countries, and what might be the reasons for varying developments. The selection of case studies is confined to selected examples due to limitations on the size of this volume, and cannot be seen as a systematic test of the diffusion and actual working of new forms of labour organisation.

In **chapter 12** *Littek* and *Heisig* explore the development of skilled white collar work using evidence gathered over several years from research projects they have conducted in Germany. Skilled white collar work previously faced a tendency towards *Taylorist fragmentation* and concomitant de-skilling with a narrow range of employee discretion during the 1960s and 1970s. This development derived from a scarcity of skilled labour and relatively low pressures from the market on quality and service in a generally growing economy. This route towards Taylorisim was also accentuated by the early use of centralised main frame computer technology in large companies. However, *Littek* and *Heisig* found that this tendency did not become predominant as it was confined only to a certain historical situation. Trends in work organisations since the mid 1970s have taken a different direction because employers developed a skill based modernisation policy which resulted in an ongoing replacement of lower by higher skilled employees and an enormous expansion of continued education. This modernisation process was the result of a convergence of several factors including changing consumer markets with growing demands on flexibility and quality in products and services, better selection chances on the labour market for employers due to lasting mass unemployment, and the expansion of education in society. In their conclusions *Littek* and *Heisig* refer to the new debate on the crisis of the German production model which is based heavily on occupational qualifications and occupational segregation. A dilemma arises because workers´

qualifications are embedded in a line organisation and inflexible departmental structures. This tends to support the optimisation of sectional productive processes but at the same time hampers the optimisation of the overall efficiency of the company.

Chapter 13 by *Tremblay* continues with a segment of mainly skilled white collar work, this time in the financial servicees. The author distinguishes between *two employment systems,* the traditional „industrial" and a „salaried" or „professional" setting. The latter, characteristic of offices, exhibits different conditions and solutions concerning work organisation. Her analysis holds that the development of Canadian banking (similar to the US) has been characterised by *technological change* in the 1970s in order to increase processing capacity, while in the 1990s *product innovation* is the main thrust of management strategy. Here again changed market conditions with increased competition is the main explanatory factor. While the early emphasis on technological change bore Taylorist traits, the shift in emphasis to product innovation is shown to have different consequences for the division of labour. The author deals with consequences of higher job complexity that require active participation of more qualified workers. In the unequal *gendered division* of labour a slow trend of women entering higher skilled positions and at the same time a reversal of the feminisation of work is observed.

In **chapter 14** *Ferreira* also deals with the occurrence of a reversal of feminisation of work in some office or business services. The observed *reversal of feminisation* in Portugal (a less industrialised European country) is shown to have arisen because of this country´s particular cultural and social background. Feminisation of office work is much lower than in for example, Canada and did not progress so quickly because of the cultural prestige of office work. A trend to be observed similarly, for example, in Germany, as outlined in chapter 12. The late introduction of new computerised office technology in Portugal also prevented the emergence of armies of data typists which in other countries has been largely responsible for the dark picture of factory-like office work in the period of centralised electronic data processing. The fragmentation of work into standardised, low-skilled jobs geared to the seemingly inevitable requirements of batch processing technology was only characteristic of this short period, which is now past history. The author, like others, also emphasises resistance to Taylorisation as a characteristic of skilled office work.

A different aspect of the division of labour is taken up in **chapter 15** by

Hoss and *Herranz* who deal with forms of regional and cooperative work organisation. Their empirical study of one of the very few working networks of *cooperatives* within an industrialised society (in Spain) demonstrates impressively the advantages of cooperatives, which include the mobilisation of labour as well as capital in a situation where the traditional preconditions for industrial work are absent (namely a skilled and experienced workforce and accumulated capital). The collaboration between small production organisations and large enterprises with know-how (especially in product design and marketing) in this network-like division of labour is conceptualised as a „learning system" and a „social pact" based upon *high trust relations*. The authors draw on similarities but also underline decisive differences compared to the model of *„industrial districts"* characterised in the 1980s by Sabel and Piore with Northern Italy as the reference. As the main disadvantages of the Galician case, the authors point out self-exploitation, relatively low wages, long working hours, quality problems, and, in some of their cases, discriminating practices by core companies towards their „peripheries".

The difficulties of cooperation beyond the boundaries of one company are also analysed in **chapter 16** by *Endres* and *Wehner*. Their empirical evidence is drawn from the just-in-time relationship between a German car manufacturer and two of its suppliers. Referring to the notion developed by Sabel about the meta-corporation, they find in new *inter-firm relations* a blurring of boundaries both between enterprises and of hierarchical distinctions within the enterprise. However, this is found to take place in reality much more slowly than is suggested. From the study of disruptions in plant-supplier relations they contend that for an understanding of the new inter-firm division of labour the emphasis must not be laid primarily on power and influence but on the structure of communications and decision-making in *consensual* processes of cooperation. With about 7000 changes occuring in the production process monthly in this case study, direct *cooperation* (based on trust) and finally *coordination* (based on common rules) from „production" to „production" are necessary to avoid time losses and lack of information. These new elements of a form of *sequential division of labour* are not yet established in German automobile industries. But developments are pointing towards organisation structures more capable of learning, and new kinds of boundaries between work processes in order to manage economic uncertainties and complexities.

The final two case studies in this volume examine changes in work organisation in more traditional industrial sectors. In **chapter 17** *Tomaney* and *Winterton* discuss the relevance of the flexible specialisation debate and new production concepts for changes in work organisation in the British coal mining industry after restructuring. Two case studies are selected — one is an older coalfield in the North East of England and the other using the most advanced technology and production methods. In the former (which has subsequently closed) productivity increases were achieved via job enlargement and work intensification following the defeat of the Miner´s Union in 1985. In the latter there was an attempt to create post-Fordist work practices but pre-strike consensus based approaches by management have been largely abandoned in recent developments which approximate more closely to a „punishment centred bureaucracy". The consequences of new forms of work organisation in the British context are less progressive for labour and more pessimistic than the findings of Kern and Schumann for „core industries" in Germany.

In **chapter 18** *Niemela* and *Leimu* present the results of their case studies on the Finnish shipbuilding Industry. Their findings provide a stark contrast to the previous chapter on British coalmining — in Finland the restructuring of Shipyards has improved the quality of work based upon a new compromise between worker´s interests and those of management. Finnish Shipbuilding was based upon craft production which, despite changes in the labour process in the direction of Taylorism after World WarII, remained until the 1980s. The one-of-a-kind production in the shipbuilding Industry and the inoperability of piece rate wage payment systems meant only a limited application of Taylorist methods until the 1980s. The labour process underwent further change in the 1990s in the direction of team work and job enlargement with job redesign. Skilled workers have benefitted from these changes as reported in their surveys due to a powerful trade union movement, the involvement of workers in job redesign and co-operative labour relations. At the same time changes in the direction of functional flexibility contrast with increased job insecurity and the resort to numerical flexibility which limit the extent to which new production concepts can be fully realised in the case of Finnish Shipbuilding.

Chapter 12
Taylorism Never Got Hold of Skilled White-Collar Work in Germany

*Wolfgang Littek and Ulrich Heisig**

Contents

1 Introduction

Contrary to widespread expectations, the development of work in white-collar functions in Germany has brought a new division of labour in relevant segments which builds on complex and comprehensive tasks, relatively high autonomy, responsibility, cooperation and motivation of employees. The development has done away in these segments of work with high fragmentation, narrow discretion, tight hierarchy, direct personal control and piecemeal incentive schemes. The segments of white-collar work we are talking about

* Some arguments of this text appeared in an article for the American journal *Work and Occupations*, Vol. 18, No. 1, 1991: pp. 4-28.

here comprise all kinds of highly skilled office work in administrative, commercial and technical functions, professional and lower management work and the like. Our own empirical findings are from white-collar work in manufacturing industry, but we include research findings from other branches and, thus, contend to give a picture of the overall development of working conditions in skilled office work in Germany.

We shall show in this chapter that trends towards Taylorist work structuring indeed emerged in the 1960s and early 1970s. This development, however, was not the inevitable result of capitalist production relations but rather a reaction to a decrease in the supply of skilled labour in a booming economy. With the increasing supply of highly skilled labour, the structures of work organisation went in the opposite direction. Intensified competition and the growing expectations of customers on the quality of goods and services led employers to administer a modernisation policy for enterprises which built decisively on the competence, initiative and self-reliance of workers.

Observations in this chapter based on our own findings are mainly from two larger reserach projects which we conducted between 1979 and 1989. They were based on qualitative methodology, which means case studies with intensive, open-ended interviewing and using other available documentary material from the enterprises studied. Our initial research project was carried out in three large enterprises of steel, consumer electronics, and office machinery industry between 1979 and 1982 (for summaries, see U. Heisig, 1989; W. Littek, 1986; W. Littek and U. Heisig, 1986). During this phase of the research, we conducted 20 expert interviews with top or middle managers and members of works councils, and 150 intensive interviews with trained and qualified white-collar employees („*Sachberabeiter*“) in bookkeeping, sales, personnel, industrial engineering, production planning, production steering, organisation and electronic data processing, software engineering and system maintenance. The fieldwork for our later project was conducted between 1988 and 1989 among office workers in a large automobile plant in Northwestern Germany. This second phase of research was based on expert interviews with heads of departments and management experts, representatives of the works council and the trade union and roughly 100 intensive interviews with white-collar employees in departments similar to those initially studied. The second research project served to amplify our initial conclusions, and to provide a more elaborate grasp of the underlying reasons why employers shifted their conception of appropriate work design models.

Both research projects made clear to us that in West Germany the *high occupational qualifications* of white-collar employees have always played and (save for a short period between the 1960s and 1970s) today play an even more central role in the structuring and restructuring of work. We shall use our empirical findings to show that West German managers in large enterprises since the recession of the late 1970s and early 1980s sought to overcome the economic crises of that period by abandoning mass production strategies that involved close direct control of the labour process, low qualifications, and low labour costs. Increasingly, employers fell back on the high educational and occupational training level of the national labour force and chose what we term a *skill oriented modernisation policy*, based on the recruitment of more and more highly qualified personnel.[1]

We contend that a confluence of micro- and macrosocial factors explains this change. The German tradition of *vocational preparation*, institutionalised within the educational system, has provided a ready supply of technically and ideologically prepared white-collar employees who can be trusted to behave in keeping with managerial goals. At the same time, employees´ possession of technical knowledge and expertise has enabled them to strike a hard bargain with their employers, implicitly shaping the job redesign process with their own interests in mind. We found, as we call it, *informal participation* and *„trading" of interests* in work rationalisation or work restructuring to be characteristic of labour relations in skilled white-collar sectors, reflecting management´s dependence on the competence and loyalty of these workers. All these are elements favourable for the emergence of *high trust relations* as the basis for work coordination (see more extensively on this, chapter 1 by U. Heisig and W. Littek in this book). In addition, although we do not explore this in depth here, the German „co-determination" system of labour relations provides a corporatist structure that aligns the interests of employers, workers, and the state and which, in turn, minimises employers´ need to exercise direct control over their employees (cf. for more details U. Heisig,

[1] For a comparative evaluation, cf. B. Mahnkopf (1989), who contrasts the West German skill-oriented modernisation policy with the British situation which (according to her) even today is still characterised by a policy of price-orientated downgrading and deskilling. In the British case, increases in the productivity of labour are still mainly due to a strengthening of managerial control and compliance, and not — as in Germany — to skill oriented human resource management and cooperation between management and labour. See also chapter 7 by T. Charles in this book for a comparative approach.

1992). These conditions in skilled white-collar work provide the stable background for the typical *individualistic* pursuit of interests and conflict regulation.

Today with a severe and tendencially growing problem of underemployment in the labour market and tight international competition the organising principles of work in the whole economy are reconsidered in Germany. In companies the current concern over *lean production* and *lean management* indicates that labour relations which we describe in this chapter will *grow* in importance, although the relative weight of its specific elements will change (for more details of the Japanese lean production/lean management concept of work organisation and its applicability in Germany, see chapter 1 by U. Heisig and W. Littek and chapter 11 by U. Jürgens in this book).

To make our findings and interpretations better understood to readers not familiar with the process of skilling and the role of occupational qualifications in Germany, we first briefly sketch the features of the German occupational structure and the system of vocational training on which it rests.[2]

2 Occupational Structure and Vocational Education in Germany

Within the German employment system, white-collar workers (*Angestellte*) form a category that is socially and legally distinct from blue-collar workers (*Arbeiter*).[3] The distinction between the two categories has a long history and finds expression in differential legal regulations mainly in two areas: social insurance (since 1911 with different institutions as bearers of insurance) and labour law (even though several efforts have been undertaken to assimilate the law and tariff regulations). Thus there exists a clear and definite „collar line“ (*Kragenlinie*) between manual and nonmanual workers. Because of the structural change in our society towards service work, the white-collar work-

[2] For a more detailed and profound analysis of the pecularities of the German occupational situation in white-collar employment, refer to C. Lane (1985, 1989, 1992) and W. Streek et al. (1987).

[3] The third category of the dependent work force are civil servants (*Beamte*), which comprises not only state administrators, but also e.g. teachers and professors etc.

ers are a constantly growing group, whereas blue-collar workers are shrinking in number. Since 1987, *Angestellte* have outnumbered *Arbeiter* in West Germany and now make up the largest group of the work force.[4] The group is so heterogeneous (from sales jobs to top management) that generalisations valid for all are impossible. However, the *core* of white-collar or service work is characterised by high skill, discretion, competent and responsible performance, and trust within cooperative social relations. In this chapter we shall draw our arguments from findings on *skilled* white-collar workers in non-managerial functions of large (industrial) enterprises. This may well be considered the core group of Angestellte, and it comprises commercial and technical functions.

The average West German skilled commercial white-collar worker must complete a 3-year period of vocational training (*Berufsausbildung*). Before becoming employed as a skilled white-collar worker in commercial or administrative functions, the individual has to complete an apprenticeship within an enterprise which is combined with formal schooling at a public vocational school (*Berufsschule*). This combination of more theoretically oriented schooling (1 or 2 days a week) with practical skill training at the enterprise (the other days of the week) is known as the „dual system" of vocational training. (It is basically the same for the training of *Facharbeiter* in the blue-collar sector.)

At the vocational school, general education also is completed. At the enterprise, training is comprehensive and includes a great variety of different commercial tasks and functions. After finishing vocational education, the person is certified as a fully educated clerk, an office, industrial, or banking salesman, or some other occupational speciality. In recent years, the average level of formal education has risen, and many of the younger business employees have university diplomas instead (or on top) of vocational training.[5]

[4] In 1993 the workforce of former West Germany was composed of 45,4% „Angestellte" (white-collar workers), 35,9% „Arbeiter" (blue-collar workers), 7,9% „Beamte" (civil servants) and 10,8% „Selbständige" (self-employed) (figures from: Statistisches Bundesamt, 1994, p. 86).

[5] Meanwhile, the educational level of those who begin a vocational training is growing higher and higher as well. Latest data show that one in five young persons beginning a vocational training (Auszubildene) in industry are graduates of a higher secondary school and have the Abitur (i.e., the qualification for university entrance). Compared with this, the proportion of young persons who only have the lowest 9- or 10- year main school education stayed relatively constant during the past years at around 28% (Be-

On the technical side, the traditional minimum precondition to become a qualified departmental technician (*Technischer Sachbearbeiter*) is 3 years of vocational training within a blue-collar trade. Additionally, the average technical employee has at least some years of practice as a qualified blue-collar worker and then further technical education in a specialised school, which is documented with a certificate comparable to that of master craftsman. In recent years, however, the educational level of technical employees has also risen dramatically in many sectors of industry. Today, the majority of younger qualified technical employees are engineers who were educated at technical colleges („Fachhochschulen") or universities.

The relevant and formally acknowledged occupational education of the commercial and technical white-collar staff has some very important implications for the organisation of white-collar work in West German enterprises. Because all skilled white-collar workers have strong occupational preparation, management can typically assume that white-collar workers will possess comprehensive production or administration knowledge and expertise. And employers can also take for granted that professional standards and normative orientations will invite employees to behave in ways that are mindful of managerial goals.

In effect, this allows work to be organized on the basis of competence, relative autonomy and responsibility. Managers typically expect that a competent white-collar employee can solve problems autonomously and is prepared to react flexibly to changing markets and clients requirements. Because of these underlying assumptions, skilled white-collar work normally is not prescribed in full detail and always includes varying margins of discretion.

This system of organising labour processes according to vocational qualifications, however, creates *problems* when the aim is no longer to optimise a single task or department, but the overall performance of an enterprise. In the current debates on business restructuring — „lean management", „business reengineering" — the shortcomings of work organisation on the basis of distinct vocations becomes more obvious. In this sense, H. Kern and Ch. Sabel

rufsbildungsbericht 1993). In some of the most attractive occupations the proportion of secondary school leavers („Abiturienten") is even higher. In banking industry in 1992 approximately 56% of apprentices who learned „Bankkaufmann/-frau" („banking salesman") had Abitur; in manufacturing industry the proportion of secondary school leavers among those who learned „Industriekaufmann/-frau" („industrial salesman") was about 40% (Bundesminister für Wissenschaft und Bildung, 1994, p. 61).

(1994) have started a discussion on „the crisis of the German production model".

Qualified employees, on the other hand, know that their employer will continue to grant them discretion only if they prove to be competent and trustworthy partners. To keep their position, skilled white-collar workers develop a personal interest in competent and sufficient performance. They come to feel responsible themselves for the successful execution of their tasks. Under such conditions, management is able to use *trust* as a basis of labour relations, and workers do their best to be trustworthy. Moreover, because it dispenses with the apparatus needed to exercise direct control over its white-collar employees, management can do without an extensive middle-management stratum, thereby saving the expense of unproductive administrative costs.

3 The Brief Career of Taylorism in White-Collar Work

When we began our first research project on white-collar workers in industry (1979-1982), the West German economy was undergoing the wrenching effects of recession for the first time since the end of the war. After 25 years of economic boom, the quantitative growth of production had come to an almost abrupt end 1973/74 which heralded the end of the golden years of mass production. Many industrial firms, especially in the old sectors of the economy (steel, shipbuilding, automobile, and traditional office machinery) had to cope with profit crises and began to restructure work processes. The effect on the labour market was an abrupt change from full employment to lasting underemployment and the experience of mass unemployment. For the first time, even qualified white-collar workers were strongly affected by technical and organisational change in connection with the widespread application of new microelectronic office technology, which occurred at the same time. Large numbers of white-collar workers were dismissed. With the new advent of the micro-computer based office technology, social scientists widely expected industrialisation of office work processes and a proletarianisation of white-collar workers (U. Briefs, 1984; U. Jaeggi and H. Wiedemann, 1966; U. Kadritzke, 1982; F. Schiefer, 1969; cf. similarly for the U.S. E. Glenn and R. Feldberg, 1979).

All three of the firms in which we conducted our research were strongly affected by the economic crisis, and all three have had to reduce their personnel in the past few years. Under these pressures for further cost reductions, we expected that white-collar employees would experience further fragmentation and dequalification of their work. The research results, however, confronted us with contrary facts: Management had begun to reduce the division of labour and to reverse its fragmentation of work. We found no empirical evidence for a destruction of skills or a reduction of work autonomy in the core areas. Besides a continuing tendency to standardise and replace simple, narrowly prescribed routinised work through automation, we found a tendency to combine work tasks into more highly creative functions, with high discretion and an increased delegation of decisions. (The main results of this research are summed up and reinterpreted in W. Littek and U. Heisig, 1987; W. Littek, 1986.) The skill requirements involved in technical and commercial work were reconstructed where they had been eroded in the years before and preserved where they were still intact. More demanding workplaces were designed in order to make better use of the qualified departmental experts. Contrary to our expectations, we found that an upgrading of work and a gradual expansion of responsible autonomy occurred and that high-trust social relations in production were stabilised or reestablished. Thus at the peak of an economic recession, we found no assimilation of work organisation and social relations in white-collar sectors to patterns existing in blue-collar sectors of work. The differences in social relations and the organisation of work between white-collar and blue-collar workers did not diminish but remained as wide as before.

We can retrospectively say that we had the luck to conduct our first research on white-collar working conditions at precisely that point in time (the late 1970s and early 1980s) when the organisational concepts which have been dominant for years were reevaluated. After nearly 2 decades of experiments with *Taylorist* modes of work organisation in commercial and technical white-collar jobs, management began to reconsider its usage of highly qualified labour power, the implementation and arrangement of new technologies, and the design of work. During this period, a new consensus began to spread: Nearly all experts and employees whom we interviewed in those days remembered, reflected, or agonised over the adverse effects of the Taylorist experiments which they experienced. Most managers reported their insight that strategies of fragmentation and deskilling of qualified white-collar work had produced disadvantages for the level of performance. Low motivation to work occurred when high expectations of workers were frustrated by low demands in work tasks. It was nearly unanimously reported in our interviews that the Taylorist restructuring of white-collar work had created more problems than it had solved.

Our interviews showed then that the situation at the end of the 1970s was the culmination of work design processes begun in the 1960s. Managers recalled that this period had been characterised by a strong expansion of productive capacities in West Germany, which caused a drastic *shortage of well skilled labour*. During this period, the skill composition of the total labour force experienced a dramatic decrease. Although most of the deskilling happened within blue-collar work, the white-collar sector was also affected by this trend. Although they usually had some occupational training, many of the white-collar employees recruited in the 1960s and early 1970s were not skilled for the specific task. In this time, the professional structure of white-collar work eroded because many people were recruited who had not been thoroughly prepared, had been trained on the job, and nevertheless were put into positions of departmental experts. In short, the labour shortage during the boom years resulted in a dearth of adequately (for the occupation) trained, experienced workers.

This development was accompanied by a rationalisation of work which produced segmentation and polarisation between different groups of white-collar workers, who had formerly been a more homogeneous body. To cope with the employment of ever growing proportions of formally low educated or occupationally untrained workers, management had to divide and standardise white-collar work extensively. It gave clear prescriptions of tasks, reduced task ranges, and cut back the discretionary content of work.

This downgrading of qualification requirements was accompanied and partly made possible by the rapid introduction of electronic data processing (EDP) equipment in the 1960s and early 1970s (U. Jaeggi and H. Wiedemann, 1966; F. Schiefer, 1969). Against the background of qualified labour shortage, the new microelectronic technologies were used mainly to simplify work. The strategy was to create tasks for less qualified personnel, and eventually to automate them. To compensate for the loss of knowledge and expertise in the middle ranks of departments, management aimed at centralising knowledge and expertise in the rising new electronic data processing (EDP) departments. This strategy of qualificational exchange failed, however, mainly because of the lack of qualified experts in the EDP field. It also became clear in the other departments that functional expertise remained essential for effective decision making in all parts of the organisational hierarchy.

In connection with the deskilling of qualified white-collar work, there arose manifold material and social problems which were unknown within white-collar sectors of West German enterprises. Respondents in our interviews were unanimous in their evaluation of that period. According to the experts interviewed, the great flexibility and adaptability which traditionally had characterised qualified white-collar work was lost; errors and mistakes increased, and the quality of goods and services declined. In general, the planning, coordination, and control of work became more difficult and expensive. These unintended consequences made it increasingly obvious to management that in essential sectors of commercial and technical service work, Tayloristic work organisation and direct control were counterproductive. The view that qualified white-collar work cannot be fragmented and organised according to Taylorist principles without losing productivity and quality gained momentum.

3.1 The Rise of a Skill-Oriented Modernisation Policy

By the end of the 1970s, a reorientation of work design in large companies began to substitute low-skilled workers with better educated and more adequately trained ones. This reorientation had two preconditions: It was strongly pushed by changes in the markets for products and services, on one hand, and by changes in the labour market, on the other. As sales markets no longer grew so quickly, as in the 1960s, and hence became increasingly competitive and oriented towards consumers´ needs, managers began to concentrate their efforts on more sophisticated high-quality products, better services, and more intelligent solutions, such as more creative marketing concepts. To improve the quality of services and to strengthen firms´ abilities to innovate, more people were needed who did not „just solve everyday problems, but who think in the long term", according to the head of the personnel department of a manufacturer of computers. These new abilities and competences, however, were and are equated with better formal education, high school diplomas, vocational certificates, and university degrees.

The chances to select better educated and experienced employees have grown dramatically since the end of the German boom period in the mid-1970s. After 20 years of labour shortages, mass unemployment became a constant feature of the labour market. White-collar workers as well were no longer saved from unemployment. Enterprises thus could be far more selective in their recruiting efforts from the external (as well as in the internal) labour market and more demanding in their qualification requirements. To avoid further losses of qualified workers and destruction of their creative, innovative, and adaptive abilities, management since the mid-1970s started to reduce fragmentation and direct control of work. As a personnel manager put it, management began „to draw reasonable frames of action, to try methods to produce creativity in order to systematically develop innovation". Management aimed at establishing „a work organisation that provides an adequate framework for employees´ activities, maintaining suitable margins of discretion while mindful of managerial goals". What happened since the late 1970s and the early 1980s was a reconstruction of the white-collar labour process which aimed at greater adaptability, more flexibility, and better quality of work.

Within this context, the introduction of decentralised computer terminals and video screens was used to decentralise control over work performance and to reestablish discretion and margins of action at the level of qualified departmental experts. In order to use the skills and competence of the qualified employees more comprehensively, management ceased using EDP technology simply as a means of automation and labour saving and began to develop EDP as an information management system to *support* the qualified workers. Departmental experts again were allowed increased discretion to actively optimise their own work performance and creatively exploit the high qualitative potentials of the new technologies for improved services.

Within management, a broad consensus emerged that these aims could be reached best if the lower skilled commercial or technical employees would be replaced by higher and more recently qualified personnel. In the commercial and technical departments, workers skilled in the old style and vocationally trained practitioners were gradually replaced by better educated and better trained professionals (for example, college- or university-trained engineers). The chances of advancement from below into the ranks of the technical „Sachbearbeiter" began to decline as fully qualified personnel were recruited from the various technical institutes („Fachhochschulen") and universities.

Although the reorientation of work organisation was not a simple process, its goals were reached quite comfortably and without high additional costs. Two factors were mainly responsible. First, an overall rise of the educational level continued, with constantly growing numbers of vocational certificates and rising university enrollments among young workers.[6] Second, the advent of lasting unemployment since the mid-1970s caused the supply of highly qualified, credentialed workers to exceed the demand in the labour market, creating new selection chances for employers.

The extent of the qualificational exchange which occurred at that time is demonstrated by the following figures: Whereas between 1978 and 1982 the total increase of employment in white-collar sectors was about 9%, the employment of university trained „academics“ at the same time increased about 22%. And while there has been little change in the proportion of white-collar employment since the early 1980s, the proportion of employees with high school and university diplomas still continues to increase (for a fuller discussion, see e.g. Imiela, 1987).[7]

The resulting process of skill upgrading allowed the spread of high-trust relations and responsible autonomy to become the dominant form in white-collar work organisation, whereas formerly, this had been practiced mainly in the small professional sectors of enterprises.

3.2 Informal Bargaining over Work Redesign: The Influence of High-Skilled Employees

The picture given thus far reveals only *half the story*, however, because it unilaterally emphasises changes in management´s preferences. Such a view puts too much emphasis on intentionality and foresightedness. It suggests that

[6] Out of the total work force:
(1) those with no formal vocational qualification („unskilled“) were 1976: 34,9%; 1991: 20,2%; and for 2010 are expected to be only about 10%;
(2) those with finished vocational education were 1976: 57,8%; 1991: 67,5%; and for 2010 are expected to be nearly 73%;
(3) those with a university or college degree were 1976: 7,3%; 1991: 12,3%; and for 2010 are expected to be approximately 17% (figures from M. Tessaring, 1994).

[7] Another example may be given from a single company: Siemens AG, an industrial manufacturer of electric and electronic goods and one of the largest employers in Germany, since 1986 in its workforce has more employees with university or college degree (in commercial and technical functions) than skilled workers.

management´s actions always are part of a rational and comprehensive strategy and thus overlooks the particular work situation and the strong mutual dependence between managers and qualified workers. To understand shifts in the organisation of white-collar work, it is essential to direct attention towards the workers, the ways in which they seek to influence management decisions by using their expertise in the labour process as resources with which to gain or defend their occupational control.

The competence of employees in handling work effectively contributes decisively to the design of workers´ jobs. Although the material outcomes of rationalisation measures are contingent on many factors, the social outcomes of restructuring processes usually favour the higher qualified groups who are essential for high performance. These groups are often successful in securing their specific interests by mobilising relevant resources and forming temporary coalitions with members of line management. For this reason, relevantly skilled groups are usually found on the side of the rationalisation winners („Rationalisierungsgewinner"), often using their already strong position to influence the outcomes of work restructuring to continue or strengthen their position, status differences, and privileges. The uneven distribution of losses and gains prevents, as we have shown elsewhere (W. Littek and U. Heisig, 1990), the formation of solidarity between different groups of workers and weakens class conflict to a level that enables the functioning of the labour process on the basis of consent (see also W. Littek, 1986).[8]

These tendencies become accentuated by strategies of lean production and lean management (in recent years). The implementation leads to screening processes for the workers. Individuals who perform well or who have the potential to perform well are kept in the process and are promoted, while low performers are removed. A redefinition of effectivity is taking place.

[8] It is because of this „strategic" behaviour that Goldthorpe (1982) identified the members of the already privileged groups of the (white-collar) service class as one of the main „conservative" elements within the social structure of advanced capitalist societies.

4 The Consolidation of New Patterns of Work Design

On the basis of our previous research, the second phase of our endeavours focussed on the connections between different skill levels, high-trust social relations in production, and modalities of control. At this point, we were interested in learning how widespread „responsible autonomy" strategies of work organisation and control had become within white-collar sectors of employment in connection with the skill-based reorganisation, and according to what criteria high trust and responsible autonomy were granted to different groups of white-collar workers. We supposed that high-trust relations and responsible autonomy were strongly connected with the qualificational level of different employee groups, and we expected that they were more strongly developed in sectors where better educated and higher qualified workers were employed (the theoretical background for these expectations is developed in greater detail in W. Littek and U. Heisig, 1990; see also our chapter 1 in this book).

The fieldwork this time was conducted in the white-collar sections of a large automobile plant in northwestern Germany in summer 1988. During the 1980s the plant had undergone a tremendous upswing and had rapidly expanded because the management of the mother company — a major West German producer of high-quality cars — had decided to build a new model car here. With about 16,000 employees, it was the largest employer in the region. Chances for a selective hiring of employees with high qualifications were particularly good, because of a regional high unemployment: the State of Bremen with up to 14% registered unemployed then had the highest rate of unemployment of all States of the former Western part of Germany.

While conducting the fieldwork, we immediately realised that in this company, high trust and responsible autonomy were the predominant strategies of white-collar work organisation. Beyond that, we found that high trust and responsible autonomy, contrary to our expectations, were granted to nearly *all* white-collar employees, largely independent of skill level. In the case of the enterprise under study, this phenomenon can be explained by a general precondition and a specific reason. The general precondition is that within this company, social relations were already traditionally based on high job security and a corporate culture which attaches great importance to cooperative relationships between capital and labour. The additional reason is that nearly all white-collar workers (and large proportions of blue-collar workers as well), even at the lower levels of the job hierarchy, are qualified with at least 3 years of relevant vocational training. A large proportion of the newly hired (commercial and technical) employees are thus highly skilled. With both factors given, the main preconditions for the application of high-trust relations in production and responsible autonomy are obviously at hand.

At first sight, it appeared that the egalitarian distribution of trust and autonomy created an overall climate of cooperation which was positively evaluated by management and employees. The high-trust pattern, however, produced unintended effects, especially within the lower-skilled sectors of white-collar work. High-trust relations, work autonomy and the absence of immediate control were often *criticised* by workers there. The lower-skilled workers felt neglected; they quite often grumbled that management did not care for their work performance, concluding that management was not interested in their efforts because it did not respect the relevance of their work. The rationale behind this apparent critique was that the lower-skilled workers felt they had no chance for career advancement within the internal labour market.

It was especially the departmental managers who were aware of this problem. Therefore, to stabilise high-trust patterns and responsible autonomy in the lower-skilled areas, they often tried to organise even comparatively simple jobs in a way that made work interesting. On the other hand, in the areas of highly skilled workers, it went without saying that their tasks must not become less interesting to any degree, lest management risk existing high-trust relations and loyal cooperation. It was not the technology but social considerations which in nearly all departments played the most decisive role in work design.

4.1 Maintaining Versus Raising Skill Levels: Three Cases of Differently Skilled White-Collar Work

To demonstrate the way in which qualified white-collar work today is organised in advanced and progressive West German enterprises, we present examples for three different skill levels of white-collar work. Our selection of the cases, moreover, is guided by the intention to show some of the social problems that may emerge within a company if the skill level of a functional group is changed substantially.

4.1.1 The Pay Clerks

We begin with the occupation of pay clerk (in the *Lohnbüro*), a comparatively low-qualified and low-salaried job which nevertheless has been and in the future will be performed by vocationally trained employees. Although the task of the pay clerk is not highly skilled, it is, however, the philosophy of the plant management and the department head that the pay clerk is doing a service job and therefore must take care that the customers, that is primarily the blue-collar workers of the plant, are always satisfied with the services delivered by the wage and salaries department. It was management´s opinion that if blue-collar workers are expected to perform good work, their fundamental interests (wage, working time, and working conditions) had to be recognised and satisfied.

Within wage accountancy, it is the commonly shared opinion that a pay clerk can only be a competent and self-confident interlocutor for workers if he or she knows the job well. Thus the work of pay clerks is designed to require dealing with a mix of all forms of wages (time, piece, premium, and so on). One clerk autonomously accounts the wages of about 800 workers and is personally responsible for all of these accounts. Although the single tasks of the pay clerk remain simple and could be performed by unskilled workers, the complete job is rather ambitious and quite interesting. It is the specific distribution and combination of tasks and the delegation of discretion which makes the pay clerk a relatively qualified, flexible, and responsible worker.

The kind of work organisation here contributes to the high satisfaction of workers. The pay clerks do not become more ambitious, since there are no opportunities for promotion in their area of work. If they are ambitious, their only chance is to apply for another task.

4.1.2 The Records Clerks

The second case is the records clerk in the parts department (within *Produktionssteuerung*). Until recently, this job was completely routinised and low paid; it was one of the lowest skilled and least respected white-collar jobs within the whole company. Records keeping was the domain of advanced blue-collar workers, and very often, it was even filled with deserving blue-collar workers who had little physical vitality and now lived on charity in the parts department.

The original task of the records clerk was and still is to transform the components of a new car from the construction plans into piece lists and to keep the piece lists of produced cars up to date if changes are made within production. In former times, it did not matter if mistakes were made within records keeping because the data remained mainly within the department and were nearly exclusively for administrative purposes. Although the single task superficially has not changed much, the relevance and meaning of the job has totally changed since computers were brought into the department. The data produced by records clerks are now directly fed into the central EDP system, which is used for the planning of production processes. These data have become an important part of the company´s „electronic text" (Zuboff, 1988), which is now used for detailed planning and decision making in several departments.

Because of the more relevant use of the parts list after the introduction of EDP, it became very important that the data were exact and up to date; the records clerk now had to make „intelligent" decisions and work hard to be in line with the changes in construction and production. To fulfill these higher demands, the records clerk, according to his superiors, now needed a far higher degree of technical knowledge, an idea of the product and awareness of the productive context, and a high degree of attentiveness and accuracy. These attributes are equated with high formal education and technical competence through relevant occupational training. Consequently, departmental managers took the changes in the functional organisation of the information and planning process as a reason for raising the skill level of the departmental staff and decided that the work of the records clerk would be redefined as an engineering job. Line managers certainly were aware that, measured against the actual task demands, engineers were overskilled, but they supposed that the employment of highly qualified personnel would give an impetus to a redesign of work processes in order to more comprehensively use the increased knowledge of the staff.

Contrary to these expectations an intense struggle ensued between the head of the records keeping and the head of the planning department about the necessity of „upskilling" the records keeping function. While the former repeatedly tried to make clear that the records clerks had become a major element in the overall planning process, the latter remained skeptical and refused to recognise the importance of record keeping. The records clerks were still viewed in the company as simply inputting data, which was seen as a simple and undemanding task because of the stronger position of the planning department.

The example clearly shows that there is a relevant difference between the enrichment of a job and the recruitment of skilled workers within a department, on the one hand, and the companywide *acknowledgment* of a job as a skilled one, on the other. It is difficult to improve the reputation of a department or type of job because of the resistance of priviledged groups in the existing structure. If the attempt for improvement is not successful, then the qualified employees will adapt their behaviour to that of the lower skilled workers who still exist in that department (see H.-D. Gondek and U. Heisig, 1991).

4.1.3 Engineers in the Planning Department

Whereas the jobs in the pay office and the parts department were situated at the lower levels of the white-collar job hierarchy, the job of the industrial engineer in the production planning department (*Produktionsplanung*) was on the top of the firm´s occupational ladder. Industrial engineers here perceived themselves as the core group of the qualified white-collar staff because it was they who decided on the introduction of robots and about the design of the work on the assembly line, and it was they who controlled the manufacturing process. Not only they but nearly everyone else believed that they were the people who made and kept the plant running. Every planning engineer was and felt personally responsible for one part (the chassis, the lacquer finish, the interior equipment, and so on) of the manufacturing process of the complete car. Within their prescribed task range, industrial engineers had a great degree of work autonomy, and they were allowed and forced to constantly make far-reaching decisions. In consequence, they were also one of the best paid groups within the company.

The job of the industrial engineer was not only ambitious and interesting but was accepted and respected by nearly all employees within the enterprise. If ambitious tasks and important new responsibilities (e.g. project management functions) were allocated within the enterprise, it was almost self-evident that one of the industrial engineers from the production planning department was given the responsibility. As such tasks were of central importance for the firm´s performance, the person doing such a job usually received attention. As industrial engineers here had the best opportunities to prove their outstanding abilities, they were the employees who within the whole enterprise had the best chances to become widely known. They not only had the most interesting tasks but had good opportunities to advance in the department or make a career within the plant or company. As a whole, industrial engineers were in full accord with the informal norms and commonly shared official values of the company.

Departmental leaders and industrial engineers shared common interests and used their already good standing and reputation to further strengthen their role and importance within the firm. In effect, the power and influence of the department was permanently growing. Because of these favourable conditions, it is not surprising that the overall work satisfaction of industrial engineers was high and that in the department a trust culture existed and worked well. However, as one consequence of good opportunities for getting an ambitious job and becoming widely known, engineers within the production planning department heavily competed with one another. But even though the competition was strong and ubiquitous, it was not dangerous for the cohesiveness of managers and workers. It was treated as an expression of the fair contest which was an inherent part of the departmental culture. The internal contest seemed to strengthen team spirit and shape the undivided outside appearance.

4.2 Some Consequences for the Skill Debate

The three examples sketched here, especially the struggle over the skill demand and value of the records keeping function, make clear that *skill* is never only a technical matter but, rather, is closely connected with commonly shared norms and values which are the reference points for the assignment of respect, status, and income. Beyond that, norms and values make sense of, account for, and culturally secure the distribution of influence and authority. If the qualifications of a group of employees are recognised and officially valued, they provide an important means of further advancing sectional interests. Likewise, it is also true that the recognition of a group as highly skilled depends on its power and the alliances that it forms within the firm as well. Skill, therefore, is always an intensely political matter within a social context (W. Littek, 1986; W. Littek and U. Heisig, 1987).

Our research on white-collar workers in industry further reveals that high-trust work relations and responsible autonomy are not as closely related to different levels of qualifications as we originally expected. Rather than simply refuting our hypotheses, the wide dissemination of trust and autonomy in work that we found may be explained by the fact that in recent years, even lower-skilled white-collar employees in many companies exhibit an overall high qualificational level. But the findings also draw attention to the fact that whereas high trust and responsible autonomy today are accorded to qualificationally very different groups of white-collar employees, they only function sufficiently if certain very specific supplementary conditions obtain.

The point is that if management wants to make adequate use of qualified labour, it has to consider the social as well as the material dimension of work. Beyond raising the technical requirements (training level, multiskilling etc.) it must take care that the high qualifications of the employees and their specific efforts are socially recognised and rewarded. Management has to be aware that highly skilled employees not only expect their work to be interesting, demanding, and ambitious but that they expect that good work performance will offer chances to create an outstanding image, to acquire status, and to advance within the internal labour market. Where the latter conditions are lacking, the employment of qualified employees leads to contradictions, discontent, frictional losses, and an implicit withdrawal of efficiency. Our interviews suggest that in departments where such stimulating opportunities are lacking, employees experience the performance of complex tasks as mere stress. By contrast, where workers are employed under conditions of responsible autonomy and enjoy thc opportunity to gain status and advancement, autonomy is experienced not as a burden but as a positive source of gratification.

5 Organisational Limits to the Efficient Use of Higher Skills

In conclusion we wish to emphasise that it would be wrong to see work organisation based on high skills to be highly productive *per se*. The struggle between departments over the valuation of work in our case shows the *limits* of the organisation of work along occupational lines, which characterises the German production model. In this model actors aim at the expansion of their distinct range of responsibilities. This usually occurs at the expense of others and leads to a rivalry between functions or departments. This means that the optimisation of the *overall* performance is not executed as the primary task, but is, in effect, undermined. This is where the Japanese model of skill formation, and of skill usage within the work process differs decisively. In order to make best use of the high German work skills it will be necessary to do away with the rigid occupational segmentation and the strong interconnection between occupations, departments and status.

References

Baethge, M. and H. Oberbeck (1986), *Zukunft der Angestellten: Neue Technologien und berufliche Perspektiven in Büro und Verwaltung*. Frankfurt/New York, Campus.

Berger, U. (1984), *Wachstum und Rationalisierung der industriellen Dienstleistungsarbeit: Zur lückenhaften Rationalität der Industrieverwaltung*. Frankfurt/New York, Campus.

Bravermann, H. (1974), *Labor and Monopoly Capital*. New York, Monthly Review Press.

Briefs, U. (1984), *Informationstechnologien und Zukunft der Arbeit*. Köln, Pahl-Rugenstein.

Bund-Länder-Kommission für Bildungsplanung und Forschungsförderung (ed.- 1987), Künftige Perspektiven von Absolventen der beruflichen Bildung im Beschäftigungssystem, Report No. 15, Bonn, Bund-Länder-Kommission für Bildungsplanung und Forschungsförderung.

Bundesminister für Bildung und Wissenschaft (1993), *Berufsbildungsbericht*. Bad Honnef, Bundesminister für Bildung und Wissenschaft.

Bundesminister für Bildung und Wissenschaft (1994), *Berufsbildungsbericht*. Bad Honnef, Bundesminister für Bildung und Wissenschaft.

Crozier, M. and E. Friedberg (1979), *Macht und Organisation: Die Zwänge kollektiven Handelns*. Kronberg/Ts., Athenäum (French original: *L'Acteur et le Systéme*. Paris, Edition du Seuil 1977).

Glenn, E.N. and R.L. Feldberg (1979), Proletarianizing Clerical Work: Technology and Organizational Control in the Office, in Zimbalist, A. (ed.), *Case Studies in the Labour Process*. New York, Monthly Review Press: 51-72.

Goldthorpe, J.H. (1982), On the Service Class, its Formation and Future, in Giddens, A. and G. MacKenzie (eds.), *Social Class and the Division of Labour*. Cambridge, Cambridge University Press: 162-185.

Gondek, H.-D. and U. Heisig (1991), Kulturelle Bewertungsmuster im Konflikt (am Beispiel von Ingenieurstätigkeiten), in Littek, W. and H.-D. Gondek (eds.), *Dienstleistungsarbeit*. Berlin, Edition Sigma: 167-186.

Hager, A., M. Kurbjuhn and L. Loop (1989), *Betriebliche Angestelltenarbeit*. (Final research report.) Berlin, Fachhochschule für Wirtschaft.

Hartmann, M. (1991), Akademiker in der Sachbearbeitung. Unsicherheitselemente in den innerbetrieblichen Sozialbeziehungen? In Littek, W., U. Heisig and H.-D. Gondek (eds.), *Dienstleistungsarbeit*. Berlin, Edition Sigma: 187-198.

Heisig, U. (1989), *Verantwortung und Vertrauen im Großbetrieb*. Konstanz, Wisslit.

Heisig, U. (1992), Vertrauensbeziehungen und Interessenvertretung im Angestelltenbereich, in Bleicher, S. and E. Fehrmann (eds.), *Autonomie und Organisation*. Hamburg, VSA: 119-142.

Heisig, U. and W. Littek (1982), Entwicklungstendenzen kaufmännischer Sachbearbeitertätigkeiten in der Industrie, in Boehm, U., W. Littek and F. Ortmann (eds.), *Rationalisierung der Büroarbeit und kaufmännische Berufsausbildung*. Frankfurt/New York, Campus: 99-117.

Imiela, U. (1987), Gewerkschaften an der Hochschule. Zunehmende Akademikerbeschäftigung in Produktion und Dienstleistung — Herausforderung an die gewerkschaftliche Hochschul- und Angestelltenpolitik. *Die Mitbestimmung*, Vol. 31, No. 8: 466-469.

Jaeggi, U. and H. Wiedemann (1966), *Der Angestellte im automatisierten Büro*. Stuttgart, Enke.

Kadritzke, U. (1982), Angestellte als Lohnarbeiter. Kritischer Nachruf auf die deutsche Kragenlinie, in Schmidt, G., H.-J. Braczyk and J. von den Knesebeck (eds.), *Materialien zur Industriesoziologie. Kölner Zeitschrift für Soziologie und Sozialpsychologie*, special issue 24: 219-249.

Kern, H. and M. Schumann (1970), *Industriearbeit und Arbeiterbewußtsein*. Frankfurt/Köln, Europäische Verlagsanstalt.

Kern, H. and M. Schumann (1984), *Das Ende der Arbeitsteilung? Rationalisierung in der industriellen Produktion*. Munich, Beck.

Kern, H. and Ch. Sabel (1994), Verblaßte Tugenden. Zur Krise des deutschen Produktionsmodells. *Soziale Welt*, Special issue No. 9: 605-624.

Lane, Ch. (1985), White Collar Workers in the Labour Process. The Case of the Federal Republic of Germany. *Sociological Review*, Vol. 33, No. 2: 298-328.

Lane, Ch. (1989), *Management and Labour in Europe: The Industrial Enterprise in Germany, Britain and France*. Aldershot, Edward Elgar.

Lane, Ch. (1992), Technologischer Wandel und kaufmänniche Angestelltenarbeit in Großbritannien. Ein Vergleich mit der deutschen Situation, in Littek, W., U. Heisig and H.-D. Gondek (eds.), *Organisation von Dienstleistungsarbeit*. Berlin, Edition Sigma: 201-218.

Littek, W. (1986), Rationalisation, Technical Change and Employee Reactions, in Purcell, K., S. Wood, A. Waton and S. Allen (eds.), *The Changing Experience of Employment*. London, Macmillan: 156-172.

Littek, W. and U. Heisig (1986), Rationalisierung von Arbeit als Aushandlungsprozess: Beteiligung bei Rationalisierungsverläufen im Angestelltenbereich. *Soziale Welt*, Vol. 37, No. 2/3: 237-262.

Littek, W. and U. Heisig (1987), *Rationalisierung und Angestellte. Papers on the Rationalization of the White Collar Work and Employee Reactions*. Bremen, University of Bremen Press.

Littek, W. and U. Heisig (1990), Work Organization under Technical Change. Sources of Differentiations and the Reproduction of Social Inequality in Processes of Change, in Clegg, S.R. (ed.), *Organization Theory and Class Analysis*. Berlin/New York, de Gruyter: 299-314.

Littek, W., U. Heisig and H.-D. Gondek (eds.- 1991), *Dienstleistungsarbeit. Strukturveränderungen, Beschäftigungsbedingungen und Interessenlagen*. Berlin, Edition Sigma.

Littek, W., U. Heisig and H.-D. Gondek (eds.- 1992), *Organisation von Dienstleistungsarbeit. Sozialbeziehungen und Rationalisierung im Angestelltenbereich*. Berlin, Edition Sigma.

Mahnkopf, B. (1989), Gewerkschaftspolitik und Weiterbildung. Chancen und Risiken einer qualifikationsorientierten Modernisierung gewerkschaftlicher (Tarif-)Politik. (Discussion Paper FS I 89-11.) Berlin, Wissenschaftszentrum.

Piore, M.J. and Ch.F. Sabel (1984), *The Second Industrial Divide: Possibilities for Prosperity*. New York, Basic Books.

Schiefer, F. (1969), *Elektronische Datenverarbeitung und Angestellte*. Meisenheim am Glan, Hain.

Statistisches Bundesamt (ed.- 1994), *Datenreport 1994*. Bonn, Bundeszentrale für politische Bildung.

Steinkühler, F. and S. Bleicher (eds.- 1988), *Zwischen Aufstieg und Rationalisierung: Die Angestellten*. Hamburg, VSA.

Streek, W., J. Hilbert, K.H. van Kevelaar, F. Maier and H. Weber (1987), The Role of the Social Partners in Vocational Training and Further Training in the Federal Republic of Germany. (Discussion paper.) Berlin, European Centre for the Promotion of Vocational Training — CEDEFOP.

Tessaring, M. (1994), Langfristige Tendenzen des Arbeitskräftebedarfs nach Tätigkeiten und Qualifikationen in den alten Bundesländern bis zum Jahr 2010. *Mitteilungen aus der Arbeitsmarkt- und Berufsforschung*, No. 1: 5-19.

Zuboff, S. (1988), *In the Age of the Smart Machine: The Future of Work and Power*. New York, Basic Books.

Chapter 13
Innovation, Employment Systems and Division of Labour: An Analysis of the Canadian Banking Sector

Diane-Gabrielle Tremblay

Contents

Over recent years, social scientists interested in technological change and work organisation have increasingly been making use of the concepts of „new production concepts" and „new division of labour". As we know, the basic analysis was developed in relation with studies of manufacturing activities. Various studies indicated that some elements of Taylorism, particularly the intensified division of labour it implied, were being abandoned in many industries. The objective of this renewed and reduced division of labour was apparently to secure the same productivity advantages which had previously been secured through Taylorism and a strong division of labour. As the intense division of labour proved less and less successful in securing the expected productivity gains, some employers turned to a new strategy, that of an „anthropocentric“ route, implying a reduced division of labour and increased importance of human resources. In the „new production concepts“ perspective, the human being is regarded as the essential lubricant in the production process, rather than the potential trouble factor which it was in the Taylorist paradigm.

In this paper, we analyze the evolution of the division of labour in the banking sector, in order to determine whether the same can be said of this sector and of service activities with regard to the new division of labour debate. The banking sector may not be exemplary for the whole of the service sector, particularly traditional services, but it is quite representative for the modern — or dynamic services, particularly other financial and business services, but also more and more of the social and commercial services (Economic Council of Canada, 1987; Rajan, 1987, 1984).

Let us add that while our case studies are based on Canada, and while there are institutional and legal differences between the Canadian and U.S. banking sectors, industrial relations, human resources management and employment systems tend to be quite similar in the two countries. The model described here is therefore characteristic of many financial and business services throughout North America. Some pecularities can be found in specific institutions such as credit unions in Canada as well as in the U.S., but the general trends described here are quite similar.

Although it has become customary to reduce „old“ production (including service production) methods to one dominant mode of production, that is Taylorism, it is in our view important to note that the employment systems of service industries were not all as tayloristic as manufacturing industries. At least, this appears to be the case with banking employment systems. In this perspective, our paper presents an analytical framework which distinguishes *two* main types of employment systems; one which is more characteristic of the service sector, while the other represents industrial settings.

Our research is based on statistical data as well as a survey based on open-ended interviews of workers and persons responsible for human resources management, technological and product innovation, as well as training, in a number of Canadian financial institutions; one particular institution was studied in more detail, while French banks were also the object of supplementary analysis. The research leads to the conclusion that product and technological innovation question some of the elements at the basis of employment systems, particularly the salaried system of banks, and bring firms to reorganise the division of labour and internal labour markets. Historical compromises are being remodelled in the salaried employment systems of banks, as they are also in many industrial systems. However, while product innovation as well as technological change exert pressure for a change in employment systems and division of labour, they do not determine a specific outcome. From a theoretical point of view, our research clearly goes against the technological determinism perspective. In the face of product and technological innovation, firms are confronted with *two* main modes of adjustment to the new division of labour, one which is based on internal offensive flexibility, calling upon a stronger development of internal labour markets, internal mobility and training, and the other based on external defensive flexibility, bringing firms to fire certain categories of personnel in order to hire employees having the newly required qualifications (Tremblay, 1991e; Zarifian, 1987).

1 Technological and Product Innovation and Division of Labour

It is useful to start by distinguishing two stages of strategic innovation in banking institutions, although most authors insist only on the first, that of technological innovation (Rajan, 1984; amongst others). Pure technological change dominated the scene during the first period (1960s to mid 1980s), while in our view, *product innovation* actually pulls the innovation process in the 1990s. It is not always easy, and may be somewhat artificial to try to separate the two forms of innovation, product and process, as they are often very closely linked. Nevertheless, from a theoretical point of view, it is important to do so, as these forms of innovation are not only different, but clearly have different impacts on division of labour and employment systems (Tremblay, 1991b, 1991c). Also, this important distinction puts into light the main factor which „pulls or pushes" (Tremblay, 1989b) innovation in a given competitive context, while considering that different forms of innovation can be associated in an innovative process, which is not unimportant.

This predominance of product innovation is all the more important in Canada and the U.S., as well as many other industrialised countries where banks cannot expect to gain new clients, given the „baby bust“. It is for this reason that they turn to product innovation, or *„diversified quality services“*, which in turn imply a new division of labour. As the number of clients cannot be expected to increase over the next decades as much as it did in the post-war years, banks have adopted the same strategy as „mature“ industries such as the steel or car manufacturing (Sorge and Streek, 1987; Coriat, 1986), which look to *„diversified quality production“* in order to maintain their profits. While the case of manufacturing industries has been quite well documented, particularly in what is referred to as the „new division of labour“ debate, there has been relatively little work done on the changes in division of labour in the service sector.

In the 1970s, *technological change* in the banking sector was aimed at an increase in the processing capacity, a reduction of the need for personnel in a context where demand for traditional banking services kept on increasing with the „baby-boomers“ getting older. The objective was to replace human resources by machines as much as possible in order to be able to keep up with the formidable increase in demand for processing services. Division of labour was based on a taylorist perspective, that is a relatively strong division of labour, established work rules and repetitive tasks for salaried workers, as well as a division between conception and execution.

In the 1990s, with the „baby-bust“ and the saturation of markets, banks are searching for new niches for profit. In this perspective, they are developing new products, new financial „packages“, in short „financial innovations“ with more value added than previous products. The main strategic objectives of banking institutions have evolved and the division of labour within firms has evolved along those lines. Taylorism has lost ground, although it has not totally disappeared from all banking environments and job categories. Different institutions have different management styles and work organisations; also, the lowest levels of jobs, such as junior clerk, tend to continue to be characterised by short repetitive tasks, although they also tend to be disappearing from job structures, as we will show later (Table 1).

In any case, product innovation, which in banks means diversified quality services, now leads competition in the banking sector; this has clear consequences in terms of the division of labour, as well as the type of human resources needed and employment systems. This new division of labour is based on the development of a certain „professionalisation“ of some categories of bank workers, who are called upon to offer a diversified set of high quality (or „high knowledge-based") services in the various fields of credit and investment, eventually in management, marketing and financial analysis. To a large extent, particularly in commercial credit activities, „professionalised knowledge" appears to be taking over on „local empirical knowledge". This type of „professional" or counselling activity used to be limited to the head office personnel, but this financial knowledge and analysis is now present at the level of local branches.

The new division of labour and associated *„professionalisation" of work* therefore call for a different work force, with more formal knowledge and experience in financial activities. They also require more sophisticated technologies which assist not only in calculations, but also in management, marketing, financial analysis, etc. (computer-aided decision systems). In this perspective, individual branches want to have access to the data on their clientele in order for their staff to do close follow-ups and to adjust their products, or financial packages, to the characteristics of their clients. These new systems are being adopted since 1990.

While traditional banking services could rely on a rather unspecialised work force, with often only high school education[1], which was limited to execution of specific tasks, the new financial packages require a more „professional" work force, which can not only execute given tasks, but also design specific financial packages, as well as do some financial analysis in a credit or investment perspective. Not all of the work force will be the object of this professionalisation, but as Automatic Teller Machines and other computerised services develop, all institutions clearly indicate that a larger part of their work force will be composed of employees having professional knowledge of the financial field (financial analysts, credit and investment specialists, etc.), jobs such as junior clerk disappearing gradually, as will be seen in Table 1. The trend is evolving quite rapidly in many Canadian institutions since the beginning of the 1990s.

[1] Detailed data in Tremblay (1989a), with similar trends being observed to a certain extent in Rajan (1984, 1987).

2 Transformations in the Nature of Work

As mentioned earlier, while the first phases of automation centered on the automation of basic non skilled tasks which had been organised along the lines of Taylorism, and therefore implied a disappearance of various manual tasks, more recent transformations imply new products and new computerised functions which require an *active participation of more qualified workers*. The workers must have a wider range of knowledge of the work process and content. Tasks that have been transformed by this more recent phase of computerisation have become more abstract, conceptual and diversified. The teller´s job is a good example of this increasing level of abstraction, conception and diversity, not to say of complexity. Credit agents´ tasks have also become more abstract and more complex, and involve more conception and responsibility.

Although it is often considered „easy work", as a lot of office work is often seen from the exterior[2], a teller´s work should in fact be considered rather complex, particularly with the recent evolution. As is the case for credit agents, job complexity has increased over the years; throughout the century, new machines and tasks were introduced (Lowe, 1986), and more recently, it is particularly the multiplication of new products and services, and the increase in quality of service required by customers, which have changed jobs[3]. Complexity is defined here on the basis of the diversity of tasks, of the level of abstraction needed to execute them, of interruptions of given tasks by other more urgent ones, and of the need to anticipate possible errors and malfunctioning of equipment, this last element being particularly important in the case of credit agents. An agent´s or teller´s work is therefore considered complex because of the level of abstraction and conception required for many of the tasks which involve work with computers, because of its increasing diversity (tasks, products and services), as well as because of the frequent interruptions of work in the case of the teller particularly.

In the case of credit agents, besides the increase in conception activities,

[2] Lowe (1985, 1986) gives some indication on traditional office work and its evolution over the years. The two books have a rather historical scope, not so much oriented towards present and future technological developments.

[3] Tremblay (1989a, 1991a, 1991e) develops on these more recent trends in Canadian banking, with a stronger accent on the question of qualification and skill.

new expert systems require a sequential integration of information and therefore exert more strain on memory. For example, if the agent does not want to have to ask the client for information which he has previously given voluntarily, in relation with another question, he or she must recall the information to be entered on the computer later on in the process. When things were done on paper, the agent just flipped the paper over and wrote down the information in the appropriate space (Tremblay, 1991d). Now, not only is the gathering of information somewhat more complex, but the work asked of the agent is also, considering it is to offer a personalised financial package.

In terms of abstraction, an important number of operations that used to be done manually are now done with computers and require the use of an increasing number of codes. A high level of mental work is needed to perform tasks such as planning of activities, analysis and filing of data, calculations, as well as various checks. All this requires a good dose of concentration and memorisation.

As concerns the diversity of work, the organisation of work in the banking sector as in many services, is usually not based on as precise a division of labour as is the case in industry. Personnel is called upon to do different tasks, to replace other workers, as „work rules" are not as rigid as is the case in the manufacturing sector. With the deregulation of the financial sector, new activities are now part of banking and this implies new tasks for the bank employees and the division of labour becomes even looser. Tasks related to investment planning, insurance, etc., are now introduced in banking branches (Economic Council of Canada, 1987). Financial agents and tellers still have to assume administrative functions, as these have not diminished with the arrival of computers. On the contrary, for tellers, controls and checks are part of the work, as are balancing cash, inter-bank compensation, putting cash in the Automated Teller Machines, etc. For credit agents, controls and checks of information given by the client with other financial institutions and with the credit bureau (reimbursement rates) are also an important part of the process.

Finally, interruptions refer to the fact that check-up phone calls with financial institutions and other activities often have to be taken up some time after having started another task, more urgent tasks sometimes temporarily interrupting the work. This implies a higher level of mental activity than is obvious at first sight, as has often been indicated by ergonomists (Teiger and Bernier, 1987).

This complexity of tellers´ and agents´ work is often hidden by the fact that management usually assumes that machines and computers will make the work easier, that tellers and agents will be able to do things more quickly and will therefore have more time to spend trying to sell new products and services to clients. This „sales“ function is a new task which has been introduced into banking work in relation with the development of diversified quality services; this part of the work is closer to conception than to pure execution. Since tellers have contact with clients when they come to deposit checks or to get cash, they are asked to inform the clients of the new products and services which banks are eager to sell in the new context of financial sector deregulation. Agents will then design specific „packages“ for specific clients. Financial analysis and planning, executive banking services (including credit and investment), brokerage services, insurance, etc. are part of the work.

3 Job Structures, Professionalisation and the New Division of Labour

The increasing importance of product diversification and package designing, related to professionalisation and a new division of labour, brings about an increase in the number of employees in the counselling and professional categories. Traditional job categories (tellers and clerks) become less important in the job structures, and often take on a new conceptual and service dimension.

3.1 The New Division of Labour

As an example of the evolution in the division of labour within the banking sector, let us note that the percentage of employees in financial counselling went from 3% in 1975 to 4% in 1980 in the main institution studied and more than doubled to 11% in 1986. Estimations indicate they represent about 15% of workers in most institutions in the 90s, some even going as high as 20%. Over the same period (1975-1986), junior clerks went from 12% to 5%, and tellers from 44% to 40%. The professionals and the technicians are the only category which has known an increase, except for office workers in small branches; in this last case, it must be noted that very small branches are becoming less numerous, but also that they imply a greater flexibility of staff, and sometimes a less extended range of financial products. As indicated in interviews, division of labour has never been very strong in small branches, due to the limited number of staff; a very strong division of labour was therefore counter-productive, if not altogether impossible. In these smaller branches, there have always been rather flat hierarchies, due to the limited staff.

Table 1: Distribution by Category, in Percentage Terms, 1975-1986 (percent)

	1975	1980	1986
Total (number)		14,000	20,000
Junior clerk	12	4	5
Teller	44	44	40
Senior clerk	11	11	16
Secretary	5	3	3
Agent (counsel)	3	4	11
Accountant	8	6	1
Directors	10	10	6
Others	7	18	18

Source: Tremblay (1989a, p. 549).

Although not affecting all of the work force in all institutions, there is a clear trend towards a „professionalisation", in the sense of a less intense division of labour, a „closing" of the internal labour market. This of course means the exclusion of workers who do not have the new qualifications required to participate in the new division of labour, to work with the new equipment and to offer customised diversified financial services and products.

At the present time, management of banking institutions still seems undecided as to the strategy it will adopt in order to obtain these *new qualifications* and develop more fully the less tayloristic work organisation, particularly since the new qualifications required are not necessarily available on the external labour market, at least not in the precise form needed by banks. In fact, banks have always been one of the sectors which does the most internal training; in this perspective, they are somewhat closer to the European tradition than to the North-American tradition, where firms generally do little training. Competition based on product innovation and diversification seems to be increasing this trend.

Management is now defining and constructing the new skills required (such as sales and communication) for tellers´ work as well as for the more specialised financial counselling. In this sense, the banking sector (as with many other financial activities) is clearly the object of a process of redefinition of the division of labour and of internal labour markets. Rather than say that the internal labour market is becoming altogether flatter, we would say it is becoming more centered on specific professional capacities, closer to the type of employment system characteristic of computer specialists for example, which is centered on professional knowledge and capacities. To a certain extent, it is also becoming somewhat flatter, as management is being reduced, particularly in small branches (Tremblay, 1989a), while technical and professional employees see their ranks growing. This is a trend which is observed in Europe (Rajan, 1987), as well as in North America (Economic Council of Canada, 1987).

3.2 Professionalisation and the Gendered Division of Labour

Detailed data by gender is not available for more recent years, but data on 1980-1984 give a good idea of the gendered division of labour in the main institution studied which, according to our contacts in banks, is quite similar in all Canadian institutions and has not changed much over recent years. As can be observed, banking is a women´s world: 80% of the workers are women, and the percentage is similar throughout all institutions in North America. However, women dominate at the bottom of the hierarchy (tellers, clerks, office supervisor), but are less present at the top (assistant director and director), although there seems to be some evolution in the new intermediate categories of counselling and current operations agent (see Table 2).

In these new categories which are increasing in numbers, such as those of credit or savings counsellor (agent-counsel), the formal knowledge requirements are important. Detailed knowledge of credit and financial activities is required. This leads to relatively less women in this category, comparatively to the tellers´ group. Of course the tables show a strong percentage of women in these categories (60-70% of women as agents) and even a rise in these professional groups, but the percentages are lower than what they are in traditional banking jobs (over 90%). This means that many men come from outside the banking industry to the professional jobs; in other words, the internal labour market is to a certain extent open to outside professionals for these jobs. Thus, although women have made some gains in the 1980s, (55% to 60% of counselling agents, 63 to 70% for other agents — cf. Table 2), the percentages observed for the new professional jobs are lower than those of traditional banking jobs. Also, relatively few women have managed to go from a teller or clerk´s job to a counselling job. As most job openings are in this type of professional job (increase from 3% in 1975 to 11% in 1986 in percentage of total workforce), this means that the *jobs of the future* are to a certain extent more often held by men than was the case previously: there are 30-40% men in these categories against less than 10% in traditional categories. Although men do not occupy the majority of professional jobs, they occupy a significant percentage, clearly higher than was the case with traditional non professional jobs such as teller or clerk. This leads to conclude that banking jobs are becoming somewhat more frequently occupied by *men*. Also, it is particularly the professional jobs that are the object of entry of men; while women are a majority in the professional jobs, they are not as dominant as they were in traditional banking, that is jobs tellers´ and clerks´ jobs (over 90% women in these categories), where they remain strongly dominant (Tremblay, 1991a).

Table 2: Workers by Job and by Gender, 1980-1984 (percent)

	1980		1984	
	Men	Women	Men	Women
Tellers	4.7	95.3	3.9	96.1
Jr clerk	6.5	93.5	7.8	92.2
Sr clerk	10.2	90.8	6.3	93.7
Office supervisor	8.1	91.9	6.9	93.1
Agent counsel	44.7	55.2	39.2	60.8
Agent current operations	33.3	63.3	29.4	70.6
Assistant director counsel	83.0	16.9	82.4	17.6
Assistant director current operations	93.0	7.0	75.9	24.1
Director	82.3	17.7	83.4	16.5
Total	21.8	78.2	19.6	80.4

Source: Tremblay (1989a, p. 550).

The professionalisation of banking exerts pressure on female bank workers, who have a somewhat lower level of schooling (less university degrees in the office category, which is mainly female). Although they are a majority, women have somewhat more difficulty entering the new job categories, that is jobs related to credit, savings and financial counselling and analysis, than they did — and still do — in traditional jobs. The traditional jobs still remain very open to women, while the newer and more professional ones are somewhat less open to them, letting more men filter into the internal labour market for these jobs.

In a situation where banks are trying to deliver customised quality services, the institution considered has to determine how far it must or can go in order to adapt to this new objective. It has to determine whether it will rely, at least to a certain extent, on the internal workforce to develop new skills or whether it will rely exclusively upon the external labour market. It has little choice in terms of the need to offer a more professional service and therefore to develop a more professional workforce. However, in order to do so, must it abandon its traditional workforce, which caused it to be firmly embedded in the local environment, and hire on the external labour market (a specialised majoritarily masculine workforce), or must it invest in a redirection of the skills of its traditionally female workforce? This is the present dilemma.

The employees who are the most firmly embedded in local environments and have more informal knowledge of clients are often those who lack the newly valued formal capacities. However, it must be noted that given the high unemployment rate in Québec and Canada over the last decade (on average 11%), the percentage of highly educated women (college level particularly) is increasing steadily. This educated workforce, often overqualified for the actual job occupied (teller), also has requirements as concerns job content, and in many branches it is observed that the process of professionalisation of the job is seen positively by individuals with a higher education.

However, women do not seem to be profitting as much as they should or could from the recent evolution of the division of labour in banking. As Table 2 shows, women are still overrepresented in office, teller and lower level jobs, and underrepresented in higher level jobs, particularly at the highest levels of management. We will return to the explanation of this situation in our concluding remarks on the gendered division of labour, for which it is useful to refer to the concepts of internal labour markets and employment systems.

4 Innovation and Employment Systems

The concepts of internal labour markets, of employment systems or of „industrial relations sub-systems“, which are considered more or less synonymous by Osterman (1984), are useful to analyse the evolution of the division of labour, in relation with product innovation and technological change. These concepts are usually called upon to analyze workers´ place and mobility in firms´ job ladders or hierarchies, and are thus central to our study of reorganisation and division of labour in the context of innovation. They are particularly useful in analysing the possible discrimination against women presently working in banks.

In this perspective, we will present an analytical framework which brings us to distinguish *two* main categories of employment systems, one which is more frequent in industrial settings, the other which is more characteristic of professional or office settings, or of the service sector in general. We will then show how the new division of labour can be attained through two different strategies, strategies which will have very different impacts on a firm´s labour force.

4.1 Internal Labour Markets

As Doeringer and Piore (1971) indicate, the main factors which contribute to the development of internal labour markets, or stable employment systems, are the specificity of qualification and technology of a firm, the desire to reinforce social cohesion of a group of workers, as well as to ensure loyalty of the workers. In other words, firms create internal labour markets in order to keep their trained qualified workers, and to ensure loyalty and cohesion within the firm (Osterman, 1984; Tremblay 1989a, 1990a, 1990b, Doeringer and Piore, 1971).

These elements are clearly present in the banking institutions´ actual objectives. The goal of such a construction as an internal or closed labour market is to attach a group of workers to the firm by organising mobility files and wages in such a way that workers possessing specific qualifications essential to the firm, and for which substitutes are not easy to find, will be inclined to remain with the firm. Those who do not possess the newly required qualifications and cannot integrate the new division of labour will be pushed out of the firm by management practices which tend to make them more unstable through non-standard forms of employment, lack of wage progression and other similar practices (Tremblay, 1990a, 1990b).

To compare employment systems of firms in different settings, it is useful to turn to Osterman´s work (1984), which distinguishes employment systems according to the following aspects: organisation of work, „work rules", guarantees in terms of stability of employment, forms of employment (full time, part time...), union practices, firms´ practices, etc. These various elements are used to draw up a broad classification consisting of two main employment systems, which are specifically designed by firms in order to attain their general goals, as identified by Doeringer and Piore (1971), that is to be able to use the specific technology of the firm, and to ensure cohesion and loyalty of workers[4].

4.2 Industrial and Professional (or Salaried) Employment Systems

The *traditional „industrial" employment system* is very characteristic of North-American manufacturing work organisations. It tends to favour a rather rigid and strong division of labour, tasks and work rules associated to each job being defined very precisely in collective agreements and being difficult to change. Wages are fixed for each job classification and the „seniority" principle (last in first out) is at the basis of this system, which is common in North-American industry (much less in Europe). The work organisation is rather hierarchical and there is a particular rule of job security attached to these jobs, firms being allowed to fire the number of workers which they wish, but having to respect the „seniority" principle.

In these industrial employment systems, seniority is the basic rule, wages increasing in relation mainly with seniority. While it cannot be considered as job security, the seniority rule of „last in, first out" regulates the system. These elements actually represent a historical „compromise" between the actors present in the firm, that is workers (possibly unions) and the employer. In such a context, workers are not asked to be particularly „loyal" to the

[4] Obviously, the social cohesion and loyalty can just as well be considered as a result (if it works) and an objective of the firm in creating specific employment systems or internal labour markets.

firm, nor to „participate“ or to assume personal responsibility for their work. Such an organisation is traditionnally associated with a Tayloristic division of labour. As has been shown in many studies of manufacturing industries, amongst which Sorge and Streek (1987), Coriat (1986) and many others, this traditional model is under pressure in many manufacturing industries and has often evolved towards what is often referred to as „lean“ production or „new production concepts“. The traditional model is still frequent in North-American manufacturing however.

In the *„salaried“ or „professional“ setting*, characteristic of offices, Taylorism is not always the rule and the division of labour has often been more diffuse than in the traditional industrial setting. Workers often have to assume a stronger „professional“ responsibility and, to a certain extent, to be „loyal“ to the firm. In exchange for these advantages, the firm offers a certain „job stability“. In other words, layoffs are generally less frequent, as they might destroy the engagement and participation which are necessary to the firm´s operations and productivity. Traditionally, the banking sector and offices in general tend to be characterised by such an employment system, which is now becoming more „professional“ still.

Ultimately, through these various stategies of employment, the main objective of firms is always to secure maximum productivity through the appropriate work organisation; productivity advantages can be gained through different work settings, inasmuch as they are coherent with the workers´ expectations. In this sense, work organisation, division of labour and employment systems are designed in different ways in different countries in order to secure the best performance, given national (legal and institutional) constraints, production requirements and worker expectations.

5 Management Strategies and the New Division of Labour

While in previous writings Braverman (1974) and Marglin (1973) indicated computerisation would result in a stronger division of labour and dequalification of all workers concerned, there is no clear trend of dequalification in the Canadian banking sector. On the contrary, over recent years, the trend towards a less tayloristic division of labour and a more qualified workforce seems to be gaining support. It is not totally uniform in all banking organisations and agencies. There is a certain diversity of evolutions observed, and this can be explained by the fact that human resources management strategies (and not just technology) largely determine the outcomes in terms of job content, of division of labour and skills, as well as the way in which these skills are obtained, i.e. through internal development of training or through the external labour market.

5.1 Two Main Management Strategies

Our analysis of employers´ strategies (in the banking sector in particular) has led us to define two main categories of human resources management strategies used to adjust to change. The first strategy is one which aims at a maximum flexibility of the employment system. It rests mainly on the use of the external labour market for access to jobs, but also on the development of particular or non typical (normal) forms of employment (short term contracts, occasional work, part time, etc.), as well as on wage reductions or elimination of cost-of-living adjustments. Resting on the use of non standard forms of employment, it often implies a more tayloristic division of labour.

The second strategy is one which aims at workers´ stabilisation in an internal labour market, their motivation and involvement in the „firm´s project". This usually means more occupational training, development of a strong internal labour market, a less Tayloristic organisation, more participation of workers in the firm´s decisions.

Both these strategies are very different in terms of methods, and of course, in terms of impact on the labour force. The first is a strategy of pure rationalisation, of cost minimisation through direct or indirect wage compressions, or through close adjustment of working hours to the volume of production (part time, occasional work, etc.) in order to ensure higher productivity of work. In our view, it is inappropriate for the development of new forms of work organisation and, indeed, it does not seem to be favoured by firms developing diversity and quality in production.

The second is a more qualitative strategy, considered more appropriate for the development of a less Tayloristic work organisation where the involvement of workers, the development of their skills and their motivation are considered determinant for productivity. The development of clear mobility paths, or internal labour markets, is also often associated with this type of strategy which facilitates the development of new skills and a non tayloristic work design within the firm.

5.2 What Future for Salaried/Professional Employment Systems?

In the context of new production concepts, of technological change, and of economic restructuring more generally, many internal labour markets are presently being destructured and remodelled. Criteria, rules and various characteristics of the internal labour markets are being destroyed and replaced by new rules or criteria; for example, the new skills required for the new less tayloristic jobs tend to impose new criteria for hiring, for internal mobility, etc. All elements of the employment systems are not destroyed instantly, but many characteristics can be modified, the relative value of different skills or qualifications changing. New production concepts and innovation attack some of the elements of the salaried/professional employment system which characterises the banking sector. In the context of the new division of labour, previous compromises on issues of work organisation and mobility need to be remodelled.

In a salaried setting such as that of the institution studied and of Canadian banks more generally, firms would sometimes like to be able to do away with workers and to hire young graduates with the new skills required by the new division of labour. However, they are quite conscious that this might very well erode the traditional „compromise" which ensures quality of work and productivity. Also, as mentioned, the educational system does not offer banks the specific knowledge needed and they generally have to complete the knowledge of new hirees. A new compromise is needed, but it is not easy to move towards such a new compromise without breaking the system of „loyalty" which not only remains essential to the firm, but must often be developed further into a more active participation of workers, in the context of product innovation and development of new customised services. If one party in the compromise or agreement no longer goes along with some elements of the agreement (job security for example), the other party can just as well decide to make a breach, and diminish its „loyalty" or responsibility, thus reducing productivity or quality of products (or service). This is obviously not what is wanted in a context of professionalisation and reduced division of labour, on the contrary. That is also why in the present context of a search for

„diversified quality services“, the expression of „professional“ employment system seems more appropriate to us, at least in the case of the banking sector.

6 Concluding Remarks on New Production Concepts and the New Division of Labour in Banking

As concerns the new production concepts and new division of labour debate more generally, the analysis of service industries such as banking is important in order to show that Taylorism is not necessarily prevalent in all economic sectors.

6.1 The New Division of Labour

In North-American banking, division of labour was often less intense than in many manufacturing industries; however, even if the service sector was not coming from as far back in terms of the intensity of the division of labour, it nevertheless is going in the direction of new production concepts which imply an even less intense division of labour than was the case before. Professionalisation and larger work scope characterise the present evolution. Considering mass production and work specialisation on the one hand, and diversifed quality production with a new division of labour on the other hand, most authors conclude that the latter holds more promise for the future of North America as well as many other Western nations.

In our view however, the debate has not stressed enough the fact that *different routes* can be taken to arrive at the new division of labour associated with the new production concepts. When we compare national traditions in terms of human resources management, we see that North America generally tends to opt for the first strategy identified above, that is external flexibility and labour cost minimisation, while European countries (particularly Sweden and Germany) tend to favour the second strategy. The latter is however emerging in some branches of the North American economy, amongst which banking, and this leads us to stress the fact that human resources management strategies are at the centre of the process of introduction of new production concepts and of work redesign. They are also determinant in the success or failure in terms of performance of the whole work organisation.

In the case of Canadian banks and services, the two strategies defined earlier are used. Some banking branches maintain or develop workers´ responsibility and participation and ensure the redirection of skills through internal training and mobility, thus bringing about the new division of labour „from within". However, some also choose to go against the „pact" based on job stability, stability of employment being in any case more and more often attacked, with the development of non-standard forms of employment in all industrialised economies, and more particularly in the service sector. This brings firms either to fire workers or to let attrition work, while at the same time stimulating job rotation (and quits) through the absence of career possibilities, etc. This strategy implies that the new division of labour comes through the introduction of personnel from outside the firm.

In any case, a new — less intense — division of labour is appearing in the banking sector as in other service sectors. It is seen in the increasing abolition of unskilled and semi-skilled occupations, as well as in the process of professionalisation which is permitted by the improved supply of qualified skilled workers, and observed in the more formal knowledge requirements, but also new job contents which imply more communication and sales capacities. Both these elements, reduction in unskilled occupations and increase in skilled occupations, as well as reduction in management jobs and increase in „professionalisation" are characteristic of the so-called new division of labour. However, as it is often forgotten, we insist that it is important to stress that the evolution towards this new division of labour can take two routes, as it does in North-American banking: that of a firing-hiring strategy, or that of a further and renewed development of professionalised employment systems, based on internal training and mobility. When analysis is concentrated mainly on *production* systems, instead of on *employment* systems, one may tend to neglect the important process of change in employment systems, and maybe consider the „new division of labour" too positively, while some groups of workers (i.e. the less skilled) may be paying a high price for this evolution, that is their exclusion from employment.

It might also be stressed that the „newness" of the so-called new division of labour is maybe not so new in Europe as it is in North America, where division of labour and Tayloristic rationalisation seem to have played a more dominant role than they did in Europe, at least in countries like Germany and Sweden, where vocational training has a long tradition. However, division of labour was also less dominant in the salaried employment systems of North America, of which banking is part.

6.2 The Gendered Division of Labour

Related to the exclusion of the less skilled, is of course the gender issue, as it is yet unclear whether women will access the new professional counselling functions as easily as they did the traditional tellers´ and clerks´ jobs. Obviously, the internal training and mobility strategy favours women´s employment, while the firing-hiring strategy favours men, who are now relatively absent (20%) in banking at the moment, although they still dominate the job hierarchy (directors´ jobs particularly).

As to the interpretation of the relatively lower representation of women in the new professional categories (compared to traditional jobs), which brings up the issue of the gendered division of labour, our interviews indicate the main reason for the entry of men and for the relatively lower percentage of women (compared to traditional jobs, let us not forget) is the fact that women in the firm often do not have the level of schooling required for the new jobs. In this context, the firm prefers to go out into the labour market to get the formal qualifications required. In so doing, it hires new graduates and professionals (mainly men) from other banking institutions.

These are at least the official reasons. In interviews, a few women indicated there might be some discrimination against women, what we would call „systemic" discrimination, that is general social discrimination against women because they are women, because women can become pregnant, decide to spend more time on kids´ education, etc. It is true however that women represent roughly half of graduates in business schools (college and university); in this perspective, based on their representation in the external labour market (external to the firm) their representation in professional categories would be considered higher than that on the labour market. However, if one considers the internal labour market of the firm, composed mainly of women, then one tends to consider they are underrepresented in professional jobs.

The main question is whether or not it is — or could be — possible to occupy these jobs on the basis of internal training and experience only. A second question is whether the women occupying tellers´ and clerks´ jobs would want to occupy the professional jobs. On these two questions, we got a few answers from different perspectives. Most managers and workers indicated the professional skills required to occupy the professional jobs had to be acquired through formal schooling, while some indicated that internal training could permit female tellers and clerks to acquire these skills. Beyond this possibility, the majority of persons interviewed indicated women had new attitudes towards work and were interested in the new professional categories, but a minority did indicate some women were not interested in the increased responsibilities which accompany the professional jobs.

It therefore is difficult to conclude, but it does not seem that the internal skill development strategy, which favours women, has been fully implemented. In our view, this has to be understood in the context of a high chronic unemployment situation in Canada over the last 10 years; given this situation, there is an important number of graduates with the required qualifications, so that the firm sees no need to invest itself in costly training programmes. Therefore, the women present in the internal labour market must acquire the new qualifications required — most often on their own — in order to gain access to the professional jobs.

As we have seen, the division of labour and gendered division of labour have evolved considerably in Canadian banking over recent years, but changes are still to come, as product and technological innovation continue to develop in an incessant flow.

References

Braverman, H. (1974), *Labor and monopoly capital.* New York, Monthly Review Press.

Coriat, B. (1986), Technologies nouvelles et modernisation: naissance d´un nouvel ordre d´usine. *Les temps modernes,* March: 55-65.

Coriat, B. (1987), L´atelier flexible. *Les Cahier français,* No. 231: 30-35.

Cossalter, C. (1984), D´une informatisation à l´autre: l´exemple des banques et des assurances. *Formation-Emploi.* Paris: La Documentation française, No. 5:18-27.

Doeringer, P. and M.J. Piore (1971), *Internal labor markets and manpower analysis.* Lexington, D.C. Heath and Co.

Economic Council of Canada (1987), *Innovation, employment, adaptation. An economic council of canada report.* Ottawa, Supply and Services Dept.

Lowe, G.S. (1986), Mechanization, feminization and managerial control in the early twentieth-century Canadian office, in Heron, C. and R. Storey (eds.), *On the Job*. Montreal, Kingston, McGill and Queen´s University Press.

Lowe, G.S. (1985), *Women in the Administrative Revolution*. Toronto, University of Toronto Press.

Marglin, S. (1973), Origines et fonctions de la parcellisation des tâches, in Tremblay, D.-G. (ed.- 1992), *Travail et société. Une introduction à la sociologie du travail.* Montréal, Editions Agence d´Arc: 153-187.

Osterman, P. (eds.- 1984), *Internal labor markets*. Cambridge, Mass., MIT Press.

Piore, M.J. and C. F. Sabel (1984), *The second industrial divide. Possibilities for prosperity.* New York, Basic Books.

Rajan, A. (1987), *Services — the second industrial revolution*. London, Butterworths.

Rajan, A. (1984), *New technology and employment in insurance, banking and building societies. Recent experience and future impact*. London, Gower Press.

Sorge, A. and W. Streek (1987), Industrial relations and technical change: The case for an extended perspective. Discussion paper No. IIM/LMP 87-1. Berlin, WZB.

Teiger, C. and C. Bernier (1987), Informatique et qualifications; les compétences masquées, in Tremblay, D.-G. (ed.), *Diffusion des nouvelles technologies: stratégies d´entreprises et évaluation sociale.* Montréal, Saint-Martin: 255-267.

Tremblay, D.-G. (1991a), Computerization, human resources management and redirection of women´s skills, in Eriksson, I., B. Kitchenham and K. Tijdens (eds.), *Women, work and computerization: understanding and overcoming bias in work and education.* Amsterdam, Elsevier Science Publishers: 129-143.

Tremblay, D.-G. (1991b), Innovation, concurrence et mobilisation de la main-d´oeuvre. L´exemple du secteur bancaire, in Gadrey, J. and N. Gadrey (eds.), *La gestion de la main-d´oeuvre dans les services et le commerce.* Paris, L´Harmattan: 183-202.

Tremblay, D.-G. (1991c), Innovation et marchés internes du travail dans le secteur bancaire. Vers un modèle multidimensionnel de l´innovation. *Technologies de l´information et société,* Vol. 4, No. 3: 351-380.

Tremblay, D.-G. (1991d), Mise à l´essai d´un système expert pour la formation et la décision en matière d´octroi de crédit. *Revue ICO,* Vol. 3, No. 1: 41-52.

Tremblay, D.-G. (1991e), Computerization and the construction of new qualifications in the context of product and process innovation in the banking sector, in Nurminen, M.I. and G.R.S. Weir (eds.), *Computer jobs and human interfaces*. Amsterdam, Elsevier Science Publishers: 113-123.

Tremblay, D.-G. (1990a), *L´emploi en devenir*. Québec, Institut québécois de recherche sur la culture, Collection Diagnostic.

Tremblay, D.-G. (1990b), *Economie du travail: les réalités et les approches théoriques*. Montréal, Editions Saint-Martin et Télé-Université.

Tremblay, D.-G. (1989a), La dynamique économique du processus d´innovation; une analyse de l´innovation et du mode de gestion des ressources humaines dans le secteur bancaire canadien. Doctoral thesis delivered to the Université de Paris I, Panthéon-Sorbonne. Paris, Université de Paris I, 2 volumes.

Tremblay, D.-G. (1989b), Technological change, internal labor markets and women´s jobs. The case of the banking sector, in Tijdens, K., M. Jennings, I. Wagner and M. Weggelaar (eds.), *Women, work and computerization. forming new alliances*. Amsterdam, Elsevier Science Publishers, North Holland Press: 263-272.

Zarifian, P. (1987), Du taylorisme au systémisme: une nouvelle approche de la qualification dans l´industrie. Cahier de recherche No. 8. Paris, GIP Mutations industrielles.

Chapter 14
Office Work, Gender and Technological Change: The Portuguese Case

Virgínia Ferreira[*]

Contents

This study deals with the changes in the sexual structure of employment in offices and their relations with the intensity and extension of office computerization. These changes will be used as an analytic device to understand the consequences of information technology (IT) on female employment, in Portugal.[1]

[*] This chapter has been through a number of drafts. I would particularly like to thank the editors of this volume, especially Wolfgang Littek, and Carlos Fortuna. In carrying out this research I have benefited from the financial support of the Instituto Nacional de Investigação Científica.

[1] Offices seem to be the best suited employment sector to study the evolution of feminization and IT diffusion in Portugal. Offices are the second most important employment sector as regards total women´s employment, they have absorbed the greatest increase in female labour force, and, finally, they have undergone the most relevant technological changes due to the introduction of IT.

1 Initial Question — Does Computerization Mean Re-Masculinization?

The starting point for this study was the evidence of the increasing number of male employees in some types of office jobs traditionally held by women. This was a small but noteworthy change that ran counter to the basic expectations produced by any of the available theoretical frameworks. Between 1970 and 1981, the rate of feminization of stenographers, typists and similar occupations decreased from 86.3% to 79%, and that of operators of automated information machines from 46.5% to 42.9% (Instituto Naçional de Estatística, 1973, 1983). The available data of the national census of 1991 led us to believe that this trend continued during the eighties.[2]

These small statistical differences gained importance in the light of information from a union leader of the sector, according to whom the number of young men entering the work force to operate computers was a major source of concern, namely because they were hired without recognition of their qualifications and underpaid. This trend brings the Portuguese society into sharp contrast with the general employment tendency shown in Western Europe and North America, where there has been a continued and generalized increase in female employment, especially in jobs more mechanized or automated.

Another singularity must be noted — in the majority of Western Europe and North America countries, the rate of feminization of office employment is around 80%, much higher than the 52% registered in Portugal in 1991.[3] In a society in which office work can hardly be defined as female, and in which qualified posts still exist, it is likely that men do not offer the resistance to

[2] It is not possible to know the evolution of each of these two occupations because the classification of occupations follows now the new rules approved during the 14th International Conference of Statisticians of Work held in Brussells in 1987. At the available level of disaggregation, the stenographers, typists and operators of computers are in one single category. The problem is that the category includes also more qualified computer professionals (as for instance data processing managers), whenever they do not possess the formal qualifications required by the posts they occupy. Examining these occupations altogether we verify a decreasing of the feminization rate from 67% in 1981 (subgroups 0,8; 3,2 and 3,4 of the CNP-1980) to 57% in 1991 (subgroups 312 and 411 of the CITP-88).

[3] In the Federal Republic of Germany and in Holland the rate of feminization of office work is also merely around 50% (Littek, 1986; Fransen and Seegers, 1985).

the use of the keyboard, stressed by Collin Gill (1985). Thus, operating technologies, which has been left to women in the more developed countries (Cockburn, 1985), may well be a symbol of prestige in a technologically less advanced society.

In view of this, one may question whether or not the introduction of information technologies will cause an inversion in the process of feminization of office employment (see hints towards similar trend in Canadian banking, due to an overall upgrading of jobs, reported in chapter 13 by Tremblay in this book). Undoubtedly, there is not a unique refutation or confirmation procedure for each of these aspects in view of the ongoing technological change. As many studies carried out during the eighties have already shown office workers´ experience of newly implemented IT is highly complex (Littek, 1986; Webster, 1990; Ramsay et al., 1991).

In opposition to the claims made by technologically determinist accounts, which stress the great influence of the *valence of technology* (in the sense of technological best way, as mentioned by Corlann Bush, 1983: 155) over work organization, it is important to acknowledge the relevance of the context in which technology is applied. The results of the study presented in this chapter suggest that the interrelatedness between office computerization and office feminization can only be addressed by taking into account the particularities of the social context in which the interaction between gender and IT takes place. The social-economic conditions in which actual social meanings of IT are structured and articulated within a society condition the impact of IT on the gendering of the employment system (see also chapter 4 by Webster in this book).

Before I turn to a presentation of the theoretical framework and the results of my study I will now provide a brief description of office employment in Portugal.

2 Growth and Feminization of Office Employment in Portugal

In Portugal, office employment has been subject to profound transformations. In 1940, office employees represented 2.1% of the active population and, forty years later, the figure reached 9.4%. Changes in the sexual composition of this work force have also been registered. In 1940 female employment in offices represented 11% of the total employment in the sector and only 1% of the total of the active female population. By 1991 these figures had risen to 52% and 12% respectively (INE, 1994). Although the number of female office employees has been increasing markedly since 1940, the definitive turning point occurred during the 1960s and the 1970s, when female employment began to rise at a greater rate (1960/1970 17.1% for men and +147% for women; 1970/1981 -48% and +107% respectively).

During the sixties, Portuguese society underwent a period marked by various phenomena which directly affected the male work-force. Firstly, there was a general increase in employment caused by industrialization, resulting from the partial repeal of the Industrial Restriction Law, which had been in effect since the early thirties, and the lifting of limitations on foreign investment. Secondly, there was a reduction in the male labour force owing to the colonial wars and emigration. Thirdly, and most important, there was an expansion of state functions and a development of administrative requirements.

These phenomena are part of a set of factors which have been considered responsible for the increase in the female labour force in offices in other countries (Glenn and Feldberg, 1977; Rotella, 1981; Davies, 1982; Bruand, 1985; Cohn, 1985; Lowe, 1987). The specificity of the situation in Portugal, however, resides in the limited character of the country´s feminization process, let alone the weak and relatively late development of industrial, commercial and financial activities (Ferreira, 1994). This is in turn the effect of the lack of technical education programmes capable of attracting a significant number of young people. The limited technical education in Portugal is also closely related to the extent to which the existing vocational training programmes outside the schools, including the Institute of Accelerated Vocational Training created in 1964, were largely ineffective, underfunded, designed primarily for adult education, and under continuous redesign. For its part, the double tracking in the secondary education system (academic and technical schools) came under severe criticism right after the revolution of

25th of April 1974. The subsequent unification of the system furthered the tendency to lower the status of technical training in Portugal. As a result of this social groups whose career paths in „normal" conditions would take some technical training directions end up being pushed into schooling. Thus, the juvenile conceptions of the plausible routes to career mobility are displaced upward and school attendance is prolonged without career prospects being clearly defined (Pinto, 1991: 27). Young men, now found in competition with young women for office jobs, have followed this route. Once the labour market is reached, they believe themselves to be too qualified to enter technical jobs as trainees, though they have no technical qualifications, whatsoever. The tendency towards the devaluation of technical careers continues to mark Portuguese society and it represents a considerable force in the remasculinization of some sectors of economic activity. We will return to this question later. For the moment we will more explicitly detail the hypotheses and methodology followed in the present study.

3 Feminization versus Computerization Predictors

In both the upgrading skills and the deskilling thesis, with the computerization of offices, the gender segregation of employment would be reinforced, with women concentrated in less qualified and more poorly paid jobs, but the consequences at the level of the feminization of employment would be rather different in each case. The upgrading thesis suggests the possibility of the remasculinization of employment, if women do not get the necessary qualifications to keep their jobs (CEDEFOP, 1986; Kaplinsky, 1987). The deskilling thesis, however, predicts the intensification of employment feminization because more opportunities would come up for women in present gendered segregated employment systems (Glenn and Feldberg, 1977; Barker and Downing, 1980).

Instead of concentrating on these generalizations, Samuel Cohn (1985) suggested that the exclusion of women from employment, since they earn lower wages, must be understood in terms of its costs to the employer, so that we can define who will be able to support such costs. Through his study of two large English publicly held companies, the author successively rejects the theses of deskilling, of human capital, of discriminatory action by male unions and of the segmentation of the labour market, and claims that discrimination against women is less likely to occur in labour-intensive enterprises and, other conditions being equal, is less tolerated in the jobs which are the basis of the labour force in an enterprise. For Cohn, the more labour-intensive enterprises are the more female labour they tend to employ in offices. The same remains true for the more white-collar labour-intensive branches of the economy (Cohn, 1985).

Following Hicks, Cohn also considers the crystallization of economic practices within enterprises, which prevent, often through inertia, any change in such practices, once the conditions which formerly justified them no longer exist. Hicks suggested, for example, that this happens in expanding enterprises, whose salaries are set at a fairly high level in order to attract workers during the first stages of economic activity. Once the initial conditions no longer apply, the enterprise´s practices tend to fossilize so that it is not possible to interpret them in terms of economic efficiency.

If we apply these predictors of the exclusion of women to the analysis of the reversal of feminization, we may expect that re-masculinization occurs in the enterprises exhibiting characteristics with a strong positive effect on segregation. We must, however, take into account computerization in its eventual association with re-masculinization.

Many studies have shown that the prematurely proclaimed revolution of the paperless office is far from becoming a reality, and that the adoption of IT is associated with certain characteristics of the enterprises.[4] For example, a survey launched in England revealed that computerization is greater in enterprises with a higher white- to blue-collar workers *ratio*. So, financial and commercial services are the most computerized, followed by retail and wholesale enterprises (McLoughling and Clark, 1988: 23-26).

The model for analysing the re-entry of male workers into offices is obtained by crossing the influential factors of feminization with those of computerization. The resulting model contains, however, a clear paradox. On the one hand, feminization increases in enterprises where the white- to blue-collar workers *ratio* is higher; on the other hand, the correlation between this *ratio* and computerization varies accordingly. The model of feminization previously discussed states that more computerization corresponds to greater

[4] See, for instance, the studies carried out in England, France, West Germany and Italy (Fondation Européenne pour l´Amélioration des Conditions de Vie et de Travail, 1984).

feminization. It is exactly in this regard that the exceptional nature of the Portuguese society becomes apparent, account taken of the possible scenario, in which offices tend to combine higher proportions of *male* workers with higher levels of computerization.

As far as research methodology is concerned, the first step of data collection was to consult yearly records of establishments´ personnel delivered to the Ministry of Employment and Social Security, in order to survey the general characteristics of offices, and of their workers. So, the sample included all establishments of enterprises or private associations with at least two clerical workers[5] and a minimum of five employees, in the District of Coimbra.[6] The records of a total of 538 establishments with almost 4,000 clerical workers in the years 1989 and 1991 were consulted.

The second phase of data collection was a telephone survey to 504 offices of those whose records had been consulted, in order to characterize the equipment in use. Finally, focused interviews — 27 individual plus 4 group interviews, in which participated another 29 office employees — provided information on office workers´ experiences relative to both training and job performance with computers.

5 All the office workers whose job designation led to the conclusion that they worked with written information have been included in the sample. Excluded, on the one hand, were telephonists, office messengers, telex operators and debt-collectors, and on the other, managerial positions, in order to limit the variety of situations regarding both work content and degree of autonomy. In this kind of data collection, it is inevitable that the classification of the employees is taken simply from that attributed by the entrepreneur, but it is recognised that this classification may be totally arbitrary.

6 The District of Coimbra is neither the most nor the least developed of the 18 districts in Continental Portugal. If we analyze it according to various indices of economic development, it almost invariably occupies an intermediate position. Its importance as sample data in this study does not derive from the possibility of taking it as a national average, which would be absurd, but from the heterogeneity of the region, which permits both traditional and advanced industries to exist in the same areas (Rodrigues, 1988). In the processes under study in this research, there are no standardizable tendencies or behaviours from a global perspective. These exist only from the specific perspective related to the sectors of economic activity, size, degrees of organizational complexity, and types of technology used. Thus, since the data are analyzed with the concern of typifying practices and orientations by sectors of economic activity, the geographic area from which the sample is taken tends to lose relevance.

4 The Study: Re-Masculinization in Business Services

Of the 1,038 workers with less than 5 years of service with their employer in 1989, 53.5% were female, which indicates that, as a rule, offices in the District of Coimbra are undergoing a slow process of feminization (see Table 1).[7] The most feminized sector is Public, Social and Personal Services (Group 9 in the Classification of Economic Activities [CEA]).[8] The Business Services (BS, from now on) is the sector (sub-group 8.3.2 of the CEA) which appears to be undergoing the reversal of feminization, since only 53.8% of workers entering the sector over the four years before 1989 were female, whereas the average rate of feminization for this sector was 56.6%. The results obtained two years later, in 1991, do confirm this trend.

Table 1: Rate of Feminization of Office Employment (in %) - District of Coimbra (1989, 1991)

Sectors of activity	All office employees		With less than 5 years	
	1989	1991	1989	1991
All sectors of activity	382.0 (N=3,786)	41.4 (N=3,806)	53.5 (N=1,038)	56.9 (N=1,153)
Public, social and personal services	58.6 (N=333)	60.7 (N=435)	69.2 (N=104)	70.2 (N=161)
Business services	56.6 (N=173)	59.4 (N=212)	53.8 (N=130)	58.8 (N=148)

Usually, male employees are on average older than female employees. The BS sector, considering the group of employees with less than 5 years of service, however, is the sector with the lowest mean age of both male and female employees and the smallest difference between them (28.9 years for men and 28.3 for women, in 1989 and 27.5 years for men and 27.2 for women, in 1991).[9]

[7] The choice of this period of service was determined by the fact that, accordingly to the results of the telephone survey, more than three quarters of the entreprises (76.6% of 385) acquired their first computer from 1985 on.

[8] The subgroup 8.3.2 of the Classification of Economic Activities includes real estate and other consulting and accounting services entreprises. Banking and insurance are not included in this subgroup.

[9] The average age of all sectors of activity had been reduced during the same period. In the case of male employees, from 31,6 years to 30,9, and, in the case of female employees, from 29 years to 28,7 years.

In turn, the proportion of the same group of workers in relation to all employees in the sector gives us a measure of the intensity of job creation or of employment turnover. In this respect, the sector of BS has the highest proportion of this group of workers. Moreover, it is the only sector in which the proportion of recently hired men (78%) is greater than that of women (68%).

Data related to these three indicators lead us to think that an intensification of hiring male employees in offices may be happening in this specific sector of economic activity. The most interesting point is that this sector is also one of the most feminized, in which the enterprises tend to have the highest *ratio* of clerical workers to total workers (around 0.61), in which the office structure is the most complex and hierarchical, computing occupations are most frequent (in 46.9% of the offices), and computerization is simultaneously the most extensive (87.8% of the offices are equipped with computers), and the most intensive (about 30% of the offices have mini computers and mainframes computers, well ahead of the sector which comes in second place — Wholesale and Retail, with only 7.2%). Lastly, this is the earliest computerized sector of all (average age of computers is 4.9 years, while the general average is 2.94 years). In short, the indicators render this BS sector an ideal model in as much as it is one of the most feminized and most computerized sectors of economic activity.

The BS sector is in great expansion indeed. Various reforms underway, as a result of modernization, administrative, accounting and fiscal systems brought about by Portugal´s entry into the EC, cause a large increase in the demand for this type of services (computing, legal, advertising) by numerous micro and small enterprises generally lacking in suitably qualified staff. This tendency is quite recent, but very marked, displaying a positive variation of employment of 41.4%, between 1981 and 1989. In our sample, in only two years, between 1989 and 1991, employment in the offices of BS had a positive variation of 23%.

In this light, the hiring of male employees could be understood as being a case where the enterprise prefers to pay higher salaries in order to attract workers (the explanation put forward by Hicks, above mentioned). However, a comparison of the average monthly salary in this sector (around US$ 345 for men and US$ 362 for women) with that of all sectors (in average, around US$ 470 for men and US$ 400 for women) does not corroborate that expectation. As a matter of fact, it confirms instead the hypothesis of payment of lower salaries, which can be explained by the fact of this being a sector where small-scale businesses prevail. In addition, the sector´s output is strongly dependent on the office output, which reinforces the low salaries rule. This is to say that, in Cohn´s terms, the BS sector should not be able to afford the exclusion of women in its employment structure.

The male/female gap in salaries seems to be the major factor contributing to the hiring of male employees. In the case of the occupations with a decreasing rate of feminization (typists and operators of automation machines), women earn more than men (see Table 2). After controlling the variables of qualifications, age and duration of service, one confirms that male typists earn less than female typists, who represent 78.3% of the total occupation. The average monthly salary of operators (with more than 55% rate of masculinization) in 1989 was still less (US$ 245) than that of their female counterparts (US$ 270), though this is not the case in general in 1991.[10] In the offices of the BS, however, this discrepancy still holds true. As Table 2 shows in these offices male operators earn US$ 324 and their female counterparts earn US$ 346 on average.

Table 2: Average Monthly Salaries of Typists and Automated Machines Operators (in US$) - District of Coimbra (1991)

Sectors of activity	Typists		Automated machines operators	
	Male	Female	Male	Female
All sectors of activity	348	353	529	432
Business services	307	400	324	346

It is understandable that men are now entering those occupations which used to pay women higher salaries once we take the line of reasoning of Cohn, which advances that discrimination is exercised mostly by those entrepreneurs who can afford the costs involved therein. As BS offices are the most labour intensive, the most computerized, and display the most numerous category of operators of all the computing professions (72.3%), it is understandable they are the most responsive to the new market trends.

From data collected, it is plausible to assume that, though still not clearly defined, a tendency towards *re-masculinization* is on its way in BS. Flis Henwood (1993) detects a similar trend in the USA, where the rate of femini-

[10] These data are corroborated by the nation-wide 1986 study carried out by the Ministry of Employment and Social Security (Duarte et al., 1989: 22).

zation of data entry clerks went from 92% in 1980 to 87% ten years later. The author argues that this re-masculinization is the outcome of the replacement of white women by both women and men of ethnic minorities. What is new, therefore, is the entry of ethnic minorities. For sociopolitical reasons, far beyond the primary subject of this paper, one has to discard the ethnic argument as an explanatory reasoning to understand the position of women in computing in Portugal. Instead, we will turn towards two specific levels of the Portuguese situation: firstly, in the overall profile of computerization prevailing in offices in Portugal; secondly, in the training programmes and policies which have guided the adaptations to IT and the characteristics of the labour market.

5 The Evolution of Computerization in Portugal and its Effects on the Feminization of Offices

Some of the peculiarities of the office work in Portugal derive from the fact that traditional batch-processing computer systems have not been widespread and have not allowed space for the creation of many deskilled positions typified as women´s jobs, and usually associated with them. That is why the image of large pools of typists or key-punch operators, who spend endless hours hunched over terminals or electronic machines, under strict supervision, has never been common in Portuguese offices. Even if this has been an accurate picture of some very few offices, it has no doubt been only the case of big companies controlled by foreign capital.

This is signaled by the relatively narrow diffusion of certain equipment, such as electronic typewriters, along with the virtual non-existence of word processors or computerized archives. All this points to the fact that those offices have not passed beyond the transition phase from the electronic data processing equipment of the sixities and early seventies to the flexible technologies of the eighties.

During the focused group interviews, people value the ability to work with a computer as a new qualification in itself regardless of the tasks performed. In truth, in the large majority of offices computers are being used only to improve productivity for some of the more routine tasks. The great prevalence of micro-computers, the weak development of telecommunications and the virtual non-existence of other more sophisticated IT conform Portuguese offices to a profile of simple mechanization of certain elementary operations with no functional integration with the information services of the organizations. Computerization admits applications which have in common the characteristic of eliminating the human work of transformation without necessarily altering the degree of functional integration of the office or changing the existing relation between it and the rest of the sub-systems of the organizations in which it is introduced. It is thus a matter of rudimentary computerization which saves time and improves the handling of tasks but does not significantly affect the organization of work in the office.

What can be concluded here is that given the characteristics of office work, namely its resistance to Taylorization,[11] we do not observe a great change in the nature of the tasks involved in office jobs brought about by computerization. This evidence is repeatedly emphasized in many studies. For instance, Wolfgang Littek stresses that while „technical" working conditions may change dramatically and visibly, the social relations in production need not be changed so much (1986: 159); Sonia Liff argues that it appears that changes are only occurring in the way a job is done rather than in what is being done (1993: 104); and Juliet Webster concludes that IT will mostly affect employment not skills (1990). In the same way, offices in Portugal have not been affected much by the feminization and deskilling effects generally associated with traditional electronic data processing machines. Firstly, small and micro-businesses whose offices have less than 5 employees, employing over 50% of the office workers in the District of Coimbra, do not organize their work on the basis of subdivided, repetitive and parcelled out tasks. Secondly, the equipment available in offices that only have microcomputers, as is the case in 190 of the 416 offices with computers, does not facilitate the adoption of such a taylorized rationale for the organization of work (Ferreira, 1993). Thirdly, it is rather clear that the „gadgetry" aspect of advanced IT in offices creates a positive identification with the skills being developed.

[11] The information that constitutes the raw material of office activities is essentially discontinuous, cyclical and irregular. These features account for the „slowness of the office Taylorization process" (Muldur, 1984) or for what has been considered a specific office „rationalization dilemma", in view of the fact that many job positions hold large „areas of uncertainty" (Littek, 1986; see also chapter 12 by Littek and Heisig in this book).

6 The Conditions of Labour Mobilization

The labour recruitment policies followed by employers are molded by a particular combination of economic, social and organizational factors. In interviews with those responsible for BS, I realized that their preferences for young male labour were connected with the generalized precarious nature of employment in the sector. This is expressed in high rates of turnover. In 1991, 69.4% of the office employees of this sector had left their 1989 employers (on the whole sample, this proportion was 20.5%). As noted by Cohn (1985), high rates of turnover may be profitable when time demanded by job learning is minimal or null. The relevance of the employment precariousness is emphasized in the Portuguese society largely because the training programmes and policies associated with elementary office automation are generally very incipient and task-specific or, simply, do not exist (in 47% of the offices surveyed, there had been no training programme at all). In this context the process of acquisition of computer skills is heavily dependent of personal diligence apart from any kind of formal training programme and sometimes beyond the working hours. As it is generally acknowledged, this is a situation that is particularly harmful for women, since their „second shift“ leaves them with less time available to make this learning by themselves. The access to training programmes is, indeed, defined by the enterprises´ inner relations of force, social power and authority, whose workings (needless to say it here) are not favourable to women (Crompton and Sanderson, 1990). In sharp contrast with this, the superior training of young men acquired through games, school activities, clubs, etc., allows them to adapt more quickly to the computer-based technologies and overcome more easily the difficulties of the job.

Young male workers tend to accept these employment conditions, precarious as they are, due to the lack of intermediate-level job positions which, in turn, has to do with the predominantly labour-intensive industrial fabric, making use of relatively backward methods of production. Moreover, as mentioned before, the high professional expectations on the part of young males who had prolonged their education without a precise definition of career prospects add up to their attraction to office jobs. Furthermore, one must not overlook the tendency towards the devaluation of technical careers existing in Portugal which contributes to the desirability assigned to office job positions.

The feminist criticism has repeatedly emphasized that the much discussed models of Atkinson (flexibility) and of Piore and Sabel (flexible specialization) imply that *women* are forced into a *peripheral, secondary*, extremely feminized segment of the labour market. It is argued that the division between core and periphery proposed by the Atkinson model is essentially one between male and female workers (Walby, 1989), and that the „flexible specialist" of the Piore and Sabel model is gender-stereotyped as male (Jenson, 1989). Apparent as this statement might be at a global level, there are situations however in which the labour market may go through exceptional changes. In the case of accentuated unemployment, especially among young male labour force, it often happens that *male* labour force takes the place of female labour force in the more precarious employment positions, in the secondary segment of the labour market. As a whole, technological changes provide social contexts akin to the emergence of these processes of labour force replacement, because they are often closely related to changes in the gender-stereotyping of jobs.

7 Conclusion

Gender and technology are both constructed in discursive practices intersecting at individual, social and symbolic levels, and producing particular and often contradictory „results" (Van Zooncn, 1992). This helps explain the *differences* we find in particular societies, labour market situations or sectors of economic activity. In the context of the Portuguese semiperipheral society, in which office job positions still hold a relatively high symbolic prestige, the process of feminization has been retarded and limited. This chapter has offered two kinds of explanations for this: (1) the lack of intermediary positions of the employment structure and the absence of an adequate technical and vocational training pushed male labour force into office jobs; and (2) the weak diffusion of mainframe computer systems prevented the creation of numerous deskilled jobs, potentially occupied by women. This background, topped by a profile of simple mechanization of certain elementary operations with no functional integration in the organizational systems, leads to an adaptation to IT with no major changes in the labour force composition. In sharp contrast with this we registered a phenomenon of re-masculinization in the

Business Sector in Portugal. Rather than revealing a substantiation of the flexible specialization model, this expresses a labour market situation characterized by deep employment precariousness, which leads to a noticeable mobilization of young male labour force.

Employment patterns, labour markets and skill requirements are shaped more by the adaptative strategies developed by the enterprises in the adaptation to technological changes. The particular dynamic of each sector of employment and the global logic of employment system constitute fundamental elements of reference to keep in mind. In the case of the Portuguese offices, this study shows that the same technology may produce different effects depending on the specific sectors of activity in which technologies are applied.

The influence of IT upon employment practices varies in accordance with the way in which each individual user, network, organization or community assimilates and makes sense of these technologies. Acknowledging that technology is *culturally conditioned* and that, as such, it accepts or aggravates the existing social norms and values, we will also have to acknowledge that it will have different consequences for men and for women. At the same time, we cannot establish *a priori* what these differences are, nor can we generalize the differences to all men or all women. The results of this study show that job feminization cannot be seen as a process directly associated with office automation. As a matter of fact, the type of change we observed is unlikely to lead to questioning of occupational gender-stereotyping.

References

Barker, Jane and Hazel Downing (1980), Word Processing and the Transformation of the Patriarchal Relations of Control in the Office. *Capital and Class* 10 (Spring): 64-99.

Bush, Corlann (1983), Women and the Assessment of Technology: To Think, To Be; To Unthink, To Free, in J. Rothschild (ed.), *Machina ex dea: Feminist Perspectives on Technology*. New York, Pergamon Press: 151-170.

Bruand, Françoise (1985), Marché du Travail et Féminisation des Emplois de Bureau. *Bref Bulletin de Recherches sur l'Emploi et la Formation* 15 (July/August): 5-11.

CEDEFOP (1986), *Nouvelles Technologies et Formation Continue dans les Emplois de Bureau*. Berlin, Centre Européen pour le Dévelopement de la Formation Professionnelle.

Cockburn, Cynthia (1985), *Machinery of Dominance — Women, Men and Technical Know-How*. London, Pluto Press.

Cohn, Samuel (1985), *The Process of Occupational Sex-Typing — The Feminization of Clerical Labor in the Great Britain*. Philadelphia, Temple University Press.

Crompton, Rosemary and Kay Sanderson (1990), *Gendered Jobs and Social Change*. London, Unwin Hyman.

Davies, Margery (1982), *Women´s Place is at the Typewriter*. Philadelphia, Temple University Press.

Duarte, Manuel João, Luis Pereira da Silva, Antun Lopes Sirmaes and José Garcia Salvador (1989), *O peso das Profissões Informáticas no Emprego e suas Perspectivas Futuras*. Lisbon, Ministério do Emprego e da Segurança Social, Colecção Estudos, Série A, No. 8.

Ferreira, Virgínia (1993), *Novas Tecnologias de Informação, Formação e Emprego das Mulheres nos Escritórios*. Coimbra, CES para IEFP.

Ferreira, Virgínia (1994), Women´s Employment in the European Semiperipheral Countries: Analysis of the Portuguese Case. *Women´s Studies International Forum* 17 (2/3): 141-155.

Fondation Européenne pour l´Amélioration des Conditions de Vie et de Travail (1984), *L´Etendue de l´Introduction des Machines Electroniques au Bureau*. Dublin, Fondation Euroéenne pour l´Améloriation des Conditions de Vie et de Travail.

Fransen, F.J.G. and H.J.L. Seegers (1985), *Technological Revolution in the Office — The Netherlands*. Dublin, European Foundation for the Improvement of Living and Working Conditions, Working Papers Series.

Gill, Collin (1985), *Work, Unemployment and the New Technology*. Cambridge, Polity Press.

Glenn, Evelyn N. and Roslyn L. Feldberg (1977), Degraded and Deskilled: The Proletarianization of Clerical Work. *Social Problems* 25 (October): 52-64.

Henwood, Flis (1993), Establishing Gender Perspectives on Information Technology: Problems, Issues and Opportunities, in Eileen Green, Jeremy Owen and Den Pain (eds.), *Gendered by Design?* London, Taylor and Francis: 31-49.

Hicks, Joseph R. (1963), *Theory of Wages*. London, MacMillan.

Instituto Nacional de Estatística (1973; 1983; 1994), *Recenseamento da População*. Lisbon, INE.

Jenson, Jane (1989), The Talents of Women, the Skills of Men: Flexible Specialization and Women, in Stephen Wood (ed.), *The Transformation of Work?* London, Unwin Hyman: 141-155.

Kaplinsky, Raphael (1987), *Micro-electronics and Employment Revisited*. Geneva, International Labour Office.

Liff, Sonia (1993), Information Technology and Occupational Restructuring in the Office, in Eileen Green, Jeremy Owen and Den Pain (eds.), *Gendered by Design?* London, Taylor and Francis: 95-110.

Littek, Wolfgang (1986), Rationalisation, Technical Change and Employee Reactions, in Kate Purcell, Allen Waton and Sheila Allen (eds.), *The Changing Experience of Employment*. London, MacMillan/British Sociological Association: 156-172.

Lowe, Graham (1987), *Women in the Administrative Revolution*. Cambridge, Polity Press.

McLoughling, Ian and Ian Clark (1988), *Technological Change at Work*. Milton Keynes/Philadelphia, Open University Press.

Muldur, Ugur (1984), La rationalisation du travail de bureau: le taylorisme avant la bureautique?, in Maurice de Montmollin and Olivier Pastré (eds.), *Le Taylorisme*. Paris, La Découverte: 227-241.

Pinto, José Madureira (1991), Considerações sobre a Produção Social de Identidade. *Revista Crítica de Ciências Sociais* 32 (June): 217-232.

Ramsay, Harvie, Chris Baldry, Anne Connolly and Cliff Lockyer (1991), Municipal Microchips: The Computerised Labour Process in the Public Sector, in Chris Smith, David

Knights and Hugh Willmott (eds.), *White-Collar Work — The Non-Manual Labour Process*. London, MacMillan: 35-63.
Rodrigues, M. João (1988), *O Sistema de Emprego em Portugal — Crise e Mutações*. Lisbon, Dom Quixote.
Rotella, Elyce (1981), *From Home to Office: U.S. Women at Work*. Ann Arbor, Mich., UMI Research.
Van Zoonen, Liesbet (1992), Feminist Theory and Information Technology, *Media, Culture and Society,* 14 (1): 9-29.
Walby, Sylvia (1989), Flexibility and the Changing Sexual Division of Labour, in Stephen Wood (ed.), *The Transformation of Work?* London, Unwin Hyman: 127-140.
Webster, Juliet (1990), *Office Automation*. London, Harvester.

Chapter 15
The Division of Labor Between Center and Periphery in Industrial Networks: The Case of Galicia, Spain

Dietrich Hoss and Roberto Herranz

Contents

1 Galicia: Another „Industrial District"?

This article deals with the building-up of a relatively stable network of small plants and production units operating on a cooperative basis in the vicinity of medium-sized enterprises, both of which are newly established and modernized in Galicia (northern Spain). We want to recompose the real productive processes which result from the new relationship between „head" and „hand" enterprises (J.J. Castillo 1988/89) by analyzing the forms in which the different social actors have „socially constructed" a specific division of labor using their limited resources (Bagnasco 1988) and the nature of exchange and cooperation relations (which can be asymmetrical or equilibriated and „trust" based) which develop between them. This investigation should contribute to the debate over the growing significance of more decentralized and flexible production structures which has developed, above all in connection with the northern Italian model, during the eighties.

It presents a reflection „on the field" in relation to the diversity of „social structures of accumulation". The international debate on the mode of their generation and the forms they adopt in a specific social context started by rediscovering the works of Marshall, which centered on analysis of the social processes which create a crystalization of stable or fluid productive networks on the base of indigenous or local resources named „industrial districts" (Marshall 1919).

In connection with his 1984 work (together with Piore), Sabel has summarized the main characteristics of an *„industrial district"* in a more recent article (1989) about „regional economies" as follows: a division of labor exists between larger companies in which economic and technological know-how (finance, design, marketing, distribution, etc.) are concentrated, and smaller enterprises essentially limited to production. This „network of flexible contractors" enjoys a kind of stability (e.g., long-term delivery contracts) that makes it possible for these smaller enterprises to gain experience and a certain independence. A minimum of continuity is the prerequisite for the maintenance of quality standards and the capacity for flexible adaptation to changing market demands. This is due to the fact that the „industrial district" as a whole presents a „learning system" which is directly connected to the national and international market and which, therefore, must be in a position to constantly up-date products and production methods. Within the individual enterprises, as well as between them, „an elaborate combination of conflict and consensus" prevails; a „social pact" based on „high trust relations". The overall system is supported by local government institutions which are transformed from social-welfare to labor policy institutions. They provide financial and technical aid, especially in the form of training programmes and „technical consulting services". Altogether the new viewpoint could be described as a „view of the region as an economic entity full of under- or unused resources that range from traditional artisanal skills to petty commerce" (Sabel 1989, p. 40).

Basing himself on the experiences of the „Third Italy", Becattini (1988/89) defined the „industrial district" as a „harmonization of the requirements of a certain organization of the productive process with the socio-cultural features (values and institutions) of a particular population which has slowly developed over the course of time". The industrial district is marked by a „particular symbiosis between production activity and community life". For Becattini, the point is to recognize that there is a diversity of possible forms of industrial development which are traceable to specific regional conditions and traditions. „History and geography count" (Becattini 1989, p. 14).

2 Small- and Medium-Sized Enterprises in Spain

Just as with regional structures, small- and medium-sized companies in Spain have also begun to be recognized for their significance as growth factors in recent years. In an exhaustive study by Castells (and others) entitled „New Technologies, Economics, and Society in Spain“, there is discussion of „new economic growth poles“ in relation to the small-company sector (Castells et al. 1986, p. 432). Apart from the large multinational corporations, and above all in the automobile and chemical industries, this sector is the „second type of export industry with dynamism and prospects for the future“. Primarily, this involves textile, garment, and shoe factories, as well as other manufacturers of consumer goods which are in a position to combine „production flexibility, low wage costs and design quality“. They frequently function „on the basis of more productive and decentralized networks of subcontractors and home-work which can answer quickly to changes in demand. In this way they accelerate capital turnover, cut administrative costs and time lost to production shutdowns“ (Castells et al. 1986, p. 458).

In fact, this small business sector in Spain can assume very differing forms. On the one hand there is the tendency „to look for the Third World at home“, as Sanchís and Pico say, meaning conditions of industrial underdevelopment and super-exploitation. This entrepreneurial orientation allows using the underground economy as an instrument to discipline the labor force, extending the life of outmoded internal forms of organization and avoiding the pressure of the world market (Sanchís/Pico 1983, p. 89).

Nevertheless, in a newer study, the authors have established that — at least in their own region of Levante — a second type of small business has also developed which can be characterized as extremely open to innovation and oriented towards quality (Sanchís et al. 1988/89). On the one hand, there are subcontractors in the metal fabrication sector which supply the larger multinational corporations (such as Ford and IBM) with their demand for high standards of quality. These standards can be achieved only through a radical renovation of productive structures. On the other hand, however, there are sectors like the ceramic industry where the old pattern of technologically advanced large enterprises contracting out to technologically and organizationally backward small businesses does not hold true. Instead, there are rather more complementary, balanced relations between enterprises operating on a similar technological-organizational level.

The results of a survey of experts carried out by the authors shows that *three types of small businesses* can be distinguished. In branches such as the shoe or furniture industries, the classical small business dominates the scene: employing workers with only primary education, little in the way of innovation, almost no investment in raising the qualifications of personnel, and seeking to compete mainly in the area of price competition. This type of business made up about half of the survey sample. An entirely different type, however, was found primarily in the metal fabrication and ceramic industries, and was described as the „modernization type". Representatives of this category had an education at the middle school, high school, or university level, and were usually the sons of small businessmen or self-employed professionals. A section of them jointly established enterprises. They sought a competitive advantage in the area of quality production, used information technology and invested in raising the qualifications of the workforce. This type, in fact, constituted only 15% of the sample. The remaining 35% combined features of both types.

3 Industrial Development in the Semi-Rural Context of Galicia

The building up of new small-enterprise structures in Galicia can be understood as a further exemplary case of the potential for the development of an industrial network in Spain which is still far from the differentiation and stability which characterizes the „industrial districts" of northern Italy. Nevertheless, only now can certain specific features characteristic of the region´s traditions and social formations be elaborated on.

During the second half of the 1980s, the decline of agricultural and industrial employment in absolute terms as a consequence of the complicated process of crisis, technological and organizational reconversion of the enterprises has been partially compensated by a strong growth of employment in the service and building sectors.

In 1990, effectively 43% of the employed workforce was engaged in the service sector, 9% in the building sector, and 32.7% in agriculture. These averaged figures conceal, however, sharp variations between the various geographical zones in Galicia.

From a working population of about 1 million persons during the second half of the 1980s, only 53.7% were considered to be „salaried employees", whereas in Spain as a whole it was about 75%. Nearly half of the working population are working as independent farmers, small businessmen, or artisans. This structure is characterized by an important part of non-wage earning population, mainly in rural areas, explaining partly the estimated lower unemployment rates in Galicia (13%) compared with the unemployment rates for the rest of Spain (21%). All observers recognize the existence of high unemployment in the rural areas of Galicia. This is why today there is still an important reservoir of employable population in these regions, disposed to offer its capacities on the labor market for rather low wages.

With this as background, the developmental conditions in two industrial branches will be described which, in contrast to crisis-shaken branches such as shipbuilding and the weak capacity for innovation of many industrial enterprises, have been marked by new growth spurts. The first branch is the *garment industry*, which has a very long tradition in this region. Up through the 1970s, a weak industrial network developed within a rather polarized structure. However, because a large amount of custom-tailoring was still being carried out at this time, there was a multitude of small handicraft dressmaking and independent „autonomously" working women („modistas" or „costureras").

With the extension of industrial mass-production and the opening of the market to international manufacturers (especially producers of cheap goods from the Far East, and also those from other countries such as Portugal), this structure fell into crisis. Neither the large factories nor the small family-run tailoring businesses were able to maintain their positions. At the beginning of the 1980s, a new structure emerged which assimilated elements of the old one — craft capabilities and technical know-how — and in a specific way, flexible diversification and decentralization. Enterprises have been established — often on the initiative and under the management of a former custom tailor — which for the first time made their appearance on the Spanish market with a specific image as a regional group. „Moda Galicia" has started to become a new trade name. In addition, these enterprises are operated according to a new system: the number of employees in the parent plant is very small, usually between 100 and 250 people (Informe Cero, p. 174). They are involved primarily with the design and first phases of production (cutting), as well as the final ones like ironing and distribution. The main part of production, the sewing, is turned over to smaller enterprises and, to an increasing degree, to *cooperatives*. The garment sector has experienced a significant upswing in the last few years with this restructuring. The new features of this division of labor will be explored in the following sections of this paper.

In contrast to the garment industry, our second area of investigation, the *electronics branch*, scarcely has a tradition in Galicia, just as the metal processing industry is almost entirely absent in this region. Nevertheless, the current structure of this branch is characterized by a similar relationship between medium-sized parent companies and the small subcontractors.

The following results of our investigation are based on case studies involving numerous interviews with experts at both management and plant levels, observations of production plants (operations) and an analysis of written data. (The study has been supported by the German „Volkswagen"-foundation.)

4 Four Case Studies: Some Cross-Industrial Results

The four companies investigated in detail by us with their respective environments of smaller production units can be seen as paradigms for the previously described new constellation of industrial development. We are dealing with medium-sized companies with around 200 employees. In the last few years, each of them has succeeded in inducing a phase of economic expansion by means of technical and organizational innovations. At the same time there are clear differences between the four companies. Both garment enterprises were established in the late 1970s, one of which is characterized by a strong family tradition. One of the electronics companies, which was founded in the 1960s, is a family business cast in a well-defined paternalistic mold as well. The other is a business taken over by a multinational corporation in 1982. These differences with regard to company traditions and management styles make it possible to identify the features common to successful modernization strategies, as well as certain divergent approaches to technical-organizational problems.

A tendency towards „diversified quality production" is common to all of these enterprises. Like a series of other Galician businesses in this sector, both garment producers have come to understand the necessity of conquering a position on the Spanish market — and to a certain degree, even on the world market — by means of attractive design and superior quality. The electronics companies are being successful in their efforts to adapt their product technology to international standards: one in the television antenna field, and the other in telecommunications equipment. Only in the latter case does the Galician company work together with the research and development (R&D) department of the parent company in Madrid. This expansion proceeded in both branches on the basis of significant technological and organizational changes in the production process. In both cases these changes were established primarily in the pre-production and pre-assembly areas: computerization of the controlling and warehousing, NC production of circuit boards in the electronics companies and use of CAD in the areas of design and cutting in the garment plants. The printing of circuit boards as well as the sewing together of garments are resistant to technical automation. Despite the use of individual semi-automated machines — e.g., the sewing of button holes or laser-guided machines for circuit board printing — the production process in both branches is still distinguished by the dominance of manual activity. In fact, with the improved technical equipping of the production-preparation areas, the acceleration and diversification of manufacturing puts the production department itself under significant pressure in terms of time and flexibility. In addition, demands for quality have risen. In both cases, time delays in delivery of production materials (e.g., cloth) as well as periodic fluctuations in the necessary quantity of labor create difficult adaptation problems. Personnel policy must take all of these requirements into account. It can generally be said that workforce policy must combine a high standardization and formalization of the work process with the greatest possible flexibility in the deployment and numbers of workers. This can be demonstrated in various respects. Given the relaxed legal standards in employee relations and the prevailing tradition of the informal small-scale economy, the labor force assembled by the companies reveals three clearly distinguishable segments:

(1) a relatively stable workforce („plantilla“) with employee status and an unlimited contract, relatively high qualifications and skills obtained through many years of work experience;

(2) a number of employees, with 3- or 6-month fixed contracts, which varies according to orders and phase of the production cycle; most have minimal qualifications;

(3) a relatively large number of workers employed in home-work, small plants cooperatives, etc., who work exclusively, or at least predominantly,

for a particular enterprise. This segment is also usually characterized by only minimal certificates of education. Through a long-term familiarization in particular processes, however, they gain greater experience-related qualifications.

The number of fixed-term workers oscillates between a fourth and a third of the total number employed by the parent company. The number of workers employed in the „periphery“ of a company is usually at least as great as those in the company itself, but it can be as much as twice as high. As a rule, only labor-intensive processes (assembly and pre-assembly in the electronics industry and the sewing together of various clothing pieces in the garment industry) are suited for the employment of fixed-term workers or allocation to the periphery. The qualification- and technology-intensive preparatory phases of the production process (manufacture of circuit boards; design and cutting of garments) as well as quality control and marketing remain with the parent plant.

Indeed, there is a certain porousness between these workforce segments in hiring and internal promotions. As long as a special formal qualification is not necessary (e.g., trained technicians), a new-hire´s first job is usually of a fixed-term nature. While in the past familial relations played a decisive role in the selection of workers (and in one of the investigated companies this still holds true), there is an increasing tendency to take into account formal education (high school and technical college diplomas). One company has begun administering systematic employment selection tests; otherwise, younger workers are given preference. After the expiration of the fixed-term labor contracts, employees may be offered the option of extended contracts (up to 2 years) — possibly with interruptions — and following that, the possibility of full-employee status or incorporation into one of the cooperatives associated with the company.

Within a company´s regularly employed labor force, there is a promotional ladder extending from jobs requiring minimal qualifications (warehouse, simple assembly or sewing jobs), to the mastering of one or more complicated tasks, to quality control and various management positions. For the graduates of this promotional ladder there is also the possibility of being placed in leading positions for the building-up and management of a cooperative. Thus, the companies are concerned primarily with training in factory-specific qualifications. This is accomplished by rotating the workforce between various jobs. This rotation is not conducted in a systematic manner, but rather (apart from the need to compensate for temporary absences), results from the necessity for frequent changeovers and adaptations in production which do not allow for rigid and long-term structuring of the productive process. In addition, the companies conduct occasional seminars and training courses, especially in the field of information technology. Many management representatives complain about a generally insufficient level of qualification among their workers, but truly critical problems appear to exist only at the higher levels of technical qualification. It is here that one most likely comes across older workers with experience acquired in foreign countries.

In all of the investigated companies, work performance is pre-structured in terms of time and more or less exactly calculated, sometimes using an information processing system. Yet, in only two companies (one electronics, one garment) did we find the use of a payment system based on standardization of labor performance (in one case the Bedeaux system) with relatively high wage incentives connected to performance. In the two other cases, both technical (calculation expenditures that are too high) and social (avoidance of conflict) reasons were given for forgoing such a payment method.

While the internal technical-organizational structure of the companies under investigation corresponds rather closely to conditions in more industrialized countries (despite some individual differences), their *„peripheries"* are organized very differently. In addition, they find themselves in a deep restructuring process. Traditionally, a part of the production in the electronics and garment branches was given over to home-workers or small shops which were mainly established in the underground economy outside of the influence of legal controls. To the same degree that production volume expanded, product diversification increased and quality standards rose, this structure became increasingly dysfunctional. The high profit margins resulting from low wages and piece-rates were less and less able to make up for uncertainties in this sphere: delivery delays, problems with quality, transportation and coordination costs, etc. Small shops operating with their own wage workers were barely in a position to respond quickly enough to the cyclically fluctuating orders of the parent company with a sufficient mobilization of labor reserves. The few numbers of workers employed are scarcely bound to the small enterprises and fluctuate continuously. The plants maintain stability mainly through the existence of familial obligations and commitments.

As far as the option for a model of „irregular" or „black market" employment in the underground economy is concerned, there is also the additional risk of legal sanctions due to non-adherence to applicable labor laws.

5 The Cooperatives — A New Production Model

These are some of the reasons for the *development of a new production model: the cooperatives*. We paid special attention to this periphery of the four companies. Since the individual members of the cooperatives usually invest a significant amount of their own capital (more or less half the total costs of about 4 million pesetas per workplace, the other half being paid by various subsidies: EC funds, state and regional subsidies), they have a more long-term interest in the development of their production facilities and a greater readiness to make short-term sacrifices for the consolidation and broadening of their own production base. Adherence to delivery schedules and quality standards are more closely controlled because of their personal stake in the operation. In this way, the parent company combines the advantages of a dispersal of production plants in the underground economy (relatively low unit costs, no social insurance obligations, either a diminution of risk or gain in flexibility in view of fluctuations in demand, avoidance of trade union and labor-protection laws) with the advantages of an employment of the workforce in a way that is usually possible only with the direct control found inside the company itself: a high degree of labor discipline and production which meets relatively high standards of quality.

Aside from these reasons, however, the cooperative model presents, above all, a path towards a significant accumulation of capital in a very short period of time. In contrast to a one-sided and simplistic view of the peripheral productive networks which put the main emphasis on mobilization of a cheap workforce under precarious labor conditions, our investigation shows that the network of subcontractors constituting themselves as *cooperatives* allows the *mobilization of a labor force as well as the necessary capital*. The goal is not only to tap the capabilities and readiness of the workers, but also the necessary financial means, in order to set the productive process in motion.

The labor force which is drawn together in very simple production and organizational structures constitutes a foundation for the parent factory to carry out its production at a very low cost and without risk. In this way they turn a profit as much from the investments made by members of the cooperatives as from their work. This solution offers the additional advantage of shifting the costs of training, procurement, and maintenance of machinery, problems in production and the overcoming of social conflicts (individual and collective) onto the cooperatives.

Thus, compared to the conventional periphery model for the parent companies, the *cooperative model* not only offers a series of advantages, but is very likely one of the factors which have contributed to the success of a company such as the „Group Zara", the biggest Galician garment company, which has been able to quickly realize a rate of growth which can only be described as spectacular in the Galician context and which has achieved a prominent position in the Spanish clothing industry. With about 1,200 employees („en plantilla"), this enterprise succeeded in obtaining the support of some 1,700 workers in 68 cooperatives during a 5-6-year time period. Altogether they accounted for sales of about 20,000 millions pesetas in 1987, whereas in 1983 the sales of the group reached only about 4,000 millions.

In a rural area where a generally underdeveloped entrepreneurial tradition accompanies a marked caution vis-à-vis activity in industrial production, it is very difficult to find people who can quickly raise the necessary capital and assemble a labor force in order to carry out production on a longer-term basis in internally well-organized structures. The lack of entrepreneurial capabilities is especially felt in the garment industry with its particular growth dynamics, including the competition that takes place between the 20 „large" parent companies. The boom experienced in the one section of the garment industry which specializes in high-quality products sparked sharp competition between the innovative parent companies, which looked for solid relations with small subcontractors characterized by professionalism and a certain technical know-how. These small plants are established either at the initiative of former low- or mid-level officials of the parent company and/or as a consequence of the dissolution of some larger enterprises which were devoted to the production of large, highly standardized lines of clothing in the 1970s, or finally by the transformation of earlier tailoring businesses. The strong rise in production has reached such a degree of saturation in the small auxiliary shops that some of the enterprises investigated have undertaken projects to build up new small enterprises outside Galicia under the management of an experienced specialist (e.g., Adolfo Dominguez).

In economic terms, it can be said that there is an inelasticity in production on the supply side. Without a doubt, an economic culture, as it is typically found in Galicia´s rural areas — scarcely innovative and primarily oriented towards agriculture and fishing — limits the development of initiative in the industrial sector. This is particularly true for the kind of initiative required for the adoption of certain production conditions and organization not commonly found in this area. Lacking here are not only certain capabilities and technical-organizational knowledge, but also the subjective disposition and social behavior necessary for engagement in industrial activity.

To these socio-cultural limitations one must add the difficulty of finding individuals who are not only willing, but in position to raise the capital necessary for setting up a garment plant. One must be clear that the founding of a small garment plant means the necessity to find a source of financing not only for fixed installations, machines, and the ongoing expenditures for materials, but the direct and indirect costs of a labor force which will be relatively unproductive during at least the first six months of their employment, due to the necessary training and familiarization process. The relative equality of a productive structure built on small (mostly agricultural) owners reduces the number of individuals and families with the capital required to found a garment plant, even in the form of a small enterprise consisting of only 15 or 20 workers. When such a unit of capital exists, it is normally applied to traditional activities such as agriculture, animal husbandry, fishing, or speculative activities in the area of construction.

In contrast, the cooperative model allows the simultaneous grouping of various work efforts, and dividing the risks among the various workers. It makes it possible to share the fixed capital necessary for the establishment of the cooperatives which have access to substantial public subsidies, financing methods, and low-interest loans.

If the possibilities of creation and stabilization of cooperatives are a result of the capacity for design and commercialization of the central enterprises, then this is a necessary but not sufficient condition. Furthermore, a labor force is needed that is disposed to accept low incomes and a distribution of irregular working time. In addition to the high female composition of the cooperatives, their allocation in rural or coastal areas, where the small farmer and fisherman constitute a base of subsistence, and who usually have a large family to support, are two factors conducive to the „socially constructed" form which is needed for the labor force.

Doubtless, the hidden employment and the general lack of employment opportunities in the local rural labor markets favor an orientation towards this type of enterprise. At the same time, the dependency of the *woman* on the family limits her geographical horizons of employment and reinforces the value of a workplace near the home. The cooperative offers the opportunity to gain additional income without having to leave her own earth (here understood as property, cultural ground, and community). The incorporation of the woman into paid work and the success of many cooperatives is based on the resources of a large family, where the members are responsible for the housework and protection of the children, as well as being a possible workforce when circumstances demand it.

Finally, the hope of earning a reasonable income is soon raised by the agent who mediates the discussions with the central enterprises, and constitutes a major factor in the decision to create a cooperative. The success of some of the first-generation cooperatives undoubtedly served as an orientation for the more recent entries. At the same time this initial confidence, partially frustrated after some time, constitutes the basis for a raising of group-consciousness of the cooperatives and the beginning of the creation of various unions and associations for the defense of the workers´ interests, regulation of the market, and for maintaining relations with the central companies.

This form of operation also offers other advantages for the workers united in the cooperatives. This kind of activity offers the benefit of legal occupational existence, rather than employment in the underground economy (legal standards for cooperatives have been in existence since 1987). Invested capital comes partly from ECU funds, local governments, and unemployment insurance funds. The directorship of the cooperative is elected by the members, and questions of production organization are resolved by common agreement. Formally, at least, there is a collective economic independence, even if it cannot be foreseen to what extent this can become a material reality vis-à-vis the real economic dependence from the parent company.

However, the *disadvantages* that this cooperative has in common with the underground economy and which could be expressed as „self-exploitation", should not be overlooked: long working hours (often 10 hours per day and Saturday mornings), overtime (including weekends) when urgent orders require it, little vacation time, and extremely low wages (ca. 30,000 pesetas ~ 250-300 US$/month) or no wages at all, until the loans for machine procurement are paid off.

In order to pay back the loans, members of the cooperative see themselves forced to raise productivity either by intensifying work performance and/or extending the work day. Under the combined pressure of payment according to the number of finished pieces (practiced by the parent companies) and the demands of the creditors, they must compensate for the weaknesses stemming from a lack of experience and a form of production organization that is often very underdeveloped. There are frequently complaints about the fact that too little attention is paid to the development of time-saving work routines and optimal utilization of the machinery.

In addition to this lack of managerial capabilities, there are also more technical reasons for the low productivity level. Cooperatives and other small enterprises that are less professionalized have some difficulties in incorporating specialized machinery and stable operating processes. This is due to the variety of the nature and the type of product ordered by the central enterprises. This attitude is especially characteristic for the enterprises affiliated with the „Group ZARA", which does not pay a great amount of attention to quality, and can be explicated by a lack of planning at the central enterprise level regarding distribution and subcontracting of work. It may be added as an hypothesis that it is also in their best interest to maintain the cooperatives in a position of dependency and to stay with production processes based on the exploitation of cheap labor.

For these reasons, cooperatives must coordinate work with the demands of the central enterprises which is not foreseen in terms of time or in the nature of the product. Given the low prices per piece, the cooperatives are obliged to accept every type of work. This policy by the central enterprises — even if they have created a certain „industrial atmosphere" — is putting an important sector of cooperatives in a position of dependency because central enterprises

(1) do not stimulate the development of apprenticeships oriented towards the production of quality goods;

(2) impede an increase in productivity; and

(3) offer no possibility to change from subcontracts for low quality products to subcontracts for higher quality products, which are the specialty of the group „Galicia Moda".

On the basis of our findings, the analysis of the different spaces of apprenticeship, as well as the segmentations and limitations which are generated within the general framework of the development of an industrial atmosphere, would be an important aspect to examine in further detail.

6 Alternatives of Future Development

In this sense we have observed differences in the way cooperatives were created and in the relationships they maintain with the central enterprises, i.e. the nature of supports and exchanges emerging between the central enterprises and cooperatives.

Even if we cannot develop a completely closed model, we can affirm the existence of two types of subcontracting:

(1) There is a first type, which has difficulties in surviving over a long period, (e.g., in replacing machinery) and which cannot, except in extraordinary cases, improve quality or productivity. The central enterprise is not interested in these aspects and has many possibilities of subcontracting low-paid work of low quality in northern Portugal, and of using this threat and other competition pressures systematically to keep cooperative enterprises in a position of dependency.

(2) The second type of subcontracting is more stable, and is characterized by the development of preferential communicational and exchange relations with the intention of improving the relationship in a long-term perspective. Even if market rules — under different forms — are still functioning, traditional terms of competition on the supply side or monopoly on the demand side are not suited to encompass the emerging complexity of exchange relation and socio-economic cooperation. The most substantial difference lies in whether the cooperative is started up at the initiative of the „parent company", or if it is the result of local efforts on the part of the workers themselves. These kinds of varying relations between the parent company and its cooperatives were also found within the investigated plants. One of the garment plants, as well as one of the electronics plants — in contrast to their counterparts — are expending a great deal for the establishment of cooperatives according to their own specific needs and their own organizational structure. They stimulated the workers to establish one or more cooperatives with the severance pay offered to them by the parent company. In this case the new cooperatives were set up with a workforce already having the necessary skills and experiences to set the production process in motion.

The garment company, which is especially interested in a product of higher quality and which seeks to distinguish itself from the rest with its „fashion style", is in this way directly involved in the *establishment and organization of the cooperatives*. Without any sort of outside mediation, it directed and controlled this process by selecting the women workers who want to participate in the cooperative; by structuring the plant and production lines according to a proven criteria, including the parent plant´s wage-incentive system; by taking over the mediation of every kind of loan or subsidy, or functioning itself as creditor to the cooperatives; by offering the women training and educational opportunities in their own plants; and finally, by offering the cooperatives advice and support with management tasks and concluding a contract with them which guarantees a long-term production relationship with the parent company.

We have found a similar model with the electronics company which manufactured antennas and other telecommunications products. This electronics company has undergone a deep transformation in the last few years. The growing automation of circuit board production has been accompanied by innovations in assembly. Specifically, robots have been introduced on the company assembly line; at the moment, however, they can only be employed for relatively simple tasks. This is one of the factors that induced the company to pave the way for strong growth (based on a flexible network of cooperatives) and a decentralization of the production process. In this case, the cooperatives were an extension of the assembly plants of the parent company which, in some instances, took over control of the electronic circuits. The majority of the cooperatives fulfilled relatively simple tasks, but two have recently been established and have brought together personnel with a marked educational level in order to carry out tasks requiring a high standard of quality. This is also the case with a small subcontractor shop with NC controlled production of circuit boards. Even if it is not a real cooperative, it has been founded by former workers of the parent plant on a relatively egalitarian basis.

By contrast, other companies refrain from playing such a forceful initiating role and more or less limit themselves to establishing joint working relations with the cooperatives in other ways, especially some of the garment plants which remain on the margins of the process of forming cooperatives. This is true for the cooperatives of the „Group Zara", which is functioning under the slogan „bueno, bonito y barato" (good, pretty, and cheap). Quantity counts for more than quality. In this situation the network was formed to a great extent on the initiative of two priests who convinced the young women living in their parishes of the possibility of establishing cooperatives. At least in the beginning, these cooperatives worked exclusively for the „Group Zara". The success of these promoters in mobilizing a total of about 1,700 workers in 68 cooperatives (Lopez/Dosil 1988) is closely bound up with the prestige and status of priests in the rural areas of Galicia. In this case, the parent company hands over all organizational problems and management of the cooperatives to the cooperatives themselves. To a large degree these tasks were resolved with the assistance of the priests.

By these differentiations, one can see how different the central enterprises can act to create a framework of new production capacities under the form of small cooperative enterprises.

Without going into detail on all of the differences brought about by the conditions of establishment specific to the various cooperatives, it should be pointed out here that at the moment, the situation of the cooperatives can be characterized by a very tight relationship of *dependency* and asymmetry to the central enterprises and in many cases, by a situation of frustration and deception of the initial hopes. The dependency and control seems to be greater in the electronic sector, even if the incomes and stability of production here are also higher than in a „softer" branch such as the garment industry. Even in the garment branch itself there are differences. The working conditions in the „fashion style" sector are better than those in lower quality production, but in the first one, as in the second one, the power relations of exchange can be ameliorated in favor of the cooperatives by the accumulation of work experiences and professional capabilities in the different unities and by the creation of a union or association of cooperatives which can homogenize their common interests and negotiate collectively with the central enterprises and the political administration. Both processes are starting up now. Some cooperatives in the garment sector have discovered the possibilities of more profitable opportunities that have appeared on the market recently. At the same time, there is the parallel process of creating cooperative unions and associations, in order to be in a position to negotiate certain minimum standards concerning unit prices, etc. In other words, they intend to gain the kind of negotiating strength necessary to make real economic autonomy at least imaginable. The first strategy of amelioration of the market position can be characterized as *„exit"* orientation, in the terminology of Hirshman, while the second is oriented on the construction of a political mechanism (*„voice"*) which regulates the market relations and the political exchange with the administration. Only in this way could the relationship between the parent company and periphery adopt some elements of a new equilibrium between conflict and consensus characteristic of the production system of an „industrial district“, as mentioned above.

7 Conclusion

In conclusion we can say that there is emerging in Galicia a „new division of labor“ in two senses: firstly a certain tendency to develop „a new division of labor“ *between* central enterprises and their periphery creating a more stable subcontracting network with preferential exchange relations to allow a diversified quality production, secondly *inside* the cooperatives new forms of enterprise organization based in principal on unhierarchical self-regulation rules. But even if there are by these aspects some similarities with the Italian model of *industrial districts*, we must say that up to now there still remain considerable differences. Only in a small sector of the new network-building the relationship between centre and periphery is based on *trust* and confidence whereas in the majority the situation of the new cooperatives is characterized by *dependency* and asymmetric power relations in favour to the centre. Nevertheless the new trends appear to be an economic and social experiment which, under given structural conditions, offers long-term employment possibilities in expanding economic branches, mainly for women, in other words, to those who are specially disadvantaged in the labor market. The new framework fits rather well to existing qualification-, labor market- and cultural structures, a necessery condition for the development of new forms of work analyzed in another context (Hoss 1986). But to structure relations between centre and periphery in a more equilibrated way and to develop the whole socio-economical potential of the cooperatives the new model needs more than in the past support by the regional and local governments, not only financial, but in technical and organizational terms — an essential prerequisite for the success of the Italian model as mentioned in the first part of this article. It would appear to be rewarding if further research on the field of cooperative development could constribute to raise public awareness in this sense.

References

Bagnasco, A. (1988), *La construzione sociale del Mercato*. Bologna, Il Mulino.

Becattini, G. (1988/89), Los distritos industriales y el reciente desarrollo italiano, in *Sociologiá del Trabajo*, No. 5: 3-17.

Castells, M., A. Barrera, P. Casal, C. Castaño, P. Escario, J. Melero and J. Nadal (1986), *Nuevas tecnologías, Economía y Sociedad en España*. Madrid, Alianza Editorial.

Castillo Alonso, J.J. (1988/89), La division del trabajo entre empresas, in *Sociologia del trabajo*, No. 5: 19-39.

Herranz, R. (1986), New Trends in Work Organization: The Case of Spain, in Grootings P., B. Gustavsen and L. Hethy (eds.), *New Forms of Work Organization in Europe*. New Brunswick and Oxford, Transaction Publishers: 175-192.

Herranz, R. and D. Hoss (1991), Division del trabajo entre centro y periferia (cooperativas y industrialisacion diffusa en Galicia), in *Sociologia del Trabajo*, No. 11: 67-91.

Hirshman, R. (1970), *Exit, Voice and Loyalty: Responses to Decline in Firms, Organizations and States*. Cambridge MA, Harvard University Press.

Hoss, D. (1986), Technology and Work in the Two Germanies. Some Comparative Remarks, in Grootings, P. (ed.), *Technology and Work, East-West Comparison*, London, Croom Helm: 231-272.

Informe Cero (1986), *A Economia Galega*. Santiago, Universdade de Santiago de Compestela.

Lopez, X. and R. Dosil (1988), O cooperativismo: un medio eficaz na promocion del emprego, in *Encrucillada, Revista galega de pensamento cristan*, No. 56: 61-66.

Marschall, A. (1919), *Industry and Trade*. London, Macmillan.

Meixide Vecino, A. (1985), El problemo del empleo en Galicia ante la integración en la C.E.E.: algunas consideraciones, in Carames, L. (coordinator), *Galicia ante el mercado comun*, Santiago de Compostela, Banco de Bilbao.

Piore, M. and Ch. Sabel (1984), *The Second Industrial Divide*. New York, Basic Books.

Pyke, F. (1988), Cooperative Practices among Small and Medium-sized Establishment, in *Work, Employment and Society*, Vol. 2, No. 3, 352-365.

Pyke, F. and W. Sengenberger (eds.- 1992), *Industrial Districts and Local Economic Regeneration*. Geneva, ILO.

Sabel, Ch. (1989), Fexible Specialization and the Re-Emergence of Regional Economies, in Hirst, P. and J. Zeitlin (eds.), *Reversing Industrial Decline?* Oxford/New York/Hamburg, Berg: 17-70.

Sanchis, E. and J. Picó (1983), La economía sumergida. El estado de la cuestión en España, in *Sociologia del Trabajo*, No 9: 65-93.

Sanchis, E., J. Picó and J.M. Olmos (1988/89), La nueva pecueña empresa de la industria Valenciana, in *Sociologia del Trabajo*, No. 5: 41-65.

Venze Deza, X. (1986), *Capitalismo e desemprego en Galicia*. Vigo, Ediciones Xerais de Galicia.

Chapter 16
Frictions in the New Division of Labor: Cooperation between Producers and Suppliers in the German Automobile Industry

*Egon Endres and Theo Wehner**

Contents

1 Introduction

Until recently, it appeared as if the „factory of the future" in the German automobile industry would be characterized essentially by different forms of computer integration and networks. It was clear that the workerless factory would remain an illusion, but the visions of future factory life were characterized more by control centers and computers than by people. This was changed little by the very lively discussion of „new production concepts" (Kern/Schumann 1984) and the challenges of „flexible specialization" (Piore/Sabel 1984) at the middle of the 1980s. The trends and visions described by the two groups of researchers were indeed recognized by many representatives of management. But they did not bring about changes worth mention-

* The work was sponsored in the framework of the City of Bremen's program „Work & Technology".

ing, neither in the factory production concepts nor in the concrete work organization.

This has changed in the meantime. The „human factor“ is now seen as the decisive resource for dealing with complex production and market events. The largest share of German automobile managers has suddenly ascribed to worker-related functions, which in the past were considered more as unpredictable disruptive factors, the capability of being able to deal with problems and disruptions most flexibly. The focus of attention is not, however, the individual worker, but the cooperation and interaction of different persons and groups. Interfaces and divisions of labor which originated in Taylorism appear to have been superseded by diverse forms of communication and cooperation.

2 Change in Supplier Relations and Inter-Firm Cooperation

The above mentioned findings hold true above all for the cooperation between suppliers and final manufacturers in the automobile industry, an area which is characterized by a high division of labor. The need for coordination appears to increase precisely at a point where an intensive division of labor exists.

The supplier relations will — in the assessment of many autombile manufacturers — develop increasingly toward partnership, cooperation, dialogue and working together. A survey of over 100 management representatives from the most important German automobile manufacturers and suppliers revealed a few years ago that they believed that their company's competitive situation could only be improved through a change in the relations between manufacturers and suppliers (cf. Wildemann 1988). At present the concepts named above are (still) little suited for describing the relationship between final manufacturers and suppliers.

Our central thesis is, however, that the traditional forms of the inter-firm division of labor will be replaced in the next few years by new forms of working together which will have a strong cooperative character and will use the experience of the *Facharbeiter* (skilled workers) more intensively than previously (cf. Wehner/Rauch/Bromme 1990).

An essential background for this is the progressive reduction of vertical integration at all German automobile producers, which will probably be speeded up through the current cost and sales problems. It does not make a difference for the actual production of a car whether the individual production steps are spread out in individual factories. On the other hand, it is important for the work systems which are affected that they be in tune with each other. However, there is an important difference between the division of labor within the factory and between firms: one of the reasons why the latter is being considered by the final manufacturer is that the firms in question (frequently small and medium sized firms) generally have a lower wage level and lower administrative overhead costs. Implicitly there is naturally also the hope that the „smaller" partner can better solve the „large" coordination problems due to its already existing lean structure.

The ever increasing allocation of manufacturing stages to suppliers is also accompanied by a polarization of delivery structures in Germany: on the one hand, a few large system suppliers arise and, on the other hand, „a multitude of smaller and highly dependent subsuppliers" (Deiß/Döhl 1992, p. 14). The more value added, logistical competence and product responsibility are shifted from the final manufacturer to system suppliers, the more intensively they have to communicate and cooperate with each other.

We can already see today that a number of disruptions and conflicts between firms cannot be traced back to differences in power and practices of domination, but to a lacking coordination of the respective organizational procedures. This contradicts a central interest of the final manufacturer in being able to better deal with flexibility problems by shifting production steps to other firms (cf. Semlinger 1989). The success of a division of labor between firms is thus primarily dependent on how permeable the existing interfaces are and how quickly they can react. This is also true for the cooperation between system suppliers and their own suppliers.

We define *cooperation* as the basic form of human consensual processes, which is tied to concrete persons, goals, and concepts. The three fundamental characteristics of cooperation are: *First*, there must be at least a partial agreement of goals and values on the part of the cooperation partners. *Second*, reciprocal contacts, communication forms, and coodination efforts are necessary. *Third*, the cooperation must have consequences or benefits; these can be both material and non-material.

There is a close connection between the division of labor and cooperation. On the one hand, Marx referred in the *Capital* to the fact that with the spread of the factories, the original „natural“ divisions of labor were no longer possible (Marx/Engels 1890/1970, p. 483). On the other hand, the industrial division of labor necessitated new forms of cooperation, because the different partial tasks could not exist alone, but produced results only through their being combined (cf. Littek/Rammert/Wachtler 1982, p. 119). In the current systemic rationalization process (cf. Altmann/Sauer 1989; Wittke 1989), existing divisions of labor between and within individual industries and companies are being dissolved to an extent previously unheard of. In the course of the computer and production technology networks connected with this, new cooperation forms are emerging whose scope cannot yet be assessed. The fact that such changes are taking place is undisputed (cf. Semlinger 1993; Sabel/Kern/Herrigel 1991; Döhl/Deiß 1992). Disagreements exists, however, in the assessments of how far the newly emerging cooperation forms extend and the extent to which they represent a break in the traditional supplier relationships.

In this context, Sabel (1991; see also chapter 2 in this volume) expects the spread of a new form of „meta-corporations“, which he also calls „Moebius-strip organizations“. A fundamental characteristic of these new production structures is that „it is impossible to distinguish their insides from their outsides“ (p. 25). The „blurring between, and the hierarchical distinctions within, firms“ is taking place much slower than Sabel suggested, however. As our own studies in the German automobile supplier industry show, this process necessitates complicated reorganization measures within and between the cooperating firms. The change in the inter-firm divisions of labor does not take place without setbacks.

In the following, we would like to present some findings from a current empirical study of the cooperation between an automobile plant for upper-middle class and luxury cars and two of its system suppliers. Supplier A constructed its plant in the direct vicinity of the final manufacturer, for which it has been delivering seats in a close computerized linkage for ten years. The supplier relationship is considered to be a prime example of a just-in-time connection.

For supplier A, the logistic competence is just as important as its production technology know-how, particularly since it produces a product with comparatively a low value added. It is expected above all from supplier A that it can handle the very broad and fluctuating model variety.

Supplier B has for a number of years produced part of the electrical cables which are completed in the factory with cables from other suppliers and assembled as cable sets. The responsibility for the preassembly or complete delivery of the taillight wiring set has recently been consigned to supplier B. This concerns above all the delivery for a sports car model which is produced in a volume of 50 units per shift. In the course of a model change the delivery of the same wiring set for the middle class vehicle, which will be produced in a volume of 250 units per shift, will now be transferred to supplier B. Both supplier relationships take place on a just-in-time basis.

Although the label just-in-time supplier can be used for both firms, there are differences, to be precise in the effects of a faulty devlivery: whereas a car can definitely be assembled in the case of a false delivery of the seats, even if they are totally missing, and the problem can be corrected at the end of assembly, a falsely delivered cable set has to be assembled in order to carry out the following assembly steps. The correction, at the end of assembly, is naturally only possible when everything else has been disassembled; with a cable set which takes around 120 minutes to assemble, this time now increases to 16 hours. We consider this reference to be necessary, because the just-in-time label without further differentiation (like the correction possibilities and the subsequent costs in the case of false deliveries) appears too superficial.

In order to obtain a realistic picture of the existing cooperation structures between the assembly plant and the two system suppliers we are carrying out analyses of disruptions. We are directing our attention at disruptions (whereby we mean unexpected events) because both their emergence and the process of dealing with them give information about the extent of existing cooperation relations (cf. Endres/Wehner 1993, p. 17). In an analysis of disruptive events in a fully mechanized axle assembly we determined that depending on the respective cooperation relations, both a different frequency of disruptions and differing lengths of time needed for dealing with them could be observed: if there was a close coordination and cooperation between production workers and mechanics or fitters, more disruptions were „allowed" and these were dealt with more rapidly (and thus more provisionally). If such a cooperation relationship did not exist, then less disruptions occurred at technically identical stations. The disruptions which occurred, however, were repaired longer (and thus more comprehensively).

3 The Connection between Firm and Inter-Firm Organizational Structures

We proceed from the assumption that there is a connection between the organizational and, with this, the cooperation structures *within* a firm and *between* firms. This connection remains almost ignored in the relevant literature on the problem of suppliers. Most studies of the relationship between final manufacturers and suppliers focus their attention primarily on the structures of power and influence between the firms. Supplier relationships are thus seen as a fully new research object — or so it appears with a few more differentiated exceptions (cf. Jürgens 1992; Sabel/Kern/Herrigel 1991; Semlinger 1989).

The consensual processes between the suppliers described above and the final manufacturer, a company with several different assembly plants, are subject to a very complex structure of communications and decision-making. There is not a single interface through which the entire supplier relationship is coordinated, but a number of different contacts. This is true both for the suppliers and the final manufacturer. The question of whether a supplier relationship will be established or continued is decided first of all by the procurement department, which is located at the company's core plant, several hundred kilometers away. The procurement department's contacts at the suppliers are, on the other hand, firm management and the sales department.

At the plant level, the suppliers work together primarily with the materials management, process control, production, and quality control departments of the automobile plant.

Two central problems of the final manufacturer come through in the relationships with the suppliers. First, there is a lack of cooperation (in the sense of agreements) between different areas and persons. These are in part competing with each other or, at the least, do not appear to have sufficient communication channels at their disposal. Second, there is a lack of on-the-spot experience which is collected, e.g. by production, and reported back to the planning areas where it can be generalized.

Both problem areas become visible precisely through just-in-time networks, as the time available for dealing with disruptions and communication problems is very limited. We do not consider „*just-in-time*" to be primarily a logistic category, though; the applications we see in practice are too different for this. „Just-in-time" is primarily interesting as a metaphor for the attempt at aligning the interfaces between firms more closely to each other.

Just-in-time supplier relationships thus aim at a redefinition of the boundaries or divisions of labor between firms.

Thus, for example, delays in the paint shop of the final manufacturer lead to the fact that supplier B receives the necessary production impulses too late. Delivery losses or delays are then unavoidable if no agreement has been reached among the areas affected in the final manufacturer as to how the supplier will be provided with the necessary information.

A further example should make clear how closely the organizational structures within and between firms can be connected. The suppliers agree with the procurement department of the automobile company on the price of a certain product with specific quality characteristics. But it happens frequently that these quality agreements contradict those of other areas like production or quality control. Certain characteristics of an electrical cable set could thus be rejected by quality control, although these corresponded exactly to the procurement agreement. Consensual processes are particularly difficult when dealing with parts for which no clear quality agreements can be made; this is especially the case for seats and upholstery. If we keep in mind the fact that the definition of quality standards already diverges for the different production shifts, then we can see how complicated quality negotiations are. Thus supplier B has the problem that the installation of the cable sets always takes place the shift after it is delivered. Thus consultation and agreements with the shifts which are affected by the respective delivery relationships can only be carried out with difficulty. This creates particular problems because the final manufacturer's two shift groups have differing assembly concepts, or, we could say, preferences. The suppliers then get into the situation of having to choose or mediate between the final manufacturer's differing quality requirements. The fact that the latter is extremely difficult is made clear in the first experiences of so-called *„Entfeinerung"* projects (the opposite of *Verfeinerung*, German for refinement). *„Entfeinerung"* is understood as the reduction of overly strict quality standards, which could achieve enormous savings potentials. An example of excessive quality is when an auto seat is reclaimed solely due to a weaving flaw at a point which is not visible to the customer. *„Entfeinerung"* attempts frequently fail because agreements on changed quality standards can often not even be achieved at the final manufacturer. In contrast to this, rigid zero error criteria hardly make cooperation necessary.

The difficulty of quality agreements between firms increases further due to the fact that both the automobile manufacturers and their suppliers relegate a good share of the responsibility for quality to the production or assembly work forces and remove centralized quality controls. At this point, changes in the division of labor in the factory produce an additional need for cooperation between firms (cf. Endres/Wehner 1995).

Most conspicuous is the inadequate flow of information and communication in the case of changes to the product, which occur in the automobile plant in question (thus by no means at the company level) around 7,000 times monthly. The particular problem in this is that a change generally necessitates further changes at other points in the product, and thus in the process chain. Thus, for example, a modification in the auto antenna could necessitate a different antenna cable, which in turn has consequences for the suppliers of the cable set and perhaps also for the body plant and paint shop.

If individual suppliers are not included sufficiently in the consensual process necessary for carrying out changes, this could result in false or defective deliveries. Changes must both be tested in regard to all consequences in the planning phase and be realized synchronously in the the production phase. This process necessitates a close communication network between firms, which presupposes intact communication relations within the firm. Thus the competence of the supplier often includes comprehending the organizational structure of the final manufacturer as adequately as possible so as to continue it in their own company. For this reason, individual persons took on respective borderline and coordination functions at the companies we investigated (cf. Pohlmann 1991, p. 15). In the case of supplier B, this extends so far that one person is continuously present in the automobile plant, above all to compensate for the internal lack of cooperation which exists there.

4 The Limits of Inter-Firm Cooperation

Many German management representatives believe that only the radical reduction of interface levels between those areas directly involved can solve the existing communication and cooperation problems with respect to the suppliers. Thus those persons for the assembly area in the automobile plant we investigated have gone over to making the contacts to supplier B themselves. They criticized the previous arrangement of supplier contacts through the areas of materials management and logistics as static and inflexible. This is why they established the *direct* connection to the production or assembly area at supplier B. At this level — from „production“ to „production“ — they speak a common language and know how to come to an understanding about problems and disruptions. In the case we described, the maxim of treating the supplier like one of their own departments (in this case pre-assembly) allowed the rapid formation of intensive contacts between the production areas of the two plants. Thus assembly workers and group foremen *(Meister)* often visited the respective other plants. Since then, problems (like faulty deliveries of cables) are discussed directly and ad hoc solutions are sought after.

This entirely local strategy does include the capacity and willingness to cooperate intensively and flexibly deal with disruptions, which is then generally successful. They neglect to trace back and preserve experiences beyond this area, however. In the case described this led to the fact that the cooperating production areas removed themselves more and more from the level of formalized exchange relations (for example, between procurement at the final manufacturer and sales at supplier B). The areas affected or uncoupled by this, whose central task is coordination and generalization, thus operate increasingly on the basis of false or inexact data. This affects, for instance, quality arrangements which are no longer systematically reported back to the quality control departments. This led in the case described to the fact that the planning and controlling areas (both at the final manufacturer and at the supplier) could less and less reconstruct the actual situation in production in their computers. For example, the production areas of the two plants agreed on a new type of electrical cable for assembly without having the respective design areas change the drawings. The formalized documentation of changed product structures was thus increasingly delayed or totally omitted.

The discrepancy between computer projections and plant reality at the final manufacturer we studied led supplier A, which was very successful in logistic matters, to prepare its own „shadow“ documentation. That means it ignored the final manufacturer´s delivery requisition data which it received weeks and months in advance. Instead, supplier A planned its materials and other resources on the basis of its own experience (especially that of production). Supplier A trusted this more than the auto manufacturer's pseudo-exact EDP specifications.

A further problem in the communication with the auto manufacturer becomes clear in the case of supplier A. There are two different codings which can be used to send orders to suppliers. The first and more simple form consists of sending the suppliers part numbers. Each part number represents a concrete and unmistakeable part of a product, for instance an electrical plug. The second, and more complicated, form consists of transmitting so-called construction model code numbers, which are determined by the sales department. This makes it possible for the customer to select between certain equipment variants. Behind each code is a product segment with different parts (and thus part numbers), thus, for example, a certain headrest.

After supplier A received false part numbers from the final manufacturer too frequently in the past, it went over to assembling seats on the basis of code numbers. Supplier A thus converts each transmitted code into part numbers itself. This procedure, which taken alone requires more time and energy, helps prevent supplier A time and again from constructing seats on the basis of incomplete or faulty information. It is a central experience of the suppliers that each faulty part which is delivered to the final manufacturer is considered first of all to be caused by the supplier. In addition, the later correction of errors places considerable logistic and flexibility demands precisely on the suppliers.

In the relationship to supplier B it has not yet been decided whether the orders will be placed on the basis of part numbers or code numbers. The decision has been delayed up to now by the auto manufacturer, as the different areas there pursue different strategies. Thus the planning and controlling areas are in favor of transmitting parts numbers, because they believe that they make possible a more exact logistical check. On the other hand, above all production (assembly) strongly supports the transmission of code numbers, as they have proved to be less likely to cause errors and more flexible.

The communication problems described are not new within plants or companies. They are aggravated, however, when the production or value-adding process is spread out over different companies with differing organizational structures. At this point both cooperation processes which are entirely decentrally oriented (from „production“ to „production“) and those which are centrally oriented (from „logistics“ to „logistics“) run the risk of structurally intensifying the inter-firm coordination problems.

5 Inter-Firm Cooperation and Coordination as a Cyclical Process

The example of inter-firm cooperation illuminates vividly that there is a close interrelation between cooperation, on the one hand, and coordination, on the other hand. Sauer (1992) refers to this connection critically as he observes that no end of mass production is emerging: instead of „flexible specialization" a trend toward „flexible standardization" (p. 50) could be recognized. We do not want to continue the discussion of the most suitable term at this point. One thing is certain, however, the interplay of cooperation and coordination in the course of the decade-long Taylorization of production and organizational structures has become fragile and no longer does justice to the *changed demands of the inter-firm division of labor*.

A highly complex production process, like that in the automobile industry, depends on coordinated organizational procedures. These procedures should develop automatisms and standardisations to help deal with demands which come up again and again or change constantly. The cooperation between different firms cannot be constantly secured anew through negotiations, but requires a high degree of regulation. Up to now, regulation has found its perfection in the establishment of EDP structures. Without them everything would come to a standstill (in the most literal sense of the word) in automobile production with its extreme division of labor. This is true both for the networking of very different production processes and for the just-in-time delivery of a multitude of materials. Many standardizations start with the modularization of assembly steps, which enables a considerable reduction in complexity (cf. Schraysshuen 1992).

Coordination is, however, only possible when results can be anticipated (cf. Table 1). This is also generally the case in the automobile industry, which is geared to changes in market requirements. Predictabilities and planning data make it possible to demarcate tasks between different persons and areas and distribute them according to an algorithm. The cooperation is then determined in the course of if-then rules. Communication is then only required in order to secure the input of information and knowledge. In addition, an exchange will take place when the rules which were jointly agreed to are no longer adequate and exact enough.

The increased allocation of production steps to just-in-time suppliers, however, makes the final manufacturer more vulnerable in regard to its sequence stability. The more production steps are spread out over different suppliers, the easier it is for delivery losses or delays to occur. This increases the importance of achieving inter-firm cooperation and rapid problem solving (cf. Endres/Wehner 1995).

Table 1: Distinguishing Criteria of Cooperation and Coordination

Criteria and forms	Cooperation	Coordination
Prerequisite	relation of trust	common rules
Mode	consensual agreement	sequential assignment
Task structure	overlapping	delimited
Syntax	symbol-oriented exchange	algorithmic methods
Use	unexpected and ad hoc occurrences	occurrences which can be anticipated
Content	knowing that	knowing how

Cooperation starts when events cannot be standardized and thus anticipated (yet) or when they take place so seldom that the development of general regulating structures would be totally out proportion to the possible isolated case. This is exactly the reason why Japanese car companies formulate relatively abstract quality requirements for their suppliers. There is only a limited specification of quality demands in the form of contracts and production drawings (Döhl/Deiß 1992, p. 42).

While coordination aims at the abstraction of interrelations, cooperation involves bringing the concrete experiences of the actors involved in tune with each other. The vagueness of Japanese quality agreements requires the capacity for cooperation if the situation requires it (cf. Mehl 1992, p. 8). This capacity for cooperation is social to the extent that it is tied to concrete persons (or groups) and that relationships of trust emerge. This does not mean, however, that a personal relationship or even a friendship is necessary. Trust aims rather at adhering to personally negotiated commitments and thus to minimize imponderables together (cf. Helper 1991). Relationships of trust are mutual and are not subject to „contracturally codified regulations“ (Gondek/Heisig/Littek 1992, p. 38).

Cooperation relations have the character of consensual agreements which, however, require that conflicts are allowed. In cooperation relations the tasks of those involved are not clearly deliminated, but overlap or coincide. Cooperation is more strongly dependent on communicative exchange than coordination is. This must not be limited to verbal communication, however, but can encompass all forms of symbol-oriented exchange. But it is not necessary for cooperation that communication constantly takes place. Communication can by all means be limited to certain phases of working together. Essential is merely the fundamental possibility of reactivating communicative exchange (cf. Engeström 1992).

Cooperation relations almost always have the goal of being able to be converted to coordination. Cooperation can then be suspended when it is possible to coordinate the work through a sequential division of labor.

The interplay between cooperation and coordination is more complicated and uneven in the inter-firm reality than can be seen from the decisions made. Thus there is already an considerable amount of friction at the level of the cooperating actors: the establishment of consensual coordination between two or more actors (like the establishment of a quality standard, for example) can take months or years. Personal relationships are formed along with the emerging cooperation relations. When people cooperate in an attempt to solve a problem they always work on themselves and their personal relationships as well. Social relationships which thus emerge can, on the one hand, achieve a communicative importance in the establishment of identity. On the other hand, they can lead to a privileged position or even a dominance in respect to ones own area or company. Both of these factors can hinder the transition from a cooperation relation to one based on coordination. This is because such a transition would devalue the know-how of the individual actor and transform it into relatively accessible planning knowledge. To this extent, the self-preservation tendencies of inter-firm cooperation networks can block the necessary development of coordination structures.

But in the inter-firm reality, it is frequently the case that not even cooperation relations can emerge, because the interacting areas or persons are in a competitive relationship with each other. Thus supplier A delivers seat covers to the automobile factory, which are then processed further to make seats in the textile area there. A close coordination between the areas would seem to be necessary for production engineering reasons. Because the automobile factory's textile area is afraid that it will eventually have to give up further production activities to supplier A, however, it is not interested in establishing a functioning cooperation relation. For this reason they demand rigid and uncompromising quality standards from supplier, which are oriented on outdated requirements. In this case it is neither possible to establish cooperation relations nor coordination structures.

A further problem makes the interplay of inter-firm cooperation and coordination more difficult. Frequently, not only the plants of the final manufacturer, but also those of the suppliers are tied into corporate groups and thus have only limited possibilities to generalize their cooperation relations in coordination structures. Thus both for the final manufacturer and for the supplier, the firms design area was not at the plant site. In the case of design changes, each plant would have to involve other plants which are involved in the production combine. This leads to the fact that cooperation experiences are frequently transferred too rapidly into coordination processes.

6 Conclusion

The empirical findings outlined above should make it clear that the redefinition of the inter-firm division of labor expected by Sabel (1991) is a contradictory process. The intensification or improvement of the division of labor between suppliers and final manufacturers will hardly be possible without the establishment of inter-firm cooperation relations. The development cannot remain at the level of decentralized cooperations, though, but requires the transfer of the experiences gained to the level of coordination or organizational structures. At the moment, however, both of these are still lacking in the German automobile industry: there is both a lack of inter-firm cooperation structures and an inability to transfer the results of cooperation into coordinated work and organizational courses. The ability of companies to deal with these two problem bundles will be increasingly decisive for the success of inter-firm lean structures, not only in the automobile industry. The economic uncertainties and complexities will no longer be able to be managed without organizational structures which are more capable of learning (Sabel/Kern/Herrigel 1991) and „new kinds of boundaries“ (Sabel 1991, p. 46).

References

Altmann, Norbert and Dieter Sauer (1989), *Systemische Rationalisierung und Zulieferindustrie. Sozialwissenschaftliche Aspekte zwischenbetrieblicher Arbeitsteilung*. Frankfurt/New York, Campus.

Deiß, Manfred and Volker Döhl (eds.- 1992), *Vernetzte Produktion. Automobilzulieferer zwischen Kontrolle und Autonomie*. Frankfurt/New York, Campus.

Döhl, Volker and Manfred Deiß (1992), Von der Lieferbeziehung zum Produktionsnetzwerk — Internationale Tendenzen in der Reorganisation der zwischenbetrieblichen Arbeitsteilung, in Deiß/Döhl (1992): pp. 5-48.

Endres, Egon and Theo Wehner (1993), Kooperation: Die Wiederentdeckung einer Schlüsselkategorie, in Jürgen Howaldt and Heiner Minssen (eds.), *Leaner...? Die Veränderung des Arbeitsmanagements zwischen Humanisierung und Rationalisierung*. Dortmund, Montania: pp. 201-222.

Endres, Egon and Theo Wehner (1995), Störungen zwischenbetrieblicher Kooperation — Eine Fallstudie zum Grenzstellenmanagement in der Automobilindustrie, in Jörg Sydow and Peter Conrad (eds.), *Managementforschung*, Vol. 5. Berlin/New York, de Gruyter: pp. 1-46.

Engeström, Yrjö (1992), Interactive Expertise. Studies in Distributed Working Intelligence. Helsinki, University of Helsinki, Department of Education, Research Bulletin 83.

Gondek, Hans-Dieter, Ulrich Heisig and Wolfgang Littek (1992), Vertrauen als Organisationsprinzip, in Wolfgang Littek, Ulrich Heisig and Hans-Dieter Gondek (eds.), *Organisation von Dienstleistungsarbeit, Sozialbeziehungen und Rationalisierung im Angestelltenbereich*. Berlin, Edition Sigma: pp. 33-55.

Helper, Susan (1991), How Much Has Really Changed between U.S. Automakers and Their Suppliers?, in *Sloan Management Review*, Summer: pp. 15-28.

Jürgens, Ulrich (1992), Synergiepotentiale der Entwicklungskooperation zwischen Zulieferern und Abnehmern — Japan als Vorbild, in Deiß/Döhl (1992): pp. 421-440.

Kern, Horst and Michael Schumann (1984), *Das Ende der Arbeitsteilung? Rationalisierung in der industriellen Produktion*. Munich, Beck.

Kern, Horst and Charles F. Sabel (1990), Gewerkschaften in offenen Arbeitsmärkten. Überlegungen zur Rolle der Gewerkschaften in der industriellen Reorganisation. Unpublished paper.

Littek, Wolfgang, Werner Rammert and Günther Wachtler (eds.- 1982), *Einführung in die Arbeits- und Industriesoziologie*. Frankfurt/New York, Campus.

Marx, Karl and Friedrich Engels (1890), Das Kapital. Kritik der politischen Ökonomie I., in Karl Marx (1970), *Werke*, Vol. 23. Berlin, Dietz.

Mehl, Rainer (1992), Wachsender Druck auf die Automobil-Zulieferindustrie, in *Blick durch die Wirtschaft*, Vol. 7, No. 1: pp. 7-8.

Mendius, Gerhard and Ulrike Wendeling-Schröder (1991), *Zulieferer im Netz. Neustrukturierung der Logistik am Beispiel der Automobilzulieferung*. Köln, Bund.

Piore, Michael and Charles F. Sabel (1984), *The Second Industrial Divide. Possibilities for Prosperity*. New York, Basic Books.

Pohlmann, Markus (1991), Macht, Recht und Vertrauen zwischen Abnehmer und Zulieferer. Report No. 98, Lüneburg, Department of Economic and Social Sciences, University of Lüneburg.

Pohlmann, Markus, Maja Apelt and Henning Martens (1992), Autonomie und Abhängigkeit — Die Voraussetzungen der Kooperation an der Schnittstelle Beschaffung-Zulieferung, in Deiß/Döhl (1992): pp. 177-207.

Sabel, Charles F. (1991), Moebius-Strip Organizations and Open Labor Markets: Some Consequences of the Reintegration of Conception and Exekution in a Volatile Economy, in Pierre Bourdieu and James S. Coleman (eds.), *Social Theory for a Changing Society*. New York, Russell Sage: pp. 23-54.

Sabel, Charles F., Horst Kern and Garry Herrigel (1989), Collaborative Manufacturing: New Supplier Relations in the Automobile Industry and the Redefinition of the Industrial Corporation. Manuscript.

Sabel, Charles F., Horst Kern and Garry Herrigel (1991), Kooperative Produktion. Neue Formen der Zusammenarbeit zwischen Endfertigern und Zulieferern in der Automobilindustrie und die Neuordnung der Firma, in Mendius/Wendeling-Schröder (1991): pp. 203-227.

Sauer, Dieter (1992), Auf dem Weg in die flexible Massenproduktion, in Deiß/Döhl (1992): pp. 49-79.

Schraysshuen, Thomas (1992), Flexibel durch Module — Die Bewältigung neuer Flexibilitätsanforderungen in unternehmensübergreifender Perspektive, in Deiß/Döhl (1992): pp. 107-140.

Semlinger, Klaus (1989), Stellung und Probleme kleinbetrieblicher Zulieferer im Verhältnis zu großen Abnehmern, in Altmann/Sauer (1989): pp. 89-118.

Semlinger, Klaus (1993), Effizienz und Autonomie in Netzwerken — zum strategischen Gehalt von Kooperationen, in Wolfgang H. Staehle and Jörg Sydow (eds.), *Managementforschung*, Vol.3. Berlin/New York, de Gruyter: pp. 309-354.

Wehner, Theo, Klaus-Peter Rauch and Rainer Bromme (1990), Über den Dialog zwischen Erfahrungs- und Planungswissen bei der Entwicklung von Arbeitssicherheitsmaßnahmen, in Carl Graf Hoyos (ed.): 5. Workshop *„Psychologie der Arbeitssicherheit"*. Heidelberg, Asanger: pp. 138-146.

Wildemann, Horst (1988), *Die deutsche Automobilindustrie — ein Blick in die Zukunft, Delphi-Studie der Arthur Andersen & Co. Unternehmensberatung GmbH*. Frankfurt, Arthur Andersen & Co.

Wittke, Volker (1989), Systemische Rationalisierung — Zur Analyse aktueller Umbruchprozesse in der industriellen Produktion, in *SOFI-Mitteilungen*, No. 17: pp. 41-52.

Womack, James P., Daniel T. Jones and Daniel Roos (1991), *Die zweite Revolution in der Automobilindustrie*. Frankfurt/New York, Campus.

Chapter 17
Technological Change and Work Relations in the British Coal Mining Industry

*John Tomaney and Jonathan Winterton**

Contents

1 Introduction

This case study assesses the relevance of the „flexible specialisation" debate to patterns of contemporary change in the British coal mining industry. Particular attention is directed to the unevenness of restructuring and to questions of industrial relations. In the work of Piore and Sabel (1984) and Kern and Schumann (1984; 1989), sectors such as coal mining are not examined for the presence of „new production concepts". The „old" industrial sectors are seen as being preoccupied with survival and are most affected by economic recession. By implication, there is little room for new production concepts because in these industries the fight for survival is characterised by capacity reduction and declining significance in the economic hierarchy (Tomaney, 1991). However, this characterisation is only partly true of the British coal industry. Colliery closures have taken place alongside the creation of entirely

* Andy Gillespie, Stephen Leman, Neil Turnbull and Ruth Winterton made helpful comments on an earlier draft of this paper presented at the 12th World Congress of Sociology, Madrid, 9-13 July 1990. We should also like to acknowledge the cooperation of miners, union officials and managers in the two coalfields.

new capacity. Moreover, this new capacity has incorporated some of the most advanced developments in production technology. The study of changing workplace relations in the traditional industries remains important because of the significance they still retain in the present economic structure and future prospects of some regions of Europe, both as direct employers and because of their extensive linkages.

The following section presents a brief outline of the production system in the British coal industry, with the emphasis on the development of new technological systems in the 1970s and 1980s. Corresponding to these technological changes were proposals on the part of the National Coal Board (NCB, renamed British Coal in March 1987) for changes in work practices. A conflict between the NCB and the National Union of Mineworkers (NUM) over the nature of the restructuring culminated in the 1984-85 miners´ strike, which had profound implications for the subsequent development of the industry. The processes of restructuring are analyzed through studies of an „old" coalfield (the north-east) and the most modern mine complex in Europe (Selby).

2 Crisis and Restructuring

The mechanisation of longwall mining reflected „the prevailing outlook of mass production engineering" (Trist et al., 1963) and from the industry´s nationalisation in 1947, coal mining production has clearly aspired to, and taken as its model, „factory" methods. The longwall mining system was developed around the coalface conveyor even under hand-getting of coal, and when coal cutting was mechanised, the division of labour was intensified. When, in the late 1950s, coal cutting and loading operations were combined in powerloading machines, the work of face teams was re-unified but also subject to more intensive managerial supervision as the industry moved towards measured day work and the allocation of labour by method study and work measurement.

Productivity grew through the 1960s as a result of powerloading, reaching a plateau in the 1970s. Studies by NCB engineers identified obstacles to further productivity increases which were both technical and social in origin. It was discovered that on the average coal face, equipment was only operating for one third of the available shift time. The remaining unproductive time was a result of technical problems, including machine breakdowns, and the practices of workers which increased the porosity of the working day. The problems were thrown into sharp relief by the industrial relations crisis which affected the industry between 1968 and 1974 in the form of a series of mass strikes over pay. These developments reflected in part the replacement of locally-determined piece-rates with day rates established by industry-wide collective bargaining under the national power loading agreement. The miners´ growing militancy was also both a cause and a consequence of the growing influence of the political left inside the NUM.

In December 1973, when the first oil shock restored much of the bargaining power miners had lost in the previous fifteen years of cheap oil, an overtime ban in support of a wages claim, which led to the 1974 strike, prompted a reassessment of industrial relations strategy at the highest level within the NCB. The management response centred on reducing the power of the miners´ unions, especially the NUM, and the pursuit of automation to reduce the role and strategic influence of labour in the production process (Winterton and Winterton, 1989: 9-12). Part of the settlement of the 1974 strike, which brought down the Conservative Government, included a tripartite agreement between the unions, the NCB and the new Labour Government to expand and modernise production. This *Plan for Coal* entailed a programme of investment in new coal mines, most notably the complex at Selby in North Yorkshire, and the development of new mining techniques to extend the life of existing mines. This confluence of factors prompted an expansion of the NCB´s research and development programme, concentrated on two major innovations: automated monitoring and control systems and heavy duty mining equipment (HDME), together known as advanced technology mining (ATM).

Automated mining, which had enjoyed only limited success during the 1960s, was facilitated by the development of the microprocessor. A microelectronic-based control and monitoring system, MINOS (Mine Operating System), was designed to provide centralised and hierarchical control of mining operations (Burns et al., 1983). Many routine tasks, such as patrolling coal clearance systems, were automated, thereby reducing labour, and continuous monitoring provided management with a qualitatively new level of knowledge of the production process (Leman, 1990). The emphasis is on coordinating and optimising the performance of the whole mine as an overall system, rather than on specific technical innovation. The key objectives of these developments have been improved machine utilisation and intensified work rates (Winterton, 1985).

The more intensive use of machinery necessitated the development of technically superior and more robust HDME, designed to achieve consistently high coalface outputs and overcome the technical limits of mining equipment identified at the end of the 1960s. Although based on the existing longwall method, the equipment is designed to cope with much higher peak loads and is typically driven by very high levels of electrical power. The principles of HDME are applied to the main coalface machinery — the shearer (coal cutting machine), the face conveyor, roof supports — and ultimately to the whole mine. Available evidence clearly indicates that the greater the presence of HDME, the better the performance. At the end of 1988, NCB statistics showed that while faces operating with conventional equipment were producing a daily output of 1,177 tonnes, the average output for HDME faces was 1,315 tonnes with one element, 1,861 tonnes with two elements, and 2,445 tonnes with all three elements. The value of a conventional coalface is in the range £3-4 million. The value of an average heavy-duty face is £6.5 million, while the average value of coalfaces in the Selby complex is £9 million. Where HDME has been introduced, it has normally been accompanied by a move from longwall advance faces to retreat faces which give a higher rate of extraction with lower personnel levels. However, the applicability of HDME, like MINOS, is limited to certain conditions.

These technological changes, according to the former NCB Chairman Sir Ian MacGregor (1986), were bringing about a transformation of the industry from a labour-intensive to a capital-intensive one (Feickert, 1987). The NCB argued that the new working practices were required in order to liberate the true productive potential of these new systems. A number of proposed changes to working practices had been formulated by the mid-1980s. These included: the extension of direct production time through multi-shift working, which was designed to increase the time for which machinery was available for production; the development of localised, highly-flexible forms of payment systems (including ad hoc payments); the fusion of the roles of fitters and electricians into a single „electro-mechanic“ (reflecting changed maintenance needs); and the transfer of certain maintenance functions to machine operators. According to the NCB, the coal industry would be smaller as a result of the changes but for those who remained a high-wage/high-productivity scenario was envisaged. Capacity began to be modernised along the lines described above, but the projected upturn in coal demand failed to materialise because of the onset of world recession, increased competition from internationally-traded coal and changes in the patterns of energy use. The consequence of productivity increases in a context of stagnant or declining markets underlay the NCB´s colliery closure programme, which led to the 1984-85 miners´ strike (Burns et al., 1985). While the proximate cause of the strike was pit closures, it was clear that wider issues, including the complete restructuring of production relations, were at stake. Indeed, following the defeat of the miners´ year-long struggle, massive restructuring has occurred as can be assessed from Table 1.

Table 1: British Coal Operating Statistics 1978-92

Year[a]	Collieries[b]	Employment[c]	Output[d]	Total OMS[e]	Face OMS[f]
1978/79	223	233.6	105.5	2.24	n.a.
1979/80	219	231.8	109.3	2.31	8.88
1980/81	211	230.7	110.3	2.32	9.09
1981/82	200	218.8	108.9	2.40	9.56
1982/83	191	208.0	104.9	2.44	10.10
1983/84	170	191.7	90.1	2.43	10.32
1984/85[g]	169	171.4	27.6	2.08	10.54
1985/86	133	138.5	88.4	2.72	12.03
1986/87	110	107.7	88.0	3.29	14.40
1987/88	94	89.0	82.4	3.62	16.20
1988/89	86	80.1	85.0	4.14	19.05
1989/90	73	65.4	75.6	4.32	20.52
1990/91	65	57.3	72.3	4.70	22.62
1991/92[h]	50	49.2	70.5	5.36	25.28

Sources: NCB, BC reports and accounts, and operating statistics (various).

[a] Financial year ended 31 March.
[b] Number of operating collieries at year end.
[c] Men on colliery books, thousands, year average.
[d] Millions of tonnes, deep-mined coal.
[e] Output per manshift, tonnes, all men on colliery books.
[f] Output per manshift, tonnes, production workers.
[g] Miners' strike.
[h] Year estimates based on weeks 26 and 39 weekly and cumulative statistics.

By September 1992, out of 170 collieries in operation immediately after the strike, 119 had closed or merged, and the future for 31 of the remaining

51 collieries is at best uncertain. Between 1984/85 and 1991/92 employment fell from 171,400 to 52,560, a contraction of 70%, while the reduction in output from 88.4 million tonnes to 70.5 million tonnes represented a contraction of only 20%. In other words, 80% of production was maintained with only 30% of the workforce. Over the same period, overall productivity rose from 2.72 to 5.36 tonnes per manshift, an increase of 97%, or 10% per annum on average. At the coal face, productivity has risen faster, from 12.03 to 25.28 tonnes per manshift, representing an increase of 110% or 11.5% per annum on average. By September 1992 overall productivity was in excess of 6 tonnes per manshift.

Only a small percentage of this productivity growth is attributable to the closure of less productive collieries (Prior and McCloskey, 1988). The remainder is due to the further application of new technologies, which both increased the rate of production and reduced labour requirements through automation (Winterton, 1988), and work intensification as a result of increased external supervision supported by surveillance systems and supervision internalized in the form of various incentive schemes (Leman and Winterton, 1991). The differential effects of restructuring are illustrated in the following accounts of these processes in the North-east and at the Selby complex.

3 The North-East: A Productivity Miracle in a Declining Coalfield

The North-east coalfield is the oldest in the world. Until very recently it contained the oldest surviving coal mine in Britain (Murton in County Durham, which closed in 1991). Despite once being the most important coal-producing area in the world, the „Great Northern Coalfield“ has been in decline throughout the twentieth century. This process intensified after the second world war. In 1947 there were 188 mines in north-east England, employing 149,000 miners. By 1981 the number of pits had fallen to 28 and the miners to 14,000. The industrial relations traditions of the north east developed over two centuries. Under private ownership labour relations were characterised by paternalism on the part of employers and moderation on the part of the official trade union. Following nationalisation, these traditions were transformed into an accommodative pattern of industrial relations. However, during this whole period, moderation at the level of the regional union bureaucracy has been complemented by traditions of rank and file militancy in some areas, often born of highly-developed systems of worker control over production, known as „cavilling". Just prior to the 1984-85 strike, control of the regional union passed into the hands of the political left, which prosecuted a vigorous, but ultimately forlorn, struggle against NCB plans to close several north-east mines. The productivity performance of north-east coal mines in the period after the miners´ strike was frequently referred to by management and the press as a „miracle". Despite being in apparent terminal decline and having production difficulties associated with undersea mining, the north-east coalfield witnessed a rapid and unprecedented increase in productivity. Between 1982/83 (the last year of normal production before the 1984-85 strike) and 1988/89, the number of collieries was reduced by 61% and employment by 47%, while output fell by less than 18%. Productivity increased by 87%. At Westoe colliery, for example, employment fell from 2,380 in 1983 to 1,536 in 1990, while productivity rose from 2.71 tonnes to 4.36 tonnes per manshift over the same period. On 13 October 1992, British Coal announced the closure of four of the remaining five collieries in the north-east. This decision was modified by the Coal Review White Paper published on 25 March 1993: Westoe and Easington were put on a „care and maintenance" basis, so could theoretically re-open, and Wearmouth was „reprieved" on the basis of market testing, while the closure of Vane Tempest was confirmed. In practice all four collieries will be closed by March 1995, leaving Ellington, which produced over 2 million tonnes in 1992/93, as the only surviving colliery in the north-east.

In general, the north-east coalfield experienced only incremental changes in technology since the strike. There was only the most limited application of heavy duty technology (due to the unsuitability of the prevailing geological conditions) and ATM. These developments cannot explain the dramatic nature of the productivity improvements which have occurred since the strike. There has been no technological breakthrough of the type which characterises the Selby complex. The main part of the productivity improvement has come through unilateral alterations to working practices imposed by local management.

The most far-reaching changes to working practices have involved extending the range of tasks to individual workers. This practice affects all categories of worker, both underground and at the surface. Examples include abolishing the position of fork-lift operator and requiring surface craft workers to operate the machines in addition to their existing tasks. Below-ground craft workers have been made responsible for maintaining a wider range of equipment. The operators of coal-getting and development machinery are now expected to undertake a wider range of ancillary tasks that were previously the responsibility of other workers. These responsibilities do not, however, extend to the area of maintenance. This latter point is an important one: the assignment of these extra responsibilities does not amount to the meaningful acquisition of additional skills. Such developments are experienced overwhelmingly by workers as a process of work intensification. In addition to these developments, there has been a major increase in the use of external contractors to perform tasks formerly undertaken internally. Although the use of contractors was widespread in some coalfields before 1984-85, their use was severely limited in the north-east because of strong opposition from the craft-workers´ union. Moreover, new technology had provided a legitimation for specialist outside contractors, and there was less installed in the north-east.

The allocation of additional tasks to workers occurred alongside the effective extension of the working day. In the coastal pits of the north-east, the coal-face workings had become remote from the shaft bottom, several miles out under the North Sea. As a consequence, an increasing proportion of the total shift time was spent in travelling to the coal face and a correspondingly reduced proportion of time was spent in coal cutting, since the Coal Mines Regulation Act 1908 stipulates that a miner can only be required to work a shift of seven and three quarter hours. In the long term, management attempted to overcome this problem of diminishing productive time by campaigning for a relaxation of the legal restrictions. In the short term, and in the face of NUM opposition to legal changes, management in the north-east instituted the practice of coal production during „voluntary" overtime. Nationally, the NUM is opposed to any extension of the working day and to the practice of coal production during overtime on grounds of health and safety. Nevertheless, despite resistance from the local miners´ union, by late 1989 management had established coal production in overtime as the norm at every colliery in the north-east, allowing improved machine utilisation rates and greater continuity of production. Despite the unpleasantness and threat to health involved in spending twelve hours or more underground, the relatively low basic wage earned by miners since the strike compels many miners to improve their standard of living through extensive overtime working.[1] Thus, in the north-east in the five years after the miners´ strike the proportion of shifts worked which were overtime shifts increased from 10% to over 20%. The intensification of craft work also allowed, in some cases, the elimination of maintenance shifts and their replacement by production shifts.

Such developments were complemented by increased levels of supervision. The weakened position of the union made direct supervision easier and management made use of microelectronic machine monitoring systems. While used ostensibly to check machine operation, the systems can be (and are) used to increase work rates by allowing surface control room personnel to maintain a high level of pressure on underground work groups to keep machines running. As such, this technology is used in an overtly Tayloristic way.

Finally, in many collieries traditions of worker self-regulation which were for generations characteristic of north-east coal mines (see Trist and Bamforth, 1951; Krieger, 1983), have been largely destroyed since the 1984-85 strike. These „cavilling" traditions had their origins in practices developed in the nineteenth century designed to give equality of earnings opportunity under piece rate systems. At Westoe, for example, up until the 1984 strike, the miners´ union retained control of a complex system of work-group selection to give all workers a fair chance of good earnings and favourable working conditions. This system also appeared to have played a role in the formation of the highly solidaristic labour practices which underlay the colliery´s reputation for extreme industrial militancy. Management at the colliery, however, were hostile to the practice, seeing it as an interference in their „right to manage" (which indeed it was) and following the strike it was abolished. At Wearmouth colliery the miners´ union controlled a system of equalizing the opportunities for overtime earnings. this too was seen by management as incompatible with the requirements of production in the post-strike period and was abolished.

The „productivity miracle", referred to earlier, was achieved largely through a highly-intensive exploitation of labour rather than through a technological breakthrough. The qualitative increase in work intensity which gave

[1] Indeed the period since the strike had been characterised by an increase in the number of workplace accidents in the north-east.

rise to the productivity increase could only have been possible with the defeat of the miners´ union, a process referred to euphemistically by management as „regaining the right to manage". The north-east coalfield could, therefore, be seen as conforming to the stereotype of a declining industry resorting to regressive labour practices to maintain ground in a period of intense competition and crisis. The success with which this strategy has been pursued is remarkable because by 1990 the coalfield was producing the cheapest deep-mined coal in the world. These events, however, do not tell the whole story of the recent changes in the British coal industry. At the opposite end of the production spectrum is the Selby complex, which is considered below.

4 Selby: A Post-Fordist Coal Mine?

At Selby the technological systems which had been gestating in the late 1970s and early 1980s were to ripen and bear fruit. The design concept for Selby was unprecedented. The complex was to consist of five vertical shafts to be used only for ventilation, materials handling and manriding. Coal was to be brought to the surface through a series of underground roadways connected to two 12 km-long parallel drifts, with according to NCB publicity of the late 1970s, „maximum use to be made of automation and remote control techniques, including the use of computers programmed to react to changes in coal flow". The Selby concept was predicated upon the application of computerised monitoring and control, heavy duty technology and retreat mining methods. When fully operational, the complex was to produce over 10 million tonnes of coal per annum; some authorities refer to 12.5 million tonnes, and local management estimate the capacity of Gascoigne Wood, where the surface coal handling facilities are located, to be 17 million tonnes. Some of the potential of the Selby complex is revealed by recent operating statistics. During 1988/89 Selby productivity averaged 8.35 tonnes per manshift (compared with a national average of 4.14 tonnes), while in 1991/92 Selby productivity was over 12 tonnes per manshift (compared with a national average of 5.36 tonnes) and individual mines in the complex achieved performances far superior to those achieved in any other European deep mine.[2]

[2] The Selby Complex has experienced some major production problems in its period of development. Nevertheless the productivity performance remains impressive and our

From an early stage in the development of the complex, the official literature of the NCB implied that the highly-integrated and capital-intensive nature of the production process there would give rise to new labour requirements. The early literature used a language which, if somewhat overblown, was akin to that which characterises some of the flexible specialisation debate:

By comparison with traditional mines, the Selby pits will be modest employers of labour — perhaps 200 or so men per shift at each. Selby is to be a high-technology development whose employees will be technicians, not labourers. Automatic monitoring, electronic alarm systems, closed-circuit television and a network of two-way telephones will make it possible to control operations from a small number of strategic points (Pollard, 1976: 105).

In the light of these requirements, it appears that in the early period of the development of the complex (1980-84) there was a real attempt by the NCB to recast the relationships which had traditionally existed between management and workers in the coal industry.

The NCB faced the fact that among existing collieries within the Yorkshire coalfield there was much modern, low-cost capacity which tended to be concentrated around the Doncaster area. This area had, and continues to have, a record of industrial militancy. By contrast, the coalfield around West Yorkshire was in decline and had, according to the NCB´s official historian, „a very long tradition of very good labour relations“ (Ashworth, 1986: 380). The NCB began recruiting workers for the Selby coalfield from West Yorkshire.

The process is exemplified by the case of Riccall, one of the five Selby mines. When Riccall was being developed in late 1983, the management there began a series of meetings with workers at Newmarket colliery, near Wakefield, which was about to close because of exhausted reserves. Newmarket conformed closely to the stereotype of West Yorkshire pits. The aim of the meetings was to attempt to persuade Newmarket miners to transfer to Riccall. The process extended to guided tours of the complex for the men and their families and the provision of special services to help them overcome the upheaval of change. Such a degree of attention on the part of management was hitherto unknown to the men and was considered indicative of the new climate of industrial relations which was to prevail at the colliery.

purpose here is merely to illustrate the principles which underlie it and the potential of the complex. For a fuller critique of the limitations arising from the technological design approach adopted, see also Burns et al. (1983); Winterton (1985).

Miners at West Yorkshire pits which were about to close were faced with the option of commuting to Selby or moving to the area. In the event, about 50% of the current workforce lives within the vicinity of the complex. Those who elected to move were offered an effective mortgage subsidy to encourage them to purchase a house, amounting to £15,000 over seven years, and which was added to the wage slip. By using the subsidy system many miners were able to trade-up in the housing market. Simultaneously, according to management sources, the NCB took „a political decision“ to prevent the formation of „a strong mining community“. Rather than building large estates for the miners, the workforce was dispersed throughout the many small farming villages of the area. In this way the NCB avoided creating traditional coal communities which were so important in fostering solidaristic relations within the Doncaster area.

Irrespective of whether men actually moved home, a powerful incentive to becoming a Selby miner was the high level of bonus payments obtained by the workforce in the period prior to and shortly after the 1984-85 miners´ strike. At this time miners could regularly earn £250 per week in addition to their basic pay. The impression given was that Selby was to be operated on the basis of a high-wage/high-productivity bargain, and was symbolic of the rhetoric of the NCB generally. (Subsequently, bonus payments fell dramatically and tended to fluctuate from week to week.)

These attempts by management to build a new relationship with its workers, however, were frustrated by intractable industrial relations problems, which reflected both local and national factors. Locally, disputes tended to reflect the workforce´s determination to ensure a consistently high level of bonus payments. This situation may appear paradoxical given the NCB´s efforts to select a workforce from moderate areas of the declining coalfield. In part the paradox reflects the assumption of positions of power within the NUM branches of well-organised, militant miners who were able to set an industrial and political climate in the complex which was at odds with NCB ambitions. Selby miners also took part in the nationally-organised overtime ban which culminated in the 1984-85 struggle against the NCB´s pit closure programme.

The 1984-85 strike represented a turning point for the Selby complex as well as for the industry nationally. While in Yorkshire as a whole there was strong support for the strike, at Selby support proved to be relatively weak. When the strike ended in March 1985, less than 5% of the workforce at pits in the heart of the Yorkshire coalfield had broken the strike, whereas in Selby the corresponding figure was over 50% (Winterton and Winterton, 1989: 202). This situation could be attributed to a sectionally-based perception of the issues held by the miners at Selby: they knew that the complex was immune from the closure pressures affecting pits elsewhere. However, it is also clear that the collapse of the strike at Selby reflected the type of production relations that had been established there. In particular, the absence of a discernible mining community to offer solidarity and the crushing burden of mortgage debt experienced by those who had bought relatively high value homes in the Selby district were crucial explanatory factors.

The defeat of the strike had important consequences for the development of production relations at Selby after 1985. The national ascendancy of management hard-liners was matched locally.[3] In the immediate aftermath of the strike, significant changes were made to the management bureaucracy. Albert Tuke was appointed Director of the North Yorkshire Area of the NCB. Tuke had been associated with that faction of the management which was opposed to a negotiated settlement of the strike and had organised strike-breaking in the Doncaster area, although with less success than Moses in Derbyshire. Managerial responsibility for the Selby complex was given to Robert Siddall, another member of the hard-line faction who, during the miners´ strike, had responded to tales of miners´ hardship by telling them to „eat grass". In this context the aspirations of the pre-strike period for a new industrial relations bargain looked unlikely to be continued. Indeed, miners at Selby walked out following Siddall´s first visit to the complex. The climate of industrial relations changed dramatically, with management using the defeat of the strike as an opportunity to „put the boot in" (i.e. to act with extreme aggression towards the workforce), according to a management source.

Following the end of the national strike, industrial relations at Selby worsened. Between January 1986 and March 1987 there were 51 unofficial disputes at the complex, which management estimated had led to losses of

[3] The ascendancy of the militant faction within management at the national level was stimulated by the appointment of Ian MacGregor as Chairman in September 1983, and became complete in the post-strike period. Moderate figures such as Geoffrey Kirk and Ned Smith quickly departed the scene, and hard-liners such as Ken Moses and John Northard were appointed to national positions, followed by Albert Wheeler, the architect of new working practices being widely introduced (Winterton and Winterton, 1989: 216).

£13 million. According to local union officials, these disputes reflected a determination to resist the new management offensive which manifested itself in the form of an attack on trade union privileges, new working practices, higher levels of supervision and reduced levels of bonus payment. The industrial relations problems of the complex received extensive coverage in the press (e.g. Sunday Times 11 October 1987) as an example of a residual militancy despite the crushing defeat of the 1984-85 strike.

However, throughout this period tensions have existed within the management between supporters of the new aggressive approach and those who favoured the more accommodative approach which had characterised the pre-strike period. One manifestation of this tension was the attempted introduction of a „quality circle“ approach to production monitoring. This initiative owed much to the pre-strike conception of how industrial relations at the complex would develop and involved large numbers of miners being taught „problem-solving“ techniques by the US management consultants Kepner Tregoe. In theory this involved miners being transformed into what management called „analytical trouble shooters“, constantly on the look-out for potential production problems and tracing faults back to originating causes to prevent a repetition of failure. The ideal hoped for by management corresponded closely to Kern and Schuman´s notion of the worker as a „scout“. It is significant that this initiative was tried at Selby and not in the north-east, but in the prevailing climate of the period, the ideal only exists in a mutated form. Other attempts by management to introduce the practice of machine operators conducting certain maintenance functions have, so far, been abandoned in the face of union opposition. However, at Selby demarcations between craft groups were eroded to a greater degree than was the case in the north-east. This may be a function of technological requirements, as the electrical and mechanical technologies converge.

Tensions within management and between management and workers appear to have been largely resolved during an incident in July 1987 when a leading trade union official at the Selby complex was dismissed following a disagreement over new working practices. The local union failed to organise a successful defence of the official and, as a result, a severe defeat was inflicted on the union. From that time the level of industrial militancy at the complex fell dramatically and „a spirit of resignation“ (Richardson, 1989) overcame the workforce with a tendency to acquiesce to management wishes. The record productivity levels at Selby have not been attained on the basis of the new consensus model, but rather on the basis of management aggression and the defeat of the NUM.

5 Conclusion

In the previous section we have attempted to show how „miraculous" productivity improvements have occurred in the British coal industry. The means to this end have been different in the two cases. In the north-east, productivity doubled after the strike, largely as a result of work intensification. This was the only option open to management there due to the inappropriateness of HDME to the prevailing conditions. To raise productivity under these circumstances, the reduction of the power of the miners´ unions was essential and this was made possible by the defeat of the 1984-85 strike. The prognosis for the coal industry in the north-east is problematic, the future for its workforce is bleak. When asked how the coal industry in the area might survive its proposed privatisation, an old miner replied, „the industry will survive if they smash the union and turn us into slaves". It is now clear that even those conditions will not secure a reprieve for the doomed pits.

The case of Selby is apparently a total contrast. Prior to the miners´ strike there is evidence that an attempt was begun to create a workforce which corresponded to the „post-Fordist" model. In rhetoric, at least, there was a correspondence between the strategies of the NCB (and British Coal) and those which Kern and Schumann describe as „new production concepts". However, the battle lines between the „modernists" and the „traditionalists" are difficult to adduce, but to the extent that these terms are meaningful in our case, the hegemony of traditionalists has come to dominate. The pre-strike experiments are pursued only half-heartedly and exist in a degenerate form. It appears that in the post-strike period consensus-oriented practices have been deemed inappropriate or inapplicable. Management initiatives to establish direct communication with the workforce represent a continuation of the union busting begun in the strike (Winterton, 1990), rather than an opportunity for workers to participate in decisions (Edwards and Heery, 1989: 56). The local management have adopted the role of a „punishment-centred bureaucracy" (Gouldner, 1954). In such conditions there is no hope of a new pact between management and labour, although some union officials out of desperation appear prepared to deal with management in the hope of making the best out of a bad situation. Claims that „there are no signs of a sustained attack on the formal institutions of representation and collective bargaining at the workplace level" (Richardson and Wood, 1989: 51), are contradicted by the evidence of a systematic management offensive since 1984 (Winterton and Winterton, 1993). The experience of the British coal industry may be said to reflect something of the British model. This response to the changing world capitalist order is based upon a relative absence of investment in fixed capital and a preference for raising productivity through the intensification of labour. This is reflected nationally in the emergence of the UK as a low-wage/low-productivity economy in the European context. Thus, the „traditional" strategy of defeating the unions and intensifying work is presented as the „modernisation" of British industry. British Coal does not totally conform to type, however, because of its evident attempt to modernise at least some of its production. However, as a whole, British Coal has replicated closely the dominant (Thatcherite) rhetoric which insists on „the reassertion of management´s right to manage". In the post-strike period Ian MacGregor, as head of British Coal, reflected the Thatcherite mentality when he stated infamously: „people are now discovering the price of insubordination and insurrection. And boy are we going to make it stick" (Winterton and Winterton, 1989: 216-7). British management, therefore, lacks a modernist wing. Although we find much in the work of Kern and Schumann which is stimulating, we tend to share the pessimism of their critics about the implications for labour of the present tendencies. Any reservations which are held about the benign effects of contemporary changes in the German context must be doubled in the British case. In the UK case it is difficult to find a place for the interests of management in any progressive strategy. Any possible strategy for labour which has any hope of success must involve a severe curtailment of the prerogatives of management, prerogatives which will not be easily given up.

References

Ashworth, W. (1986), *History of the British coal industry, Vol.5, 1946-82. The Nationalised Industry*. Oxford, Oxford University Press.

Burns, A., D. Feickert, M. Newby and J. Winterton (1983), The miners and new technology. *Industrial Relations Journal*, 14, 4: 7-20.

Burns, A., M. Newby and J. Winterton (1985), The restructuring of the British coal industry. *Cambridge Journal of Economics,* 9: 93-110.
Edwards, C. and E. Heery (1989), *Management control and union power, a study of labour relations in coal mining.* Oxford, Clarendon.
Feickert, D. (1987), The midwife of mining. *Capital and Class,* 31: 7-15.
Gouldner, A. (1954), *Patterns of industrial bureaucracy.* New York, Free Press.
Kern, H. and M. Schumann (1984), *Das Ende der Arbeitsteilung*? Munich, Beck.
Kern, H. and M. Schumann (1989), New concepts of production in West German plants: the pursuit of flexible specialisation in Britain and West Germany. *Work, Employment and Society,* 2 (2).
Krieger, J. (1983), *Undermining capitalism: State ownership and the dialectic of control in the British coal industry.* Princeton, NJ, Princeton University Press.
Leman, S. (1990), Wisdom, knowledge or information? Work monitoring in the coal mining, clothing manufacture and mail order industries. *Industrial Tutor,* 5, 2: 63-77.
Leman, S., and J Winterton (1991), New technology and the restructuring of pit-level industrial relations in the British coal industry. *New Technology, Work and Employment,* 6, 1: 54-64.
MacGregor, I. (1986), *The enemies within, the story of the miners´ strike, 1984-5.* London, Collins.
Piore, M.J. and C. F. Sabel (1984), *The second industrial divide.* New York, Basic Books.
Pollard, M. (1976), Selby — the mine, in Vielvoye, R. (ed.), *Coal: energy for Britain´s future.* London, Macmillan.
Prior, M. and G. McCloskey (1988), *Coal on the market: can British Coal survive privatization?* London, Financial Times Business Information.
Richardson, G. (1989), *Selby coalfield industrial chaplaincy: Annual report 1988/9.* Selby, Selby Coalfield Industrial Chaplaincy.
Richardson, R. and S. Wood (1989), Productivity change in the coal industry and the new industrial relations. *British Journal of Industrial Relations,* 27, 1: 33-55.
Tomaney, J. (1991), Technical change and the transformation of work: The case of British coalmining. PhD thesis. Newcastle, University of Newcastle.
Trist, E.L. and K.W. Bamforth (1951), Some social and psychological consequences of the longwall method of coal getting. *Human Relations,* 4, 1: 3-38.
Trist, E.L., G.W. Higgin, H. Murray and A.B. Pollock (1963), *Organizational choice.* London, Tavistock.
Winterton, J. (1985), Computerized coal: New technology in the mines, in H. Beynon (ed.), *Digging deeper: Issues in the miners´ strike.* London, Verso: 231-43.
Winterton, J. (1988), The effect of new technologies on the productivity and production costs of the British coal mining industry. Report No.12, Bradford, University of Bradford Working Environment Research Group.
Winterton, J. (1990), Private power and public relations: the effects of privatisation upon industrial relations in British Coal, in M. Poole and G. Jenkins (eds.), *New forms of ownership.* London, Routledge: 134-50.
Winterton, J. and R. Winterton (1989), *Coal, crisis and conflict: The 1984-85 miners´ strike in Yorkshire.* Manchester, Manchester University Press.
Winterton, J. and R. Winterton (1993), Coal, in A. Pendleton and J. Winterton (eds.), *Public enterprise in transition: Industrial relations in state and privatized corporations.* London, Routledge: 69-99.

Chapter 18
Job Redesign at Finnish Shipyards — Causes and Consequences

Jukka Niemelä and Heikki Leimu

Contents

1 Introduction

The thesis of flexible specialization (Piore and Sabel, 1984) and its position on the causes and consequences of job redesign has become very familiar during the last ten years. It has aroused a lot of debate and criticism (see for instance Wood, 1989; and Pollert, 1991). From the point of view of our research the following criticism is relevant.

Customized quality goods can be produced economically efficiently within various forms of work organizations. We agree with Sorge and Streeck (1988: 42), who have argued that management has no need to „challenge industrial relations rigidities" if existing product strategy and organizational structures yield „satisfactory results by the firm´s culturally and politically defined performance standards". Most of the Finnish shipyards studied by us began the one-off production of customized vessels in the 1970s. For almost ten years this new product strategy was associated with the work organization influenced by craft traditions and Taylorist features. It was not until the mid-1980s that management began to redesign work tasks. The management of the Finnish shipyards had no incentive to redesign jobs because the contraction of international ship markets hit Finnish yards later than other Western yards.

In previous studies of work reorganization it has been observed that the rigidities and economic inefficiency of the preceding work process constituted some of the most important causes of job redesign (see for instance Dankbaar, 1988; Düll, 1989; Gustavsen and Hethy, 1989). The same reasons have triggered reorganization at the Finnish yards. However, it was not until the mid 1980s, when both the prices and markets for vessels declined substantially, that management moved into action. Finnish shipyards exemplify the case in which management can tolerate for years costs caused by rigidities of the labour process if these costs do not threaten the market position of the firm. In order to analyze how the rigidities and contradictions of the work process — the crisis of the labour process — emerged we will therefore outline the development of the product strategy and work organization of Finnish shipbuilding after the Second World War.

We agree with Pollert (1991: 18) who has stated that the concept of technological paradigm is

> based on an oversimplified conception both of mass production and of craft production as the dual characteristic forms of production of twentieth century capitalism. Even within the large and technologically advanced firms associated with the primary sector and mass production, a variety of technologies and productions systems co-existed and continue to do so.

Finnish shipyards carry on the traditions of craft production, but at the same time apply mass production techniques in many parts of the production process.

The flexible specialization thesis overemphasizes the flexible quality of the new computer based production technology at the expense of other factors such as factory layouts, disposable tools and product design (Wood, 1989: 16). In the shipbuilding industry these factors have had far more impact on production processes, the quality of work and skill levels than any computer controlled machinery.

The position of the flexible specialization thesis on the causes and consequences of job redesign is excessively optimistic. So far empirical studies on the reorganization of work have not indicated a radical rupture in the deployment of labour in industry, but evidence is available of incremental change, modest task enlargement and even of an intensification of work (see, for instance Wood, 1989; Düll, 1989; Elger, 1991; Alasoini, 1991; Tomaney, 1990). The thesis of flexible specialization does not analyze the conditions under which work reorganization leads to a general improvement and up-skilling of work (O´Reilly, 1992). In the conclusion of this chapter we consider why job redesign has improved the quality of work at Finnish shipyards.

Compared to shipbuilding in other countries, Finnish shipbuilding managed well until the mid-1980s (Todd, 1985: 362). The exceptional success of the Finnish shipyards was due to two basic factors: firstly, the Finnish yards have concentrated upon the construction of technologically advanced special vessels and secondly, orders from the former Soviet Union were substantial and, before the mid-1980s, they even predominated at some yards. Since 1984 the level of employment has decreased by about 50% so that by the end of 1992 the Finnish shipyards employed a total labour force of about 6,700 persons.[1] The contraction of Finnish shipbuilding was primarily an outcome of the collapse of exports to the former Soviet Union and of the larger subsidies granted by other states to their shipbuilders. In Finland only the normal export credit facilities within the rules of the OECD have been conceded.

Our data consists of qualitative interviews of blue collar workers and officials (white collar workers) (N = 80) and survey questionnaires of blue collar workers (N = 618) and officials (N = 531). In this chapter we will not use the data on officials. This chapter is a part of our extensive research project on Finnish shipyards, their subcontractors and their joint regional employment effects, which was funded by the Academy of Finland between 1990-93. The study is concerned with the two largest Finnish shipbuilding companies, Kvaerner Masa-Yards and Finnyards, which together employ 5,500 people. Masa-Yards was founded in November 1989 after the bankcruptcy of the then largest Finnish shipbuilding company, Wärtsilä Marine, in order to continue shipbulding at the Helsinki and Turku yards. In 1991 Masa-Yards was bought by the Norwegian company Kværner, which in 1992 was the largest shipbuilder in Europe and the fourth largest in the world. In 1991 and 1992 Masa-Yards was one of the most profitable enterprises within the Kværner group of industries. At the beginning of 1993 Masa-Yards obtained orders totalling more than 1 billion US dollars, for a luxury cruise

[1] Redundancies took place mostly in the 1980s. Most of the redundant shipbuilding workers easily found new jobs in the good labour market situation of the 1980s (Jusi, 1989). Redundancies did not cause labour market segmentation, the modern version of polarization (cf. Kern and Schumann, 1984: 300-320).

liner from Japan and for four LNG-tankers from Abu Dhabi despite stiff competition from primarily Japanese shipyards. The other major Finnish shipbuilder, Finnyards is situated in Rauma from where it operates two yards. At the end of 1992 Finnyards had a total of 1900 employees. Finnyards was founded in 1992 when Rauma Yards and Hollming were merged with the aid of a minor state subsidy.

Referring to the German shipbuilding industry, Kern and Schumann (1984: 308) argued a decade ago that new production concepts do not help workers in shipbuilding, because their jobs are prey to the global, sectoral and even regional collapse of shipping markets. The situation in the 1990s is different. The trough of the current worldwide-crisis of the shipbuilding industry has been reached and, according to market forecasts, a favourable period is to be expected in the 1990s. Most of the tankers and bulk carriers that were built in the 1970s will have to be scrapped and replaced during the 1990s.

2 The Crisis of the Labour Process in the Finnish Shipbuilding Industry

It is well documented that shipbuilding took the form of craft production in Finland and other countries before the Second World War. Products were customer-specific and the level of mechanization was low. The organization of work usually rested upon a system of craft control. Management relied on hierarchical divisions of manual labour to control the day-to-day process of production. Squads led by craftsmen had an essential role in organizing the work (Andersen, 1986; Lorenz, 1983; Reid, 1991; Schumann, et al. 1982; Svensson, 1983; Teräs, 1985).

After the Second World War management introduced standardized ships, welding, and section building as well as prefabrication methods. Moreover Finland was fortunate in having had a speciality in respect of shipbuilding. The metal industry in general and Finnish shipbuilding in particular grew very rapidly after the War because Finland built hundreds of ships for the former Soviet Union as part of its war indemnities. The war indemnities were paid off by 1952 but the batch production of technically simple cargo carriers, tankers and bulk carriers for the Soviet Union continued during the 1950s.

The production strategy and the organization of work at the Finnish shipyards moved in a „Taylorist" direction. Although Taylorism was applied to shipbuilding, there are limits to the mechanization and routinization of the work undertaken at certain stages of the shipbuilding production process. Mass production techniques are best applied during the early stages of hull assembly and in the batch production of super tankers, standard cargo vessels and bulk carriers. The fitting out of ships and the production of customized ships is quite another thing altogether. Here the work has tended to retain more of its craft character (Lorenz, 1983: 166).

However, Taylorist methods never became as strongly implanted in the Finnish shipbuilding industry as they did, for instance, in the Swedish yards in their golden period during the 1950s and 1960s. At that time, the methods used in Sweden for the batch production of ships were perhaps the most advanced in the world (Svensson, 1983: 302-305; cf. Kuuse, 1983). Finnish shipyards were too small to become ship factories in the Swedish sense of being designed to construct a long series of large, highly standardized ships. However, the era of batch production of standardized vessels left its imprint on work organization within the Finnish shipyards in the form of a mixture of Taylorism and craft principles. Taylorism could be observed in the gap that existed between production and planning departments, in the fragmentation of work by piece rates and in the attempt by management to standardize operations and to plan and control work in detail. Taylorism as a piece-rate system followed the boundaries set by different crafts. In this way, wages based upon piece-work supported traditional craft demarcations. As in the craft era of shipbuilding, each trade had its own piece-rate but now piece-rates were more precisely calculated and were based on systematic work measurement.

In many ways the craft tradition in Finnish shipbuilding was still alive at the beginning of the 1980s. Craftsmen with extensive work experience, who were also highly ranked in terms of skills and wages, were placed at the top of the workers´ hierarchy. Next in the hierarchy came the category of other skilled workers and apprentices. Finally, auxiliary workers (cleaners, etc.) were to be found at the bottom of the hierarchy. Apprentices were socialised into the craft identity by working in pairs with skilled workers. The workers saw themselves primarily as members of for example, the same trade (as pipefitters and shipwrights) and only secondarily as shipbuilders.

The electricians are the only group to be organized into a craft union whilst the other shipbuilding trades are organised into a single industrial union —

the metal workers union. However, at the level of the individual shipyard, the craft unions were very important actors. Until the end of the 1980s, each trade had its own shop steward and wage competition existed between the crafts. Most stoppages were wild-cat strikes undertaken by members of single trades. In the 1970s and at the beginning of the 1980s, shipbuilding was the most strike-prone branch in the engineering sector as well as of the whole Finnish economy (Kauppinen and Alasoini, 1985: 31).

A crisis of the labour process arose at the Finnish shipyards as a result of their historical development. The nature of the crisis can be conceptualized with the aid of notions developed by a German research project, Automation and Qualification (PAQ, 1987). In order to investigate changes in the labour process PAQ analyzes the tensions between the demands of the forces of production, work tasks and work activities. By „demands of the forces of production" PAQ refers to technological demands which place limits on the type of work organization possible. These demands are transformed into tasks (the organization of work) defined by the employer. By work activities PAQ means the activities which workers actually do. Workers interpret and react to situations that are conditioned by the work tasks and demands relating to the forces of production. There are no deterministic relations between the demands of the forces of production, work tasks and work activities. It is important to study their interrelationships where the changing of one element alters the others and, at the same time, disturbs the balance for the whole. PAQ sees development as a process of crises and breaks (PAQ, 1987: 18-23; Haug, 1985: 84-86).

When we apply the theoretical notions of PAQ to Finnish shipbuilding we can notice first that the demands of forces of production changed when the product strategy and production methods developed. From the 1970s, the yards in Helsinki and Turku and the former Hollming Yards in Rauma (a predecessor to Finnyards) changed their product strategy from a concentration on the batch production of standardized vessels to the production of customized and more sophisticated vessels. Changing the product strategy, shortening the production time and the introduction of new production methods (e.g. section fitting and the increased use of prefabrication) are developments which led to a greater stress being placed upon the significance of departmental and craft based cooperation in shipbuilding.

The work organization, which was a mixture of Taylorism and craft organization, was in tension with this increased demand for cooperation. A number of factors including skill demarcations, the hierarchical divisions of manual labour, the nature of supervision based on occupational groups, the impact of piecework related pay, the gap between planning and production and the existence of strict divisions between the largest production departments (particularly between hull construction and fitting) conflicted with the demands for cooperation. At the levels of work activities, these factors also led to a lack of overall responsibility, to coordination difficulties, „job reworking“,[2] a waste of material, planning „bugs“, piece rate disputes and strikes.

It became very difficult to maintain a piece work system in respect of the one-off production of ships, because the production conditions were so variable. In this kind of production environment piece-rates bore little relation to productivity and ceased to act as an incentive (cf. Svensson, 1983: 343-348, 357-361). In addition the piece-rate system had a negative influence upon industrial relations.

Hungarian sociologists have elaborated the concept of „quasi-Taylorism“. This concept is appropriate to describe the labour process at the Finnish shipyards in the 1970s and 1980s. By „quasi-Taylorism“ Hungarian sociologists mean a situation in which formal features of Taylorism are present but they are heavily modified by the reality of a production process, where there is neither standardization of production nor any stability in respect of either the conditions of, or rewards for, more intensive work. In this kind of situation, workers and shop-floor managers ... „are compelled to break away from the formal prescriptions and to violate official regulations in the interest of uninterrupted production. As a consequence of the many operational disturbances, workers have to organize production and cooperation themselves“, as Lado and associates argue (Lado et al., 1989: 31).

[2] A lot of the work carried out at the Finnish shipyards has to be redone because of problems of coordination which arise either at different phases in the work process, or between different departments and occupational groups. Often such changes are also a result of revised customer specifications for vessels. Given the lack of an established term to describe such wasteful repetiton of work, we use the term „job reworking“. In the mid-1980s it was estimated that up to one third of all work had to be re-done at the yard in Turku.

3 The Repertoire of Job Redesign

When it comes to the Finnish yards the term polyvalency is most commonly discussed in the context of job redesign. According to interview findings, polyvalency has been implemented in the following ways: firstly, by means of lateral job enlargement, secondly, through downwards job enlargement, thirdly, by recourse to a secondary occupation and fourthly, by resort to group work.

According to Child (1985: 138), polyvalency takes the form of (1) a removal of skill demarcations and (2) job enlargement. At the Finnish shipyards these routes to polyvalency are intertwined. Skilled work can be enlarged by attaching to it tasks, the performance of which does not require special skills, only certain basic skills. Pipe fitting may be cited as an example of a development, where work has been enlarged to encompass parts of machine fitting, welding and shipwright work so that it includes the fitting of gadgets attached to piping and the welding of supports. Simultaneously, the dividing line separating pipe fitting from welding and shipwright work has become less marked. A similar process of job enlargement has also taken place in respect of other occupational groups.

Another way to enlarge traditionally defined vocational tasks is to add various auxiliary tasks to them. Examples of such tasks include cleaning up after work activities and general tasks related to the arrangement of work (e.g. arranging lighting, ventilation, air conditioning and heating, transportation and minor scaffolding). The partial combination of auxiliary jobs with skilled jobs is a common practice among firms striving to increase their functional flexibility and productivity (Thompson and McHugh, 1990: 198).

In its most developed form, polyvalency means that a worker has the knowledge and capabilities to work in two or more trades. In our terminology this is referred to as „secondary occupation“. The shipyards have resorted to subcontracting and to transferring labour from one department to another in order to even out work load variations and to maintain employment. These personnel transfers require secondary skills and training.

Shipbuilding has always involved the use of at least some work squads, although Taylorism has greatly decreased the autonomy and number of these squads. Until the 1990s, group work meant the deployment of work squads at the Finnish shipyards. In the 1990s, Masa-Yards in particular has tried to modernize and to develop the squad tradition of shipbuilding. Group work has been discussed and implemented under the heading team work. Through team work, management has tried to enlarge tasks, remove skill demarcations and to improve communication and co-operation between the production departments and other departments. Under team work the ship is divided into work units (covering an area, a system and a given section) and a team comprised of a production engineer, a foreman, a planner and a group of workers is responsible for production within the work unit. The teams are not autonomous nor are the traditional tasks of supervision of work transferred to the workers.

In the mid 1980s management started the introduction of job enlargement in new departments because opposition to job redesign was very heavy in the old departments. This reorganization contradicted craft identities, traditional skill demarcations and the moral code evolved by skilled workers. According to Shaiken (1985: 28), four central concerns comprise the moral code of skilled workers: „pride of craftsmanship, independence on the job, a sensitivity to changes in skill and job content, and a strong sense of collective action". The skilled workers at the shipyards were afraid that polyvalency would degrade their jobs. In addition, conflictual industrial relations (especially at the yards in Turku and Helsinki) and the piece-rate wage system were major impediments to the reorganization of work (Niemelä and Leimu, 1991).

Polyvalency was not rational from the workers point of view in so far as it related to the piece-rate system. The piece-rate system encourages a worker to train for a particular task and impeded co-operation between workers. Every worker was encouraged by the system to consider only his or her own situation. A worker could do well within a piece work system but at the same time cause extra work for other workers. Coordination of work between different trades is a common problem in shipbuilding (see, for example, Brown and Brannen, 1970; The National Shipbuilding Research Programme, 1987; Svensson, 1983).

The piece-rate wage system was abandoned at the Finnish yards in the early 1990s. The following reasons may be noted: firstly, the piece rate system did not fit well with functional flexibility; secondly, the piece work system became technically unsuitable when the product strategy changed from batch production to the one-off production of ships and, thirdly, the piece work system had a negative influence on industrial relations.

Nowadays Masa-Yards and Finnyards operate time payment systems together with different kinds of production bonuses, which are paid if certain economic results are achieved during the production process. According to our qualitative interviews and survey data time payment systems have improved the level of co-operation between crafts.In addition, changing the payment systems has decreased worker resistance to job redesign. In 1988, when the system of piece work was in operation, 52% of Turku shipyard workers were against polyvalency with only 32% in support of it (Kevätsalo, 1991, N = 334). By the time of our 1992 survey, attitudes had reversed to such an extent that only 28% were against polyvalency and 54% supported the idea (N = 207). In addition, the radical change from confrontation to co-operation that has taken place since 1989 in industrial relations at Masa-Yards has decreased the resistance of workers to job redesign (Niemelä and Leimu, 1991).

Job redesign no longer arouses hard resistance at the yards and the local unions accept functional flexibility. In Masa-Yards, the union has even been active in reorganization issues which runs against long established traditions of shipyard trade unionism. In Finland as in many other European countries (Alasoini, 1991: 63; Levie and Sandberg, 1991) unions in general have been passive with respect to job redesign issues.

4 The Scope and Scale of Job Redesign

In this section, we study how work reorganization has influenced Finnish shipyard workers. Our starting point is to ask how extensive and intensive job redesign has been at the Finnish shipyards. In Table 1 the prevalence of the various forms of work reorganization can be observed. The statistics are based on our own survey of shipyard personnel.

It may be observed that the most modest version of job redesign, downward job enlargement, is the most common version. The most profound version of work reorganization, the secondary occupation, is the rarest. We constructed a summative scale comprised of these five questions designed to measure the degree of job redesign encountered by respondents. The scale is divided up into low, medium and high values. High values were ascribed to those workers who had answered „yes“ to the question on secondary jobs or „yes“ to the four other questions concerning job redesign. The replies „no“

and „don´t know“ were combined. The value „low“ was ascribed to workers who had answered „no“ to all five questions or „yes“ to only one of the questions other than the question about a secondary job. The value „medium“ was ascribed to all other workers.

Table 1: Have any of the Following Ways of Organizing Work Been Applied to Your Job? (in %)

	Yes	No	Don´t know	Total	N
Downward job enlargement	60	31	9	100	597
Lateral job enlargement	55	34	11	100	584
Polyvalency	40	49	11	100	590
Work groups	57	35	8	100	588
Secondary occupation	23	64	13	100	583

The distribution of workers according to the degree of job redesign was as follows: low 32%, medium 40% and high 28%. Can we speak of the rise of a multiskilled craftsman or is it merely job enlargement that has taken place? According to these figures it appears that change for the majority of shipyard workers has been solely restricted to job enlargement. However, a significant minority of workers may be considered as belonging to the group of multiskilled craftsmen. The group of multiskilled craftsmen consists of those workers, who obtain the highest value on our scale of job redesign (28%) The great majority of these workers (74%) have a secondary occupation.

Referring back to the debate on flexible specialization (see for instance Pollert, 1991; Wood, 1989), it may be asked whether functional flexibility is directed at those shipyard workers whose jobs are already relatively skilled? Job redesign at the Finnish shipyards is less directed to workers with no vocational schooling and low levels of skill than to other workers. If those workers without vocational schooling (15 %) or those in the lowest skill group (17 %) are excluded, the level of job redesign extends rather evenly to all other skill groups. In other words, differences between skill groups are not statistically significant once the groups mentioned above have been excluded. Measured by the official classification of skill used in the Finnish metal industry, the skill level at the yards is higher than that found in the metal industry on average. Functional flexibility at the Finnish shipyards is mostly directed towards relatively skilled workers who form the great majority of all workers.

At Masa-Yards job redesign has been combined with team work which has improved the level of co-operation between different crafts and the co-operation between production and the design department The management at Masa-Yards has thus succeeded in its aspirations to enlarge jobs and improve the level of co-operation by team work.

One may ask how job redesign has affected other aspects of the quality of work. Has it increased skill requirements, the variety of tasks, and work autonomy? We studied first how job redesign has influenced the skill requirements in different skill groups. The dependent variable is based on the survey question: „Have the skill requirements of your work increased, remained the same or decreased during the last five years?“ Only a couple of% of workers at every level of skill reported a decrease in skill requirements. In a loglinear analysis almost a half (46%) of the workers in our survey reported an increase in skill requirements, using the same variable of job redesign that we used earlier. In order to measure levels of skill we employed the official classification of skills used by the Finnish metal industry.

We found two statistically significant associations: (1) between the degree of job redesign (R) and the increase (I) of skill requirements ($p = 0.001$); and (2) between the level of skill (S) and the increase (I) of skill requirements ($p = 0.006$). Job redesign has increased the skill requirements of the work. At every level of skill the percentage of respondents reporting an increase in skill requirements becomes larger when the degree of job redesign increases. For instance, at medium level of skill this association is the following: About 30% of workers at low levels of job redesign report that the skill requirements of their work have increased. Among the workers at high levels of job redesign the corresponding percentage is about 50. Workers at the highest level of skill report more often the increase of skill requirements than workers at lower levels of skill. This is at least partly due to the fact that skilled workers have a habit of emphasizing their high levels of working knowledge.

We also found out that both job redesign and upskilling are connected to retraining, which has been organised in the vocational schools of the shipyards. Work has become more versatile at all levels of skill. The higher the degree of job redesign the higher the increase in the degree of interest in work and the greater the variety of tasks at all skill levels. It is not suprising that, according to our loglinear analysis, work has become more interesting when skill requirements, autonomy of work and worker influence on decision making have increased. It is more relevant that the association between job redesign and increased interest in work did not vanish even when we used these other indicators as control variables.

According to our survey many workers reported an increase in work pace (54%) and stress (27%). There is no direct association between job redesign on the one hand and increased stress and the pace of work on the other hand. The indirect association is mediated by increased skill requirements, which are connected to increased stress and the work pace. In this way, new organizational forms have ambiguous effects on working conditions — a finding which has been obtained in other studies (see for instance, Düll, 1989: 214).

Has job redesign increased the influence of workers on decision-making? The dependent variable was dichotomized (remained the same — increased). Only very few workers (a couple of%) reported a decrease in influence and 29% reported the opposite change.The independent variables in the logit log-linear analysis were the following: degree of job redesign, level of skill and the change of skill requirements. According to this analysis, there is statistically significant ($p = 0.000$) interaction between the variables decision making, job redesign and the change of skill requirements.

Job redesign is connected to increased worker influence on decision making only when there has been increase of skill requirements. In addition we found a statistically significant association ($p = 0.004$) between worker influence on decision making and the level of skill. The higher the level of skill the more the worker´s influence has increased. It is not suprising that both variables of skill are associated with changes in worker influence. It is one of the classical findings of industrial sociology that skill gives power to workers.

5 Conclusions

The experience of the majority of workers at the Finnish shipyards is that job redesign has improved the quality of working life. How can this observation be explained?

O´Reilly (1992: 369) has argued that

the concept of functional flexibility fails to make a clear distinction between a deliberate strategy to enhance skills and training, in contrast to where task enlargement has developed in an ad hoc manner, as a result of restructuring.

She further argues that only the adoption of such a deliberate strategy can lead to a general improvement and up-skilling of work. At the Finnish shipyards there has been a deliberate strategy by management to broaden tasks and increase training and workers´ skills since the mid 1980s. The opportunities for the Finnish yards to organize supplementary training for their labour force are good because they already run vocational schools of their own. Child (1985: 138) maintains that one important condition for the implementation of polyvalent strategies is the existence of a craft or professional tradition and an emphasis by management on the training and development of their workers. Finnish shipyards exemplify this type of organization.

Negrelli (1988: 96) distinguishes four different types of management strategies (or union-management negotiating cultures) with regard to reorganization issues. The neo-pluralist strategy and the strategy of concession bargaining assume that unions are a hindrance to technological and organizational change. Both approaches lead management to press unions to accept concessions as well as to seek a reduction in union bargaining power. In an integrative strategy as well as in participative strategies, management does not merely see unions as a threat or as a barrier but as a partner. According to the integrative strategy, management makes limited concessions in exchange for worker support for company goals. The participative strategy creates new structures for the resolution of specific problems such as technological and organizational innovation and management gives workers and unions an opportunity to participate in the planning of the company´s development.

At the Finnish shipyards (particularly at Masa-Yards), management has adopted both integrative and participative strategies. There are several reasons for this kind of management approach. The metal workers´ union is one of the largest and most powerful unions in Finland and the shipyard workers have a militant tradition. The neo-pluralist and the concession strategy would have led to severe industrial conflicts. In the prevailing highly competitive and declining product market, the employer could not risk a dispute with, or open opposition from, its workers as a result of the assertion of managerial authority. In fact, shipyard management had an incentive to gain the co-operation of the workforce. Both management and labour were forced to cooperate in a situation, where their survival was at stake (cf. Hartley, 1991: 118-119). This is particularly true of the yards in Turku and Helsinki, which went bankrupt before their reorganization as parts of Masa-Yards.[3] As in many other Western countries, the shipbuilding crisis in Finland has led to an improvement in management — labour co-operation rather than to increased working class militancy (cf. Stråth, 1987).

It may be argued that the participation of worker representatives in the planning of job redesign has reduced workers´ resistance to reorganization. On the basis of previous research (Berggren, 1994; Parker and Slaughter, 1988; Turner, 1990) we may also assume that job redesign has had a positive influence upon the content of shipyard jobs because the adoption of participative systems has meant that, at least to some extent, the interests of workers have been taken into account.

In brief, the following factors help us to understand why job redesign has improved the quality of work at Finnish shipyards:

(1) because of the craft traditions of shipbuilding, there are a lot of skilled and autonomous workers;

(2) a deliberate strategy of management to enhance skills together with the vocational schooling of the shipyards;

(3) a powerful trade union movement with militant traditions;

(4) cooperative industrial relations as a result of a severe crisis of the industry which made both management and labour dependent on each others good will;

(5) integrative and participative management strategies in reorganization issues.

However, even in these conditions job redesign at the shipyards has meant job enlargement for a great majority of workers. Only a minority of workers (23 %) have a secondary occupation and can be called multi-skilled craftsmen. In the short run economic reasons prevent secondary jobs from being more prevalent at the yards. The widespread distribution of such jobs would require more vocational supplementary training than any other form of job re-

[3] Now that the operations of Masa-Yards have stabilized following the uncertainty and difficulties experienced during the early days of the company, distrust between the management and the union seems to be on the increase. Once the company´s operations are secure neither party depends as much on the willingness of the other party to co-operate as was the case at the start of Masa-Yards.

design. Management compares costs arising from training and long training times to costs arising from the use of subcontracted labour. In this respect it is clear that fully trained subcontracted workers are able to do the same job faster and more effectively than the shipbuilding workers who are just starting to acquire skills needed in a secondary job. The simultaneous use of subcontracted labour and lay-offs among the core workforce have caused some conflicts between management and labour at the shipyards. The case of the Finnish shipyards exemplifies the fact that numerical flexibility achieved through the use of external labour places limits upon the degree of functional flexibility that can be achieved in the internal labour market of the firm.

References

Alasoini, T. (1991), Modernization Strategies in Finnish Manufacture: Past Experiences, Prospects for the ´90´s, in Kasvio, A., C. Mako and M. McDaid (eds.), *Work and Social Innovations in Europe*, Proceedings of a Finnish-Hungarian Seminar in Helsinki, September 11th-13th 1990, Tampere, University of Tampere, Research Institute for Social Sciences. Work Research Centre, Working Papers 25/1991: 39-68.

Andersen, H. W. (1986), *Fra det britiske til det amerikanske produksjonsideal. Forandringer i teknologi og arbeid ved Aker mek. Verksted og i norsk skipsbyggingsindustri 1935-1970* (From British to American Production Ideals at Norwegian Shipyards — in Norwegian only). Trondheim, Centre of Science, Technology and Society.

Berggren, C. (1994), *The Volvo Experience. Alternatives to Lean Production in the Swedish Auto Industry*. London, Macmillan.

Brown, R. and P. Brannen (1970), Social Relations and Social Perspectives Amongst Ship building Workers — A Preliminary Statement, Part Two, *Sociology*, Vol. 4 (2): 197-212.

Child, J. (1985), Managerial Strategies, New Technology and the Labour Process, in Knights, D., H. Willmot, and D. Collinson (eds.), *Job Redesign: Critical Perspectives on the Labour Process*, Aldershot, Gower: 107-141.

Dankbaar, B. (1988), *New Production Concepts, Management Strategies and the Quality of Work. Work, Employment & Society,* Vol. 2 (1): 25-50.

Düll, K. (1989), New Forms of Work Organization: Case Studies from the Federal Republic of Germany, France and Italy, in Grootings, P., B. Gustavsen and L. Hethy (eds.), *New Forms of Work Organization in Europe*. New Brunswick, New Jersey, Transaction Publishers: 193-216.

Elger, T. (1991), Task Flexibility and the Intensification of Labour in UK Manufacturing in the 1980s, in Pollert, A. (ed.), *Farewell to Flexibility?* Oxford, Cambridge, Massachusetts, Basil Blackwell: 46-68.

Gustavsen, B. and L. Hethy (1989), An Overview, in Grootings, P., B. Gustavsen and L. Hethy (eds.), *New Forms of Work Organization in Europe*. New Brunswick, New Jersey, Transaction Publishers: 1-26.

Hartley, J. (1991), Industrial Relations and Job Insecurity: A Social Psychological Framework, in Hartley, J., D. Jacobson, B. Klandermans and T. van Vuuren (eds.), *Job Insecurity. Coping with Jobs at Risk.* London, Newbury Park, New Delhi, Sage, 104-122.

Haug, F. (1985), Automation as a Field of Contradictions, in Gustavson, B.O., J.C. Karlsson and C. Räftegård. (eds.), *Work in the 1980s: Emancipation and Derogation, Papers from the Karlstad Symposium on Work.* Brookfield, Vermont, Gower: 83-92.

Jusi, K. (1989), *Vuosaaren telakan sulkeminen ja työvoimahallinnon toiminta* (The Closing of Vuosaari Yard and Action Resorted to by Department of Labour — in Finnish only). Helsinki, Ministry of Labour, Studies in Labour Relations, no. 84.

Kauppinen. T. and T. Alasoini (1985), Työtaistelut telakoilla. Yhteenveto Wärtsilän ja Rauma-Repolan telakkakohtaisten työtaistelututkimusten tuloksista. Helsinki, Työelämän suhteiden neuvottelukunta (Summary: Labour disputes at the shipyards of Oy Wärtsilä Ab and Rauma-Repola Oy). Helsinki, Committee for Labour Relations, Studies in Labour Relations, no. 1.

Kern, H. and M. Schumann (1984), *Das Ende der Arbeitsteilung? Rationalisierung in der industriellen Produktion.* Munich, Beck.

Kevätsalo, K. (1991), *Ammattiyhdistysliike ja työelämän muutos. Ammattiyhdistysliikkeen toiminta 5 työpaikan muutoksessa* (The Unions and Changes in Working Life — in Finnish only). Helsinki, The Metal Workers´ Union.

Kuuse, J. (1983), *Varven och underleverantörerna. Förandringar i fartygsbyggandets industriella länkeffekter* (Shipyards and subcontractors — in Swedish only). Gothenburg, Svenska Varv.

Lado, M., A. Simonyi and F. Toth (1989), From Taylorism to New Forms of Work Organization in Hungary, in Grootings, P., B. Gustavsen and L. Hethy (eds.), *New Forms of Work Organization in Europe.* New Brunswick, New Jersey, Transaction Publishers: 27-40.

Levie, H. and Å. Sandberg (1991), Trade Unions and Workplace Technical Change in Europe, *Economic and Industrial Democracy,* Vol 12 (2): 231-258.

Lorenz, E.H. (1983), The Labour Process and Industrial Relations in the British and French Shipbuilding Industries from 1880 to 1970. Two Patterns of Development. Unpublished doctoral dissertation, Cambridge, University of Cambridge.

Miller, D. C. and W. H. Form (1964), *Industrial Sociology: The Sociology of Work Organizations.* New York, Evanston, London, Harper & Row.

The National Shipbuilding Research Programme (1987), Multiskilled, Self-Managing Work Teams in a Zone-Construction Environment. New York, The U.S. Department of Transportation, The U.S. Department of Maritime Administration and the U.S. Navy in Co-operation with the Marine Construction Division of the Bethlehem Steel Corporation.

Niemelä, J. and H. Leimu (1991), From Industrial Conflict towards Flexible Specialization? A Case Study of Finnish Shipyards, in Kasvio, A., C. Mako and M. McDaid (eds.), *Work and Social Innovations in Europe.* Proceeding of a Finnish-Hungarian Seminar in Helsinki, September 11th-13th 1990. Tampere, University of Tampere, Research Institute for Social Sciences. Work Research Centre, Working Papers 25/1991: 79-100.

Negrelli, S. (1988), Management Strategy: Towards New Forms of Regulation, in Hyman, R. and W. Streeck, (eds.), *New Technology and Industrial Relations.* Oxford, Basil Blackwell: 89-100.

O´Reilly, J. (1992), Where Do You Draw the Line? Functional Flexibility, Training & Skill in Britain & France, *Work, Employment & Society,* Vol 6 (3): 369-396.

Parker, M. and J. Slaughter (1988), *Choosing Sides. Unions and the Team Concept.* Boston, South End Press.

PAQ, Projektgruppe Automation und Qualifikation (1987), *Widersprüche der Automationsarbeit: Ein Handbuch.* Berlin, Das Argument.

Piore, M.J. and C.F. Sabel (1984), *The Second Industrial Divide: Possibilities for Prosperity.* New York, Basic Books.

Pollert, A. (1991), The Orthodoxy of Flexibility, in Pollert, A. (ed.), *Farewell to Flexibility?* Oxford, Cambridge, Massachusetts, Basil Blackwell: 3-31.

Reid, A. (1991), Employers´ Strategies and Craft Production: The British Shipbuilding industry 1870-1950, in Tolliday, S. and J. Zeitlin (eds.), *The Power to Manage? Employers and Industrial Relations in Comparative-Historical Perspective.* London, New York, Routledge: 35-51.

Schumann, M., E. Einemann E., C. Siebel-Rebell and K.P. Wittemann (1982), *Rationalisierung, Krise, Arbeiter. Eine empirische Untersuchung der Industrialiserung auf der Werft.* Frankfurt-on-Main, Europäische Verlagsanstalt.

Shaiken, H. (1985), *Work Transformed: Automation and Labour in the Computer Age.* New York, Holt, Rinehart & Winston.

Sorge, A. and W. Streeck (1988), Industrial Relations and Techical Change: The Case for an Extended Perspective, in Hyman, R. and W. Streeck (eds.), *New Technology and Industrial Relations.* Oxford, Basil Blackwell: 19-47.

Streeck, W. (1987), Industrial Relations and Industrial Change: The Restructuring of the World Automobile Industry in the 1970s and 1980s. *Economic and Industrial Democracy,* Vol 8 (4): 437-462.

Stråth, B. (1987), *The Politics of De-industrialization. The Contraction of West European Shipbuilding Industry.* London, New York, Sydney, Croom Helm.

Svensson, T. (1983), *Från ackord till månadslön. En studie av lönepolitiken, fackföreningarna och rationaliseringarna inom svensk varvsindustri under 1900-talet* (Summary: From Piece-rates to Monthly Wages: A Study of Wages Policy, Trade Unions and Rationalization within the Swedish Shipbuilding Industry During the Twentieth Century). Gothenburg, Svenska Varv.

Teräs, K.(1985), *Verstasliikkeistä suurtaisteluihin. Metalli 49:n historia vuosilta 1894-1930* (From Workshops to Great Battles, the History of Branch 49 of the Metal Workers´ Union in 1894-1930 — in Finnish only). Tampere, Kirjayhtymä.

Thompson, P. and D. McHugh (1990), *Work Organizations. A Critical Introduction.* London, MacMillan.

Todd, D. (1985): *The World Shipbuilding Industry.* London, Sydney, Croom Helm.

Tomaney, J. (1990), The Reality of Workplace Flexibility, *Capital & Class,* (40): 29-60.

Turner, L. R. (1990), *The Politics of Work Reorganization: Industrial Relations under Pressure in Contemporary World Markets.* Ann Arbor, Michigan, UMI Dissertation Services.

Wood, S. (1989), The Transformation of Work? In Wood, S. (ed.), *The Transformation of Work? Skill, Flexibility and the Labour Process.* London, Unwin: 1-43.

Notes on Contributors

Volker Baethge-Kinsky is a Research Assistant at SOFI (Soziologisches Forschungs-Institut), University of Göttingen, and collaborative author of *Trendreport Rationalisierung* (1994) under the direction of Michael Schumann.

Dieter Bögenhold is a "Privatdozent" in the Department of Sociology at the University of Bielefeld (Germany). He is author of *Die Selbständigen* (1985), *Der Gründerboom* (1987), *Von Dämonen zu Demiurgen*? (1994) and currently working on a book which has an international comparative focus on service sector developments.

Tony Charles is Professor of Sociology and Director of the School of Social and International Studies at the University of Sunderland. He was previously Senior Research Fellow at FAST in the European Commission (1991-93) and Head of Sociology at Staffordshire University. He has published on new technology and work organisation, industrial policy and the sociology of work in Europe, Japan and the U.S.A.

Pierre Dubois is Professor of Sociology at the University Paris X (Nanterre/France). He has been engaged in different cross-national studies on organisational and technical changes in Eastern and Western European enterprises. At present, he is Director of the research group Travail et Mobilités.

Egon Endres is Research Fellow at the Technical University of Hamburg-Harburg. He has been conducting research in the area of industrial relations, union organisation and work organisation. He is author of *Macht und Solidarität. Beschäftigungsabbau in der Automobilindustrie* (2nd ed. 1991) and several articles on work organisation and industrial relations.

Virgínia Ferreira teaches Sociology of Work and Employment in the Faculty of Economics at the University of Coimbra (Portugal). Her main research interests are in office automation, clerical work restructuring, women's employment, and the workings of the gendered division of labour. She has published in various journals of Social Sciences and Women's Studies. She is a member of the Editorial Board of *The European Journal of Women's Studies*.

Dirk Geldof is Lecturer in the Department of Political and Social Sciences at the University of Antwerp and he has published on poverty and labour market issues.

Richard Gordon is Associate Professor of Politics and Director of the Silicon Valley Research Group at the University of California, Santa Cruz. His research focuses on diverse aspects of the political and economic transformation of capitalism in historical and contemporary contexts. He is author of a forthcoming work on *Silicon Valley, Global High Technology and the Politics of Economic Change.*

Martin Heidenreich teaches industrial and organisational sociology at the university of Bielefeld (Germany). His major research topic is the cross-national study of organisations, especially in France, Italy, West and East Germany and in the post-socialist countries of Central Europe.

Ulrich Heisig is a Scientific Advisor at the Chamber of White-Collar Employees (Angestelltenkammer) in Bremen. He has been conducting qualitative research on working conditions and social relations in white-collar sectors of manufacturing firms and has taught at the universities of Bremen and Erlangen-Nuremberg. He has published a book on *Verantwortung und Vertrauen im Großbetrieb* (1989) and several articles on trust relations, work restructuring and interest representation in white-collar sectors of employment. He is currently doing research on public sector service work and is engaged in the transfer of research findings to trade union representatives and works councils.

Robert Herranz is currently teaching sociology at the University of Santiago de Compostela (Spain). He has been conducting several studies on professional training and industrial network-building in Spain.

Dietrich Hoss is Professor of Sociology at the University of Lyon II, France. He previously conducted research at the Institute for Social Research (Frankfurt/Main) in the field of organisational and technical restructuring in both Western and Eastern European industry for more than a decade.

Ulrich Jürgens is Senior Researcher at the Science Centre Berlin for Social Research. He studied Political Science and Economics at the Free University

Berlin and completed his PhD (Dr.rer.pol.) in 1978. He has published in the field of labour policy, industrial relations and work organisation with a focus on the automobile industry.

Martin Kuhlmann is a Research Assistant at SOFI (Soziologisches Forschungs-Institut) at the University of Göttingen and collaborative author of *Trendreport Rationalisierung* (1994) under the direction of Michael Schumann.

Constanze Kurz is a Research Assistant at SOFI (Soziologisches Forschungs-Institut) at the University of Göttingen and collaborative author of *Trendreport Rationalisierung* (1994) under the direction of Michael Schumann.

Michele La Rosa is Professor of Sociology and Director of the International Documentation and Research Centre on Problems of Work at the University of Bologna (Italy). He is editor of the journal *Sociologia del Lavoro*. His major research topics are the quality of work and technical and organisational changes in West European countries.

Heikki Leimu is Fellow of Sociology at the University of Turku and Docent of Economic Sociology at Turku School of Economics, University of Vaasa. He has coordinated research projects on Small Manufacturing and Finnish Shipyards both funded by the Academy of Finland. His main fields of interest include sociology of work, small business and their employees, industrial organisation, security policy.

Wolfgang Littek is Professor of Sociology at the University of Bremen and previously at Munich. His research focuses on working conditions of employees, work organisation, technology, and on changes in the social and employment structure at large. He has published in Germany and internationally books and articles on the sociology of work, service work, development of skills, and organisational concepts (among others: *Einführung in die Arbeits- und Industriesoziologie*, 1984; *Dienstleistungsarbeit*, 1991; *Organisation von Dienstleistungsarbeit*, 1992 - with co-authors). He is currently writing a book on the *Sociology of Service Work* (with Ulrich Heisig).

Marc Maurice is Research Director Emeritus, CNRS based at LEST (Laboratoire d'Economie et Sociologie du Travail) at Aix-en-Provence. He has been researching organisational and technological change in France, England and Japan. He is author of many books and articles including *Politique d'economie et organisation industrielle au France et en Allemagne* (1982, with F. Sellin and J. Liberte). He is a member of the editorial board of *Sociologie du Travail*.

Albert L. Mok is Professor of Business Policy at the University of Antwerp (Belgium) and the Agricultural University Wageningen (Netherlands). He has published articles and books on general sociology, occupations and professions, labour market segmentation, management culture and service work.

Uwe Neumann is a Research Assistant at SOFI (Soziologisches Forschungs Institut) at the University of Göttingen and collaborative author of *Trendreport Rationalisierung* (1994) under the direction of Michael Schumann.

Jukka Niemelä has worked as a researcher in the Knowledge and Work Project 1985-1988 and in the Finnish Shipyards Project 1990-1993, both funded by the Academy of Finland. He is Scientific Assistant in Economic Sociology, Turku School of Economics since 1993. He is writing a dissertation on industrial relations and work organisation in Finnish shipyards.

Charles F. Sabel is Ford International Professor of Social Science at the Massachusetts Institute of Technology, Cambridge, USA, where he has been on the faculty since 1978. He is the author of *Work and Politics* (1982) and co-author, with Michael Piore, of *The Second Industrial Divide* (1984), as well as numerous articles.

Gert Schmidt is Professor of Sociology at the University of Nuremberg, Germany, and chairman of the international research group 'GIFT'. He is editor of the German *Soziologische Revue* and is co-editor of the journal *Zeitschrift für Soziologie*. He has been engaged in cross-national studies of organisational and technological changes in different West and East European countries.

Michael Schumann is Professor of Sociology and Director of SOFI (Soziologisches Forschungs-Institut) at the University of Göttingen. He is author of *Industriearbeit und Arbeiterbewußtsein* (1970, with Horst Kern),

Ende der Arbeitsteilung? (1984, with Horst Kern) and *Trendreport Rationalisierung* (1994, with associates at SOFI).

John Tomaney is a researcher in the Centre for Urban and Regional Development Studies, University of Newcastle-upon-Tyne. His research interests include industrial restructuring in traditional industries and the development prospects of Europe's less favoured regions. Recently he has co-edited, with Ash Amin, a book on social and economic cohesion in Europe called *Behind the Myth of the European Union* (1995).

Diane-Gabrielle Tremblay is Professor of Labour Economics and Sociology of Work at the Télé-Université (Open University) of the University of Québec. She is author of two textbooks in these fields: *Economie du travail: Les réalités et approaches théoriques* and *Travail et société: une introduction á la sociology travail.* She is also member of the Centre for Research on Science and Technology (CIRST) at the University of Québec in Montréal and is conducting comparative research on innovation and work organisation in Canada, Sweden and Japan.

Juliet Webster is a Senior Lecturer in the Department of Innovation Studies at the University of East London. She has been conducting research in the area of technological change and the labour process in manufacturing and office work for over a decade. She is the author of *Office Automation: the Labour Process and Women's Work in Britain* (1990), and currently working on a second book, *Gender and Technology at Work*, which will provide an overview of research and debate in this area.

Theo Wehner is Professor of Psychology at the Technical University of Hamburg-Harburg. He has been conducting research in the areas of safety, work-accidents, critical incidents and human errors in industrial work. He is author and editor of *Sicherheit als Fehlerfreundlichkeit. Arbeits - und sozialpsychologische Befunde für eine kritische Technikbewertung* (1992).

Jonathan Winterton is Senior Lecturer in Industrial Relations and Coordinator of the Work Organisation Research Unit at the University of Bradford Management Centre. His main research areas are restructuring in the coal mining and clothing industries, and innovative forms of work organisation, on which he has published extensively. His major books are *Coal, Crisis and Conflict: the 1984-85 Miners' Strike in Yorkshire* (with Ruth Winterton, 1989), *Public Enterprise in Transition: Industrial Relations in State and Privatized Corporations* (with Andrew Pendleton, 1993) and *Managing Human Resources* (with Chris Molander, 1994).